Reliable Distributed Systems

Kenneth P. Birman

Reliable Distributed Systems

Technologies, Web Services,
and Applications

 Springer

Kenneth P. Birman
Cornell University
Department of Computer Science
Ithaca, NY 14853
U.S.A.
ken@cs.cornell.edu

Mathematics Subject Classification (2000): 68M14, 68W15, 68M15, 68Q85, 68M12

Based on *Building Secure and Reliable Network Applications*, Manning Publications Co., Greenwich, ©1996.

ISBN-10 0-387-21509-3   Springer New York, Heidelberg, Berlin
ISBN-13 978-0-387-21509-9   Springer New York, Heidelberg, Berlin

Printed in the United States of America.   (KeS/HP)

9 8 7 6 5 4 3 2 1   SPIN 10969700

springeronline.com

Contents

Preface

This is a new book whose origins are in a 1996 work entitled *Building Secure and Reliable Network Applications*. This earlier book eventually went out of print, and when I set out to revise it during the summer of 2003, I quickly recognized that a tremendous amount of material was outmoded. This new (shorter) text retains some material from the earlier one, but drops some of the old content and includes a treatment of such recent topics as "Web Services," "Grid Computing" and "Autonomic Computing."

Much of the work reported here was made possible by grants from the U.S. Department of Defense through its Advanced Research Projects Agency, DARPA (administered by the Office of Naval Research, Rome Laboratories, and NASA), the Air Force Office of Scientific Research, AFRL Rome Laboratories, and by infrastructure grants from the National Science Foundation. Grants from a number of corporations have also supported this work, including Microsoft, IBM Corporation, Reliable Network Solutions, Isis Distributed Systems, Inc., Siemens Corporate Research (Munich and New Jersey), and GTE Corporation. I wish to express my thanks to all of these agencies and corporations for their generosity. Many individual program directors fought hard for the funding that enabled the research reported here, which involved teams at universities and laboratories nationwide and has resulted in tremendous gains for industry and many impressive successes. All of us in the field owe a tremendous debt to these funding officers, who often went out on the limb for us. Without funding, research into high assurance simply cannot advance.

The techniques, approaches, and opinions expressed here are my own; they may not represent positions of the organizations and corporations that have supported this research.

Many people offered suggestions and comments on the earlier book that contributed towards the current version. These include Paul Francis, Werner Vogels, Robbert van Renesse and Fred Schneider. Paul Francis and Yair Amir used the textbook in their respective classes during Fall 2003, and the feedback was invaluable. I also owe an incredible debt of gratitude to Bo Mings of Microsoft Corporation, and to the whole team responsible for Microsoft Word. Over the years during which this book was edited, something damaged the underlying index files. Bo and his teammates salvaged the book using a beta version of Office 11, and without their help, I honestly don't know that the project could have been completed! Others who provided useful comments and feedback include Jon Weissman. Esha Molette did an outstanding editing job, with the help of several work-study students whose names, unfortunately, were never passed to me. Bill Hogan picked up with Esha left off. I'm very grateful to the whole "team."

I remain grateful to those who reviewed and commented on the earlier edition as well, including my colleagues at Cornell, Isis Distributed Systems, and worldwide for their help in this undertaking. I am also grateful to Paul Jones of Isis Distributed Systems and to François

Barrault and Yves Eychenne of Stratus France and Isis Distributed Systems, France, for providing me with resources needed to work on this book during a sabbatical that I spent in Paris (in fall of 1995 and spring of 1996). Cindy Williams and Werner Vogels provided invaluable help in overcoming some of the details of working at such a distance from home. A number of reviewers provided feedback on early copies of this text. Thanks are due to Marjan Bace, David Bakken, Robert Cooper, Yves Eychenne, Dalia Malkhi, Raghu Hudli, David Page, David Plainfosse, Henrijk Paszt, John Warne, and Werner Vogels. Raj Alur, Ian Service, and Mark Wood provided help in clarifying some thorny technical questions and are also gratefully acknowledged. Bruce Donald's e-mails on idiosyncrasies of the Web were extremely useful and had a surprisingly large impact on treatment of that topic in this text.

Kermeth P. Birman
Cornell University
February 2004

Introduction

Despite more than 30 years of progress towards ubiquitous computer connectivity, distributed computing systems have only recently emerged to play a serious role in industry and society. Perhaps this explains why so few distributed systems are reliable in the sense of tolerating failures automatically, or guaranteeing properties such as high availability, or having good performance even under stress, or bounded response time, or offer security against intentional threats. In many ways the engineering discipline of reliable distributed computing is still in its infancy.

Reliability engineering is a bit like alchemy. The field swirls with competing schools of thought. Profound arguments erupt over obscure issues, and there is little consensus on how to proceed even to the extent that we know how to solve many of the hard problems. In fact, if there is agreement on anything today, it seems to be an agreement to postpone thinking seriously about reliability until tomorrow! But of course, not everyone can deliberately take that risk. This book is aimed at those who find themselves in an unfortunate bind. How can we build reliable systems over a widely popular but unreliable substrate?

One might be tempted by a form of circular reasoning, concluding that reliability must not be all that important in distributed systems (otherwise, the pressure to make such systems reliable would long since have become overwhelming). Yet, it seems more likely that we have only recently begun to see the kinds of distributed computing systems in which the pressure to guarantee reliability is so critical that the developer simply has no alternative. At any rate, there is much evidence that reliability *does* matter to those building the standards; the new Web Services standard, about which we will have a great deal to say, includes a component called WS_RELIABILITY and, as one might hope, this explains how one should tackle reliability issues in the context of a platform supporting the Web Services architecture. WS_RELIABILITY would not be there if there were not a significant commercial demand for a reliability solution.

The problem is that if one delves deeper, this particular form of reliability has serious limits—limits that might preclude solving the great majority of what one would most naturally term "reliability problems." WS_RELIABILITY turns out to be about reliably passing documents down a pipeline with intermediary processing and queuing components in it—a form of reliability analogous to what we see when ordering a product on the Web. You place the order and it enters a pending order subsystem. Later, when availability has been confirmed, you learn that now your order is in "fulfillment," and still later, that it has been shipped and you have been billed. WS_RELIABILITY formalizes and standardizes this kind of protocol.

This is all well and good, but reliability means something specific in the context of, say, a critical care application in a hospital. "Change the digitalis dosage for Mr. Smith in room

219" does not mean "sooner or later." An air traffic controller who wants US Airways flight 29 to climb to 25,000 feet does not mean "and tell the pilot eventually." Thus a pipelined, queued, sooner-or-later guarantee might not do the trick in these kinds of settings. For them, reliability implies high availability, and perhaps other properties as well, such as real-time guarantees or security.

Web Services are not the only game in town, and a developer faced with such an issue might consider implementing the system using the CORBA architecture instead. CORBA, which predated Web Services and is more object oriented (Web Services are "document" oriented) has a fault-tolerance standard, FTOL. At a glance the match with the problem as stated is somewhat better. But now we encounter a different problem: it has not been widely implemented, and the CORBA community finds it overly constraining. In particular, the CORBA FTOL standard limits itself to solving one specific high availability problem, and only when the application satisfies certain properties (notably, determinism) that many applications cannot guarantee (notably, because of multi-threading, I/O from multiple channels, and asynchronous event handling). In particular, the medical and air traffic control applications probably couldn't manage within these kinds of constraints.

Why not cast an even wider net? Some of the world's most demanding distributed systems were built using reliable "process group" architectures. For example, in this text we will learn about the technologies underlying the New York Stock Exchange overhead quote and trade reporting system. The same technology is used to full replicate the Swiss Stock Exchange so that every trader has a complete replica of the state of the entire exchange on his or her workstation. And it was used to implement Air Traffic Control by the French as part of their PHIDIAS console clustering architecture, and to support inter-airport communication as well. It runs the AEGIS Naval Warship, and if ever there was a system that needs to "take a licking and keep on ticking," that's the one. So, why not use the same technology to solve our problem?

The response to such a question highlights an issue event tougher than the purely technical one: to a growing extent, standards like Web Services and CORBA are the only games in town. While rolling one's own system (as did the enterprises just cited) was an option in the early 1990s, doing so is expensive and means that the developers are unable to exploit the best productivity tools and technologies. So most development teams are now compelled to work within widely accepted standards. But as we just saw, where reliability is concerned, these standards are quite limited. The designer faces a tough problem: Pragmatic considerations force him or her to work with platforms that lack support for reliability, yet the application demands stronger guarantees. How then can one circumvent the limitations without building a "non-standard" application?

To the extent that existing mission- and even life-critical applications rely on distributed software, the importance of reliability has perhaps been viewed as a narrow, domain-specific issue. One could argue that hospitals and air traffic control centers *should* use special-purpose software designed to address their specialized requirements. Why should everyone pay for platform features that are only needed in obscure, specialized, applications? On the other hand, as distributed software is placed into more and more critical applications, where safety or financial stability of large organizations depends on the reliable operation of complex distributed applications, the inevitable result will be that some of these will require exactly the same reliability mechanisms needed in those hospital and air traffic control systems. It is time to tackle distributed systems reliability in a serious manner. To fail to do so today is to invite catastrophic computer systems failures tomorrow.

Web Services are likely to amplify this new concern about reliability. The *service-oriented computing* movement makes it much easier to reuse existing functionality in new ways: to build a new application that talks to one or more old applications. As this trend plays out, we are seeing a slow evolution towards elaborate, poorly understood, interdependency between applications. Developers are discovering that the failure of a component that they did not even know was "involved" in their application may have performance or availability implications in remote parts of the system. Even when a dependency is evident, the developer may have no clue as to what some components do. Thus, finding ways to guarantee the availability of critical subsystems and components may be the only way for platform vendors to avoid some very unhappy customer experiences.

Perhaps with this in mind, many vendors insist that reliability is a high priority for their internal development teams. The constraint, they explain, is that they are uncomfortable with any approach to reliability that has visibility to the developer or end user. In effect, reliability is important, but the mechanisms must be highly "transparent." Moreover, they insist that only generally accepted, best of breed solutions can be considered for inclusion in their standards.

Unfortunately, for three decades, the computing industry has tried (and failed) to make the mechanisms of reliable, secure distributed computing transparent. Moreover, as noted earlier, there is considerable confusion about just what the best of breed solutions actually are in this field; we will see why in Part III of the book.

Now, perhaps the experts who have worked in this field for almost three decades have missed some elegant, simple insight . . . if so, it would not be the first time. On the other hand, perhaps we cannot achieve transparency and are faced with deep tradeoffs, so that there simply isn't any clear best of breed technology that can make all users happy.

Thus while these distributed computing experts have all kinds of interesting technologies in their "tool kits," right now the techniques that make reliability, and security, and stability possible in massive settings can't be swept under a rug or concealed from the developer. On the contrary, to succeed in this new world, developers need to master a diversity of powerful new ideas and techniques, and in many cases may need to implement variants of those techniques specialized to the requirements of their specific application. There just isn't any sensible way to hide the structure of a massive, and massively complex, distributed system scattered over multiple data centers.

We need to learn to expose system structure, to manage it intelligently but explicitly, and to embed intelligence right into the application, so that each application can sense problems, develop a suitable application-specific strategy for reacting to those problems, and ride out the disruption. One can certainly wish that greater transparency were an option, and maybe someday we will gain such a sophisticated understanding of the matter that we will be able to do better. But today the best hope is to standardize the best mechanisms we can bring to bear on the problem, while also exposing those mechanisms so that a developer who understands them well can either customize his/her behavior or work around their limitations.

The confluence of these trends forces universities to offer new kinds of courses: courses aimed at educating students in some esoteric, hard to understand, hard to use technologies, and in the "reliability mindset" required to apply them appropriately. In fact, a reliability engineering program should include several such courses: courses in security, in system management, in large-scale system structure and risk analysis, and in software techniques for building reliable applications. Some of these topics can be integrated into existing courses; this is how we handle the challenge at Cornell. The present textbook will be useful mostly for the last of these needs: teaching students the specific technology options available to them in situations where reliability is a clear requirement.

If we do not educate the next generation of developers to deal with the challenge, they simply won't be prepared when they start to encounter puzzling questions: "But how should the application react if that request times out?" "What might happen if the load surges?" "What is causing our periodic 90-second network "storms?" We owe it to our students to equip them for the world in which they will live and work!

But there is also some good news here. The experience of teaching courses on reliability and security and "information assurance" has been quite positive. What looks hard at first glance starts to make sense when explained slowly and clearly. Simple exercises can go a long way towards helping students master the technologies involved. And while the material is not easy, it is not impossibly complex either.

True, it would be better if the most important technologies were part of standard platforms, but even if something cannot be purchased from Microsoft, it may still be available to those willing to download and work with free packages. Even if a protocol is not trivial, a good programming team may be able to implement it once someone explains it clearly. We will see that reliability engineering is as much a mindset as a "technology", and one can teach a mindset and work through examples to see how a way of thinking can translate into actions. It is not unreasonable to expect *every* student to gain at least a broad appreciation of the issues and the challenges. And it turns out that a great many students should be able to gain a real mastery of the state of the art, and even some hands-on experience.

The instructor teaching from this book, or the professional reading the book to catch up on developments, will find that it is organized into multiple "parts." The early parts are somewhat remedial in nature: they review technologies that any student has probably seen in other settings, and even when a part consists of four or five chapters, these early chapters probably do not merit more than one lecture in a semester-long class. They are included because even the basic technologies have some surprising reliability and performance characteristics, and one cannot plunge directly into more advanced technologies without an appreciation of the basics. But any course that devotes more than cursory attention to these parts of the book is probably using the wrong text. For example, when the author teaches from this textbook, pretty much all the important material in Parts I and II is covered during the first two lectures, revisiting one or two topics a bit later in the semester.

As we move forward, notably in Part III, IV and V of the book, we encounter the conceptual core of the subject. Replication, for example, is a fundamental need in any reliable system: if a system depends on some service, or some dataset, and we fail to replicate it, our system will be down when that service or dataset is unavailable. But unless the service or the information is completely static (unchanging), we need to worry about how to deal with updates, how to deal with failures while updates are happening, what to do when two conflicting updates are issued concurrently, how to deal with network problems that might present themselves as transient failures, and what kinds of consistency guarantees we can offer.

A seemingly simple reliability requirement thus unleashes a number of technical challenges. Part III of the book tackles these challenges and shows how they can be solved. Indeed, we end up with a family of solutions that differ in their costs and properties. Parts IV and V build on this base and then explore other related problems and solutions.

Let us get a bit more specific, by looking briefly at the replication problem and asking what makes a problem like this so hard to solve. As just noted, replication of an important service or an important data set is at the core of the difficulty of making a system reliable. Lacking replicas, if that critical service crashes, the rest of the system may be stuck (or may begin to fail in some sort of a cascade of failures, triggered by the core outage but less and less "obviously" related to it). With replicas, we can just *fail over* from the faulty server to a healthy one. Of course, doing this (failing over) does entail detecting the failure and knowing where to find a healthy backup.

Before we try to solve this problem, let us start by pinning down some terminology and stating our objectives more explicitly. As we use the term here, a *computer network* is a communication technology supporting the exchange of messages among computer programs executing on computational nodes. Computer networks are *data movers,* providing capabilities for sending data from one location to another, dealing with mobility and changing topology, and automating the division of available bandwidth among contending users. Computer networks have evolved dramatically over the past few decades. Today, wireless networks are shifting the landscape yet again.

Modern networks span such a range of technologies and configurations that one cannot really make any blanket claims about them. It is rare to see a network that can guarantee that messages will get through in a timely manner, or one that is not subject to occasional disruptive events. Indeed, some technologies such as firewalls and network address translators can wall off sets of computers, so that not every computer can communicate to every other. Even if we have the chance to design a network by hand (say, in a hospital), one cannot preclude a future upgrade (perhaps, to add wireless connectivity) that would change the "properties" of the original hand-designed system.

But let us move on. In our terminology, a *distributed computing system* refers to computing systems and applications that cooperate to coordinate actions at multiple locations while communicating over a network. Rather than adopting a perspective in which conventional (non-distributed) application programs access data remotely over a network, a distributed system includes multiple application programs that communicate over the network, but

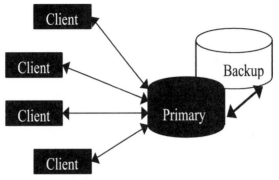

Figure 1. An idealized client/server system with a backup server for increased availability. The clients interact with the primary server; in an air traffic application, the server might provide information on the status of air traffic sectors, and the clients may be air traffic controllers responsible for routing decisions. The primary server keeps the backup up to date, so that if a failure occurs, the clients can switch to the backup and resume operation with minimal disruption.

that take action at the multiple locations where the application run. Despite the widespread availability of networking since early 1980, distributed computing has only become common in the 1990s. This lag reflects a fundamental issue: distributed computing turns out to be much harder than non-distributed or network computing applications, especially if reliability is required.

A subsystem that replicates a critical service or dataset is an instance of a distributed computing system. What does it mean to talk about guaranteeing reliability for such a system? Consider the design of an air traffic control software system, which (among other services) provides air traffic controllers with information about the status of air traffic sectors (Figure 1). Web sophisticates may want to think of this system as one that provides a Web-like interface to a database of routing information maintained on a server. Thus, the controller would be presented with a depiction of the air traffic situation, with push-button style interfaces or other case-specific interfaces providing access to additional information about flights, projected trajectories, possible options for rerouting a flight, and so forth. To the air traffic controller these are the commands; the Web user might think of them as active hyperlinks.

A controller who depends on a system such as this needs an absolute assurance that if the service reports that a sector is available and a plane can be routed into it, this information is correct and no other controller has been given the same information in regard to routing some other plane. An optimization criterion for such a service would be that it minimizes the frequency with which it reports a sector as being occupied when it is actually free. A fault-tolerance goal would be that the service remains operational despite limited numbers of failures of component programs, and perhaps that it takes a component off-line if it somehow falls out of synchronization with regard to the states of other components.

Goals of the type just enumerated would avoid scenarios such as the one illustrated in Figure 2, where the system state has become dangerously inconsistent as a result of

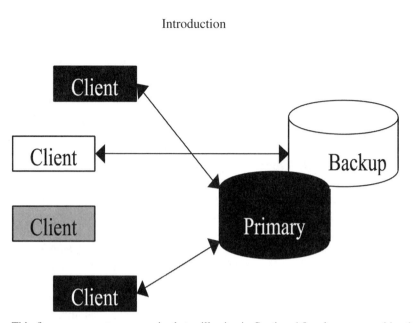

Figure 2. This figure represents a scenario that will arise in Section 4.8, when we consider the use of a standard remote procedure call methodology to build a client/server architecture for a critical setting. In the case illustrated, some of the client programs have become disconnected from the primary server, perhaps because of a transient network failure (one that corrects itself after a brief period during which message loss rates are very high). In the resulting system configuration, the primary and backup servers each consider itself to be in charge of the system as a whole. There are two clients still connected to the primary server (black), one to the backup server (white), and one client is completely disconnected (gray). Such a configuration exposes the application user to serious threats. In an air traffic control situation, it is easy to imagine that accidents could arise if such a situation were encountered. The goal of this book is two-fold: to assist the reader in understanding why such situations are a genuine threat in modern computing systems, and to study the technical options for building better systems that can prevent such situations from occurring. The techniques presented will sometimes have limitations, which we will attempt to quantify and to understand any reliability implications. While many modern distributed systems have overlooked reliability issues, our working hypothesis will be that this situation is changing rapidly and that the developer of a distributed system has no choice but to confront these issues and begin to use technologies that respond to them.

a network failure that fools some clients into thinking the primary server has failed, and similarly fools the primary and backup into mutually believing one another to have crashed.

Why might inconsistency arise? One big problem concerns the difficulty of detecting a failure. If a computer crashes, attempts to communicate with applications running on it will time out. But this can also happen if the network experiences a transient disconnection, or for any number of other reasons. Thus a failure might be "mistakenly" detected. From such seemingly minor concerns a tremendous number of higher level issues arise.

We could evade these issues by just making the rule that (1) an application will retry requests indefinitely until a response is received; and (2) any failed component will be restarted, eventually. But it is easy to see that while this might give us a form of reliability, it will not work in an air traffic control system where we need to take actions within fractions of a second; restarting a crashed computer could take hours and certainly won't take less than minutes. Thus when reliability also entails *high availability* we are in trouble. WS_RELIABILITY is an example of a technology aimed at applications willing to accept the rule just outlined. This book covers that technology . . . but also dozens of other technologies addressing such needs as high availability, special kinds of consistency or recoverability, real-time data delivery, and so on.

But now suppose that the techniques of this book were used to construct such a service, using the best available technological solutions, combined with rigorous formal specifications of the software components involved and the best possible quality process. Theoretical results assure us that inconsistencies such as the one in Figure 2 cannot concur. Years of testing might yield a very high degree of confidence in the system, yet the service remains a large, complex software artifact. Even minor changes to the system, such as adding a feature, correcting a very simple bug, or upgrading the operating system version or hardware, could introduce serious problems long after the system was put into production. The question then becomes: Can complex software systems ever be used in critical settings? What should be the social process surrounding the system: how should we manage it, and what issues arise when humans are part of the loop. Are the issues seen when building distributed systems somehow worse than in other settings, or are the issues similar?

Whereas we do treat the technical issues here, this book does not give very much attention to the "social" considerations seen in this question. Reliability demands far more than just technology, and any designer worth his or her salt will need to become good at thinking through the broader usage cases surrounding the systems they build, the management policies that will be applied, the way that reliability and security will be presented to the end-user. Such topics arise in any setting where software is used to solve problems people might construe as "mission critical," and lead to a whole risk-analysis mindset that could be the subject of another book. But this is not that book. Here, we will limit ourselves to walking through some scenarios in a step-by-step manner illustrative of the broader process.

Nonetheless, through the material in this book, the developer will be guided to appropriate design decisions, appropriate development methodologies, and to an understanding of the reliability limits on the solutions that result from this process. No book can expect to instill the experience and sense of balance that a reader may need to draw upon in order to make such decisions wisely, but one hopes that computer systems engineers, like bridge builders and designers of aircraft, are highly motivated to build the best and most reliable systems possible. Given such a motivation, appropriate development methodology, and appropriate software tools, extremely reliable distributed software can be implemented and deployed even into critical settings.

Perhaps this book can serve a second purpose in accomplishing its primary one. Many highly placed industry leaders have commented to me that until reliability is forced upon them, their companies will *never* take the issues involved seriously. The investment needed is simply viewed as very large, and likely to slow the frantic rate of progress on which computing as an industry has come to depend. I believe that the tide is now turning in a way that will, in fact, force change, and that this book can contribute to what will, over time, become an overwhelming priority for the industry.

Given that we can solve the technical side of these kinds of problems, why are reliability technologies not more common in the marketplace today? For that matter, why do so many otherwise state-of-the-art corporations and development groups wander into the trap of building and deploying mission-critical applications using inadequate platforms and tools, without even tackling the broader management and life-cycle issues just mentioned?

One possibility is that reliability is often viewed by developers as an expensive goal, requiring systems that are complex and costly, much as the phrase "robust bridge" conjures up a vision of a massive, expensive, and ugly artifact. If this is the case, it probably reflects the slightly ad hoc development methodology that has become entrenched in industry. Rather than designing systems before building them, we often plunge in, adding functionality as a product slowly evolves, and often doing so by coupling new functions to old components running elsewhere in the network. Reliability, in software built this way, is an organic process: a system grows, evolves, suffers illnesses, recovers. Telling a developer to build a reliable system is thus a bit like telling him or her to "do your job better."

If we believe this, part of the job of this book and of the instructors who teach from it will be to give students a sense of the elegance and "rightness" of the solutions under study. A student who becomes comfortable with the core ideas – not the superficial expressions of those ideas, but the real underlying technology – will also be freed from the mindset just summarized. Such a student will realize that yes, the techniques in question are a bit complicated, but they are not particularly ugly. Yes, one needs to design them into an application, but this need not bring enormous complexity or cost to the development process. The Golden Gate Bridge is quite robust. But it is not ugly, and if it cost more to make it robust, well, that is a price we accept to avoid the alternative of an even more costly failure.

Indeed, if those of us who train the next generation of developers do not do *our* jobs well, we are sending our students into the field without the technical knowledge to do *their* jobs well. Thus by starting to teach students to think about reliability issues and to approach problems with reliability as one goal among many, perhaps we are creating the very problem that we decry. Conversely, as the general level of demonstrated knowledge concerning how to make systems reliable rises, the expectation of society and government that vendors will employ such technologies is also likely to rise. And this could spur the emergence of a broader, deeper, product suite.

The challenge of engineering reliability in distributed computing systems is perhaps the unavoidable challenge of the coming decade, just as performance was the challenge of the past decade. By accepting this challenge, we also gain new opportunities, new commercial markets, and help create a future in which technology is used responsibly for the broad benefit of society. There will inevitably be real limits on the reliability of the distributed systems we can build, and consequently there will be types of distributed computing systems that should not be built because we cannot expect to make them adequately reliable. However, we are far from those limits: in many circumstances deploying technologies known to be fragile in ways that actively encourage their use in critical settings. Ignoring this issue, as occurs too often today is irresponsible and dangerous and increasingly unacceptable. Reliability challenges us as a community: It now falls upon us to respond.

A User's Guide to This Book

In this section I simply want to recap a point made in the introduction, concerning the right way to approach this text and to structure a course around it. The book was written with several types of readers in mind, and consequently weaves together material that may be of greater interest to one type of reader than that aimed at another type of reader.

Although the book is intended to be readable from start to finish, in fact the real meat of the subject does not begin until parts III, IV and V. Parts I and II are basically remedial and should not be the subject of more than a few lectures in a class based on this text; the author covers most of that material in his first two lectures, returning only now and then to topics from these parts later in the semester.

Specifically, Parts I and II review communication standards and Web Services, point to reliability and performance issues commonly encountered when using those technologies, and (hopefully) level the playing field. In a how-to textbook, such a treatment would be littered with very detailed examples: "push this button and you will see the following pop-up box. Now type the code shown below into the box. Next pull down the "compile and run" menu and click on run."

I am not trying to compete with the how-to textbooks; the small number of code samples included here are provided for clarity of exposition, but not with the intent that the user "type this in and run it."

An instructor who teaches from this text should plan to devote a lot of time to the fundamental protocols and conceptual material; the reward for doing so is that students will gain both an insight into the reliability "mindset" and also very useful understanding of technologies such as the ones in the Ensemble system or the Spread Toolkit. And this focus on fundamentals needs to be evident even in the first lectures of a course, both to set the expectations of the students appropriately, and also to get them hooked on the topic.

Thus, as mentioned above, I recommend that instructors limit themselves to a lecture or two each on the material in Parts I and II, and let the students read the rest of those chapters offline. Moreover, even these introductory lectures need to drill right down by emphasizing basic, deep quandaries. For example, in the introduction we saw that replication is a basic need in distributed systems that offer reliability guarantees (actually, "high availability guarantees" would be more accurate; a system can be designed to recover reliably from failures, and this does not necessarily involve replicating anything). Reliability, in turn, raises deep questions: how should failure be detected? How can data be accessed while updates are underway? How should failures be handled if an update was happening when the failure takes place? How should a process joining a group be initialized?

At the outset of a course, it can be very helpful to get the students talking about these kinds of goals and debating what might be needed in one setting or another. Get the students to point out that a failed machine is indistinguishable from an inaccessible machine (until the network heals itself!) and to think about some of the kinds of inconsistency that can result. How would they replicate data in the face of such considerations? What tradeoffs can they identify?

There is a seductive nature to such questions, and students who start to wrestle with them in the first days of a course will quickly be drawn into the real core of the book. This, in my view, is found in Parts III, IV and V, which look squarely at a great variety of reliability technologies. Instructors should plan to devote several weeks to this material: each chapter is the basis for several lectures in my classes at Cornell, and at that pace, one can tease out the detail and be sure that the students really understand how the various protocols work and why they have the structure being used.

Having said this, I should also make it clear that a reader who wishes to skip the detail and focus on practical tools may want to skim through Part III (Chapters 14 through 18), which get into the details of some fairly complex protocols and programming models. I have written the book so that later chapters do not rely very much on the details covered in those in Part III, and that material unquestionably challenging. This said, in light of the poor platform support for reliability in most products, I think that even a battle-hardened professional might benefit from the material covered in these chapters. At the time of this writing, there is sometimes no alternative but to roll up one's sleeves and "do it from scratch."

The remainder of the book is relatively independent (Chapters 14 through 18). Chapter 19 recaps some of the material in 14–18, hence a reader who skips those should be able to find his or her footing by reading this one. Chapters 20 and 21 explore reliability-enhancing tools through an approach based on wrappers, and Part V, consisting of Chapters 22 through 26, looks at related issues concerning such topics as real-time systems, security, peer-to-peer computing, transactions, and system management. The content is practical and the material is intended to be of a hands-on nature. Chapter 27 surveys research projects relevant to the topics covered in the book.

Where possible, the book includes general background material, but in comparison to the 1996 work, I have cut quite a bit of this basic information out in response to comments. Readers of the previous book basically found this material too scanty to be of real value. For example, the earlier book included a section on ATM networks, and that was droppped from the current book. Our treatment of CORBA, J2EE and .NET is probably too shallow to serve as a real introduction to this topic, and is intended more as a level-setting discussion than as an introduction to any of these three important platforms. And it had a chapter on cluster computing, but one that was not really particularly deep. I recommend the textbook by Tannenbaum and van Steen to those who need a more systematic treatment of the basic technologies. Instructors will want to cover this background material at a rapid clip. As for grid and cluster computing, there is a well known book on the Global Grid by Ian Foster, and it would be the obvious place to start.

Instructors putting together a course based on this book are more then welcome to borrow from my slides for Cornell's CS514 class. You will find a link on http://www.cs.cornell.edu/ken. I bring the slide set up to date periodically, and will be doing so for the Spring 2005 semester. Of course, teaching from someone else's slide set can be a challenge. This is particularly so for distributed computing: I have worked in the area of reliability for most of my career, and most of the techniques presented here have been invented by my colleagues and myself. Having experienced them first hand, don't hesitate to drop me a note if you have any questions or comments.

A final comment regarding references: To avoid encumbering the discussion with a high density of references, the book cites relevant work the first time a reference to it occurs in the text, or where the discussion needs to point to a specific reference, but may not do so in subsequent references to the same work. These can be found in the bibliography. References are also collected at the end of each chapter into a short section on related reading. It is hard to do adequate justice to such a large and dynamic area of research with a limited number of citations, but every effort has been made to be fair and complete. I should also add that the field is faddish and that this is reflected in the references. A decade ago, for example, the hot topic was performance of multicast systems; today, scalability seems to be the main issue (especially using peer-to-peer techniques). This results in clusters of references. Where the issue is especially significant, I will point it out in the "further readings" section. And of course the lack of recent evaluations of multicast performance on various platforms also points to research opportunities for experimentally-oriented students, especially where access to lab stocked with state-of-the-art hardware is an option. Such a student could evaluate a package like "Spread", then try to tune it for the latest and best hardware and re-evaluate after doing so, and could end up with a really interesting (and publishable) result. People who do publish on topics relevant to the treatment here should not hesitate to show me their work and to provide appropriate citations; I would be happy to include references to the best recent results in future revisions of this text.

Trademarks

Unix is a Trademark of Santa Cruz Operations, Inc. CORBA (Common Object Request Broker Architecture) and OMG IDL are trademarks of the Object Management Group. ONC (Open Network Computing), NFS (Network File System), Solaris, Solaris MC, XDR (External Data Representation), Jaa, J2EE, Jini and JXTA are trademarks of Sun Microsystems, Inc. DCE is a trademark of the Open Software Foundation. XTP (Xpress Transfer Protocol) is a trademark of the XTP Forum. RADIO is a trademark of Stratus Computer Corporation. Isis Reliable Software Developer's Kit, Isis Reliable Network File System, Isis Reliable Message Bus, and Isis for Databases are trademarks of Isis Distributed Computing Systems, Inc. Orbix is a trademark of Iona Technologies Ltd. Orbix+Isis is a joint trademark of Iona and Isis Distributed Computing Systems, Inc. TIB (Teknekron Information Bus) and Subject Based Addressing are trademarks of TIBCO (although we use subject based addressing in a more general sense in this text). Chorus is a trademark of Chorus Systems, Inc. Power Objects is a trademark of Oracle Corporation. Netscape is a trademark of Netscape Communications. OLE, COM, DCOM, Windows, Windows XP, .NET, Visual Studio, C#, and J# are trademarks of Microsoft Corporation. Lotus Notes is a trademark of Lotus Computing Corporation. Purify is a trademark of Highland Software, Inc. Proliant is a trademark of Compaq Computers, Inc. VAXClusters, DEC MessageQ, and DECsafe Available Server Environment are trademarks of Digital Equipment Corporation. MQSeries and SP2 are trademarks of International Business Machines. PowerBuilder is a trademark of PowerSoft Corporation. Ethernet is a trademark of Xerox Corporation. Gryphon and WebSphere are trademarks of IBM. WebLogic is a trademark of BEA, Inc.

Other products and services mentioned in this document are covered by the trademarks, service marks, or product names as designated by the companies that market those products. The author respectfully acknowledges any that may not have been included.

Reliable Distributed Systems

PART I

Basic Distributed Computing Technologies

Although our treatment is motivated by the emergence of the World Wide Web, object-oriented distributed computing platforms such as J2EE (for Java), .NET (for C# and other languages) and CORBA, the first part of the book focuses on the general technologies on which any distributed computing system relies. We review basic communication options and the basic software tools that have emerged for utilizing them and for simplifying the development of distributed applications. In the interests of generality, we cover more than just the specific technologies embodied in the Web as it exists at the time of this writing, and, in fact terminology and concepts specific to the Web are not introduced until Part II. However, even in this first part, we discuss some of the most basic issues that arise in building reliable distributed systems, and we begin to establish the context within which reliability can be treated in a systematic manner.

1

Fundamentals

1.1 Introduction

Reduced to the simplest terms, a *distributed computing system* is a set of computer programs, executing on one or more computers, and coordinating actions by exchanging *messages*. A *computer network* is a collection of computers interconnected by hardware that directly supports message passing. Most distributed computing systems operate over computer networks, but one can also build a distributed computing system in which the components execute on a single multitasking computer, and one can build distributed computing systems in which information flows between the components by means other than message passing.

Moreover, there are new kinds of parallel computers, called clustered servers, which have many attributes of distributed systems despite appearing to the user as a single machine built using rack-mounted components. With the emergence of what people are calling "Grid Computing," clustered distributed systems may surge in importance. And we are just starting to see a wave of interest in wireless sensor devices and associated computing platforms. Down the road, much of the data pulled into some of the world's most exciting databases will come from sensors of various kinds, and many of the actions we'll want to base on the sensed data will be taken by actuators similarly embedded in the environment. All of this activity is leading many people who do not think of themselves as distributed systems specialists to direct attention to distributed computing.

We will use the term "protocol" in reference to an algorithm governing the exchange of messages, by which a collection of processes coordinate their actions and communicate information among themselves. Much as a *program* is a set of instructions, and a *process* denotes the execution of those instructions, a *protocol* is a set of instructions governing the communication in a distributed program, and a distributed computing system is the result of executing some collection of such protocols to coordinate the actions of a collection of processes in a network.

This text is concerned with *reliability* in distributed computing systems. Reliability is a very broad term that can have many meanings, including:

- *Fault tolerance*: The ability of a distributed computing system to recover from component failures without performing incorrect actions.
- *High availability*: In the context of a fault-tolerant distributed computing system, the ability of the system to restore correct operation, permitting it to resume providing services during periods when some components have failed. A highly available system may provide reduced service for short periods of time while reconfiguring itself.
- *Continuous availability*: A highly available system with a very small recovery time, capable of providing uninterrupted service to its users. The reliability properties of a continuously available system are unaffected or only minimally affected by failures.
- *Recoverability*: Also in the context of a fault-tolerant distributed computing system, the ability of failed components to restart themselves and rejoin the system, after the cause of failure has been repaired.
- *Consistency*: The ability of the system to coordinate related actions by multiple components, often in the presence of concurrency and failures. Consistency underlies the ability of a distributed system to emulate a non-distributed system.
- *Scalability*: The ability of a system to continue to operate correctly even as some aspect is scaled to a larger size. For example, we might increase the size of the network on which the system is running—doing so increases the frequency of such events as network outages and could degrade a "non-scalable" system. We might increase numbers of users, or numbers of servers, or load on the system. Scalability thus has many dimensions; a *scalable system* would normally specify the dimensions in which it achieves scalability and the degree of scaling it can sustain.
- *Security*: The ability of the system to protect data, services, and resources against misuse by unauthorized users.
- *Privacy*: The ability of the system to protect the identity and locations of its users, or the contents of sensitive data, from unauthorized disclosure.
- *Correct specification*: The assurance that the system solves the intended problem.
- *Correct implementation*: The assurance that the system correctly implements its specification.
- *Predictable performance*: The guarantee that a distributed system achieves desired levels of performance—for example, data throughput from source to destination, latencies measured for critical paths, requests processed per second, and so forth.
- *Timeliness*: In systems subject to real-time constraints, the assurance that actions are taken within the specified time bounds, or are performed with a desired degree of temporal synchronization between the components.

Underlying many of these issues are questions of tolerating failures. Failure, too, can have many meanings:

- *Halting failures*: In this model, a process or computer either works correctly, or simply stops executing and crashes without taking incorrect actions, as a result of failure. As the model is normally specified, there is no way to detect that the process has halted except by timeout: It stops sending "keep alive" messages or responding to "pinging" messages and hence other processes can deduce that it has failed.
- *Fail-stop failures*: These are accurately detectable halting failures. In this model, processes fail by halting. However, other processes that may be interacting with the faulty process also have a completely accurate way to detect such failures—for example, a fail-stop environment might be one in which timeouts can be used to monitor the status of processes, and *no timeout occurs unless the process being monitored has actually crashed*. Obviously, such a model may be unrealistically optimistic, representing an idealized world in which the handling of failures is reduced to a pure problem of how the system should react when a failure is sensed. If we solve problems with this model, we then need to ask how to relate the solutions to the real world.
- *Send-omission failures*: These are failures to send a message that, according to the logic of the distributed computing systems, should have been sent. Send-omission failures are commonly caused by a lack of buffering space in the operating system or network interface, which can cause a message to be discarded after the application program has sent it but before it leaves the sender's machine. Perhaps surprisingly, few operating systems report such events to the application.
- *Receive-omission failures*: These are similar to send-omission failures, but they occur when a message is lost near the destination process, often because of a lack of memory in which to buffer it or because evidence of data corruption has been discovered.
- *Network failures*: These occur when the network loses messages sent between certain pairs of processes.
- *Network partitioning failures*: These are a more severe form of network failure, in which the network fragments into disconnected sub-networks, within which messages can be transmitted, but between which messages are lost. When a failure of this sort is repaired, one talks about *merging* the network partitions. Network partitioning failures are a common problem in modern distributed systems; hence, we will discuss them in detail in Part III of this book.
- *Timing failures*: These occur when a temporal property of the system is violated—for example, when a clock on a computer exhibits a value that is unacceptably far from the values of other clocks, or when an action is taken too soon or too late, or when a message is delayed by longer than the maximum tolerable delay for a network connection.
- *Byzantine failures*: This is a term that captures a wide variety of other faulty behaviors, including data corruption, programs that fail to follow the correct protocol, and even malicious or adversarial behaviors by programs that actively seek to force a system to violate its reliability properties.

An even more basic issue underlies all of these: the meaning of computation, and the model one assumes for communication and coordination in a distributed system. Some examples of models include these:

- *Real-world networks*: These are composed of workstations, personal computers, and other computing devices interconnected by hardware. Properties of the hardware and software components will often be known to the designer, such as speed, delay, and error frequencies for communication devices; latencies for critical software and scheduling paths; throughput for data generated by the system and data distribution patterns; speed of the computer hardware, accuracy of clocks; and so forth. This information can be of tremendous value in designing solutions to problems that might be very hard—or impossible—in a completely general sense.

  A specific issue that will emerge as being particularly important when we consider guarantees of behavior in Part III concerns the availability, or lack, of accurate temporal information. Until the late 1980s, the clocks built into workstations were notoriously inaccurate, exhibiting high drift rates that had to be overcome with software protocols for clock resynchronization. There are limits on the quality of synchronization possible in software, and this created a substantial body of research and lead to a number of competing solutions. In the early 1990s, however, the advent of satellite time sources as part of the global positioning system (GPS) changed the picture: For the price of an inexpensive radio receiver, any computer could obtain accurate temporal data, with resolution in the sub-millisecond range. However, the degree to which GPS receivers actually replace quartz-based time sources remains to be seen. Thus, real-world systems are notable (or notorious) in part for having temporal information, but of potentially low quality.

  The architectures being proposed for networks of lightweight embedded sensors may support high-quality temporal information, in contrast to more standard distributed systems, which "work around" temporal issues using software protocols. For this reason, a resurgence of interest in communication protocols that use time seems almost certain to occur in the coming decade.

- *Asynchronous computing systems*: This is a very simple theoretical model used to approximate one extreme sort of computer network. In this model, no assumptions can be made about the relative speed of the communication system, processors, and processes in the network. One message from a process p to a process q may be delivered in zero time, while the next is delayed by a million years. The asynchronous model reflects an assumption about time, but not failures: Given an asynchronous model, one can talk about protocols that tolerate message loss, protocols that overcome fail-stop failures in asynchronous networks, and so forth. The main reason for using the model is to prove properties about protocols for which one makes as few assumptions as possible. The model is very clean and simple, and it lets us focus on fundamental properties of systems without cluttering up the analysis by including a great number of practical considerations. If a problem can be solved in this model, it can be solved at least as well in a more realistic one. On the other hand, the converse may not be true: We may be able to do things in realistic systems by making use of features not available in the asynchronous model, and in this way may be able to solve problems in real systems that are impossible in ones that use the asynchronous model.

- *Synchronous computing systems*: Like the asynchronous systems, these represent an extreme end of the spectrum. In the synchronous systems, there is a very strong concept of time that all processes in the system share. One common formulation of the model can be thought of as having a system wide gong that sounds periodically; when the processes in the system hear the gong, they run one round of a protocol, reading messages from one another, sending messages that will be delivered in the next round, and so forth. And these messages *always* are delivered to the application by the start of the next round, or not at all.

  Normally, the synchronous model also assumes bounds on communication latency between processes, clock skew and precision, and other properties of the environment. As in the case of an asynchronous model, the synchronous one takes an extreme point of view because this simplifies reasoning about certain types of protocols. Real-world systems are not synchronous—it is impossible to build a system in which actions are perfectly coordinated as this model assumes. However, if one proves the impossibility of solving some problem in the synchronous model, or proves that some problem requires at least a certain number of messages in this model, one has established a sort of lower bound. In a real-world system, things can only get worse, because we are limited to weaker assumptions. This makes the synchronous model a valuable tool for understanding how hard it will be to solve certain problems.

- *Parallel-shared memory systems*: An important family of systems is based on multiple processors that share memory. Unlike for a network, where communication is by message passing, in these systems communication is by reading and writing shared memory locations. Clearly, the shared memory model can be emulated using message passing, and can be used to implement message communication. Nonetheless, because there are important examples of real computers that implement this model, there is considerable theoretical interest in the model per-se. Unfortunately, although this model is very rich and a great deal is known about it, it would be beyond the scope of this book to attempt to treat the model in any detail.

1.2 Components of a Reliable Distributed Computing System

Reliable distributed computing systems are assembled from basic building blocks. In the simplest terms, these are just processes and messages, and if our interest was purely theoretical, it might be reasonable to stop at that. On the other hand, if we wish to apply theoretical results in practical systems, we will need to work from a fairly detailed understanding of how practical systems actually work. In some ways, this is unfortunate, because real systems often include mechanisms that are deficient in ways that seem simple to fix, or inconsistent with one another, but have such a long history (or are so deeply embedded into standards) that there may be no way to improve on the behavior in question. Yet, if we want to actually build reliable distributed systems, it is unrealistic to insist that we will only do so in idealized environments that support some form of theoretically motivated structure. The real world is heavily committed to standards, and the task of translating our theoretical insights into practical tools that can interplay with these standards is probably the most important challenge faced by the computer systems engineer.

It is common to think of a distributed system as operating over a layered set of network services (see Table 1.1). It should be stated at the outset that the lower layers of this hierarchy make far more sense than the upper ones, and when people talk about ISO compatibility or the ISO layering, they almost always have layers below the "session" in mind, not the session layer or those above it. Unfortunately, for decades, government procurement offices didn't understand this and often insisted on ISO "compatibility." Thankfully, most such offices have finally given up on that goal and accepted that pure ISO compatibility is meaningless because the upper layers of the hierarchy don't make a great deal of sense.

Table 1.1. OSI Protocol Layers

Application	The program using the communication connection
Presentation	Software to encode application data into messages and to decode on reception
Session	The logic associated with guaranteeing end-to-end properties such as reliability
Transport	Software concerned with fragmenting big messages into small packets
Network	Routing functionality, usually limited to small- or fixed-size packets
Data Link	The protocol used to send and receive packets
Physical	The protocol used to represent packets on the wire

Each layer corresponds to a software abstraction or hardware feature, and may be implemented in the application program itself, in a library of procedures to which the program is linked, in the operating system, or even in the hardware of the communication device. As an example, here is the layering of the International Organization for Standardization (ISO) Open Systems Interconnection (OSI) protocol model (see Comer, Comer and Stevens [1991, 1993], Coulouris et al., Tanenbaum):

- *Application*: This is the application program itself, up to the points at which it performs communication operations.
- *Presentation*: This is the software associated with placing data into messages in a format that can be interpreted by the destination process(es) to which the message will be sent and for extracting data from messages in the destination process.
- *Session*: This is the software associated with maintaining connections between pairs or sets of processes. A session may have reliability properties and may require some form of initialization or setup, depending on the specific setting with which the user is working. In the OSI model, the session software implements any reliability properties, and lower layers of the hierarchy are permitted to be unreliable—for example, by losing messages.

- *Transport*: The transport layer is responsible for breaking large messages into smaller packets that respect size limits imposed by the network communication hardware. On the incoming side, the transport layer reassembles these packets into messages, discarding packets that are identified as duplicates, or messages for which some constituent packets were lost in transmission.
- *Network*: This is the layer of software concerned with routing and low-level flow control on networks composed of multiple physical segments interconnected by what are called bridges and gateways.
- *Data link*: The data-link layer is normally part of the hardware that implements a communication device. This layer is responsible for sending and receiving packets, recognizing packets destined for the local machine and copying them in, discarding corrupted packets, and other interface-level aspects of communication.
- *Physical*: The physical layer is concerned with representation of packets on the wire—for example, the hardware technology for transmitting individual bits and the protocol for gaining access to the wire if multiple computers share it.

It is useful to distinguish the types of guarantees provided by the various layers: *end-to-end* guarantees in the case of the session, presentation, and application layers and *point-to-point* guarantees for layers below these. The distinction is important in complex networks where a message may need to traverse many links to reach its destination. In such settings, a point-to-point property is one that holds only on a per-hop basis—for example, the data-link protocol is concerned with a single hop taken by the message, but not with its overall route or the guarantees that the application may expect from the communication link itself. The session, presentation, and application layers, in contrast, impose a more complex logical abstraction on the underlying network, with properties that hold between the end points of a communication link that may physically extend over a complex substructure. In Part III of this book we will discuss increasingly elaborate end-to-end properties, until we finally extend these properties into a completely encompassing distributed communication abstraction that embraces the distributed system as a whole and provides consistent behavior and guarantees throughout. And, just as the OSI layering builds its end-to-end abstractions over point-to-point ones, we will need to build these more sophisticated abstractions over what are ultimately point-to-point properties.

As seen in Figure 1.1, each layer is logically composed of transmission logic and the corresponding reception logic. In practice, this often corresponds closely to the implementation of the architecture—for example, most session protocols operate by imposing a multiple session abstraction over a shared (or multiplexed) link-level connection. The packets generated by the various higher-level session protocols can be thought of as merging into a single stream of packets that are treated by the IP link level as a single customer for its services.

One should not assume that the implementation of layered protocol architecture involves some sort of separate module for each layer. Indeed, one reason that existing systems deviate from the ISO layering is that a strict ISO-based protocol stack would be quite

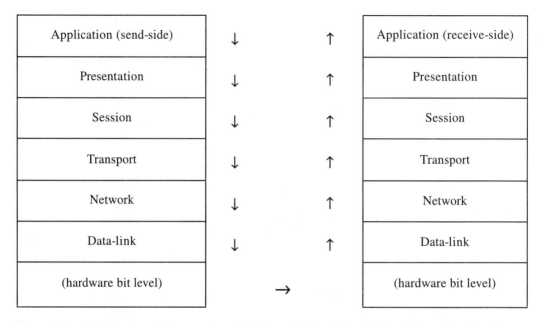

Figure 1.1.   Data flow in an OSI protocol stack. Each sending layer is invoked by the layer above it and passes data off to the layer below it, and conversely on the receive-side. In a logical sense, however, each layer interacts with its peer on the remote side of the connection—for example, the send-side session layer may add a header to a message that the receive-side session layer strips off.

inefficient in the context of a modern operating system, where code-reuse is important and mechanisms such as IP tunneling may want to reuse the ISO stack "underneath" what is conceptually a second instance of the stack. Conversely, to maximize performance, the functionality of a layered architecture is often compressed into a single piece of software, and in some cases layers may be completely bypassed for types of messages where the layer would take no action—for example, if a message is very small, the OSI transport layer wouldn't need to fragment it into multiple packets, and one could imagine a specialized implementation of the OSI stack that omits the transport layer. Indeed, the pros and cons of layered protocol architecture have become a major topic of debate in recent years (see Abbott and Peterson, Braun and Diot, Clark and Tennenhouse, Karamcheti and Chien, Kay and Pasquale).

Although the OSI layering is probably the best known such architecture, layered communication software is pervasive, and there are many other examples of layered architectures and layered software systems. Later in this book we will see additional senses in which the OSI layering is outdated, because it doesn't directly address multiparticipant communication sessions and doesn't match very well with some new types of communication hardware, such as asynchronous transfer mode (ATM) switching systems. In discussing this point we will see that more appropriate layered architectures can be constructed, although they don't match the OSI layering very closely. Thus, one can think of layering as a methodology matched to the particular layers of the OSI hierarchy. The former perspective is a popular one that is only gaining importance with the introduction of object-oriented distributed computing environments, which have a natural form of layering associated with object classes and subclasses. The latter form of layering has probably become hopelessly incompatible with standard practice by the time of this writing, although many companies and governments continue to require that products comply with it.

It can be argued that layered communication architecture is primarily valuable as a *descriptive abstraction*—a model that captures the essential functionality of a real communication system but doesn't need to accurately reflect its implementation. The idea of abstracting the behavior of a distributed system in order to concisely describe it or to reason about it is a very important one. However, if the abstraction doesn't accurately correspond to the implementation, this also creates a number of problems for the system designer, who now has the obligation to develop a specification and correctness proof for the abstraction; to implement, verify, and test the corresponding software; and to undertake an additional analysis that confirms that the abstraction accurately models the implementation.

It is easy to see how this process can break down—for example, it is nearly inevitable that changes to the implementation will have to be made long after a system has been deployed. If the development process is really this complex, it is likely that the analysis of overall correctness will not be repeated for every such change. Thus, from the perspective of a user, abstractions can be a two-edged sword. They offer appealing and often simplified ways to deal with a complex system, but they can also be simplistic or even incorrect. And this bears strongly on the overall theme of reliability. To some degree, the very process of cleaning up a component of a system in order to describe it concisely can compromise the reliability of a more complex system in which that component is used.

Throughout the remainder of this book, we will often have recourse to models and abstractions, in much more complex situations than the OSI layering. This will assist us in reasoning about and comparing protocols, and in proving properties of complex distributed systems. At the same time, however, we need to keep in mind that this whole approach demands a sort of meta-approach, namely a higher level of abstraction at which we can question the methodology itself, asking if the techniques by which we create reliable systems are themselves a possible source of unreliability. When this proves to be the case, we need to take the next step as well, asking what sorts of systematic remedies can be used to fight these types of reliability problems.

Can well structured distributed computing systems be built that can tolerate the failures of their own components, or guarantee other kinds of assurance properties? In layerings such as OSI, this issue is not really addressed, which is one of the reasons that the OSI layering won't work well for our purposes. However, the question is among the most important ones that will need to be resolved if we want to claim that we have arrived at a workable methodology for engineering reliable distributed computing systems. A methodology, then, must address descriptive and structural issues, as well as practical ones such as the protocols used to overcome a specific type of failure or to coordinate a specific type of interaction.

1.2.1 Communication Technology

The most basic communication technology in any distributed system is the hardware support for message passing. Although there are some types of networks that offer special properties, most modern networks are designed to transmit data in *packets* with some fixed, but small, maximum size. Each packet consists of a *header*, which is a data structure containing information about the packet—its destination, route, and so forth. It contains a *body*, which are the bytes that make up the content of the packet. And it may contain a *trailer*, which is a second data structure that is physically transmitted after the header and body and would normally consist of a checksum for the packet that the hardware computes and appends to it as part of the process of transmitting the packet.

When a user's message is transmitted over a network, the packets actually sent on the wire include headers and trailers, and may have a fixed maximum size. Large messages are sent as multiple packets. For example, Figure 1.2 illustrates a message that has been fragmented into three packets, each containing a header and some part of the data from the original message. Not all fragmentation schemes include trailers, and in the figure no trailer is shown.

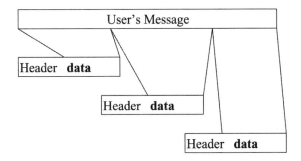

Figure 1.2. Large messages are fragmented for transmission.

Modern communication hardware often permits large numbers of computers to share a single communication fabric. For this reason, it is necessary to specify the address to which a message should be transmitted. The hardware used for communication will therefore normally support some form of *addressing capability*, by which the destination of a message can be identified. More important to most software developers, however, are addresses supported by the transport services available on most operating systems. These *logical addresses* are a representation of location within the network, and are used to route packets to their destinations. Each time a packet makes a "hop" over a communication link, the sending computer is expected to copy the hardware address of the next machine in the path into the outgoing packet. Within this book, we assume that each computer has a logical address, but will have little to say about hardware addresses.

Readers familiar with modern networking tools will be aware that the address assigned to a computer can change over time (particularly when the DHCP protocol is used to dynamically assign them), that addresses may not be unique (indeed, because modern firewalls and network address translators often "map" internal addresses used within a LAN to external ones visible outside in a many-to-one manner, reuse of addresses is common), and that there are even multiple address standards (IPv4 being the most common, with IPv6

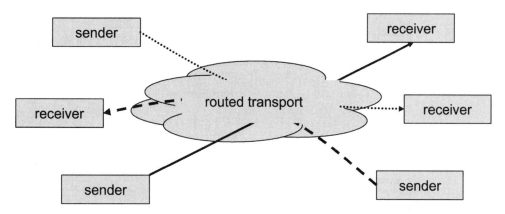

Figure 1.3. The routing functionality of a modern transport protocol conceals the network topology from the application designer.

promoted by some vendors as a next step). For our purposes in this book, we'll set all of these issues to the side, and similarly we'll leave routing protocols and the design of high speed overlay networks as topics for some other treatment.

On the other hand, there are two addressing features that have important implications for higher-level communication software. These are the ability of the software (and often, the underlying network hardware) to *broadcast* and *multicast* messages. A broadcast is a way of sending a message so that it will be delivered to all computers that it reaches. This may not be all the computers in a network, because of the various factors that can cause a receive omission failure to occur, but, for many purposes, absolute reliability is not required. To send a hardware broadcast, an application program generally places a special logical address in an outgoing message that the operating system maps to the appropriate hardware address. The message will only reach those machines connected to the hardware communication device on which the transmission occurs, so the use of this feature requires some knowledge of network communication topology.

A multicast is a form of broadcast that communicates to a subset of the computers that are attached to a communication network. To use a multicast, one normally starts by creating a new multicast group address and installing it into the hardware interfaces associated with a communication device. Multicast messages are then sent much as a broadcast would be, but are only accepted, at the hardware level, at those interfaces that have been instructed to install the group address to which the message is destined. Many network routing devices and protocols watch for multicast packets and will forward them automatically, but this is rarely attempted for broadcast packets.

Chapter 2 discusses some of the most common forms of communication hardware in detail.

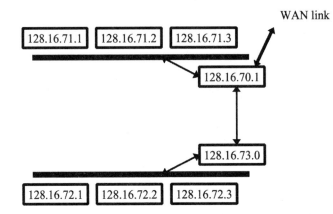

Figure 1.4. A typical network may have several interconnected sub networks and a "wide area" link to the Internet. Here, each computer is represented by its IP address; the various arrows and heavy lines represent communication devices – Ethernets, other types of point-to-point connections, and a wide area or "WAN" connection. Although one can design applications that take advantage of the unique characteristics of a specific communications technology, such as a wireless link, it is more common to ignore the structure and routing used within a network and simply treat all the machines within it as being capable of communication with all others, albeit at varying speeds, with varied reliability properties, and perhaps subject to firewalls and network address translation constraints.

1.2.2 Basic Transport and Network Services

The layer of software that runs over the communications layer is the one most distributed systems programmers deal with. This layer hides the properties of the communication hardware from the programmer (see Figure 1.3). It provides the ability to send and receive messages that may be much larger than the ones supported by the underlying hardware (although there is normally still a limit, so that the amount of operating system buffering space needed for transport can be estimated and controlled). The transport layer also implements logical addressing capabilities by which every computer in a complex network can be assigned a unique address, and can send and receive messages from every other computer.

Although many transport layers have been proposed, almost all vendors have adopted one set of standards. This standard defines the so-called "Internet Protocol" or IP protocol suite, and it originated in a research network called the ARPANET that was developed by the U.S. government in the late 1970s (see Comer, Coulouris et al., Tanenbaum). A competing standard was introduced by the ISO organization in association with the OSI layering cited earlier, but has not gained the sort of ubiquitous acceptance of the IP protocol suite. There are also additional proprietary standards that are widely used by individual vendors or industry groups, but rarely seen outside their community—for example, most PC networks support a protocol called NetBIOS, but this protocol is not common in any other type of computing environment.

All of this is controlled using *routing tables*, as shown in Table 1.2. A routing table is a data structure local to each computer in a network—each computer has one, but the contents will generally not be identical from machine to machine. Routing mechanisms differ for wired and wireless networks, and routing for a new class of "ad hoc" wireless networks is a topic of active research, although beyond our scope here. Generally, a routing table is indexed by the logical address of a destination computer, and entries contain the hardware device on which messages should be transmitted (the next hop to take). Distributed protocols for dynamically maintaining routing tables have been studied for many years and seek to optimize performance, while at the same time attempting to spread the load evenly and routing around failures or congested nodes. In local area networks, static routing tables are probably more common; dynamic routing tables dominate in wide-area settings. Chapter 3 discusses some of the most common transport services in more detail.

1.2.3 Reliable Transport Software and Communication Support

A limitation of the basic message passing services discussed in Section 1.2.2 is that they operate at the level of individual messages and provide no guarantees of reliability. Messages can be lost for many reasons, including link failures, failures of intermediate machines on a complex multi-hop route, noise that causes corruption of the data in a packet, lack of buffering space (the most common cause), and so forth. For this reason, it is common to layer a reliability protocol over the message-passing layer of a distributed communication architecture. The result is called a *reliable communication channel*. This layer of software is the one that the OSI stack calls the session layer, and it corresponds to the TCP protocol of the Internet. UNIX and Linux programmers may be more familiar with the concept from their use of pipes and streams (see Ritchie).

The protocol implementing a reliable communication channel will typically guarantee that lost messages will be retransmitted and the out-of-order messages will be re-sequenced and delivered in the order sent. Flow control and mechanisms that choke back the sender when data volume becomes excessive are also common in protocols for reliable transport (see Jacobson [1988]). Just as the lower layers can support one-to-one, broadcast, and multicast communication, these forms of destination addressing are also potentially interesting

Table 1.2. A sample routing table, such as might be used by computer 128.16.73.0 in Figure 1.4

Destination	Route Via	Forwarded By	Estimated Distance
128.16.72. *	Outgoing link 1	(direct)	1 hop
128.16.71. *	Outgoing link 2	128.16.70.1	2 hops
128.16.70.1	Outgoing link 2	(direct)	1 hop
..*.* *	Outgoing link 2	128.16.70.1	(infinite)

in reliable transport layers. Moreover, some systems go further and introduce additional reliability properties at this level, such as authentication (a trusted mechanism for verifying the identity of the processes at the ends of a communication connection), data integrity checking (mechanisms for confirming that data has not been corrupted since it was sent), or other forms of security (such as trusted mechanisms for concealing the data transmitted over a channel from processes other than the intended destinations).

1.2.4 Middleware: Software Tools, Utilities, and Programming Languages

The most interesting issues that we will consider in this book are those relating to programming environments and tools that live in the middle, between the application program and the communication infrastructure for basic message passing and support for reliable channels.

Examples of important middleware services include the naming service, resource discovery services, the file system, the time service, and the security key services used for authentication in distributed systems. We will be looking at all of these in more detail later, but we review them briefly here for clarity.

A naming service is a collection of user-accessible directories that map from application names (or other selection criteria) to network addresses of computers or programs. Name services can play many roles in a distributed system, and they represent an area of intense research interest and rapid evolution. When we discuss naming, we'll see that the whole question of what a name represents is itself subject to considerable debate, and raises important questions about concepts of abstraction and services in distributed computing environments. Reliability in a name service involves issues such as trust—can one trust the name service to truthfully map a name to the correct network address? How can one know that the object at the end of an address is the same one that the name service was talking about? These are fascinating issues, and we will discuss them in detail later in the book (see, for example, Sections 6.7 and 10.5).

A related topic concerns resource discovery. In large networks there is more and more interest in supporting self-configuration and self-repair mechanisms. For example, one would wish that a universal controller (for VCRs, televisions, etc) could automatically discover the media devices in a room, or that a computer might automatically discover printers in the vicinity. Some programming environments, such as the JINI environment for Java programmers, provide a form of ICQ ("I seek you") functionality, although these are not standard in other kinds of Internet environments. As we move to a world with larger and larger numbers of computers, new kinds of small mobile devices, and intelligence embedded into the environment, this type of resource discovery will become an important problem and it seems likely that standards will rapidly emerge. Notice that discovery differs from naming: discovery is the problem of finding the resources matching some criteria in the area, hence of generating a list of names. Naming, on the other hand, is concerned with rules for how names are assigned to devices, and for mapping device names to addresses.

From the outset, though, the reader may want to consider that if an intruder breaks into a system and is able to manipulate the mapping of names to network addresses, it will be possible to interpose all sorts of snooping software components in the path of communication from an application to the services it is using over the network. Such attacks are now common on the Internet and reflect a fundamental issue, which is that most network reliability technologies tend to trust the lowest-level mechanisms that map from names to addresses and that route messages to the correct host when given a destination address.

A time service is a mechanism for keeping the clocks on a set of computers closely synchronized and close to real time. Time services work to overcome the inaccuracy of inexpensive clocks used on many types of computers, and they are important in applications that either coordinate actions using real time or that make use of time for other purposes, such as to limit the lifetime of a cryptographic key or to timestamp files when they are updated. Much can be said about time in a distributed system, and we will spend a considerable portion of this book on issues that revolve around the whole concept of before and after and it's relation to intuitive concepts of time in the real world. Clearly, the reliability of a time service will have important implications for the reliability of applications that make use of time, so time services and associated reliability properties will prove to be important in many parts of this book.

Authentication services are, perhaps surprisingly, a new technology that is lacking in most distributed computing environments. These services provide trustworthy mechanisms for determining who sent a message, for making sure that the message can only be read by the intended destination, and for restricting access to private data so that only authorized access can occur. Most modern computing systems evolved from a period when access control was informal and based on a core principle of trust among users. One of the really serious implications is that distributed systems that want to superimpose a security or protection architecture on a heterogeneous environment must overcome a pervasive tendency to accept requests without questioning them, to believe the user-Id information included in messages without validating it, and to route messages wherever they may wish to go.

If banks worked this way, one could walk up to a teller in a bank and pass that person a piece of paper requesting a list of individuals that have accounts in the branch. Upon studying the response and learning that W. Gates is listed, one could then fill out an account balance request in the name of W. Gates, asking how much money is in that account. And, after this, one could withdraw some of that money, up to the bank's policy limits. At no stage would one be challenged: The identification on the various slips of paper would be trusted for each operation. Such a world model may seem strangely trusting, but it is the model from which modern distributed computing systems emerged.

1.2.5 Distributed Computing Environments

An important topic around which much of this book is oriented concerns the development of general purpose tools from which specialized distributed systems can be constructed. Such tools can take many forms and can be purely conceptual—for example, a methodology or theory that offers useful insight into the best way to solve a problem or that can help the developer confirm that a proposed solution will have a desired property. A tool can offer practical help at a very low level—for example, by eliminating the relatively mechanical steps required to encode the arguments for a remote procedure call into a message to the server that will perform the action. A tool can embody complex higher-level behavior, such as a protocol for performing some action or overcoming some class of errors. Tools can even go beyond this, taking the next step by offering mechanisms to control and manage software built using other tools.

It has become popular to talk about distributed systems that support *distributed operating environments*—well-integrated collections of tools that can be used in conjunction with one another to carry out potentially complex distributed programming tasks. Examples of the current generation of distributed programming environments include Microsoft's .NET technology, the Java Enterprise Edition (J2EE), Sun's JINI system for mobile computing and CORBA. Older environments still in wide use include the Open Network Computing (ONC) environment of Sun Microsystems, the Distributed Computing Environment (DCE) of the Open Software Foundation, and this is just a partial list. Some environments are especially popular for users of specific languages—for example, the Java community tends to favor J2EE, and the C# community (a language almost identical to Java) is more familiar with .NET. C++ programmers tend to work with CORBA-compliant programming tools. Layered over these environments one sometimes finds middleware tools that extend the basic environment with additional features. Examples that will be discussed in this text include the Isis and Spread Toolkits—the former was developed by my colleagues and me and will be discussed in Chapter 21, while the latter is a more modern system developed at John Hopkins University by Yair Amir, but with similar features. (This is anything but a complete list!)

Distributed systems architectures undertake to step even beyond the concept of a distributed computing environment. An architecture is a general set of design principles and implementation standards by which a collection of compliant systems can be developed. In principle, multiple systems that implement the same architecture will interoperate, so that if vendors implement competing solutions, the resulting software can still be combined into a single system with components that might even be able to communicate and cooperate with one another. Despite the emergence of .NET and J2EE, which are more commercially important at the time of this writing, the Common Request Broker, or CORBA, is probably still the best-known distributed computing architecture. CORBA is useful for building systems using an object-oriented approach in which the systems are developed as modules that cooperate. Thus, CORBA is an architecture, and the various CORBA-based products that comply with the architecture are distributed computing environments. .NET and J2EE are CORBA's younger siblings; both inherit a great many features directly from CORBA, while also supporting very powerful mechanisms for building applications that access databases— a specialization lacking in CORBA until fairly recently, when that architecture began to lose ground to these new upstarts.

Looking to the future, many analysts are now claiming that the most important architecture of all will be the new Web Services standards, aimed at promoting direct computer-to-computer interactions by standardizing all aspects of naming, invocation, making sense of data, and so forth. While these predictions (much like predictions of the "vintage of the century") need to be viewed with skepticism, there is no question that Web Services are both extremely ambitious and extremely interoperable—designers promise that these standards will, for the first time, let almost anything talk to almost anything else. This is just a first step: If you speak French and I speak English, I may be able to talk to you, but you won't necessarily understand me. Similarly, Web Services will need to be supported by standards for, say, communicating with a pharmacy inventory system, or requesting a quote on a batch of machine parts. Nonetheless, such standards can certainly be defined in many settings. Vendors supporting .NET and J2EE tout the ease of building Web Services systems when using their products, and a great many vendors have announced plans to support this architecture. On the other hand, the architecture is ill-suited for some purposes: Web Services have a confused notion of reliability and will definitely not be appropriate for building very high availability systems (at least for the first few years), or for supporting applications like very large-scale information monitoring systems, or large-scale sensor architectures. Indeed, it may be best to think of Web Services (for the time being) as the likely winner in the battle for architectures by which a client connects to a single database at a time, although perhaps as part of a longer series of operations involving transactions on multiple databases (e.g., to purchase a plane ticket, then reserve a hotel room, then reserve a car, etc). For these sorts of pipelined, relatively asynchronous applications, Web Services seem like an outstanding development. Were one focused on the development of a new military platform aimed at integrating all the computer-controlled devices on a battlefield, Web Services would seem much less appropriate for the need.

1.2.6 End-User Applications

One might expect that the end of the line for a layered distributed system architecture would be the application level, but this is not necessarily the case. A distributed application might also be some sort of operating system service built over the communication tools that we have been discussing—for example, the distributed file system is an application in the sense of the OSI layering, but the user of a computing system might think of the file system as an operating system service over which applications can be defined and executed. Within the OSI layering, then, an application is any freestanding solution to a well-defined problem that presents something other than a point-to-point communication abstraction to its users. The distributed file system is just one example among many. Others include message bus technologies, distributed database systems, electronic mail, network bulletin boards, and the Web. In the near future, computer-supported collaborative work systems, sensor networks, and multimedia digital library systems are likely to emerge as further examples in this area.

An intentional limitation of a layering such as the OSI hierarchy is that it doesn't really distinguish these sorts of applications, which provide services to higher-level distributed applications, from what might be called end-user solutions—namely, programs that operate over the communication layer to directly implement commands for a human being. One would like to believe that there is much more structure to a distributed air traffic control system than to a file transfer program, yet the OSI hierarchy views both as examples of applications. We lack a good classification system for the various types of distributed applications.

In fact, even complex distributed applications may merely be components of even larger-scale distributed systems—one can easily imagine a distributed system that uses a distributed computing toolkit to integrate an application that exploits distributed files with one that stores information into a distributed database. In an air traffic control environment, availability may be so critical that one is compelled to run multiple copies of the software concurrently, with one version backing up the other. Here, the entire air traffic control system is at one level a complex distributed application in its own right, but, at a different meta level, is just a component of an over-arching reliability structure visible on a scale of hundreds of computers located within multiple air traffic centers.

These observations point to the need for further research on architectures for distributed computing, particularly in areas relevant to high assurance. With better architectural tools we could reason more effectively about large, complex systems such as the ones just mentioned. Moreover, architectural standards would encourage vendors to offer tools in support of the model. Ten years ago, when the earlier book was written, it would have seemed premature to argue that we were ready to tackle this task. Today, though, the maturity of the field has reached a level at which both the awareness of the problem is broader, and the options available for solving the problem are better understood. It would be a great shame if the community developing Web Services architectures misses this unique chance to really tackle this pressing need. As this revision was being prepared, there were many reasons to feel encouraged—notably, a whole series of Web Services "special interest groups" focused on these areas. However, a discussion is one thing, and a widely adopted standard is quite another. Those of us looking for mature standards backed by a variety of competing tools and products will need to watch, wait, and hope that these efforts are successes.

1.3 Critical Dependencies

One of the major challenges to building reliable distributed systems is that computer networks have evolved to have a great many dependencies on a variety of technologies. Some of the major ones are identified in Figure 1.5; however the set is growing steadily and this figure is not necessarily complete. In fact it deliberately omits all sorts of components associated with network routing, dynamic allocation of IP addresses, and mapping host names to IP addresses in settings with firewalls or network address translators. When an organization builds a "mission-critical" application, that application may add new servers and critical components not shown in the figure. Also, the figure does not treat dependencies on hardware components of the distributed infrastructure, such as the communication network itself, power supply, or hardware routers. Indeed, the telecommunication infrastructure

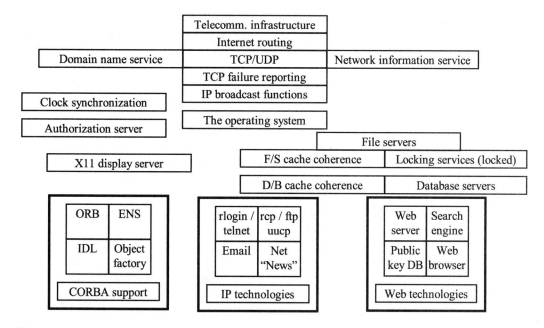

Figure 1.5. Technologies on which a distributed application may depend in order to provide correct, reliable behavior. The figure is organized so that dependencies are roughly from top to bottom (the lower technologies being dependent upon the upper ones), although a detailed dependency graph would be quite complex. Failures in any of these technologies can result in visible application-level errors, inconsistency, security violations, denial of service, or other problems. These technologies are also interdependent in complex and often unexpected ways—for example, some types of UNIX and Linux workstations will hang (freeze) if the NIS (network information service) server becomes unavailable, even if there are duplicate NIS servers that remain operational. Moreover, such problems can impact an application that has been running normally for an extended period and is not making any explicit new use of the server in question.

underlying a typical network application is itself a complex network with many of the same dependencies, together with additional ones such as the databases used to resolve mobile telephone numbers or to correctly account for use of network communication lines. One can easily imagine that a more complete figure might cover a wall, showing level upon level of complexity and interdependency.

Of course, this is just the sort of concern that gave rise to such panic about the year 2000 problem, and as we saw at that time, dependency isn't always the same as vulnerability. Many services are fairly reliable, and one can plan around potential outages of such critical services as the network information service. The Internet is already quite loosely coupled in this sense. A key issue is to understand the technology dependencies that can impact reliability issues for a specific application and to program solutions into the network to detect and work around potential outages. In this book we will be studying technical options for taking such steps. The emergence of integrated environments for reliable distributed computing will, however, require a substantial effort from the vendors offering the component technologies:

An approach in which reliability is left to the application inevitably overlooks the problems that can be caused when such applications are forced to depend upon technologies that are themselves unreliable for reasons beyond the control of the developer.

1.4 Next Steps

While distributed systems are certainly layered, Figure 1.5 makes it clear that one should question the adequacy of any simple layering model for describing reliable distributed systems. We noted, for example, that many governments tried to mandate the use of the ISO layering for description of distributed software, only to discover that this is just not feasible. Moreover, there are important reliability technologies that require structures inexpressible in this layering, and it is unlikely that those governments intended to preclude the use of reliable technologies. More broadly, the types of complex layerings that can result when tools are used to support applications that are in turn tools for still higher-level applications are not amenable to any simple description of this nature. Does this mean that users should refuse the resulting complex software structures, because they cannot be described in terms of the standard? Should they accept the perspective that software should be used but not described, because the description methodologies seem to have lagged behind the state of the art? Or should governments insist on new standards each time a new type of system finds it useful to circumvent the standard?

Questions such as these may seem narrow and almost pointless, yet they point to a deep problem. Certainly, if we are unable to even describe complex distributed systems in a uniform way, it will be very difficult to develop a methodology within which one can reason about them and prove that they respect desired properties. On the other hand, if a standard proves unwieldy and constraining, it will eventually become difficult for systems to adhere to it.

Perhaps for these reasons, there has been little recent work on layering in the precise sense of the OSI hierarchy: Most researchers view this as an unpromising direction. Instead, the concepts of structure and hierarchy seen in the OSI protocol have reemerged in much more general and flexible ways: the object-class hierarchies supported by technologies in the CORBA framework, the layered protocol stacks supported in operating systems like UNIX and Linux or the x-Kernel, or in systems such as Isis, Spread and Horus. We'll be reading about these uses of hierarchy later in the book, and the OSI hierarchy remains popular as a simple but widely understood framework within which to discuss protocols.

Nonetheless, particularly given the energy being expended on Web Service architectures, it may be time to rethink architectures and layering. If we can arrive at a natural layering to play the roles of the OSI architecture but without the constraints of its simplistic, narrow structure, doing so would open the door to wider support for high assurance computing techniques and tools. An architecture can serve as a roadmap both for technology developers and for end users. The lack of a suitable architecture is thus a serious problem for all of us interested in highly assured computing systems. Research that might overcome this limitation would have a tremendous, positive, impact.

1.5 Related Reading

General discussion of network architectures and the OSI hierarchy: (see Architecture Projects Management Limited [1989, April 1991, November 1991], Comer, Comer and Stevens [1991, 1993], Coulouris et al., Cristian and Delancy, Tanenbaum, XTP Forum).

Pros and cons of layered architectures: (see Abbott and Peterson, Braun and Diot, Clark and Tennenhouse, Karamcheti and Chien, Kay and Pasquale, Ousterhout [1990], van Renesse et al. [1988, 1989]).

Reliable stream communication: (see Comer, Comer and Stevens [1991, 1993], Coulouris et al., Jacobson [1988], Ritchie, Tanenbaum).

Failure models and classifications: (see Chandra and Toueg [1991], Chandra et al. [1992], Cristian [February 1991], Christian and Delancy, Fischer et al. [April 1985], Gray and Reuter, Lamport [1978, 1984], Marzullo [1990], Sabel and Marzullo, Skeen [June 1982], Srikanth and Toueg).

2

Basic Communication Services

2.1 Communication Standards

A communication standard is a collection of specifications governing the types of messages that can be sent in a system, the formats of message headers and trailers, the encoding rules for placing data into messages, and the rules governing format and use of source and destination addresses. In addition to this, a standard will normally specify a number of protocols that a provider should implement.

Examples of communication standards that are used widely, although not universally, are:

- *The Internet protocols*: These protocols originated in work done by the Defense Department's Advanced Research Projects Agency, or DARPA, in the 1970s, and have gradually grown into a wider-scale high-performance network interconnecting millions of computers. The protocols employed in the Internet include IP, the basic packet protocol, and UDP, TCP and IP-multicast, each of which is a higher-level protocol layered over IP. With the emergence of the Web, the Internet has grown explosively since the mid-1990s.
- *SOAP (Simple Object Access Protocol)*: This protocol has been proposed as part of a set of standards associated with Web Services, the architectural framework by which computers talk to other computers much as a browser talks to a Web site. SOAP messages are encoded in XML, an entirely textual format, and hence are very verbose and rather large compared to other representations. On the other hand, the standard is supported by a tremendous range of vendors.
- *Proprietary standards*: Many vendors employ proprietary standards within their products, and it is common to document these so that customers and other vendors can build compliant applications.

But just because something is a standard doesn't mean that it will be widely accepted. For example, here are some widely cited standards that never cut the mustard commercially:

- *The Open Systems Interconnect protocols*: These protocols are similar to the Internet protocol suite, but employ standards and conventions that originated with the ISO organization. We mention them only because the European Union mandated the use of these protocols in the 1980's. They are in fact not well supported, and developers who elect to employ them are thus placed in the difficult situation of complying with a standard and yet abandoning the dominant technology suite for the entire Internet. In practice, the EU has granted so many exceptions to its requirements over the past two decades that they are effectively ignored—a cautionary tale for those who believe that simply because something is "standard," it is preferable to alternatives that have greater commercial support.
- *The Orange Book Security Standard*: Defined by the United States Department of Defense, the Orange Book defined rules for managing secure information in US military and government systems. The standard was very detailed and was actually mandatory in the United States for many years. Yet almost every system actually purchased by the military was exempted from compliance because the broader industry simply didn't accept the need for this kind of security and questioned the implicit assumptions underlying the actual technical proposal. At the time of this writing, Orange Book seems to have died.

During the 1990s, open systems—namely, systems in which computers from different vendors could run independently developed software—emerged as an important trend, gaining a majority market share on server systems; simultaneously, Microsoft's proprietary Windows operating system became dominant on desktops. The two side-by-side trends posed a dilemma for protocol developers and designers. Today, we see a mix of widely-accepted standards within the Internet as a whole and proprietary standards (such as the Microsoft file-system access protocol) used within local area networks. In many ways, one could suggest that "best of breed" solutions have dominated. For example, the Microsoft remote file access protocols are generally felt to be superior to the NFS protocols with which they initially competed. Yet there is also a significant element of serendipity. The fact is that any technology evolves over time. Windows and the open (Linux) communities have basically tracked one-another, with each imitating any successful innovations introduced by the other. In effect, market forces have proved to be far more important than the mere fact of standardization, or laws enforce within one closed market or another.

The primary driver in favor of standards has been *interoperability*. That is, computing users need ways to interconnect major applications and to create new applications that access old ones. For a long time, interoperability was primarily an issue seen in the database community, but the trend has now spread to the broader networking and distributed systems arena as well. Over the coming decade, it seems likely that the most significant innovations will emerge in part from the sudden improvements in interoperation, an idea that can be traced to the CORBA community. Interoperability was initially given somewhat reduced emphasis by the Java community, because its early focus on a "single universal language." In recent years, interoperability was championed by Microsoft in its .NET product line, and this emphasis soon motivated the J2EE community to invest more effort in the question as well. Today, one of the most important reasons for having standards is to promote interoperability.

The Web Services architecture seeks to carry out this goal, at least for the basic issues of matching a client program with the services it needs, and permitting it to invoke operations in a platform and location independent manner. For this latter purpose, the SOAP protocol is employed, giving SOAP a uniquely central role in the coming generation of distributed applications. SOAP is a layered standard: it expresses rules for encoding a request, but not for getting messages from the client to the server. In the most common layering, SOAP runs over HTTP, the standard protocol for talking to a Web site, and HTTP in turn runs over TCP, which emits IP packets.

The remainder of this chapter touches briefly on each of these components. Our treatment omits all sorts of other potentially relevant standards, and is intended more as "a taste" of the topic than as any sort of exhaustive treatment. The reader is referred to the Web sites maintained by the W3 consortium, and by vendors such as IBM or Microsoft, for details of how SOAP and HTTP behave. Details of how the IP suite is implemented can be found in Comer, Comer and Stevens (1991, 1993).

2.2 Addressing

The *addressing* tools in a distributed communication system provide unique identification for the source and destination of a message, together with ways of mapping from symbolic names for resources and services to the corresponding network address, and for obtaining the best route to use for sending messages.

Addressing is normally standardized as part of the general communication specifications for formatting data in messages, defining message headers, and communicating in a distributed environment.

Within the Internet, several address formats are available, organized into classes aimed at different styles of application. However, for practical purposes, we can think of the address space as a set of 32-bit identifiers that are handed out in accordance with various rules. Internet addresses have a standard ASCII representation, in which the bytes of the address are printed as unsigned decimal numbers in a standardized order—for example, this book was edited on host gunnlod.cs.cornell.edu, which has Internet address 128.84.218.58. This is a class B Internet address (should anyone care), with network address 42 and host ID 218.58. Network address 42 is assigned to Cornell University, as one of several class B addresses used by the University. The 218.xxx addresses designate a segment of Cornell's internal network—namely the Ethernet to which my computer is attached. The number 58 was assigned within the Computer Science Department to identify my host on this Ethernet segment.

A class D Internet address is intended for special uses: IP multicasting. These addresses are allocated for use by applications that exploit IP multicast. Participants in the application join the multicast group, and the Internet routing protocols automatically reconfigure themselves to route messages to all group members. Unfortunately, multicast is not widely deployed—some applications do use it, and some companies are willing to enable multicast for limited purposes, but it simply isn't supported in the Internet as a whole. IP multicast falls into that category of standards that seemed like a good idea at the time, but just never made it commercially—an ironic fate considering that most network routers do support IP multicast, and a tremendous amount of money has presumably been spent building those mechanisms and testing them.

The string gunnlod.cs.cornell.edu is a symbolic name for the IP address. The name consists of a machine name (gunnlod, an obscure hero of Norse mythology) and a suffix (cs.cornell.edu), designating the Computer Science Department at Cornell University, which is an educational institution (Cornell happens to be in the United States, and as a practical matter .edu is largely limited to the USA, but this is not written in stone anywhere). The suffix is registered with a distributed service called the domain name service, or DNS, which supports a simple protocol for mapping from string names to IP network addresses.

Here's the mechanism used by the DNS when it is asked to map my host name to the appropriate IP address for my machine. DNS basically forwards the request up a hierarchical tree formed of DNS servers with knowledge for larger and larger parts of the naming space: above gunnold.cs.cornell.edu is a server (perhaps the same one) responsible for cs.cornell.edu, then cornell.edu, then the entire edu namespace, and finally the whole Internet—there are a few of these "root" servers. So, perhaps you work at foosball.com and are trying to map cs.cornell.edu. Up the tree of DNS servers your request will go, until finally it reaches a server that knows something about .edu domains—namely the IP address of some *other* server that can handle cornell.edu requests. Now the request heads back down the tree. Finally, a DNS server is reached that actually knows the current IP address of gunnold.cs.cornell.edu; this one sends the result back to the DNS that made the initial request. If the application that wanted the mapping hasn't given up in boredom, we're home free.

All of this forwarding can be slow. To avoid long delays, DNS makes heavy use of caching. Thus, if some DNS element in the path already knows how to map my host name to my IP address, we can short-circuit this whole procedure. Very often, Internet activity comes in bursts. Thus, the first request to gunnold may be a little slow, but from then on, the local DNS will know the mapping and subsequent requests will be handled with essentially no delay at all. There are elaborate rules concerning how long to keep a cached record, but we don't need to get quite so detailed here.

DNS can manage several types of information, in addition to host-to-IP address mappings. For example, one kind of DNS record tells you where to find an e-mail server for a given machine. In fact, one could devote a whole chapter of a book like this to DNS and its varied capabilities, and perhaps a whole book to the kinds of programs that have been built to exploit some of the more esoteric options. However, our focus is elsewhere, and we'll just leave DNS as an example of the kind of protocol that one finds in the Internet today.

Notice, however, that there are many ways the DNS mapping mechanism can stumble. If a host gets a new IP address (and this happens all the time), a DNS cache entry may become stale. For a period of time, requests will be mapped to the old IP address, essentially preventing some systems from connecting to others—much as if you had moved, mail isn't being forwarded, and the telephone listing shows your old address. DNS itself can be slow or the network can be overloaded, and a mapping request might then time out, again leaving some applications unable to connect to others. In such cases, we perceive the Internet as being unreliable, even though the network isn't really doing anything outside of its specification. DNS, and the Internet, is a relatively robust technology, but when placed under stress, all bets are off, and this is true of much of the Internet.

The Internet address specifies a machine, but the identification of the specific application program that will process the message is also important. For this purpose, Internet addresses contain a field called the port number, which is at present a 16-bit integer. A program that wants to receive messages must bind itself to a port number on the machine to which the messages will be sent. A predefined list of port numbers is used by standard system services, and has values ranging from 0 to 1,023. Symbolic names have been assigned to many of these predefined port numbers, and a table mapping from names to port numbers is generally provided—for example, messages sent to gunnlod.cs.cornell.edu that specify port 53 will be delivered to the DNS server running on machine gunnlod. E-mail is sent using a subsystem called Simple Mail Transfer Protocol (SMTP), on port 25. Of course, if the appropriate service program isn't running, messages to a port will be silently discarded. Small port numbers are reserved for special services and are often trusted, in the sense that it is assumed that only a legitimate SMTP agent will ever be connected to port 25 on a machine. This form of trust depends upon the operating system, which decides whether or not a program should be allowed to bind itself to a requested port.

Port numbers larger than 1,024 are available for application programs. A program can request a specific port, or allow the operating system to pick one randomly. Given a port number, a program can register itself with the local Network Information Service (NIS) program, giving a symbolic name for itself and the port number on which it is listening. Or, it can send its port number to some other program—for example, by requesting a service and specifying the Internet address and port number to which replies should be transmitted.

The randomness of port selection is, perhaps unexpectedly, an important source of security in many modern protocols. These protocols are poorly protected against intruders, who could attack the application if they were able to guess the port numbers being used. By virtue of picking port numbers randomly, the protocol assumes that the barrier against attack has been raised substantially and that it need only protect against accidental delivery of packets from other sources (presumably an infrequent event, and one that is unlikely to involve packets that could be confused with the ones legitimately used by the protocol

2.1 *Internet Brownouts: Power Failures on the Data Superhighway?*

The data superhighway is experiencing serious growing pains. Growth in load has vastly exceeded the capacity of the protocols used in the Internet and World Wide Web. Issues of consistency, reliability, and availability of technologies, such as the ones that support these applications, are at the core of this book.

Beginning in late 1995, clear signs emerged that the Internet was beginning to overload. One reason is that the root servers for the DNS architecture are experiencing exponential growth in the load of DNS queries that require action by the top levels of the DNS hierarchy. A server that saw ten queries per minute in 1993 was up to 250 queries per second in early 1995, and traffic was doubling every three months. Such problems point to fundamental aspects of the Internet that were based on assumptions of a fairly small and lightly loaded user population repeatedly performing the same sorts of operations. In this small world, it makes sense to use a single hierarchical DNS structure with caching, because cache hits are possible for most data. In a network that suddenly has millions of users, and that will eventually support billions of users, such design considerations must be reconsidered: Only a completely decentralized architecture can possibly scale to support a truly universal and worldwide service.

The near-exponential growth of the network lagged in 1999 as the .com boom abruptly ended. Simultaneously the widespread use of network address translators allowed re-use of IP addresses, essentially eliminating the threat that the IP address space would soon be exhausted. Yet as this text was being revised in 2003, there were signs that rapid growth may be reemerging, fueled by cellular telephones and other small devices with network connectivity.

These problems of scale have visible but subtle impact on the Internet user: They typically cause connections to break, or alert boxes to appear on your Web browser warning you that the host possessing some resource is unavailable. There is no obvious way to recognize that the problem is not one of local overload or congestion, but in fact is an overloaded DNS server or one that has crashed at a major Internet routing point. Unfortunately, such problems have become increasingly common: The Internet is starting to experience brownouts. Indeed, the Internet became largely unavailable for many hours during one crash in September of 1995, and this was hardly an unusual event. As the data superhighway becomes increasingly critical, such brownouts represent increasingly serious threats to reliability.

Conventional wisdom has it that the Internet does not follow the laws of physics, there is no limit to how big, fast, and dense the Internet can become. As with the hardware itself, which seems outmoded almost before it reaches the market, we assume that the technology of the network is also speeding up in ways that exceed demand. But the reality of the situation is that the *software architecture* of the Internet is in some basic ways *not* scalable. Short of redesigning these protocols, the Internet won't keep up with growing demands. In some ways, it already can't.

Internet scalability problems don't imply some form of catastrophic collapse. Rather, they take the form of visible quality disruptions that prevent applications with strong "quality of service" requirements from operating smoothly. Paradoxically, this means that even as the Internet degrades from the perspective of one category of users, it may seem to be working better and better for a different category of users whose needs are less stringent. In particular, since browsing Web pages is an activity that doesn't demand particularly extreme reliability in any case, Web users may be quite happy with the status quo. Yet developers of high assurance applications would have good reason to feel frustrated, because they find that the Internet is offering higher and higher bandwidth when it works well, but that it continues to suffer from unpredictable outages and to offer no real options for applications needing steady guarantees of higher quality communications connectivity.

Here's an example of the sort of thing a developer of a mission-critical networked application might want. Suppose that the application depends on sending a megabyte of data per minute from server A to server B, and that the normal bandwidth of the Internet is more than adequate to sustain this data rate. The developer will still be forced to ask how the application can survive a transient network overload during which the bandwidth available might drop well below the desired level. A few ideas come to mind: perhaps she could make multiple connections, or perhaps even ask the network to route the data on more than one path. But as it turns out, multiple connections between identical endpoints would almost certainly route over the same paths within the Internet, hence experiencing correlated outages. And there isn't any way to obtain "path independent routes" within the Internet today. That developer, then, would encounter a dead-end.

Thus, today's Internet is alive and well, for many purposes, and yet can be a frustrating environment for those seeking to construct high assurance applications.

on the port). Later, however, we will see that such assumptions may not always be safe: Modern network hackers may be able to steal port numbers out of IP packets; indeed, this has become a serious enough problem so that many kinds of Internet control messages are encrypted (IPSec), and there have been proposals to use encryption even more extensively in IPv6, a "next generation" Internet protocol standard that may, however, never be deployed.

Finally, each network service publishes information specifying the protocol to use when communicating with it: TCP, when communicating with the UUCP service; UDP when communication with the TFTP service (a file transfer program); and so forth. Some services support multiple options, such as the domain name service.

2.3 Network Address Translation

All of the above discussion presumes that any computer can be addressed by any other. However, this is not the case. In the modern Internet, devices called "Network Address Translators" are widely employed. As the name suggests, these serve to translate from an "internal" IP address and port number used within a local area network to an external address and port number, used for routing in the wider public Internet.

Network address translators first emerged as a response to the shortage of network addresses mentioned earlier. With such a translator, it becomes possible for a user to define a private domain containing a potentially large number of computers, using an internal convention to assign IP addresses within that domain. When a machine within the private domain wishes to connect to the external network, it "punches" a new hole through the network address translation devices. More specifically, the device substitutes its own IP address and a unique port number for the IP address and port number used by the application. As responses are received, the box translates addresses and ports on the fly. This creates the ability to make connections from the inside of the private network to the outside world—but not in the reverse direction, because the address translation box will only route packets on behalf of connections it knows about, and it learns about connections only when packets first traverse it in an outward direction.

This limitation has recently been overcome by a protocol called STUN. STUN permits applications to discover one-another and form connections even when one or both are behind network address translators and hence cannot address each other directly. The protocol makes use of a trusted third party—a STUN "server," addressable on the Internet, which informs the endpoints of their "external" addresses, permitting them to tunnel through most forms of network address translation and firewall mechanisms during a brief connection-establishment period. With STUN, it is possible for most applications to exchange UDP messages (but not TCP messages), even if one or both endpoints reside behind firewalls or NATs—for such applications, anything normally possible in the absence of network address translation becomes possible again, albeit with a small set-up delay while running the STUN protocol, and with an extra obligation to send "keep alive" messages periodically (otherwise, the network address translation box will close the connection and recycle its IP address and port number pair). On the other hand, there are a small number of especially "smart" firewalls and NATs that would be able to defeat STUN. Thus until the IETF community designates STUN as a standard (which would encourage all firewall manufacturers to comply), the technology may have limited impact.

Network address translators create a complex world, in which the majority of Internet-enabled computers can't communicate directly without running STUN or a proprietary equivalent, but where the risk of running out of IP addresses is essentially eliminated. On the other hand, these devices have become ubiquitous, permitting huge numbers of home computing enthusiasts to link multiple home computers to a single Internet connection, freeing companies from the need to obtain large numbers of IP addresses in support of their large internal networks, and relieving what was fast becoming an intolerable stress on the Internet as a whole. Indeed, there is a real possibility that network address translation, in conjunction with STUN, could eliminate most of the rationale for deployment of IPv6.

An interesting historical footnote: IPv6 is a consensus standard, created by merging several proposals; we'll discuss it in the next subsection. One of these standards was authored by Paul Francis, who is thus a co-author of the IPv6 standard. But Paul is also the inventor of network address translation. Thus, the NAT story may be a rare instance of a high impact invention killed off by an even higher impact invention by the same individual! As the saying goes, if someone is going to eat your lunch, it might as well be you!

2.4   IP Tunnelling

A technique called IP tunneling creates further confusion for those who might have preferred to think of IP addresses as unique identifiers for individual computers. Basically, an IP tunnel is a piece of software that takes packets from some source, encapsulates them into other packets (perhaps fragmenting them to do so), and then ships them to a counterpart elsewhere in the network, where the packets are de-encapsulated and retransmitted in the local network. IP tunnels are often used to route packets from one local addressing region of the network, across some form of large-scale link, and then back into a remote portion of the same private network. With tunneling, machines that might not normally have been able to talk to one-another can potentially do so. Moreover, one can potentially tunnel over all sorts of technologies. For example, there are "silly" IP tunnels that can run through e-mail messages, or over instant messenger protocols. One can even tunnel using the DNS service (the packet content would be stored as the "value" field of a DNS record monitored by the remote de-encapsulation process).

IP tunneling is not necessarily a good thing. While there are good reasons to tunnel, for example when connecting disparate components of a corporate network, or routing messages to a mobile device that may change its IP address as it moves around, tunnels are also a mechanism for evading security and in some cases, evading billing policies. Indeed, there are products designed specifically to monitor communication flows in an effort to try to discover tunnels (however, encryption will defeat most such mechanisms).

2.5   Internet Protocols

This section presents the three major components of the Internet protocol suite: the IP protocol, on which the others are based, and the TCP and UDP protocols, which are the ones normally employed by applications. We also discuss some recent extensions to the IP protocol layer in support of IP multicast protocols. There has been considerable discussion of security for the IP layer, but no single proposal has gained wide acceptance as of the time of this writing, and we will say very little about this ongoing work for reasons of brevity.

2.5.1   Internet Protocol: IP layer

The lowest layer of the Internet protocol suite is a connectionless packet transmission protocol called IP. IP is responsible for unreliable transmission of variable-size packets from the sender's machine to the destination machine. Although IP actually can support fairly large packet sizes, there is normally an upper limit of 1,518 bytes. IP packets are required to conform to a fixed format consisting of a variable-length packet header and a variable-length body. The actual lengths of the header, body, and trailer are specified through length fields, which are located at fixed offsets in the header. An application that makes direct use of the IP is expected to format its packets according to this standard. However, direct use of IP is normally restricted by the operating system because of security issues raised by the prospect of applications that might exploit such a feature to mimic some standard protocol, such as the Transmission Control Protocol (TCP), doing this in a nonstandard manner that could disrupt the remote machines or create security loopholes.

Implementations of IP normally provide routing functionality, using either a static or dynamic routing architecture. The type of routing used will depend upon the complexity of the installation and its configuration of the Internet software, and this is a topic beyond the scope of this book.

In 1995, IP was enhanced to provide a security architecture, whereby packet payloads can be encrypted to prevent intruders from determining packet contents, and to provide options for signatures or other authentication data in the packet trailer.

2.5.2 Transmission Control Protocol: TCP

TCP is a name for the connection-oriented protocol within the Internet protocol suite. TCP users start by making a TCP connection, which is done by having one program set itself up to listen for and accept incoming connections, while the other program connects to it. A TCP connection guarantees that data will be delivered in the order sent, without loss or duplication, and will report an end of file if the process at either end exits or closes the channel. TCP connections are byte-stream oriented: Although the sending program can send blocks of bytes, the underlying communication model views this communication as a continuous sequence of bytes. TCP is thus permitted to lose the boundary information between messages, so that what is logically a single message may be delivered in several smaller chunks, or delivered together with fragments of a previous or subsequent message (however, always preserving the byte ordering). If very small messages are transmitted, TCP will delay them slightly to attempt to fill larger packets for efficient transmission; the user must disable this behavior if immediate transmission is desired.

Applications that involve concurrent use of a TCP connection must interlock against the possibility that multiple write operations will be done simultaneously on the same channel; if this occurs, then data from different writers can be interleaved when the channel becomes full.

2.5.3 User Datagram Protocol: UDP

UDP is a message or datagram-oriented protocol. With this protocol, the application sends messages, which are preserved in the form sent and delivered intact, or not at all, to the destination. No connection is needed and there are no guarantees that the message will get through, or that messages will be delivered in any particular order, or even that duplicates will not arise. The operating system associates a size limit on each UDP socket, typically 8 KB. Thus, an application needing to send a large message must increase this OS controlled limit, or break the message into multiple packets. Moreover, there is a 64 KB limit on the maximum possible UDP packet size.

Internally, UDP will normally fragment a message into smaller pieces, which match closely with the maximum-size packet that an Ethernet can transmit in a single hardware packet. If a UDP packet exceeds the maximum packet size, the UDP packet is sent as a series of smaller IP packets. On reception, these are reassembled into a larger packet. If any fragment is lost, the UDP packet will eventually be discarded.

The reader may wonder why this sort of two-level fragmentation scheme is used—why not simply limit UDP to 1,518 bytes, too? To understand this design, it is helpful to start with a measurement of the cost associated with a communication system call. On a typical operating system, such an operation has a minimum overhead of twenty thousand to fifty thousand instructions, regardless of the size of the data object to be transmitted. The idea, then, is to avoid repeatedly traversing long code paths within the operating system. When an 8 KB UDP packet is transmitted, the code to fragment it into smaller chunks executes deep within the operating system. This can save tens of thousands of instructions. On the other hand, no effort is made to ensure that IP packets get through, and UDP packets consume a scarce resource: kernel memory. Thus one doesn't want a UDP packet size limit to become too large, because the risk that at least one IP fragment will be lost rises (in this case the whole UDP packet has to be discarded), and because the amount of memory required would become prohibitive. While 8KB seems a bit small by modern standards, this became the accepted default size limit in the late 1980's.

One might also wonder why communication needs to be so expensive in the first place. In fact, this is a very interesting and rather current topic, particularly in light of recent work that has reduced the cost of sending a message (on some platforms) to as little as six instructions. In this approach, which is called *Active Messages* (see von Eicken et al. [1992, 1995]), the operating system is kept completely off the message path, and if one is willing to pay a slightly higher price, a similar benefit is possible even in a more standard communication architecture (see Section 7.4). Commercial operating systems products offering comparably low latency and high throughput became available in the late 1990s. However, the average operating system will certainly not catch up with the leading-edge approaches for many years. Thus, applications may have to continue to live with huge and in fact unnecessary overheads for the time being.

2.5.4 Multicast Protocol

IP multicast was a relatively late addition to the Internet protocol suite (see Deering [1988, 1989], Deering and Cheriton). With IP multicast, UDP or IP messages can be transmitted to groups of destinations, as opposed to a single point-to-point destination. The approach extends the multicast capabilities of the Ethernet interface to work even in complex networks with routing and bridges between Ethernet segments.

IP multicast is a session-oriented protocol: Some work is required before communication can begin. The processes that will communicate must create an IP multicast address, which is a class D Internet address containing a multicast identifier in the lower 28 bits. These processes must also agree upon a single port number, which all will use for the communication session. As each process starts, it installs IP address into its local system, using system calls that place the IP multicast address on the Ethernet interface(s) to which the machine is connected. The routing tables used by IP, discussed in more detail below, are also updated to ensure that IP multicast packets will be forwarded to each destination and network on which group members are found.

Once this setup has been done, an IP multicast is initiated by simply sending a UDP packet with the IP multicast group address and port number in it. As this packet reaches a machine that is included in the destination list, a copy is made and delivered to local applications receiving packets on the port. If several are bound to the same port on the same machine, a copy is made for each.

Like UDP, IP multicast is an unreliable protocol: Packets can be lost, duplicated, or delivered out of order, and not all members of a group will see the same pattern of loss and delivery. Thus, although one can build reliable communication protocols over IP multicast, the protocol itself is inherently unreliable.

When used through the UDP interface, a UDP multicast facility is similar to a UDP datagram facility, in that each packet can be as long as the maximum size of UDP trans-missions, which is typically 8 KB. However, when sending an IP or UDP multicast, it is important to remember that the reliability observed may vary from destination to destination. One machine may receive a packet that others drop because of memory limitations or corruption caused by a weak signal on the communication medium, and the loss of even a single fragment of a large UDP message will cause the entire message to be dropped. Any application that uses this transport protocol should carefully instrument loss rates, because the effective performance for small messages may actually be better than for large ones due to this limitation.

When large numbers of senders simultaneously send IP multicast packets, episodes of very high loss rates are sometimes observed. Termed "broadcast storms" or "multicast storms," these arise when the capacity overwhelmed by bursts of back-to-back incoming packets. Applications that run on IP multicast must therefore limit themselves to data rates lower than the threshold at which this might occur.

2.6 Routing

Routing is the method by which a communication system computes the path by which packets will travel from source to destination. A routed packet is said to take a series of *hops*, as it passes from machine to machine. The algorithm used is generally as follows:

- An application generates a packet, or a packet is read from a network interface.
- The packet destination is checked and, if it matches with any of the addresses that the machine accepts, delivered locally (one machine can have multiple addresses—a feature that is sometimes exploited in networks with dual hardware for increased fault tolerance).
- The *hop count* of the message is incremented. If the message has a maximum hop count and would exceed it, the message is discarded. The hop count is also called the *time to live*, or TTL, in some protocols.

- For messages that do not have a local destination, or class D multicast messages, the destination is used to search the routing table. Each entry specifies an address, or a pattern covering a range of addresses. The outgoing interface and a physical next-hop address are identified for the message (or a list of them, if the message is a class D multicast). For a point-to-point message, if there are multiple possible routes, the least costly route is employed. For this purpose, each route includes an estimated cost, in hops.
- The packet is transmitted on interfaces in this list, other than the one on which the packet was received.

A number of methods have been developed for maintaining routing tables. The most common approach is to use *static routing*. In this approach, the routing table is maintained by system administrators, and is never modified while the system is active.

Dynamic routing employs a class of protocols by which machines can adjust their routing tables to benefit from load changes, route around congestion and broken links, and reconfigure to exploit links that have recovered from failures. In the most common approaches, machines periodically distribute their routing tables to nearest neighbors, or periodically broadcast their routing tables within the network as a whole. For this latter case, a special address is used, which causes the packet to be routed down every possible interface in the network; a hop-count limit prevents such a packet from bouncing endlessly.

The introduction of IP multicast has resulted in a new class of routers, which are static for most purposes, but that maintain special dynamic routing policies for use when an IP multicast group spans several segments of a routed local area network. In very large settings, this *multicast routing daemon* can take advantage of the *multicast backbone*, or *mbone* network to provide group communication or conferencing support to sets of participants working at physically remote locations. However, most use of IP multicast is limited to local area networks at the time of this writing, and wide area multicast remains a somewhat speculative research topic.

Finally, we are now seeing the emergence of a new class of routing protocols designed to support mobile devices and physically fixed devices using wireless links. These protocols must deal with rapidly changing connectivity, and some are additionally designed to support "ad hoc" networking, where a set of mobile machines cooperate to route one-another's wireless traffic. However, although the topic is a fascinating one, it lies outside the scope of this book.

2.7 End-to-End Argument

The reader may be curious about the following issue. The architecture described above permits packets to be lost at each hop in the communication subsystem. If a packet takes many hops, the probability of loss would seem likely to grow proportionately, causing the reliability of the network to drop linearly with the diameter of the network. There is an alternative approach in which error correction would be done hop by hop. Although packets could still be lost if an intermediate machine crashes, such an approach would have loss rates that are greatly reduced, at some small but fixed background cost (when we discuss the details of reliable communication protocols, we will see that the overhead need not be very high). Why, then, do most systems favor an approach that seems likely to be much less reliable?

In a classic paper, Jerry Saltzer and others took up this issue in 1984 (see Saltzer et al). This paper compared end-to-end reliability protocols, which operate only between the source and destination of a message, with hop-by-hop reliability protocols. They argued that even if reliability of a routed network is improved by the use of hop-by-hop reliability protocols, it will still not be high enough to completely overcome packet loss. Packets can still be corrupted by noise on the lines, machines can crash, and dynamic routing changes can bounce a packet around until it is discarded. Moreover, they argued, the measured average loss rates for lightly to moderately loaded networks are extremely low. True, routing exposes a packet to repeated threats, but the overall reliability of a routed network will still be very high on average, with worst-case behavior dominated by events like routing table updates and crashes that hop-by-hop error correction would not overcome. From this the authors conclude that since hop-by-hop reliability methods increase complexity and reduce performance, and must still be duplicated by end-to-end reliability mechanisms, one might as well use a simpler and faster link-level communication protocol. This is the end-to-end argument and has emerged as one of the defining principles governing modern network design.

Saltzer's paper revolves around a specific example, involving a file transfer protocol (FTP). The paper makes the point that the analysis used is in many ways tied to the example and the actual reliability properties of the communication lines in question. Moreover, Saltzer's interest was specifically in reliability of the packet transport mechanism: failure rates and ordering. These points are important because many authors have come to cite the end-to-end argument in a much more expansive way, claiming that it is an absolute argument against putting any form of property or guarantee within the communication subsystem. Later, we will be discussing protocols that *need* to place properties and guarantees into subsystems, as a way of providing system-wide properties that would not otherwise be achievable. Thus, those who accept the generalized end-to-end argument would tend to oppose the use of these sorts of protocols on philosophical (one is tended to say "religious") grounds.

A more mature view is that the end-to-end argument is one of those situations where one should accept a very general insight, but with a degree of skepticism. On the one hand, the end-to-end argument is clearly correct in situations where an analysis comparable to Saltzer's original one is possible. However, the end-to-end argument cannot be applied blindly: There are situations in which low-level properties are beneficial and genuinely reduce complexity and cost in application software, and, for these situations, a pure end-to-end approach might be inappropriate, leading to more complex applications that are error prone or, in a practical sense, impossible to construct.

In a network with high link-level loss rates, or one that is at serious risk of running out of memory unless flow control is used link to link, an end-to-end approach may result in near-total packet loss, while a scheme that corrects packet loss and does flow control at the link level could yield acceptable performance. This, then, is a case in which Saltzer's analysis could be applied as he originally formulated it, but it would lead to a different conclusion. When we look at the reliability protocols presented in Part III of this book, we will see that certain forms of consistent distributed behavior (such as is needed in a fault-tolerant coherent caching scheme) depend upon system-wide agreement, which must be standardized and integrated with low-level failure-reporting mechanisms. Omitting such a mechanism from the transmission layer merely forces the application programmer to build it as part of the application; if the programming environment is intended to be general and extensible, this may mean that one makes the mechanism part of the environment or gives up on it entirely. Thus, when we look at distributed programming environments such as the CORBA architecture, discussed in Chapter 5, there is in fact a basic design choice to be made. Either such a function is made part of the architecture, or, by omitting it, no application can achieve this type of consistency in a general and interoperable way except with respect to other applications implemented by the same development team. These examples illustrate that like many engineering arguments, the end-to-end approach is highly appropriate in certain situations, but not uniformly so.

2.8 OS Architecture Issues: Buffering and Fragmentation

We have reviewed most stages of the communication architecture that interconnects a sending application to a receiving application. But what of the operating system software at the two ends?

The communication software of a typical operating system is modular, organized as a set of components that subdivide the tasks associated with implementing the protocol stack or stacks in use by application programs. One of these components is the *buffering* subsystem, which maintains a collection of kernel memory buffers that can be used to temporarily store incoming or outgoing messages. On most UNIX and Linux systems, these are called *mbufs*, and the total number available is a configuration parameter, which should be set when the system is built. Other operating systems allocate buffers dynamically, competing with the disk I/O subsystem and other I/O subsystems for kernel memory. All operating systems share a key property, however: The amount of buffering space available is limited.

The TCP and UDP protocols are implemented as software modules that include interfaces up to the user, and down to the IP software layer. In a typical UNIX or Linux implementation, these protocols allocate some amount of kernel memory space for each open communication socket, at the time the socket is created. TCP, for example, allocates an 8 KB buffer, and UDP allocates two 8 KB buffers, one for transmission and one for reception (both can often be increased to 64 KB). The message to be transmitted is copied into this buffer (in the case of TCP, this is done in chunks if necessary). Fragments are then generated by allocating successive memory chunks for use by IP, copying the data to be sent into them, prepending an IP header, and then passing them to the IP sending routine.

Some operating systems avoid one or more of these copying steps, but this can increase code complexity, and copying is sufficiently fast that many operating systems simply copy the data for each message multiple times. Finally, IP identifies the network interface to use by searching the routing table and queues the fragments for transmission. As might be expected, incoming packets trace the reverse path.

An operating system can drop packets or messages for reasons unrelated to the hardware corruption or duplication. In particular, an application that tries to send data as rapidly as possible, or a machine that is presented with a high rate of incoming data packets, can exceed the amount of kernel memory that can safely be allocated to any single application. Should this happen, it is common for packets to be discarded until memory usage drops back below threshold. This can result in unexpected patterns of message loss—for example, consider an application that simply tests packet loss rates. One might expect that as the rate of transmission is gradually increased, from one packet per second to ten, then 100, then 1,000, the overall probability that a packet loss will occur would remain fairly constant; hence, packet loss will rise in direct proportion to the actual number of packets sent. Experiments that test this case, running over UDP, reveal quite a different pattern.

In practice, packet loss rate is a serious problem when processes send messages rapidly. In such situations, one sees bursty behavior, in which some groups of packets are delivered and others are completely lost. Moreover, the aggregate throughput can be quite low in these overloaded cases, and the operating system often reports no errors at all for the sender and destination. On the sending side, the loss occurs after UDP has accepted a packet, when it is unable to obtain memory for the IP fragments. On the receiving side, the loss occurs when UDP packets turn out to be missing fragments, or when the queue of incoming messages exceeds the limited capacity of the UDP input buffer.

The quantized scheduling algorithms used in multitasking operating systems such as Windows, UNIX, and Linux probably account for the bursty aspect of the loss behavior. These operating systems tend to schedule processes for long periods, permitting the sender to send many packets during congestion periods, without allowing the receiver to run to clear its input queue in the local case or giving the interface time to transmit an accumulated backlog in the remote case. The effect is that once a loss starts to occur, many packets can be lost before the system recovers. Interestingly, packets can also be delivered out of order when tests of this sort are done, presumably reflecting some sort of stacking mechanisms deep within the operating system. The same measurements might yield different results on other versions of the same systems, or other operating systems. However, with the exception of special-purpose, communication-oriented operating systems such as QNX (a real-time system for embedded applications), one would expect a similar result for most of the common platforms used in distributed settings today.

TCP behavior is much more reasonable for the same experiments, presumably because the sender is forced to sleep when the TCP window becomes full, but there are other types of tests for which TCP can behave poorly—for example, if one process makes a great number of TCP connections to other processes, and then tries to transmit multicast messages on the resulting one-to-many connections, the measured throughput drops worse than linearly, as a function of the number of connections, for most operating systems. This is a result of a mechanism called TCP "slow start," whereby a TCP connection that has been idle for more than a few hundred milliseconds starts sending at a very low data rate, just in case the network has become congested while the connection was idle. Moreover, if groups of processes are created and TCP connections are opened between them, pairwise, performance is often found to be extremely variable—latency and throughput figures can vary wildly even for simple patterns of communication. Even a single point-to-point link often behaves very differently in one direction than in the other.

UDP or IP multicast (in practice, these are the same thing) gives the same behavior as UDP. However, the user of multicast should also keep in mind that packet loss can result in very varied patterns of reliability across the different receivers in the IP multicast group. For example, one destination of a multicast transmission may experience high loss rates even if many other destinations receive all messages with no losses at all. There may also be conditions under which every transmission incurs some loss, yet the loss is scattered, with different receivers experiencing problems on different packets. Problems such as this are potentially difficult to detect and are very hard to deal with in software; they often force the developer to design an acknowledgement into their protocol, creating a many-to-one flow of packets that can overwhelm the sender, and requiring one-to-one retransmissions that can defeat the purpose of using IP multicast. Indeed, many IP-multicast based protocols have been shown to scale no better than protocols where one sender uses UDP or TCP to send to lots of receivers—and most such protocols scale poorly! Later in this book, we'll look closely at scalability and we'll see that while there are ways to build very reliable, very scalable protocols, they aren't trivial. A naïve protocol design is likely to result in a solution that scales rather poorly, even if it tries to make clever use of IP multicast or other "tricks."

2.9 Next Steps

The astonishing vigor of the TCP protocol, more than 30 years after its introduction, has been both a blessing and a curse to developers of Internet applications. The positive story is surely the more important one: applications able to obtain the guarantees they need using end-to-end protocols, and for which TCP performance is adequate, have been the fuel driving the engine of the Internet. Moreover, Internet performance has risen steadily for the entire period, hence applications such as streaming audio are increasingly practical even in light of the limitations of TCP and UDP. Web browsers rapidly evolved to offer sensible behavior despite the potential of unexpected disconnections and erratic through-put. Indeed, as one who believes that computers should be reliable, the modern Internet stands in mute testimony to the power of a mostly reliable mechanism. The solution may not be perfect but it is good enough and flexible enough to accommodate a vast array of applications.

TCP has evolved in many ways since its original introduction. What most people refer to as TCP today is a version, developed by Van Jacobson, that incorporates a mechanism to treat packet loss as a sign of Internet congestion by rapidly scaling down the transmission rate, then slowly ratcheting it back up later when conditions improve. This usual version of TCP also employs a mechanism called "slow start," meaning that after any pause in transmission of more than a few hundred milliseconds, the sending rate will throttle down to a very low number. Standard TCP also makes use of a keep-alive mechanism, sending small packets every few seconds to keep connections alive (an important feature because network address translators might otherwise recycle the associated internet addresses and ports for other purposes). However, at least a dozen non-standard TCPs have been proposed, tackling such issues as real-time guarantees, offering properties useful for sending audio or video, etc. Within the Internet as a whole, one sees little use of these variants, but they are relatively common in products designed to run within proprietary settings or on high-quality local area networks.

So all of this is good news. But the story has two sides. Arguing in the negative, one could point to the rigidity of the Internet model for purposes other than e-mail, file transfers and Web browsing. Internet addresses reveal very little about location, hence applications have a tough time predicting likely behavior or planning strategies for efficient movement of large data objects. It is essentially impossible to guarantee that data will get through, even under conditions where the Internet "as a whole" has nearly unlimited numbers of paths on which to send it. Applications seeking real-time behavior must struggle with the style of network congestion control that works best for TCP, even when their own needs would be far better served by some other mechanism. And the network addressing infrastructure has gravitated more and more strongly towards a kind of client to server model that precludes many other styles of communication, at least in the absence of a mechanism like STUN. For an application seeking to download data from a web server hosted in the public Internet, the model is nearly ideal. Given an application with almost any structure other than this, and limitations on the model may prove prohibitive.

It is important to appreciate that there isn't any right or wrong in this story. The Internet is a tremendous success, and the limitations associated with the network stem directly from the same features that made it so successful. Indeed, the open question—one that I personally would love to see answered—is whether there are other ways to build a network that would scale equally well and yet provide useful guarantees (ones stronger than those with which we struggle today). Meanwhile, lacking an answer to this deeper question, the good news is that performance really can overcome many kinds of problems. The Internet continues to get faster and faster, and raw speed often leaves applications with the breathing room to overcome what would otherwise have led to debilitating problems. Some classes of applications will continue to need dedicated, private networks, where conditions can be tightly controlled—military battlefield systems, for example, or systems to control the electric power grid or telephone network. But for the vast majority of purposes, the Internet, warts and all, seems to be quite adequate. And after all, if the network made reliability too easy, those of us who work on high assurance computing for a living would be out of business!

2.10 Related Reading

On the Internet protocols: (see Comer, Comer and Stevens [1991, 1993], Coulouris et al., Tannebaum).

Network Address Translators: see RFC 3022 (Srisuresh and Egevang).

Performance issues for TCP and UDP: (see Brakmo et al., Comer, Comer and Stevens [1991, 1993], Hunt, Kay and Pasquale, Partridge and Pink).

IP Multicast: (see Deering [1988, 1989], Deering and Cheriton, Frank et al., Hunt).

Active Messages: (see von Eicken et al. [1992, 1995].

End-to-end argument: (see Saltzer et al.).

STUN: see RFC 3489 (Rosenberg et al.).

3

High Assurance Communication

3.1 Notions of Correctness and High Assurance Distributed Communication

In the introduction to this text we discussed some of the many forms of "high assurance" one might seek in a mission-critical computing system. These range from guarantees that the system will remain continuously available despite minor disruptions (such as transient communication disruptions or overloads) to stronger requirements, such as rapid restart of failed components or even rapid rollover from a failed platform to a healthy one, with service continuously maintained for applications. Our goal in this brief chapter is to look at the issue of reliability in fairly basic terms: reliability as a goal in the context of the Internet (either a local network or a wide-area one). Higher level techniques for achieving these reliability goals will be topics of entire chapters, but much later in this text.

3.2 The Many Dimensions of Reliability

When we talk about reliability for an application that runs over an unreliable communications infrastructure, there is a sense in which we are setting out to do the impossible. Consider a very simple reliability goal. Perhaps, we would like to build a system consisting of a banking computer that tracks account balances, and a set of cash dispensers. We would like to know that cash is only dispensed appropriately, even if communication between the two units breaks down, and even if one or the other fails.

It shouldn't be hard to see that the problem, as posed, really can't be solved. Suppose that I walk up to a cash dispenser and request $100 from my account. The machine verifies the account balance, but now communication is suddenly lost between the dispenser and the bank. Should the bank assume that the link failed but that the cash was dispensed? Or might the ATM itself have failed, in which case the money is still in the bank? Shortly after this occurs, I walk up to a second dispenser and try to empty my bank account. Should the bank assume that I received the $100, or should it run the risk of error and allow me to withdraw that cash "a second time"?

Clearly, in such a scenario we're stuck either way. If the bank denies my request for that last $100, an unlucky bank manager may soon see me in their office, complaining that first their ATM system died, and now the bank itself won't let me access my account balance. Short of retrieving the records of the failed ATM unit and perhaps even physically counting the money in its cash box, they may have no way to determine what actually occurred. The converse scenario is also easy to understand: having received my cash, I unplugged the ATM. The bank lets me withdraw my $100 a second time, and only later discovers the problem.

In any distributed computing system, we're forced to struggle with uncertainty. Application processes know their own state, and they know what state other processes were in "recently." But they don't have any way to know one-another's *current* state—they lack the equivalent of shared memory. They lack accurate ways to detect failures, or to distinguish a communication failure from a computer failure.

Indeed, all the components of the basic Internet infrastructure can fail in irritating ways:

IP and UDP: These basic Internet technologies don't make any pretense of offering reliability. In one early version of a communication toolkit I built, I discovered to my chagrin that under some conditions, the operating system would let my system send a UDP packet without reporting any errors, but then would discard that packet instantly, without ever "trying" to send it at all! We used to joke that UDP was the "unreliable" datagram protocol, and in that case, willfully so. In fact, studies have concluded that UDP and IP packets are transmitted quite reliably in the backbone of the Internet, but that they are often lost near the edges—in routers close to the sender or receiver, or in the computing system of the sender or receiver. Thus, when a packet is sent, there is absolutely no justification for assuming it will be received, and if an acknowledgement is received, the process that sent the acknowledgement is uncertain about that status of the acknowledgement.[1] Moreover,

---

[1] Here's a small brain-teaser. Suppose that Joe and Anne like to meet for lunch. Since it often rains, they meet indoors unless Anne, who has an office window, sees that the weather is good. If so, she sends an email to Joe to tell him that they should meet outside. Now, assume that e-mail has the properties of UDP: mail can silently vanish. Can Joe and Anne overcome this unreliability using an acknowledgement protocol, where Joe acknowledges Anne's mail, and Anne acknowledges Joe's acknowledgement message, etc? For example, suppose that Anne sends the message "let's meet outside" and Joe acks this message, and she acks the ack, and so forth, until finally a message is actually lost.

For example, perhaps things stopped after Joe's 1021'st ack—Anne either didn't get that ack, or her reply to it was lost.

Astonishingly, if Joe and Anne are logical people, they will meet *inside*. Explain why. *(Hint: what happens if, when the protocol stops, Anne's machine hasn't received even a single acknowledgement? What happens if Anne received one acknowledgement, but Joe hasn't seen the acknowledgement to that acknowledgement? Can Joe distinguish these two cases?)*

Now, we all know that people aren't really very logical thinkers. Joe and Anne will probably enjoy their lunch outside. But computers do need to follow logical rules. So this little puzzle illustrates a way that unreliable communication, combined with elementary logic, can cause quite a mess!

one finds that for a stream of UDP packets, loss rate and delay can vary unpredictably, messages can sometimes arrive out of order, and individual messages may even be delivered in duplicate.

IP multicast: Not only can IP multicast fail in the same ways that UDP can fail, individual receivers will usually see different patterns of loss and different delay characteristics. It may be that your machine will drop two thirds of the packets in some IP multicast stream while mine gets them all. Making matters worse, there's the issue of multicast storms mentioned in Section 2.5.4. As a result, while we might like to think of IP multicast as a quick way to get messages to lots of destinations with reasonable reliability, the actual experience is very mixed—some messages may reach no destinations at all, while others get to most or all destinations, and the sender will have no way to detect the outcome. Making IP multicast reliable is no small matter, since the Internet won't do it for us (recall the end-to-end argument). We're faced with adding mechanisms that somehow feed the outcome back to the sender, and also that track the "set" of receivers (otherwise the sender has no way to know who should have received a copy), and then resending any lost packets. By the end of the day, one arrives at a rather complex set of protocols that may not gain much in performance despite their use of IP multicast to send packets "at the outset."

TCP: Although TCP is obviously more reliable than UDP, the protocol is ultimately at risk of failing in many of the same ways. TCP uses acknowledgements and retransmission to detect and repair loss, but it can't overcome longer communication outages that disconnect the sender from the receiver for long enough to defeat the retransmission strategy—normally, the maximum tolerable disconnection period is between 30 and 90 seconds. TCP could sometimes signal a failure and give up when both end-points are quite healthy. And, at best, TCP won't transmit data any faster than the network is willing to let it through, hence congestion or temporarily high loss rates can cause TCP to throttle its rate down to a trickle. Indeed, there are conditions (such as running TCP over a noisy wireless link) where TCP will misinterpret packet loss as a sign of congestion, and slow itself down, even though the actual problem is best addressed by retransmitting as rapidly as possible!

In addition to these issues, we also need to cope with firewalls that may disrupt messages from passing between certain pairs of machines links that only work in one direction, or that have much higher speeds in one direction than another machine addresses that change but where the old, stale, IP address is the only one that we can find and a whole range of similar oddities. The Internet is a frustrating place to work, because when push comes to shove, it really doesn't guarantee anything. The fact is that *most* of the time, things work perfectly well, but *some* of the time the network behaves in a disrupted way, manifested as anything from high rates of packet loss or slow throughput to outright disconnection. There is enough hardware involved so that the risk of something failing is always significant, and the network is a sufficiently "black box" to make it very difficult to diagnose problems if they do occur.

Yet another set of issues stem from the way that the Internet handles routing and congestion control. In the current network architecture, there is only a single route from any given source to any given destination, and routing adapts rather slowly if at all, when a network overload occurs. Moreover, overload is often "signaled" by packet loss; in some approaches, a router will deliberately drop packets to warn the endpoints that an overload situation is beginning to develop. Thus a degree of unreliability and route inflexibility is built into the current network. Were one to want more than one route from a source to a destination, as a backup in the event of a problem, there is no network-level mechanism for requesting such a setup or using it. An application that can't change its data rate when packet loss is detected nonetheless is subjected to the same policy that works well for TCP. In effect, we live in a one-size-fits-all world, and unfortunately, reliable applications are not the primary target.

In contrast, while the same API is normally used both for WAN communication and for local communication, the properties of a local area network or of communication entirely contained within a single machine are often far stronger. In these latter settings one can sometimes eliminate packet loss and avoid the kinds of disruptions just described. We can build very high quality monitoring mechanisms that have a good chance of correctly interpreting problems that occur, so that applications can detect them and react in a coordinated manner. Indeed, within a single machine, communication is normally completely reliable, failure detection is completely trustworthy (unless an application simply goes into an infinite loop, at least), and we even can share memory when communication delays might otherwise lead to ambiguity concerning the current state. All of this means that software running in a single machine, or in a local area network, can often do things that aren't possible in a wide area network. In a WAN, a Web browser epitomizes the very best we can do. A LAN is a simpler, more powerful environment. In effect, the single communication API has different semantics depending on where the endpoints are running, and developers are often very much aware of this.

As we begin to enumerate reliability requirements for applications running in these tougher environments, we move dangerously close to asking for the impossible. Often, tradeoffs are unavoidable. The bank may simply need to accept the risk of giving out that $100 twice or, if that risk is unacceptable, may have to live with some irate customers from time to time. We can try to make the undesirable case unlikely, and all sorts of tricks suggest themselves for doing so. Yet, ultimately, the nature of the network may compel us to accept some forms of limitations.

Later in this book, we'll explore a number of notions of reliability and look closely at the tradeoffs involved in approximating various properties, or guaranteeing those properties, even when network problems loom. It turns out that there are a surprising number of practical options for building high reliability systems. Some of the tradeoffs made to do so are rather minor—for example, we can accurately detect failures simply by compelling a "failed" computer to restart, even if that computer thinks it was perfectly healthy the whole time, and we can avoid the risk of absurd scenarios by requiring a majority vote on failures. If most of us agree that your computer is down, it's down and that's that. At the cost of a rare "forced reboot," the rest of the system can achieve consistent agreement on the status, healthy or faulty, of its members. In a similar sense, a wide range of seemingly impossible barriers can sometimes be evaded by slightly redefining our goals in ways that do have costs—but tolerable costs, or ones rarely encountered, and that seem acceptable in the infrequent cases where they must be incurred.

3.3 Scalability and Performance Goals

One of the most important issues looming before the high-assurance computing community concerns the poor scalability of many of the most common, popular technologies. As mentioned earlier, by scalability we mean the capacity of a system to continue to function correctly when the size of the network is increased or the number of participants increases, or at least to show a growth of load proportional to the growth in request rate that the users present to the system. One might assume that with twice the rate of requests, a system should have twice as much to do, but experience with complexity analysis for algorithms and data structures stands as a reminder that it isn't quite so simple.

In fact, while many problems do have scalable solutions, there are surprisingly many others that pose serious scalability challenges. For example, we might wish to run a database system on behalf of a large enterprise. Discovering that the load on the system is too high for the computer to keep up with, a decision is made to split the database over n servers. We should now have n times the capacity, right?

Not necessarily. If the database is almost entirely used for read-only tasks, this type of scalability isn't hard to achieve. The approach is called "soft state" replication—now and then (but not too often, or we're in a different world), copy the database to create n replicas. Spread the requests over the replicas in a uniform way, and each should end up doing a roughly equivalent share of the work.

But most databases change from time to time. Unless we are willing to use stale data to respond to requests, our simple scheme won't work very well with a database that changes. To compensate for such a problem, one could update all the copies at the same time using a form of reliable multicast—but this might not scale well, particularly when doing the update is hard work. One could somehow partition the database into n separate databases, for example by hashing data items into the set $[0, n - 1]$ and directing requests to the corresponding server. However, not all databases can be so conveniently split.

In practice, modern computing systems can be partitioned roughly into three categories. One class is easy: it consists of systems with the character of our read-only database and these can scale without limit rather easily. Unfortunately, though, this class is of limited value— most data changes sooner or later, and many of the most interesting systems have data that changes rather often. The second class of systems are easily partitioned, and these scale well too, up to the limit of our ability to design a suitable partitioning function. But unfortunately, there are many cases where this approach is problematic—cases such as systems needing a fairly strong reliability property (a partitioned system will have many single points of failure, since the handling of any specific data item becomes the job of a single server). The third class of systems are the hard ones: they demand non-trivial protocols to replicate information, overcome conflicts when more than one update is directed simultaneously to the same data item, and so forth. Much of this book is concerned with the challenges of building these kinds of systems. They are perhaps less common than the others, but they are also the ones that demand the most effort and, in many cases, the ones that also bring the highest payoffs.

The dilemma, then, is that sometimes we need the toughest forms of reliability. Yet the mechanisms available for providing strong properties often scale poorly, and we also need scalability. As we will see in the later chapters of this book, for the first time, researchers are beginning to offer a compelling story in response to these seemingly irreconcilable goals. Unfortunately, for nearly two decades, we've faced a choice between offering the reliability properties needed in demanding applications, and providing the performance and scalability expected by the user.

Additional and very different issues are seen if we look at performance issues of the sort needed for media player applications, such as Internet-based collaborative work tools, radio, video, and so forth. In these settings, guarantees of steady throughput and low variability of inter-packet delays may be more important than other properties such as raw reliability. Unfortunately, however, the Internet is no better at providing these guarantees than it is at offering reliability. Packet delays in the network are extremely variable and while applications can easily download files for replay later, streaming audio or video remains quite problematic.

Again, there may finally be a plausible story in this area—namely, a type of "virtual" network called an overlay, where a single set of hardware is used to host more than one network side-by-side, not all using the Internet protocols to manage themselves. Overlay networks could emerge as a vehicle for addressing the needs of applications with special requirements, such as the need to send media data with steady rates and low variability in latency. However, this is a speculative suggestion; the feasibility of doing such a thing has only recently been established, and we are far from seeing commercial network platforms that might actually offer these kinds of options to users.

3.4 Security Considerations

Security is a vital background question for the topics covered in this book; indeed, it deserves a book in its own right, and this is part of our reason for covering it in a rather cursory manner here. Nonetheless, we should note the many ways in which the existing Internet infrastructure is insecure, and the implications of this insecurity for applications seeking a high degree of robustness. First, unless one explicitly uses IPSec (as, for example, in the case of a VPN) IP itself lacks any way to authenticate sender and destination information once a packet departs from the origin computing system, making it easy for a sender to misrepresent its address and easy to spray packets to destinations as a part of an attack on the network infrastructure or on specific Web sites. Although IPSec does provide security for the core infrastructure of the Internet—the routing tables, and the DNS mappings it uses—this security mechanism has known limits and is also dependent upon a relatively small number of core servers. Attacks, particularly if mounted from a compromised Internet Service Provider, remain a serious concern. A single compromised router, for example, could easily disrupt an IP packet flow and, if well positioned, might be able to shut down large parts of the Internet as a whole simply by claiming it can reach certain address ranges cheaply, then dropping the packets.

The infrastructure isn't the whole problem. To build a secure application, it would be important to protect against compromised data, denial of service attacks, and other forms of intrusion. Yet TCP, UDP and IP leave such matters to the application. The application is expected to select its own security mechanisms, distribute security keys (securely) to the participants, track the participant set and update keys as needed, encrypt and decrypt data, etc. One can argue that this is appropriate; the security needs of different applications are often quite distinct from one-another and any standard solution risks imposing undesired strictures on applications having their own needs. Yet there has been a great deal of success for so-called *virtual private networks* in which all communication is signed so that intruders are unable to introduce packets without access to the key. Clearly, the market is eager for certain kinds of broadly useful, powerful tools. Lacking them, many applications are forced to abandon security simply because the effort of implementing security is too high.

The situation is somewhat better for Web Services, which benefit from the existing secure Web protocols, HTTPS (which runs over SSL, the "secure sockets layer"). However, these mechanisms are limited in scope: they secure connections, but do not help the application enforce authentication, verify that users are authorized to perform the actions they are taking, or tackle other kinds of multiparty security policy issues.

3.5 Next Steps

Throughout the remainder of this book, the desire to build highly robust, secure applications will motivate much of the treatment and help us decide what topics to drill down on and what topics to set to the side. We'll pursue high availability, for example, in considerable detail—despite the lack of industry standards and the relatively poor support for high availability systems in modern platforms. On the other hand, we'll provide relatively little detail on widely used industry platforms such as J2EE and .NET, because the robustness properties of these platforms are similar to those of CORBA and Web Services, and there is little to be gained by exploring them in great detail.

For the research community, robustness of network applications stands as something of a conundrum. To pursue these properties runs against the commercial current; indeed, the problem today is not so much that we don't know how to overcome the limitations of the Internet (although not all limits can be overcome), but that overcoming these limitations is "non-standard" and requires significant extensions to the major computing platforms. As researchers, we can tackle the next set of reliability issues—for example, the design of technologies with which a system can monitor itself, or automatically adapt parameters and configuration as conditions change (an approach called "Autonomic Computing"), or security mechanisms for mobile users, or representation of security policy. Yet while solutions to such problems are needed, they would then join a collection of solutions which are well in hand, and yet not being exploited.

We can also consider the converse approach, by building useable solutions and either contributing them to open source repositories or launching companies to commercialize them. By and large, doing so runs into a problem of perceived value. Everyone wants reliability and security, but not to such a degree that there is a really large associated market. Fundamentally, what developers want is for commercial platforms to offer the needed tools. Yet at the same time, developers want high performance, ease of development and debugging, and a host of other practical properties. Up to the present, offering better reliability has not been a useful market differentiator. These conditions squeeze the market so that the security or reliability vendor is faced with very limited revenue opportunities and serious issues of being "non-standard."

The next step, then, is to find a way through this thicket of potential problems. My own belief is that Web Services offers the best hope for change. With Web Services, a large commercial community is, for the first time, discovering a real need for strong properties. The associated market will be enormous, and vendors will be highly motivated to attract the biggest, most important commercial customers—precisely the ones having the strongest requirements. However, at the time of this writing, we are still in the very early days for Web Services systems, and it is not at all clear how the matter will play out.

3.6 Related Reading

To learn more about the Internet, see Keshav [1997] or Comer (a 3-volume series treating all aspects of the IPv4 and IPv6 protocol suite).

For recent work on overlay networks (see Anderson [2001]).

IPSec is documented in the RFC archives and by IETF.org.

Unfortunately, the author is not aware of any detailed treatment of high assurance on the existing Internet infrastructure.

4

Remote Procedure Calls and the Client/Server Model

4.1 The Client/Server Model

The emergence of real distributed computing systems is often identified with the *client/server* paradigm and a protocol called *remote procedure call* (RPC), which is normally used in support of this paradigm. The basic idea of a client/server system architecture involves a partitioning of the software in an application into a set of *services*, which provide a set of operations to their users, and *client programs*, which implement applications and issue requests to services as needed to carry out the purposes of the application. In this model, the application processes do not cooperate directly with one another, but instead share data and coordinate actions by interacting with a common set of servers and by the order in which the application programs are executed.

There are a great number of client/server system structures in a typical distributed computing environment. Some examples of servers include the following:

- *File servers*: These are programs (or, increasingly, combinations of special-purpose hardware and software) that manage disk storage units on which file systems reside. The operating system on a workstation that accesses a file server acts as the client, thus creating a two-level hierarchy: The application processes talk to their local operating system. The operating system on the client workstation functions as a single client of the file server, with which it communicates over the network.
- *Database servers*: The client/server model operates in a similar way for database servers, except that it is rare for the operating system to function as an intermediary in the manner that it does for a file server. In a database application, there is usually a library of procedure calls with which the application accesses the database, and this library plays the role of the client in a client/server communication protocol to the database server.

- *Network name servers*: Name servers implement some form of map from a symbolic name or service description to a corresponding value, such as an IP address and port number for a process capable of providing a desired service.

- *Network time servers*: These are processes that control and adjust the clocks in a network, so that clocks on different machines give consistent time values (values with limited divergence from one another). The server for a clock is the local interface by which an application obtains the time. The clock service, in contrast, is the collection of clock servers and the protocols they use to maintain clock synchronization.

- *Network security servers*: Most commonly, these consist of a type of directory in which public keys are stored, as well as a key generation service for creating new secure communication channels.

- *Network mail and bulletin board servers*: These are programs for sending, receiving, and forwarding e-mail and messages to electronic bulletin boards. A typical client of such a server would be a program that sends an e-mail message or that displays new messages to a user who is using a newsreader interface.

- *WWW servers*: As we learned in the introduction, the World Wide Web is a large-scale distributed document management system developed at CERN in the early 1990s and subsequently commercialized. The Web stores hypertext documents, images, digital movies and other information on *Web servers*, using standardized formats that can be displayed through various browsing programs. These systems present point-and-click interfaces to hypertext documents, retrieving documents using Web document locators from Web servers, and then displaying them in a type-specific manner. A Web server is thus a type of enhanced file server on which the Web access protocols are supported.

- *Web Services*: A Web server that handles documents and can be browsed using a Web browser is really just an instance of a more general kind of server implementing the "Web Services" architecture. We'll be looking at this architecture in some detail later in the book, and it promises to have an enormous impact on the way that distributed computing systems are designed and implemented. Broadly, though, Web Services systems are a form of computer-accessible Web site that lets client computing systems access databases, file servers, or other kinds of services within the server's computing platform. A Web Service, then, is a form of computer-accessible front end. Web Services, at a minimum, have a description of the available services encoded as a WSDL document and support access via a protocol called SOAP, the Standard Object Access Protocol. They may also advertise themselves using forms of name services and with a protocol called UDDI employed to represent naming information.

- *Grid Computing Services*: One of the hot topics for modern distributed systems researchers involves building a kind of parallel supercomputer out of resources scattered over the Internet. In this so-called "grid computing" architecture, companies or individuals offer computing systems to participate within a new kind of computing service, which can be accessed over the network by clients having appropriate permissions (in the commercial case, fee-paying clients). Grid computing systems are forms of Web Services, but specialized to offer computing and storage capabilities to potential users. We'll visit this topic in more detail later in the book.

In most distributed systems, services can be instantiated multiple times—for example, a distributed system can contain multiple file servers or multiple name servers. We normally use the term *service* to denote a set of servers. Thus, the *network file system service* consists of the network file servers for a system, and the *network information service* is a set of servers, provided on UNIX and Linux systems, that maps symbolic names to ASCII strings encoding values or addresses. An important question to ask about a distributed system concerns the binding of applications to servers.

We say that a *binding* occurs when a process that needs to talk to a distributed service becomes associated with a specific server that will perform requests on its behalf. Various binding policies exist, differing in how the server is selected. For an NFS distributed file system, binding is a function of the file path name being accessed—in this file system protocol, the servers all handle different files, so that the path name maps to a particular server that owns that file. A program using the UNIX network information server (NIS) normally starts by looking for a server on its own machine. If none is found, the program broadcasts a request and binds to the first NIS that responds, the idea being that this NIS representative is probably the least loaded and will give the best response times. (On the negative side, this approach can reduce reliability: Not only will a program now be dependent on availability of its file servers, but it may be dependent on an additional process on some other machine, namely the NIS server to which it became bound). The CICS database system is well known for its explicit load-balancing policies, which bind a client program to a server in a way that attempts to give uniform responsiveness to all clients.

Web Services have a standardized binding mechanism. In this model, the client system will normally start by searching for the desired service in some form of name space. Information about servers is encoded using the UDDI standard, and can be searched to find an exact match or using a form of pattern match. The model is designed for flexibility and one can anticipate years of research on the best ways to do this pattern matching. Very likely, we'll end up with different stories in different settings: searching for resources in a mobile application poses questions remote from the ones seen in a database application operating over a network. Having found the service, a Web Services application will normally form an initial connection using TCP, sending requests over that connection using SOAP to encode the requests and HTTP to actually send them. However, SOAP and HTTP are both slow, verbose encodings and even a very simple, small request can bloat into an enormous object. Accordingly, many Web Services systems finish their binding operation by switching to a less general but more efficient connection between client and server. Where the performance of the client/server application is important there seems to be no simpler way to get both the generality of the Web Services standard and performance competitive with that of a more specialized solution. On the other hand, computers and communications hardware continue to get faster and faster, and for many purposes, the speed of a standard Web Services interaction may be adequate. In these cases, the last steps of the binding process outlined above could be skipped, yielding a slower but more general application.

Algorithms for binding, and for dynamically rebinding, represent an important topic to which we will return in Chapter 20, once we have the tools at our disposal to solve the problem in a concise way.

A distributed service may or may not employ *data replication*, whereby a service maintains more than one copy of a single data item to permit local access at multiple locations or to increase availability during periods when some server processes may have crashed—for example, most network file services can support multiple file servers, but they do not replicate any single file onto multiple servers. In this approach, each file server handles a partition of the overall file system, and the partitions are disjoint from one another. A file can be replicated, but only by giving each replica a different name, placing each replica on an appropriate file server, and implementing handcrafted protocols for keeping the replicas coordinated. Replication, then, is an important issue in designing complex or highly available distributed servers.

Caching is a closely related issue. We say that a process has *cached* a data item if it maintains a copy of that data item locally, for quick access if the item is required again. Caching is widely used in file systems and name services, and permits these types of systems to benefit from locality of reference. A *cache hit* is said to occur when a request can be satisfied out of cache, avoiding the expenditure of resources needed to satisfy the request from the *primary store* or *primary service*. The Web uses document caching heavily, as a way to speed up access to frequently used documents. Web Services systems will use caching even more extensively, and one study, by IBM researchers C. Mohan and G. Cuomo, suggests that there may be dozens of situations in which Web Services systems will depend heavily on caching mechanisms. Caching is similar to replication, except that cached copies of a data item are in some ways second-class citizens. Generally, caching mechanisms recognize the possibility that the cache contents may be stale, and they include a policy for validating a cached data item before using it. Many caching schemes go further, and include explicit mechanisms by which the primary store or service can invalidate cached data items that are being updated, or refresh them explicitly. In situations where a cache is actively refreshed, caching may be identical to replication. Such a cache is said to be "coherent."

However, "generally" does not imply that this is always the case. The Web, for example, has a cache validation mechanism but does not actually require that Web proxies validate cached documents before providing them to the client; the reasoning is presumably that even if the document were validated at the time of access, nothing prevents it from changing immediately afterwards and hence being stale by the time the client displays it. Thus, a periodic refreshing scheme in which, cached documents are refreshed every half hour or so is in many ways equally reasonable. A caching policy is said to be *coherent* if it guarantees that cached data is indistinguishable to the user from the primary copy. The Web caching scheme is thus one that does not guarantee coherency of cached documents.

4.2 RPC Protocols and Concepts

The most common communication protocol for communication between the clients of a service and the service itself is a Remote Procedure Call. The basic idea of an RPC originated in work by Birrell and Nelson in the early 1980s (see Birrell and Nelson). Nelson worked in a group at Xerox PARC that was developing programming languages and environments to simplify distributed computing. At that time, software for supporting file transfer, remote login, electronic mail, and electronic bulletin boards had become common. PARC researchers, however, had ambitious ideas for developing other sorts of distributed computing applications, with the consequence that many researchers found themselves working with the lowest-level-message-passing primitives in the PARC distributed operating system, which was called Cedar.

Much like a more modern operating system, message communication in Cedar supported three communication models:

- Unreliable datagram communication, in which messages could be lost with some (hopefully low) probability
- Broadcast communication, also through an unreliable datagram interface
- Stream communication, in which an initial connection was required, after which data could be transferred reliably

Programmers found these interfaces hard to work with. Any time a program, p, needed to communicate with another program, s, it was necessary for p to determine the network address of s, encode its requests in a way that s would understand, send off the request, and await a reply. Programmers soon discovered that certain basic operations needed to be performed in almost any network application and that each developer was developing his or her own solutions to these standard problems. Some programs used broadcasts to find a service with which they needed to communicate; others stored the network address of services in files or hard-coded them into the application, and still others supported directory programs with which services could register themselves, supporting queries from other programs at run time. Not only was this situation confusing, it turned out to be difficult to maintain the early versions of PARC software: A small change to a service might break all sorts of applications that used it, so that it became hard to introduce new versions of services and applications.

Surveying this situation, Bruce Nelson started by asking what sorts of interactions programs were really needed in distributed settings. He concluded that the problem was really no different from a function or procedure call in a non-distributed program that uses a pre-supplied library; that is, most distributed computing applications would prefer to treat other programs with which they interact much as they treat pre-supplied libraries, with well-known, documented, procedural interfaces. Talking to another program would then be as simple as invoking one of its procedures—a remote procedure call.

The idea of remote procedure call is compelling. If distributed computing can be transparently mapped to a non-distributed computing model, all the technology of non-distributed programming could be brought to bear on the problem. In some sense, we would already know how to design and reason about distributed programs; how to show them to be correct; how to test, maintain and upgrade them; and all sorts of preexisting software tools and utilities would be readily applicable to the problem.

Unfortunately, the details of supporting a remote procedure call turn out to be nontrivial, and some aspects result in visible differences between remote and local procedure invocations. Although this wasn't evident in the 1980s when RPC really took hold, the subsequent ten or 15 years saw considerable theoretical activity in distributed computing, out of which ultimately emerged a deep understanding of how certain limitations on distributed computing are reflected in the *semantics*, or properties, of a remote procedure call. In some ways, this theoretical work finally lead to a major breakthrough in the late 1980s and early 1990s, when researchers learned how to create distributed computing systems in which the semantics of RPC are precisely the same as for local procedure calls (LPC). In Part III of this book, we will study the results and necessary technology underlying such a solution, and we will see how to apply it to RPC. We will also see that such approaches involve subtle tradeoffs between the semantics of the RPC and the performance that can be achieved; the faster solutions also weaken semantics in fundamental ways. Such considerations ultimately lead to the insight that RPC cannot be transparent, however much we might wish that this was not the case.

Making matters worse, during the same period of time a huge engineering push behind RPC elevated it to the status of a standard—and this occurred *before* it was understood how RPC could be made to accurately mimic LPC. The result of this is that the standards for building RPC-based computing environments (and, to a large extent, the standards for object-based computing that followed RPC in the early 1990s) embody a nontransparent and unreliable RPC model, and this design decision is often fundamental to the architecture in ways that the developers who formulated these architectures probably did not appreciate. In the next chapter, when we study stream-based communication, we will see that the same sort of premature standardization affected the standard stream technology, which as a result also suffers from serious limitations that could have been avoided had the problem simply been better understood at the time the standards were developed.

In the remainder of this chapter, we will focus on standard implementations of RPC, with two specific standards in mind—the SOAP standard used in Web Services systems and the CORBA standard, which predates and serves as a form of template for RPC in industry platforms such as .NET and J2EE. As it happens, the details of these varied standards won't enter into the remainder of this chapter, because our interest is primarily in the basic steps by which a program RPC is coded in a program, how that program is translated at compile time, and how it becomes bound to a service when it is executed. Then, we will study the encoding of data into messages and the protocols used for service invocation and for collecting replies. Finally, we will try to pin down a semantic for RPC: a set of statements that can be made about the guarantees of this protocol and that can be compared with the guarantees of LPC. The details of exactly how a piece of data is represented in a message, or exactly how the RPC specifies that the client wants to involve the "database lookup" function of the server as opposed to some other function, are examples of the sort of aspect for which the standards are very different, but that we won't be looking at in any detail. Interested readers, however, will find SOAP particularly easy to understand because the encoding is entirely in ASCII, and all aspects are accessible from a standard Web browser. Thus one can literally walk through every step by which a client finds a Web Services system, binds to it, sends it requests and decodes the replies, using a browser to inspect the information that would normally be hidden inside packets exchanged directly from an application on one computer with an application on a second one. Doing so is a useful exercise in demystification of this important class of technologies.

It should be noted that, while SOAP is rapidly stealing the stage, CORBA (the Common Object Request Broker Architecture) really deserves the credit for introducing many of the basic mechanisms used today. Web Services-oriented platforms such as .NET and J2EE actually trace more of their functionality to CORBA than to any other prior technology, and precisely because SOAP is verbose and very general, it is also a very slow performer. CORBA is more representative of the kinds of RPC that can really be used to build complex, high-speed applications.

The use of RPC leads to interesting problems of reliability and fault handling, shared among all major RPC platforms. As we will see, it is not hard to make RPC work if most or all components within a system are working well. When a system malfunctions, however, RPC can fail in ways that leave the user with no information at all about what has occurred and with no evident strategy for recovering from the situation. There is nothing new about the situations we will be studying—indeed, for many years, it was simply assumed that RPC was subject to intrinsic limitations, and since there was no obvious way to improve on the situation, there was no reason that RPC shouldn't reflect these limitations in its semantic model. As we advance through the book, however, and it becomes clear that there *are* realistic alternatives that might be considered, this point of view becomes increasingly open to question. To this author's taste, it is a real shame that modern RPC platforms, such as .NET, J2EE and SOAP, have missed the boat by failing to take advantage of some of the options available to us today. Doing so wouldn't be very difficult and might lead to big reliability benefits in applications hosted on the technology.

The good news is that the Web Services community has launched a whole series of projects aimed at developing a new set of standards for distributed computing. But the bad news is that there is absolutely no evidence that these standards will actually fix the problems, because the communities developing them have not approached the underlying issues in a systematic way, at least at the time of this writing in 2003. For example, we'll see that a central issue underlying almost every aspect of reliability concerns the manner in which a system detects failures and reports them. Standard ways of solving this problem could have a huge impact and can transform the options for solving other problems. However, the Web Services community has tended to accept the basic Web architecture as a given, and as any user of a Web browser can confirm, failure detection and reporting in the Web is very haphazard. This, then, feeds into an overall mindset in which Web Services are expected to cope with (rather than to overcome) a great many problems associated with the unreliability and inconsistency of lower-level event reporting. Overall, the only conclusion one can draw is that existing standards are flawed, and the failure of the standards community to repair these flaws has erected an enormous barrier to the development of reliable distributed computing systems. In a technical sense, these flaws are not tremendously hard to overcome—although the solutions would require some reengineering of communication support for RPC in modern operating systems. The challenge is more of an educational one: a wider range of leaders from the relevant industry sectors needs to come to grips with the nature of the problem and the most promising options.

Interestingly, were these conceptual blocks overcome, one could build a greatly improved RPC environment that would have few, if any, user-visible incompatibilities with the usual approaches—it would look similar but work better. The issue then is one of education—the communities that control the standards need to understand the issue better, and they need to understand the reasons that this particular issue represents such a huge barrier to progress in distributed computing. They would also need to recognize that the opportunity vastly outweighs the reengineering costs that would be required to seize it. With this goal in mind, let's take a close look at RPC.

4.3 Writing an RPC-based Client or Server Program

The programmer of an RPC-based application employs what is called a *stub-generation* tool. Such a tool is somewhat like a macro preprocessor: It transforms the user's original program into a modified version; which can be linked to an RPC run-time library. Different systems come with different forms of stub generators. Thus, on a UNIX or Linux system running CORBA, a stub generator is a program that one runs separately, whereas in Microsoft's .NET framework, users of Visual Studio C# automatically obtain the needed stubs simply by declaring that their applications are using external objects.

From the point of view of the programmer, a server or client program looks much like any other program, although it may be necessary to code the program in a somewhat stylized manner. Normally, the program will *import* or *export* a set of interface definitions, covering the remote procedures that will be obtained from remote servers or offered to remote clients, respectively. A server program will also have a name and a version, which are used to connect the client to the server. Once coded, the program is compiled in two stages: First the stub generator is used to map the original program into a standard program with added code to carry out the RPC, and then the standard program is linked to the RPC run-time library for execution.

RPC-based application or server programs are coded in a programming style very similar to certain kinds of non-distributed programs, namely those written to interact through some form of graphical user interface (GUI). There is no explicit use of message passing, and the program is structured to register a variety of "callback" procedures, which will be invoked by the runtime system as events occur and need to be handled (this is a familiar model for anyone who has written a program using a standard GUI package). However, there is an important aspect of RPC programming that differs from programming with local procedure calls: the separation of the service interface definition, or IDL[2], from the code that implements it. In an RPC application, a service is considered to have two parts. The interface definition specifies the way that the service can be located (its name), the data types used in issuing requests to it, and the procedure calls that it supports. A *version number* is included to provide for evolution of the service over time—the idea being that if a client is developed to use version 1.1 of a service, there should be a way to check for compatibility if it turns out that version 1.0 or 2.3 is running when the client actually gets executed. These checks are often automated, and in some systems (notably the Microsoft .NET environment) there are mechanisms for automatically downloading versions of services needed by an application, and even for running two different versions of the same service side-by-side in support of a set of clients having varied requirements.

The basic actions of the RPC library were described earlier. In the case of a server program, the library is responsible for registering the program with the RPC directory service program, which is normally provided as part of the RPC run-time environment. An RPC client program will automatically perform the tasks needed to query the directory to find this server and to connect to it, creating a client/server binding. For each of the server operations it invokes, code will be executed to marshal a representation of the invocation into a message—that is, information about the way that the procedure was called and values of the parameters that were passed. Code is included to send this message to the service and to collect a reply; on the server side, the stub generator creates code to read such a message, invoke the appropriate procedure with the arguments used by the remote caller, and to marshal the results for transmission back to the caller. Issues such as user-id handling, security and privacy, and handling of exceptions are often packaged as part of a solution. Finally, back on the caller side, the returning message will be demarshaled and the result made to look like the result of a local procedure.

Although much of this mechanism is automatic and hidden from the programmer, RPC programming differs from LPC programming in many ways. Most noticeable is that most RPC packages limit the types of arguments that can be passed to a remote server, and some also limit the size (in bytes) of the argument information—for example, suppose that a local procedure is written to search a list, and an LPC is performed to invoke this procedure, passing a pointer to the head of the list as its argument. One can ask whether this should work in an RPC environment—and, if so, how it can be supported. If a pointer to the head of the list is actually delivered to a remote program, that pointer will not make sense in the remote address space where the operation will execute. So, it would be natural to propose that the pointer be de-referenced, by copying the head of the list into the message. Remotely, a pointer to the copy can be provided to the procedure. Clearly, however, this will only work if one chases *all* the pointers in question—a problem because many programs

---

[2]It is common to call the interface to a program its IDL, although IDL actually is a shorthand for Interface Definition Language, which is the name of the language used to write down the description of such an interface when using CORBA. Thus one often reads about the "IDL" of a Web Services application, despite the fact that such applications describe their interfaces as part of the WSDL document.

that use pointers have some representation for an un-initialized pointer, and the RPC stub generator may not know about this.

In building a balanced tree, it is common to allocate nodes dynamically as items are inserted. A node that has no descendents would still have left and right pointer fields, but these would be initialized to *nil* and the procedure to search nodes would check for the nil case before dereferencing these pointers. If an RPC marshalling procedure were to automatically make a copy of a structure to send to the remote server (see Figure 4.1), it would need to realize that for this particular structure, a pointer value of nil has a special meaning and should not be chased.

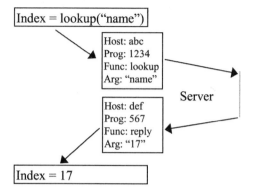

Figure 4.1. Remote procedure call involves creating a message that can be sent to the remote server, which unpacks it, performs the operation, and sends back a message encoding the result.

The RPC programmer sees issues such as these as a set of restrictions. Depending on the RPC package used, different approaches may be used to attack them. In many packages, pointers are simply not legal as arguments to remote procedures. In others, the user can control some form of argument-copying mechanism, and in still fancier systems, the user must provide general-purpose structure traversal procedures, which will be used by the RPC package to marshal arguments. Further complications can arise if a remote procedure may modify some of its arguments. Again, the degree to which this is supported at all, and the degree to which the programmer must get involved, varies from package to package.

Perhaps ironically, RPC programmers tend to complain about this aspect of RPC no matter how it is handled. If a system is highly restrictive, the programmer finds that remote procedure invocation is annoying, because one is constantly forced to work around the limitations of the invocation package—for example, if an RPC package imposes a size limit on the arguments to a procedure, an application that works perfectly well in most situations may suddenly fail because some dynamically defined object has grown too large to be accepted as an RPC parameter. Suddenly, what was a single RPC becomes a multi-RPC protocol for passing the large object in chunks, and a perfectly satisfied programmer has developed distinct second thoughts about the transparency of RPC. At the other extreme are programming languages and RPC packages in which RPC is extremely transparent. These, however, often incur high overheads to copy information in and out, and the programmer is likely to be very aware of these because of their cost implications—for example, a loop that repeatedly invokes a procedure having one changing parameter as well as others (including a pointer to some large object) may be quite inexpensive to invoke in the local case. But if the large object will be copied to a remote program on every invocation, the same loop may cost a fortune when coded as part of a distributed client/server application, forcing the program to be redesigned to somehow pass the object to the remote server prior to the computational loop. These sorts of issues make programming with RPC quite different from programming with LPC.

RPC also introduces error cases that are not seen in LPC, and the programmer needs to deal with these. An LPC would never fail with a binding error, or a version mismatch, or a timeout. In the case of RPC, all of these are possibilities—a binding error would arise if the server were not running when the client was started. A version mismatch might occur if a client was compiled against version 1 of a server, but the server has now been upgraded to version 2. A timeout could result from a server crash, a network problem, or even a problem on the client's computer. Many RPC applications would view these sorts of problems as unrecoverable errors, but fault-tolerant systems will often have alternative sources for critical services and will need to fail-over from a primary server to a backup. The code to do this is potentially complex, and in most RPC environments, it must be implemented by the application developer on a case-by-case basis.

The worst error-handling case arises when an application needs to know the precise outcome of a request in order to take the next step after a failure incapacitates the server with which it was communicating. For example, suppose that an application process requests that a ticket-selling server check for a seat in the orchestra of the local opera is available and, if so, record the sale. When this request fails by timing out, the application has no way to know whether or not the seat was available. Although there may be other servers to which the request can be reissued, doing so runs some risk that the client will be sold two orchestra seats instead of one. This is typical of a situation in which RPC's "semantics" are too weak to address the needs of the application.

4.4 The RPC Binding Problem

The *binding* problem arises when an RPC client program needs to determine the network address of a server capable of providing some service it requires. Binding can be approached from many perspectives, but the issue is simplified if issues associated with the name service used are treated separately, as we do here.

The first step in binding involves asking the naming service for a form of "handle" that can be used to contact the server. This interaction is highly specific to the platform: naming in CORBA is quite different from naming in .NET, J2EE or Web Services. However, the basic principle is the same: a library procedure is provided and the client application invokes this procedure with the name of the desired service, the host on which it is running, a list of properties it should have, or some other form of pattern that can be used to find the best matching server within a potentially longer list. Back comes a handle (in practice, an IP address and port number) or an error code. At this stage binding takes place, and consists primarily of a protocol for establishing a connection to the server and verifying compatibility between the client and server version numbers.

The compatibility problem is important in systems that will operate over long periods of time, during which maintenance and the development of new versions of system components will inevitably occur. Suppose that a client program, c, was developed and tested using server s, but that we now wish to install a new version of s, c, or both. Upgrades such as these create a substantial risk that some old copy of c will find itself talking to a new copy of s, or vice versa—for example, in a network of workstations it may be necessary to reload c onto the workstations one by one, and if some machines are down when the reload occurs, an old copy of c could remain on its disk. Unless c is upgraded as soon as the machine is rebooted—and this may or may not occur, depending on how the system is administered—one would find an old c talking to an upgraded s. It is easy to identify other situations in which problems such as this could occur.

It would be desirable to be able to assume that all possible versions of s and c could somehow communicate with all other versions, but this is not often the case. Indeed, it is not necessarily even desirable. Accordingly, most RPC environments support a concept of *version number,* which is associated with the server IDL. When a client program is compiled, the server IDL version is noted in software. This permits the inclusion of the client's version of the server interface directly in the call to the server. When the match is not exact, the server could reject the request as being incompatible, perform some operation to map the old-format request to a new-format request, or even preserve multiple copies of its functionality, running the version matched to the caller.

Connection establishment is a relatively mechanical stage of binding. Depending on the type of client/server communication protocol that will be used, messages may be transmitted using unreliable datagrams or over reliable communication streams such as TCP. Unreliable datagram connections normally do not require any initial setup, but stream connections typically involve some form of open or initialization operation. Having identified the server to which a request will be issued, the binding mechanism would normally perform this open operation.

The binding mechanism is sometimes used to solve two additional problems. The first of these is called the factory problem and involves starting a server when a service has no currently operational server. In this approach, the first phase of binding looks up the address of the server and learns that the server is not currently operational (or, in the connection phase, a connection error is detected and from this the binder deduces that the server has failed). The binder then issues a request to a "factory", namely a service in which the system designer has stored instructions for starting a server up when needed. The factory will now manufacture an instance of the desired object. After a suitable pause, the binder cycles back through its first phase, which presumably succeeds.

The second problem arises in the converse situation, when the binder discovers multiple servers that could potentially handle this client. The best policy to use in such situations depends very much on the application. For some systems, a binder should always pick a server on the same machine as the client, if possible, and should otherwise pick randomly. Other systems require some form of load-balancing, while still others may implement an affinity policy under which a certain server might be especially well suited to handling a particular client for reasons such as the data it has cached in memory or the type of requests the client is expected to issue once binding has been completed.

Binding is a relatively expensive operation—for example, in a Web Services RPC environment, binding can be more than ten times as costly as RPC. However, since binding only occurs once for each client/server pair, this high cost is not viewed as a major problem in typical distributed computing systems.

4.5 Marshalling and Data Types

The purpose of a data marshalling mechanism is to represent the caller's arguments in a way that can be efficiently interpreted by a server program. In the most general cases, this mechanism deals with the possibility that the computer on which the client is running uses a different data representation than the computer on which the server is running.

Marshalling has been treated at varying levels of generality. Web Services, for example, make use of the Extensible Markup Language (XML) to represent data and data types. XML leads to a verbose representation, but a very general one. In contrast, major vendors have adopted data representations of their own, such as Sun Microsystem's External Data Representation (XDR) format, which is used in the widely popular Network File System (NFS) protocol. Indeed, some vendors, such as Microsoft, support multiple marshalling mechanisms in order to provide compatibility with a variety of "foreign" platforms while also offering the highest possible performance when Windows platforms interact.

The basic issues that arise in a data marshalling mechanism are as follows. First, integer representations vary for the most common CPU chips. On some chips the most significant byte of an integer is also the low byte of the first word in memory, while on others the most significant byte is stored in the high byte of the last word of the integer. These are called little endian and big-endian representations. At one point in the 1980s, computers with other representations—other byte permutations—were on the market, but at the time of this writing I am not aware of any other surviving formats.

A second representation issue concerns data alignment. Some computers require that data be aligned on 32-bit or even 64-bit boundaries, while others may have weaker alignment rules—for example, by supporting data alignment on 16-bit boundaries. Unfortunately, such issues are extremely common. Compilers know about these rules, but the programmer is typically unaware of them. However, when a message arrives from a remote machine that may be using some other alignment rule, the issue becomes an important one. An attempt to fetch data directly from a message without attention to this issue could result in some form of machine fault, or it could result in retrieval of garbage. Thus, the data representation used in messages must encode sufficient information to permit the destination computer to find the start of an object in the message, or the sender and destination must agree in advance on a packed representation that will be used for messages on the wire even if the sender and destination themselves share the same rules and differ from the standard. Needless to say, this is a topic capable of generating endless debate among computer vendors whose machines use different alignment or data representations.

A third issue arises from the existence of multiple floating-point representations. Although there is an IEEE standard floating point representation, which has become widely accepted, some older computers used nonstandard representations for which conversion would be required. These still live on, hence their representations remain relevant. Even within computers using the IEEE standard, byte-ordering issues can still arise.

A fourth issue concerns pointers. When transmitting a complex structure in which there are pointers, the marshalling mechanism needs to either signal that the user has requested something illegal, or somehow represent these pointers in a way that will permit the receiving computer to fix them upon reception of the request. This is especially tricky in languages like LISP, which requires pointers and hence cannot easily legislate against them in RPC situations. On the other hand, passing pointers raises additional problems: Should the pointed-to object be included in the message, transferred only upon use (a "lazy" scheme), or handled in some other way?

Finally, a marshalling mechanism may need to deal with incompatibilities in the basic data types available on computers (see Figure 4.2)—for example, a pair of computers supporting 64-bit integers in hardware may need to exchange messages containing 64-bit integer data. The marshalling scheme should therefore be able to represent such integers. On the other hand, when this type of message is sent to a computer that uses 32-bit integers the need arises to truncate the 64-bit quantities so that they will fit in the space available, with an

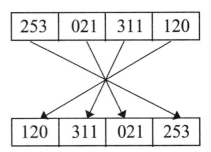

Figure 4.2. The same number (here, a 32-bit integer) may be represented very differently on different computer architectures. One role of the marshalling and demarshalling process is to modify data representations (here, by permuting the bytes) so that values can be interpreted correctly upon reception.

exception being generated if data would be lost by such a truncation. Yet, if the message is merely being passed through some sort of intermediary, one would prefer that data not be truncated, since precision would be lost. In the reverse direction, sign extension or padding may need to be performed to convert a 32-bit quantity into an equivalent 64-bit quantity, but only if the data sent is a signed integer. Thus, a completely general RPC package needs to put a considerable amount of information into each packet, and it may need to do quite a bit of work to represent data in a universal manner. On the other hand, such an approach may be much more costly than one that supports only a very limited set of possible representations, or that compiles the data marshalling and demarshalling operations directly into in-line code.

The approach taken to marshaling varies from RPC package to package. The Web Service XML approach is extremely general, but this generality comes at a high cost: all data is converted to a printable ASCII representation for transmission and converted back on reception. Less general schemes can gain enormous efficiency at the price of certain kinds of cross-platform incompatibilities.

As a general rule of thumb, users will want to be aware that the more general solutions to these problems are also more costly. If the goal is extreme speed, it may make sense to design the application itself to produce data in a form that is inexpensive to marshal and demarshal. The cost implications of failing to do so can be surprising, and, in many cases, it is not difficult to redesign an interface so that RPCs to it will be inexpensive.

4.6 Associated Services

No RPC system lives in isolation. As we will see, RPC is often integrated with a security mechanism and security keys, often using timestamps that in turn depend upon a clock synchronization mechanism. For this reason, one often talks about distributed computing environments that include tools for implementing client/server applications such as an RPC mechanism, security services and time services. The most elaborate environments, such as J2EE and Microsoft .NET, go well beyond this, including system instrumentation, management interfaces and tools, fault-tolerant tools, and so-called Fourth-Generation Language (4GL) tools for building applications using graphical user interfaces (GUIs). Such approaches can empower even unskilled users to develop sophisticated distributed solutions. In this section we briefly review the most important of these services.

4.6.1 Naming Services

A naming service maintains one or more *mappings* from some form of name (normally symbolic) to some form of value (normally a network address). Naming services can operate in a very narrow, focused way—for example, the Domain Naming Service of the TCP/IP protocol suite maps short service names, in ASCII, to IP addresses and port numbers, requiring exact matches. At the other extreme, one can talk about extremely general naming services, which are used for many sorts of data, allow complex pattern matching on the name, and may return other types of data in addition to, or instead of, an address. The Web Services standard specifies a whole language for "naming," called UDDI (the Universal Description, Discovery and Integration language). One can even go beyond this to talk about secure naming services, which could be trusted to only give out validated addresses for services and dynamic naming services, which deal with applications such as mobile computing systems in which hosts have addresses that change constantly.

In standard computer systems at the time of this writing, three naming services are widely supported and used. As previously mentioned, the Domain Name Service (DNS) offers limited functionality, but is very widely used. It responds to requests on a standard network port address, and for the domain in which it is running can map ASCII names to Internet port numbers. DNS is normally used for static services, which are always running when the system is operational and do not change port numbers at all—for example, the e-mail protocol uses DNS to find the remote mail daemon capable of accepting incoming e-mail to a user on a remote system. Although there are a number of extensions to the basic DNS functionality, and some applications have tried to use DNS in a very dynamic way (notably, the Akamai web hosting system), not all implementations of DNS comply with these more "esoteric" uses, and they have consequently found limited uptake in the field. Indeed, some members of the governing organization of the Internet, IETF, have complained about the Akamai use of DNS, arguing that DNS wasn't really designed to support rapid updates and that Akamai's pattern of use was disrupting DNS for other purposes and also imposing an unreasonably high load.

On UNIX and Linux systems, the Network Information Service (NIS), previously called Yellow Pages (YP), is considerably more elaborate. NIS maintains a collection of maps, each of which has a symbolic name (e.g., hosts, services, etc.) and maps ASCII keywords to an ASCII value string. NIS is used on UNIX systems to map host names to Internet addresses, service names to port numbers, and so forth. Although NIS does not support pattern matching, there are ways for an application to fetch the entire NIS database, one line at a time, and it is common to include multiple entries in an NIS database for a single host that is known by a set of aliases. NIS is a distributed service that supports replication: The same data is normally available from any of a set of servers, and a protocol is used to update the full set of servers if an entry changes. However, NIS is not designed to support rapid updates: The assumption is that NIS data consists of mappings, such as the map from host name to Internet address, which change very rarely. A 12-hour delay before NIS information is updated is not unreasonable given this model—hence, the update problem is solved by periodically refreshing the state of each NIS server by having it read the contents of a set of files in which the mapping data is actually stored. As an example, NIS is often used to store password information on UNIX and Linux systems.

Microsoft obtains NIS-like functionality from a very elaborate naming service called the "active registry." Within a local area network running Windows, the registry functions as a vast database storing everything from the list of documents a user most recently opened to the location on the display where Word's window was most recently positioned. The application is notified when this information changes.

There are a number of standards for naming services such as DNS. The community that gave us the ISO standards defined X.500, an international standard that many expect will eventually replace NIS. This service, which is designed for use by applications running the ISO standard remote procedure call interface and ASN.1 data encoding, operates much like an NIS server. No provision has been made in the standard for replication or high-performance update, but the interface does support some limited degree of pattern matching. As might be expected from a standard of this sort, X.500 addresses a wide variety of issues, including security and recommended interfaces. However, reliability issues associated with availability and consistency of the X.500 service (i.e., when data is replicated) have not yet been tackled by the standards organization.

The more successful standard is called LDAP. LDAP is supported by most platforms and vendors, and is flexible enough to be compatible with emerging naming mechanisms, such as the UDDI naming scheme employed by Web Services. X.500, in contrast, probably can't be stretched quite so far. Nonetheless, there is considerable interest in using LDAP or X.500 to implement general-purpose White-Pages (WP) servers, which would be explicitly developed to support sophisticated pattern matching on very elaborate databases with detailed information about abstract entities. Rapid update rates, fault-tolerance features, and security are all being considered in these proposals. At the time of this writing, it appears that the Web will require such services and that work on universal resource naming for use in the Web will be a major driving force for evolution in this overall area. One might speculate that LDAP will ultimately prevail in the battle to be the successful standard for naming services, but X.500 can't be ruled out, and it is also possible that Web Services will give rise to new kinds of naming services and new, even more general, standards.

Last but (someday) most important in this list are name services for Web Services applications. As this book was being written, there was a tremendous amount of commercial competition to offer such services and each of the major vendors (IBM, BEA, Microsoft, etc) had its own proprietary product line with a specialized, high-value feature set. Eventually, it seems likely that a small set of winners will emerge to dominate this space, and that a new naming standard will then be defined, combining best-of-breed features from the most popular solutions.

4.6.2 Time Services

With the launch of the so-called Global Positioning System satellites, microsecond accuracy became possible in workstations equipped with inexpensive radio receivers. Unfortunately, however, accurate clocks remain a major problem in the most widely used computer workstations and network technologies. We will discuss this in more detail in Chapter 23, but some background may still be useful here.

At the time of this writing, the usual clock for a PC or workstation consists of a quartz-based chip much like the one in a common wristwatch, accurate to within a few seconds per year. The initial value of such a clock is either set by the vendor or by the user, when the computer is booted. As a result, in any network of workstations, clocks can give widely divergent readings and can drift with respect to one another at significant rates. For these reasons, there has been considerable study of algorithms for clock synchronization, whereby the clocks on individual machines can be adjusted to give behavior approximating that of a shared global clock. In Chapter 23, we will discuss some of the algorithms that have been proposed for this purpose, their ability to tolerate failures, and the analyses used to arrive at theoretical limits on clock accuracy.

However, much of this work has a limited lifetime. GPS receivers can give extremely accurate time, and GPS signals are transmitted frequently enough so that even inexpensive hardware can potentially maintain time accurate to microseconds. By broadcasting GPS time values, this information can be propagated within a network of computers, and although some accuracy is necessarily lost when doing so, the resulting clocks are still accurate and comparable to within tens of microseconds. This development can be expected to have a major impact on the way that distributed software is designed—from a world of asynchronous communication and clocks that can be inaccurate by many times the average message latency in the network, GPS-based time could catapult us into a domain wherein time skews are considerably smaller than the average latency between sending a message and when it is received. Such developments make it very reasonable to talk about synchronous (time-based) styles of software design and the use of time in algorithms of all sorts.

Even coarsely synchronized clocks can be of value in distributed software—for example, when comparing versions of files, microsecond accuracy is not needed to decide if one version is more current than another: Accuracy of seconds or even tens of seconds may be adequate. Security systems often have a concept of expiration associated with keys. One can thus attack these by attacking the clock—although an intruder would need a way to set a clock back by days, not fractions of a second. And, although we will see that RPC protocols use time to detect and ignore very old, stale messages, as in the case of a security mechanism a clock would need to be extremely inaccurate for such a system to malfunction.

4.6.3 Security Services

In the context of an RPC environment, security is usually concerned with the *authentication* problem. Briefly stated, this is the problem of providing applications with accurate information about the user-ID on behalf of which a request is being performed. Obviously, one would hope that the user-ID is related in some way to the user, although this is frequently the weak link in security architecture. Given an accurate source of user identifications, the basic idea is to avoid intrusions that can compromise user-ID security through break-ins on individual computers and even replacements of system components on some machines with versions that have been compromised and hence could malfunction. As in the case of clock services, we will look more closely at security later in the textbook (Chapter 22) and hence limit ourselves to a brief review here.

To accomplish authentication, a typical security mechanism (e.g., the Kerberos security architecture for DCE [see Schiller, Steiner et al.]) will request some form of password or one-time key from the user at login time, and periodically thereafter, as keys expire on the basis of elapsed time. This information is used to compute a form of secure user identification that can be employed during connection establishment. When a client binds to a server, the security mechanism authenticates both ends, and also (at the option of the programmer) arranges for data to be encrypted on the wire, so that intruders who witness messages being exchanged between the client and server have no way to decode the data contained within them. (Unfortunately, however, this step is so costly that many applications disable encryption and simply rely upon the security available from the initial connection setup.) Notice that for such a system to work correctly, there must be a way to trust the authentication server itself: The user needs a way to confirm that it is actually talking to the authentication server and to legitimate representatives of the services it wishes to use. Given the anonymity of network communication, these are potentially difficult problems.

In Chapter 22, we will look closely at distributed security issues (e.g., we will discuss Kerberos in much more detail) and also at the relationship between security and other aspects of reliability and availability—problems that are often viewed as mutually exclusive, since one replicates information to make it more available, and the other tends to restrict and protect the information to make it more secure. We will also look at emerging techniques for protecting privacy, namely the true user-ID of programs active in a network. Although the state of the art does not yet support construction of high performance, secure, private applications, this should be technically feasible within the not-too-distant future. Of course, technical feasibility does not imply that the technology will become widely practical and therefore useful in building reliable applications, but at least the steps needed to solve the problems are increasingly understood.

4.6.4 Threads packages

A fourth component of a typical RPC system is the lightweight threads package, which enables a single program to handle multiple tasks at the same time. Although threads are a general concept and indeed have rather little to do with communication per se, they are often viewed as necessary in distributed computing systems because of the potential for deadlock if threads are *not* present.

To understand this point, it is helpful to contrast three ways of designing a communication system. A single-threaded, message-based approach would correspond to a conventional style of programming extended directly to message passing. The programmer would use system calls like *sendto* and *recvfrom* as desired to send and receive messages. If there are several things happening at the same time in a program structured this way, however, the associated bookkeeping can be a headache (see Break-out 4.1).

Threads offer a simple way to eliminate this problem: Each thread executes concurrently with the others, and each incoming request spawns a new thread to handle it. While an RPC is pending, the thread that issues it blocks (waits) in the procedure call that invoked the RPC. To the degree that there is any bookkeeping to worry about, the associated state is represented directly in the local variables of this procedure and in the call itself: When the reply is received, the procedure returns (the thread resumes execution), and there is no need to track down information about why the call was being done—this is obvious to the calling procedure. Of course, the developer does need to implement adequate synchronization to avoid concurrency-related bugs, but in general this is not a difficult thing to do. The approach overcomes many forms of problems that are otherwise difficult to address.

Consider a situation in which an RPC server is also the client of some other server, which is in turn the client of still additional servers. It is entirely possible that a cycle could form, in which RPC a by process x on process y leads to an RPC b by y on z, and so forth, until finally some process in the chain makes a request back to the original process, x. If these calls were LPC calls, such a sequence would simply be a form of recursion. For a single-threaded RPC system, however, x will be busy performing RPC a and hence would be unresponsive, creating a deadlock. Alternatively, x would need to somehow save the information associated with sending RPC a while it is handling this new incoming request. This is the bookkeeping problem alluded to above.

Yet a third option is known as event dispatch and is typical of windowing systems, in which each action by the user (mouse motion or clicks, keyboard entries) results in delivery of an event record to a central dispatching loop. The application program typically registers a set of procedure callbacks to perform when events of interest are received: If the left mouse button is pressed, invoke *left_button ()*. Arguments to these callbacks tell the program exactly what occurred: The cursor was at position 132,541 when the mouse button was pressed; this is inside such and such a window, and so forth. One can use the same approach to handle event dispatch in message-based systems: Incoming messages are treated as events and result in callbacks to handler procedures.

The approaches can also be combined: Event dispatch systems can, for example, fork a new thread for each incoming message. In the most general approach, the callback is registered with some indication of how it should be performed: by forking a thread, by direct procedure call, or perhaps even by some other method, such as enqueuing the event on an event queue. This last approach is used in the Horus system, which we will discuss in Chapter 21.

At the time of this writing, although this is not universally the case, many RPC systems are built directly over a lightweight threads package. Each incoming RPC is handled by a new thread, eliminating the risk of deadlock, but forcing the programmer to learn about lightweight threads, preemption, mutual exclusion mechanisms, and other issues associated with concurrency. In this book, we will present some protocols in which processes are assumed to be multithreaded, so that the initiator of a protocol can also be a participant in it. However, we will not explicitly discuss threads packages or make use of any special features of particular packages.

The use of threads in this manner remains debatable. UNIX programs have heavily favored this approach, and the UNIX community generally understands the issues that must be addressed and minimizes their difficulty. Similarly, the Java and C# languages have built-in thread support and for some purposes, such as designing GUIs, a user may be forced to work with threads. Moreover, with experience, threaded programming is not all that difficult. One merely needs to get in the habit of enforcing necessary synchronization using appropriate interlocks. However, the PC community tends to work with an event-based model that lacks threads, in which the application is visualized as a dispatcher for incoming events and all callbacks are by procedure invocation. Thus, the PC community has its own style of programming, and it is largely nonthreaded. Windows NT further complicates this picture: It supports threads, and yet uses an event-oriented style of dispatching throughout the operating system; if a user wants to create a thread to handle an event, this is easily done but not forced upon the programmer. When a thread really is required (for example, to ensure that a window will remain responsive to the "stop" or the "exit" buttons even while processing a request) the use may be almost trivial. Thus a great many people use threads and yet surprisingly few people understand how to use them correctly. This situation is a source of far more problems and bugs than is commonly recognized.

4.1. Threads: A Personal Perspective

Many user-interface systems, such as Windows Frames or the UNIX X-Windows library, are based on "event dispatchers," in which the application registers event handling procedures with the system, and then when events occur, the system issues a callback to the handler. In many respects, event dispatch and thread creation compete, playing similar roles. Thus it can be awkward to have both mechanisms in one environment, as often happens in modern systems.

Rather than choosing between threads and event dispatch, an approach that supports threads as an option over event dispatch offers more flexibility to the developer. That is, the user should have a way to indicate whether a call to an event handler should be done as a separate thread, or as a simple procedure call. Speaking from personal experience, I have mixed feelings on the issue of threads (versus events dispatch). Early in my career I worked with protocols implemented directly over a UDP datagram model. This turned out to be very difficult: Such a system needs to keep track of protocol state in some form of table, matching replies with requests, and is consequently hard to program. For example, suppose that a distributed file server is designed to be single-threaded. The file server may handle many applications at the same time, so it will need to send off one request, perhaps to read a file, but remain available for other requests, perhaps by some other application that wants to write a file. The information needed to keep track of the first request (the read that is pending) will have to be recorded in some sort of pending activities table, and later matched with the incoming reply from the remote file system. Having implemented such an architecture once, I would not want to do it again.

This motivated me to move to RPC-style protocols, using threads. We will be talking about the Isis Toolkit, which is a system that I implemented (with help from others!) in the mid 1980s, in which lightweight threads were employed extensively. Many Isis users commented to me that they had never used threads before working with Isis, and they were surprised at how much the approach simplified things. This is certainly the case: In a threaded system, the procedure handling the read would simply block waiting for the reply, while other procedures can be executed to handle other requests. The necessary bookkeeping is implicit: The blocked procedure has a local state consisting of its calling stack, local variables, and so forth. Thus there is no need to constantly update a table of pending activities.

Of course, threads are also a potential source of insidious programming bugs. In Isis, the benefits of threads certainly outweighed the problems associated with them, but it is also clear that this model requires a degree of programming sophistication that goes somewhat beyond standard single-threaded programming. It took me at least a year to get in the habit of thinking through the potential reentrance and ordering issues associated with concurrency and to become comfortable with the various styles of locking needed to overcome these problems. Many users report the same experience. Isis, however, is perhaps an unusually challenging case because the order in which events happen is very important in this system, for reasons that we will study in Part III.

In more recent work, I have teamed up with Robbert van Renesse, who is the primary author of the Horus system (we discuss this in considerable detail in Chapter 19). Horus, like Isis, was initially designed to use threads and is extremely sensitive to event ordering. But when testing very demanding applications, van Renesse found that threads were a serious a source of overhead and code bloat: overhead because a stack for a thread consumes 16 KB or more of space, which is a lot of space in a system that can handle tens of thousands of messages per second, and excess code because of the necessary synchronization. Yet, as in the case of Isis, Horus sometimes needs threads: They often make it easy to do things that would be very hard to express in a nonthreaded manner.

van Renesse eventually extended Horus to use an event dispatch model similar to the one in Windows NT, which offers threads as an option over a basic event dispatch mechanism. This step, which substantially simplified many parts of Horus, left me convinced that supporting threads over an event dispatch architecture is the right way to go. For cases in which a thread is needed, it is absolutely vital that it be available. However, threads bring a considerable amount of baggage, which may be unnecessary in many settings. An event dispatch style of system gives the developer freedom to make this choice and has a light-weight and fast default behavior. I am, however, still convinced that event dispatch systems that lack the option of forking a thread when one is needed are often unwieldy and very difficult to use. This approach should be avoided.

4.6.5 Transactions

Later in this book we'll discuss a programming model from the database community, in which applications are structured as "transactions" that operate on databases or other forms of persistent data storage. Databases are extremely important in commercial computing settings, and transactions are often closely integrated with RPC environments. For example, the J2EE system was developed as a very general purposed Java runtime environment, but has gradually become more and more popular for database applications encapsulated as "Java Beans." In support of this style of programming, J2EE provides an elaborate transactional package. Similarly, Microsoft's .NET system has a very comprehensive database subsystem called ADO.NET. Applications using this package gain automatic access to a transactional mechanism integrated with the basic .NET remote procedure call.

Web Services systems include perhaps the most elaborate transactional mechanisms ever, supporting two forms of transactions. One form matches the "operation on a database" model just mentioned. The other is aimed at a broader problem, namely support for applications that will do a series of the basic style of transactions over a long period of time. These so-called "business transactions" raise all sorts of additional reliability issues. For example, suppose that a travel agent wants to book a request for a plane ticket, a rental car and a hotel. In the abstract this is a single transaction, but in practice each involves talking to a separate application and those applications are not likely to cooperate. Accordingly, each request will probably be performed as a separate transaction—an RPC to the appropriate kind of Web Service with "transactional properties"—but the set will be treated as a business transaction—a series of transactions that should all be performed. If one fails, for example because no hotel rooms are available, it may be necessary to back the others out and return control to the user.

Later we'll be looking closely at transactional mechanisms, and this is not the place to launch into that discussion. However, it is important for RPC programmers to be aware that many packages are designed with a model in mind. Developers should always be attentive to the styles of examples provided by the vendor or organization promoting a given package and, even before starting to use that package, confirm that those examples are very closely matched with the needs of the application being constructed.

4.7 The RPC Protocol

The discussion up to this point has focused on client/server computing and RPC from the perspective of the user. A remote procedure call *protocol* is concerned with the actual mechanism by which the client process issues a request to a server and by which the reply is transmitted back from the server to the client. We now look at this protocol in more detail. We'll focus on RPC as it arises in systems like J2EE and .NET rather than in Web Services, where RPC (SOAP) runs over HTTP which in turn runs on TCP—the resulting layering is very complex, and because TCP lives at the bottom of the stack, many issues seen in other RPC settings simply don't arise for Web Services systems. On the other hand, Web Services run like molasses when compared with these other "native" implementations.

Abstractly, the remote procedure call problem, which an RPC protocol undertakes to solve, consists of emulating LPC using message passing. LPC has a number of properties—a single procedure invocation results in exactly one execution of the procedure body, the result returned is reliably delivered to the invoker, and exceptions are raised if (and only if) an error occurs.

Given a completely reliable communication environment, which never loses, duplicates, or reorders messages, and given client and server processes that never fail, RPC would be trivial to solve. The sender would merely package the invocation into one or more messages and transmit these to the server. The server would unpack the data into local variables, perform the desired operation, and send back the result (or an indication of any exception that occurred) in a reply message. The challenge, then, is created by failures.

Were it not for the possibility of process and machine crashes, an RPC protocol capable of overcoming limited levels of message loss, disorder, and even duplication would be easy to develop (Figure 4.3). For each process to which it issues requests, a client process maintains a message sequence number. Each message transmitted carries a unique sequence number, and (in most RPC protocols) a time stamp from a global clock—one that returns roughly the same value throughout the network, up to clock synchronization limits. This

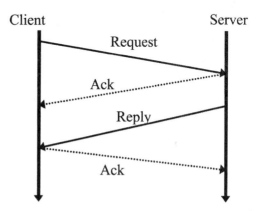

Figure 4.3. Simple RPC interaction, showing packets that contain data (thick) and acknowledgements (dotted).

information can be used by the server to detect very old or duplicate copies of messages, which are discarded, and to identify received messages using what are called *acknowledgment protocol messages.*

The basic idea, then, is that the client process transmits its request and, until acknowledgments have been received, continues to retransmit the same messages periodically. The server collects messages and, when the full request has been received, performs the appropriate procedure invocation. When it transmits its reply, the same sort of reliable communication protocol is used. Often, the acknowledgement is delayed briefly in the hope that the reply will be sent soon, and can be used in place of a separate acknowledgement.

A number of important optimizations have been proposed by developers of RPC-oriented distributed computing environments—for example, if one request will require the transmission of multiple messages, because the request is large, it is common to inhibit the sending of acknowledgments during the transmission of the burst of messages. In this case, a *negative acknowledgement* is sent if the receiver detects a missing packet; a single acknowledgement confirms reception of the entire burst when all packets have been successfully received (Figure 4.4).

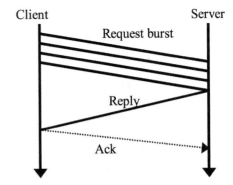

Figure 4.4. RPC using a burst protocol; here the reply is sent soon enough so that an acknowledgement to the burst is not needed.

Process and machine failures, unfortunately, render this very simple approach inadequate. The essential problem is that because communication is over unreliable networking technologies, when a process is unable to communicate with some other process, there is no way to determine whether the problem is a network failure, a machine failure, or both (if a process fails but the machine remains operational the operating system will often provide some status information, permitting this one case to be accurately sensed).

When an RPC protocol fails by timing out, but the client or server (or both) remains operational, it is impossible to know what has occurred. Perhaps the request was never received, perhaps it was received and executed but the reply was lost, or perhaps the client or server crashed while the protocol was executing. This creates a substantial challenge for the application programmer who wishes to build an application that will operate reliably despite failures of some of the services upon which it depends.

A related problem concerns the issue of what are called *exactly once semantics.* When a programmer employs LPC, the invoked procedure will be executed exactly once for each invocation. In the case of RPC, however, it is not evident that this problem can be solved. Consider a process, c, that issues an RPC to a service offered by process s. Depending upon the assumptions we make, it may be very difficult even to guarantee that s performs this request *at most* once. (Obviously, the possibility of a failure precludes a solution in which *s* would perform the operation exactly once.)

To understand the origin of the problem, consider the possible behaviors of an arbitrary communication network. Messages can be lost in transmission, and as we have seen this can prevent process *c* from accurately detecting failures of process *s*. But, the network might also misbehave by delivering a message after an unreasonably long delay—for example, suppose that a network router device fails by jamming up in such a manner that until the device is serviced, the software within it will simply wait for the hardware to be fixed. Obviously, there is no reason to simply assume that routers won't behave this way, and in fact it is known that some routers definitely could behave this way. Moreover, one can imagine a type of attack upon a network in which an intruder records messages for future replay.

One could thus imagine a situation in which process *s* performs a request from *c*, but then is presented with the same request after a very long delay (Figure 4.5). How can process *s* recognize this as a duplicate of the earlier request?

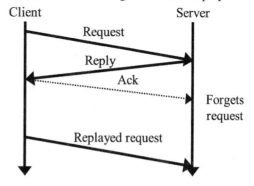

Depending upon the specific protocol used, an RPC package can use a variety of barriers to protect itself against replays of long-delayed messages—for example, the package might check timestamps in the incoming messages, rejecting any that are very old. Such an approach, however, presumes that clocks are syn-

Figure 4.5. If an old request is replayed, perhaps because of a transient failure in the network, a server may have difficulty protecting itself against the risk of re-executing the operation.

chronized to a reasonable degree and that there is no danger that a message will be replayed with a modified timestamp—an action that might well be within the capabilities of a sophisticated intruder. The server could use a connect-based binding to its clients, but this merely pushes the same problem into the software used to implement network connections—and, as we shall see shortly, the same issues occur and remain just as intractable at that level of a system. The server might maintain a list of currently valid users, and could insist that each message be identified by a monotonically increasing sequence number—but a replay could, at least theoretically, re-execute the original binding protocol.

Analyses such as these lead us to two possible conclusions. One view of the matter is that an RPC protocol should take reasonable precautions against replay but not be designed to protect against extreme situations such as replay attacks. In this approach, an RPC protocol might claim to guarantee *at most once semantics*, meaning that provided that the clock synchronization protocol has not been compromised or some sort of active attack been mounted upon the system, each operation will result in either a single procedure invocation or, if a communication or process failure occurs, in no invocation. An RPC protocol can similarly guarantee at least once semantics, meaning that if the client system remains operational indefinitely, the operation will be performed at least once but perhaps more than once. Notice that both types of semantics come with caveats: conditions (hopefully very unlikely ones) under which the property would still not be guaranteed. In practice, most RPC environments guarantee a weak form of at most once semantics: Only a mixture of an extended network outage and a clock failure could cause such systems to deliver a message twice, and this is not a very likely problem.

A different approach, also reasonable, is to assume a very adversarial environment and protect the server against outright attacks that could attempt to manipulate the clock, modify messages, and otherwise interfere with the system. Security architectures for RPC applications commonly start with this sort of extreme position, although it is also common to weaken the degree of protection to obtain some performance benefits within less hostile subsets of the overall computing system. We will return to this issue and discuss it in some detail in Chapter 22.

At the start of this subsection, we commented that Web Services support SOAP RPC over TCP and hence avoid many of the issues just mentioned. It is important to realize that this positioning doesn't eliminate those issues. For example, TCP is a "reliable" protocol in the sense that it checks for and retransmits lost messages, but this form of reliability has limits. TCP can't detect end-point failures and can't distinguish host crashes from transient network outages. Thus while TCP tries to be reliable, as a practical matter it is not able to be any more reliable than a hand-coded protocol running directly on UDP. In effect, all of the same issues just cited arise in Web Services RPC too, although the sources of the problems are buried in layer upon layer of abstractions.

4.8 Using RPC in Reliable Distributed Systems

The uncertainty associated with RPC failure notification and the weak RPC invocation semantics seen on some systems pose a challenge to the developer of a reliable distributed application.

A reliable application would typically need multiple sources of critical services, so that if one server is unresponsive or faulty the application can re-issue its requests to another server. If the server behaves as a read-only information source, this may be an easy problem to solve. However, as soon as the server is asked to deal with dynamically changing information, even if the changes are infrequent compared to the rate of queries, a number of difficult consistency and fault-tolerance issues arise. Even questions as simple as load-balancing, so that each server in a service spanning multiple machines will do a roughly equal share of the request processing load, can be very difficult to solve.

Suppose that an application will use a primary-backup style of fault tolerance, and the requests performed by the server affect its state. The basic idea is that an application should connect itself to the primary, obtaining services from that process as long as it is operational. If the primary fails, the application will fail-over to the backup. Such a configuration of processes is illustrated in Figure 4.6. Notice that the figure includes multiple client processes, since such a service might well be used by many client applications at the same time.

Consider now the design of a protocol by which the client can issue an RPC to the primary-backup pair such that if the primary performs the operation, the backup learns of the associated state change. In principle, this may seem simple: The client would issue an RPC to the server, which would compute the response and then issue an RPC to the backup, sending

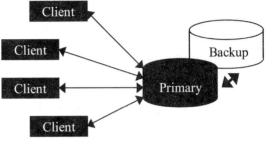

Figure 4.6. Idealized primary-backup server configuration. Clients interact with the primary and the primary keeps the backup current.

it the request it performed, the associated state change, and the reply being returned to the client. Then the primary would return the reply, as shown in Figure 4.7.

This simple protocol is, however, easily seen to be flawed if the sorts of problems we discussed in the previous section might occur while it were running (see Birman and Glade). Take the issue of timeout (see Figure 4.8). In this solution, two RPCs occur, one nested within the other. Either of these, or both, could fail by timeout, in which case there is no way to know with certainty in what state

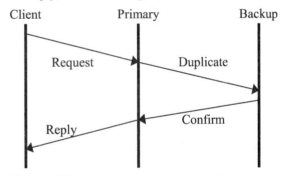

Figure 4.7. Simplistic RPC protocol implementing primary-backup replication.

the system was left. If, for example, the client sees a timeout failure, there are quite a few possible explanations: The request may have been lost, the reply may have been lost, and either the primary or the primary and the backup may have crashed. Fail-over to the backup would only be appropriate if the primary were indeed faulty, but there is no accurate way to determine if this is the case, except by waiting for the primary to recover from the failure—not a "highly available" approach.

The line between easily solved RPC applications and very difficult ones is not a clear one—for example, one major type of file server accessible over the network is accessed by an RPC protocol with very weak semantics, which can be visible to users. Yet this protocol, called the Network File System protocol, is widely popular and has the status of a standard, because it is easy to implement and widely available on most vendor computing systems. NFS is discussed in some detail in Section 5.3 and so we will be very brief here.

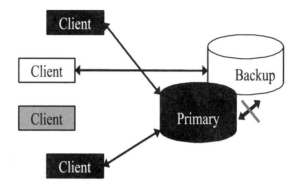

Figure 4.8. RPC timeouts can create inconsistent states, such as this one, in which two clients are connected to the primary, one to the backup, and one is disconnected from the service. Moreover, the primary and backup have become disconnected from one another—each considers the other faulty. In practice, such problems are easily provoked by transient network failures. They can result in serious application-level errors—for example, if the clients are air traffic controllers and the servers advise them on the safety of air traffic routing changes, this scenario could lead two controllers to route different planes into the same sector of the airspace! The matter is further complicated by the presence of more than one client. One could easily imagine that different clients could observe different and completely uncorrelated outcomes for requests issued simultaneously but during a period of transient network or computer failures. Thus, one client might see a request performed successfully by the primary, another might conclude that the primary is apparently faulty and try to communicate with the backup, and yet a third may have timed out both on the primary *and* the backup! We use the term "inconsistent" in conjunction with this sort of uncoordinated and potentially incorrect behavior. An RPC system clearly is not able to guarantee the consistency of the environment, at least when the sorts of protocols discussed above are employed, and hence reliable programming with RPC is limited to very simple applications.

One example of a way in which NFS behavior reflects an underlying RPC issue occurs when creating a file. NFS documentation specifies that the file creation operation should return the error code EEXISTS if a file already exists at the time the create operation is issued. However, there is also a case in which NFS can return error EEXISTS even though the file did not exist when the create was issued. This occurs when the create RPC times out, even though the request was in fact delivered to the server and was performed successfully. NFS automatically re-issues requests that fail by timing out and will retry the create operation, which now attempts to re-execute the request and fails because the file is now present. In effect, NFS is unable to ensure at most once execution of the request, and hence can give an incorrect return code. Had NFS been implemented using LPC (as in the local file system), this behavior would not be possible.

NFS illustrates one approach to dealing with inconsistent behavior in an RPC system. By weakening the semantics presented to the user or application program, NFS is able to provide acceptable behavior despite RPC semantics that create considerable uncertainty when an error is reported. In effect, the erroneous behavior is simply redefined to be a feature of the protocol.

A second broad approach that will interest us here involves the use of agreement protocols by which the components of a distributed system maintain consensus on the status (operational or failed) of one another. A rigorous derivation of the obligations upon such consensus protocols, the limitations on this approach, and the efficient implementation of solutions will be discussed later in this book (Section 14.3). Briefly, however, the idea is that any majority of the system can be empowered to vote that a minority (often, just a single component) be excluded on the basis of apparently faulty behavior. Such a component is cut off from the majority group: If it is not really faulty, or if the failure is a transient condition that corrects itself, the component will be prevented from interacting with the majority system processes, and will eventually detect that it has been dropped. It can then execute a rejoin protocol, if desired, after which it will be allowed back into the system.

With this approach, failure becomes an abstract event—true failures can trigger this type of event, but because the system membership is a self-maintained property of the system, the inability to accurately detect failures need not be reflected through inconsistent behavior. Instead, a conservative detection scheme can be used, which will always detect true failures while making errors infrequently (discussed in more detail in Section 15.3).

By connecting an RPC protocol to a group membership protocol that runs such a failure consensus algorithm, a system can resolve one important aspect of the RPC error-reporting problems discussed above. The RPC system will still be unable to accurately detect failures; hence, it will be at risk of incorrectly reporting operational components as having failed. However, the behavior will now be consistent throughout the system: If component a observes the failure of component b, than component c will also observe the failure of b, unless c is also determined to be faulty. In some sense, this approach eliminates the concept of failure entirely, replacing it with an event that might be called exclusion from membership in the system. Indeed, in the case where b is actually experiencing a transient problem, the resulting execution is much like being exiled from one's country: b is prevented from communicating with other members of the system and learns this. Conversely, the concept of a majority allows the operational part of the system to initiate actions on behalf of the full membership in the system. The system now becomes identified with a rigorous concept: the output of the system membership protocol, which can itself be defined formally and reasoned about using formal tools.

As we move beyond RPC to consider more complex distributed programming paradigms, we will see that this sort of consistency is often required in non-trivial distributed applications. Indeed, there appears to be a dividing line between the distributed applications that give nontrivial coordinated behavior at multiple locations, and those that operate as completely decoupled interacting components, with purely local correctness criteria. The former type of system requires the type of consistency we have encountered in this simple case of RPC error reporting. The latter type of system can manage with error detection based upon timeouts, but is potentially unsuitable for supporting any form of consistent behavior.

4.9 Layering RPC over TCP

It is increasingly common to run RPC protocols over stream protocols such as TCP, to simplify the implementation of the RPC interaction itself. In this approach, the RPC subsystem establishes a stream connection to the remote server and places it into an urgent transmission mode, whereby outgoing data is immediately transmitted to the destination. The reliability mechanisms built into the TCP protocol now subsume the need for the RPC protocol to implement any form of acknowledgement or retransmission policy of its own. In the simplest cases, this reduces RPC to a straightforward request-response protocol. When several threads multiplex the same TCP stream, sending RPCs over it concurrently, a small amount of additional code is needed to provide locking (so that data from different RPC requests are not written concurrently to the stream, which could interleave the data in some undesired manner) and to demultiplex replies as they are returned from the server to the client.

The most widely cited example of a layering of RPC over TCP arises in object-oriented architectures such as CORBA and Web Services. In CORBA, this is part of the "inter-ORB" protocol by which one CORBA system can talk to another CORBA system. Web Services use SOAP RPC over HTTP over TCP to transport most of its requests. Thus the reliability of the RPC protocol becomes a question of the reliability of TCP. A CORBA "remote" request or a Web Services object invocation will fail if the TCP connection breaks or times out, and neither architecture is very clear about what the application programmer should do in this situation.

It is important to appreciate that the reliability associated with TCP will not normally improve (or even change) the reliability semantics of an RPC protocol superimposed upon it. A TCP stream would report a broken connection under essentially the same conditions where an RPC protocol would fail by timing out, and the underlying acknowledgement and retransmission protocol will not affect these semantics in any useful way. The major advantage of running RPC over a stream is that by doing so, the amount of operating system software needed in support of communication is reduced: Having implemented flow control and reliability mechanisms for the stream subsystem, RPC becomes just another application-level use of the resulting operating system abstraction. Such an approach permits the operating system designer to optimize the performance of the stream in ways that might not be possible if the operating system itself were commonly confronted with outgoing packets that originate along different computational paths. On the other hand, the user is left in a confusion situation: if a request fails, just as we saw earlier, it is unclear what state the server was left in. Generally, the application will either toss up its hands and let the (human) user sort things out, or engage in some sort of application-specific resynchronization whereby connection to the server (or to a backup) is cautiously reestablished, and then the state of the interrupted request is determined by some form of interrogation of the server. This isn't trivial, and standards for reconnecting after a disruption are sorely needed.

To reiterate a point made earlier, the situation need not be such a mess. In work with Brad Glade, some years ago, we discovered that if RPC and TCP failure reporting was "rewired" to use a failure detection and agreement service, a considerable degree of consistency could be superimposed on the RPC layer. This could have widespread benefits throughout the system, and isn't all that hard to do—TCP's timeout mechanism is controlled by a parameter, the so-called KEEPALIVE value, and can be disabled by the user, at which point some other failure sensing mechanism can be introduced. Nonetheless, even if the mechanism is available, such a change wouldn't be minor, and unless the vendors who build the major operating systems platforms decide to take this step, we'll all have to live with the very confusing outcomes that arise when doing RPC to a service over a protocol that employs timeout for failure detection.

In some situations, standards are intentionally designed to leave vendors room to innovate, and that's a good thing. Here, though, we see a situation where the standard in some sense defines the only acceptable behavior for the protocol. An ill-considered and yet absolute standard can be very dangerous, and the rather careless introduction of the TCP timeout mechanism into the Internet (David Clark has told the author that it was added "one night" by a developer at Berkeley and that many IETF members would have preferred an end-to-end solution) is a case in point! If Professor Clark's recollection is accurate, we have a good instance here of a poorly considered mechanism, tossed into the system rather thoughtlessly, which has now emerged as central source of unreliability for the entire Internet!

4.10 Related Reading

A tremendous amount has been written about client/server computing, and several pages of references could easily have been included here. Good introductions into the literature, including more detailed discussions of DCE and ASN.1, can be found in Birrell and Nelson, Comer and Stevens (1993), Coulouris et al., Tanenbaum.

On RPC performance, the classic reference is Shroeder and Burrows. Critiques of the RPC paradigm appear in Birman and van Renesse, Tanenbaum and van Renesse.

On the problem of inconsistent failure detection with RPC and TCP: (see Birman and Glade).

Other relevant publications include Bal et al. (1992), Bellovin and Merritt, Berners-Lee et al. (1994, 1995), Birrelland Nelson, Braun and Diot, Brockschmidt, Engler et al., Govindran and Anderson, Heidemann and Popek (1994), Jacobsen (1988, 1990), Mullender et al., Rashid, Shroeder and Burrows, Thekkanth and Levy, von Eicken et al. (1995).

A good reference to DCE is Open Software Foundation and to OLE-2 is Brockschmidt. Readers interested in CORBA will find Doug Schmidt's ACE/TAO web sites useful: http://www.cs.wustl.edu/~schmidt/; these are popular CORBA platform technologies (ACE is the "distributed computing environment" and TAO is a CORBA Object Request Broker implemented over ACE).

Web Services and SOAP RPC are documented at www.w3.org and in extensive online repositories maintained by the major vendors in the field, such as IBM, Microsoft, BEA, etc.

Kerberos is discussed in Bellovin and Merritt, Schiller, Steiner et al.

5

Styles of Client/Server Computing

5.1 Stateless and Stateful Client/Server Interactions

Up to now, this book has focused on the communication protocols used to implement RPC, architectures for integrating RPC into larger applications (Chapter 6 tackles this in greater detail), and on the semantics provided when a failure occurs. Independent of the way that a communication technology is implemented, however, is the question of how the programming paradigms that employ it can be exploited in developing applications, particularly if reliability is an important objective. In this chapter, we examine client/server computing technologies, assuming that the client/server interactions are by RPC, perhaps implemented directly; perhaps issued over TCP. Our emphasis is on the interaction between the architectural structure of the system and the reliability properties of the resulting solutions. This topic will prove particularly important when we begin to look closely at the Web, where both browsing and the more recent Web Services architecture employ a stateless client/server computing paradigm, implemented over TCP connections to Web servers. The weakness of this model poses significant challenges to the programmer—challenges that browsers more or less ignore, but that demand much greater effort from the Web Services programmer, who may need to "overcome" problems emerging from deep within the system in order to achieve the strong guarantees required by a mission-critical application.

5.2 Major Uses of the Client/Server Paradigm

The majority of client/server applications fall into one of two categories, which can be broadly characterized as being the file server, or *stateless,* architectures, and the database-styled transactional, or *stateful*, architectures. Although there are a great many client/server systems that neither manage files nor any other form of database, most such systems share a very similar design with one or the other of these. Moreover, although there is an important middle ground consisting of stateful distributed architectures that are not transactional (including stateful file servers). These kinds of applications can usually be understood as "enhanced stateless" architectures.

For example, Microsoft's NTFS file system looks stateful to the user, but is implemented as a "mostly stateless" system using event notification mechanisms to warn the client when events occur on the server that might be important to it; the client quickly rereads the changed data and, with any luck at all, applications running on it won't even notice the temporary inconsistency. If one understands the basic ideas behind stateless system designs, a file system such as this can be understood as starting from a stateless approach and then cleverly adding mechanisms that hide many of the usual issues encountered in stateless designs—an approach that gives the Microsoft system substantial robustness, and that readers of this book might want to think of as an especially good model to follow when building applications of their own. For example, the Web Services architecture invites one to follow a similar development path.

This chapter focuses on extreme cases: purely stateless file systems, and strongly stateful database systems. By doing this, we'll gain familiarity with the broader technology areas of which each is representative and of the state of practice at the time of this writing. Part III of this book, starting with Chapter 14, discusses distributed systems architectures in more general terms and in much more detail, and will look at some systems that don't fit quite so cleanly into one category or the other, but in doing so will also move away from the sorts of technologies that one finds prepackaged into modern application builder tools into a class of technologies that aren't as widely supported, and hence can only be exploited by sophisticated developers who are prepared to do quite a bit more of the nuts-and-bolts implementation.

A *stateless client/server architecture* is one in which neither the clients nor the server needs to maintain accurate information about one another's status. This is not to say that the clients cannot cache information obtained from a server; indeed, the use of caches is one of the key design features that permit client/server systems to perform well. Moreover, the server might include some form of call-back or event notification mechanism to warn its clients that information has changed and should be re-read. However, even without such a notification mechanism, cached information must *always* be understood as potentially stale, and any time an operation is performed on the basis of data from the cache, some sort of validation scheme must be used to ensure that the outcome will be correct even if the cached data has become invalid.

More precisely, a stateless client/server architecture has the property that servers do not need to maintain an accurate record of their current set of clients and can change state without engaging in a protocol between the server and its clients. If a server does track its clients, it may view that information as a kind of cache as well: the list of clients is understood to be an "approximation," and could list some machines that have since become disconnected from the network or that have been shut down. In a stateless architecture, when state changes occur on the server, even though the client systems will have data that lags the changes, their "correct behavior" must not be affected. That is, the client system can only used the cached data in ways that are cautious enough to avoid problems if that data turns out to be stale.

The usual example of a stateless client/server architecture is one in which a client caches records copied from a name server. These records might, for example, map from ASCII names of bank accounts to the internal account numbers and branch identification for the bank server maintaining that account. Should the account be reassigned to a different branch (i.e., if the customer moves to a different city but stays with the same bank), requests that access that account will be directed to the wrong server. Since the transfer of the account is readily detected, this request will fail and the client will realize that its cached branch record has become stale. It can then refresh its cache record by looking up the account's new location. The request can then be reissued and should now reach the correct server. This is illustrated in Figure 5.1. Notice that the use of cached data is transparent to (concealed from) the application program, which benefits through improved performance when the cached record is correct, but is unaffected if an entry becomes stale and must be refreshed at the time it is used. This style of caching is extremely common; indeed, one unpublished study of Web Services by C. Mohan and G. Cuomo, senior technical leaders in the Web Services area for IBM, concluded that a typical commercial Web Services application might include as many as ten to fifteen different caches, all needed to accelerate performance, and with each differing slightly from the others. The authors concluded that caching plays a central role in modern architectures, but also found tremendous variability in the mechanisms used to detect staleness and recover when stale data is accessed. Moreover, while most of the validation mechanisms are simple, a small subset of them are remarkably complex.

One implication of a stateless design is that the server and client are independently responsible for ensuring the validity of their own states and actions. In particular, the server makes no promises to the client, except that the data it provides was valid at the time they were provided. The client, for its part, must carefully protect itself against the risk that the data it obtained from the server subsequently became stale. Applications that can't be designed to behave this way shouldn't use a stateless approach.

Notice that a stateless architecture does not imply that there is no form of state shared between the server and its clients. On the contrary, such architectures often share state through the cache, as seen in Figure 5.1. The server might keep an approximate list of its clients, and that's also a form of shared state. The fundamental property of the stateless paradigm is that correct function doesn't require that such shared information be *accurate*.

The reader familiar with what are called "race conditions" in concurrent operating system code may recognize that stateless architectures embody a kind of race condition. Suppose that a client tries to access a record x by first checking to make sure that the cached copy, x', is still valid, and then permitting the client operation to proceed. On the server, x won't be locked against changes during the period between the validation operation and the completion of the client's operation, hence x could change just as this protocol executes. The client will then validate the record, and yet will access stale data, perhaps resulting in some sort of visible misbehavior in the eyes of an end-user. This is fundamental to

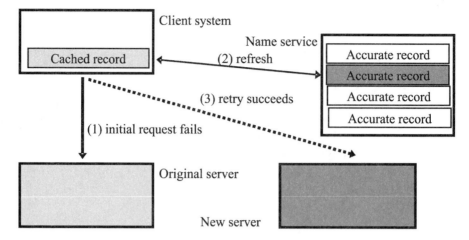

Figure 5.1. In this example, a client of a banking database has cached the address of the server handling a specific account. If the account is transferred, the client's cached record is said to have become stale. Correct behavior of the client is not compromised, however, because it is able to detect staleness and refresh the cached information at run time. Thus, if an attempt is made to access the account, the client will discover that it has been transferred (step 1) and will look up the new address (step 2), or it will be told the new address by the original server. The request can then be reissued to the correct server (step 3). The application program will benefit from improved performance when the cached data is correct, which is hopefully the normal case, but it never sees incorrect or inconsistent behavior if the cached data is incorrect. The key to such an architecture lies in the ability to detect that the cached data has become stale when attempting to use this data, and in the availability of a mechanism for refreshing the cache transparent to the application.

stateless designs: they lack strong synchronization mechanisms (such as locking) and for that reason, applications may glimpse inconsistencies. The approach can only be used when the consequences of such anomalies are felt to be minor.

Despite its limitations, the stateless client/server paradigm is one of the most successful and widely adopted tools for building distributed systems. File servers, perhaps the single most widely used form of distributed system, are typically based on this paradigm, with the caveat noted earlier: arguably the most important file system, Windows NTFS, uses a stateless underpinning but then layers various callback and notification mechanisms over it to give the illusion of a fairly tightly coupled, stateful approach. The Web is based on stateless servers, and this is often cited as one of the reasons for its rapid success. Moreover, many of the special-purpose servers developed for individual applications employ a stateless approach.

However, as we'll see momentarily, stateless architectures also carry a price: Systems built this way often exhibit strange reliability or consistency problems under what one hopes will be unlikely scenarios. Moreover, there is rarely any way to be sure that the troublesome scenarios will always be rare. For example, many stateless systems malfunction during network partitioning events. Networks normally work well, hence this kind of malfunction might never be experienced during development and may also be uncommon in practice.

Even a developer aware of the risk could conclude that these events just don't occur. However, if something occurs to make network partitioning more common (a transient hardware failure, for example), the associated application-level problems could suddenly be both common and costly. An application that was perceived as working well will now be seen as buggy. Such considerations often preclude stateless architectures in settings where correct behavior is really important, such as medical systems or applications where human life or property could be placed at risk. As corporations move new generations of increasingly vital applications to computers, it seems likely that the stateless approach to server design will be less and less adequate.

The first setting in which this issue is encountered may be associated with the deployment of mission-critical Web Services applications. As we've noted, Web Services emerged from Web browser standards, and of course extreme reliability is just not needed when using a browser. Browsers are thus quite successful with a stateless caching model. Yet in Web Services applications, reliability is an important goal, and loose forms of consistency may not be good enough. The mismatch in expectations is likely to result in many nasty surprises in the coming decade.

A *stateful architecture* is one in which information is shared between the client and server in such a manner that the client may take local actions under the assumption that this information is correct. In the example of Figure 5.1, this would have meant that the client system would never need to retry a request. Clearly, to implement such a policy, the database and name mapping servers would need to track the set of clients possessing a cached copy of any record that is about to be transferred. The system would need to somehow lock these records against use during the time of the transfer or invalidate them so that clients attempting to access the transferred record would first look up the new address. The resulting protocol would guarantee that if a client is permitted to access a cached record, that record will be accurate; however, it would do so at the cost of complexity (in the form of the protocol needed when a record is transferred) and delay (namely, delays visible to the client when trying to access a record that is temporarily locked, and/or delays within the servers when a record being transferred is found to be cached at one or more clients).

Later in this text we will see that stateful systems are, at their core, systems which depend upon replicated data, although the nature of the replicated information may not be immediately obvious. In effect, "state" really comes down to shared state, and what distinguishes these systems from the stateless ones is that we want the shared (replicated) state to mimic the behavior of a system in which the data in question isn't replicated but instead resides at a single, highly available, server. A stateful system, then, replicates certain aspects of application state so as to mimic the behavior of a system that uses the identical information but doesn't replicate it.

To achieve this mimicry, stateful architectures invariably require locking mechanisms or other distributed synchronization protocols, permitting them to tightly synchronize the client with the server. If a client of a stateful system is modifying data, it must lock the data (potentially waiting until any pending readers or prior writers have finished), read an accurate copy, modify it, and check it back in. This behavior may be hidden from the developer or embedded into higher level mechanisms, such as transactions, but the core functionality is invariably present. Stateful systems thus embrace a more complex style of interaction between client and server and may need to accept reduced server availability as part of the price: if the client is temporarily unreachable but has locked some data, the server can't allow other client systems to access that data. Such systems often work around the resulting limitations, for example by having the client ship operations to the server (the so-called "three-tier" architecture); by doing so, any availability issues that arise are shifted into the server, where it may be possible to use special hardware to minimize the impact of outages. But of course the application designer is now working in a model remote from more familiar distributed object and remote method invocation approaches. Existing platforms lack a widely accepted, well-supported, solution for the case where the application programmer needs high availability and consistency, and yet isn't able to move to a transactional model.

Our comments on the Windows NTFS file server made it clear that a stateless system can become fairly complex, with layers of mechanisms designed to minimize the scenarios in which clients might realize that the system is ultimately not providing guaranteed consistency. Nonetheless, these mechanisms are often simple ones: caching, perhaps some form of event notification to warn clients that data has changed, etc. In contrast, stateful architectures often become extremely complex, because they really *do* provide strong guarantees. They also require a different style of application development. This is a cost we accept in situations, like a hospital or an air traffic control application, where those guarantees matter and make the complexity seem like a reasonable price to pay.

Stateful systems can also be associated with "coherent caching," in which the client system can cache data with confidence that the cached copy won't become stale. As we will see, this problem is solvable, although necessary mechanisms are rarely available to developers. The issue turns out to reflect a tradeoff between performance and properties. It is clear that a client system with a coherently cached data item will obtain performance benefits by being able to perform actions correctly using local data (hence, avoiding a round-trip delay over the network) and may therefore be able to guarantee some form of real-time response to the application. However, the system as a whole will see reduced performance because locking and other forms of synchronization are typically conservative, preventing some actions even when they would have been legal. Moreover, the associated mechanisms make the underlying platform more complex. Platform developers have apparently concluded that most users value higher performance more than they value strong guarantees and hence have opted for a simpler, faster architecture.

For applications in which the cost of communicating with a server is very high, or where there are relatively strict real-time constraints, coherent caching could offer extremely useful guarantees—for example, an air traffic controller contemplating a proposed course change for a flight would not tolerate long delays while checking with the database servers in the various air sectors that flight will traverse, but also can't run the risk of giving out the wrong answer. Such a system accepts performance that may be quite a bit slower "on average" to avoid these very costly penalties. Similar issues are seen in many real-time applications, such as computer-assisted conferencing systems and multimedia playback systems. But these kinds of examples are atypical, and the "usual" client/server system wouldn't have such stringent requirements. Vendors tend to follow the majority of the market, hence until we see large-scale demand for coherent caching, the necessary mechanisms will probably remain non-standard.

There is one way to offer clients some of the benefits of stateful architecture, but without requiring that remotely cached data be maintained in a coherent state. The key is to use some form of abort or backout mechanism to roll back actions taken by a client on a server. Rollback occurs if the server detects that the client's state is inconsistent with its own state. This forces the client to roll back its own state and, presumably, retry its operation with refreshed or corrected data. This is sometimes called an "optimistic" replication or caching approach, because its benefits are achieved primarily when the optimistic assumption that the cached data hasn't become stale turns out to be valid. Optimistic caching is common in transactional database systems, perhaps the most common of the stateful client/server architectures.

The basic idea in a transactional system is that the client's requests are structured into clearly delimited transactions. Each transaction begins, encompasses a series of *read* and *update* operations, and then ends by *committing* in the case where the client and server consider the outcome to be successful or *aborting* if either client or server has detected an error. An aborted transaction is backed out both by the server, which erases any effects of the transaction, and by the client, which will typically restart its request at the point of the original begin, or report an error to the user and leave it to the user to decide if the request should be retried. A transactional system is one that supports this model, guaranteeing that the results of committed transactions will be preserved and that aborted transactions will leave no trace.

The connection between transactions and statefulness is as follows. Suppose that a transaction is running, and a client has read a number of data items and issued some number of updates. Often it will have locked the data items in question for reading and writing, a topic we discuss in more detail in Chapter 24. These data items and locks can be viewed as a form of shared state between the client and the server: The client basically trusts the server to ensure that the data it has read is valid until it commits or aborts and releases the locks that it holds. Just as our cached data was copied to the client in the earlier examples, all of this information can be viewed as knowledge of the server's state that the client caches. And the relationship is mutual: The server, for its part, holds an image of the client's state in the form of updates and locks that it maintains on behalf of the partially completed transactions.

Now, suppose that something causes the server's state to become inconsistent with that of the client, or vice versa. Perhaps the server crashes and then recovers, and in this process some information that the client had provided to the server is lost. Or, perhaps it becomes desirable to change something in the database without waiting for the client to finish its transaction. In a stateless architecture we would not have had to worry about the state of the client. In a transactional implementation of a stateful architecture, on the other hand, the server can exploit the abort feature by arranging that the client's transaction be aborted, either immediately, or later when the client tries to commit it. This frees the server from needing to worry about the state of the client. In effect, an abort or rollback mechanism can be used as a tool by which a stateful client/server system is able to recover from a situation where the client's view of the state shared with the server has been rendered incorrect.

In the remainder of this chapter, we review examples of stateless file server architectures from the research and commercial community, stateful file server architectures (we will return to this topic in Chapter 24), and stateful transactional architectures as used in database systems. As usual, our underlying emphasis is on reliability implications of these architectural alternatives.

5.3 Distributed File Systems

We have discussed the stateless approach to file server design in general terms. In this section, we look at some specific file system architectures in more detail, to understand the precise sense in which these systems are stateless, how their statelessness may be visible to the user, and the implications of statelessness on file system reliability.

Client/server file systems normally are structured as shown in Figure 5.2. Here, we see that the client application interacts with a cache of file system blocks and file descriptor objects maintained in the client workstation. To illustrate these points, let's briefly review the implementation of the Network File System (NFS) client/server architecture. NFS wasn't the first network file system, but it was surely one of the most successful. The basic idea is

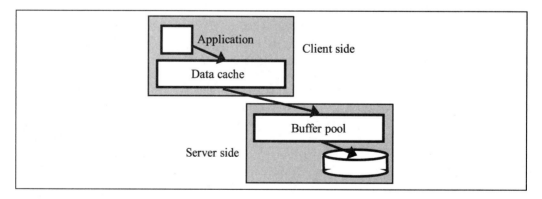

Figure 5.2. In a stateless file system architecture, the client may cache data from the server. Such a cache is similar in function to the server's buffer pool, but is not guaranteed to be accurate. In particular, if the server modifies the data that the client has cached, it has no record of the locations at which copies may have been cached and no protocol by which cached data can be invalidated or refreshed. The client side of the architecture will often include mechanisms that partially conceal this limitation—for example, by validating that cached file data is still valid at the time a file is opened. In effect, the cached data is treated as a set of hints that are used to improve performance but should not be trusted in an absolute sense.

to emulate the way that a UNIX operating system handles mounted disk file systems, but to do so in a way that doesn't require that the disk be attached to the client's computer.

A UNIX file system can be understood in terms of several basic data structures. An *inode* is a small data structure representing the on-disk information by which a file is defined. The inode contains identification information for the file's owner, a small access control vector, dates of file creation and last modification, file size, the file "type," and pointers to the data (depending on the size of the file, the inode may simply list the data blocks containing the file data, or may be "indirection" blocks that themselves list the data blocks). A disk has a *freelist* listing the blocks that are available for allocation. A *directory* is a type of file containing a list of file names and associated inode numbers.

To access a file system on a local disk, a UNIX user first issues a *mount* operation that associates the root directory of the mounted file system with some existing pathname. The user then issues the file operation; perhaps, a file *create* followed by a *write*. To perform the *create* operation, UNIX first searches the file system to ensure that the desired file doesn't already exist; if it does, an error (EEXISTS) is returned to the user. This behavior is widely exploited by applications that need a simple way to obtain locks in a UNIX setting: they *create* a "lock file," interpreting EEXISTS as an indication that the file is already locked, and otherwise performing the desired task and then releasing the lock by deleting the file. A successful *create* causes the file inode to be loaded into kernel memory, it's reference counter to be incremented, and a file handle returned to the application. The application then specifies the file handle when issuing write operations.

The remote case is designed to closely parallel the local case. A remote *mount* operation is implemented by forming a message that encodes the parameters of the *create* into a standard byte order. NFS uses a self-describing representation called XDR (external data representation) for this purpose (NFS was designed in the early 1980's, long before the emergence of the SOAP and XML standards). The request is then transmitted to the server on which the file system resides.

On the server system, a *mount* request is checked for validity: the requested file system must be available and the client's user-id must be one permitted to perform a mount operation. NFS has two mechanisms for checking user-id's; one is based on a cryptographic authentication protocol, and provides fairly strong protection. The other, more commonly used, mechanism simply trusts the client operating system to set the client-id and group-id fields of the message correctly. In this mode, if my computer wishes to access a file system on your computer, I simply tell you what user-id I'm using, and you check to see if that user is permitted to perform the operation. Nothing stops a client from cycling through user id's until one is found that will be accepted by the server, and indeed some virus programs exploit this as a way to break into UNIX file systems. As it turns out, the stronger authentication mechanism is rarely enabled, in part because it employs proprietary protocols and hence is incompatible with hardware and software from certain vendors. A result is that UNIX file systems are often poorly protected. We'll see more examples of this momentarily.

It is interesting to realize that nothing requires the "server" to be a vendor-supplied UNIX implementation of NFS. A mount operation can be handled by *any* application, and in fact it is common for applications to implement the NFS protocol, running in user-mode and perhaps even running on the same machine where the client doing the mount is active! This feature is very convenient for researchers who are developing new NFS-like file systems; they can build a user-level file server and debug it, and yet client software will see what appears to be a completely standard file system no different from any disk-resident one. Students using this textbook have often seized upon this ability to mount a fake file system implemented by an application as a "hook" enabling the introduction of sophisticated functionality without changing the operating system. For example, one can implement file systems that construct data on demand, file systems that use replication to obtain high availability, and so forth.

At any rate, a successful mount operation returns a file-handle to the client system, which stores it in the remote mount table. The client is now ready to issue file system operations, such as file *open* or *create* requests. Let's consider a *create* in order to maintain the similarity between our local and remote cases. The arguments to a *create* request are the pathname of the file to be created and the access rights that should be used. The client file system will recognize that the desired file is on a remote-mounted disk while scanning the pathname, by encountering a pathname prefix that leads to a file system mount point. When this occurs, the suffix of the pathname and the access permission information are marshalled into an XDR message, which is sent with the mount handle to the remote server. Again, there are two modes; in one, the XDR request is signed cryptographically (permitting the remote server to protect against attacks); in the other more common mode, any request with a valid mounted volume handle is trusted, and no attempt is made to verify the user-id or group-id information. The remote server will receive the *create* request, perform the operation, package up the result into an XDR reply message, and send the reply back to the client system.

Remote procedure calls aren't transported reliably, leading to one of the more peculiar issues seen with a stateless file system architecture. If our *create* operation times out, the client system will reissue it, and if that happens, no action occurs on the server side to detect repeat requests. Thus, a scenario can arise in which a *create* is issued, is performed successfully, and then the reply is lost. Should this happen, the request will be issued a second time, but will now fail, since the file was created on the first try! If we are using files as locks, the user's application would incorrectly conclude that the file is locked, when in fact the lock request succeeded. This is a good example of a case where a stateless approach sometimes malfunctions, but where the problem is normally rare enough to be ignored. When it does occur, however, a part of the system could go down until an administrator takes remedial action. In UNIX, this problem is sometimes seen when using printer spooling software, and an administrator may need to manually remove the lock file to unjam the printer.

If successful, operations like *create* and *open* return what is called a *virtualized inode* or *vnode* structure, providing the client operating system with basic information about the file and also a file handle that can be used in subsequent *read* or *write* requests. The client system will typically cache vnodes and also some subset of the blocks of the file itself, using what is called a *write through* policy under which writes modify the client cache (hence client applications will "see their own writes" instantly), then are written back to the server as bandwidth permits. A substantial time lag can easily arise, with the client system knowing about great numbers of updates that have yet to reach the server, and hence would be lost if the client system crashes or becomes disconnected from the network.

When performing NFS *read* and *write* operations, the split between authenticated and non-authenticated operations mentioned earlier arises again: in the non-authenticated case, any request with a valid file mount handle and vnode handle will be accepted by the server, which keeps no records of which clients have mounted the volume or opened a given file. Thus, an intruder can easily "spoof" the file system into permitting a mount operation and permitting file access with falsified user-id and group-id credentials. It is child's play to build the client-side software needed to exploit this form of UNIX attack, and unless the site administrator enables file system authentication, UNIX offers no real defense against the attacker.[3]

For example, suppose that a hospital system were to use a mixture of NFS-based file servers and client systems from many vendors, and for this reason found it impractical to use NFS authentication. Any teenage patient with a laptop and some time to kill could potentially connect the laptop to the hospital network, use a packet "sniffer" application to capture and examine some packets passing by, discover the identity of the hospital file servers and a few common user-ids, and then construct faked file system requests for those same servers using these same user-ids. He or she would be granted unrestricted access to the hospital's files, and could even modify records. It is disturbing to realize that there must be literally hundreds of hospitals (and other similarly sensitive systems) exposed to such attacks. Even worse, administrators are often forced to deploy NFS insecurely, because the industry has been unable to reach agreement on cryptographic security standards, making file system security a largely proprietary matter. Small wonder that we read of major security intrusions on a regular basis!

Lest this all seem very dire, it is important to realize that file systems such as NFS with authentication enabled, Microsoft NTFS, or Carnegie Mellon's Andrew File System and CODA file system all use stronger authentication protocols and are far more secure. In these systems, the client system must authenticate itself and obtain cryptographic credentials, which are used to sign subsequent requests. The file server is able to reject falsified requests because they lack appropriate credentials, and to detect and rejected tampered requests because they won't have a correct signature. It is unfortunate that these stronger authentication protocols have not been unified into a single standard; had this occurred, file system security would today be far stronger than is commonly the case. Microsoft NTFS, Andrew and CODA are also more stateful than UNIX NFS: the server tracks the files open on clients, using this information to prevent inconsistency when a file is modified while

---

[3]The author describes this means of attacking an NFS system with some trepidation. Yet the security problem outlined here is so well known, and NFS deployments that disable strong security are so common, that only the most naïve hacker would be unaware of the issue. With this in mind, it seems more important to warn the next generation of system architects about the risk, even knowing that some particularly uninformed hackers could learn of this security hole from this textbook!

some client systems have it open for reading and may have cached the contents. As noted earlier, NTFS ultimately treats such information as a hint, presumably because the designers didn't want to leave files locked on a server in the event that a client using them crashes or becomes disconnected from the network. Andrew and CODA, in contrast, *do* leave such files locked, although administrative commands can be used to manually release locks if necessary.

Notice that statelessness and a relaxed approach to authentication are two separate issues, although in practice they often go hand-in-hand. What makes NFS stateless is a server design in which the server doesn't worry about copies of vnodes or file blocks on client systems. The UNIX client protocol is responsible for noticing staleness (in practice, applications are expected to use locking if they want to avoid potential problems). Even when NFS runs with authentication enabled, it remains a stateless architecture. Microsoft's file system, and the two CMU-developed file systems, employ not just stronger authentication mechanisms, but also forms of statefulness. One "sees" the statelessness of the NFS file system in many situations: when a *create* operation returns EEXISTS and yet the file didn't exist before the request was issued, when a file read returns a stale cached file block rather than the most recently updated version, or when a change visible on a client system is nonetheless not seen by the server, perhaps for a long time.

NFS does what it can to conceal its statelessness from the client. As we've seen, client-side cached file blocks and vnodes in the cache represent the main form of state present in an NFS configuration. The approach used to ensure that this information is valid represents a compromise between performance objectives and semantics. Each time a file is opened, NFS verifies that the cached vnode is still valid. The file server, for its part, treats a request as invalid if the file has been written (by some other client system) since the vnode and its associated file handle was issued. Thus, by issuing a single open request, the client system is able to learn whether the data blocks cached on behalf of the file are valid or not and can discard them in the latter case.

This approach to cache validation poses a potential problem, which is that if a client workstation has cached data from an open file, changes to the file that originate at some other workstation will not invalidate these cached blocks, and no attempt to authenticate the file handle will occur. For example, suppose that process q on client workstation a has file F open, and then process p on client workstation b opens F, writes modified data into it, and then closes it. Although F will be updated on the file server, process q may continue to observe stale data for an unlimited period of time, because its cache subsystem has no occasion to check for staleness of the vnode. Indeed, short of closing and reopening the file, or accessing some file block that is not cached, q might *never* see the updates!

One case where this pattern of behavior can become visible to a UNIX NFS user arises when a pipeline of processes is executed with each process on a different computer. If p is the first program in such a pipeline and q is the second program, p could easily send a message down the pipe to q telling it to look into the file, and q will now face the stale data problem. UNIX programmers often encounter problems such as this and work around them by modifying the programs to use *fflush* and *fsync* system calls to flush the cache at p and to empty q's cache of cached records for the shared file.

NFS vendors provide a second type of solution to this problem through an optional locking mechanism, which is accessed using the *flock* system call. If this optional interface is used, the process attempting to write the file would be unable to open it for update until the process holding it open for reads has released its read lock. Conceptually, at least, the realization that the file needs to be unlocked and then relocked would sensitize the developer of process p to the need to close and then reopen the file to avoid access anomalies, which are well documented in NFS. At any rate, file sharing is not all that common in UNIX, as demonstrated in some studies (see Ousterhout et al. [1985]), where it was found that most file sharing is between programs executed sequentially from the same workstation.

The NFS protocol is thus stateless but there are quite a few situations in which the user can glimpse the implementation of the protocol because its statelessness leads to weakened semantics compared to an idealized file system accessed through a single cache. Moreover, as noted in the previous chapter, there are also situations in which the weak error reporting of RPC protocols is reflected in unexpected behavior, such as the file *create* operation of Section 4.8, which incorrectly reported that a file couldn't be created because a reissued RPC fooled the file system into thinking the file already existed.

Similar to the basic UNIX file system, NFS is designed to prefetch records when it appears likely that they will soon be needed—for example, if the application program reads the first two blocks of a file, the NFS client-side software will typically fetch the third block of that file without waiting for a read request, placing the result in the cache. With a little luck, the application will now obtain a cache hit and be able to start processing the third block even as the NFS system fetches the fourth one. One can see that this yields performance similar to that of simply transferring the entire file at the time it was initially opened. Nonetheless, the protocol is relatively inefficient in the sense that each block must be independently requested, whereas a streaming style of transfer could avoid these requests and also handle acknowledgements more efficiently. In the following text, we will look at some file systems that explicitly perform whole-file transfers and that are able to outperform NFS when placed under heavy load.

For developers of mission-critical applications, the reliability of the file server is of obvious concern. One might want to know how failures would affect the behavior of operations. With NFS, as normally implemented, a failure can cause the file server to be unavailable for long periods of time, can partition a client from a server, or can result in a crash and then reboot of a client. The precise consequences depend on the way the file system was being used just prior to the crash. For the situations where a server becomes unreachable or crashes and later reboots, the client program may experience timeouts, which would be reported to the application layer as errors, or it may simply retry its requests periodically, for as long as necessary until the file server restarts. In the latter case, an operation will be reissued after a long delay, and there is some potential for operations to behave unexpectedly, as in the case of *create*. Client failures, on the other hand, are completely ignored by the server.

Because the NFS client-side cache uses a write-through policy, in such a situation a few updates may be lost but the files on the server will not be left in an extremely stale state. The locking protocol used by NFS, however, will not automatically break locks during a crash—hence, files locked by the client will remain locked until the application detects this condition and forces the locks to be released, using commands issued from the client system or from some other system. There is a mode in which failures automatically cause locks to be released, but this action will only occur when the client workstation is restarted, presumably to avoid confusing network partitions with failure/reboot sequences.

Thus, while the stateless design of NFS simplifies it considerably, the design also introduces serious reliability concerns. Our discussion has touched on the risk of processes seeing stale data when they access files, the potential that writes could be lost, and the possibility that a critical file server might become unavailable due to a network or computer failure. If you are building an application for which reliability is critical, any of these cases could represent a very serious failure. The enormous success of NFS should not be taken as an indication that reliable applications can in fact be built over it, but rather as a sign that failures are really not all that frequent in modern computing systems and that most applications are not particularly critical! In a world where hardware was less reliable or the applications were more critical, protocols such as the NFS protocol might be considerably less attractive.

Our discussion has focused on the case of a normal NFS server. There are versions of NFS that support replication in software for higher availability: R/NFS and Deceit (see Siegel), HA-NFS (see Bhide et al.), and Harp (see Ladin et al., Liskov et al.), as well as dual-ported NFS server units in which a backup server can take control of the file system. The former approaches employ process-group communication concepts of a sort we will discuss later, although the protocol used to communicate with client programs remains unchanged. By doing this, the possibility for load-balanced read access to the file server is created, enhancing read performance through parallelism. At the same time, these approaches allow continuous availability even when some servers are down. Each server has its own disk, permitting tolerance of media failures. And, there is a possibility of varying the level of the replication selectively, so that critical files will be replicated and non-critical files can be treated using conventional nonreplicated methods. The interest in such an approach is that any overhead associated with file replication is incurred only for files where there is also a need for high availability, and hence the multiserver configuration comes closer to also giving the capacity and performance benefits of a cluster of NFS servers. Many users like this possibility of paying only for what they use.

The dual-ported hardware approaches, in contrast, primarily reduce the time to recovery. They normally require that the servers reside in the same physical location, and are intolerant of media failure, unless a mirrored disk is employed. Moreover, these approaches do not offer benefits of parallelism: One pays for two servers, or for two servers and a mirror disk, as a form of insurance that the entire file system will be available when needed. These sorts of file servers are, consequently, expensive. On the other hand, their performance is typically that of a normal server—there is little or no *degradation* because of the dual configuration.

Clearly, if the performance degradation associated with replication can be kept sufficiently small, the mirrored server and/or disk technologies will look expensive. Early generations of cluster-server technology were slow, hence software performed relatively poorly when compared with mirroring. However, the trend seems to be for this overhead to become smaller and smaller, in which case the greater flexibility and enhanced read performance, due to parallelism, would argue in favor of the NFS cluster technologies.

Yet another file system reliability technology has emerged into prominence over the past decade or so. It involves the use of clusters or arrays of disks to implement a file system that is more reliable than any of the component disks. Such so-called RAID file systems (see Paterson et al.) normally consist of a mixture of hardware and software: the hardware for mediating access to the disks themselves, and the software to handle the buffer pool, oversee file layout, and optimize data access patterns. The actual protocol used to talk to the RAID device over a network would be the same as for any other sort of remote disk: It might be the NFS protocol or some other remote file access protocol. The use of RAID in the disk subsystem itself would normally not result in protocol changes.

RAID devices typically require physical proximity of the disks to one another (this is needed by the hardware). The mechanism that implements the RAID is typically constructed in hardware and employs a surplus disk to maintain redundant data in the form of parity for sets of disk blocks; such an approach permits a RAID system to tolerate one or more disk failures or bad blocks, depending on the way the system is configured. A RAID is thus a set of disks that mimics a single more reliable disk unit with roughly the summed capacity of its components, minus overhead for the parity disk. However, even with special hardware, management and configuration of RAID systems can require specialized software architectures (see Wilkes et al.).

Similar to the case for a mirrored disk, the main benefits of a RAID architecture are high availability in the server itself, together with large capacity and good average seek time for information retrieval. In a large-scale distributed application, the need to locate the RAID device at a single place, and its reliance on a single source of power and software infrastructure, often means that in practice such a file server has the same distributed reliability properties as any other form of file server. In effect, the risk of file server unavailability as a source of downtime is reduced, but other infrastructure-related sources of file system unavailability remain to be addressed. In particular, if a RAID file system implements the NFS protocol, it would be subject to all the limitations of the NFS architecture.

5.4 Stateful File Servers

The performance of NFS is limited by its write-through caching policy, which has led developers of more advanced file systems to focus on improved caching mechanisms and, because few applications actually use the optional locking interfaces, on greater attention to cache validation protocols. In this section, we briefly discuss some of the best-known stateful file systems. Breakout 5.1 discusses the Andrew File System.

5.1. *The Andrew File System (AFS)*

The Andrew File System (AFS) is widely cited for its strong security architecture and consistency guarantees. It was developed at Carnegie Mellon University and subsequently used as the basis of a worldwide file system product offered by Transarc, Inc. (see Satynarayanan et al., Spasojevic and Satyanarayanan). The basic ideas in Andrew are easily summarized.

AFS was built with the assumption that the Kerberos authentication technology would be available. We present Kerberos in Chapter 22, and therefore limit ourselves to a brief summary of the basic features of the system here. When a user logs in (and, later, periodically, if the user remains connected long enough for timers to expire), Kerberos prompts for a password. Using a secure protocol, which employs DES to encrypt sensitive data, the password authenticates the user to the Kerberos server, which will now act as a trustworthy intermediary in establishing connections between the user and the file servers he or she will access. The file servers similarly authenticate themselves to the Kerberos authentication server at startup.

File system access is by whole-file transfer, except in the case of very large files, which are treated as sets of smaller ones. Files can be cached in the AFS subsystem on a client, in which case requests are satisfied out of the cached information whenever possible (in fact, there are two caches—one of file data and one of file status information—but this distinction need not concern us here). The AFS server tracks the clients that maintain cached copies of a given file, and, if the file is opened for writing, uses callbacks to inform those clients that the cached copies are no longer valid. Additional communication from the client to the server occurs frequently enough so that if a client becomes disconnected from the server, it will soon begin to consider its cached files to be potentially stale. (Indeed, studies of AFS file server availability have noted that disconnection from the server is a more common source of denial of access to files in AFS than genuine server downtime.)

AFS provides a strong form of security guarantee, based on access control lists at the level of entire directories. Because the Kerberos authentication protocol is known to be highly secure, AFS can trust the user identification information provided to it by client systems. Short of taking over a client workstation, an unauthorized user would have no means of gaining access to cached or primary copies of a file for which access is not permitted. AFS destroys cached data when a user logs out or an authorization expires and is not refreshed (see Bellovin and Merritt, Birrell, Lampson et al., Satyanarayanan, Schiller, Steiner et al.).

In its current use as a wide area file system, AFS has expanded to include some 1,000 servers and 20,000 clients in ten countries—all united within a single file system name space (see Spasojevic and Satyanarayanan). Some 100,000 users are believed to employ the system on a regular basis. Despite this very large scale, 96 percent of file system accesses are found to be resolved through cache hits, and server inaccessibility (primarily due to communication timeouts) was as little as a few minutes per day. Moreover, this is true even when a significant fraction of file references is to remote files. AFS users are reported to have had generally positive experiences with the system, but (perhaps not surprisingly) they complain about poor performance when a file is not cached and must be copied from a remote file server. Their subjective experience presumably reflects the huge difference in performance between AFS in the case where a file is cached and that when a copy must be downloaded over the network.

Work on stateful file systems architectures can be traced in part to an influential study of file access patterns in the Sprite system at Berkeley (see Baker et al.). This work sought to characterize the file system workload along a variety of axes: read/write split, block reuse frequency, file lifetimes, and so forth. The findings, although not surprising, were at the same time eye-openers for many of the researchers in this field. In this study, it was discovered that all file access was sequential, and that there was very little sharing of files between different programs. When file sharing was observed, the prevailing pattern was the simplest one: One program tended to write the file, in its entirety, and then some other program would read the same file. Often (indeed, in most such cases), the file would be deleted shortly after it was created. In fact, most files survived for less than ten seconds or longer than 10,000 seconds. The importance of cache consistency was explored in this work (it turned out to be quite important, but relatively easy to enforce for the most common patterns of sharing), and the frequency of write/write sharing of files was shown to be so low that this could almost be treated as a special case. (Later, there was considerable speculation that on systems with significant database activity, this finding would have been challenged.) Moreover, considerable data was extracted on patterns of data transfer from server to client: rate of transfer, percentage of the typical file that was transferred, and so forth. Out of this work came a new generation of file systems that used closer cooperation between client and file system to exploit such patterns.

Best known among existing stateful file systems is the Windows file system, although as noted earlier, Windows is in some ways more of a stateless than a stateful system. Basically, NTFS starts with an NFS-like client/server structure, although using cryptographic authentication to prevent unauthorized file access. Layered over this basic mechanism, however, is an event notification subsystem that will notify applications when parts of the file system that they are using change. For example, a program displaying a file system directory (a folder) can register itself to receive an event notifying it if that directory changes, and then redisplay the modified contents. Moreover, the Windows file system has a coherent caching mechanism, so that a file cannot be modified by more than one program at a time without using a special locking interface, and any program reading a file will see the most current data. (This can be very irritating, of course, if a program crashes without unlocking the file). Unfortunately, however, relatively little has been written about the detailed design and performance of the Windows file system (see Vogels [1999]). Rather than speculate, we'll instead look closely at some other systems for which a great deal of detail is available.

Examples of well-studied file systems that employ a stateful approach to provide increased performance (as opposed to availability) are AFS (see Howard et al., Satyanarayanan, Satyanarayanan et al.) and Sprite (see Ousterhout et al. [1988], Srinivasan and Mogul), a research file system and operating system developed at University of California, Berkeley. On the availability side of the spectrum, the Coda project (see Kistler and Satyanarayanan, Mummert et al.), a research effort at Carnegie Mellon University, takes these ideas one step further, integrating them into a file system specifically for use on mobile computers that operate in a disconnected, or partially connected, mode. Ficus, a project at

UCLA, uses a similar approach to deal with file replication in very wide area networks with nonuniform connectivity and bandwidth properties. To varying degrees, these systems can all be viewed as stateful ones in which some of the information maintained within client workstations is guaranteed to be coherent. The term stateful is used a little loosely here, particularly in comparison with the approaches we will examine in Chapter 18. Perhaps it would be preferable to say that these systems are "more stateful" than the NFS architecture, gaining performance through the additional state. Among the four, only Sprite actually provides strong cache coherence to its clients. The other systems provide other forms of guarantees, which are used either to avoid inconsistency or to resolve inconsistencies after they occur. Finally, we will briefly discuss XFS, a file system developed at the University of California, Berkeley, which exploits the file system memory of client workstations as an extended buffer pool, paging files from machine to machine over the network to avoid the more costly I/O path from a client workstation over the network to a remote disk.

Both AFS and Sprite replace the NFS write-through caching mechanism and file handle validation protocols with alternatives that reduce costs. The basic approach in AFS is to cache entire files, informing the server that a modified version of a file may exist in the client workstation. Through a combination of features, such as whole-file transfers on file open and for write back to the server, and by having the file server actively inform client systems when their cached entries become invalid, considerable performance improvements are obtained with substantially stronger file access semantics than for NFS. Indeed, the workload on an AFS server can be an order of magnitude or more lower than that for an NFS server, and the performance observed by a client is comparably higher for many applications. AFS was commercialized subsequent to the initial research project at CMU, becoming the component technology for a line of enterprise file systems (worldwide file systems) marketed by Transarc, a subsidiary of IBM.

Sprite, which caches file system blocks (but uses a large 4KB block size), takes the concept of coherent caching one step further, using a protocol in which the server actively tracks client caching, issuing callbacks to update cached file blocks if updates are received. The model is based on the caching of individual data blocks, not whole files, but the client caches are large enough to accommodate entire files. The Sprite approach leads to such high cache hit rates that the server workload is reduced to almost pure writes, an observation that triggered some extremely interesting work on file system organizations for workloads that are heavily biased towards writes. Similar to AFS, the technology greatly decreases the I/O load and CPU load on the servers that actually manage the disk.

Sprite is unusual in two ways. First, the system implements several different caching policies depending upon how the file is opened: One policy is for read-only access; a second and more expensive one is used for *sequential write access,* which occurs when a file is updated by one workstation and then accessed by a second one later (but in which the file is never written simultaneously from several systems); and a third policy is used for *concurrent write access*, which occurs when a file is written concurrently from several sources. This last policy is very rarely needed because Sprite does not cache directories and is not often used in support of database applications. Second, unlike NFS, Sprite does not use a write-through policy. Thus, a file that is opened for writing, updated, then closed and perhaps reopened by another application on the same machine, read, and then deleted, would remain entirely in the cache of the client workstation. This particular sequence is commonly seen in compilers that run in multiple passes and generate temporary results and in editors that operate on an intermediate copy of a file, which will be deleted after the file is rewritten and closed. The effect is to greatly reduce traffic between the client and the server relative to what NFS might have, but also to leave the server out of date with respect to a client system that may be writing cached files.

Sequential write sharing is handled using version numbers. When a client opens a file, the server returns the current version number, permitting the client to determine whether or not any cached records it may have are still valid. When a file is shared for concurrent writing, a more costly but simple scheme is used, whereby none of the clients are permitted to cache it. If the status of a file changes because a new open or close has occurred, Sprite issues a callback to other clients that have the file open, permitting them to dynamically adapt their caching policy in an appropriate manner. Notice that because a stateless file system such as NFS has no information as to its current client set, this policy would be impractical to implement within NFS. On the other hand, Sprite faces the problem that if the callback RPC fails, it must assume that the client has genuinely crashed; the technology is thus not tolerant of communication outages that can partition a file server from its clients. Sprite also incurs costs that NFS can sometimes avoid: Both *open* and *close* operations must be performed as RPCs, and there is at least one extra RPC required (to check consistency) in the case where a file is opened, read quickly, and then closed.

The recovery of a Sprite server after a crash can be complicated, because some clients may have had files opened in a cache for writing mode. To recover, the server makes use of its knowledge of the set of clients that had cached files for writing, which is saved in a persistent storage area, and of the fact that the consistency state of a file cannot change without the explicit approval of the server. This permits the server to track down current copies of the files it manages and to bring itself back to a consistent state.

The developers of Sprite commented that most of the complexity in the recovery mechanism comes in detecting crashes and reboots, rather than in rebuilding state. This is done by tracking the passage of RPC packets, and using periodic keep-alive packets to detect when a client or server has crashed or rebooted: The same mechanism also suffices to detect network partitions. There is a cost to tracking RPC packets, but a reliable crash and reboot detection mechanism is of course useful for other purposes besides recovering file server state (see Srinivasan and Mogul). This may at first seem confusing, because we have seen that RPC mechanisms cannot reliably detect failures. However, Sprite is not subject to the restrictions we cited earlier because it can deny access to a file while waiting to gain access to the most current version of it. Concerns about RPC arose in trying to determine the cause of an RPC failure in real time. A system that is able to wait for a server to recover is fortunate in not needing to solve this problem: If an apparent failure has occurred, it can simply wait for the problem to be repaired if doing otherwise would violate file system consistency guarantees.

Experiments have shown the Sprite cache-consistency protocols to be highly effective in reducing traffic to the file server and preserving the illusion of a single copy of each file. Performance of the system is extremely good, utilization of servers very low, and the anomalous behaviors that can arise with NFS are completely avoided. However, the technology relies on the veracity of user-ID's, and hence suffers from some of the same security concerns that we will discuss in relation to NFS in Chapter 22.

Coda is a file system for disconnected use. It can be understood as implementing a very generalized version of the whole-file caching methods first introduced in AFS: Whereas AFS caches individual files, Coda caches groups of files and directories so as to maintain a complete cached copy of the user's entire file system or application. The idea within Coda is to track updates with sufficient precision so that the actions taken by the user while operating on a cached copy of part of the file system can be merged automatically into the master file system from which the files were copied. This merge occurs when connection between the disconnected computer and the main file system server is reestablished.

Much of the sophistication of Coda is concerned with tracking the appropriate sets of files to cache in this manner and with optimizing the merge mechanisms so that user intervention can be avoided when possible. (See Breakout 5.2)

The Ficus system, developed by Jerry Popek's group at UCLA (see Reiher et al.), explores a similar set of issues but focuses on an enterprise computing environment similar to the world-wide file system problems to which AFS has been applied in recent years. (For brevity we will not discuss a previous system developed by the same group, Locus [see Walter et al.].) In Ficus, the model is one of a large-scale file system built of file servers that logically maintain replicas of a single file system image. Communication connectivity can be lost and servers can crash—hence, at any point, a server will have replicas of some parts of the file system and will be out of touch with some other replicas for the same data. This leads to an approach in which file type information is used both to limit the updates that can be performed while a portion of the file system is disconnected from other segments, and to drive a file merge process when communication is reestablished (see Heidemann and Popek [1995]). Where Coda is focused on disconnected operation, however, Ficus emphasizes support for patterns of communication seen in large organizations that experience bandwidth limits or partitioning problems that prevent servers from contacting each other for brief periods of time. The resulting protocols and algorithms are similar to the ones used in Coda, but place greater attention on file-by-file reconciliation methods, whereas Coda is oriented towards mechanisms that deal with groups of files as an ensemble.

All of these systems are known for additional contributions beyond the ones we have discussed. Coda, for example, makes use of a recoverable virtual memory mechanism, which offers a way to back out changes made to a segment of virtual memory, using a logging facility that performs replay on behalf of the user. Ficus is also known for work on stackable file systems, in which a single file system interface is used to provide access to a variety of types of file-like abstractions. These contributions, and others not cited here, are beyond the scope of our present discussion.

5.2. *Mobile File Access in Coda*

The challenge faced by Coda is easily appreciated when the following example is considered. Suppose that Fred and Julia are collaborating on a major report to an important customer of their company. Fred is responsible for certain sections of the report and Julia for others, but these sections are also cited in the introductory material and boilerplate used to generate the report as a whole. As many readers of this book will appreciate, there are software tools with varying degrees of ease of use for this type of collaborative work. The most primitive tools provide only for locking of some sort, so that Julia can lock Fred out of a file while she is actually editing it. More elaborate ones actually permit multiple users to concurrently edit the shared files, annotating one another's work, and precisely tracking who changed what through multiple levels of revisions. Such tools typically view the document as a form of database and keep some type of log or history showing how it evolved through time.

If the files in which the report are contained can be copied onto portable computers that become disconnected from the network, however, these annotations will be introduced independently and concurrently on the various copies. Files may be split or merged while the systems are disconnected from each other, and even the time of access cannot be used to order these events, since the clocks on computers can drift or be set incorrectly for many reasons. Thus, when copies of a complex set of files are returned to the file system from which they were removed, the merge problem becomes a nontrivial one both at the level of the file system itself (which may have to worry about directories that have experienced both delete and add operations of potentially conflicting sorts in the various concurrent users of the directory) and at the level of the application and its concept of file semantics.

Not surprisingly, systems such as Coda and Ficus incorporate special-purpose programming tools and applications that are well matched to their styles of disconnected and partially connected operation (see Mummert et al., Reiher et al.). These tools include, for example, e-mail systems that maintain logs of actions taken against mailboxes, understanding how to delete mail that has been deleted while in a disconnected mode, or merging e-mails that arrived separately in different copies of a mailbox that was split within a large-scale distributed environment. One can speculate that, over time, a small and fairly standard set of tools might emerge from such research and that developers would implement specialized disconnected applications, which rely on well-tested reconciliation methods to recorrect inconsistencies that occur during periods of disconnected interaction.

The last of the stateful file systems mentioned at the start of this section is XFS, a Berkeley project that seeks to exploit the memory of the client workstations connected to a network as a form of distributed storage region for a high-performance file server (see Anderson et al.). XFS could be called a "serverless network file system," although in practice the technology would more often be paired to a conventional file system, which would serve as a backup storage region. The basic idea of XFS, then, is to distribute the contents of a file system over a set of workstations so that when a block of data is needed, it can be obtained by a direct memory-to-memory transfer over the network rather than by means of a request to a disk server, which, having much less memory at its disposal, may then need to delay while fetching it from the disk itself.

XFS raises some very complex issues of system configuration management and fault tolerance. The applications using an XFS need to know what servers belong to it, and this set changes dynamically over time. Thus, there is a membership management problem that needs to be solved in software. Workstations are reliable, but not completely reliable— hence, there is a need to deal with failures. XFS does this by using a RAID-style storage scheme in which each set of n workstations is backed by an $n+1$ machine, which maintains a parity block. If one of the $n+1$ machines fails, the missing data can be regenerated from the other n. Moreover, XFS is dynamically reconfigurable, creating some challenging synchronization issues. On the positive side, all of this complexity brings with it a dramatic performance improvement when XFS is compared with more traditional server architectures. It should be noted that XFS draws heavily on the log-structured file system (see Rosenblum and Ousterhout), a technology that is beyond the scope of this book.

The reliability properties of these stateful file systems go well beyond those of NFS. For AFS and Sprite, reliability is limited by the manner in which the servers detect the failure of clients, since a failed client clears its cache upon recovery and the server needs to update its knowledge of the state of the cache accordingly. In fact, both AFS and Sprite detect failures through timeouts—hence, there can be patterns of failure that would cause a client to be sensed incorrectly as having failed, leaving its file system cache corrupted until some future attempt to validate cache contents occurs, at which point the problem would be detected and reported. In Sprite, network partition failures are considered unlikely because the physical network used at Berkeley is quite robust and, in any case, network partitions cause the client workstations to initiate a recovery protocol. Information concerning the precise handling of network partitions, or about methods for replicating AFS servers, was not available at the time of this writing. XFS is based on a failure model similar to that of AFS and Sprite, in which crash failures are anticipated and dealt with in the basic system architecture, but partitioning failures that result in the misdiagnosis of apparent crash failures is not an anticipated mode of failure.

Coda and Ficus treat partitioning as part of their normal mode of operation, dealing with partitioning failures (or client and server failures) using the model of independent concurrent operation and subsequent state merge that was presented earlier. Such approaches clearly trade higher availability for a more complex merge protocol and greater sophistications within the applications themselves. (See Breakout 5.3.)

5.5 Distributed Database Systems

Distributed database systems represent another use of client/server architectures in distributed systems. Unlike the case of distributed file systems, however, database technologies use a special programming model called the *transactional approach* and support this through a set of special protocols (see Gray [1979], Gray and Reuter). The reliability and concurrency

5.3. *Lotus Notes*

The Lotus Notes system is a commercial database product that uses a client/server model to manage collections of documents, which can draw upon a great variety of applications (word processing, spreadsheets, financial analysis packages, etc.). The system is widely popular because of the extremely simple sharing model it supports and its close integration with e-mail and chat facilities, supporting what has become known as a groupware collaboration model. The term "computer-supported collaborative work," or CSCW, is often used in reference to activities that are supported by technologies such as Lotus Notes.

Notes is structured as a client/server architecture. The client system is a graphical user interface, which permits the user to visualize information within the document database, create or annotate documents, "mine" the database for documents satisfying some sort of a query, and exchange e-mail or send memos which can contain documents as attachments. A security facility permits the database to be selectively protected using passwords, so that only designated users will have access to the documents contained in those parts of the database. If desired, portions of especially sensitive documents can be encrypted so that even a database administrator would be unable to access them without the appropriate passwords.

Lotus Notes also provides features for replication of portions of its database between the client systems and the server. Such replication permits a user to carry a self-contained copy of the desired documents (and others to which they are attached) and update them in a disconnected mode. Later, when the database server is back in contact with the user, updates are exchanged to bring the two sets of documents back into agreement. Replication of documents is also possible among Notes servers within an enterprise, although the Notes user must take steps to limit concurrent editing when replication is employed. (This is in contrast with Coda, which permits concurrent use of files and works to automatically merge changes.) At the time of this writing, Notes did not support replication of servers for increased availability, but treated each server as a separate security domain with its own users and passwords.

Within the terminology of this chapter, Lotus Notes is a form of partially stateful file server, although presented through a sophisticated object model and with powerful tools oriented towards cooperative use by members of workgroups. However, many of the limitations of stateless file servers are present in Notes, such as the need to restrict concurrent updates to documents that have been replicated. The Notes user environment is extremely well engineered and is largely successful in presenting such limitations and restrictions as features that the skilled Notes user learns to employ. In effect, by drawing on semantic knowledge of the application, the Lotus Notes developers were able to work around limitations associated with this style of file server. The difficulty encountered in distributed file systems is precisely that they lack this sort of semantic knowledge and are consequently forced to solve such problems in complete generality, leading to sometimes surprising or nonintuitive behavior, reflecting their distributed infrastructure.

semantics of a database are defined by this model, and its efficient implementation is a major topic of research—and an important arena for commercial competition. For the purposes of this chapter, we will simply discuss the main issues, returning to implementation issues in Chapter 24.

Transactional systems are based upon a premise that applications can be divided into client programs and server programs, such that the client programs have minimal interactions with one another. Such an architecture can be visualized as a set of wheels, with database servers forming the hubs to which client programs are connected by communication pathways—the spokes. One client program can interact with multiple database servers, but although the issues this raises are well understood, such multi-database configurations are relatively uncommon in commercial practice. Existing client/server database applications consist of some set of disjoint groups, each group containing a database server and its associated clients, with no interaction between client programs except through sharing a database, and with very few, if any, client programs that interact with multiple databases simultaneously. Moreover, although it is known how to replicate databases for increased availability and loadbalancing (see Bernstein et al., Gray and Reuter), relatively little use is made of this option in existing systems. Thus, the hubs of distributed database systems rarely interact with one another. (We'll see why this is the case in Part III; ultimately, the issue turns out to be one of performance.)

A central premise of the approach is that each interaction by a client with the database server can be structured as a *begin* event, followed by a series of database operations (these would normally be database queries, but we can think of them as *read* and *update* operations and ignore the details), followed by a *commit* or *abort* operation. Such an interaction is called a *transaction*, and a client program will typically issue one or more transactions, perhaps interacting with a user or the outside world between the completion of one transaction and the start of the next. A transactional system should guarantee the persistence of committed transactions, although we will see that high-availability database systems sometimes weaken this guarantee to boost performance. When a transaction is aborted, on the other hand, its effects are completely rolled back, as if the transaction had never even been issued.

Transactional client/server systems are stateful: Each action by the client assumes that the database remembers various things about the previous operations done by the same client, such as locking information that comes from the database concurrency control model and updates that were previously performed by the client as part of the same transaction. The clients can be viewed as maintaining coherent caches of this same information during the period while a transaction is active (not yet committed).

The essential property of the transactional execution model, which is called the *serializability model*, is that it guarantees isolation of concurrent transactions. Thus, if transactions T_1 and T_2 are executed concurrently by client processes p and q, the effects will be as if T_1 had been executed entirely before T_2, or entirely after T_2—the database actively prevents them from interfering with one another. The reasoning underlying this approach is that it will be easier to write database application programs to assume that the database is idle at the time the program executed. Rather than force the application programmer to cope with real-world scenarios in which multiple applications simultaneously access the database, the database system is only permitted to interleave operations from multiple transactions if it is certain that the interleaving will not be noticeable to users. At the same time, the model frees the database system to schedule operations in a way that keeps the server as busy as possible on behalf of a very large number of concurrent clients. (See Figure 5.3)

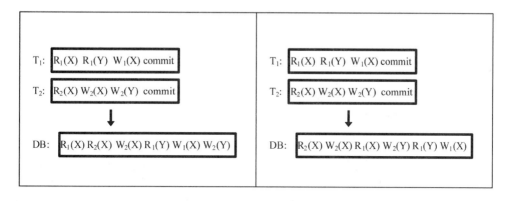

Figure 5.3. A nonserializable transaction interleaving (left), and one serializable in the order T2, T1 (right). Each transaction can be understood as a trace, which records the actions of a program that operates on the database, oblivious to other transactions that may be active concurrently. In practice, of course, the operations become known as the transaction executes, although our example shows the situation at the time these two transactions reach their commit points. The database is presented with the operations initiated by each transaction, typically one by one, and schedules them by deciding when to execute each operation. This results in an additional trace or log, showing the order in which the database actually performed the operations presented to it. A serializable execution is one that leaves the database in a state that could have been reached by executing the same transactions one by one, in some order, and with no concurrency.

Notice that simply running transactions one at a time would achieve the serializability property.[4] However, it would also yield poor performance, because each transaction may take a long time to execute. By running multiple transactions at the same time, and interleaving their operations, a database server can give greatly improved performance, and system utilization levels will rise substantially, just as a conventional uniprocessor can benefit from multitasking. Even so, database systems sometimes need to delay one transaction until another completes, particularly when transactions are very long. To maximize performance, it is common for client/server database systems to require (or at least strongly recommend) that transactions be designed to be as short as possible. Obviously, not all applications fit these assumptions, but they match the needs of a great many computing systems.

There are a variety of options for implementing the serializability property. The most common is to use locking—for example, by requiring that a transaction obtain a read-lock

---

[4]An important special case arises in settings where each transaction can be represented as a single operation, performing a desired task and then committing or aborting and returning a result. Many distributed systems are said to be transactional but, in fact, operate in this much more restrictive manner. However, even if the application perceives a transaction as being initiated with a single operation, the database system itself may execute that transaction as a series of operations. These observations motivate a number of implementation decisions and optimizations, which we discuss in Chapter 24.

on any data item that it will read, and a write-lock on any data item it will update. Read-locks are normally nonexclusive: Multiple transactions are typically permitted to read the same objects concurrently. Write-locks, however, are mutually exclusive: An object with a write lock cannot have any other locks on it (either write or read). In the most standard locking protocol, called *two-phase locking*, transactions retain all of their locks until they commit or abort, and then release them as a group. It is easy to see that this achieves serializability: If transaction T_b reads from T_a, or updates a variable after T_a does so, T_b must first acquire a lock that T_a will have held exclusively for its update operation. Transaction T_b will therefore have to wait until T_a has committed and will be serialized after T_a. Notice that the transactions can obtain read-locks on the same objects concurrently, but because read operations commute, they will not affect the serialization order (the problem gets harder if a transaction may need to upgrade some of its read-locks to write-locks).

Concurrency control (and hence locking) mechanisms can be classified as *optimistic* or *pessimistic*. The locking policy described above is a pessimistic one, because each lock is obtained before the locked data item is accessed. An optimistic policy is one in which transactions simply assume that they will be successful in acquiring locks and perform the necessary work in an opportunistic manner. At commit time, the transaction also verifies that its optimistic assumption was justified (that it got lucky, in effect), and aborts if it now turns out that some of its lock requests should in fact have delayed the computation. As one might expect, a high rate of aborts is a risk with optimistic concurrency-control mechanisms, and they can only be used in settings where the granularity of locking is small enough so that the risk of a real locking conflict between two transactions is actually very low.

The pessimistic aspect of a pessimistic concurrency-control scheme reflects the assumption that there may be frequent conflicts between concurrent transactions. This makes it necessary for a pessimistic locking scheme to operate in a more conventional manner, by delaying the transaction as each new lock request occurs until that lock has been granted; if some other transaction holds a lock on the same item, the requesting transaction will now be delayed until the lock-holding transaction has committed or aborted.

Deadlock is an important concern with pessimistic locking protocols—for example, suppose that T_a obtains a read-lock on x and then requests a write-lock on y. Simultaneously, T_b obtains a read-lock on y and then requests a write-lock on x. Neither transaction can be granted its lock, and in fact one transaction or the other (or both) must now be aborted. At a minimum, a transaction that has been waiting a very long time for a lock will normally abort; in more elaborate schemes, an algorithm can obtain locks in a way that avoids deadlock or can use an algorithm that explicitly detects deadlocks when they occur and overcomes them by aborting one of the deadlocked transactions. Deadlock-free concurrency-control policies can also be devised—for example, by arranging that transactions acquire locks in a fixed order or by using a very coarse locking granularity so that any given transaction requires only one lock. We will return to this topic, and related issues, in Chapter 24, when we discuss techniques for actually implementing a transactional system.

Locking is not the only way to implement transactional concurrency control. Other important techniques include so-called timestamped concurrency control algorithms, in which each transaction is assigned a logical time of execution, and its operations are performed as if they had been issued at the time given by the timestamp. Timestamped concurrency-control is relatively uncommon in the types of systems that we consider in this book—hence, for reasons of brevity, we omit any detailed discussion of the approach. We do note, however, that optimistic timestamped concurrency control mechanisms have been shown to give good performance in systems where there are few true concurrent accesses to the same data items, and that pessimistic locking schemes give the best performance in the converse situation, where a fairly high level of conflicting operations result from concurrent access to a small set of data items. Additionally, timestamped concurrency-control is considered preferable when dealing with transactions that do a great deal of writing, while locking is considered preferable for transactions that are read-intensive. It has been demonstrated that the two styles of concurrency control cannot be mixed: One cannot use timestamps for one class of transactions and locks for another on the same database. However, a hybrid scheme, which combines features of the two approaches and works well in systems with mixtures of read-intensive and write-intensive transactions, has been proposed.

It is common to summarize the properties of a client/server database system so that the mnemonic ACID can be used to recall them:

- *Atomicity*: Each transaction is executed to completion, or not at all. The term *atomic* will be used throughout this text to refer to operations that have multiple suboperations but that are performed in an all-or-nothing manner. If a failure interrupts an atomic transaction it may be necessary to back out (roll back) any partially completed work.
- *Concurrency*: Transactions are executed so as to maximize concurrency, in this way maximizing the degrees of freedom available within the server to schedule execution efficiently (e.g., by doing disk I/O in an efficient order).
- *Independence*: Transactions are designed to execute independently from one another. Each client is written to execute as if the entire remainder of the system were idle, and the database server itself prevents concurrent transactions from observing one another's intermediate results. This is also referred to as *isolation*.
- *Durability*: The results of committed transactions are persistent.

Notice that each of these properties could be beneficial in some settings but could represent a disadvantage in others—for example, there are applications in which one wants the client programs to cooperate explicitly. The ACID properties effectively constrain such programs to interact using the database as an intermediary. Indeed, the overall model makes sense for many classical database applications, but is less suited to message-based distributed systems consisting of large numbers of servers and in which the programs coordinate their actions and cooperate to tolerate failures. All of this will add up to the perspective that complex distributed systems need a mixture of tools, which should include database technology but not legislate that databases be used to the exclusion of other technologies.

We turn now to the question raised earlier: the sense in which transactional systems are stateful, and the implications that this has for client/server software architectures.

A client of a transactional system maintains several forms of state during the period that the transaction executes. These include the transaction ID by which operations are identified, the intermediate results of the transactional operation (values that were read while the transaction was running or values that the transaction will write if it commits), and any locks or concurrency-control information that has been acquired while the transaction was active. This state is shared with the database server, which for its part must keep original values of any data objects updated by noncommitted transactions; keep updates sorted by transactional-ID to know which values to commit if the transaction is successful; and maintain read-lock and write-lock records on behalf of the client, blocking other transactions that attempt to access the locked data items while allowing access to the client holding the locks. The server thus knows which processes are its active clients, and must monitor their health in order to abort transactions associated with clients that fail before committing (otherwise, a failure could leave the database in a locked state).

The ability to use commit and abort is extremely valuable in implementing transactional systems and applications. In addition to the role of these operations in defining the scope of a transaction for purposes of serializability, they also represent a tool that can be used directly by the programmer—for example, an application be designed to assume that a certain class of operations (such as selling a seat on an airline) will succeed, and to update database records as it runs under this assumption. Such an algorithm would be optimistic in much the same sense as a concurrency-control scheme can be optimistic. If, for whatever reason, the operation encounters an error condition (no seats available on some flight, customer credit card refused, etc.), the operation can simply abort and the intermediate actions that were taken will be erased from the database. Moreover, the serializability model ensures that applications can be written without attention to one another: Transactional serializability ensures that if a transaction would be correct when executed in isolation, it will also be correct when executed concurrently against a database server that interleaves operations for increased performance.

The transactional model is also valuable from a reliability perspective. The isolation of transactions from one another avoids inconsistencies that might occur if one transaction were to see the partial results of some other transaction—for example, suppose that transaction T_a increments variable x by 1 and is executed concurrently, with transaction T_b, which decrements x by 1. If T_a and T_b read x concurrently they might base their computations on the same initial value of x. The *write* operation that completes last would then erase the other update. Many concurrent systems are prone to bugs because of this sort of mutual-exclusion problem; transactional systems avoid this issue using locking or other concurrency control mechanisms that would force T_b to wait until T_a has terminated, or the converse. Moreover, transactional abort offers a simple way for a server to deal with a client that fails or seems to hang: It can simply timeout and abort the transaction that the client initiated. (If the client is really alive, its attempt to commit will eventually fail: Transactional systems never guarantee that a commit will be successful). Similarly, the client is insulated from the effects of server failures: It can modify data on the server without concern that an inopportune server crash could leave the database in an inconsistent state.

There is, however, a negative side to transactional distributed computing. As we will see in Chapter 24, transactional programming can be extremely restrictive. The model basically prevents programs from cooperating as peers in a distributed setting, and although extensions have been proposed to overcome this limitation, none seems to be fully satisfactory—that is, transactions really work best for applications in which there is a computational master process, which issues requests to a set of slave processors on which data is stored. This is, of course, a common model, but it is not the only one. Any transactional application in which several processes know about each other and execute concurrently is difficult to model in this manner.

Moreover, transactional mechanisms can be costly, particularly when a transaction is executed on data that has been replicated for high availability or distributed over multiple servers. The locking mechanisms used to ensure serializability can severely limit concurrency, and it can be very difficult to deal with transactions that run for long periods of time, since these will often leave the entire server locked and unable to accept new requests. It can also be very difficult to decide what to do if a transaction aborts unexpectedly: Should the client retry it or report to the user that it aborted? Decisions such as these are very difficult, particularly in sophisticated applications in which one is essentially forced to find a way to roll forward.

For all of these reasons, although transactional computing is a powerful and popular tool in developing reliable distributed software systems, it does not represent a complete model or a complete solution to all reliability issues that occur.

5.6 Applying Transactions to File Servers

Transactional access to data may seem extremely well matched to the issue of file server reliability. Typically, however, file servers either do not implement transactional functionality, or do so only for the specific case of database applications. The reasons for this illustrate the sense in which a mechanism such as transactional data access may be unacceptably constraining in nontransactional settings.

General-purpose computing applications make frequent and extensive use of files. They store parameters in files, search directories for files with special names, store temporary results in files that are passed from phase to phase of a multiphase computation, implement ad hoc structures within very large files, and even use the existence or nonexistence of files and the file protection bits as persistent locking mechanisms, compensating for the lack of locking tools in operating systems such as UNIX .

As we saw earlier, file systems used in support of this model are often designed to be stateless, particularly in distributed systems—that is, each operation by a client is a complete and self-contained unit. The file system maintains no memory of actions by clients, and although the clients may cache information from the file system (such as handles pointing to open file objects), they are designed to refresh this information if it is found to be stale when referenced. Such an approach has the merit of extreme simplicity. It is certainly not the only approach: Some file systems maintain coherent caches of file system blocks within client systems, and these are necessarily stateful. Nonetheless, the great majority of distributed file systems are stateless.

The introduction of transactions on files thus brings with it stateful aspects that are otherwise avoided, potentially complicating an otherwise simple system architecture. However, transactions pose more problems than mere complexity. In particular, the locking mechanisms used by transactions are ill-matched to the pattern of file access seen in general operating systems applications.

Consider the program that was used to edit this book. When started, it displays a list of files that end with the extension ".doc," and waited for me to select the file on which I wished to work. Eventually, the file selected and opened, an extended editing session ensued, perhaps even appearing to last overnight or over a weekend if some distraction prevented me from closing the file and exiting the program before leaving for the evening. In a standard transactional model, each of the read accesses and each of the write accesses would represent an operation associated with the transaction, and transactional serialization ordering would be achieved by delaying these operations as needed to ensure that only serializable executions are permitted—for example, with locks.

This now creates the prospect of a file system containing directories that are locked against updates (because some transaction has read the contents), files that are completely untouchable (because some transaction is updating, or perhaps even deleting the contents), and of long editing sessions that routinely end in failure (because locks may be broken after long delays, forcing the client program to abort its transaction and start again from scratch). It may not seem obvious that such files should pose a problem, but suppose that a transaction's behavior was slightly different as a result of seeing these transient conditions? That transaction would not be correctly serialized if the editing transaction were now aborted, resulting in some other state. No transaction should have been allowed to see the intermediate state.

Obviously, this analysis could be criticized as postulating a clumsy application of transactional serializability to the file system. In practice, one would presumably adapt the model to the semantics of the application. However, even for the specific case of transactional file systems, the system has been less than convincing—for example, at Xerox the early versions of the Clearinghouse software (a form of file system used for e-mail and other user-profile information) offered a fully transactional interface. Over time, this was greatly restricted because of the impracticality of transactional concurrency-control in settings that involve large numbers of general-purpose applications.

Moreover, many file-based applications lack a practical way to assign a transaction-ID to the logical transaction. As an example, consider a version control software system. Such a system seems well matched to the transactional model: A user checks out a file, modifies it, and then checks it in; meanwhile, other users are prevented from doing updates and can only read old copies. Here, however, many individual programs may operate on the file over the period of the transaction. What is lacking is a practical way to associate an identifier with the series of operations. Clearly, the application programs themselves can do so, but one of the basic principles of reliability is to avoid placing excessive trust in the correctness of individual applications; in this example, the correctness of the applications would be a key element of the correctness of the transactional architecture, a very questionable design choice.

On the other hand, transactional file systems offer important benefits. Most often cited among these are the atomic update properties of a transaction, whereby a set of changes to files is made entirely, or not at all. This has resulted in proposals for file systems that are transactional in the limited sense of offering failure atomicity for updates, but without carrying this to the extreme of also providing transactional serializability. Hagmann's use of group commit to reimplement the Cedar file system (see Hagmann) and IBM's QuickSilver file system (see Schmuck and Wyllie) are examples of a research efforts that are viewed as very successful in offering such a compromise. However, transactional atomicity remains uncommon in the most widely used commercial file system products because of the complexity associated with a stateful file system implementation. The appeal of stateless design, and the inherent reliability associated with an architecture in which the clients and servers take responsibility only for their own actions and place limited trust in information that they don't own directly, continues to rule the marketplace.

The most popular alternative to transactions is the atomic rename operation offered by many commercially standard file systems. For complex objects represented as a single file, or as a rooted graph of files, an application can atomically update the collection by creating a new root object containing the modifications, or pointing to modified versions of other files, and then rename the result to obtain the equivalent effect of an atomic commit, with all the updates being installed simultaneously. If a crash occurs, it suffices to delete the partially modified copy; the original version will not be affected. Despite having some minor limitations, designers of fairly complex file systems applications have achieved a considerable degree of reliability using operations such as rename, perhaps together with an *fsync* operation that forces recent updates to an object or file out to the persistent disk storage area.

In conclusion, it is tempting to apply stateful mechanisms and even transactional techniques to file servers. Yet similar results can be obtained, for this particular application, with less costly and cumbersome solutions. Moreover, the simplicity of a stateless approach has enormous appeal in a world where there may be very little control over the software that runs on client computers, and in which trust in the client system will often be misplaced. In light of these considerations, file systems can be expected to remain predominantly stateless even in settings where reliability is paramount.

More generally, this point illustrates an insight to which we will return repeatedly in this book. Reliability is a complex goal and can require a variety of tools. While a stateless file system may be adequately reliable for one use, some other application may find its behavior hopelessly inconsistent and impossible to work around. A stateful database architecture works wonderfully for database applications, but it turns out to be difficult to adapt to general purpose operating systems applications that have less structure, or that merely have a nontransactional structure. Only a diversity of tools, integrated in an environment that encourages the user to match the tool to the need, can possibly lead to reliability in the general sense. No single approach will suffice.

5.7 Message-Queuing Systems

An emerging area of considerable commercial importance, *message-queuing systems* are concerned with extending the client/server paradigm so that clients and servers can be operated asynchronously. This means, for example, that a client may be able to send requests to a server that is not currently operational for batch processing later and that a server may be able to schedule requests from a request queue without fear of delaying a client application that is waiting for a reply. We discuss Message-Queuing systems and other forms of Message-Oriented Middleware Systems (MOMS) in Chapter 11, in conjunction with other distributed computing paradigms that depart from the strict, synchronous-style, client/server architectures that are the focus of this chapter.

5.8 Related Topics

The discussion of this chapter has merely touched upon a very active area for both commercial products and academic research. Although the Windows File System (NTFS) and Sun's Network File System (NFS) are probably the most widely used distributed file system technologies, other major products are doing well in the field—for example, Transarc's AFS product (based on a research system developed originally at Carnegie Mellon University) is widely cited for its advanced security and scalability features and is marketed by IBM. AFS is often promoted as a secure, worldwide file system technology. Later, when we discuss NFS security, it will become clear that this is potentially a very important property and represents a serious reliability exposure in distributed computing configurations that use NFS.

Stateful database and transactional technologies represent one of the largest existing markets for distributed computing systems. Major database products include System-R, SQL-server, and ORACLE; all of these include client/server architectures. There are dozens of less well-known but very powerful technologies. OnLine Transaction Processing (OLTP) technologies, which permit transaction operations on files and other special-purpose data structures, are also a major commercial market: Well-known products include Tuxedo and Encina; and there are many less well known but very successful similar technologies available in this market.

On the research side of the picture, much activity centers around the technical possibilities created by broadband communication, which is bringing extremely high bandwidths and low latencies to systems that were originally designed to operate as autonomously as possible back in the days of slow telephone modems. File systems that page data over high speed network and that treat the client buffer pools as a large distributed buffering resource shared by all clients are being developed: Such systems gain enormous performance benefits from the resulting substantial enlargement in the file system buffer pool and because the latency incurred when fetching data over the network is orders of magnitude lower than that of fetching data from a remote disk. Examples of this style of research include the XFS project at Berkeley (see Anderson et al.), the Global Memory project at University of Washington (see Feeley et al.), and the CRL project at MIT (see Johnson et al.). Such architectures create interesting reliability and consistency issues, which are closely related to the technologies we will be discussing in Part III.

In the past, file systems and database servers saw a mixed read-write load with a bias toward read operations, and they were organized accordingly. But as the percentage of active data resident in the buffer pools of clients has risen, the percentage of read requests that actually reach the server has dropped correspondingly. A modern file system server sees a workload that is heavily biased towards update traffic. Best known of the work in this area is Rosenblum's log-structured file system (LFS) (see Rosenblum and Ousterhout), developed as part of Ousterhout's Sprite project at Berkeley. LFS implements an append-only data structure (a log), which it garbage collects and compacts using background scavenger mechanisms. Fast indexes permit rapid read access to the file system but because most of the disk I/O is in the form of writes to the log, the system gains a tremendous performance boost. Similar issues have been studied in the context of database systems and have shown that similar benefits were possible. One can anticipate that the technology trends now seen in the broad marketplace will continue to shift basic elements of the low-level file system architecture creating further opportunities for significant improvements in average data access latencies and in other aspects of client/server performance.

5.9 Related Reading

I am not aware of any good general reference on NFS itself, although the standard is available from Sun Microsystems and is widely supported.

The definitive paper on performance of the Berkeley File System is McKusick *et. al.* (2000). A "contrary" view on file system performance can be found in Ganger (2000).

NFS performance and access patterns is studied in Ousterhout (1985) and extended to the Sprite file system in Baker et al.

References to NFS-like file systems supporting replication include Bhide et al., Digital Equipment Corporation, Kronenberg et al., Ladin et al., Liskov et al., Siegal.

Topics related to the CMU file system work that lead to AFS are covered in Bellovin and Merritt, Birrell, Howard et al., Lampson et al., Satyanarayanan, Satyanarayanan et al., Schiller, Spector, Steiner et al.

Coda is discussed in Kistler and Satyanarayanan, Mummert et al. The definitive paper on the CODA file system was published in ACM TOCS: see Satayanarayanan 2003.

MIT's Rover Toolkit is discussed in Joseph (1995).

RAID is discussed in Paterson et al. Sprite is discussed in Nelson et al., Ousterhout et al., Srinivasan and Mogul. Ficus is discussed in Reiher et al., Locus in Heidemann and Popek (1995), Walter et al.

XFS is discussed in Anderson et al.

The world's largest distributed file system (35,000 computers at last count) is operational at Google, and described in Ghemawat (2003).

Additional important work on file systems includes Ganger et al., Rosenblum et al., McKusick et al., Hartman et al. and Santry et al. A clever way to reduce the bandwidth needed by mobile file systems is described in Muthitacharoen et al. Frangiapani, a scalable distributed file system based on group communication mechanisms, is described in Thekkath et al. and is worth reading both as an interesting paper and because the Paxos mechanisms employed in the core of this system have been embraced by Microsoft Corporation for internal purposes and hence could someday become visible to developers using that company's platforms.

Work on global memory is covered in Feeley et al., Johnson et al.

Database references for the transactional approach are studied in Bernstein et al., Gray (1979), Gray and Reuter.

Tandem's system is presented in Bartlett et al.

Nomadic transactional systems are covered in Alonso and Korth, Amir.

Transactions on file systems are discussed in Hagmann, Schmuck and Wyllie.

Related work is treated in Liskov and Scheifler, Liskov et al., Macedo et al., Moss.

6

CORBA: The Common Object Request Broker Architecture

With the emergence of object-oriented programming languages, such as Modula and C++, came a recognition that object-orientation could play a role similar to that of the OSI hierarchy for complex distributed systems. In this view, one would describe a computing system in terms of the set of objects from which it was assembled, together with the rules by which these objects interact with one another. Object-oriented system design became a major subject for research, with many of the key ideas pulled together for the first time by a British research effort, called the Advanced Network Systems Architecture group, or ANSA. In this chapter, we will briefly discuss ANSA, and then focus on a more recent standard, called CORBA, which draws on some of the ideas introduced by ANSA, and has emerged as a widely accepted standard for objected-oriented distributed computing. Finally, we touch briefly on J2EE and .NET, two modern object-oriented environments that make extensive use of ideas from CORBA.

A common and popular implementation of the CORBA model is the TAO system, developed by Doug Schmidt at the University of California, Irvine (previously, he worked at Washington University in St. Louis). The system exists both as a free platform that can be downloaded from http://www.cs.wustl.edu/~schmidt/, and as a commercial product from a company Schmidt subsequently launched to support and extend the basic system. TAO runs over a remote procedure call and "execution environment" technology called ACE. Readers of this text who wish to experiment with CORBA and are using a Linux platform for development are encouraged to download ACE and TAO.

6.1 The ANSA Project

The ANSA project, headed by Andrew Herbert, was the first systematic attempt to develop technology for modeling complex distributed systems (see Architecture Projects

Management Limited [1989, April 1991, November 1991]). ANSA was intended as a technology base for writing down the structure of a complex application or system and then translating the resulting description into a working version of that system in a process of stepwise refinement.

Abstractly, ANSA consists of a set of models, which deal with various aspects of distributed systems design and representation problems. The *enterprise model* is concerned with the overall functions and roles of the organizational structure within which the problem at hand is to be solved—for example, an air-traffic control system would be an application within the air traffic control organization, an enterprise. The *information model* represents the flow of information within the enterprise; in an air traffic application this model might describe flight control status records, radar inputs, radio communication to and from pilots, and so forth. The *computation model* is a framework of programming structures and program development tools that are made available to developers. The model deals with such issues as modularity of the application itself, invocation of operations, parameter passing, configuration, concurrency and synchronization, replication, and the extension of existing languages to support distributed computing. The *engineering and technology models* reduce these abstractions to practice, providing the implementation of the ANSA abstractions and mapping these to the underlying run-time environment and its associated technologies.

In practical terms, most users viewed ANSA as a set of rules for system design, whereby system components could be described as objects with published interfaces. An application with appropriate permissions could obtain a handle on the object and invoke its methods using the procedures and functions defined in this interface. The ANSA environment would automatically and transparently deal with such issues as fetching objects from storage, launching programs when a new instance of an object was requested, implementing the object invocation protocols, and so forth. Moreover, ANSA explicitly included features for overcoming failures of various kinds, using transactional techniques drawn from the database community, as well as process group techniques in which sets of objects are used to implement a single highly available distributed service. We will consider both types of technology in considerable detail in Part III of the book.

ANSA treated the objects that implement a system as the concrete realization of the enterprise computing model and the enterprise information model. These models captured the essence of the application as a whole, treating it as a single abstraction even if the distributed system as implemented necessarily contained many components. Thus, the enterprise-computing model might support the abstraction of a collision-avoidance strategy for use by the air traffic control enterprise as a whole, and the enterprise data model might define the standard data objects used in support of this service. The actual implementation of the service would be reached by a series of refinements in which increasing levels of detail are added to this basic set of definitions. In effect, one passes from the abstraction of a collision-avoidance strategy to the more concrete concept of a collision-avoidance subsystem located at each set of primary sites and linked to one another to coordinate their actions (see Figure 6.1). This concept evolved to one with further refinements, defining the

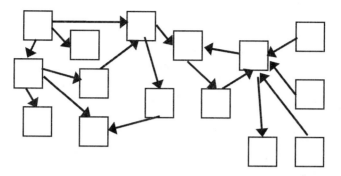

Figure 6.1. Distributed objects abstraction. Objects are linked by object references, and the distributed nature of the environment is hidden from users. Access is uniform even if objects are implemented to have special properties or internal structure, such as replication for increased availability or transactional support for persistence. Objects can be implemented in different programming languages, but this is invisible to users.

standard services composing the collision-avoidance system as used on a single air traffic control workstation, and then evolved still further to a description of how those services could be implemented.

In very concrete terms, the ANSA approach required the designer to write down the sort of knowledge of distributed system structure that, for many systems, is implicit but never encoded in a machine-readable form. The argument was that by writing down these system descriptions, a better system would emerge: one in which the rationale for the structure used was self-documenting and in which detailed information would be preserved about the design choices and objectives that the system carries out; in this manner the mechanisms for future evolution could be made a part of the system itself. Such a design

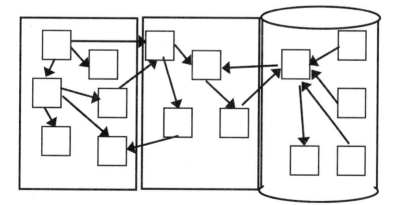

Figure 6.2. In practice, the objects in a distributed system execute on machines or reside in storage servers. The run-time environment works to conceal movement of objects from location to location and to activate servers when they are initially referenced after having been passively stored. The environment also deals with fault-tolerance issues, the life-cycle of an object, garbage collection, and other issues that span multiple objects or sites.

promotes extensibility and interoperability, and offers a path to system management and control. Moreover, ANSA designs were expressed in terms of objects, whose locations could be anywhere in the network, with the actual issues of location developing only after the design was further elaborated, or in specific situations where location of an object might matter (Figure 6.2). This type of object-oriented, location-transparent design has proved very popular with distributed systems designers.

6.2 Beyond ANSA to CORBA

While the ANSA technology per se never gained a wide following, these ideas have had a huge impact on the view of system design and function adopted by modern developers. In particular, as the initial stages of the ANSA project ended, a new project was started by a consortium of computer vendors. Called the Common Object Request Broker Architecture, CORBA defines a range of standards permitting interoperation between complex object-oriented systems potentially built by diverse vendors (see Object Management Group and X/Open). CORBA has become a widely used, important platform. At the time of this writing, the J2EE and .NET platforms have become dominant, and CORBA receives somewhat less attention. Web Services are just emerging. Yet CORBA will be with us for many years into the future. Moreover, essentially all aspects of CORBA have analogs within J2EE and .NET.

CORBA represents a consensus developed within an industry standards organization called the Object Management Group, or OMG. The mission of OMG was to develop architecture standards promoting interoperability between systems developed using object-oriented technologies—the stress, then, is on getting legacy applications to talk to one-another and to new applications. In some ways, this represents a less-ambitious objective than the task with which ANSA was charged, since ANSA set out both to develop an all-encompassing architectural vision for building enterprise-wide distributed computing systems, and to incorporate reliability technologies into its solutions. However, ANSA was sometimes criticized for its emphasis on new generations of systems and its inattention to the difficulties of legacy integration. CORBA's early success was almost certainly related to the good treatment of this topic. Moreover, as CORBA has evolved, it has begun to tackle many of the ANSA's original topics.

At the time of this writing, CORBA was basically a framework for building distributed computing environments and letting applications running in one CORBA environment issue requests to applications running in another. Notice that different vendors might offer their own CORBA solutions with differing properties. Nonetheless, adherence to the CORBA guidelines should permit such solutions to interoperate. For example, a distributed system programmed using a CORBA product from Hewlett-Packard should be useful from within an application developed using CORBA products from Sun Microsystems, IBM, or some other CORBA-compliant vendor.

A common and popular implementation of the CORBA model is the TAO system, developed by Doug Schmidt at the University of California, Irvine (previously, he worked at Washington University in St. Louis). The system exists both as a free platform that can be downloaded from http://www.cs.wustl.edu/~schmidt/TAO.html, and as a commercial product from a company Schmidt subsequently launched to support and extend the basic system. TAO runs over a remote procedure call and "execution environment" technology called ACE. Readers of this text who wish to experiment with CORBA and are using a Linux platform for development are encouraged to download ACE and TAO.

Interoperability has steadily grown in importance over the decade since CORBA was first introduced. In fact, it is quite striking to discover that in some ways, J2EE and .NET have replayed the same questions that initially distinguished CORBA from ANSA. J2EE (Java version 2 Enterprise Edition) is a "commercial strength" runtime environment for Java applications—specifically, Java applications that talk to databases and other forms of servers (they are constructed using what is called the "Java Beans" component of the overall architecture). Initially, the vision of the Java community was that Java would sweep other languages to the side. As a result, much of the early effort in the Java development activities at SUN and elsewhere concentrated on pure Java applications, with interoperability arising only in the binding between a Java Bean and the server (normally, database server) to which it was connected. J2EE incorporated most aspects of the CORBA framework and all aspects of the CORBA database architecture.

J2EE was tremendously successful right from the outset, and this motivated Microsoft to fight back with a J2EE-like environment of its own. Microsoft needed a distinguishing product focus, however, hence while .NET includes analogous database and server functionality to J2EE (in the architectural framework called ADO.NET), the platform goes much further in its handling of integration issues. .NET promotes a tremendous range of integration and legacy systems features, including full language interoperability, easy mechanisms for binding a new system to a specific instance of an old system and a means for making sure that the right versions are running at the same time, cross-language debugging tools, and so forth. This position was an immediate success within the Microsoft market, and J2EE almost immediately began to lose market share. Accordingly the J2EE developers responded by developing a new "object adaptor" framework for J2EE, offering all of the kinds of interoperability available for .NET users.

J2EE is a framework aimed at Java users, and Microsoft is often portrayed as an opponent of Java. In fact, however, .NET embraces the Java language in many ways. First, .NET supports a completely standard version of Java, so Java applications can migrate easily to .NET. Secondly, however, .NET introduces a new programming language called C# (C-sharp), which is nearly identical to Java with the exception of some very minor syntactic decisions and some rather obscure aspects of the base object class. The C# runtime environment, however, departs in dramatic ways from the J2EE runtime environment, offering native (but supposedly secure) access to all sorts of Windows primitives and permitting very comprehensive use of all aspects of the Windows environment, particularly through the "builder" system, called Visual Studio .NET for C#.

The effect of all of this activity is that .NET seems to have firmed Microsoft's hold on the desktop, where SUN had initially hoped to see J2EE emerge as a major player. J2EE and CORBA are dominant on enterprise servers and within the corporate network backbone.

6.3 Web Services

As this book was being written, Web Services were poised to shake things up yet again. These standards can be seen as unifying features common to CORBA, .NET and J2EE, but also as limiting themselves (at least for now) through their focus on interoperability between client and server systems. In contrast, .NET, J2EE, and CORBA are perhaps more focused on new applications and are best seen as comprehensive runtime environments. Part II of the book focuses on the Web Services model and looks at a variety of fault-tolerance and reliability issues that arise in this architecture. The same sort of analysis could have been applied to .NET, J2EE or CORBA, and the findings would be essentially identical. However, Web Services are likely to be the common denominator for a wide range of technologies and systems, and many Web Services developers are likely to confront the sorts of reliability and "high assurance" goals we consider here.

The best way to understand Web Services (and indeed, .NET or J2EE) is to first understand CORBA, hence this chapter focuses on the CORBA model.

6.4 The CORBA Reference Model

The key to understanding the structure of a CORBA environment is the *Reference Model*, which consists of a set of components that a CORBA platform should typically provide. These components are fully described by the CORBA architecture, but only to the level of interfaces used by application developers and functionality. Individual vendors are responsible for deciding how to implement these interfaces and how to obtain the best possible performance; moreover, individual products may offer solutions that differ in offering optional properties such as security, high availability, or special guarantees of behavior that go beyond the basics required by the model.

At a minimum, a CORBA implementation must supply an *Object Request Broker*, or ORB, which is responsible for matching a requestor with an object that will perform its request, using the object reference to locate an appropriate target object (see Figure 6.3). The implementation will also contain translation programs, responsible for mapping implementations of system components (and their IDLs) to programs that can be linked with a run-time library and executed. A set of *object services* provide the basic functionality needed to create and use objects: These include such functions as creating, deleting, copying, or moving objects; giving them names that other objects can use to bind to them; and providing security. An interesting service, which we will discuss in more detail, is the *Event Notification Service* or ENS: This allows a program to register its interest in a class of events. All events in that class are then reported to the program. It thus represents a communication technology different from the usual RPC-style or stream-style of connection. A set of *Common Facilities* contains a collection of standardized applications that most CORBA implementations are expected to support, but that are ultimately optional: These include, for example, standards for system management and for electronic mail that may contain objects. And, finally, of

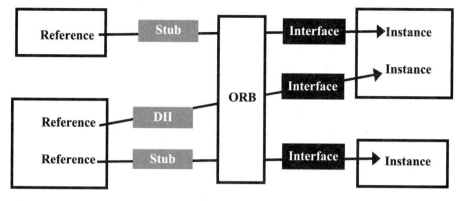

Figure 6.3. The conceptual architecture of CORBA uses an object request broker as an intermediary that directs object invocations to the appropriate object instances. There are two cases of invocations; the static one, which we focus on in the book, and the dynamic invocation interface (DII), which is more complex to use and hence not discussed here.

course, there are *Application Objects* developed by the CORBA user to solve a particular problem.

In many respects the Object Request Broker is the core of a CORBA implementation. Similar to the function of a communication network or switching system, the ORB is responsible for delivering object invocations that originate in a client program to the appropriate server program, and routing the reply back to the client. The ability to invoke an object, of course, does not imply that the object that was invoked is being used correctly, has a consistent state, or is even the most appropriate object for the application to use. These broader properties fall back upon the basic technologies of distributed computing that are the general topic of this book; as we will see, CORBA is a way of *talking about* solutions but not a *specific set of prebuilt solutions*. Indeed, one could say that because CORBA worries about syntax but not semantics, the technology is largely superficial: a veneer around a set of technologies. However, this particular veneer is an important and sophisticated one, and it also creates a context within which a principled and standardized approach to distributed systems reliability becomes possible.

For many users, object-oriented computing means programming in Java, C++ or C#, although SmallTalk and Ada are also object-oriented languages, and one can develop object interfaces to other languages like FORTRAN and COBOL. Nonetheless, Java and C++ are the most widely used languages, and most Java programmers focus on J2EE, while C# programmers tend to use .NET. Thus for illustration of CORBA it makes sense to employ C++, since the average CORBA programmer would work in this language. Our examples are drawn directly from the programmer's guide for Orbix, an extremely popular CORBA technology at the time of this writing.

An example of a CORBA object interface, coded in the Orbix interface definition language (IDL), is shown in Figure 6.4. This interface publishes the services available from a grid server, which is intended to manage two-dimensional tables such as are used in spreadsheets or relational databases (apologies to those who were hoping that this example is from the Grid Computing world). The server exports two read-only values, width and height, which can be used to query the size of a grid object. There are also two operations that can be performed upon the object: "set," which sets the value of an element, and

```
// grid server example for Orbix
// IDL – in file grid.idl
interface grid {
        readonly attribute short height;
        readonly attribute short width;

        void set(in short w, in short h, in long value);
        long get(in short w, in short h);
}
```

Figure 6.4. IDL interface to a server for a grid object coded in Orbix, a popular CORBA-compliant technology.

"get," which fetches the value. Set is of type void, meaning that it does not return a result, get, on the other hand, returns a long integer.

To build a grid server, the user would need to write a C++ program that implements this interface. To do this, the IDL compiler is first used to transform the IDL file into a standard C++ header file in which Orbix defines the information it will need to implement remote invocations on behalf of the client. The IDL compiler also produces two forms of stub files—one that implements the client side of the get and set operations; the other implements the server side. These stub files must be compiled and linked to the respective programs. (See Figure 6.5.)

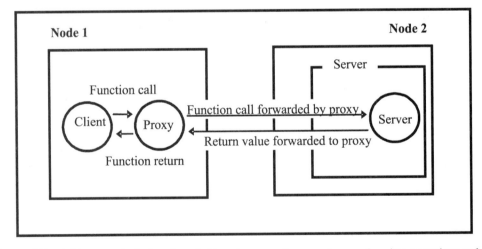

Figure 6.5. Orbix conceals the location of objects by converting remote operations into operations on local proxy objects, mediated by stubs. However, remote access is not completely transparent in standard CORBA applications if an application is designed for reliability—for example, error conditions differ for local and remote objects. Such issues can be concealed by integrating a reliability technology into the CORBA environment, but transparent reliability is not a standard part of CORBA, and solutions vary widely from vendor to vendor.

If one were to look at the contents of the header file produced for the grid IDL file, one would discover that width and height have been transformed into functions; that is, when the C++ programmer references an attribute of a grid object, a function call will actually occur into the client-side stub procedures, which can perform an RPC to the grid server to obtain the current value of the attribute.

We say RPC here, but in fact a feature of CORBA is that it provides very efficient support for invocations of local objects, which are defined in the same address space as the invoking program. The significance of this is that although the CORBA IDL shown in Figure 6.4 could be used to access a remote server that handles one or more grid objects, it can also be used to communicate to a completely local instantiation of a grid object, contained entirely in the address space of the calling program. Indeed, the concept goes even further: In Orbix+Isis, a variation of Orbix, the grid server could be replicated using an object group for high availability. And in the most general case, the grid object's clients could be implemented by a server running under some other CORBA-based environment, such as IBM's DSOM product, HP's DOMF or ObjectBroker, Sun's DOE, or other object-oriented environments with which CORBA can communicate using an adapter, such as

```
// Implementation of grid class
#include "grid_i.h"

grid_i::grid_i(short h, short w) {
        m_height = h;
        m_width = w;
        m_a = new long* [h];
        for (int i = 0; i < h; i++)
                m_a[i] = new long [w];
}
grid_i::~grid_i() {
        for (int i = 0; i < m_height; i++)
                delete[ ] m_a[i];
        delete[ ] m_a;
}
short grid_i::width(CORBA::Environment &) {
        return m_width;
}
short grid_i::height(CORBA::Environment &) {
        return m_height;
}
void grid_i::set(short w, short m, long value, CORBA::Environment &) {
        m_a[n][m] = value;
}
long grid_i::get(short n, short m, CORBA::Environment &) {
        return m_a[n][m];
}
```

Figure 6.6.   Server code to implement the grid_i class in Orbix

```
#include "grid_i.h"
#include <iostream.h>

void main() {
        grid_imyGrid(100,100);
        // Orbix objects can be named but this is not
        // needed for this example
        CORBA::Orbix.impl_is_ready();
        cout <<"server terminating" << endl;
}
```

Figure 6.7. Enclosing program to declare a grid object and accept requests upon it.

```
#include "grid_h.h"
#include <iostream.h>

void main() {
        grid *p;

        p = grid::_bind(":gridSrv");
        cout << "height is " << p->height() << endl;
        cout << "width is " << p->width() << endl;
            p->set(2, 4, 123);
        cout << "grid(2, 4) is " << p->get(2, 4) << endl;
            p->release();
}
```

Figure 6.8. Client program for the grid object—assumes that the grid was registered under the server name "gridSrv." This example lacks error handling; an elaborated version with error handling appears in Figure 6.10.

Microsoft's OLE. CORBA implementations thus have the property that object location, the technology or programming language used to build an object, and even the ORB under which it is running can be almost completely transparent to the user.

What exactly would a grid server look like? If we are working in C++, a grid would be a C++ program that includes an implementation class for grid objects. Figure 6.6 shows the code that might be used to implement this abstract data type, again drawing on Orbix as a source for our example. The "Environment" parameter is used for error handling with the client. The BOAImpl extension ("gridBOAImpl") designates that this is a Basic Object Adaptor Implementation for the grid interface.

Finally, our server needs an enclosing framework: the program itself that will execute this code. The code in Figure 6.7 provides this; it implements a single grid object and declares itself to be ready to accept object invocations. The grid object is not named in this example, although it could have been, and indeed the server could be designed to create and destroy grid objects dynamically at run time.

```
#include "grid_h.h"
#include <iostream.h>

void main() {
        grid *p;

        TRY {
                p = grid::_bind(":gridSrv");
        }
        CATCHANY {
                cerr << "bind to object failed" << endl;
                cerror << "Fatal exception " << IT_X << endl;
                exit(1);
        }
        TRY {
                cout << "height is " << p->height() << endl;
        }
        CATCHANY {
                 cerr << "call to height failed" << endl;
                cerror << "Fatal exception " << IT_X << endl;
                exit(1);
        }
        ... etc ...
}
```

Figure 6.9. Illustration of Orbix error-handling facility. Macros are used to catch errors; if one occurs, the error can be caught and potentially worked around. Notice that each remote operation can potentially fail—hence, exception handling would normally be more standardized. A handler for a high-availability application would operate by rebinding to some other server capable of providing the same functionality. This can be concealed from the user, which is the approach used in systems like Orbix+Isis or Electra, a CORBA technology layered over the Horus distributed system.

The user can now declare to Orbix that the grid server is available by giving it a name and storing the binary of the server in a file, the path name of which is also provided to Orbix (see Figure 6.9). The Orbix life-cycle service will automatically start the grid server if an attempt is made to access it when it is not running.

CORBA supports several concepts of reliability. One is concerned with recovering from failures—for example, when invoking a remote server. A second reliability mechanism is provided for purposes of reliable interactions with persistent objects, and is based upon what is called a transactional architecture. We discuss transactions elsewhere in this book and will not digress onto that subject at this time. However, the basic purpose of a transactional architecture is to provide a way for applications to perform operations on complex persistent data structures, without interfering with other concurrently active but independent operations, in a manner that will leave the structure intact even if the application program or server fails while it is running. Unfortunately, as we will see in Chapter 24, transactions are primarily useful in applications that are structured as database systems on which programs operate using read and update requests. Such structures are important in distributed systems, but there are many distributed applications that match the model poorly, and, for them, transactional reliability is not a good approach.

Outside of its transactional mechanisms, CORBA offers relatively little help to the programmer concerned with reliability or high availability. For example, Orbix can be notified that a server application can be run on one of a number of machines. When a client application attempts to use the remote application, Orbix will automatically attempt to bind to each machine in turn, selecting at random the first machine that confirms that the server application is operational. However, Orbix does not provide any form of automatic mechanisms for recovering from the failure of such a server after the binding is completed. The reason for this is that a client process that is already communicating with a server may have a complex state that reflects information specific to that server, such as cached records with record identifiers that came from the server, or other forms of data that differ in specific ways even among servers able to provide the same functionality. To rebind the client to a new server, one would somehow need to refresh, rebuild, or roll back this server-dependent state. And doing so is potentially very difficult; at a minimum, considerable detailed knowledge of the application will be required.

The same problems can also arise in the server itself. For example, consider a financial trading service, in which the prices of various stocks are presented. Now, suppose that this data is extremely dynamic due to rapidly changing market data. The server may need to have some form of setup that it uses to establish a client profile, and it may need to have an internal state that reflects the events that have occurred since the client first bound to it. Even if some other copy of the server is available and can provide the same services, there could be a substantial time lag when rebinding and there may be a noticeable discontinuity if the new server, lacking this state of the session, starts its financial computations from the current stream of incoming data. Such events will not be transparent to the client using the server and it is unrealistic to try and hide them.

The integration of a wider spectrum of reliability-enhancing technologies with CORBA represents an important area for research and commercial development, particularly if reliability is taken in the broad sense of security, fault tolerance, availability, and so forth. High-performance, commercially appealing products will be needed to demonstrate the effectiveness of the architectural features that result: When we discuss transactions on distributed objects, for example, we will see that merely supporting transactions through an architecture is not likely to make users happy. Even the execution of transactions on objects raises deeper issues that would need to be resolved for such a technology to be accepted as a genuinely valid reliability-enhancing tool—for example, the correct handling of a transactional request by a non-transactional service is unspecified in the architecture.

More broadly, CORBA can be viewed as the ISO hierarchy for object-oriented distributed computing: It provides us with a framework within which such systems can be described and offers ways to interconnect components without regard for the programming language or vendor technologies used in developing them. Exploiting this to achieve critical reliability in distributed settings, however, stands as a more basic technical challenge that CORBA does not directly address. CORBA tells us how to structure and present these technologies, but not how to build them.

6.5 IDL and ODL

IDL is the language used to define an object interface (in the TINA standard, there is an ODL language that goes beyond IDL in specifying other attributes of the object, and in allowing each object to export more than one interface). (See Figure 6.10.) CORBA defines an IDL for the various languages that can be supported: C++, SmallTalk, Ada95, and so forth. The most standard of these is the IDL for C++, and the examples given above are expressed in C++ for that reason. However, expanded use of IDL for other programming languages is likely in the future.

The use of C++ programs in a CORBA environment can demand a high level of sophistication in C++ programming. In particular, the operator overload functionality of C++ can conceal complex machinery behind deceptively simple interfaces. In a standard programming language one expects that an assignment statement such as $a = b$ will execute rapidly. In C++ such an operation may involve allocation and initialization of a new abstract object and a potentially costly copying operation. In CORBA such an assignment may

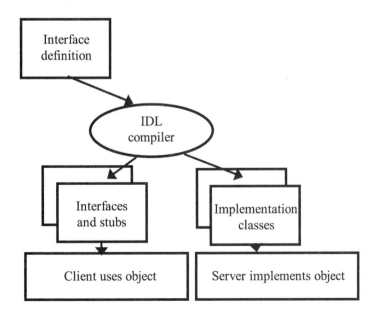

Figure 6.10. From the interface definition, the IDL compiler creates stub and interface files, which are used by clients that invoke the object and by servers that implement it.

involve costly remote operations on a server remote from the application program that executes the assignment statement. To the programmer, CORBA and C++ appear as a mixed blessing: Through the CORBA IDL, operations such as assignment and value references can be transparently extended over a distributed environment, which can seem like magic. But the magic is potentially tarnished by the discovery that a single assignment might now take seconds (or hours) to complete!

Such observations point to a deficiency in the CORBA IDL language and, perhaps, the entire technology as currently conceived. IDL provides no features for specifying *behaviors* of remote objects that are desirable or undesirable consequences of distribution. There is no possibility of using IDL to indicate a performance property (or cost, in the above example) or to specify a set of fault-tolerant guarantees for an object that differ from the ones normally provided in the environment. Synchronization requirements or assumptions made by an object, or guarantees offered by the client, cannot be expressed in the language. This missing information, potentially needed for reliability purposes, can limit the ability of the programmer to fully specify a complex distributed system, while also denying the user the basic information needed to validate that a complex object is being used correctly.

One could argue that the IDL should be limited to specification of the interface to an object and that other types of services would manage any behavioral specifications. Indeed, in the case of the life-cycle service, one has a good example of how the CORBA community approaches this problem: The life-cycle aspects of an object specification are treated as a special type of data managed by this service, and are not considered to be a part of the object interface specification. Yet this information often belongs in the interface specification, in the sense that these types of properties may have direct implications for the user that accesses the object and may be information of a type that is important in establishing that the object is being used correctly. The specification of an object involves more than the specification of its interfaces, and indeed the interface specification involves more than just the manner in which one invokes the object. In contrast, the CORBA community considers behavior to be orthogonal to interface specification, and hence it relegates behavioral aspects of the object's specification to the special-purpose services directly concerned with that type of information. Unfortunately, it seems likely that much basic research will need to be done before this issue is addressed in a convincing manner.

6.6 ORB

An Object Request Broker, or ORB, is the component of the run-time system that binds client objects to the server objects they access, and that interprets object invocations at run time, arranging for the invocation to occur on the object that was referenced. (CORBA is thus the OMG's specification of the ORB and of its associated services). ORBs can be thought of as switching systems through which invocation messages flow. A fully compliant CORBA implementation supports interoperation of ORBs with one another over TCP connections, using what is called the Internet Inter-ORB Protocol (IIOP) protocol. In such an interoperation mode, any CORBA server can potentially be invoked from any CORBA client, even if the server and client were built and are operated on different versions of the CORBA technology base.

Associated with the ORB are a number of features designed to simplify the life of the developer. An ORB can be programmed to automatically launch a server if it is not running when a client accesses it (this is called factory functionality), and can be asked to automatically filter invocations through user-supplied code that automates the handling of error conditions or the verification of security properties. The ORB can also be programmed to make an intelligent choice of an object if many objects are potentially capable of handling the same request; such a functionality would permit, for example, load-balancing within a group of servers that replicate a particular database.

6.7 Naming Service

A CORBA naming service is used to bind names to objects. Much as a file system is organized as a set of directories, the CORBA naming architecture defines a set of *naming contexts*, and each name is interpreted relative to the naming context within which that name is registered. The CORBA naming architecture is potentially a very general one, but, in practice, many applications are expected to treat it as an object-oriented generalization of a traditional naming hierarchy. Such applications would build hierarchical naming context graphs (directory trees), use ASCII style path names to identify objects, and standardize the sets of attributes stored for each object in the naming service (e.g., size, access time, modification time, owner, permissions, etc.). The architecture, however, is sufficiently flexible to allow a much broader concept of names and naming.

A CORBA name should not be confused with an object reference. In the CORBA architecture, an object reference is essentially a pointer to the object. Although a reference need not include specific location information, it does include enough information for an ORB to find a path to the object, or to an ORB that will know how to reach the object. Names, in contrast, are symbolic ways of naming these references. By analogy to a UNIX file system, a CORBA object name is similar to a path name (and, as with a path name, more than one name can refer to the same object). A CORBA object reference is similar to a UNIX *vnode* reference: a machine address and an identifier for a file *inode* stored on that machine. From the name one can lookup the reference, but this is a potentially costly operation. Given the object reference one can invoke the object, and this (one hopes) will be quite a bit cheaper.

6.8 ENS—The CORBA Event Notification Service

The CORBA Event Notification Service, or ENS, provides for notifications of asynchronous events to applications that register an interest in those events by obtaining a handle, to which events can be posted and on which events can be received. Reliability features are optionally supplied. The ENS is best understood in terms of what is called the *publish/subscribe* communication architecture[5]. In this approach, messages are produced by *publishers* that label each new message using a set of *subjects* or *attributes*. Separately, applications that wish to be informed when events occur on a given subject will *subscribe* to that subject or will poll for messages relating to the subject. The role of the ENS is to reliably bind the publishers to the subscribers, ensuring that even though the publishers do not know who the subscribers will be, and vice versa, messages are promptly and reliably delivered to them. (See Figure 6.11.)

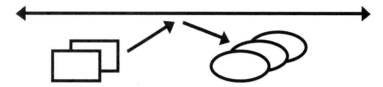

Figure 6.11. The CORBA ENS is a form of message bus that supports a publish/subscribe architecture. The sources of events (boxes) and consumers (ovals) need not be explicitly aware of one another, and the sets can change dynamically. A single object can produce or consume events of multiple types, and, in fact, an object can be both producer and consumer.

Two examples will make the value of such a model more clear. Suppose that one were using CORBA to implement a software architecture for a large brokerage system or a stock exchange. The ENS for such an environment could be used to broadcast stock trades as they occur. The events in this example would be named using the stock and bond names that they describe. Each broker would subscribe to the stocks of interest, again using these subject names, and the application program would then receive incoming quotes and display them to the screen. Notice that the publisher program can be developed without knowing anything about the nature of the applications that will use the ENS to monitor its outputs: It need not have compatible types or interfaces except with respect to the events that are exchanged between them. And the subscriber, for its part, does not need to be bound to a particular publisher: If a new data source of interest is developed, it can be introduced into the system without changing the existing architecture.

A second example of how the ENS can be useful would arise in system management and monitoring. Suppose that an application is being developed to automate some of the management functions occurring in a VLSI fabrication facility. As time goes by, the developers expect to add more and more sources of information and introduce more and more applications that use this information to increase the efficiency and productivity of the factory. An ENS architecture facilitates doing so, because it permits the developers to separate the *information architecture* of their application from its *implementation architecture*. In such an example, the information architecture is the structure of the ENS event space

---

[5]It should be noted, however, that the ENS lacks the sort of subject mapping facilities that are central to many publish-subscribe message-bus architectures, and is in this sense a more primitive facility than some of the message bus technologies that will be discussed later in this book, such as the TIBCO Information Bus (TIB).

itself: The subjects under which events may be posted, and the types of events that can arise in each subject. The sources and consumers of the events can be introduced later, and will in general be unaware of one another. Such a design preserves tremendous flexibility and facilitates an evolutionary design for the system. After basic functionality is in place, additional functions can be introduced in a gradual way and without disrupting existing software. Here, the events would be named according to the aspect of factory function to which they relate: status of devices, completion of job steps, scheduled downtime, and so forth. Each application program would subscribe to those classes of events relevant to its task, ignoring all others by not subscribing to them.

Not all CORBA implementations include the ENS—for example, the basic Orbix product described above lacks an ENS, although the Orbix+Isis extension makes use of a technology called the Isis Message Distribution Service to implement ENS functionality in an Orbix setting. This, in turn, was implemented using the Isis Toolkit, which we will discuss in more detail in Chapter 20.

6.9 Life-Cycle Service

The Life-Cycle Service, or LCS, standardizes the facilities for creating and destroying objects, and for copying them or moving them within the system. The service includes a *factory* for manufacturing new objects of a designated type. The Life-Cycle Service is also responsible for scheduling backups, periodically compressing object repositories to reclaim free space, and initiating other life-cycle activities. To some degree, the service can be used to program object-specific management and supervisory functions, which may be important to reliable control of a distributed system.

6.10 Persistent Object Service

The Persistent Object Service, or POS, is the CORBA equivalent of a file system. This service maintains collections of objects for long-term use, organizing them for efficient retrieval and working closely with its clients to give application-specific meanings to the consistency, persistency, and access-control restrictions implemented within the service. This permits the development of special-purpose POSs—for example, to maintain databases with large numbers of nearly identical objects organized into relational tables, as opposed to file system-style storage of very irregular objects.

6.11 Transaction Service

Mentioned earlier, the transaction service is an embedding of database-style transactions into CORBA architecture. If implemented, the service provides a *concurrency control* service for synchronizing the actions of concurrently active transactions; *flat* and (optionally) *nested* transactional tools, and special-purpose persistent object services, which implement the transactional *commit* and *abort* mechanisms. The transaction service is often used with the *relationship service*, which tracks relationships among sets of objects—for example, if they are grouped into a database or some other shared data structure. We looked at the transactional execution model in Section 5.6, and return to it in Chapter 24.

6.12   Interobject Broker Protocol

The IOB, or Interobject Broker Protocol, is a protocol by which ORBs can be interconnected. The protocol is intended for use between geographically dispersed ORBs from a single vendor and to permit interoperation between ORBs developed independently by different vendors. The IOB includes definitions of a standard object reference data structure by which an ORB can recognize a foreign object reference and redirect it to the appropriate ORB, as well as definitions of the messages exchanged between ORBs for this purpose. The IOB is defined for use over a TCP channel; should the channel break or not be available at the time a reference is used, the corresponding invocation will return an exception.

6.13   Properties of CORBA Solutions

While the CORBA architecture is impressive in its breadth, the user should not be confused into believing that CORBA therefore embodies solutions for the sorts of problems that were raised in the first chapters of this book. To understand this point, it is important to again stress that CORBA is a somewhat superficial technology in specifying the way things *look* but not *how they should be implemented*. In language terminology, CORBA is concerned with syntax but not semantics. This is a position that the OMG adopted intentionally, and the key players in that organization would certainly defend it. Nonetheless, it is also a potentially troublesome aspect of CORBA, in the sense that a correctly specified CORBA application may still be underspecified (even in terms of the interface to the objects) for purposes of verifying that the objects are used correctly or for predicting the behavior of the application.

Another frequently cited concern about CORBA is that the technology can require extreme sophistication on the part of developers, who must at a minimum understand exactly how the various object classes operate and how memory management will be performed. Lacking such knowledge, which is not an explicit part of the IDL, it may be impossible to use a distributed object efficiently. Even experts complain that CORBA exception handling can be very tricky. Moreover, in very large systems there will often be substantial amounts of old code that must interoperate with new solutions. Telecommunication systems are sometimes said to involve millions or tens of millions of lines of such software, perhaps written in outmoded programming languages or incorporating technologies for which source code is not available. To gain the full benefits of CORBA, however, there is a potential need to use CORBA *throughout* a large distributed environment. This may mean that large amounts of old code must somehow be retrofitted with CORBA interfaces and IDLs—neither a simple nor an inexpensive proposition.

The reliability properties of a particular CORBA environment depend on a great number of implementation decisions that can vary from vendor to vendor and often will do so. Indeed, CORBA is promoted to vendors precisely because it creates a level playing field within which their products can interoperate but compete: The competition would revolve around this issue of relative performance, reliability, or functionality guarantees. Conversely, this implies that individual applications cannot necessarily count upon reliability properties of CORBA if they wish to maintain a high degree of portability: Such applications must in effect assume the least common denominator. Unfortunately, in the CORBA architectural specification this least level of guarantees is quite weak: Invocations and binding requests can fail, perhaps in inconsistent ways, corresponding closely to the failure conditions we identified for RPC protocols that operate over standard communication architectures. Security, being optional, must be assumed not to be present. Thus, CORBA creates a framework within which reliability technologies can be standardized, but, as currently positioned, the technology base is not necessarily one that will encourage a new wave of reliable computing systems.

6.14 Performance of CORBA and Related Technologies

A large number of middleware, network infrastructure and operating systems choices are available to designers and builders of distributed systems. Yet there is limited data available that permits potential users and researchers to understand actual, measured real-time performance of various technologies. Lockheed Martin Advanced Technology Labs has, over many years, carried out systematic evaluations of operating system determinism, network transport behavior, and middleware performance. The company and the researcher who headed this effort, Dr. Gautam Thaker, have made their findings available to the public and also provided some representative data for use in this textbook.

Thaker's methodology has been, to the extent possible, to use identical test conditions (application, hardware etc.) which permits comparisons to reveal performance differences between various systems. The graph seen in Figure 6.12 shows measured roundtrip latencies to exchange a "n" byte message between two processes on a 2 node SMP as one progresses from shared memory to TCP (in C and Java), ORB (TAO), RMI, and EJB. Shared memory communication, as expected, is the fastest means of message exchange as there are no protocol stacks to traverse and speed is dominated by operating system process synchronization efficiency and memcpy speed. However, shared memory architectures are inflexible, and for this reason many systems are built on top of a network transport such as TCP/IP. As we can observe in the graph, moving from shared memory to TCP/IP costs almost an order of magnitude in roundtrip latencies, although the TCP/IP configuration has increased flexibility and generality.

As we move up to higher levels of abstractions, CORBA and RMI, we see the costs associated with the extra software layers required. CORBA and RMI both utilize TCP/IP in the configuration evaluated here. Also, we note that at the TCP/IP level the difference between C and Java implementations is about 10 usec, but that the difference between TAO

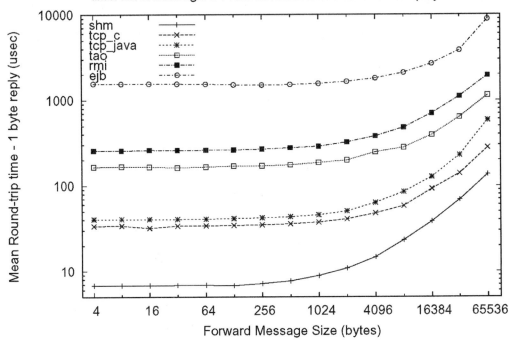

Figure 6.12. Comparison of round-trip delay when performing a method invocation using a variety of common technologies. The graph is designed to highlight the incremental overheads associated with various technology layerings. As we work our way up to higher and higher levels of abstraction (in this graph, the extreme case is Enterprise Java Beans implemented using Jboss on the TAO CORBA object request broker), we pay higher costs but gain power and flexibility. This graph, and graphs 6.13 and 6.14, were provided by Dr. Gautam Thaker, Lockheed Martin ATL.

(an ORB implemented in C) and RMI (implemented in Java) is about 100 usec. Finally, moving to Enterprise Java Beans ("EJB"), the most popular database access technology for Java users (here, the EJB implementation was Jboss 3.2.1) adds almost another order of magnitude delay over RMI. ATL reports that these tradeoffs continue to hold as one moves from two processes on a single node to two processes on two nodes interconnected via a highspeed (100 Mbps) network.

Figure 6.13 compares a CORBA Component Model (CCM) implemenation's round-trip latencies using both the TCP/IP based IIOP and SCTP/IP based SCIOP protocols mappings. Here we observe that benefits of SCTP – a specialized version of TCP that provides network fault tolerance by path multiplexing, come with just a slight increase in latency. The ATL site includes similar studies of a great many other TCP variants.

In addition to tests under unloaded conditions, numerous tests were performed with background stress on the system, revealing some surprising problems. An example of this is

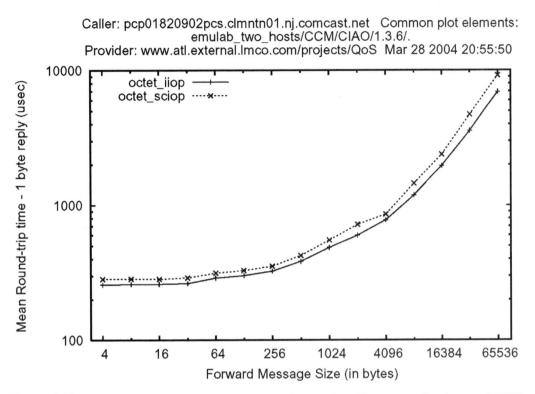

Figure 6.13. The cost of improved fault-tolerance can be very low. Here we see that the use of STCP, a protocol that maintains duplicate TCP channels to reduce the risk of a lost connection, introduces only a negligible overhead.

seen in Figure 6.14. Knowledge of average latencies isn't always good enough. Developers of distributed, real-time, embedded systems often need to anticipate maximum latency values. Figure 6.14 shows range of latencies recorded for TCP/IP based on a Timesys RTOS node in presense of very heavy disk interrupt load. We observe that under these conditions use of real-time support from the underlying operating system makes a crucial difference in holding down the maximum latencies.

Beyond the results summarized in Figure 6.12–6.14., a large amount of experimental data is available from ATL through a web interface to its web site (www.atl.external.lmco.com/projects/QoS). In most tests a very large number of samples (typically 1 million) were collected. Careful histograms are maintained and the website permits examination of not just the mean latencies but also entire distribution (including the maximum.) Sophisticated "Comparator" utilities (known as "MW_Comparator" and "Jitter Comparator") are available on the website. These permit the viewer to select a subset of collected data and to generate charts that overlay these results for easy visual and tabular comparison.

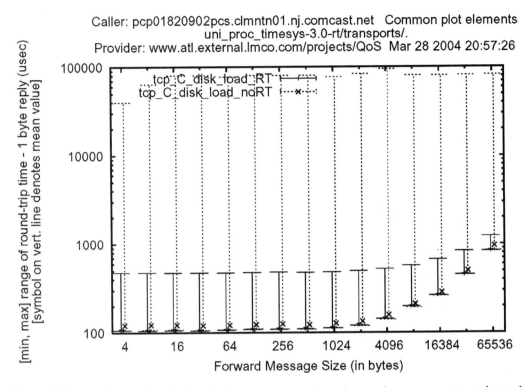

Figure 6.14. Developers of applications that incorporate some form of responsiveness guarantee need to track not just the average response delay but also the worst case delay. Here we see that when performing method invocations on a machine with some background load (the TCP-C benchmark suite), delays can be very large. Use of an operating system with real-time scheduling capabilities reduces this delay substantially.

6.15 Related Reading

On the ANSA project and architecture: (see Architecture Projects Management Limited [1989, April 1991, November 1991]). Another early effort in the same area was Chronus: (see Gurwitz et al., Schantz et al.).

On CORBA: (see Object Management Group and X/Open). Other publications are available from the Object Management Group, a standards organization; see their Web page, http://www.omg.org.

For the CORBA products cited, such as Orbix, the reader should contact the relevant vendor. Documentation for ACE and TAO, Doug Schmidt's Open Source CORBA platform, can be found at http://www.cs.wustl.edu/~schmidt/; this system is an excellent choice for readers wishing to work with a good quality CORBA implementation on Linux or other popular platforms.

7

System Support for Fast Client/Server Communication

After so much discussion of object oriented architectures, issues relating to performance may seem out of place. None of the object-oriented architectures we've reviewed places a particularly high premium on performance, nor is performance the first metric by which one would evaluate them. However, as client/server computing pushes toward lower levels of the system, of course, the situation changes. Whereas a CORBA or Web Services application will often be developed to link a new application to a legacy system, and hence may not see much "traffic" or be particularly important to the performance of the system as a whole, within systems such as J2EE or .NET, one might find objects with far more performance-critical roles, and for which the speed of method invocation is actually quite important to the overall behavior of the system. This issue was first recognized almost two decades ago, and has occasioned quite a bit of work on performance for client/server interactions. Not much of this work will benefit the developer of a Web Services system running over a long-distance Internet link, but it can be central to the behavior of a .NET application using Web Services internally, where RPC-style interactions glue the entire operating system together. This is the style of interaction on which we'll focus in the remainder of the present chapter.

The performance of a communication system is typically measured in terms of the latency and throughput for typical messages that traverse that system, starting in a source application and ending at a destination application. Accordingly, these issues have received considerable scrutiny within the operating systems research community, which has developed a series of innovative proposals for improving performance in communication-oriented applications. In the following text, we review some of these proposals.

There are other aspects of communication performance that matter a great deal when building a reliable distributed application, but these have received considerably less attention. Prominent among these are the loss characteristics of the communication subsystem.

In typical communication architectures, messages are generated by a source application, which passes them to the operating system. As we saw early in this book (Figure 1.1), such messages will then travel down some form of protocol stack, eventually reaching a device driver that arranges for the data to be transmitted on the wire. Remotely, the same process is repeated.

Such a path offers many opportunities for inefficiency and potential message loss. Frequently, the layer-to-layer hand-offs that occur involve copying the message from one memory region or address space to another, perhaps with a header prepended or a suffix appended. Each of these copying operations will be costly (even if other costs such as scheduling are even more costly), and if a layer is overloaded or is unable to allocate the necessary storage, a message may be lost without warning. Jointly, the consumption of CPU and memory resources by the communication subsystem can become very heavy during periods of frequent message transmission and reception, triggering overload and high rates of message loss. In Chapter 3 we saw that such losses can sometimes become significant (recall, for example, the issue of "broadcast storms"). Thus, while we will be looking at techniques for reducing the amount of copying and the number of cross-address space control transfers needed to perform a communication operation, the reader should also keep in mind that by reducing copying, these techniques may also be reducing the rate of message loss that occurs in the protocol stack.

The *statistical properties* of communication channels offer an extremely important area for future study. Most distributed systems, and particularly the ones intended for critical settings, assume that communication channels offer identical and independent quality-of-service properties to each packet transmitted—for example, it is typically implicit in the design of a protocol that if two packets are transmitted independently, then the observed latency, data throughput, and probability of loss will be identical. Such assumptions match well with the properties of communication hardware during periods of light, uniform load, but the layers of software involved in implementing communication stacks and routing packets through a complex network can seriously distort these underlying properties.

Within the telecommunication community, bandwidth sharing and routing algorithms have been developed that are fair in the sense of dividing available bandwidth fairly among a set of virtual circuits of known expected traffic levels. But the problem of achieving fairness in a packet switched environment with varying loads from many sources is understood to be hard: fair queuing algorithms are expensive and not widely deployed. One way to think about this problem is to visualize the operating system layers through which packets must travel, and the switching systems used to route packets to their destinations, as a form of filter, which can distort the distribution of packets in time and superimpose errors on an initially error-free data stream. Such a perspective leads to the view that these intermediary software layers introduce noise into the distributions of intermessage latency and error rates.

This is readily confirmed by experiment. The most widely used distributed computing environments exhibit highly correlated communication properties: If one packet is delayed, the next will probably be delayed too. If one packet is dropped in transmission, the odds are higher that the next will be dropped as well. As one might expect, however, such problems are a consequence of queuing, combined with the same memory constraints and layered architectures that also introduce the large latency and performance overheads that the techniques presented below are designed to combat. Thus, although the techniques discussed in this chapter were developed to provide higher performance, and were not specifically intended to improve the statistical properties of the network, they would in fact be expected to exhibit better statistical behavior than the standard distributed system architecture does simply by eliminating layers of software that introduce delays and packet loss.

7.1 Lightweight RPC

Performance of remote procedure calls has been a major topic of research since RPC programming environments first became popular. Several approaches to increasing RPC performance have had particularly significant impact.

The study of RPC performance as a research area surged in 1989 when Schroeder and Burrows undertook to precisely measure the costs associated with RPC on the Firefly operating system (see Schroeder and Burrows). These researchers started by surveying the costs of RPC on a variety of standard platforms. Their results have subsequently become outdated because of advances in systems and processor speeds, but the finding that RPC performance varies enormously even in relative terms probably remains true today. In their study, the range of performance was from 1.1 ms to do a null RPC (equivalent to 4,400 instructions) on the Cedar system, highly optimized for the Dorado multiprocessor, to 78 ms (195,000 instructions) for a very general version of RPC running on a major vendor's top-of-the-line platform (at that time). One interesting finding of this study was that the number of instructions in the RPC code path was often high (the average in the systems they looked at was approximately 6,000 for systems with many limitations and about 140,000 for the most general RPC systems). Thus, faster processors would be expected to have a big impact on RPC performance, which is one of the reasons that the situation has improved somewhat since the time of this study.

Using a bus analyzer to pin down costs to the level of individual machine cycles, this effort led to a tenfold performance improvement in the RPC technology under investigation, which was based originally on the Berkeley UNIX RPC. Among the optimizations that had the biggest impact were the elimination of copying within the application address space by marshalling data directly into the RPC packet using an in-line compilation technique, and the implementation of an RPC fast path, which eliminated all generality in favor of a hand-coded RPC protocol using the fewest instructions possible, subject to the constraint that the normal O/S protection guarantees would be respected.

Soon after this work on Firefly RPC was completed, researchers at the University of Washington became interested in other opportunities to optimize communication paths in modern operating systems. Lightweight RPC originated with the observation that as computing systems adopt RPC-based architectures, the use of RPC in *nondistributed* settings is rising as rapidly as is RPC over a network. Unlike a network, RPC in the nondistributed case can accurately sense many kinds of failures, and because the same physical memory is potentially visible to both sender and destination, the use of shared memory mechanisms represents an appealing option for enhancing performance. Bershad and others set out to optimize this common special case (see Bershad et al.).

A shared memory RPC mechanism typically requires that messages be allocated within pages, starting on page boundaries and with a limit of one message per page. In some cases, the pages used for message passing are from a special pool of memory maintained by the kernel; in others, no such restriction applies but there may be other restrictions, such as limits on passing data structures that contain pointers. When a message is sent, the kernel modifies the page table of the destination to map the page containing the message into the address space of the destination process. Depending on the operating system, the page containing the message may be mapped out of the memory of the sender, modified to point to an empty page, or marked as read-only. In this last approach (where the page is marked as read-only) some systems will trap write-faults and make a private copy if either process attempts a modification. This method is called "copy on write," and was first supported in the Mach microkernel (see Rashid).

If one studies the overheads associated with RPC in the local, shared memory case, the cost of manipulating the page tables of the sender and destination and of context switching between the sending and receiving processes emerges as a major factor. The University of Washington team focused on this problem in developing what they called a *Lightweight Remote Procedure Call* facility (LRPC). In essence, this approach reduces time for local RPC both by exploiting shared memory and by avoiding excess context switches. Specifically, the messages containing the RPC arguments are placed in shared memory, while the invocation itself is done by changing the current page table and flushing the TLB so that the destination process is essentially invoked in coroutine style, with the lowest overhead possible given that virtual memory is in use on the machine. The reply from the destination process is similarly implemented as a direct context switch back to the sender process.

Although LRPC may appear to be as costly as normal RPC in the local case, the approach actually achieves substantial savings. First, a normal RPC is implemented by having the client program perform a message send followed by a separate message receive operation, which blocks. Thus, two system calls occur, with the message itself being copied into the kernel's data space, or (if shared memory is exploited) a message descriptor being constructed in the kernel's data space. Meanwhile, the destination process will have issued a receive request and would often be in a blocked state. The arrival of the message makes the destination process runnable, and on a uniprocessor this creates a scheduling decision, since the sender process is also runnable in the first stage of the algorithm (when it has sent its request and not yet performed the subsequent receive operation). Thus, although the user might expect the sender to issue its two system calls and then block, causing the scheduler to run and activate the destination process, other sequences are possible. If the scheduler runs right after the initial send operation, it could context switch to the RPC server leaving the client runnable. It is now possible that a context switch back to the client will occur, and then back to the server again, before the server replies. The same sequence may then occur when the reply is finally sent.

We thus see that a conventional operating system requires four system calls to implement an LRPC operation, and that although a minimum of two context switches must occur, it is easily possible for an additional two context switches to take place. If the execution of the operating system scheduler represents a significant cost, the scheduler may run two or more times more than the minimum. All of these excess operations are potentially costly.

Accordingly, LRPC is implemented using a special system call whereby the client process combines its send and receive operations into a single request, and the server (which will normally delay waiting for a new RPC request after replying to the client) issues the reply and subsequent receive as a single request. Moreover, execution of the scheduler is completely bypassed.

As in the case of RPC, the actual performance figures for LRPC are of limited value because processor speeds and architectures have been evolving so rapidly. One can get a sense of the improvement by looking at the number of instructions required to perform an LRPC. Recall that the Schroeder and Burrows study had found that thousands of instructions were required to issue an RPC. In contrast, the LRPC team calculated that only a few hundred instructions are required to perform an LRPC—a small enough number to make such factors as TLB misses (caused when the hardware cache associated with the virtual memory mapping system is flushed) emerge as important determinants of performance. LRPC was, in any case, somewhat more expensive than the theoretical minimum: about 50 percent slower measured in terms of round-trip latency or instructions executed for a null procedure call. Nonetheless, this represents a factor of at least five when compared to the performance of typical RPC in the local case, and ten or more when the approach is compared to the performance of a fairly heavyweight vendor supported RPC package.

This effect is so dramatic that some operating systems vendors began to support LRPC immediately after the work was first reported. Others limited themselves to fine-tuning their existing implementations or improving the hardware used to connect their processors to the network. At the time of this writing, RPC performances have improved somewhat, but faster processors are no longer bringing commensurate improvements in RPC performance. Vendors tend to point out that RPC performance, by itself, is only one of many factors that enter into overall system performance, and that optimizing this one case to an excessive degree can bring diminishing returns. They also argue for generality even in the local case: that LRPC is undesirable because it requires a different RPC implementation than the remote case and thus increases the complexity of the operating system for a scenario that may not be as common in commercial computing settings as it seems to be in academic research laboratories.

To some degree, these points are undoubtedly valid ones: When an RPC arrives at a server, the program that will handle it may need to be scheduled, it may experience page faults, buffering and caching issues can severely impact its performance, and so forth. On the other hand, the performance of a null RPC or LRPC is entirely a measure of operating system overhead, and hence is wasted time by any reasonable definition.

Moreover, the insights gained in LRPC are potentially applicable to other parts of the operating system: Bershad, for example, demonstrated that the same idea can be generalized using a concept of *thread activations* and *continuations*, with similarly dramatic impact on other aspects of operating system performance (see Bershad et al.). This work seems not to have impacted the commercial operating systems community, at least at the time of this writing.

7.2   fbufs and the x-Kernel Project

During the same period, the University of Arizona, under Larry Peterson, developed a series of innovative operating system extensions for high-performance communication. Most relevant to the topic of this chapter are the x-Kernel, a stand-alone operating system for developing high speed communication protocols, and the *fbufs* architecture (see Drushel and Peterson), which is a general-purpose technique for optimizing stack-structured protocols to achieve high performance. While these extensions were developed based on the context of a particular operating system, but they are potentially applicable to most standard vendor-supported operating systems.

The x-Kernel (see Peterson et al.) is an operating system dedicated to the implementation of network protocols for experimental research on performance, flow control, and other issues. The assumption that x-Kernel applications are purely communication-oriented greatly simplified the operating system design, which confines itself to addressing those issues encountered in the implementation of protocols, while omitting support for elaborate virtual memory mechanisms, special-purpose file systems, and many of the other operating facilities that are considered mandatory in modern computing environments.

Recall from the early chapters of this book that many protocols have a layered structure, with the different layers having responsibility for different aspects of the overall communication abstraction. In x-Kernel, protocols having a layered structure are represented as a partially ordered graph of modules. The application process involves a protocol by issuing a procedure call to one of the root nodes in such a graph, and control then flows down the graph as the message is passed from layer to layer. x-Kernel includes built-in mechanisms for efficiently representing messages and managing their headers and for dynamically restructuring the protocol graph or the route that an individual message will take, depending upon the state of the protocols involved and the nature of the message. Other x-Kernel features include a thread-based execution model, memory management tools, and timer mechanisms.

Using the x-Kernel, Peterson implemented several standard RPC and stream protocols, demonstrating that his architecture was indeed powerful enough to permit a variety of such protocols to co-exist and confirming its value as an experimental tool. Layered protocol architectures are often thought to be inefficient, but Peterson suggested a number of design practices that, in his experience, avoided overhead and permitted highly modular protocol implementations to perform as well as the original monolithic protocols on which his work was based. Later, researchers such as Tennenhouse confirmed that standard implementations of layered protocols, particularly in the UNIX stream architecture, have potentially high overheads, but also that appropriate design techniques can be used to greatly reduce these costs.

Peterson's interest in layered protocols subsequently led him to look at performance issues associated with layered or pipelined architectures, in which modules of a protocol operate in protected memory regions (Figure 7.1). To a limited degree, systems such as UNIX and NT have an architecture similar to this—UNIX streams, for example, are based on a modular architecture, which is supported directly within the kernel. As an example, an incoming message is passed up a stack that starts with the device driver and then includes each of the stream modules that have been pushed onto the stream connection, terminating finally in a cross-address space transfer of control to the application

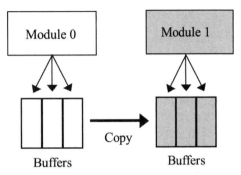

Figure 7.1. In a conventional layered architecture, as messages pass from layer to layer (here shown from left to right), messages and headers may need to be copied repeatedly. This contributes to high overhead. In this illustration, the white and gray buffers are independent regions in virtual memory.

program. UNIX programmers think of such a structure as a form of pipe implemented directly in the kernel. Unfortunately, like a pipe, a stream can involve significant overhead.

Peterson's *fbufs* architecture focuses on the handling of memory in pipelined operating systems contexts such as these. An *fbuf* is a memory buffer for use by a protocol; it will typically contain a message or a header for a message. The architecture concerns itself with the issue of mapping such a buffer into the successive address spaces within which it will be accessed and with the protection problems that arise if modules are to be restricted so that they can only operate on data that they own. The basic approach is to cache memory bindings, so that a protocol stack that is used repeatedly can reuse the same memory mappings for each message in a stream of messages. Ideally, the cost of moving a packet from one address space to another can be reduced to the flipping of a protection bit in the address space mappings of the sending and receiving modules (Figure 7.2). The method completely eliminates copying, while retaining a fairly standard operating system structure and protection boundaries.

7.3 Active Messages

At the University of California, Berkeley, and Cornell University, researchers explored techniques for fast message passing in parallel computing systems. Culler and von Eicken observed that operating system overheads are the dominant source of overhead in message-

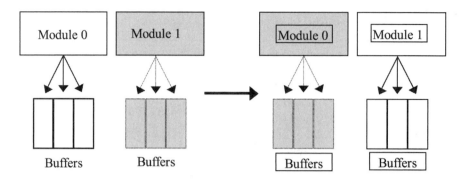

Figure 7.2. In Peterson's scheme, the buffers are in fact shared using virtual memory, exploiting protection features to avoid risk of corruption. To pass a buffer, access to it is enabled in the destination address space and disabled in the sender's address space. (In the figure, the white buffers represent real pointers and the gray ones represent invalid page-table entries pointing to the same memory regions but with access disabled.) When the buffer finally reaches the last module in the pipeline, it is freed and reallocated for a new message arriving from the left. Such an approach reduces the overhead of layering to the costs associated with manipulation of the page table entries associated with the modules comprising the pipeline.

oriented parallel computing systems (see Thekkanth and Levy, von Eicken et al. [1992]). Their work resulted in an extremely aggressive attack on communication costs, in which the application interacts directly with an I/O device and the overhead for sending or receiving a message can be reduced to as little as a few instructions. The CPU and latency overhead of an operating system is slashed in this manner, with important impact on the performance of parallel applications. Moreover, as we will see, similar ideas can be implemented in general-purpose operating systems.

An *active message* is a type of message generated within a parallel application that takes advantage of knowledge that the program running on the destination node of a parallel computer is precisely the same as the program on the source node to obtain substantial performance enhancements. In this approach, the sender is able to anticipate much of the work that the destination node would normally have to do if the source and destination were written to run on general-purpose operating systems. Moreover, because the source and destination are the same program, the compiler can effectively short circuit much of the work and overhead associated with mechanisms for general-purpose message generation and for dealing with heterogeneous architectures. Finally, because the communication hardware in parallel computers does not lose messages, active messages are designed for a world in which message loss and processor failure do not occur.

The basic approach is as follows. The sender of a message generates the message in a format that is preagreed between the sender and destination. Because the destination is running the same program as the sender and is running on the same hardware architecture, such a message will be directly interpretable by the destination without any of the overhead for describing data types and layout that one sees in normal RPC environments. Moreover, the sender places the address of a handler for this particular class of message into the header of the message—that is, a program running on machine *A* places an address of a handler that resides within machine *B* directly into the message. On the reception machine, as the message is copied out of the network interface, its first bytes are already sufficient to transfer control to a handler compiled specifically to receive messages of this type. This reduces the overhead of communication from the tens of thousands of instructions common on general-purpose machines to as few as five to ten instructions. In effect, the sender is able to issue a procedure call directly into the code of the destination process, with most of the overhead associated with triggering an interrupt on the destination machine and with copying data into the network on the sending side and out of the network on the receiving side. In some situations (e.g., when the destination node is idle and waiting for an incoming request) even the interrupt can be eliminated by having the destination wait in a tight polling loop.

Obviously, active messages make sense only if a single application is loaded onto multiple nodes of a parallel computer and hence has complete trust in those programs and accurate knowledge of the memory layout of the nodes with which it communicates. In practice, the types of systems that use the approach normally have identical programs running on each node. One node is selected as the master and controls the computation, while the other nodes, its slaves, take actions on the orders of the master. The actual programming model visible to the user is one in which a sequential program initiates parallel actions by invoking parallel operations, or procedures, which have been programmed to distribute work among the slaves and then to wait for them to finish computing before taking the next step. This model is naturally matched to active messages, which can now be viewed as optimizing normal message passing to take advantage of the huge amount of detailed information available to the system regarding the way that messages will be handled. In these systems, there is no need for generality, and generality proves to be expensive. Active messages are a general way of optimizing to extract the maximum performance from the hardware by exploiting this prior knowledge. (See Figure 7.3.)

Active messages are useful in support of many programming constructs. The approach can be exploited to build extremely inexpensive RPC interactions, but is also applicable to direct language support for data replication or parallel algorithms in which data or computation is distributed over the modes of a parallel processor. (See Figure 7.4) Culler and von Eicken have explored a number of such options and reported particular success with language-based embedding of active messages within a parallel version of the C programming language they call "split C," and in a data-parallel language called ID-90.

7.4 Beyond Active Messages: U-Net

At Cornell University, von Eicken continued the work begun in his study of active messages, looking for ways of applying the same optimizations in general-purpose operating systems connected to shared communication devices. U-Net is a communication architecture designed for use within a standard operating system such as UNIX or NT; it is intended

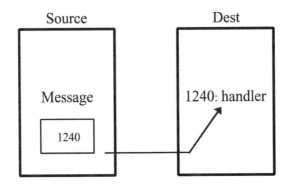

Figure 7.3. An active message includes the address of the handler to which it should be passed directly in the message header. In contrast with a traditional message-passing architecture, in which such a message would be copied repeatedly through successively lower layers of the operating system, an active message is copied directly into the network adapter by the procedure that generates it in the application program. It is effectively transferred directly to the application-layer handler on the receiving side with no additional copying. Such a zero copy approach reduces communication latencies to a bare minimum and eliminates almost all overhead on the messages themselves. However, it also requires a high level of mutual trust and knowledge between source and destination, a condition that is more typical of parallel supercomputing applications than general distributed programs.

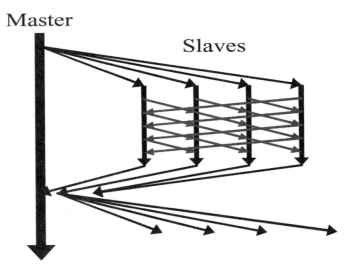

Figure 7.4. A typical parallel program employs a sequential master thread of control, which initiates parallel actions on slave processors and waits for them to complete before starting the next computational step. While computing, the slave nodes may exchange messages, but this too tends to be both regular and predictable. Such applications match closely with the approach to communication used in active messages, which trades generality for low overhead and simplicity.

to provide the standard protection guarantees taken for granted in these sorts of operating systems (see von Eicken et al. [1995]). These guarantees are provided, however, in a way that imposes extremely little overhead relative to the performance that can be attained in a dedicated application that has direct control over the communication device interface. U-Net gains this performance using an implementation that is split between traditional software functionality integrated into the device driver and nontraditional functionality implemented directly within the communication controller interfaced to the communication device. Most controllers are programmable—hence, the approach is more general than it may sound, although it should also be acknowledged that existing systems very rarely reprogram the firmware of device controllers to gain performance!

The U-Net system (see Figure 7.5) starts with an observation we have made repeatedly in prior chapters, namely that the multiple layers of protocols and operating system software between the application and the communication wire represent a tremendous barrier to performance, impacting both latency and throughput. U-Net overcomes these costs by restructuring the core operating system layers that handle such communication so that channel setup and control functions can operate out of band, while the application interacts directly with the device itself. Such a direct path results in minimal latency for the transfer of data from source to destination, but it raises significant protection concerns: If an application can interact directly with the device, there is no obvious reason that it will not be able to

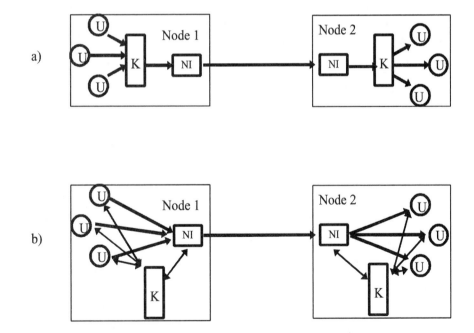

Figure 7.5. In a conventional communication architecture, all messages pass through the kernel before reaching the I/O device (a), resulting in high overheads. U-Net bypasses the kernel for I/O operations (b), while preserving a standard protection model.

subvert the interface to violate the protection on memory controlled by other applications or break into communication channels that share the device but were established for other purposes.

The U-Net architecture is based on a concept of a *communication segment*, which is a region of memory shared between the device controller and the application program. Each application is assigned a set of pages within the segment for use in sending and receiving messages, and is prevented from accessing pages not belonging to it. Associated with the application are three queues: one pointing to received messages, one to outgoing messages, and one to free memory regions. Objects in the communication segment are of fixed size, simplifying the architecture at the cost of a small amount of overhead. (See Figure 7.6.)

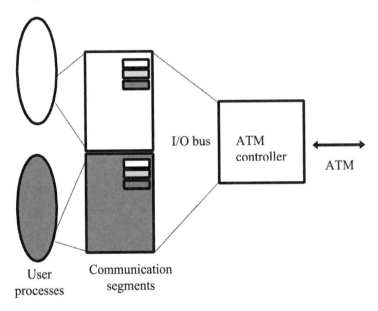

User processes   Communication segments   I/O bus   ATM controller   ATM

Figure 7.6. U-Net shared memory architecture permits the device controller to directly map a communication region shared with each user process. The send, receive and free message queues are at known offsets within the region. The architecture provides strong protection guarantees and yet slashes the latency and CPU overheads associated with communication. In this approach, the kernel assists in setup of the segments but is not interposed on the actual I/O path used for communication once the segments are established.

Each of these communication structures is bound to a U-Net channel, which is a communication session for which permissions have been validated, linking a known source to a known destination over an established communication channel. The application process plays no role in specifying the hardware communication channels to which its messages will be sent: It is restricted to writing in memory buffers that have been allocated for its use and update the send, receive, and free queue appropriately. These restrictions are the basis of the U-Net protection guarantees cited earlier.

U-Net maps the communication segment of a process directly into its address space, pinning the pages into physical memory and disabling the hardware caching mechanisms so that updates to a segment will be applied directly to that segment. The set of communication segments for all the processes using U-Net is mapped to be visible to the device controller over the I/O bus of the processor used; the controller can thus initiate DMA or direct memory transfers in and out of the shared region as needed and without delaying any setup. A limitation of this approach is that the I/O bus is a scarce resource shared by all devices on a system, and the U-Net mapping excludes any other possible mapping for this region. However, on some machines (e.g., cluster-style multiprocessors), there are no other devices contending for this mapping unit, and dedicating it to the use of the communication subsystem makes perfect sense.

The communication segment is directly monitored by the device controller. U-Net accomplishes this by reprogramming the device controller, although it is also possible to imagine an implementation in which a kernel driver would provide this functionality. The controller watches for outgoing messages on the send queue; if one is present, it immediately sends the message. The delay between when a message is placed on the send queue and when sending starts is never larger than a few microseconds. Incoming messages are automatically placed on the receive queue unless the pool of memory is exhausted; should that occur, any incoming messages are discarded silently. Specifically, U-Net was implemented using an ATM network controller. With this device, it only needs to look at the first bytes of the incoming message, which give the ATM channel number on which it was transmitted. (this could just as easily be a MAC address in the case of Ethernet). These are used to index into a table maintained within the device controller that gives the range of addresses within which the communication segment can be found, and the head of the receive and free queues are then located at a fixed offset from the base of the segment. To minimize latency, the addresses of a few free memory regions are cached in the device controller's memory.

Such an approach may seem complex because of the need to reprogram the device controller. In fact, however, the concept of a programmable device controller is a very old one (IBM's channel architecture for the 370 series of computers already supported a similar programmable channel architecture nearly 20 years ago). Programmability such as this remains fairly common, and device drivers that download code into controllers are not unheard of today. Thus, although unconventional, the U-Net approach is not actually unreasonable. The style of programming required is similar to that used when implementing a device driver for use in a conventional operating system.

With this architecture, U-Net achieves impressive application-to-application performance. The technology easily saturates an ATM interface operating at the OC3 performance level of 155 MB/sec, and measured end-to-end latencies through a single ATM switch are as low as 26 μs for a small message. These performance levels are also reflected in higher-level protocols: Versions of UDP and TCP have been layered over U-Net and shown capable of saturating the ATM for packet sizes as low as 1 KB; similar performance is achieved with a standard UDP or TCP technology only for very large packets of 8 KB or more. Overall, performance of the approach tends to be an order of magnitude or more better than with a conventional architecture for all metrics not limited by the raw bandwidth of the ATM: throughput for small packets, latency, and computational overhead of communication. Such results emphasize the importance of rethinking standard operating system structures in light of the extremely high performance that modern computing platforms can achieve.

Vendors saw these numbers and became very interested in doing something comparable in commodity operating systems. As a result, an initiative called the VIA (Virtual Interface Architecture) effort was launched, eventually resulting in a U-Net like technology that can be hidden under conventional interfaces such as Unix or Windows sockets (although Winsock Direct, as the latter is known, loses some of the performance benefits of VIA). VIA operates today over many faster technologies, such as Infiniband, gigabit Ethernet, and fiber switches; an evaluation of the performance of the standard can be found in Liu [1998]. This is a good example of a successful transition of a clever idea from research into mainstream products!

Returning to the point made at the beginning of this chapter, a technology such as U-Net also improves the statistical properties of the communication channel. There are fewer places at which messages can be lost; hence reliability increases and, in well-designed applications, may approach perfect reliability. The complexity of the hands-off mechanisms employed as messages pass from application to controller to ATM and back up to the receiver is greatly reduced—hence, the measured latencies are much tighter than in a conventional environment, where dozens of events could contribute towards variation in latency. Overall, then, U-Net is not just a higher-performance communication architecture; it is also one that is more conducive to the support of extremely reliable distributed software.

7.5 Protocol Compilation Techniques

U-Net seeks to provide very high performance by supporting a standard operating system structure in which a nonstandard I/O path is provided to the application program. A different direction of research, best known through the results of the SPIN project at University of Washington (see Bershad et al.), is concerned with building operating systems that are dynamically extensible through application programs coded in a special type-safe language and linked directly into the operating system at run time. In effect, such a technology compiles the protocols used in the application into a form that can be executed close to the device driver. The approach results in speedups that are impressive by the standards of conventional operating systems, although less dramatic than those achieved by U-Net.

The key idea in SPIN is to exploit dynamically loadable code modules to place the communication protocol very close to the wire. The system is based on Modula-3, a powerful modern programming language similar to C++ or other modular languages, but type safe. Among other guarantees, type safety implies that a SPIN protocol module can be trusted not to corrupt memory or to leak dynamically allocated memory resources. This is in contrast with, for example, the situation for a stream module, which must be trusted to respect such restrictions.

SPIN creates a run-time context within which the programmer can establish communication connections, allocate and free messages, and schedule lightweight threads. These features are sufficient to support communication protocols such as the ones that implement typical RPC or stream modules, as well as for more specialized protocols such as those used to implement file systems or to maintain cache consistency. The approach yields latency and throughput improvements of as much as a factor of two when compared to a conventional user-space implementation of similar functionality. Most of the benefit is gained by avoiding the need to copy messages across address space boundaries and to cross protection boundaries when executing the short code segments typical of highly optimized protocols. Applications of SPIN include support for stream-style extensibility in protocols, but also less traditional operating system features, such as distributed shared memory and file system paging over an ATM between the file system buffer pools of different machines.

Perhaps more significant is the fact that a SPIN module has control over the conditions under which messages are dropped because of a lack of resources or time to process them. Such control, lacking in traditional operating systems, permits an intelligent and controlled degradation if necessary—a marked contrast with the more conventional situation in which as load gradually increases, a point is reached where the operating system essentially collapses, losing a high percentage of incoming and outgoing messages, often without indicating that any error has occurred.

Like U-Net, SPIN illustrates that substantial performance gains in distributed protocol performance can be achieved by concentrating on the supporting infrastructure. Existing operating systems remain single-user centric in the sense of having been conceived and implemented with dedicated applications in mind. Although such systems have evolved successfully into platforms capable of supporting distributed applications, they are far from optimal in terms of overhead imposed on protocols, data loss characteristics, and length of the I/O path followed by a typical message on its way to the wire. As work such as this enters the mainstream, significant reliability benefits will spill over to end users, who often experience the side-effects of the high latencies and loss rates of current architectures as sources of unreliability and failure.

7.6 Related Reading

For work on kernel and microkernel architectures for high-speed communication: Amoeba (see Mullender et al., van Renesse [1988, 1989]), Chorus (see Armand et al., Rozier et al. [Fall 1988, December 1988]), Mach (see Rashid), QNX (see Hildebrand), Sprite (see Ousterhout et al. [1988]).

Issues associated with the performance of threads are treated in Anderson et al.

Packet filters are discussed in the context of Mach in Mogul et al.

The classic paper on RPC cost analysis is Shroeder and Burrows, but see also Clark and Tennenhouse.

TCP cost analysis and optimizations are presented in Clark et al., Jacobson (1988, 1990).

Lightweight RPC is treated in Bershad et al. (1989).

Active Messages are covered in Thekkanth and Levy, von Eicken et al. (1992), and U-Net is discussed in von Eicken et al. (1995). An evaluation of VIA, the industry standard "Virtual Interface Architecture" based on the U-Net architecture, can be found in Liu 1999.

Fbufs and the *x*-Kernel are discussed in Abbott and Peterson, Drushel and Peterson, Peterson et al. A really interesting piece of follow-on work is the I/O Lite system described in Pai et al. 1999. This system implements an exceptionally efficient framework for building applications that make extensive use of message-passing.

An architecture for building very high speed Web servers and other event-driven systems is discussed in Welsh [2001]. Called SEDA, the approach is offered by Welsh as an alternative to extensive multi-threading and has been controvertial because it requires a change in programming style on the part of developers.

SPIN is treated in Bershad et al. (1995).

PART II

Web Technologies

Part II focuses on the technologies that make up the World Wide Web, but in a broad sense. In addition to Web Sites and browsers, we'll look closely at the Web Services architecture and, a bit less closely at support for these kinds of technologies in major industry platforms such as .NET and J2EE. Standard tools such as instant messaging, e-mail, and news really belong here too, although we'll have less to say about them. Our discussion is detailed enough to provide the reader with a good understanding of the key components of the technology base and the manner in which they are implemented—without going to such an extreme level of detail as to lose track of our broader agenda, which is to understand how reliable distributed computing services and tools can be introduced into the sorts of critical applications that may soon be placed on the Web.

8

The World Wide Web

8.1 The World Wide Web

As recently as 1993, it was common to read of a *coming* revolution in communication and computing technologies. Distributed Computing was dominated by e-mail and manual file transfers, but experts writing in trade publications confidently predicted a future information economy, the emergence of digital libraries and newspapers, the prospects of commerce over the network, and so forth. At the same time, though, the extent of the disconnect between what we actually saw on our desktops and what the pundits were predicting triggered waves of skeptical articles, suggesting that although there might well be a trend towards an information superhighway, it seemed to lack on-ramps accessible to normal computer users.

In an astonishingly short period of time, this situation reversed itself. By assembling a relatively simple client/server application using mature, well-understood technologies, a group of researchers at CERN and at the National Center for Supercomputing Applications (NCSA) developed a system for downloading and displaying documents over a network. They employed an object-oriented approach in which their display system could be programmed to display various types of objects: audio, digitized images, text, hypertext documents represented using the HyperText Markup Language (HTML) (a standard for representing complex documents), and other data types. They agreed upon a simple resource location scheme, capable of encoding the information needed to locate an object on a server and the protocol with which it should be accessed. Their display interface integrated these concepts with easily used, powerful graphical user interface (GUI) tools. And suddenly, by pointing and clicking, a completely unsophisticated user could access a rich collection of data and documents over the Internet. Moreover, authoring tools for hypertext documents already existed, making it surprisingly easy to create elaborate graphics and sophisticated hypertext materials. By writing simple programs to track network servers, checking for changed content, and following hypertext links, substantial databases of Web documents were assembled, against which sophisticated information retrieval tools could be applied. Overnight, the long-predicted revolution in communication took place.

Today, there seems to be no end to the predictions for the potential scope and impact of the information revolution. We are poised to extend the scope of the Web beyond human-oriented browsing to include computer to computer interactions using essentially the same underlying technology, but modified to automate most elements of these operations. Thus, HTML has been redefined as an instance of XML, the Extensible Markup Language, and this latter standard is being used to encode all sorts of machine-readable information, even inside remote procedure calls. A Web Services RPC standard has been defined, called SOAP: it defines the way to encode an RPC request into a packet represented using XML, and a way to send that request to a Web Service using the same HTTP protocol employed when a browser requests a document from a Web Site. (In fact, this layered encoding is so inefficient that other options are explicitly anticipated by the standard and will surely emerge as important alternatives to the basic SOAP over HTTP approach). We also have an IDL for Web Services, again using XML, called WSDL: the Web Service Description Language, and even a standard for representing naming and other discovery data in naming services, UDDI. All are discussed later in this part of the book.

Realistic predictions of the size of the consumer-to-business marketplace in 2003 placed it in the low billions of dollars annually, and growing steadily. Web browsers and Web Sites are serious business. However, predictions of the potential size of the direct business-to-business sector come in at approximately 3 trillion dollars by the end of the decade and rising rapidly. Obviously, the dollars transacted over a technology don't translate directly into dollars earned by the vendors selling that technology. Yet there is surely a spill-over effect. Some part of those trillions will be used as investment in the underlying infrastructure, and Web Services will rapidly become a dominant theme for most computing vendors. Indeed, there may even be reason to hope that this trend will reignite the stalled technology sector of the world economy.

One is reminded of the early days of the biotechnology revolution, during which dozens of companies were launched, fortunes were earned, and the world briefly overlooked the complexity of the biological world in its unbridled enthusiasm for a new technology. Of course, initial hopes can be unrealistic. A decade or two later, the biotechnology revolution is beginning to deliver on some of its initial promise, but the popular press and the individual in the street have long since become disillusioned—or, perhaps, more realistic. The situation for Web related technologies highlights an even greater gap between expectations and reality. During the peak of the dotcom boom, the sector became tremendously overheated, precisely because technical analysts correctly judged the longer-term implications of what was happening. Investors, however, expected very quick returns on the technology, and were also dismayed by a wave of what can best be described as dishonest businesses selling smoke and snake oil at very inflated prices. Yet even after the dotcom boom and bust, the reality remains largely unchanged: the Web really does represent the future of business and the best hope for big productivity gains. Web Services really will be a big deal. The main issue, in fact, isn't even one appreciated by the community at large, namely that these early Web Services systems may lack the sorts of assurance properties that are really required by the companies deploying them. And this, of course, is our agenda in the present textbook: to understand what can be done, and how best to do it. Highly Assured Web Services applications could transform the way that companies do business, creating a new kind of "real-time enterprise" in which computers interacting over Web Services become a standard for doing just about anything one might wish to do in a distributed setting, with much greater interoperability and integration than is possible in today's world of proprietary standards and home-brew interconnects.

The biotechnology experience highlights the gap that often forms between the expectations of the general populace and the deliverable reality of a technology area. We face a comparable problem in distributed computing today, particularly after the deflation of the dotcom bubble. On the one hand, the public seems convinced that the information society has arrived, and in fact may even believe that the revolution is largely behind us. Popular expectations for this technology have passed through a hugely inflated stage and then through a crushing disappointment, and all of this confuses the reality, which is that Web technologies continue to roll out at a rate and on a scale that is surely unprecedented in the history of technology. Yet, the fundamental science underlying Web applications is in many ways very limited. The vivid graphics and ease with which hundreds of thousands of data sources can be accessed obscures more basic technical limitations, which may prevent the use of the Web for many of the uses that the popular press currently anticipates. Break-out 8.1 discusses several Web applications.

8.2 The Web Services Vision

Why are people so excited about Web Services? After all, it may seem that merely providing a way for computers to talk to one-another over Web standards is hardly a revolutionary advance given that we already had CORBA, J2EE, .NET, and dozens of less–well-known standards.

The opportunity reflects two considerations. First, we continue to spend enormous amounts of money connecting new applications to older systems and servers. Web Services could reduce costs by creating a widely accepted standard for interconnection that would span a wide-enough swath of systems to really cut these costs and also justify the development of a new generation of more powerful development environments and tools. So Web Services could be a major shot in the arm for those seeking to integrate new functions with older systems.

Yet Web Services also bring very high overheads. Although one can negotiate between a client program and a server to get the SOAP and HTML layers out of the way, most Web Services systems will be running over very verbose standards (meaning that even small messages bloat into enormous objects), through layers and layers of intermediary software (each handoff can slow things up dramatically), and perhaps running through not just the Web Services front end and the back-end server, but also some form of intermediary message

8.1 Web Applications

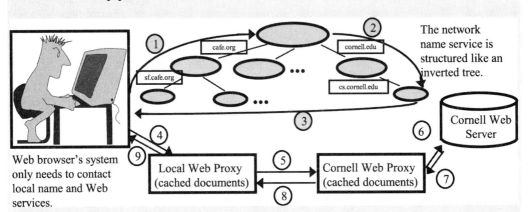

The network name service is structured like an inverted tree.

Web browser's system only needs to contact local name and Web services.

When used by a human behind a browser, the Web operates like a postal service. Computers have names and addresses, and communication is by the exchange of electronic letters (messages) between programs. Individual systems don't need to know how to locate all the resources in the world. Instead, many services, such as the name service and Web document servers, are structured to pass requests via local representatives, which forward them to more remote ones, until the desired location or a document is reached.

To retrieve the Web document www.cs.cornell.edu/Info/Projects/HORUS a browser must first map the name of the Web server, www.cs.cornell.edu, to an address. If the address is unknown locally, the request will be forwarded up to a central name server and then to one at Cornell (1–3 in figure above). The request to get the document itself will often pass through one or more Web proxies on its way to the Web server (4–9). These intermediaries save copies of frequently used information in short-term memory. Thus, if many documents are fetched from Cornell, the server address will be remembered by the local name service, and if the same document is fetched more than once, one of the Web proxies will respond rapidly using a saved copy. The term "caching" refers to the hoarding of reused information in this manner.

Our Web surfer looks irritated, perhaps because the requested server "is overloaded or not responding." This common error message is actually misleading because it can be provoked by many conditions, some of which don't involve the server at all—for example, the name service may have failed or become overloaded, or this may be true of a Web proxy, as opposed to the Cornell Web server itself. The Internet addresses for any of these may be incorrect or stale (e.g., if a machine has been moved). The Internet connections themselves may have failed or become over-loaded.

Although caching dramatically speeds response times in network applications, the Web does not track the locations of cached copies of documents, and offers no guarantees that cached documents will be updated. Thus, a user may sometimes see a stale (outdated) copy of a document. If a document is complex, a user may even be presented with an inconsistent mixture of stale and up-to-date information.

With wider use of the Web and other distributed computing technologies, particularly through the Web Services architecture (which automates the tasks mentioned above), critical applications requiring stronger guarantees are shifting to the Web. For example, many applications depend upon correct, consistent, secure, and rapid responses. If an application relies on rapidly changing information, stale responses may be misleading, incorrect, or even dangerous, as in the context of a medical display in a hospital, or the screen image presented to an air traffic controller.

One way to address such concerns is to arrange for cached copies of vital information, such as resource addresses, Web documents, and other kinds of data, to be maintained consistently and updated promptly. By reliably replicating information, computers can guarantee rapid response to requests, avoid overloading the network, and avoid single points of failure. The same techniques also offer benefits from scalable parallelism, where incoming requests are handled cooperatively by multiple servers in a way that balances load to give better response times. We'll explore these and other options in the remaining chapters of the book.

queuing system. Given so many handoffs and layers and encodings, it is a miracle that early versions of the Web Service platform are providing relatively tolerable RPC round-trip times on fast hardware—one reads of round-trip latencies as low as 25 to 50 ms, which is really quite respectable under the circumstances. Yet when we compare such numbers with the 1 or 2 ms latencies achievable with state of the art platforms for talking to high-end database servers, obviously we're looking at a relatively slow and balky technology.

The promise, though, is much broader than just letting computers talk to computers. Here's an example of where things are headed. Suppose that your favorite online store were to go to a Web Services model. Today, people need to use a Web Browser to manually surf to their site to purchase items. Tomorrow, with Web Services, any computing application, built by any third party, could potentially tap into that online store's systems. In effect, their middle-tier and back-end technologies would suddenly become accessible through web-service interfaces talking to thousands of new applications, most built by third parties. Those applications gain the ability to sell the user a needed object with a single click—the full power of online shopping without the risk of trying to create the next drugs.com. Meanwhile, the online store can offer all sorts of back-end business services too: business logic, supply-chain solutions, logistical planning, financial services, inventory, you name it. In fact, it can even offer plug-ins to let third-party developers access these services—applets, completely analogous to the ones used to make Web pages extensible. The back-end company sees huge growth in its market, and the small software developer who really needed a way to help a doctor's office reorder needed supplies wins too.

Thus, Web Services also point to a world in which online organizations of all kinds can start to offer completely new kinds of business support to applications exploiting them. In that future world, small software developers might be able to incorporate functionality demanding big back-end facilities in their software, while the back-end company suddenly extends its reach into a tremendous number of settings that might have otherwise been inaccessible. Such a step is more than incremental—it would truly be transformative, representing the sort of dramatic advance that could ignite a new dotcom revolution, although perhaps without the inflated stock valuations!

This is the real importance of the Web Services architecture—it offers the first chance, since the Web browser revolution, to really impact the whole world in a dramatic way.

In what follows, we'll look at Web Services fairly closely, and also at some of the major technical thrusts that push beyond the basic Web Services ideas to do creative things with the architecture. These include Grid Computing, an architecture many are promoting for doing high performance computing on the Web, and Autonomic Computing, a new concept for automating the configuration of complex applications, so that they can automatically sense their environments, set parameters appropriately, and adapt as conditions change over time. Autonomic tools could open the door both to better behavior in Web Services systems (lacking such tools, we risk a scenario in which our new Web Services applications wedge unexpectedly just as Web sites can do so, but where the resulting problems cripple entire corporate computing infrastructures). They could also make it possible to build exciting new kinds of applications, including ones that are far more mobile and adaptive than anything seen thus far, and applications like sensor networks, which would need to organize themselves in smart ways to conserve power and deal with erratic or limited connectivity.

8.3 Web Security and Reliability

As we will see, the basic functionality of the Web can be understood in terms of a large collection of independently operated servers. A Web browser is little more than a graphical interface capable of issuing remote procedure calls to such a server, or using simple protocols to establish a connection to a server by which a file can be downloaded. In the Web Services model, the browser is replaced by a client computer, using rather similar methods to request that operations be performed—the "document" fetched by a browser and the response to such a request are treated analogously in the architecture, and in fact a Web browser's interaction with a Web server is best described as an instance of the more general case of a Web Services client talking to an instance of a Web Services server.

The model is stateless: Each request is handled as a separate interaction, and if a request times out, a browser error message is displayed. On the other hand, the simplicity of the underlying model is largely concealed from the user, who has the experience of a session and a strong sense of continuity and consistency when all goes well—for example, a user who fills in a graphical form seems to be in a dialog with the remote server, although the server, such as an NFS server, would not normally save any meaningful state for this dialog. This illusion is tied together through the use of cookies: small notes that the server can leave for itself on the client's computing system, permitting the server to relate a subsequent action to the state established by the previous one. The stateless nature of the model, though, is such that the server never depends upon the cookie (although it will trust a properly signed cookie), and the client system is given very little in the way of reliability guarantees.

The reason that this should concern us becomes clear when we consider some of the uses to which Web servers are being put. Commerce over the Internet is being aggressively pursued by many companies. Such commerce will someday take many forms, including direct purchases and sales between companies, and direct sales of products and information to users. Today, the client of a Web server who purchases a product provides credit card billing information, and trusts the security mechanisms of the browser and remote servers to protect these data from intruders. But, unlike a situation in which this information is provided by telephone, the Web is a shared packet-forwarding system in which a number of forms of intrusion are possible.

The introduction of encryption technologies has eliminated some of the most extreme deficiencies in this situation. Yet data security alone is just one element of a broader set of requirements. As the reader should recall from the first chapters of this text, RPC-based systems have the limitation that when a timeout occurs, it is often impossible for the user to determine if a request has been carried out, and if a server sends a critical reply just when the network malfunctions, the contents of that reply may be irretrievably lost. Moreover, there are no standard ways to guarantee that an RPC server will be available when it is needed, or even to be sure that an RPC server purporting to provide a desired service is in fact a valid representative of that service—for example, when working over the Web, how can a user convince him or herself that a remote server offering to sell jewelry at very competitive prices is not in fact fraudulent? Indeed, how can the user become convinced that the Web page for the bank down the street is in fact a legitimate Web page presented by a legitimate server, and not some sort of a fraudulent version that has been maliciously inserted onto the Web? Now pose the same questions with the understanding that the user is a computer that will depend upon the responses it receives for its own correct behavior. Clearly, there is at least a serious potential for major problems. Without using the overheated language we all recall from the Year 2000 episode, it should be evident that the Web security architectures embody at most partial responses to these concerns, and that security problems may plague the Web Services architecture for years if not decades.

Full-service banking and investment support over the Web is a good example of the sort of activity that is inhibited by the current situation. Many banks are offering a wide range of functions to their customers through Web interfaces, and are developing Web-based investment tools for internal use, in which remote servers price equities and bonds, provide access to financial strategy information, and maintain information about overall risk and capital exposure in various markets. These same institutions are looking at the Web Services architecture as a tool for integrating their internal systems to a greater degree, and for building new kinds of applications in which banking systems talk to their counterparts over the network. Yet, these same tools also potentially expose these organizations to new forms of criminal activity: insider trading and fraud. Traditionally banks have kept their money in huge safes, buried deep underground. Here, one faces the prospect that billions of dollars will be protected primarily by the communication protocols and security architecture of the Web. We should ask ourselves if these are understood well enough to be trusted for such a purpose.

Web interfaces are extremely attractive for remote control of devices. How long will it be before such an interface is used to permit a plant supervisor to control a nuclear power plant from a remote location, or permit a physician to gain access to patient records or current monitoring status from home? Indeed, a hospital could potentially place all of its medical records onto Web servers, including everything from on-line telemetry and patient charts to x-rays, laboratory data, and billing. But when this development occurs, how will we know whether or not hackers could also, gain access to these databases, perhaps even manipulating the care plans for patients?

A trend towards critical dependence on information infrastructure and applications is already evident within many corporations. There is an increasing momentum behind the idea of developing corporate knowledge bases in which the documentation, strategic reasoning, and even records of key meetings would be archived for consultation and reuse. It is easy to imagine the use of a Web model for such purposes, and this author is aware of several efforts directed to developing products based on this concept.

Taking the same idea one step further, the military sees the Web as a model for future information-based conflict management systems. Such Global Information Grid systems (GIGs) would gather data from diverse sources, integrating this data and assisting all levels of the military command hierarchy in making coordinated, intelligent decisions that reflect the rapidly changing battlefield situation and that draw on continuously updated intelligence and analysis. The outcome of battles may someday depend on the reliability and integrity of information assets. Each of the US military services is developing its own architecture for these applications—the Air Force is developing the Joint Battlespace Infosphere or JBI, the Army is exploring Future Combat Systems or FCS, the Navy is exploring Network Centric Warfare or NCW, and the list goes on. Yet all have a tremendous amount in common with the Web and Web Services architectures and it wouldn't be a bad bet to speculate that once the dust settles, militarized Web Services systems will operate a great deal of the world's future military information systems.

Libraries, as well as publishers of newspapers, journals and books, are increasingly looking to the Web as a new paradigm for publishing the material they assemble. In this model, a subscriber to a journal or book would read it through some form of Web interface, being charged either on a per-access basis, or provided with some form of subscription. The library becomes a Web site in the eyes of the user, while library systems talk to one-another using the Web Services architecture and standards.

The list goes on. What is striking is the extent to which our society is rushing to make the transition, placing its most critical activities and valuable resources on the Web. A perception has been created that to be a viable company, it is necessary to make as much use of this new technology as possible. Obviously, such a trend presupposes that Web servers and interfaces are reliable enough to safely support the envisioned uses.

Many of the applications cited above have extremely demanding security and privacy requirements. Several involve situations in which human lives might be at risk if the envisioned Web application malfunctions by presenting the user with stale or incorrect data; in others, the risk is that great sums of money could be lost, a business might fail, or a battle lost. Fault tolerance and guaranteed availability are likely to matter as much as security: One wants these systems to protect data against unauthorized access, but also to guarantee rapid and correct access by authorized users.

Today, trustworthiness of the Web is often taken as a synonym for *data security*. When this broader spectrum of potential uses is considered, however, it becomes clear that reliability, consistency, availability, and trustworthiness will be at least as important as data security if critical applications are to be safely entrusted to the Web or the Internet. Unfortunately, however, these considerations rarely receive attention when the decision to move an application to the Web is made. In effect, the enormous enthusiasm for the potential information revolution has triggered a great leap of faith that it has already arrived. And, unfortunately, it already seems to be too late to slow, much less reverse, this trend. Our only option is to understand how Web applications can be made sufficiently reliable to be used safely in the ways that society now seems certain to employ them.

This situation seems very likely to deteriorate before any significant level of awareness that there is even an issue here will be achieved. As is traditionally the case in technology areas, reliability considerations are distinctly secondary to performance and user-oriented functionality in the development of Web Services. If anything, the trend seems to a form of latter-day gold rush, in which companies are stampeding to be first to introduce the critical servers and services on which Web commerce will depend. Digital cash servers, signature authorities, special-purpose Web search engines, and services that map from universal resource names to locations providing those services are a few examples of these new dependencies; they add to a list that already included such technologies as the routing and data transport layers of the Internet, the domain name service, and the dialup user authentication. To a great degree, these new services are promoted to potential users on the basis of functionality, not robustness. Indeed, the trend at the time of this writing seems to be to stamp "highly available" or "fault tolerant" on more or less any system capable of rebooting itself after a crash. As we have already seen, recovering from a failure can involve much more than simply restarting the failed service.

The trends are being exacerbated by the need to provide availability for "hot Web sites," which can easily be swamped by huge volumes of requests from thousands or millions of potential users. To deal with such problems, Web servers are turning to a variety of ad hoc replication and caching schemes, in which the document corresponding to a particular Web request may be fetched from a location other than its ostensible home. Major companies such as Akamai are making their money hosting this kind of content, while also playing a role in collecting advertising revenue, customizing data for specific categories of users, and similar tasks. Yet with each level of caching and replication, the end-user is that much more removed from the actual server and has that much less reason for confidence that the data is current. For Web applications where a bit of staleness doesn't matter, we hardly notice—newspapers, online reporting of sports events, etc. But for demanding commercial uses, the picture changes. Here, the prospect thus created is of a world within which critical data is entrusted to Web servers, which replicate these data for improved availability and performance, but without necessarily providing strong guarantees that the information in question will actually be valid (or detectably stale) at the time it is accessed. Moreover, standards such as HTTP V1.0 remain extremely vague (and perhaps necessarily) as to the conditions under which it is appropriate to cache documents and when they should be refreshed if they have become stale.

Broadly, the picture would seem to reflect two opposing trends. On the one hand, as critical applications are introduced into the Web, users may begin to depend on the correctness and accuracy of Web servers and resources, along with other elements of the Internet infrastructure, such as its routing layers, data transport performance, and so forth. To operate safely, these critical applications will often require a spectrum of behavioral *guarantees*. On the other hand, the modern Internet offers guarantees in none of these areas, and the introduction of new forms of Web Services, many of which will rapidly become indispensable components of the overall infrastructure, is only exacerbating the gap. Recalling our list of potential uses in commerce—banking, medicine, the military, and others—the potential for very serious failures becomes apparent. We are moving towards a world in which the electronic equivalents of the bridges that we traverse may collapse without warning, in which road signs may be out of date or intentionally wrong, and in which the agents with which we interact over the network may sometimes be clever frauds controlled by malicious intruders.

Strangely, the issue isn't confined to the network itself. A second trend, occurring in parallel with the one just described, involves the growth of interdependencies between various forms of physical infrastructure. Thus, the telephone system is dependent upon the electric power grid, but the grid is becoming dependent upon computerized information systems that may themselves operate over the Internet, which of course is built from the phone system. Obviously, these dependencies don't leap out at us—some would only become noticeable if a very long disruption occurred, lasting several days. Yet the broad direction seems to be one in which more and more "nationally critical infrastructure" is migrating both towards dependency on the Internet and on interdependency with other forms of critical infrastructure. We don't know enough about modeling interdependent systems to make strong statements about how such snarls behave, although clearly we wouldn't be taking such steps if doing so created extreme problems. The need, then, is for Web systems that work "well enough" to support these kinds of uses, under the assumption that if they do work well, problems won't arise; and also some reason to believe that if they break down in an extended way, perhaps under attack, the result won't cripple some huge range of mission-critical services.

As a researcher, one can always adopt a positive attitude towards such a situation, identifying technical gaps as research opportunities or open questions for future study. Many of the techniques presented in this book could be applied to Web browsers and servers, and doing so would permit those servers to overcome some (not all!) of the limitations identified above. Yet it seems safe to assume that by the time this actually occurs, many critical applications will already be operational using technologies that are only superficially appropriate.

Short of some major societal pressure on the developers and customers for information technologies, it is very unlikely that the critical Web applications of the coming decade will achieve a level of reliability commensurate with the requirements of the applications. In particular, we seem to lack a level of societal consciousness of the need for a reliable technical base and a legal infrastructure that assigns responsibility for reliability to the developers and deployers of the technology. Lacking both the pressure to provide reliability and any meaningful concept of accountability, there is very little to motivate developers to focus seriously on reliability issues. Meanwhile, the prospect of earning huge fortunes overnight has created a near hysteria to introduce new Web-based solutions in every imaginable setting.

8.4 Computing Platforms

The Web has had such a sweeping impact that many "platform" vendors have redesigned their basic computing systems around Web technologies. Examples include Microsoft, with its .NET platform, and Sun, the main force behind J2EE. Each of these systems is a comprehensive environment for building distributed applications, and each is tightly integrated with the Web. Both also offer very carefully crafted 3-tier database architectures, so that database application developers can easily pull data into their programs and perform transactional updates.

Although platform integration was not enormously important prior to the mid 1990's, modern computing systems succeed or fail to the degree that applications can be developed easily, are easy to test and debug, and can be maintained throughout their life cycle. Lacking good "stories" in each of these areas, the best new technical idea will nonetheless languish on the shelves. Thus, platform support for Web technologies is in many respects at the very core of the success of the overall technology area. Moreover, precisely because it is so easy to develop Web systems in these and other platforms, the overall quality of the average Web site or Web Services system is far higher than if users were forced to cobble together mechanisms of their own, even if the various tools they needed could be found "on the shelf."

Later in this part of the book, we'll look closely at both J2EE and .NET, and will also compare the capabilities both of the underlying languages (Java and C#) and the platforms themselves.

8.5 Related Reading

On the Web: (Berners-Lee et al. [1992, 1994, 1995], Gosling and McGilton [1995a, 1995b]).

There is a large amount of on-line material concerning the Web—for example, in the archives maintained by BEA, IBM and Microsoft. The World Wide Web (W3) Consortium (www.w3.org) is probably the best source of information concerning current standardization efforts.

9

Major Web Technologies

9.1 Components of the Web

This chapter briefly reviews the component technologies of the World Wide Web (see Berners-Lee [1992, 1994]), but not the associated technologies, such as e-mail and network bulletin boards, which are discussed in Chapter 11, or Web Services, the topic of Chapter 10. The Web draws on the basic client/server and stream protocols discussed earlier—hence, the issue here is how those technologies can be applied to a distributed problem, not the development of a new or different technology base. In the case of the Web, there are three broad technology areas (see Figure 9.1). A *Web browser* is a program for interfacing to a *Web site*, which is an instance of the more general Web Services architecture but with an orientation towards documents. There are various kinds of browsers, but the most widely used are based on graphical windowing displays, which permit the display of textual material, including sophisticated formatting directives and graphical images, and implement access through hypertext links on behalf of the user. Web browsers also have a concept of an object type and will run the display program appropriate to a given type when asked to do so. This permits a user to download and replay a video image file, audio file, or other forms of sophisticated media. Depending on the browser, there may also be ways to treat a single window as if it contained multiple separate Web pages ("frames"), to dynamically create multiple windows, to track data as is updated in real-time, and so forth.

Web servers and the associated concept of Web proxies (which are intermediaries that can act as servers by responding to queries using cached documents) represent the second major category of Web technologies. This is the level at which issues such as coherent replication and caching arise, and in which the Web authentication mechanisms are currently implemented.

A third major technology area underlying the Web consists of the *search engines*, which locate Web documents and index them in various ways, implementing query-style

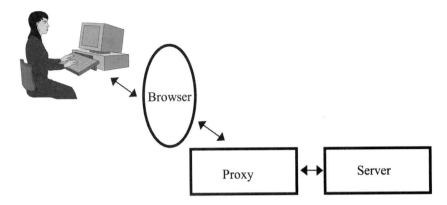

Figure 9.1. Components of a typical Web application. The user interacts with a graphical browser, which displays HTML documents and other graphical objects and issues HTTP commands to the servers on which objects needed by the user are stored. A proxy may be used to cache responses. Historically, HTTP applications have not fully specified what is or is not a cacheable response—hence, the use of this feature varies depending upon the origin of the proxy. Individual browsers may be capable of specialized display behaviors, such as rasterized display of graphical images or execution of pseudo-code programs written in languages such as Java or Visual BASIC. Although not shown above, there may be more than one level of proxy between the browser and server, and requests may "tunnel" through one or more firewalls before reaching the server. Moreover, messages passing over the Internet are relatively insecure and could be intercepted, read, and even modified on the path in either direction, if a Web security architecture is not employed.

access on behalf of a Web user. The largest search company, Google, implements searching by maintaining a "shallow" copy of the whole Web on its computers, from which it builds index structures, serving search requests through a farm said to contain some 100,000 inexpensive computers. Other search engines are hosted on large databases or other types of dedicated hardware, and some are specialized to narrower tasks, such as searching the corpus of published papers, or searching digital libraries. Search engines have two sides to them: a user-interface side, in which they accept queries from a Web user and identify Web resources that match the specified request, and a document-finding side, which visits Web servers and follows hyperlinks to locate and index new documents.

In the early days of the Web, few users viewed search engines as a particularly critical element of the overall technology area. This has changed dramatically, to the point that the most widely used search engine, Google, is now used as a verb: to "google" someone or something, meaning to look it up on the Web. Search technology is central to our ability to track down needed information, and the ordering of the displayed results can have a huge impact on what the user is able to find. Search companies sell their services in many ways: by indexing corporate knowledge bases, promising to rank a company's pages high within the search results, etc. One can easily imagine a future in which a financial analyst would become completely reliant upon such interfaces, as might a military mission planner, an air traffic controller, or a news analyst.

These technologies are supplanted by other less visible ones. Security and authentication services, provided by various vendors, play a key role in establishing trustworthy links between Web users and companies from which they purchase services; these security features include data encryption, digital signatures with which the identity of a user can be validated, and tools for performing third-party validation of transactions whereby an intermediary trusted by two parties mediates a transaction between them. Several companies have offered forms of digital cash and digital banking integrated with the Web; on the whole, however, these have not emerged as much of a challenge to more traditional credit card transactions.

Beyond these kinds of infrastructure technologies, one finds the usual panoply of Web-based commercial sites. Web implementations of "auction" facilities have become tremendously popular: eBay is a household term, and even major auction houses are turning to the Web as a way to expand their reach. Completely digital stock exchanges, on the other hand, have not been a huge success, presumably because a traditional stock exchange brings so many forms of value beyond the buying and selling aspects, such as validation of the creditworthiness of the participants, market liquidity, and so forth. Yet expanded integration of stock exchanges with Web Services and Web trading interfaces may also be a technology that will grow in importance over the coming decades.

Today, the Web is still in its early days, and remains primarily focused on a paradigm of remote access and retrieval. The future will bring the Web closer and closer to a true virtual environment, endowed with rich media content and offering new forms of social interaction and commerce. Web browsing may not turn out to have been the real key to the Internet Revolution, yet as Web Services roll out, the network and the Web in all its forms will surely play a larger and larger role in our daily lives. As this trend slowly plays out, Web sites may become more important in a diversity of ways: the overhead display of train arrival and departure times in the local train station will be a Web page, as will the patient status display in a medical critical care unit, or the map of enemy troop locations and potential targets being used by a military commander in the field. We're slowly integrating the Web with the real world, and the resulting new electronic worlds will depend upon a wide variety of critical services to function correctly and reliably.

9.2 HyperText Markup Language

The Hypertext Markup Language (HTML) is a standard for representing textual documents and the associated formatting information needed to display them. HTML is quite sophisticated, and includes such information as text formatting attributes (font, color, size, etc.), a means for creating lists and specifying indentation, and tools for implementing other standard formats. HTML also has conditional mechanisms, methods for displaying data in a concise form that can later be expanded upon request by the user. The HTML standard envisions various levels of compliance, and the most appropriate level for use in the Web has become a significant area of debate within the community.

HTML offers ways of *naming* locations in documents, and for specifying what are called *hypertext links* or *metalinks*. These links are textual representations of a document, a location in a document, or a service that the reader of a document can access. There are two forms of HTML links: those representing embedded documents, which are automatically retrieved and displayed when the parent document is displayed, and conditional links, which are typically shown in the form of some sort of "button," which the user can select to retrieve the specified object. These buttons can be true buttons, regions within the document text (typically highlighted in color and underlined), or regions of a graphical image. This last approach is used to implement touch-sensitive maps and pictures.

9.3 Extensible Markup Language

XML, the Extensible Markup Language, generalizes HTML to cover a wider variety of data types, and indeed can represent any kind of data that a computer might be used to process, together with a tremendous amount of meta-data giving semantic meaning to these data items. Today, a computer might represent my name, age and salary as a string, an integer, and a decimal number. Tomorrow, using XML, this same record might also be annotated to indicate that the name field is a "name," and that the age field represents an "age." Researchers have begun to talk about the semantic Web, a term for the Web of linkages between objects that relates various kinds of objects and explains their "meanings," at least in terms that a computer might find useful.

XML is a verbose representation, using ASCII both to encode the values of objects and to encode all of this meta information. A complex record that might require 1000 bytes to store in a database, containing 100 fields of various kinds and with varied values, could easily expand to 50,000 bytes or more in an XML encoding, where the values must be spelled out together with all of this meta information. On the other hand, that XML object is fully self-describing, while the original record is highly machine-specific and function-specific.

XML is unlikely to push other representations to the side, simply because the inefficiency of the encoding is of such a degree that other representations will almost always win when performance or size is a consideration. Yet the big advantage of XML, namely its ubiquity and interoperability, promise a shining future for XML as a language and also for XML-oriented software tools, aimed at helping the user create, store and read XML objects, compressing XML objects for greater efficiency, and integrating XML with standard databases or other kinds of servers so that new applications can "speak" to those legacy systems through XML-based interfaces.

9.4 Uniform Resource Locators

When a document contains a hypertext link, that link takes the form of a universal resource locator, or URL. A URL specifies the information needed by a Web server to track down a specified document. This typically consists of the protocol used to find that document (e.g. FTP or HTTP, the hypertext transfer protocol), the name of the server on which the document resides (e.g. www.cs.cornell.edu), an optional Internet port number to use when contacting that server (otherwise the default port number is used), and a path name for the resource in question relative to the default for that server.

Cornell's Horus research project maintains a World Wide Web page with URL http://www.cs.cornell.edu/Info/Projects/Horus.html, meaning that the hypertext transfer protocol should be used over the Internet to locate the server www.cs.cornell.edu and to connect to it using the default port number. The document Info/Projects/Horus.html can be found there. The extension .html tells the Web browser that this document contains HTML information and should be displayed using the standard html display software. The "://" separator is a form of syntactic convention and has no special meaning. Variant forms of the URL are also supported—for example, if the protocol and machine name are omitted, the URL is taken to represent a path. Such a path can be a network path ("//" followed by a network location), an absolute path ("/" followed by a file name in the local file system), or a relative path ("a file name which does not start with a "/" and that is interpreted relative to the directory from which the browser is running). In some cases a port number is specified after the host name; if it is omitted (as above), port number 80 is assumed.

Most Web users are familiar with the network path form of URL, because this is the form that is used to retrieve a document from a remote server. Within a document, however, the relative path notation tends to be used heavily, so that if a document and its subdocuments are all copied from one server to another, the subdocuments can still be found.

Web Services architects are now pushing for adoption of a Universal Resource Naming (URN) standard, in which resources have location-independent names. It is not at all clear, however, that developers are prepared to bet on this approach.

9.5   HyperText Transport Protocol

The HyperText Transport Protocol (HTTP) is one of the standard protocols used to retrieve documents from a Web server (see Berners-Lee [1995]). In current use, HTTP and FTP are by far the most commonly used file transfer protocols and are supported by all Web browsers. In the future, new transfer protocols implementing special features or exploiting special properties of the retrieved object may be introduced. HTTP was designed to provide lightness (in the sense of ease of implementation) and speed, which is clearly necessary in distributed, collaborative, hypermedia applications. However, as the scale of use of the Web has expanded, and load upon it has grown, it has become clear that HTTP does not really provide either of these properties. This has resulted in a series of "hacks" that improve performance but also raise consistency issues, notably through the growing use of Web proxies that cache documents.

Web browsers typically provide extensible interfaces: New types of documents can be introduced, and new forms of display programs and transfer protocols are therefore needed to retrieve and display them. This requirement creates a need for flexibility at multiple levels:

search, front-end update options, annotation, and selective retrieval. For this purpose, HTTP supports an extensible set of methods, which are typically accessed through different forms of URL and different document types (extensions like .txt, .html, etc.). The term "URI" (Universal Resource Identifier) has become popular to express the idea that the URL may be a locator but may also be a type of name, indicating the form of abstract service that should be consulted to retrieve the desired document. As we will see shortly, this permits an HTTP server to construct documents upon demand, with content matched to the remote user's inquiry.

The hypertext transfer protocol itself is implemented using a very simple RPC-style interface, in which all messages are represented as user-readable ASCII strings, although often containing encoded or even encrypted information. Messages are represented in the same way that Internet mail passes data in messages. This includes text and also a form of encoded text called the Multipurpose Internet Mail Extensions, or MIME (the HTTP version is "MIME-like" in the sense that it extends a normal MIME scheme with additional forms of encoding). However, HTTP can also be used as a generic protocol for contacting other sorts of document repositories, including document caches (these are often called proxies), gateways that may impose some form of firewall between the user and the outside world, and other servers that handle such protocols as Gopher, FTP, NNTP, SMTP, and WAIS. When this feature is used, the HTTP client is expected to understand the form of data available from the protocol it employs and to implement the necessary mechanisms to convert the resulting data into a displayable form and to display it to the user.

In the normal case, when HTTP is used to communicate with a Web server, the protocol employs a client/server style of request-response, operating over a TCP connection that the client makes to the server and later breaks after its request has been satisfied. Each request takes the form of a request method or command, a URI, a protocol version identifier, and a MIME-like message containing special parameters to the request server. These may include information about the client, keys or other proofs of authorization, arguments that modify the way the request will be performed, and so forth. The server responds with a status line, which gives the message's protocol version and outcome code (success or one of a set of standard error codes), and then a MIME-like message containing the content associated with the reply. In normal use the client sends a series of queries over a single connection and receives a series of responses back from the server, leaving the connection open for a while just in case it is needed again. More complicated situations can occur if a client interacts with an HTTP server over a connection that passes through proxies, which can cache replies, gateways, or other intermediaries; we return to these issues in Section 10.7.

HTTP messages can be compressed, typically using the UNIX compression tools "gzip" or "compress." Decompression is done in the browser upon receipt of a MIME-like message indicating that the body type has compressed content. The HTTP commands consist of:

Get: The get command is used to retrieve a document from a Web server. Normally, the document URL is provided as an argument to the command, and the document itself is returned to the server in its response message. Thus, the command "GET

//www.cs.cornell.edu/Info.html HTTP/1.0" could be used to request that the document "Info.html" be retrieved from "www.cs.cornell.edu," compressed and encoded into a MIME-like object, and returned to the requesting client. The origin of the resource is included but does not preclude caching: If a proxy sees this request it may be able to satisfy it out of a cache of documents that includes a copy of the Info.html previously retrieved from www.cs.cornell.edu. In such cases, the end-user will be completely unaware that the document came from the proxy and not from the server that keeps the original copy, although the browser itself does have a way to detect documents that were served out of a cache.

There are some special cases in which a get command behaves differently. First, there are cases in which a server should calculate a new HTML document for each request. These are handled by specifying a URL that identifies a program in a special area on the Web server called the cgi-bin area and encodes arguments to the program in the path-name suffix (the reader can easily observe this behavior by looking at the path name generated when a search request is issued to one of the major Web search engines, such as Lycos or Yahoo!). A Web server that is asked to retrieve one of these program objects will instead run the program, using the path-name suffix as an argument and creating a document as output in a temporary area that is then transmitted to the client. Many form-fill queries associated with Web pages use this approach, as opposed to the "post" command, which transmits arguments in a manner that requires slightly more sophisticated parsing and hence somewhat more effort on the part of the developer (put is also common).

A second special case arises if a document has moved; in this case, the get command can send back a redirection error code to the client that includes the URL of the new location. The browser can either reissue its request or display a short message indicating that this document has moved *here*. A conditional form of get, called *If-Modified-Since*, can be used to retrieve a resource only if it has changed some specified data. It is often used to refresh a cached object: If the object has not changed, minimal data is moved.

The get operation does not change the state of the server, and (in principle) the server will not need to retain any memory of the get operations that it has serviced. In practice, many servers cheat on the rules in order to prefetch documents likely to be needed in future get operations, and some servers keep detailed statistics about the access patterns of clients. We will return to this issue; it raises some serious concerns about both privacy and security of Web applications.

Head: The head command is similar to get, but the server must not send any form of entity body in the response. The command is typically used to test a hypertext link for validity or to obtain accessibility and modification information about a document without actually retrieving the document. Thus, a browser that periodically polls a document for changes could use the head command to check the modification time of the document and only issue a get command if the document indeed has changed.

Put: This command is analogous to get, but is used to store a document on a server, presumably triggering some form of action. Put is more common than the "post" operation, which is normally used to perform a database query or some other form of complex operation.

Post: The post command is used to request that the destination server accept the information included in the request as a new subordinate of the resource designated by the path. This command is used for annotating existing resources (the client posts a note on the resource); posting of a conventional message to an e-mail destination, bulletin board, mailing list, or chat session; providing a block of data obtained through a form-fill; or extending a database or file through an append operation.

This set of commands can be extended by individual servers—for example, a growing number of servers support a subscription mechanism by which each update to a document will automatically be transmitted for as long as a connection to the server remains open. This feature is needed by services that dynamically send updates to displayed documents—for example, to provide stock market quotes to a display that shows the market feed in real time. However, unless such methods are standardized through the Internet Task Force they may only be supported by individual vendors. Moreover, special-purpose protocols may sometimes make more sense for such purposes: The display program that displays a medical record could receive updates to the EKG part of the displayed document, but it could also make a connection to a specified EKG data source and map the incoming data onto the part of the document that shows the EKG. The latter approach may make much more sense than one in which updates are received in HTTP format, particularly for data that are compressed in unusual ways or for which the desired quality of service of the communication channels involves unusual requirements or a special setup procedure.

Status codes play a potentially active role in HTTP. Thus, in addition to the standard codes ("created," "accepted," "document not found") there are codes that signify that a document has moved permanently or temporarily, and providing the URL at which it can be found. Such a response is said to redirect the incoming request, but it can also be used in load-balancing schemes—for example, certain heavily used Web sites are implemented as clusters of computers. In these cases, an initial request will be directed to a load-balancing server, which redirects the request using a temporary URL to whichever of the servers in the cluster is presently least loaded. Because the redirection is temporary, a subsequent request will go back to the front-end server.

There has been quite a bit of work on what is called Web "hosting," in which a company farms out some of its Web pages to another company that maintains huge numbers of hosting computers all over the world, with the hope of speeding up access. When this is done, the real company normally rewrites the URLs for the hosted data (normally, the hosted data would be relatively static images and other unchanging files, perhaps with slots into which advertising can be dropped). The modified URLs would typically point to the hosting company, and that company would then load-balance requests to direct them to the least loaded and most appropriate server.

In early versions of HTTP, the client process was expected to open and later close a separate TCP connection for each command performed on the server. If retrieval of a document involves multiple get operations, multiple channels would be opened: one for each request. This resulted in obvious inefficiencies, so HTTP was ultimately extended to allow reuse of a single connection for multiple requests. In effect, the connection was treated as something that could be cached. Moreover, HTTP was also modified to permit a server to return a sequence of responses; the idea was to support the equivalent of a news-feed or a stock ticker. There are pros and cons associated with both the original design and this extended one. In the original design, a server didn't maintain any state on behalf of a client after serving its document request. Although there was a connection establishment overhead, the cost brought the benefit of greater server-side efficiency. With the change just described, a server might end up with thousands of open connections even if very few of the associated clients actually plan to issue additional requests. On the other hand, when multiple requests are issued to the server, the connection establishment cost is eliminated.

9.6 Representations of Image Data

Several standards are employed to compress image data for storage in Web servers. These include Graphics Interchange Format (GIF), an encoding for single images; Motion Picture Experts Group (MPEG) and Joint Photographic Experts Group (JPEG), which encode video data consisting of multiple frames; and a growing number of proprietary protocols. Text documents are normally represented using HTML, but PostScript is also supported by many browsers, as is the "rich text format" used by Microsoft's text processing products.

In the most common usage, GIF files are retrieved using a rasterized method in which a low-quality image can be rapidly displayed and then gradually improved as additional information is retrieved. The idea is to start by fetching just part of the data (perhaps every fourth raster of the image), and to interpolate between the rasters using a standard image interpolation scheme. Having finished this task, half of the remaining rasters will be fetched and the interpolation recomputed using these additional data; now, every other raster of the image will be based on valid data. Finally, the last rasters are fetched and the interpolation becomes unnecessary. The user is given the impression of a photographic image that gradually swims into focus. Depending on the browser used, this scheme may sweep from top of the image to bottom as a form of "wipe," or some sort of randomized scheme may be used. Most browsers permit the user to interrupt an image transfer before it finishes, so that a user who accidentally starts a very slow retrieval can work with the retrieved document even before it is fully available.

This type of retrieval is initiated using options to the get command, and may require compatibility between the browser and the server. A less-sophisticated browser or server may not support rasterized retrieval, in which case the rasterization option to get will be ignored and the image displayed top to bottom in the standard manner. The most sophisticated browsers now on the market maintain a type of device driver, which is used to customize their style of retrieval to the type of Web server and code version number from which a document is retrieved.

In contrast to the approach used for GIF files, MPEG and JPEG files and documents represented in formats other than HTML are normally transferred to a temporary space on the user's file system for display by an appropriate viewer. In these cases, the file object will typically be entirely transferred before the viewer can be launched, potentially resulting in a long delay before the user is able to see the video data played back or the contents of the text document.

The Web is designed to be extensible. Each type of object is recognized by its file extension, and each Web server is configured with *viewer* programs for each of these types. It is expected that new file types will be introduced over time, and new types of viewers developed to display the corresponding data. However, although such viewers can often be downloaded over the network, users should be extremely cautious before doing so. A Web document viewer is simply a program that the user downloads and runs, and there is nothing to prevent that program from taking actions that have nothing at all to do with the ostensible display task. The program could be a form of virus or worm, or it could be designed to damage the user's computer system or to retrieve data from it and send it to third parties. For this reason, the major vendors of Web browsers are starting to offer libraries of certified viewers for the more important types of Web data. Their browsers will automatically download these types of viewers, which are in some ways similar to dynamically loaded executables in a standard operating system. When the user attempts to configure a new and nonstandard viewer, on the other hand, the browser may warn against this or even refuse to do so.

An important class of viewers is those that use their own data retrieval protocols to fetch complex image data. These viewers are typically launched using very small, compact image descriptions that can be understood as domain-specific URLs. Once started, the viewer uses standard windowing primitives to discover the location of its display window on the screen, and it then begins to retrieve and display data into this location in real time. The advantage of such an approach is that it avoids the need to download the full image object before it can be displayed. Since an image object may be extremely large, there are enormous advantages to such an approach, and it is likely that this type of specialized image display will become more and more common in the future.

9.7 Authorization and Privacy Issues

Certain types of resources require that the Web browser authenticate its requests by including a special field with the request. This field provides *credentials* containing the authentication information that will be used to decide if permission for the request should be granted. Credentials are said to be valid within a *realm*.

The original ("basic") HTTP authentication scheme was based on a model in which the user must present a user-ID and password to obtain credentials for access to a realm (see Berners-Lee [1995]). The user-ID and password are transmitted in a slightly obscured but insecure mode: They are translated to a representation called base64, encoded as an ASCII string of digits, and sent over the connection to the server. This approach is only secure to the degree that the communication channel to the server is secure; if an intruder were to capture such an authorization request in transit over the network (e.g., by installing a "packet sniffer" at a gateway), the same information could later be presented to the same realm and server to authenticate access by the intruder. Nonetheless, the basic authentication scheme is required from all servers, including those that can operate with stronger protection. Browsers that communicate with a server for which stronger security is available will often warn the user before sending a message that performs basic authentication. Basic HTTP security is about as secure as writing your credit card information on the wall of a telephone booth. Fortunately, it was rapidly supplanted by SSL security (the protocol used for URL's that start with https://www....). Basic security is probably still around, but hopefully will soon be a long-forgotten wrong turn on the route to the Web.

When transferring genuinely sensitive information, Web applications typically make use of a trusted intermediary that provides session keys, using what is called public key encryption to authenticate channels and then a secret key encryption scheme to protect the data subsequently sent on that channel (the so-called *secure sockets layer* is described more fully in Internet Engineering Task Force and Denning and Branstad). At the core of this approach is a technology for publishing keys that can be used to encrypt data so that it can be read only by a process that holds the corresponding private key. The basic idea is that the public keys for services to be used by a client can be distributed to that client in some way that is hard to disrupt or tamper with, and the client can then create messages that are illegible to any process other than the desired server. A client that has created a key pair for itself can similarly publish its public key, in which case it will be able to receive messages that only it can read (the most common e-mail systems now support this feature). Because public key cryptography is costly, the recommended approach involves using a public key handshake to generate a secret key with which the data subsequently exchanged on the channel can be encrypted; in this manner, a faster protocol such as DES or RC4 can be employed for any large objects that need to be transferred securely.

We discuss security architectures for distributed systems more fully in Chapter 22. For the purposes of this section, however, one can understand the key handling mechanism of SSL in the following way. When a browser is first downloaded, it has a built-in "public key" for the company that provided it. Using this key, it is possible to go back to the parent company to obtain public keys for a variety of *directory servers* listing public keys for other companies and organizations. Having looked up the public key for a company or organization (or a person), the client is able to encrypt data in such a manner that only the designated receiver—the destination company—can read it. The effect is that if one trusts the key in the browser—say, the key for Microsoft Corporation, one can obtain a trustworthy key for the target company—say, Amazon.com, and use that to encrypt one's order. The encrypted request includes key information used to encrypt the reply. Even if the body of a request isn't encrypted, one can sign a message to confirm that no tampering has occurred between when it was generated and when it was delivered, and that it was generated by an individual having the private key corresponding to some public key.

There are ways to attack this sort of security architecture, but they are potentially difficult to mount. If an intruder can break or steal the private keys used by the client or server, it may be possible to misrepresent itself as one or the other and initiate secured transactions at leisure. Another option is to attack the stored public key information, in order to replace a public key with a falsified one that would permit a faked version of a server to mimic the real thing. Realistically, however, these would be very difficult types of attacks to engineer without some form of insider access to the systems on which the client and server execute or without having a fast way of breaking the cryptographic system used to implement the session keys. In practice, it is generally believed that although the basic authentication scheme is extremely fragile, the stronger Web security architecture should be adequate for most commercial transactions between individuals, provided, however, that the computer on which the client runs can be trusted. Whether the same schemes are adequate to secure transactions between banks, or military systems that transmit orders to the battlefield, remains an open question.

Table 9.1 outlines some real-world scenarios and looks at their mapping to the kinds of security available using the SSL protocol and the HTTPS mechanisms. What stands out is that there are many kinds of trust and role relationships in the real world, and that Web architectures currently focus on just one kind of security—the kind needed to safely provide your credit card data to a vendor "blessed" by a security service that, in turn, was "blessed" by the manufacturer of your Web browser. As Web Services penetrate the real

Table 9.1. If the world was a Web Service...

Action	Comment
I'll take this copy of "Fine Wines of Bulgaria." Here's my visa card.	If you trust the merchant, SSL security lets you look up her "public" key, encrypt your visa card and order information so that only she can read it, transmit it to her Web site, and receive back an encrypted response that could only have come from that merchant and could only be read by you.
Uncle Sal told me that Cousin Vinny knows all the trustworthy pawnbrokers in town, and Vinny gave me this torn dollar bill. If you have the other half, I'll trust you.	That torn bill is like a key-pair. You obtain a public key by asking a trusted parent for the key of a directory, and then asking that directory for a site's public key. The site can prove it has the private key without revealing it, by decrypting data encrypted with the public key or by signing a document using the private one.
My name is Bill Gates and I'll be your instructor today.	Unless the University lists public names and keys for instructors, the usual Web Services/SSL security model doesn't really let you confirm either that Bill Gates is the designated instructor, nor that the person in front of you is actually Bill Gates. (By the way, want to buy a bridge?)
Captain Townshed ordered me to drive over and pick up ten rocket propelled grenade launchers and five crates of ammo.	The Web Services security architecture lacks standard representations for security policies or these kinds of transitive trust and "orders" relationships. One could solve such problems with public and private keys, but only if every part of the system agrees to use the scheme.

Table 9.1. Continued

Action	Comment
I'm your IBM Service representative. Our online service system tells us that one of your RAID file servers needs to have a disk unit swapped. Can you show me the way to the machine room?	WS/SSL security doesn't tackle this sort of thing hence Web Services, at the outset, won't either. You can't confirm that the person represents IBM, that IBM got a message from your RAID file server, or that this is the person IBM dispatched to handle the problem!
Hi. My name is Vice President Frank Jones, and I'm calling from Bechtel Corporation about our bid to rebuild the oil field in the Al Amok region of Iraq. We're going to need to raise our bid by $100M because of some new security concerns. And by the way, can I see the documentation on our bid? I just want to make sure the files didn't get corrupted in transmission or anything.	There isn't any standard way to represent the security issues raised by such a statement. Does this person really represent Bechtel? Is this a legitimate change in the bid price on the contract? Or might this be an employee of Greasy Guys Pipelines and Sewers trying to knock Bechtel out of the bidding? Even if Jones works for Bechtel, does he really have permission to see the bid document, or to change it?
Here's a prescription Dr. Jones wrote for my morphine refill. Can I leave it now and pick up the tablets on my way out?	Did Dr. Jones really write the prescription? Has the prescription been changed? Is Jones a legitimate doctor in this state, and is this the patient for whom he wrote it? SSL security only addresses some of these questions.

world, we'll run into more and more computer analogs of these sorts of real-world problems, and developers will find it frustrating that they either need to implement their own solutions (often impractical since most developers control only a tiny corner of the application), or implement solutions that are less secure than the existing mechanisms they replace.

Let's look at these scenarios in more detail and see where things break down:

1. *I'll take this copy of "Fine Wines of Bulgaria." Here's my visa card.* This example mimics the usual manner in which users interact with Web sites. Keep in mind that one property of a visa credit card is that the card itself offers insurance against fraudulent use. Thus, the user has a high degree of protection simply because of the insurance. The goal, of course, is to ensure that the order and visa card information are passed to the correct merchant and to offer the merchant a secure way to respond—precisely the characteristics of SSL encryption.

2. *Uncle Sal told me that Cousin Vinny knows all the trustworthy pawnbrokers in town, and Vinny gave me this torn dollar bill. If you have the other half, I'll trust you.* The example is phrased in a way that evokes the image of a chain of trust: I trust my Uncle Sal, and Uncle Sal told me to trust Vinny. Accordingly, I trusted Vinny, who gave me the list of pawnbrokers and the torn bill—a public key. Now I'll trust you if you can demonstrate that you have the corresponding private key. In a similar sense, your

browser trusts the AOL or Microsoft server, which provided the key and address of a trustworthy directory server, from which a certificate containing the public key of Amazon.com was obtained. Thus the example maps nicely to the way that Web site authentication is done. On the other hand, the Web doesn't currently offer simple, standard, ways to use authentication *other* than for transactions against the Web. Thus while the model is right, as a practical matter one might find it hard to implement code that uses this model for non-standard purposes.

3. *My name is Bill Gates and I'll be your instructor today*. This statement asks me to trust that the speaker is Bill Gates. But how can that be confirmed? In a distributed system, one can't really confirm identity (without some form of physical or biometric proof, at least)—all we can do is confirm that the speaker has Bill Gates' password, or secret key. What of the statement that "I'll be your instructor today"? Here, we're offered a statement about the relationship of the speaker to the educational institution. To confirm such a claim, we would need a trustworthy way to ask the educational institution to verify that this instructor is indeed the correct one for the current class. Now we have a set of problems. First, the SSL security model doesn't really concern itself with delegation of authority—the example being the delegation of the right to instruct the class. So this already involves departing from the standard. Worse, if we adopt a representation of such relationships, how would we then implement the mechanisms using SSL technology? There has been work on this problem, notably the SPKI/SDSI architecture developed by Rivest's group at MIT. But we lack generally accepted standards, hence the real world leaves every application to its own resources!

4. *Captain Townshed ordered me to drive over and pick up ten rocket propelled grenade launchers and five crates of ammo*. Most of our comments about scenario 3 can be repeated here. Did Captain Townshed issue such an order? Was this the person he issued the order to? Is Townshed himself authorized to take this action? When did he issue the order—today, or last year? We need an elaborate infrastructure to validate such a request, and we need it to be standardized so that applications developed independently can still interact securely. Unfortunately, right now we lack both aspects.

5. *I'm your IBM Service representative. Our online service system tells us that one of your RAID file servers needs to have a disk unit swapped. Can you show me the way to the machine room?* This problem restates problem 4 in a less extreme setting. The same concerns apply. Notice, though, that we also have a new element: two different organizations are presumably interacting in this case. On the one side we have the company running the RAID server, and on the other IBM's service organization. While problems like the ones in scenarios 3 and 4 can be solved using mechanisms such as SPKI/SDSI, problems involving interactions between multiple organizations are much tougher, particularly if one or both wishes to hide most details of its internal policies. This problem is sometimes called "automated trust negotiation."

6. *Hi. My name is Vice President Frank Jones, and I'm calling from Bechel Corporation about our bid to rebuild the oil field in the Al Amok region of Iraq. We're going to need*

to raise our bid by $100M because of some new security concerns. And by the way, can I see the documentation on our bid? I just want to make sure the files didn't get corrupted in transmission or anything. Frankly, I wouldn't trust Frank! But before a computer system does so, it needs to confirm that Frank is actually a VP at Bechtel, that this actually is Frank, that Frank is authorized to update the bid, that Frank's change is authorized by Bechtel, etc. Probably there is no point in going so far as to try and verify the claimed justification—perhaps Bechtel is worried about security, but perhaps he update (if legitimate) reflects some other concerns Frank doesn't care to mention. As for the worry about file corruption, though, one would normally require that the bid document be signed by the bidding corporation—Bechtel, that is, would sign using its private key. Asking to see a copy would be a very curious request.

7. *Here's a prescription Dr. Jones wrote for my morphine refill. Can I leave it now and pick up the tablets on my way out?* Here, the question raises not merely the sorts of worries cited above, but the further possibility that someone may have tampered with the prescription (prescriptions for morphine are probably not very common), and also the concern that the individual who returns to pick the prescription up might not be the same one who dropped off the prescription. A secure system would need to anticipate all such problems and actively take measures to protect itself—perhaps quite a tough job!

From these examples it should be evident that Web technologies raise a number of privacy issues going well beyond the concerns one may have about connection security. Many HTTP requests either include sensitive information, such as authentication credentials, or include fields that reveal the identity of the sender, URIs of documents being used by the sender, or software version numbers associated with the browser or server. These forms of information all can be misused. Moreover, many users employ the same password for all their authenticated actions; therefore, a single corrupt server that relies on the basic authentication scheme might reveal a password that can be used to attack secure servers that use the basic scheme.

Web servers are often considered to be digital analogs of libraries. In the United States, it is illegal for a library to maintain records of the documents that a client has examined in the past: Only current locations of documents may be maintained in the records. Web servers that keep logs of accesses may thus be doing something that would be illegal if the server were indeed the legal equivalent of a library. Nonetheless, it is widely reported that such logging of requests is commonly done, often to obtain information on typical request patterns. The concern, of course, is that information about the private reading habits of individuals is deemed to be personal and protected in the United States, and logs that are gathered for a purpose such as maintaining statistics on frequency of access to parts of a document base might be abused for some less acceptable purpose (note, however, that these types of statistics may be maintained without storing information about specific individuals).

Access patterns are not the only issue here. Knowledge of a URI for a document within which a pointer to some other document was stored may be used to gain access to the higher level document by following the link backwards. This higher level document may, however, be private and sensitive to the user who created it. With information about the version numbers of software on the browser or server, an intruder may be able to attack one or both using known security holes. A proxy could be subverted and modified to return incorrect information in response to get commands; to modify data sent in put commands; or to replay requests (even encrypted ones), which will then be performed more than once to the degree that the server was genuinely stateless. These are just a few of the most obvious concerns that one could raise about HTTP authentication and privacy.

These considerations point to the sense in which we tend to casually trust Web interfaces in ways that may be highly inappropriate. In a literal sense, use of the Web is a highly public activity today: Much of the information passed is basically insecure, and even the protection of passwords may be very limited. Although security is improving—for example HTTPS running on SSL is now standard—the very strongest security mechanisms are not yet standard. Even if one trusts the security protocol implemented by the Web, one must also trust many elements of the environment—for example, one may need to trust that the copy of a secure Web browser that one has downloaded over the network wasn't modified in the network on the way to the user's machine, or modified on the server itself from which it was retrieved. How can the user be sure that the browser that he or she is using has not been changed in a way that will prevent it from following the normal security protocol?

One thinks of the network as anonymous, but user-ID information is present in nearly every message sent over it. Patterns of access can be tracked and intruders may be able to misrepresent a compromised server as one that is trusted using techniques that are likely to be undetectable to the user. Yet the familiarity and comfort associated with the high quality of graphics and easily used interfaces to Web browsers and key services lulls the user into a sense of trust. Because the system "feels" private, much like a telephone call to a mail-order sales department, one feels safe in revealing credit card information or other relatively private data.

Within the Web community, the general view of these issues is that they represent fairly minor problems. The Web security architecture (the cryptographic one) is considered reasonably strong, and although the various dependencies cited above are widely recognized, it is also felt that they do not correspond to gaping exposures or "show stoppers" that could prevent digital commerce on the Web from taking off. The laws that protect private information are reasonably strong in the United States (although the recent Kazaa/RIAA/Verizon lawsuit suggests that the situation is changing), and it is assumed that these offer recourse to users who discover that information about themselves is being gathered or used inappropriately. Fraud and theft by insiders is generally believed to be a more serious problem, and the legal system again offers the best recourse to such problems. For these reasons, most members of the Web community would probably feel more concerned about overload, denial of services due to failure, and consistency than about security.

I believe that the bottom line is not yet clear. It would be nice to believe that security is a problem of the past, but a bit more experience with the current Web security architecture will be needed before one can feel confident that it has no unexpected problems that clever intruders might be able to exploit. In particular, it is troubling to realize that the current security architecture of the Web depends upon the integrity of software that will increasingly be running on unprotected PC platforms, and that may have been downloaded from unsecured sites on the Web. While Java and other interpreted languages could reduce this threat, it seems unlikely to go away soon. In the current environment, it would be surprising *not* to see the emergence of computer viruses that specialize in capturing private keys and revealing them to external intruders without otherwise damaging the host system. This sort of consideration (and we will see a related problem when we talk about non-PC systems that depend upon standard file systems like NFS) can only engender some degree of skepticism about the near-term prospects for real security in the Web.

9.8 Web Proxy Servers

In Figure 9.1 a *server proxy* was shown between the browser and document server. Such proxies are a common feature of the World Wide Web, and are widely perceived as critical to the eventual scalability of the technology. A proxy is any intermediary process through which HTTP operations pass on their way to the server specified in the document URL. Proxies are permitted to cache documents or responses to certain categories of requests, and in future systems may even use cached information to dynamically construct responses on behalf of local users.

This leads to a conceptual structure in which each server can be viewed as surrounded by a ring of proxies that happen to be caching copies of documents associated with it (Figure 9.2). However, because the Web is designed as a stateless architecture, this structure is not typically represented: One could deduce a possible structure from the log of requests to the server, but information is not explicitly maintained in regard to the locations of copies of documents. Thus, a Web server would not typically have a means by which it could inform proxies that have cached documents when the primary copy changes. Instead, the proxies periodically refresh the documents they manage by using the head command to poll the server for changes or the conditional get command to simply pull an updated copy if one is available.

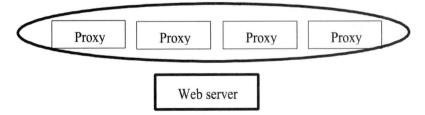

Figure 9.2.   Conceptually, the proxies that cache a document form a "distributed process group," although this group would not typically be explicitly represented, one of several consequences of the stateless philosophy used in the overall Web architecture.

In Part III of this book, we will be looking at techniques for explicitly managing groups of processes that need to coherently replicate data, such as Web documents. These techniques could be used to implement coherent replication within a set of Web proxies, provided that one is prepared to relax the stateless system architecture normally used between the proxies and the primary server. It is likely that Web documents of the future will be more and more dynamic in many settings, either rendering caches less and less useful, or making such coherency a problem of growing importance to the community selling Web-based information that must be accurate to have its maximum value.

In the most common use of Web proxies today, however, their impact is to increase availability at the cost of visible inconsistency when documents are updated frequently. Such proxies reduce load on the Web server and are often able to respond to requests under conditions when a Web server might be inaccessible, crashed, or overloaded. However, unless a Web proxy validates every document before returning a cached copy of it, which is not a standard behavior, a proxy may provide stale data to its users for a potentially unbounded period of time, decreasing the perceived reliability of the architecture. Moreover, even if a proxy does refresh a cached record periodically, the Web potentially permits the use of multiple layers of proxy between the user and the server that maintains the original document. Thus, knowing that the local proxy has tried to refresh a document is not necessarily a strong guarantee of consistency. Head operations cannot be cached; if this command is used to test for freshness there is a reasonable guarantee that staleness can be detected. But the network can be balky, hence in the modern Web, even if a document is known to be stale, there may be no practical way to force an uncooperative proxy to pass a request through to the primary server.

9.9 Web Search Engines and Web Crawlers

Web *search engines* permit the user to retrieve URLs and short information summaries about documents of potential interest. Such engines typically have two components. A *Web Crawler* is a program that hunts for new information on the Web and revisits sites for which information has been cached, revalidating the cache and refreshing information that has changed. Such programs normally maintain lists of Web servers and URLs. By retrieving the associated documents, the Web crawler extracts keywords and content information for use in resolving queries and also obtains new URIs that can be exploited to find more documents. As mentioned earlier, some search engines, such as Google, are actually implemented by making a snapshot of the entire Web and then building indices for every possible search term, every pair of terms, and so forth. At the price of maintaining an enormous computing facility, Google gains tremendous performance benefits.

A Web search engine is a program that performs queries to a database of document descriptions maintained by a Web crawler. Such search engines accept queries in various forms (written language, often English, is the most popular query language) and then use document selection algorithms that attempt to match the words used in the query against the contents of the documents. Considerable sophistication within the search engine is required to ensure that the results returned to the user will be sensible ones and to guarantee rapid response. A consequence is that information retrieval, already an important research topic in computer science today, has become a key to the success of the Web.

Future Web search programs are likely to offer customizable search criteria by which documents can be located and presented to the user based on ongoing interests. An investor might have an ongoing interest in documents that predict future earnings for companies represented in a stock portfolio, a physician in documents relating to his or her specialization, and a lover of fine wines in documents that review especially fine wines or in stores offering those wines at particularly good prices. Increasingly, Web users will be offered these services by the companies that today offer access to the Internet and its e-mail, chat, and bulletin board services.

9.10 Browser Extensibility Features: Plug-in Technologies

An important problem with existing Web browsers (including those that support Java or other agent languages) is that certain types of new features require that the browser itself be extended. Not all of these can be expressed in the somewhat constrained style that Java permits. This has led the major Web browser providers to support browser extensibility.

The basic idea of a plug-in is similar to that of a dynamically linked and loaded module in a conventional operating system, except that the module is fetched over the network. Usually, the need for a plug-in is detected when a user downloads a Web page that makes use of an extensibility feature—for example, the Web page may contain a Java applet that imports the interface of a browser extension. Such an extension tells the browser to bind the applet to the interface if it is already loaded, but it also includes a URL, which can be used to fetch a copy if the extension is not available on the host machine. If the browser lacks the necessary extension, it asks the user to fetch and install it, after which the Web document can be displayed. Once downloaded, the extension becomes an executable component of the Web browser, providing new "native" interfaces that the Java applet can exploit. The same idea is also used to support new document types.

There are arguments for and against Web browser extensibility. Ideally, if all extensions could be expressed in Java or some other agent language, one would favor doing so because of the security benefits. However, these languages all have built-in limitations, and there are some types of extensions that are intrinsically insecure because they require direct access to the hardware of the computer or to the communication network.

The ability to extend the Web browser itself overcomes this type of limitation. Indeed, the Web browser can be understood as a sort of remote operating system, which loads and executes arbitrary applications upon request. Moreover, plug-ins offer a way for a technology provider to sell technology: The sale is often integrated with the plug-in procedure, so that the user purchases and is billed for the technology in a single step, integrated with the act of downloading it. On the downside, plug-ins offer no security at all: A hostile plug-in has essentially unrestricted access both to the user's computer and to the network.

In the short term, it seems likely that as long as the Web continues to explode with new applications and new functionality, heavy use of plug-in technology will be unavoidable. Indeed, over time, plug-ins could become the most common way to purchase new software for use on PCs and workstations! However, in the longer term, the security issues created by plug-ins may force many organizations to limit their use. It seems likely that the corporate network of the future will restrict the use of plug-ins to technologies that can be found in some sort of a corporate repository. Doing so would limit the types of applications that can be imported into the corporate network and allow the corporation to check the imported technologies for potential threats. The legal protections that are now used to prosecute individuals who break into computing systems may eventually be found applicable to developers of malicious plug-ins and applications. This would also represent a step toward increased safety when downloading software over a network. However, as long as the overall technology area remains volatile, plug-ins are likely to be widely used, and serious security concerns are simply inevitable.

9.11 Future Challenges for the Web Community

Although the explosive popularity of the Web makes it clear that the existing functionality of the system is more than adequate to support useful applications, evolution of the broader technology base will also require further research and development. Some of the major areas for future study include:

Improved GUI builders and browsers: Although the first generation of browsers has already revolutionized the Web, the second wave of GUI builder technologies promises to open distributed computing to a vastly larger community. This development could revolutionize computing—increasing the use of networking by orders of magnitude and tremendously amplifying the existing trend towards critical dependency upon distributed computing systems.

Particularly interesting is the trend to treat Web browsers as "components" that can be employed relatively casually within larger applications. This trend (which fits well with the overall thinking behind Web Services), could lead to systems in which little glimpses of the Web occur everywhere—in banners at the tops of windows, in documents, and even in vendor-supplied logos. More broadly, with Web Services, we may start to see Web-enabled applications become more or less ubiquitous.

Yet as this happens, we must also keep in mind that not all computers are continuously connected to the Internet, and that many are misconfigured, poorly protected, and poorly administered. The servers providing all of this Web content may be unavailable, or could be compromised or attacked. Thus while the trends favor greater and greater integration of the Web into almost every form of application, this also promotes growing dependency on Web mechanisms that are not built to provide high availability or high security.

Thus, we see a tradeoff here that may only become more clear with increased experience. My feeling is that wider use of the Web will create growing pressure to do something about network reliability and security and that the latter topic is receiving more serious attention than the former. This could make reliability, in the sense of availability, consistency, manageability, and timely and guaranteed responsiveness, emerge as one of the major issues of the coming decade. But it is also possible that 90 percent of the market will turn out to be uninterested in such issues, with the exception of their need to gain sufficient security to support electronic commerce, and that the vendors will simply focus on that 90 percent while largely overlooking the remaining 10 percent. This could lead us to a world of secure banking tools imbedded into inconsistent and unreliable application software.

The danger, of course, is that if we treat reliability issues casually, we may begin to see major events in which distributed systems unreliability has horrific consequences, in the sense of causing accidents, endangering health and privacy, bringing down banks, or other similarly frightening outcomes. Should terrorism ever become a major problem on the network, one could imagine scenarios in which that 10 percent exposure could suddenly loom as an immense problem. As discussed in the introduction, we already face considerable risk through the increasing dependence of our telecommunication, power, banking, and air traffic control systems on the network, and this is undoubtedly just the beginning of a long-term trend.

If there is a light at the end of this particular tunnel, it is that a number of functionality benefits turn out to occur as side effects of the most effective reliability technologies, discussed in Part III. It is possible that the desire to build better groupware and conferencing systems, better electronic stock markets and trading systems, and better tools for mundane applications such as document handling in large organizations will drive developers to look more seriously at the same technologies that also promote reliability. If this occurs, the knowledge base and tool base for integrating reliability solutions into GUI environments and elaborate agent programming languages could expand substantially, making reliability both easier and more transparent to achieve and more widely accessible.

Universal Resource Locators (URLs): Uniform resource locators suffer from excessive specificity: They tell the browser precisely where a document can be found. At the same time, they often lack information that may be needed to determine which version of a document is desired. Future developments will soon result in the introduction of uniform resource locators capable of uniquely identifying a document regardless of where it may be cached, including additional information to permit a user to validate its authenticity or to distinguish between versions. Such a universal resource name would facilitate increased use of caching within Web servers and proxies other than the originating server where the original copy of the document resides. Important issues raised by this direction of research include the management of consistency in a world of replicated documents that may be extensively cached.

Security and Commerce Issues: The basic security architecture of the Web is very limited and rather trusting of the network. As noted earlier, a number of standards have been proposed in the areas of Web security and digital cash. These proposals remain difficult to evaluate and compare with one another, and considerable work will be needed before widely acceptable standards are available. These steps are needed, however, if the Web is to become a serious setting for commerce and banking.

Availability of critical Web data: Security is only of the reliability issues raised by the Web. Another important concern is availability of critical resources, such as medical documents that may be needed in order to treat patients in a hospital, banking records needed in secure financial applications, and decision-support documents needed for split-second planning in settings such as battlefields. Current Web architectures tend to include single points of failure, such as the Web server responsible for the original copy of a document, and the authentication servers used to establish secure Web connections. When these resources are inaccessible or down, critical uses of the Web may be impossible. Thus, technologies permitting critical resources to be replicated for fault tolerance and higher availability will be of growing importance as critical applications are shifted to the Web.

9.12 Consistency and the Web

Mechanisms for caching Web documents and replicating critical resources raise questions about the degree to which a user can trust a document to be a legitimate and current version of the document that was requested. With existing Web architectures, the only way to validate a document is to connect to its home server and use the head command to confirm that it has not changed since it was created. Moreover, there is no guarantee that a set of linked documents about to be retrieved will not be simultaneously updated on the originating server. Such a situation could result in a juxtaposition of stale and current documents, yielding a confusing or inconsistent result. More broadly, we need to understand what it means to say that a document or set of documents is seen in mutually consistent states, and how this property can be guaranteed by the Web. Where documents are replicated or cached, the same requirement extends to the replicas. In Chapter 20 we will consider solutions to these sorts of problems, but their use in the Web remains tentative and many issues will require further research, experimentation, and standardization.

9.13 Related Reading

On the Web: (see Berners-Lee et al. [1992, 1994, 1995]).

   For Java: (see Gosling and McGilton [1995a, 1995b]).

   For TACOMA: (see Asplin and Johansen, Johansen et al. [May 1995, June 1995, 1996]).

   There is a large amount of on-line material concerning the Web—for example in the archives maintained by Netscape Corporation, http://www.netscape.com.

10

Web Services

10.1 What is a Web Service?

A *Web Service* is a form of client/server system structured to make as much use as possible of Web standards. In the most common configurations, a Web Service is actually a front-end to a database server or some other enterprise server (or to a collection of them), functioning as an intermediary between client applications and a legacy system managed by the enterprise. However, there are other possible Web Service configurations. For example, Microsoft has explored supporting Web Service interfaces to a great variety of servers used internally by the Windows XP and .NET platform; in this use, the server would often be a rather small program or even a system module. There has been talk about using Web Services architectures to standardize communication to small sensors and other devices, such as a home entertainment system, or even a coffee maker or a bread baking machine. These kinds of applications share one important element: for the kinds of uses that are anticipated, rapid response is not a likely requirement. This is good news because, as we'll see, while Web Services may seem like a good match for almost any client/server application, in reality the technology is much more appropriate for client/server systems with modest performance needs than for those having more demanding requirements. Experiments with early versions of the Web Service API reveal that multisecond round-trip times for simple, small, RPC requests are not unusual. This is not a technology to imagine using on a time-critical path within a high-performance application!

The simplest Web Services systems consist of a small set of components (Figure 10.1). These are:

A Request Dispatch Module. This "router" accepts connections (usually, in the form of TCP connections on which HTTP will be used to issue the actual requests), decodes the request (it will be encoded using the SOAP standard), and dispatches the request to an appropriate server or other back-end process (most often, the server will be external to the request dispatcher, although perhaps on the same computing platform).

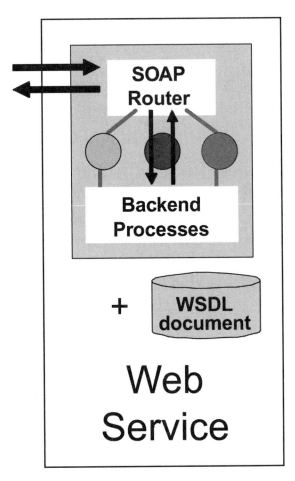

Figure 10.1. Web Services are software components described via WSDL which are capable of being accessed via standard network protocols such as SOAP over HTTP.

A Web Service Description Language (WSDL) Document. This document provides clients and other Web Services applications and tools with a description of the Web Service. The description lists the interfaces available, their authentication requirements, the types of arguments they accept, and the types of results returned. The WSDL language uses XML to actually represent the information. One of the standard operations possible on a Web Service is to fetch its WSDL document. There is much talk about extending WSDL to include information about performance and reliability guarantees, preferences the server may have, alternative ways of connecting to the server, etc.

The Server itself. The Web Services dispatch module is not normally linked into the address space of the server (most often, a single machine will support more than one Web Service application hence the dispatcher must run on behalf of all of them). The server must support SOAP, but it is common to solve this problem by "wrapping" some other server—perhaps, a database platform or some kind of legacy application—using a small SOAP-based server that accepts incoming Web Service requests, decodes them, invokes the database or legacy system using the appropriate "raw" technology, then encodes the result and sends it back.

Thus, a bare-bones Web Service could be an extremely simple affair. However, there are a variety of additional Web Services standards, and in practice, most systems will make use of at least a few of them. First among these is the standard for "naming" or "finding" a Web Services application, UDDI. UDDI, the Universal Description, Discovery and Integration standard, is a language for describing a service in terms of its name, attributes, and other properties. For example, perhaps "playroom-TV" is the name of a television set that has a cable and Internet connection, a wide-screen of a particular size, etc. With this sort of information, a device hunting for "playroom-TV" could find it, but so could an application looking for a display device capable of displaying wide-screen video.

UDDI is not, however, a standard for storing naming information. The idea is that the application might store a UDDI record in some other naming service, such as the DNS, an X.500-compatible service, a Jini or JXTA-style rendezvous service, or in a home-brew naming subsystem. UDDI information could be saved into an XML database and queried. Thus UDDI is about representing naming information and querying it, but not about where that information should be stored.

Beyond UDDI, we encounter a fairly messy collections of standards and associated technology packages. These can be loosely understood as falling into categories.

- *Asynchronous messaging.* These are technologies aimed at converting Web Services systems into reliable but asynchronous "offline" processing elements. The idea is that one could hide the poor latency of the technology and also gain important performance benefits by organizing asynchronous pipelines that accept requests at one end (and make promises to the client: the requests won't be lost, the result will be sent back within such-and-such a delay, etc), pass them to the server (perhaps in batches for greater efficiency), collect the results and pipeline those back to the various clients.

- *Reliability.* There has been a great deal of work on supporting transactional reliability in the Web Services model, focused on two styles of transactions—the sort of short-running transactions we saw earlier, and a longer-running form of transaction called a "business" transaction, where requests are issued to a set of Web Services systems over an extended period of time. The usual example is that, to plan my trip to the Carribean, I'll need to rent a house, purchase a plane ticket, rent a car, and so forth. These applications might individually be accessed through a transaction interface, but rather than tie the whole lot together into a very long-running big transaction, a business transaction treats them as a series of separate but related transactions. To get an all-or-nothing effect, there needs to be a way to either roll back, or to guarantee that progress can definitely be made even in the event that a transaction fails somewhere in the sequence.

- *Fault-tolerance and Load Balancing.* Web Services systems will need ways to restart failed servers (perhaps rolling functionality from the failed server to a healthy one), and, more broadly, will need ways of spreading load across clusters of servers. Work in these areas seeks to define standards for assisting a client in reestablishing a broken connection and resynchronizing with a server, and to assist the server itself in setting the load-balancing or fail-over policies that should be used. Keep in mind, however, that these standards are "external" ones, aimed at the client/server interaction path. Far less clear is the question of how a Web Service server might replicate the necessary state and perform the needed fault-detection and synchronization actions. Of course, in part, such issues are internal to the servers being handled—indeed, there are good arguments that Web Services systems per-se should be stateless "hot potato" forwarding modules that do as little work as possible. But in practice, the transactional mechanisms are already complex and stateful, hence it seems that this battle may have been lost even before it was really fought.

- *Security*. There is a major effort underway to define security standards for Web Services. These seek to build on Web security standards like HTTPS and SSL, but go beyond the basic Web model. At the time of this writing, it was not yet clear what form these additional guarantees might take, but there is much interest in issues of security "policy," particularly in collaborative scenarios where two companies work together on a given task, yet might not work together for other purposes. The participants thus need to share information relevant to the task without providing each-other with unfettered system access. However, this is just one of many scenarios under consideration.

- *Quality of Service*. This area within the Web Services community is focused on applications involving media playback, where quality of service guarantees both from the Web Service system and the network become important considerations. Issues here range from sharing the appropriate media coding and decoding module (the "Codec") to negotiating a QoS level that makes sense given the destination device and the bandwidth available to it.

- *Business Logic*. These are a set of "higher level" standards for encoding the overall logic of a transaction in a high-level form. The idea is that rather than assuming that the application itself understands the series of operations requested by the enterprise Web Service platform, the options might instead be encoded in a business logic language. For example, to purchase such and such a model of computer, one first does a reservation transaction on the computer itself, then on the monitor, etc, and ultimately on the shipping subsystem. The individual transactions can then be compiled from the specification and executed as a business transaction. This approach reduces the risk of a coding error or some other violation of the intended business logic.

Our list could continue, but this rough grouping should already convey the broad outlines of an area that has emerged at lightning speed to capture the attention and enthusiasm of a wide swath across the distributed systems community. Web Services are going to be too slow and clunky for many purposes, but where performance is simply not the main issue (and interoperability, on the other hand, has high value), the technology is clearly going to have an enormous impact.

The remainder of this chapter touches on each of the elements of the Web Services architecture in more detail.

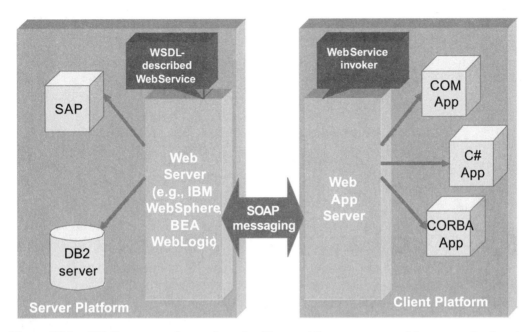

Figure 10.2. Web Servers are often configured as "front ends" or wrapers, permitting new applications to interact with legacy servers. In this figure, the legacy systems are shown on the left and the new applications on the right.

10.2 Web Service Description Language: WSDL

The role of the Web Services Description Language, WSDL, is to document the interfaces to Web Services objects. In effect, WSDL is the IDL for Web Services applications, although there has been discussion of including a number of features into WSDL not normally found in an IDL. WSDL documents are currently used by object assembly, code generation, debugging, inspection, and other tools and may also drive security policy mechanisms.

The following example illustrates the contents of a small WSDL document. This particular example was drawn from a sample Web Services application placed onto the Web by a public standards organization called XMethods.net, which was founded to promote web services standards such as SOAP, WSDL and UDDI. This site is a "virtual laboratory" for developers, listing publicly available web services and showcasing new ways this technology can be applied. The service shown below consists of a thermometer, to which one can issue temperature read requests.

The WSDL document should be largely self-explanatory. At the top we see a series of definitions giving the versions of various Web Services specifications on which the body of the WSDL document was based. Next we see the definitions for the two categories of SOAP messages supported: getTempRequest and getTempResponse. The request includes

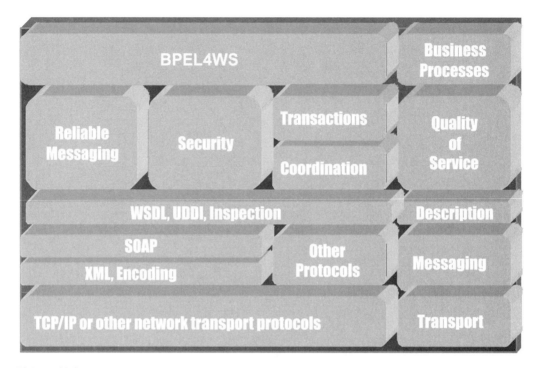

Figure 10.3. The Web Services "stack." Major architectural components of the Web Service Model are organized here to correspond, roughly, to an ISO layering. The components included here are examples; many other proposed components and standards have been omitted, and in fact the business process language mentioned here (BPEL4WS) is being promoted primarily by IBM; other companies such as Microsoft and BEA favor alternatives that differ in many ways from the IBM proposal.

a string, namely the zipcode argument, and the response consists of a floating point number. Next we see the rules for finding the port at which the Web Service is listening for these requests, the binding of this RPC rest to the HTTP transport protocol (recall that HTTP over TCP is just "the most standard" option for connecting to a Web Service, not the only option), and finally the definition of the service itself. As noted earlier, WSDL documents are normally published for use by client systems. This document was downloaded from http://www.xmethods.net/sd_ibm/TemperatureService.wsdl, within a site maintained as a public resources for those who seek to develop Web Services platforms or, like us, just want to understand the public elements of the architecture.

10.3 Simple Object Access Protocol: SOAP

The WSDL document defines the format of the SOAP request that can be issued to the temperature service. The following is an automatically generated document illustrating this information, extracted directly from the WDSL document seen above:

```xml
<?xml version="1.0" ?>
<definitions name="TemperatureService"
targetNamespace="http://www.xmethods.net/sd/TemperatureService.wsdl"
   xmlns:tns="http://www.xmethods.net/sd/TemperatureService.wsdl"
   xmlns:xsd="http://www.w3.org/1999/XMLSchema"
   xmlns:soap="http://schemas.xmlsoap.org/wsdl/soap/"
   xmlns="http://schemas.xmlsoap.org/wsdl/">
<message name="getTempRequest">
<part name="zipcode" type="xsd:string"/>
   </message>
<message name="getTempResponse">
<part name="return" type="xsd:float"/>
   </message>
<portType name="TemperaturePortType">
<operation name="getTemp">
<input message="getTempRequest" name="getTemp"/>
<output message="getTempResponse" name="getTempResponse"/>
   </operation>
   </portType>
<binding name="TemperatureBinding" type="TemperaturePortType">
<soap:binding style="rpc" transport="http://schemas.xmlsoap.org/soap/http"/>
<operation name="getTemp">
<soap:operation soapAction=""/>
<input>
<soap:body use="encoded" namespace="urn:xmethods-Temperature"
   encodingStyle="http://schemas.xmlsoap.org/soap/encoding/"/>
   </input>
<output>
<soap:body use="encoded" namespace="urn:xmethods-Temperature"
   encodingStyle="http://schemas.xmlsoap.org/soap/encoding/"/>
   </output>
   </operation>
   </binding>
<service name="TemperatureService">
<documentation>Returns current temperature in a given U.S. zipcode</documentation>
<port name="TemperaturePort" binding="TemperatureBinding">
<soap:address location="http://services.xmethods.net:80/soap/servlet/rpcrouter"/>
   </port>
</service>
</definitions>
```

Figure 10.4. WSDL document for a Temperature Service that, given a US zipcode, returns the current temperature for that region.

Detailed Description

> Current temperature in a given U.S. zipcode region.

Usage Notes

```
Request Parameter Schema:
<element name="zipcode" type="string" />

Response Parameter Schema:
<element name="return" type="float" />

Encoding Style for both request and response:
http://schemas.xmlsoap.org/soap/encoding

------------------------------------------------------------

Sample Request envelope:

<SOAP-ENV:Envelope
xmlns:SOAP-ENV="http://schemas.xmlsoap.org/soap/envelope/"
xmlns:xsi="http://www.w3.org/1999/XMLSchema-instance"
xmlns:xsd="http://www.w3.org/1999/XMLSchema">
<SOAP-ENV:Body>
<ns1:getTemp xmlns:ns1="urn:xmethods-Temperature"
SOAP-ENV:encodingStyle="http://schemas.xmlsoap.org/soap/
encoding/">
<zipcode xsi:type="xsd:string">94041</zipcode>
</ns1:getTemp>
</SOAP-ENV:Body>
</SOAP-ENV:Envelope>


------------------------------------------------------------

Sample Response Envelope:

<SOAP-ENV:Envelope
xmlns:SOAP-ENV="http://schemas.xmlsoap.org/soap/envelope/"
xmlns:xsi="http://www.w3.org/1999/XMLSchema-instance"
xmlns:xsd="http://www.w3.org/1999/XMLSchema">
```

```
<SOAP-ENV:Body>
<ns1:getTempResponse xmlns:ns1="urn:xmethods-Temperature"
SOAP-ENV:encodingStyle="http://schemas.xmlsoap.org/soap/
encoding/">
<return xsi:type="xsd:float">68.0</return>
</ns1:getTempResponse>
</SOAP-ENV:Body>
</SOAP-ENV:Envelope>
```

Notice that the SOAP request identifies the version of the SOAP specification on which the request message format was based, then species that the request is an invocation of getTemp, the temperature service. The argument is a zip code, 94041 in this case. The response, shown just below, is the floating point value 68.0. A natural question concerns the handling of floating point values that have no exact decimal representation. In fact, the "float" representation is just one of several XML representations for floating point data, and one could even define new representations to extend the base set. However, working purely within the most common options, such a value would be returned to the user only to the precision captured by this print representation.

10.4 Talking to a Web Service: HTTP over TCP

When an application wishes to talk to a Web Service, it normally must start by establishing a binding and then it can issue requests over the resulting connection. We say "normally" because the specification is extensible and one could certainly define a Web Service interface in which binding doesn't require actually creating a connection—indeed, there are already Web Service interfaces to many services, such as the Internet DNS service, that use UDP communication and require no special binding actions at all. At any rate, our temperature service *does* require a binding. This is implied by its use of HTTP as the communication protocol specified by the WSDL document.

Accordingly, the application will normally look up the port number at which the Web Service can be found (or use a default value), create a TCP connection binding to the service at that port, then use HTTP to issue its request, much as if the "request" was a document description and the "response" was the fetched document. Indeed, a Web browser can be used to manually invoke the temperature service seen above, even though the intended use is for a computer that knows the URL to obtain temperatures while running over the Web.

HTTP over TCP is a relatively slow protocol, and SOAP is quite a verbose one. Thus many Web Services will either support other options through the WSDL declaration, or offer a way to "swap" the original TCP connection for a new connection (or at least a new encoding) offering greater efficiency. At present, such a step would likely depart from the Web Services standards, but it is expected that this efficiency consideration will become such a common worry, over time, that standard ways of replacing slow, inefficient connection with faster but less general ones may become a part of the Web Services standard fairly rapidly. Very likely the first generation of such extended standards will reflect existing 3-tier database and enterprise server architectures and protocols, since those are mature and the software for them already exists. Within a single machine one would expect local RPC protocols to be used: COM and DCOM, for example, in the case of .NET on Windows. Down the road, a best standard practice solution is likely to emerge to take its place beside the SOAP over HTTP over TCP option. Nonetheless, developers need to be aware that for the foreseeable future, the "average" Web Services interaction may be quite slow and quite verbose.

10.5   Universal Description, Discovery and Integration Language: UDDI

The role of UDDI is to represent the name of the service but also other forms of descriptive information for registration in a name service such as DNS. A UDDI specification is composed of several documents. The API specification describes the SOAP APIs, which allow you to perform discovery and publishing operations. Request/response semantics and error handling are described. There is also substantial information on conventions and usage. Companion documents include the Data Structure specification and the API Schema, which define the message and data semantics.

The following is a summary of the operations supported by version 1 of the UDDI specification:

```
Inquiry Operations:        Publishing Operations:
Find                          Save
     find_business                save_business
     find_service                 save_service
     find_binding                 save_binding
     find_tModel                  save_tModel
Get details                   Delete
     get_businessDetail           delete_business
     get_serviceDetail            delete_service
     get_bindingDetail            delete_binding
     get_tModelDetail             delete_tModel
     get_registeredInfo           get_registeredInfo
                              Security
                                   get_authToken
                                   discard_authToken
```

The intention of the UDDI development community is that one might use these API's to search for a specific service, browse in a more general way to find a service matching some set of goals, or drill down on a service found in this more general way to look closely at its detailed specification.

Version 2 of the UDDI specification, recently released, extends the basic UDDI model with additional interfaces. These are intended to model a "business" in greater detail. The broad trend is to move towards a world in which companies can advertise themselves on the Web through UDDI documents, can browse the Web for sources of desired goods or services, and then can enter into transactions with matching vendors—all automatically. Of course, many Web Services systems will use only a tiny subset of this full model, yet one can see that in its complete generality, the model is an extremely powerful one that could transform the ways that organizations interact with one-another. This ambitious view of the Web Services world is, however, some distance in the future, and a great deal of technology development will need to occur before it becomes a commonplace reality.

Readers interested in learning more about UDDI version 2 are encouraged to consult "Understanding UDDI," a document developed by IBM to assist its customers in appreciating the power of this emerging model. The document can be found at http://www-106.ibm.com/developerworks/library/ws-featuddi/.

10.6 Other Current and Proposed Web Services Standards

Corporate users of Web Services are expected to place a very high premium on reliability of the overall architecture and of the specific platforms on which they build. For this reason, reliability has received a considerable degree of attention in the Web Services community. Nonetheless, as this book was being revised, the Web Services reliability model was far from decided. In what follows, we summarize the state of the standard as of late 2003, recognizing that some elements of this discussion will rapidly become outmoded.

10.6.1 WS_RELIABILITY

The WS_RELIABILITY standard defines a basic synchronization protocol (in effect, 2-phase commit) and its use in support of two transactional protocols, one aimed at short-running transactions against a database or some other server, and the other at longer running business transactions. WS_RELIABILITY will soon be extended, however, to deal with other types of reliability guarantee, notably for applications that issue transactions asynchronously through some form of queuing or MOMS software, with the response separated in time from the original request invocation. In such cases, WS_RELIABILITY provides for automated reissue of a request that may have been delayed by a failure, and offers a means to detect duplicate requests (to avoid executing them more than once). As mentioned in the introduction of this chapter, pipelined, asynchronous transactions are likely to be more successful than interactive transactions against Web Services simply because the Web Services model is slow and balky, and also because it presupposes a physical "web" of interconnected legacy systems that may be very extensive and hence have rather unpredictable performance. In an asynchronous model, one expects batchy performance and delays. Yet one also expects a "guarantee" from the platform that one's request won't be misplaced, and a well-defined interface for canceling a pending request, checking status, being informed of exceptions, etc.

10.6.2 WS_TRANSACTIONS

WS_TRANSACTIONS is the most mature of the existing Web Service reliability specifications. The basic transactional model defines the rules by which an interaction between an application and a Web Service can obtain the classic ACID guarantees. Below we illustrate a client/server application without and then with this standard in use.

Notice that the WS_TRANSACTION specification requires a considerable number of additional protocol steps and messages, and also a forced log write to a disk. All of this

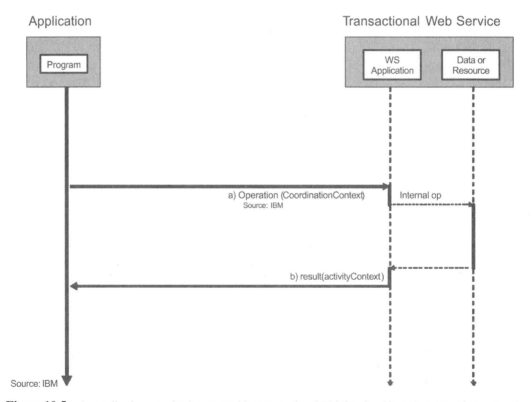

Figure 10.5. An application program interacts with a transactional Web Service. Here, the transaction protocol has been omitted and we see only the communication path of the application itself. Step a) is the issuing of the request, which is dispatched by the Web Services dispatch module (shown in this figure as the "WS application"), and then handled by a database or some other back-end resource. The result is returned.

overhead makes the specification somewhat slow, and it is likely that for many purposes, transactional reliability could be costly in this model.

A presumption of the WS_TRANSACTION specification is that applications will issue only short-running transactions to relatively small numbers of servers (perhaps more than the single server illustrated in Figure 10.5, of course, but still a small number, like two or three, not dozens). For longer-running transactions, the specification recommends that the developer think in terms of "business transactions," which are sequences of the smaller transactions illustrated above, linked by business logic and perhaps even described in a business process language. Such a pipeline of transactions would visit a series of servers in succession, performing operations on each. The integrity of the overall sequence is addressed by mechanisms for backing out of a failed series of transactions or for moving forward in "alternative" ways that might include compensation for failed requests. Such an approach has a great deal in common with a type of transactional model called the "Saga" model.

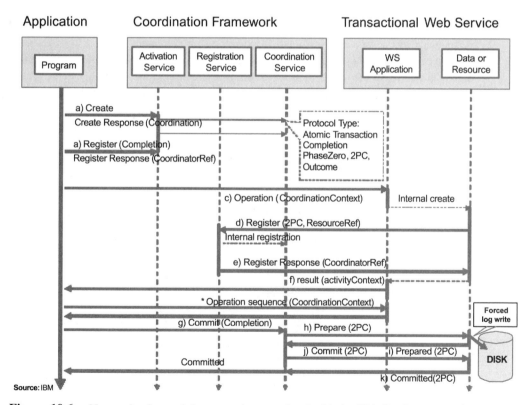

Figure 10.6. Now we've inserted the messaging associated with the Web Services transaction protocol. Notice that a new server has been added, namely the "configuration framework," and that it in turn contains three separate sub-systems. The transactional commit protocol includes a forced log write, so the "disk" on which this log resides has also been included in the figure.

10.6.3 WS_RELIABILITY

Although the Web Services architecture includes a reliability specification and an underlying reliable message passing component, the details of these parts of the framework are still a subject of debate. To understand the approach taken in WS_RELIABILITY, it helps to appreciate that most transactional applications need recoverability, but not high availability. That is, these systems *do* need a way to repair themselves and resume operations after a component fails, but the repair *does not* need to happen particularly rapidly. Indeed, even if we set the issue of failures and recovery to the side, there are many kinds of systems in which components only run periodically. WS_RELIABILITY targets such scenarios. Its role is to provide the developer with help in situations where a client may not be able to interact directly with the service on which it needs to perform an operation.

WS_RELIABILITY tackles these problems by introducing a message queuing intermediary between the client and the server (this could be the Web Services dispatch application itself, or it could be some other product). Readers may find it easiest to imagine such an intermediary as a kind of mailbox. Rather than assume that the server is operational when the client needs it, we build our application to send requests as e-mail, through a mailbox polled periodically by the server, and to handle replies in a similar manner. WS_RELIABILITY is a specification for talking to a mailbox, and reflects a basic assumption that we can provide high availability for the mailbox, at which point all we need is recoverability in the server.

The model should be familiar to anyone who frequently orders products off the Web: one places an order (this enqueues it for eventual processing), the order is then accepted, the product ships, etc. From time to time, the user may want to check on the status of the operation, but it is increasingly rare to expect instant responses from the overall system. Similarly, the WS_RELIABILITY specification doesn't assume that we mean instant availability. The goal is simply to ensure that if a client's request matters, it will eventually get processed.

WS_RELIABILITY works as follows. The client starts by labeling the operation in a way that will permit it to be uniquely identified later; for example, the name could be a tuple consisting of the machine name on which the client is running and the current wall-clock time, or a counter that increments each time a request is issued. Next, the client hands the request off to the intermediary, specifying the desired behavior in the event that a failure delays processing: should the request be performed at most once, at least once, or exactly once? (Exactly once would be the obvious choice, but is often impractical to support; at most once is next-most expensive, and at-least-once is cheapest). The queuing subsystem acknowledges the request, typically after storing a copy in a log server. The client application can now move on to other tasks, polling from time to time to check on progress, much as a human user polls Web sites to see if an order has shipped yet. In principle, the client can cancel a long-delayed request. On the other hand, it isn't clear how that might be done if the intermediary itself crashes and is down when the client checks for request status, pointing to just one of many "fuzzy" areas in the specification.

Now, in the best of worlds, the server is up and polls the intermediary, asking for enqueued requests much as your e-mail client checks for e-mail in the local e-mail server. It will be passed a copy of the request, and an indication of how the application requested that it be handled. Servers complying with the full specification will now check for duplicate requests and, potentially, will send a copy of a previous reply (just in case a reply gets lost and the request is reissued later). On the other hand, the specification recognizes that not all servers will support the full range of options. A server can, for example, refuse a request that desires an exactly-once guarantee because it is unable to guarantee exactly once execution (exactly-once execution normally requires a history mechanism in the server).

Obviously, we're not in a high-performance, high-availability domain here. When a failure occurs, there could be a delay before the server and message queuing intermediary are back in operation. WS_RELIABILITY isn't aimed at high availability, hence this delay is considered to be a part of the game—a cost of using the mechanism. Indeed, the basic queuing cost is treated as just part of the overhead associated with obtaining the reliability guarantees offered by the specification. If the intermediary logs requests to disk (as is likely), reliability thus can come at a substantial cost in terms of delay both in the basic case where all components are operational, and with the risk of far longer delays if some are faulty. Thus WS_RELIABILITY is about "eventual" reliability in applications that can afford delays and that are comfortable with a pipelined execution style in which throughput (operations per second) but not round-trip time are the performance metrics of interest.

What about WS_TRANSACTIONS? As noted earlier, the WS_TRANSACTIONS targets applications that are issuing a stream of related requests to one or more transactional server, and presumes that aborting the actions is a suitable approach if a failure occurs during such a sequence of actions. Business transactions are used for longer-running activities. WS_RELIABILITY references WS_TRANSACTIONS but it is not at all clear that the two mechanisms would ever be used simultaneously. Indeed, most of the discussion in the WS_RELIABILITY specification focuses on the case of a single operation, and WS_TRANSACTIONS doesn't have any work to do if the client is doing just singleton operations. In effect the specifications aim at orthogonal aspects of the problem.

Not all applications will be satisfied with WS_RELIABILITY and WS_TRANSACTIONS. Both reflect an assumption that Web Services are mostly concerned with heavyweight applications that mimic three-tier applications with a database at the core, or human interactions with Web sites. In contrast, one can imagine a style of application where Web Services specifications might be used between smaller, lighter-weight distributed objects. Indeed, Microsoft .NET makes it almost trivial to create such distributed objects: one takes an object and indicates that ASP.NET should be used to make it available as a Web Service, and the platform does the rest. Yet while it is easy to create and launch such an application, the reliability "model" of the architecture doesn't have them in mind. This, then, offers a research opportunity for us: can we extend the basic Web Services architecture to permit the development of lightweight, highly-available (fault-tolerant) distributed objects? In Chapter 26, we'll see that there is good reason to believe that this can be done. The coming years should witness a wave of products aimed at such problems. And it also points to a problem: lacking commercial-quality solutions that integrate with major products and platforms, the Web Services community may be inviting corporations and other enterprises to move mission-critical applications into the Web Services model with only a partial story for those concerned with reliability. This is a real shame, since it seems likely that many applications will stumble over the question, and yet it wouldn't be all that difficult to offer better reliability solutions in the major platforms.

10.6.4 WS_MEMBERSHIP

A good example of the sort of mechanism *not* considered to be a part of the standard Web Services architecture is any kind of service to track the status of components or to detect failures. Earlier, we had a glimpse of the importance of this issue when discussing the risk of "split brain" behavior in systems that detect failures inconsistently. As we saw then, a system that makes mistakes in its failure reporting can partition internally, so that half its components end up connected to a primary server and the other half to a backup that believes itself to be the new primary. This is just one of many scenarios in which a system becomes confused about its state. When such problems arise, the application is unlikely to overcome the resulting confusion and may visibly malfunction.

Werner Vogels has a long history of interest in issues arising in complex data centers, including the failure detection and handling problem. An early paper of his looked at the many forms of status reporting available in modern systems and the ways that these can be exploited to obtain much better quality failure detection than might otherwise be possible. Vogels has also worked on technologies for system-wide agreement on component status (e.g., when a situation is ambiguous, ensuring that a consistent decision is reached) and on the best ways to report such events. A recent proposal by Vogels and his research group suggests that the Web Services community might want to standardize a service incorporating these membership tracking functions, which he proposes to call WS_MEMBERSHIP.

WS_MEMBERSHIP could have a dramatic impact on the reliability of Web Services platforms, but seems unlikely to be accepted by the community any time soon. There are many reasons for this, but the most basic reason is also in some ways the most trivial one: WS_MEMBERSHIP relates to an area that most developers understand in very limited ways and, for this reason, has attracted a tremendous number of confusing and often confused proposals. In effect, Web Services tries to be a best-of-breed standardization group and is quite effective in this respect when there is a best-of-breed option readily at hand. Where standard, off-the-shelf solutions are less mature or simply not available, though, the Web Services community (the W3 consortium) is not equipped to deal with what now becomes a form of research. WS_MEMBERSHIP is an example of the needed answer, but until the W3 consortium poses the right questions, Web Services may continue to lack the needed reliability properties.

10.7 How Web Services Deal with Failure

So, how *do* Web Services handle failures? Such a question could be raised at many levels: one might ask about failures of basic Web Service components such as the request dispatch module or a UDDI-based naming service, failures of the backend servers, failures of clients that might be running transactions or business transactions—or that might be doing non-transactional requests, and failures of the network. Unfortunately, there is no simple answer to any of these questions. Although Web Services platforms may offer standardized ways of reporting exceptions, the actual information available is limited and of potentially low quality.

Just as other RPC technologies have difficulty distinguishing transient network outages from outright crashes, Web Services lack a mechanism for accurate failure detection and may report a "failure" whenever a timeout occurs. Timeout, of course, could occur at many levels of the architecture. Thus when a Web Services system reports an exception, the user will often lack information about the precise cause.

There are several standard observations one might make about this property of the Web Services infrastructure. The first is that lacking a service such as WS_MEMBERSHIP, the risk of unreliable failure reporting is simply a property of distributed computing and hence something that must be accepted and dealt with.

A second observation basically restates the end-to-end principle. If the client desires reliability, perhaps the client will simply need to play a role in achieving the desired result. To this end, there has been considerable work on adding forms of "session state" identification and persistence to the Web Services architecture. We saw an instance of this idea in the WS_RELIABILITY specification, used in support of at-most-once and exactly-once operation semantics.

But the idea of channel persistence goes much further. The basic thinking is that if the client and server can agree on the name by which "session state" will be known, then a client that becomes disconnected from a server can potentially reconnect (perhaps to a backup) and resynchronize its state with the server state. The synchronization mechanism, however, becomes complex and we lack standards for solving this problem, particularly if fail-over to a new server occurs (in that case, session state must potentially be replicated between the primary and its possible backups, and the fail-over cannot proceed until the backup is fully synchronized with the state of the failed primary, which could take some time). Thus while persistent session state may sound appealing, the devil is in the details.

Yet a third observation focuses on the server side. There has been work on transparent fail-over mechanisms of many kinds, and in fact we'll be looking at some of these mechanisms in Part III of this text. In this third approach, one asks if the server can't somehow conceal failure from the client. To the extent that servers save all their state on disk, for example in log files or a database, one can design systems using shared disks that are very unlikely to fail (a dual-ported RAID disk has this characteristic). Now, while a server might fail, some other server can potentially pick up right where the failed one left off. To a degree, this way of thinking tracks a CORBA standard called the "fault tolerant objects" architecture. However, the CORBA FTOL architecture was never widely adopted and there are criticisms that while the idea is good, the details of the CORBA standard lead to inefficient solutions and also restrict the technique so that many servers simply can't make use of it.

We are left with the transactional mechanisms, the asynchronous queuing mechanisms assumed by WS_RELIABILITY, or perhaps some hypothetical marriage of the two. In this approach, clients concerned with reliability structure their applications as transactions against transactional servers. In the event of a failure, the transaction would normally abort. A failure that occurs right in the middle of a commit, of course, is more of a problem, but in this case the client can check with the transactional service and learn the outcome once communication is reestablished. Such a solution won't provide high availability and might even be fairly slow, but does offer a story to the average developer. For the time being, this is the only real form of reliability available in the Web Services architecture.

10.8 The Future of Web Services

Web Services are still in their infancy, and have a tremendous future before them. Indeed, some analysts have suggested that within a decade, trillions of dollars in transactions will occur on Web Services platforms. If these predictions are even in the right ballpark, Web Services will be big business for technology suppliers too, since some of that money will end up being spent on infrastructure.

Yet even while we acknowledge the awesome potential of the technology, we should also consider the many problems it may cause if the community that needs highly assured solutions is unable to develop them on the available platforms. It isn't hard to imagine a future of insecure hospitals leaking sensitive medical data, of power grid hackers who can trigger large-scale blackouts with ease, air traffic control systems that hang inexplicably after seemingly minor failures, or any of a host of other problems. For Web Services to represent the tremendously positive step they *could* be, we'll need ways to build high assurance solutions with the security, availability, quality of service and other properties needed to know that they will be operational and correct when and where needed. This desirable state is far from the current situation and it isn't at all clear how to get from here to there, particularly since some of the core problems are consequences of the Internet architecture.

I personally am hoping that the problems we're identifying will be just as evident to customers as they are to us in the context of this textbook. After all, the CIO's of the world's large corporations are smart people, and one would have to assume that they will hesitate before entrusting the health of their companies to an untrustworthy technology. With any luck at all, enough CIO's will balk on using Web Services for enough purposes to scare the vendors. The vendor community is, ultimately, driven by market forces, and high assurance could easily emerge as an important marketing consideration for these platforms. If so, the need could easily trigger a cycle of innovation that would lead to real progress—indeed, one that might not stop within the Web Services platform, but extend into the underlying operating systems and even to the Internet itself. Web Services could prove to be a catalyst that brings us real progress on this important front.

10.9   Grid Computing: A Major Web Services Application

Grid Computing is an example of an emerging application for the Web Services platform. Readers will surely be aware that over the course of two decades, supercomputing has shifted from the massive computers of the past to vast clusters of less costly computers linked by high speed communication devices. The next step in this progression, for at least some applications, may be a move into the Web.

The Grid Computing community is working to develop Web Services-based standards and platforms to let computers offer computing cycles over the Web, with provisions for charging for resources, securing data, placing both intermediary results and computations on the best available machine, and letting users monitor the status of their jobs and control them remotely. Examples of major Grid Computing include Globus, which seeks to be compatible with the Web Services standards and Netsolve, a package aimed more squarely at certain classes of applications and using its own, non-standard, protocols and platforms while promising eventual Web Services compatibility.

Grid Computing has yet to establish itself as a commercially viable technology, and we will not be looking at the details of the emerging models in this book. Some have suggested that the Grid Computing concept is deeply flawed: it presumes, in effect, that users will either share computers or will treat cycles as a costly resource and communication as free. Yet in the real world, computing and storage increasingly seems to be free, while communication remains a bottleneck and a costly one, too. A typical scenario presented by the Grid Computing community involves a hospital, unable to budget the funds for a dedicated supercomputer, that instead exploits Grid Computing for its computationally intensive tasks. Yet until we can build Highly Assured Web Services, it seems doubtful that a hospital would entrust the health of critically ill patients to such a system. Moreover, there aren't really all that many applications that need tremendously powerful computing platforms and it is unclear that, even taken in the aggregate, they represent a serious market.

But even if we accept such criticisms, it is hard to overlook the success stories that early Grid Computing systems are beginning to report. SETI@Home may not yet have turned up proof of extraterrestrial intelligence, but is managing to process the data being collected even faster than radio telescopes are producing it. Computational genomics involves massive computations of a type that can sometimes be broken up into a form suitable for Grid Computing, and doing so has already turned up candidate drugs for treatment of anthrax and smallpox. It seems likely that Grid Computing will succeed, even if not for the purposes most often cited by the community developing the technology. Moreover, IBM is said to be considering offering a kind of "outsourcing" capability to computing users who would prefer not to operate their own in-house data centers. The idea is that Web Services and Grid Computing standards might be used to interface client applications to off-site servers, with IBM providing the computing platforms and its partners offering high-speed, very reliable, communications. It is easy to believe that with paying customers, IBM could make such a vision work. Notice that IBM isn't focused on supercomputing. The idea here is that mundane, normal kinds of computing might migrate to Web-based data centers administered by IBM, with that company keeping the software healthy, doing the backups, and upgrading hardware as needed. The client company no longer needs anything more than relatively "thin" front-end computers capable of issuing Web Services requests.

Grid Computing may not emerge as a true breakthrough. Yet I, for one, am hesitant to write the idea off. My guess is that Grid Computing will hit the limitations mentioned above, and perhaps many others as well, and yet that the approach will still prove to be a big success. Perhaps we won't get to the point of thinking of computing cycles as a commodity like telephone service or electricity (the metaphor often used by IBM). Nonetheless, computing on the Grid seems like an idea whose time has come, and also just the right application to really jump-start the Web Services architecture and platform development efforts.

10.10 Autonomic Computing: Technologies to Improve Web Services Configuration Management

The Web Services examples given earlier in this chapter share a common characteristic. All involve rather simple interactions between a single client and a single server, or perhaps a small number of servers. The diagrams are all "Web Server centric," with the Web Service dispatch module in the center and the backend servers relegated to nice neat boxes. But the reality of a modern corporate computing system is remote from this placid vision.

Real-world computing systems are more similar to the tangles of wiring one finds in a telephone switching office, or the spaghetti of interconnections evident when a computer chip is enlarged. That "back end server" may well consist of many systems, talking to one-another over a plethora of technologies, and including some components that date back to days of mainframes and batch processing. To suddenly expect such a ball of yarn to behave in a reliable, trustworthy manner is quite a leap. Thus, Web Services pose something of a dilemma: they suggest that this snarl of internal complexity should be presented to outside clients through a standard, simple, RPC-style interface. Any system administrator will immediately see the problem: it just won't work, and when things hang or break, it will be nearly impossible for the client system to diagnose the underlying cause—now we won't just be worried about the crash of a single system or an errant communications link, but about all the ways that a myriad of complex programs might misbehave when suddenly used in ways that they have never been used before.

This situation has many consequences. Administrators are finding that the cost of ownership for new technologies like Web Services are prohibitively high, because they are forced to hire specialists just to monitor the systems. Developers find these technologies harder to work with, because there are many ways that an application might seem to fail— for example by hanging, or terminating unsuccessfully with a vague error message—that might reflect poorly on their work, and yet are very hard to work around or solve in any kind of automated manner. And end-users are likely to find Web Services unreliable.

IBM is promoting a new initiative that, the company hopes, could overcome these kinds of problems. The idea of the Autonomic Computing effort is to develop a new generation of technical solutions that might help systems in automating more and more aspects of management that currently require human intervention. An Autonomic system would (one hopes), automatically set itself up, monitor status and detect conditions that require new parameter settings or other kinds of reconfiguration, and in general adapt behavior to match the detected runtime situation.

The IBM vision relates Autonomic Computing to two everyday behaviors. The one for which the technology is named is the body's autonomic control systems—the internal regulatory mechanisms that tell the heart how fast to beat, make you sweat when you get too warm, and so forth. On the more practical side, Autonomic Computing specialists point to RAID file servers, where a failed unit is detectable by a red light on a rack of disks, and can be repaired by simply pulling the faulty disk out and plugging in a healthy one. Obviously, RAID isn't fool-proof, and stories abound about maintenance people who pulled the wrong disk or otherwise caused the technology to fail. Yet RAID is certainly an appealing model.

Nonetheless, RAID is a very simplistic analogy to a complex Web Services platform. RAID systems are racks of hardware, while a Web Services system is a collection of interdependent software platforms, some of which may be rather old, hard to track down, and poorly instrumented. IBM's leaders for the area are pointing to new ways of using monitoring and system management technologies as a response to such needs, and there is no doubt that these kinds of options have a significant appeal. Nonetheless, until applications have routine access to the kinds of platform-level mechanisms needed to actually recover after a disruptive failure or some other event occurs, and to react in a consistent, coordinated way, when problems are detected, it is very hard to see a path that could accomplish the broad goals of this vision. In the remainder of this book we'll see some of the needed components, but no single company is really in a position to carry out such an ambitious change to the way that computing is done, hence it seems unlikely that we'll soon be able to wave an Autonomic wand at our most challenging High Assurance problems and see them magically evaporate!

10.11 Related Readings

Web Services are a new area, and quite an important commercial one. Although at the time of this writing, few books had been published on the topic, one can confidently predict that the shelves will be filled with treatments of the basic technologies in short order.

At this time, the most comprehensive sources of information include the web site of the World Wide Web consortium (http://www.w3.org), and the sites maintained by major vendors including IBM, Microsoft, and BEA. Autonomic Computing and Grid Computing have been championed by IBM, and that company maintains extensive Web information repositories on both topics.

11

Related Internet Technologies

The Web is just the latest of a series of Internet technologies that have gained extremely wide acceptance. In this chapter we briefly touch on some of the other important members of this technology family, including both old technologies such as mail and file transfer and new ones such as high-speed message bus architectures and security firewalls.

11.1 File Transfer Tools

The earliest networking technologies were those supporting file transfer in distributed settings. These typically consisted of programs for sending and receiving files, commands for initiating transfers and managing file transfer queues during periods when transfers backed up, utilities for administering the storage areas within which files are placed while a transfer is pending, and policies for assigning appropriate ownership and access rights to transferred files.

The most common file transfer mechanism in modern computer systems is that associated with the File Transfer Protocol (FTP), which defines a set of standard message formats and request types for navigating in a file system, searching directories, and moving files. FTP includes a security mechanism based on password authentication; however, these passwords are transmitted in an insecure way over the network, exposing them to potential attack by intruders. Many modern systems employ nonreusable passwords for this reason.

Other well-known file transfer protocols include the UNIX-to-UNIX copy program (UUCP) and the file transfer protocol standardized by the OSI protocol suite. Neither protocol is widely used, however, and FTP is a de facto standard within the Internet. However, file transfer over the Web conceals the FTP protocol under a layer of browser technology, so the user doesn't see the login mechanism unless anonymous login fails, and won't normally have access to the various FTP commands for controlling the transfer type (binary or text) and checking on status. This is probably a good thing; the functionality of FTP has been outmoded by twenty years of progress and few users would want to access the command layer of the application.

11.2 Electronic Mail

Electronic mail was the first of the Internet applications to gain wide popularity, and remains a dominant technology at the time of this writing. Mail systems have become steadily easier to use and more sophisticated over time, and e-mail users are supported by increasingly sophisticated mail-reading and composition tools. Indeed, in a somewhat bizarre twist, e-mail has even been used as a means of computer-to-computer communication, with the user's mailbox serving as a form of message queuing middleware! Doing this can potentially allow an application to create an IP tunnel that works around firewall and NAT restrictions, although obviously at a high cost. E-mail has also become so integrated with the web that it is now possible to e-mail interactive Web pages and other forms of dynamic content to cooperative users.

Underlying the e-mail system is a small collection of very simple protocols, of which the Simple Mail Transfer Protocol, or SMTP, is the most widely used and the most standard. The architecture of a typical mailing system is as follows. The user composes a mail message, which is encoded into ASCII (perhaps using a MIME representation) and then stored in a queue of outgoing e-mail messages. Periodically, this queue is scanned by a mail daemon program, which uses SMTP to actually transmit the message to its destinations. For each destination, the mail daemon establishes a TCP connection, delivers a series of e-mail messages, and receives acknowledgments of successful reception after the received mail is stored on the remote incoming mail queue. To determine the location of the daemon that will receive a particular piece of mail, the DNS for the destination host is queried. (See Figure 11.1.)

Users who depend upon network mail systems will be aware that the protocol is robust but not absolutely reliable. E-mail may be lost after it has been successfully acknowledged— for example, if the remote machine crashes just after receiving an e-mail. E-mail may be delivered incorrectly—for example, if the file system of a mail recipient is not accessible at the time the mail arrives and hence forwarding or routing instructions are not correctly applied. Virus and spam filters may modify or delete an e-mail. Further, there is the risk that e-mail will be inappropriately deleted if a crash occurs as the user starts to retrieve it from a mailbox. Thus, although the technology of e-mail is fairly robust, experienced users learn not to rely upon it in a critical way. To a limited degree, the return receipt mechanisms of modern mailers can overcome these difficulties, but heterogeneity prevents these from representing a completely satisfactory solution. Similarly, use of the more sophisticated e-mail mechanisms, such as HTML e-mail and e-mail with attached files, remains limited by incompatibilities between the mail reception processes that must interpret the incoming data.

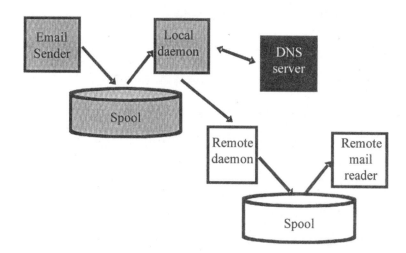

Figure 11.1. Steps in sending an e-mail. The user composes the e-mail and it is stored in a local spool for transmission by the local mail daemon. The daemon contacts the DNS to find the remote SMTP daemon's address for the destination machine, then transfers the mail file and, when an acknowledgment is received, deletes it locally. On the remote system, incoming mail is delivered to user mailboxes. The protocol is relatively reliable but can still lose mail if a machine crashes while transferring messages into or out of a spool or under other unusual conditions such as when there are problems forwarding an e-mail.

11.3 Network Bulletin Boards (Newsgroups)

Network bulletin boards evolved in parallel with the e-mail system and hence share many of the same properties. Bulletin boards differ primarily in the way that messages are viewed and the way that they are distributed.

As most readers are aware, a bulletin board is typically presented to the user as a set of articles, which may be related to one another in what are called "conversations" or "threads." These are represented by special fields in the message headers that identify each message uniquely and permit one message to refer to another. Messages are typically stored in some form of directory structure and the programs used to view them operate by displaying the contents of the directory and maintaining a simple database in which the messages each user has read are tracked.

The news distribution protocol, implemented by the NNTP daemon, is simple but highly effective. (See Figure 11.2.) It is based on a concept of flooding and uses a protocol sometimes referred to as "gossip." Each news message is posted to a news group. Associated with each newsgroup is a graph representing the connections between machines that wish to accept copies of postings to the group. To post a message, the user creates it and enqueues it in an outgoing news area, where the news daemon will eventually find it. The daemon for a given machine will periodically establish contact with some set of machines adjacent to it in the news distribution graph, exchanging messages that give the current set of available

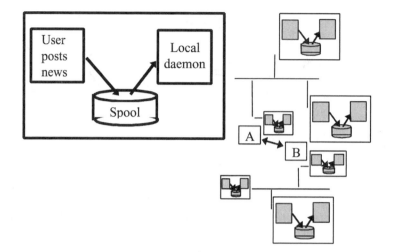

Figure 11.2. The network news protocol, NNTP, floods the network by gossip between machines that have news articles and machines that have yet to receive them. In this example, a message posted by a user reaches a forwarding node, *A*, which gossips with *B* by exchanging messages indicating the news-groups for which each has recently received new postings. If *B* has not yet received the posting *A* just received, and is interested in the newsgroup, it will pull a copy from *A*. Failures of the network or of intermediate forwarding nodes can prevent articles from reaching their destinations quickly, in which case they will expire and may never reach some destinations. Thus, the protocol is quite reliable but not always reliable.

postings and their subjects. If a daemon connects to an adjacent daemon that has not yet received a copy of some posting, it forwards it over the link, and vice versa. This is the gossip aspect: daemon A sends a message to daemon B asking if B has received postings 125–131 for group cornell.class.cs514, and B sends a message to A requesting any postings it lacks, while also offering news from its own repository. However, the gossip is rather structured: news servers talk only to servers listed in a control file that would normally be configured by a human administrator, and the gossip mechanism runs primarily along the links of a forwarding tree rooted at one of a small number of news distribution sites. Notice that the same protocol could be used on an arbitrary graph—we'll see how this turns out to be important in Part III of the book.

The basic news protocol is fairly reliable, but not absolutely so. Similar to the case of e-mail, an ill-timed crash can cause a machine to lose a copy of a recently received news posting after it has been confirmed, in which case there may be a gap in the news sequence for the corresponding group unless some other source happens to offer a copy of the same message on a different connection. Messages that are posted concurrently may be seen in different orders by different readers, and if a posting does not explicitly list *all* of the prior postings on which it is dependent, this can be visible to readers, because their display programs will not recognize that one message predates another. The display algorithms can also be fooled into displaying messages out of order by clock synchronization errors, which can erroneously indicate that one message is earlier than another.

The news protocol is known to suffer from a variety of security problems. It is trivial to forge a message by simply constructing what appears to be a legitimate news message and placing it in the reception area used by the news daemons. Such messages will be forwarded even if they misrepresent the name of the sender, the originating machine, or other information. Indeed, scripts for *spamming* newsgroups have become popular: These permit an individual to post a single message to a great number of newsgroups. To a very limited degree, the news distribution protocol has improved with time to resist such attacks, but for a user with even a small degree of sophistication, the technology is open to abuse.

Thus, while news systems are generally reliable, it would be inappropriate to use them in critical settings. In any use for which the authenticity of messages is important, the context in which they were sent is significant, or the guarantee that postings will definitely reach their destinations is required, the technology is only able to provide partial solutions.

11.4 Instant Messaging Systems

During the late 1990's and early 2000's *instant messaging* achieved explosive popularity, growing from a common but little-noticed technology available on most local-area network systems into what may be the most widely used networking application of them all. The basic capabilities of these systems should be familiar to most readers.

Instant messaging systems are typically implemented as client/server infrastructures. Each user's IM client logs into a server picked by the vendor to map "friends" to the same server if possible. This establishes a connection from the user to the server. Messages sent by the user are transmitted to the server, which echoes them back on the connections of other users who should see copies. If desired, the IM server may provide a logging capability, so that users joining a group can catch up with the recent dialog. Much like an email system, IM systems generally support a rich message encoding (XML is becoming standard) and can accept attachments, Web content, etc. With the exception of the last hop, to the end-user, extremely high data rates are possible, vastly exceeding the data rates associated with human input. One can therefore predict that these technologies will see vigorous evolution in coming years as broadband connectivity becomes prevalent. Indeed, Apple Computer has begun to bet heavily on a "rich" IM technology called "Rendezvous," seeing this as a springboard for a new generation of remote collaboration technologies aimed not just at teenagers staying in touch with their friends, but also at a new generation of mobile office workers for whom collaboration and joint work may cease to require collocation.

The most difficult challenge facing the developers of IM servers relate to latency and data replication. The latency issue may fade in importance as Internet backbone latencies drop, but at present still forces the largest vendors to operate data centers at multiple geographic locations and to map users to the center having the lowest latency with respect to their Internet access point. The problem of replication arises because it is not always possible to ensure that every group of "friends" can be bound to a single server. Lacking such a guarantee, one ends up with a tree-like architecture in which a group of friends will often map to two or more servers. To link the resulting groups, the servers then log into one-another. The author is not aware of any more elaborate IM server architectures or any major effort to provide strong reliability and security guarantees for IM applications. Presumably, however, if IM technology penetrates into business settings in a major way, such issues will grow in importance.

11.5 Message-Oriented Middleware Systems (MOMS)

Most major distributed systems vendors offer products in what has become known as the message oriented middleware, or MOMS, market. Typical of these products are HP's (originally Digital Equipment Corporation's) MessageQ product line, IBM's MQSeries products, and the so-called "asynchronous message agent technology" available in some object-oriented computing systems—for example, CORBA Event Notification Services are likely to be positioned as MOMS products. IBM is the overall market leader within this sector. In a somewhat curious "footnote," more and more applications are using e-mail as a form of message queuing intermediary, presumably because e-mail is ubiquitously available and provides the basic middleware functionality needed by many applications. We won't look closely at this case here, but if the use of e-mail as a message queuing mechanism continues to grow, future versions of this textbook may need to devote more attention to the technology.

Broadly, these products fall into two categories. One very important area is concerned with providing network access to mainframe systems and other forms of batching or delayed message delivery when a client may want to send a message to a server that is busy or not currently running. IBM's MQSeries product is focused on this problem, as are perhaps a dozen comparable products from a variety of vendors, although MQSeries can also be useful in other settings. Technologies of this sort typically present a "remote service" interface abstraction, which permits the distributed systems application developer to use a client/server architecture to develop their applications; today, we are seeing a major effort to extend this functionality to deal with Web Services through the basic Web Services API. These architectures are frequently asynchronous in the sense that the sending of a request to the remote server is decoupled from the handling of its reply—much as if one were sending mail to the server, which will later send mail back containing the results of some inquiry. This is very convenient in older systems, which tended to run in a batched manner and are hence poorly adapted to the remote procedure call model.

The message queuing system lives between the clients and the server, accepting the outgoing messages, transmitting them to the server using the protocols appropriate for the mainframe operating system, arranging for the requests to be executed in a reliable manner (in some cases, even launching the associated application, if it is not already running), and then repeating the sequence in the opposite direction when the reply is sent back. Their early success in dealing with mainframe connectivity made them widely popular and widely available, but today many systems use them as front ends to conventional servers running on network nodes or workstations, and the Web Services trends may make these technologies even more important in years to come.

The second broad category of products uses a similar architecture but is intended more as a high-level message-passing abstraction for direct use in networked applications. In these products, of which HP's MessageQ is perhaps typical, the abstraction presented to the user is of named mailboxes to which messages can be sent by applications on the network, much as user's send e-mail to one another. Unlike e-mail, the messages in question contain binary data, but the idea is very similar. Later, authorized applications dequeue the incoming messages for processing, sending back replies if desired or simply consuming them silently. As one might expect, these products contain extensive support for such options as priority levels (so that urgent messages can skip ahead of less-critical ones), flow control (so that message queues won't grow without limit if the consumer process or processes are slow), security, queue management, load-balancing (when several processes consume from the same queues), data persistence, and fault-tolerance (for long-running applications).

If the model of this second category of message-queuing products is that of an e-mail system used at a program-to-program level, the performance is perhaps closer to that of a special-purpose file system. Indeed, many of these systems work very much as a file system would work: Adding a message to a queue is done by appending the message to a file representing the queue, and dequeuing a message is done by reading from the front of the file and freeing the corresponding disk space for reuse.

The growing popularity of message-oriented middleware products is typically due to their relative ease of use when compared to datagram style message communication. Applications that communicate using RPC or datagrams need to have the producer and consumer processes running at the same time, and they must engage in a potentially complex binding protocol whereby the consumer or server process registers itself and the producer or client process locates the server and establishes a connection to it. Communication is, however, very rapid once this connection establishment phase has been completed. In contrast, a message-oriented middleware system does not require that the producer and consumer both be running at the same time, or even that they be knowledgeable of one another: A producer may not be able to predict the process that will dequeue and execute its request, and a consumer process may be developed long before it is known what the various producers of messages it consumes will be. For settings like Web Services, where the best performance may require a pipelined style of asynchronous invocations and asynchronous replies, the match between the model and the application is quite good. The downside of the model is that these products can be very slow in comparison to direct point-to-point communication over the network (perhaps by a factor of hundreds!) and that they can be hard to manage, because of the risk that a queue will leak messages and grow very large or that other subtle scheduling effects will cause the system to become overloaded and to thrash.

There is a good on-line source of additional information on middleware products, developed by the Message-Oriented Middleware Association, (MOMA), a group that now operates under the oversight of the International Middleware Association (imwa.org). Information on specific products should be obtained from their vendors.

11.6 Publish-Subscribe and Message Bus Architectures

Starting with the V operating system in 1985 (see Cheriton and Zwaenepoel) and the Isis news application in 1987 (see Birman and Joseph [November 1987]), a number of distributed systems have offered a bulletin board style of communication directly to application programs; MIT's Zephyr system followed soon after (see DellaFera et al.). In this technology, which is variously called message bus communication, message queues, subject-based addressing, or process group addressing, processes register interest in message subjects by *subscribing* to them. The same or other processes can then send out messages by *publishing* them under one or more subjects. The message bus system is responsible for matching publisher to subscriber in a way that is efficient and transparent to both: The publisher is typically unaware of the current set of subscribers (unless it wishes to know) and the subscriber is typically not aware of the current set of publishers (again, unless it has some reason to ask for this information). (See Figure 11.3.)

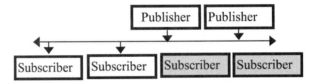

Figure 11.3. Message-bus architectures (also known as publish/subscribe systems) originated as an application of process groups in the V system, and a fault-tolerant version was included in early versions of the Isis Toolkit. These technologies subsequently became commercially popular, particularly in financial and factory-floor settings. A benefit of the architecture is that the subscriber doesn't need to know who will publish on a given subject, or vice-versa. As shown, messages on the "white" subject will reach the "white" but not the "gray" subscribers—a set that can change dynamically and that may grow to include applications not planned at the time the publishers were developed. A single process can publish upon or subscribe to multiple subjects. This introduces desirable flexibility in a technology that can also achieve extremely high performance by using hardware multicast or broadcast, as well as fault tolerance or consistency guarantees if the technology base is implemented with reliability as a goal. An object-oriented encapsulation of message bus technology is provided as part of CORBA, through its Event Notification Service (ENS). In this example the application is divided into publishers and subscribers, but in practice a single process can play both roles, and can subscribe to many subjects. Wide area extensions normally mimic the gossip scheme used in support of network bulletin boards. Within J2EE, the JMS subsystem offers functionality very similar to the CORBA ENS.

Message bus architectures are in most respects very similar to network bulletin boards. An application can subscribe to many subjects, just as a user of a bulletin board system can monitor many bulletin board topics. Both systems typically support some form of hierarchical name space for subjects, and both typically allow one message to be sent to multiple subjects. The only significant difference is that message bus protocols tend to be optimized for high speed, using broadcast hardware if possible, and they typically deliver messages as soon as they reach their destination, through some form of *upcall* to the application process. In contrast, a bulletin board system usually requires a polling interface, in which the reader checks for new news and is not directly notified at the instant a message arrives.

The usual example of a setting in which a message bus system might be used is that of a financial trading application or stock exchange. In such systems, the subjects to which the messages are sent are typically the names of the financial instruments being traded: /equities/ibm, or /bonds/at&t. Depending on the nature of the message bus, reliability guarantees may be nonexistent, weak, or very strong. The V system's process group technology illustrates the first approach: an application subscribed by joining a process group and published by sending to it, with the group name corresponding to the subject. V multicasts to process groups lacked any sort of strong reliability guarantees—hence, such an approach usually will deliver messages but not always. V transmitted these messages using hardware multicast features of the underlying transport technology, or point-to-point transport if hardware was not available.

The TIBCO Information Bus (TIB) (see Okie et al.) and Isis Message Distribution System (MDS) (see Glade) are good examples of modern technologies that support the V system with stronger reliability properties. TIB (a product of TIBCO) is extremely popular in support of trading floors and has had some success in factory automation environments. Isis was a competitor with TIB in the early 1990's and is still used in settings where reliability is an especially important attribute: the New York and Swiss Stock Exchange systems, the French Air Traffic Control System, the US Navy AEGIS warship, and some other "mission-critical" computing settings. However, Isis is no longer available as a product.

TIBCO's TIB architecture is relatively simple, but is still sufficient to provide high performance, scalability, and a considerable degree of fault tolerance when publishers fail. In this system, messages are typically transmitted by the publisher using hardware broadcast with an overlaid retransmission mechanism, which ensures that messages will be delivered reliably and in the order they were published provided that the publisher doesn't fail. Point-to-point communication is used if a subject has only a small number of subscribers. Much as for a stream protocol, overload or transient communication problems can cause exceptional conditions in which messages could be lost. However, such conditions are uncommon in the settings where TIB is normally used.

The TIB system provides a fail-over capability if there are two or more equivalent publishers for a given class of subjects. In such a configuration, subscribers are initially connected to a primary publisher; the backup goes through the motions of publishing data, but TIB in fact inhibits the transmission of any data. However, if the primary publisher fails, the TIB system will eventually detect this. Having done so, the system will automatically reconfigure so that the subscriber will start to receive messages from the other source. In this manner, TIB is able to guarantee that messages will normally be delivered in the order they are sent, and will normally not have gaps or out-of-sequence delivery. These properties can, however, be violated if the network becomes severely overloaded, a failure occurs on the publisher site, or the subscriber becomes temporarily partitioned away from the network.

In these cases a gap in the sequence of delivered messages can occur during the period of time required for the fail-over to the operational server.

The Isis Message Distribution System (MDS) is an example of a message bus that provides very strong reliability properties. This system is implemented using a technology based on reliable process groups (discussed in Chapters 14 through 20), in which agreement protocols are used to ensure that messages will be delivered to all processes that are subscribing to a subject, or to none. The approach also permits the active replication of publishers, so that a backup can provide precisely the same sequence of messages as the primary. By carefully coordinating the handling of failures, MDS is able to ensure that even if a failure does occur, the sequence of messages will not be disrupted: All subscribers that remain connected to the system will see the same messages, in the same order, even if a publisher fails, and this order will not omit any messages if the backup is publishing the same data as the primary.

MDS is implemented over hardware multicast but uses this feature only for groups with large fanout; point-to-point communication is employed for data transport when the number of subscribers to a subject is small or when the subscribers are not on the same branch of a local area network. The resulting architecture achieves performance comparable to that of TIB in normal cases, but under overload, when TIB can potentially lose messages, Isis MDS will typically choke back the publishers and, if the load becomes extreme, may actually drop slow receivers from the system as a way to catch up. These different design choices are both considered to represent reliable behavior by the vendors of the two products; clearly, the real issue for any given application will be the degree of match between the reliability model and the needs of the applications that consume the data. Were it still available as a product (and it is not), MDS would be preferable in a system where ordering and guaranteed delivery are very important to the end user; TIB might be favored in a setting where continued flow of information is ultimately valued more than the ordering and reliability properties of the system.

The reader may recall that the CORBA Event Notification Service (ENS) uses a message bus architecture. TIB is in fact notable for supporting an object-oriented interface similar to the one required for implementations of this service, and the TIBCO company has emerged as a market leader in offering this type of functionality within a range of event-oriented systems architectures.

Both systems also provide a form of message spooling and playback facility. In TIB, this takes the form of a subscriber that spools all messages on specified subjects to disk, replaying them later upon request. MDS also includes a spooling technology, which can store messages for future replay to a process. The MDS implementation of this playback technology preserves the ordering and reliability attributes of the basic publication mechanism, and is carefully synchronized with the delivery of new messages so that a subscriber can obtain a seamless playback of spooled messages followed by the immediate delivery of new messages—in a correct order and without gaps or duplication.

Both the TIB and MDS architectures can be extended to large-scale environments using a protocol much like the one described in the previous section for network bulletin boards.

A new generation of hardware-assisted publish subscribe technologies are now positioned to have dramatic impact. These are typically deployed to intercept incoming message traffic to a Web Service platform or data center and then to route messages in accordance with a simple predicate over their contents (the use of XML for content encoding facilitates such tasks). Best known among these products are IBM's Gryphon router, but other examples include XML "Content" routers from companies like Sarvega, DataPower Technology Inc., Metapa Inc., Bang Networks; Flamenco Networks.; Grand Central Communications; Kenamea; KnowNow, Slam Dunk Networks and Swingtide. Vendors with products focused on security include Forum Systems and Hitachi Computer Products (America).

Among these, only IBM Gryphon router is also intended to support a true publish-subscribe interface; Gryphon can be employed as the basis of a sophisticated internal LAN, in which applications cooperate by publishing information into the router network and subscribing to topics of interest. Gryphon is closely integrated with IBM's MQ Series message queuing middleware product, and hence can benefit from a management framework and tools for application development, debugging, and runtime monitoring.

11.7 Internet Firewalls and Network Address Translators

Internet Firewalls have recently emerged to play a nearly ubiquitous role in Internet settings. We discuss firewalls in more detail in Chapter 22, and consequently limit ourselves to some very brief comments here. This section also touches on a related technology first mentioned in Chapter 2, namely Network Address Translators, or NAT boxes. Often, firewall and NAT functionality are integrated in a single product.

A firewall is a message-filtering system. It resides at the perimeter of a distributed system, where messages enter and leave it from the broader Internet. The specific architecture used may be that of a true packet filter, or one that permits application-level code to examine the incoming and outgoing packets (so-called application-level proxy technology). Although firewalls are not normally considered to be distributed programs, if a network has multiple access points, the firewall will be instantiated separately at each. Considered as a set, the collection of firewall programs will then be a distributed system, although the distributed aspect may be implicit.

Firewall programs typically operate by examining each message on the basis of source, destination, and authentication information (if enabled). Messages are permitted to pass through only if they satisfy some criteria controlled by the system administrator, or, in the case of an application-level proxy technology, if the application programs that compose the firewall consider the message to be acceptable. In this manner, a network can be made porous for network bulletin board and e-mail messages, but opaque to incoming FTP and remote log-in attempts. It can also be made to accept only packets digitally signed by an acceptable user or originating machine.

A Network Address Translator or NAT is a special type of firewall focused on issues relating to addressing ranges. In the early Internet, all nodes were identified with IPv4 addresses. The address space is too small, hence a means of assigning internal IP addresses was devised by the mid 1980's. At first, the idea was that IP addresses with prefixes like 10 (e.g., 10.*.*.*) would be understood to be private to an organization. However, a problem now arose: when these nodes needed to connect to a server outside their addressing range, since these addresses are not unique, there was no way to route to them. A NAT box solves the problem by sitting between such a computer and the external network, translating internal addresses into its own address and back. Thus, 10.0.1.3 might be "externally" addressed as 128.84.61.6, assuming that this is the address of the NAT box. Port numbers can also be remapped by a NAT, in the same manner, and the mapped address will be recycled by the NAT when it believes it is no longer in use.

Today, most firewalls contain NAT functionality. This protects a site against random probing by potential intruders, since a NAT will reject packets to unmapped destinations, and also packets that make no sense to it (for example, NATs often reject UDP traffic to TCP ports and vice versa). NATs open the internal address space up: an organization can potentially exploit a huge internal address range, while limiting itself to a very small number of "public" NAT IP addresses. This, in turn, has taken most pressure off the IPv4 address space.

For typical Internet sites, the combination of firewalls and NATs provides the only real security. Although passwords are still employed within the firewall, such systems may be open to other forms of attack if an intruder manages to breach the firewall or to tunnel through the NAT. Nonetheless, these represent relatively strong barriers to intrusion. Whereas systems that lack gateways and NATs report frequent penetrations by hackers and other agents arriving over the network, firewalls and NATs considerably reduce such attacks. They do not create a completely secure environment, but they do offer an inexpensive way to repel unsophisticated attackers.

11.8 Related Reading

Most Internet technologies are documented through the so-called Request for Comments (RFC) reports, which are archived at various sites within the network, notably on a server maintained by SRI Corporation.

Recent work on XML content routing includes Aguilera et al. [1998] (an analysis of the Gryphon protocols), Carzaniga [2001] (a wide area publish-subscribe architecture) and Snoeren [2001]. To learn more about the product areas cited above, such as XML content routing or publish-subscribe, readers should consult the Web pages for the major vendors and products (IBM, TIBCO, Sarvega, etc).

12

Platform Technologies

A number of companies compete to offer comprehensive, integrated platforms with which developers can easily build distributed computing applications. Among the leaders are Microsoft with its .NET system and Sun with the J2EE Java platform. These are not the only players by even a remote stretch of the imagination: database and information management companies like Oracle, SAP, BEA and PeopleSoft all offer their own platforms. IBM and HP have extensive technology offerings that lead within their respective markets, and the list goes on and on. Nonetheless, .NET is probably the most visible platform for desktop and PC computing, while J2EE is probably the most widely known platform for use on servers of various kinds, having displaced CORBA. For this reason, and in the interest of brevity, this chapter focuses on just these two platforms, and also offers a short comparison of the two.

Cutting to the chase, one finds that systems like .NET and J2EE are in many ways quite similar. Both offer extensive functionality aimed at applications performing database access, both have very powerful Web integration solutions, and both have comprehensive support for a wide range of general purpose applications. While J2EE was developed with a focus on Java, and .NET with a focus on a new language called C# (and a second called J#, using Java syntax), neither is really "language centric" at the time of this writing. Where the two systems differ, ultimately, is in their focus. J2EE was created with the hope that Java and J2EE might push other forms of enterprise computing languages to the side, and was surprisingly effective in doing just that. This leads many J2EE developers to think in terms of pure-Java solutions to their applications. In contrast, .NET was introduced when J2EE had been in the market for a long time, and Microsoft positioned the platform to emphasize its integration and cross-language capabilities. The result of this was that, at the time .NET was first offered, many customers jumped to it out of frustration with the challenges they had experienced in integrating Java software with legacy applications. Within a year, J2EE offered an enhanced "object adaptor" technology that seems to have leveled the playing field. Yet even in the wake of this, J2EE continues to have the feel of a single-language platform, if for no other reason than that the documentation mostly predates this slight shift in emphasis. Yet .NET clearly favors a pure Microsoft environment, and while there are ways to export .NET technology for use on non-.NET platforms, those are somewhat limited and have an unnatural feel to the typical Linux developer.

Today, of course, both communities are mostly focused on Web Services and the battle for supremacy in the emerging market is anything but decided; indeed, other players such as BEA, IBM or HP may well emerge as dominant once the dust finally settles. End users and developers judge these platforms in many dimensions: ease of application development, interoperability, stability and security, total cost of ownership (meaning the cost of managing the platform once it is deployed), and so forth. The whole idea of using a single solution is in many respects dubious, because the whole purpose of these kinds of platforms is to promote interoperability between existing, rather diverse platforms and legacy applications.

Thus our focus in this chapter isn't intended as a detailed look at two best-of-breed solutions and isn't aimed at recommending one over the other. Rather, our purpose is to look at the way that two major vendors have responded to perceived market pressures by incorporating the kinds of mechanisms we've been reading about into their flagship product lines.

12.1 Microsoft's .NET Platform

12.1.1 .NET Framework

The .NET Framework is the infrastructure for the overall .NET Platform. It includes base class libraries, like ADO.NET and ASP.NET, as well as a common language runtime. The framework provides basic functionality available to all .NET applications—one can think of it as the operating system and the associated libraries rolled into a single package and integrated with a (large) variety of standard servers and services found in the Internet as a whole or exclusively in the Windows world.

Microsoft promotes use of a number of programming languages, and is increasingly inclined to view all systems as assemblies of objects, where the language implementing an object is the choice of the developer. Thus .NET promotes a new language called C# (it resembles Java but with some syntactic differences, mostly very minor, and many differences to the runtime package), but also supports a tremendous range of other languages, including J# (a Microsoft variant of Java with identical syntax but using the C# libraries), Visual Basic (a surprisingly object-oriented version of the Basic language), C++, C, Cobol, SmallTalk, Pascal, ML, etc. Personally, I'm waiting for the revival of Snobol, but in the mean time, I've started to work in C#. Several of these languages are extremely well supported through Microsoft's premier application development environment, Visual Studio.

As mentioned earlier, the most important target communities for .NET tend to need extremely clean access to database systems and are focused on producing Web Services or Web interfaces to their applications. ADO.NET provides database access to the .NET programmer, through a very simple, clean, virtual database environment that can be linked to the "real" database of one's choice. ASP.NET provides an easy way to turn a .NET application into a Web Services system or a Web Server for more traditional document management. ASP.NET also makes it easy to issue requests to a remote Web Service system from within a .NET application.

The CLR, or Common Language Runtime, provides an execution environment for .NET applications, irrespective of their programming language (this means, for example, that within .NET one can issue function calls directly from C# to Visual Basic and from there into COBOL, a feature that facilitates interoperation between new applications and legacy systems). The CLR provides a just-in-time compilation capability (the idea being that languages compile into an intermediate programming language that looks like machine code but is in fact platform-independent, and then this language is in turn compiled into real machine code at the last moment), memory management and garbage collection (I've never been fond of garbage collection because of the unpredictable costs, but such a capability certainly reduces bugs). The CLR also understands assemblies and can actually track down and launch multiple side-by-side versions of libraries when, as is common, one wants to run two applications and they are based on different versions of an important system library. Traditionally, loading the newer application would upgrade the library and risk causing problems for the older one. With the Microsoft approach, one does run into issues if the application itself has some sort of database and can't support multiple versions of its code side-by-side, but the risk that an upgrade will disrupt older applications is at least minimized.

Perhaps the greatest strength of the .NET platform is its Visual Studio development environment, which is also integrated with tutorials and a tremendous amount of online help for the full range of supported languages and technologies, including cut-and-paste examples. While this doesn't make application development trivial, it can smooth a new user past the rough spots and tremendously improves productivity. Moreover, Visual Studio has powerful integrated debugging and runtime analysis tools. Despite the absence of performance analysis mechanisms and technologies for promoting high assurance, the Visual Studio .NET packaging steers developers towards solutions likely to have good robustness properties and that are likely to be natural fits (hence well supported) with other elements of the .NET platform. Of course, this easy integration doesn't extend to non-Windows platforms and "standard" Java, which Microsoft supports but isn't promoting. Yet the fact remains that Visual Studio .NET is an extremely attractive entrée into the Microsoft product vision and an example to other companies showing how very complex new technologies can be introduced relatively painlessly to a very large audience.

12.1.2 XML Web Services

As we've seen, an XML Web service is a unit of application logic providing data and services to other applications. Applications access XML Web Services via ubiquitous Web protocols and data formats such as HTTP, XML, and SOAP. In .NET, one can build new Web Services trivially by telling the platform that a new system will use the ASP.NET (Application Service Provider) template. An application can either be a pure Web Services system or, more commonly, can combine Web Services interfaces with use of Microsoft's primitive COM and DCOM functionality for better performance.

12.1.3 Language Enhancements

.NET is notable for its clean integration of development tools with new languages and new distributed computing features. As noted earlier, Visual Studio .NET includes high quality development and debugging support for Visual Basic, Visual C#, and Visual C + +, as well as a new programming language, Visual J#. Developers can easily mix and match.

12.1.4 Tools for Developing for Devices

Although distributed computing remains centered on traditional wired infrastructures with client systems on desktops and servers in the data center, we're seeing more and more interest and use of smaller mobile devices and a new wave of tiny sensors is just around the corner. Microsoft has long been fascinated with such devices, and offers a stripped-down version of its Windows operating system for them.

Visual Studio .NET provides integrated support for the .NET Compact Framework, enabling developers to use Visual Studio .NET to program Pocket PCs and Windows CE .NET Powered devices using Visual Basic .NET or Visual C# .NET. Visual Studio .NET also includes integrated ASP.NET mobile controls that work with more than 150 Internet-enabled mobile devices. The idea, then, is that one can fairly easily construct applications that move some functions to mobile devices. The easiest style of application to build mimics the check-in that occurs when you return a rental car: the mobile device is out in the parking lot running a small, dedicated check-in application—perhaps it reads a bar code or the user types in a name—then issues RPC requests to servers back on the corporate data center to pull up details of the rental contract, upload data (actual miles driven, gas tank level), and finally download and print a final copy of the rental contract.

Completely new styles of mobile computing pose greater challenges. Students using this textbook will surely be eager to play with ad-hoc routing protocols and to build peer-to-peer applications that run directly between mobile devices over wireless communication channels. Such applications depart from the basic model that .NET seeks to support, hence require greater effort by the developer. Nonetheless, the tools are available to build such systems, and students looking for an exciting (but challenging) project should certainly consider attempting something along these lines.

12.1.5 Integrated Development Environment

Microsoft is particularly proud of the combination of all of these technologies in a single package. By offering an integrated development environment (IDE), developers who become proficient in the Microsoft tools and technology platform can build solutions faster by drawing on any of the tools, wizards, designers, and editors accessible from any Visual Studio .NET language. However, this integration also makes the environment a remarkably large and rather complex one, almost deceptively simple for the new developer who sets out to build a simple Windows "Form" (an application using a Windows GUI) to display data fetched from a Web Service, and yet with enormous complexity lurking just behind the surface.

This enormous complexity stands as a barrier to building the kinds of highly assured applications readers of this textbook are presumably aiming for. The application that seeks to make aggressive use of Windows XP features within .NET will discover literally dozens of available servers reporting on contents of the file system, database, providing easy access to spreadsheets and the user's e-mail repository and contacts information, and the list goes on and on. While Microsoft's solutions are notable for their self-configuration capabilities, there are so many runtime parameters in these complex environments and so many ways that a necessary service could fail (and not relaunch itself) that the resulting environment is inevitably fragile precisely because of its high degree of integration.

Here we see the basic dilemma faced by Microsoft and shared by their user community. Integration is a good thing for those seeking to develop new applications. But interdependency also can introduce fragility and hence render those applications fragile and hard to maintain. Microsoft's platform, like all the others, lacks the kinds of Autonomic Computing capabilities IBM has been calling for—but has yet to actually develop. Lacking these, we arrive at delicate, interconnected, interdependent applications with marvelous functionality and yet prone to failure and potential security exposures. Lacking integration support, on the other hand, applications may have to "do it all" themselves and are often vastly more difficult to build, debug and deploy. Are we better off in a world where we simply can't build the systems we need, or in a world where it is easy to build them but hard to keep them running? Microsoft is betting heavily that it can encourage integration and, down the road, deliver technology to keep things robust as well. But the jury won't be in on that bet for many years.

12.2   Java Enterprise Edition

The Java 2 Platform, Enterprise Edition, combines the Java language into an environment with a component based model intended to simplify enterprise development and deployment. The J2EE platform manages the infrastructure of a complex distributed application, and also supports Web Services to enable development of secure, robust and interoperable business applications. Just as Microsoft's .NET technology is at the core of its Web Services strategy, J2EE embodies Sun's platform strategy.

12.2.1   J2EE Framework

The Java 2 Platform, Enterprise Edition (J2EE) plays a role analogous to the .NET framework. J2EE is the Java standard for developing multi-tier enterprise applications. The most current release of the platform introduces support for the Web Services protocols stack, including XML data encoding and decoding, SOAP RPC formats and the ability to import object interfaces through WSDL documents. J2EE also includes a powerful collection of object Management and Deployment APIs, support for JavaServer Pages, Enterprise JavaBeans, and Connector APIs, and provides easy access to databases. All of this has established J2EE as one of the premier Web Services and enterprise application intergration platforms.

The J2EE framework differs in some ways from .NET, and these differences point to a difference in early design philosophy. When Java was first introduced, Sun promoted the language for its interoperability (meaning that a Java program should be able to run on any platform supporting the runtime environment and framework) and security (a Java program should not be capable of accessing the platform outside of the capabilities defined by the platform, and within the restrictions imposed by user-defined security policies). In contrast, .NET and Microsoft's C# effort have far less of a focus on security and portability. In these two respects, Microsoft relies on Windows. C# (like Java) is a type safe language, but because of the .NET focus on interoperability, falls back onto the basic Windows architecture for security purposes. As for portability, while there is a .NET portability library, Microsoft is far less interested than Sun in this property. Whereas Sun sells enterprise servers for use from a diversity of client systems, many running on PC environments, and hence views portability as central to its philosophy, Microsoft promotes its technology throughout the entire enterprise and portability is far less of a central requirement.

Thus, one reads a great deal about security policy in the J2EE tutorial and in the Java programming language specification itself. Security decisions dictated many of the J2EE architectural design features and continue to pervade the architecture as a whole. Moreover, this philosophy has been broadly successful; there are relatively few security problems with pure Java applications, and indeed the largest security holes in a Java-based system is often found to reside in the operating system on which the Java platform runs and the servers that the applications talk to. Based on early reports of .NET security problems, it seems likely that the Microsoft platform is more exposed to attack and less security-conscious, on the whole, than is J2EE. This would seem to be the price of interoperability.

12.2.2 Java Application Verification Kit (AVK)

Sun continues to promote a "pure Java" mindset, and also places a premium on the use of its open Java environment standards. Microsoft's J# represents a sharp challenge to this mindset, permitting the Java programmer to gain very fine-grained control over Windows platforms at the expense of this type of interoperability and portability. Accordingly, J2EE includes a verification kit to assist the developer in avoiding proprietary and hence non-portable environment features. Recent versions of the Java AVK also include portability tests for Web Services applications.

12.2.3 Enterprise JavaBeans Specification

The Enterprise JavaBeans (EJB) architecture plays a role analogous to the ADO.NET component of .NET. EJB is aimed at standardizing the development of application components that access databases and other transactional services in business settings. The EJB server-side model simplifies the development of middleware applications by providing integrated support for services such as transactions, security, and database connectivity. Starting with release 2.1, EJB also supports Web Services.

12.2.4 J2EE Connectors

As noted in the introduction, the core of Microsoft's marketing campaign for .NET was centered around the interoperability features of the platform, and this resonated with a user community that has been struggling for decades to integrate new functionality into existing systems and legacy applications. J2EE "Connectors" (based on CORBA object "adaptors") are the J2EE response to this problem. Through connectors, a pure Java application can form a gateway to a legacy system running a non-Java technology. For many years J2EE connectors were deemphasized by the J2EE community because the whole idea of connection is anathema to the "pure Java" goals of many developers. Reality, though, has a way of intruding and displacing even the most laudable goals and J2EE connectors are now considered to be a centerpiece of the architecture.

The J2EE 1.4 Tutorial is intended for programmers interested in developing and deploying J2EE applications on the J2EE 1.4 SDK Beta 2 release. The tutorial describes how to use Web Services technologies and the new versions (Servlet 2.4, JSP 2.0, EJB 2.1, JMS 1.1, J2EE Connector 1.5) of existing J2EE technologies.

12.2.5 Web Services

J2EE also provides a technology Sun calls the Java Web Services Developer Pack (Java WSDP). Java WSDP plays a role similar to that of Microsoft's ASP.NET, offering an integrated toolset that in conjunction with the Java platform allows Java developers to build, test and deploy XML applications, Web Services, and Web applications. The technologies comprising this release of the Java WSDP include the Java APIs for XML, Java Architecture for XML Binding (JAXB), JavaServer Faces, JavaServer Pages Standard Tag Library (JSTL), Registry Server, Ant build Tool, and Apache Tomcat container.

12.2.6 Other Java Platforms

J2EE is only one of three major Java platforms. Others include Sun's Jini platform, aimed at supporting ad-hoc networks in the home, and JXTA, an experimental platform aimed at peer-to-peer collaboration applications. JXTA has not been a huge commercial success, and while Jini was initially very popular, and ultimately quite successful for applications in telephony, the system has not gained the sort of commercial weight of J2EE. In the interests of brevity, we won't say more about either system here.

12.3 .NET and J2EE Comparison

The forgoing discussion should make it apparent that .NET and J2EE are extremely similar technologies, and indeed that both have tremendous similarity to CORBA. Where they differ is in core focus. J2EE emerged from a "pure Java" community with a strong security emphasis, and for this reason didn't place nearly as much emphasis on enterprise integration tasks as perhaps should have been the case. J2EE rapidly became popular, in part because of its use of Java as the core programming language and in part because security was a dominant concern of the development community in the timeframe when J2EE was introduced.

With success comes obligations, and in the case of Java and J2EE, the obligation was that of integration and support for the major enterprise servers, database platforms and other kinds of existing legacy applications. Microsoft played into this dynamic by emphasizing integration features in .NET, J2EE responded with a new Java Connectors architecture, and the marketplace shifted. Both then reacted to the market's enormous interest in Web Services by providing comprehensive Web Services packages.

Today, one might argue, the onus is shifting. Independent of the commercial stature of the two packages, .NET and J2EE both invite the developer to create complex, interdependent, tightly integrated applications. Keeping these applications running is emerging as the major challenge of the coming decade, and securing highly integrated, multi-component applications as an equally important and equally critical need. J2EE may have a slight edge in this respect, simply because of its long legacy of focus on security considerations. Microsoft, however, has loudly committed itself to tackling security in a major way.

High availability and other aspects of reliability are probably the toughest issue confronting the two architectures. Here, Microsoft would point to its data center architecture, which includes easy tools for restarting a failed service on a healthy node, mechanisms for administering shared disks, and transactional technologies to promote easy cleanup after a crash. This makes a great deal of sense, but doesn't lead to high availability; in such an architecture one would expect that a crash, the restart of the failed server, and the fail-over of access to a shared disk (if any) could take many minutes. Thus one has a way to handle failures, but not a very fast one. Moreover, as we've seen over the past chapters, failure detection in this architecture is by timeout and hence can give very inconsistent results.

For its part, Sun's strategy emphasizes multiprocessor servers and hardware fault-tolerance features, but the bottom line is similar. Neither .NET nor J2EE really has the features needed to promote high availability or other kinds of quality of service guarantee, and one might speculate that as Web Services really take hold, these kinds of features will emerge as key to the next stage of competition between the platforms.

12.4 Further Reading

A great many comparisons between J2EE and .NET can be found in the trade literature. This is a shifting and rapidly evolving landscape, hence interested readers should consult the most up-to-date sources possible before drawing conclusions and even then should keep in mind that conclusions will have very limited lifetimes.

PART III

Reliable Distributed Computing

In this third part of the book, we ask how distributed computing systems can be made reliable—motivated by our review of servers used in Web settings, but seeking to generalize beyond these specific cases to include future servers that may be introduced by developers of new classes of critical distributed computing applications. Our focus is on communication technologies, but we do review persistent storage technologies based on the transactional computing model, particularly as it has been generalized to apply to objects in distributed environments. Part III develops the core mechanisms needed; the fourth and final part of the book applies these mechanisms to Web Services and explores some related topics.

13

How and Why Computer Systems Fail

Throughout this part of the book, we will be concerned with technologies for making real distributed systems reliable (see Birman and van Renesse [1996]). Before undertaking this task, it will be useful to briefly understand the reasons that distributed systems fail. Although there are some dramatic studies of the consequences of failures (see, for example, Peterson [1995]), our treatment draws primarily from work by Jim Gray (see Gray [1990], Gray and Reuter, Gray et al.), who studied the question of *why* systems fail while he was working at Tandem Computers, and on presentations by Anita Borr (see Borr and Wilhelmy), Joel Bartlett, a developer of Tandem's transactional system architecture (see Bartlett), and Ram Chilaragee, who has studied the same question at IBM (see Chilaragee). All three researchers focused on systems designed to be as robust as possible and might have drawn different conclusions had they looked at large distributed systems that incorporate technologies built with less-stringent reliability standards. Unfortunately, there seems to have been relatively little formal study of failure rates and causes in systems that were *not* engineered with reliability as a primary goal, despite the fact that a great number of systems used in critical settings include components with this property.

13.1 Hardware Reliability and Trends

Hardware failures were a dominant consideration in architecting reliable systems until late in the 1980s. Hardware can fail in many ways, but as electronic packaging has improved and the density of integrated circuits increased, hardware reliability has grown enormously. This improved reliability reflects the decreased heat production and power consumption of smaller circuits, the reduction in the number of off-chip connections and wiring, and improved manufacturing techniques. A consequence is that hardware-related system down-time is fast becoming a minor component of the overall reliability concerns faced in a large, complex distributed system. Obviously, hardware failure does remain a factor, particularly on small handheld devices, devices dependent upon battery power, and laptop or desktop computers, all of which tend to be treated more roughly than servers. However, the frequency of hardware failures is down across the board, and dramatically so on server platforms.

To the degree that hardware failures remain a significant reliability concern today, the observed problems are most often associated with the intrinsic limitations of connectors and mechanical devices. Thus, computer network problems (manifested through message loss or partitioning failures, where a component of the system becomes disconnected from some other component) are high on the list of hardware-related causes of failure for any modern system. Disk failures are also a leading cause of downtime in systems dependent upon large file or database servers, although RAID-style disk arrays can protect against such problems to a considerable degree. Of course, even RAID disks fail (rather often because of foolish repair mistakes, such as pulling the wrong module when servicing a RAID unit that has experienced a single failure). However, disk failures of all kinds are down by at least an order of magnitude compared with the situation seen in the 1980s.

A common hardware-related source of downtime has very little to do with failures, although it can seriously impact system availability and perceived reliability. Any critical computing system will, over its life cycle, live through a series of hardware generations. These can force upgrades, because it may become costly and impractical to maintain old generations of hardware. Thus, routine maintenance and downtime for replacement of computing and storage components with more modern versions must be viewed as a planned activity that can emerge as one of the more serious sources of system unavailability if not dealt with through a software architecture that can accommodate dynamic reconfiguration of critical parts of the system while the remainder of the system remains on-line. This issue of planning for future upgrading, expansion, and for new versions of components extends throughout a complex system, encompassing all its hardware and software technologies.

13.2 Software Reliability and Trends

Early in this book, we observed that software reliability is best understood as a process, encompassing not just the freedom of a system from software bugs, but also such issues as the software design methodology, the testing and life-cycle quality assurance process used, the quality of self-checking mechanisms and of user interfaces, the degree to which the system implements the intended application (i.e., the quality of match between system specification and problem specification), and the mechanisms provided for dealing with anticipated failures, maintenance, and upgrades. This represents a rich, multidimensional collection of issues, and few critical systems deal with them as effectively as one might wish. Software developers, in particular, often view software reliability in simplified terms, focusing exclusively on the software specification that their code must implement and on its correctness with regard to that specification.

This narrower issue of correctness remains an important challenge; indeed, many studies of system downtime in critical applications have demonstrated that even after rigorous testing, software bugs account for a substantial fraction of unplanned downtime (figures in the range of 25 percent to 35 percent are common), and that this number is extremely hard to reduce (see, for example, Peterson [1995]). Jim Gray and Bruce Lindsey, who studied reliability issues in transactional settings, once suggested that the residual software bugs in mature systems can be classified into two categories, which they called *Bohrbugs* and *Heisenbugs* (see Gray and Reuter, Gray et al.). (See Figure 13.1.)

A Bohrbug is a solid, reproducible problem: If it occurs, and one takes note of the circumstances, the scenario can be reproduced and the bug will repeat itself. The name is intended to remind us of Bohr's model of the atomic nucleus: a small hard object, well localized in space. Gray and Lindsey found that as systems mature, the relative frequency of Bohrbugs drops steadily over time, although other studies (notably by Anita Borr) suggest that the population of Bohrbugs is periodically replenished when a system must be upgraded or maintained over its life cycle.

Heisenbugs are named for

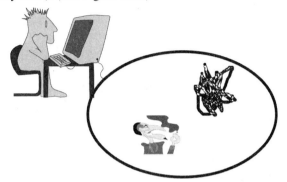

Figure 13.1. Developers are likely to discover and fix Bohrbugs, which are easily localized and reproducible sources of errors. Heisenbugs are fuzzy and hard to pin down. Often, these bugs are actually symptoms of some other bug, which doesn't cause an immediate crash; the developer will tend to work around them but may find them extremely hard to fix in a convincing way. The frequency of such bugs diminishes very slowly over the life cycle of an application.

the Heisenberg model of the nucleus: a complex wave function that is influenced by the act of observation. These bugs are typically side-effects of problems that occurred much earlier in an execution, such as overrunning an array or accidentally dereferencing a pointer after the object to which it points has been freed. Such errors can corrupt the application in a way that will cause it to crash, but not until the corrupted data structure is finally referenced, which may not occur until long after the bug actually was exercised. Because such a bug is typically a symptom of the underlying problem, rather than an instance of the true problem itself, Heisenbugs are exquisitely sensitive to the order of execution. Even with identical inputs, a program that crashed once may run correctly back in the laboratory.

Not surprisingly, the major source of crashes in a mature software system turns out to be Heisenbugs. Anita Borr's work actually goes further, finding that most attempts to fix Heisenbugs actually make the situation worse than it was in the first place. This observation is not surprising to engineers of complex, large software systems: Heisenbugs correspond to problems that can be tremendously hard to track down, and are often fixed by patching around them at run time. Nowhere is the gap between theory and practice in reliable computing more apparent than in the final testing and bug correction stages of a major software deployment that must occur under time pressure or a deadline.

Better programming languages can help enormously. Starting with the introduction of Java and now continuing with languages like C#, for the first time we are seeing large numbers of programmers moving towards languages that enforce strong type-checking, automatically handle garbage collection, and will detect and flag problematic control structures and other possible signs of mistakes. Computing platforms like J2EE and .NET reach beyond the individual application by tracking dependencies upon specific versions of external services and libraries, and at runtime will enforce these dependencies. Runtime monitoring and debugging tools have taken enormous steps forward (earlier, we mentioned that Microsoft's Visual Studio .NET is an especially good example, but there are many such systems, manufactured by dozens of vendors). All of these steps really can help.

Nonetheless, it isn't particularly hard to make mistakes in Java or C#, or to trigger an unrecoverable runtime exception. An infinite loop is still an error, no matter what the language, and object-oriented languages bring problems of their own, such as challenges in simply making a copy of an object. As programmers familiar with these languages rapidly learn, a deep copy is made by copying the object and all other objects to which it is linked, recursively, while a shallow copy retains linked-to objects, with the effect that a single physical object may now be accessed by multiple paths, possibly including some unintended ones. Yet it is far easier to create shallow copies, and this accounts for many bugs and programming errors. New languages are not about to eliminate software reliability problems.

13.3 Other Sources of Downtime

Jointly, hardware and software downtime, including downtime for upgrades, is typically said to account for some two-thirds of system downtime in critical applications. The remaining one-third of downtime is attributable to planned maintenance, such as making backups, and environmental factors, such as power outages, air conditioning or heating failures, leaking pipes, and other similar problems.

Although there may be little hope of controlling these forms of downtime, the trend is to try and treat them using software techniques that distribute critical functionality over sufficient numbers of computers, and separate them to a sufficient degree so that redundancy can overcome unplanned outages. Having developed software capable of solving such problems, downtime for hardware maintenance, backups, or other routine purposes can often be treated in the same way as other forms of outages. Such an approach tends to view system management, monitoring, and on-line control as a part of the system itself: A critical system should, in effect, be capable of modeling its own configuration and triggering appropriate actions if critical functionality is compromised for any reason. In the chapters that follow, this will motivate us to look at issues associated with having a system monitor its own membership (the set of processes that compose it) and, dynamically, adapting itself in a coordinated, consistent manner if changes are sensed. Although the need for brevity will prevent us from treating system management issues in the degree of detail that the problem deserves, we will develop the infrastructure on which reliable management technologies can be implemented, and will briefly survey some recent work specifically on the management problem.

13.4 Complexity

Many developers would argue that the single most serious threat to distributed systems reliability is the *complexity* of many large distributed systems. Indeed, distributed systems used in critical applications often interconnect huge numbers of components using subtle protocols, and the resulting architecture may be extremely complex. The good news, however, is that when such systems are designed for reliability, the techniques used to make them more reliable may also tend to counteract this complexity.

In the chapters that follow we will be looking at replication techniques that permit critical system data and services to be duplicated as a way to increase reliability. We'll also look at new-age technologies for tracking system status and reacting to problems if they arise at runtime. When these kinds of mechanisms are used appropriately, the replicas will be consistent with one another and the system as a whole can be thought of as containing just a single instance of the replicated object, but one that happens to be more reliable or more secure than any single object normally would be. If the object is active (a program), it can be *actively replicated* by duplicating the inputs to it and consolidating the outputs it produces. These techniques lead to a proliferation of components but also impose considerable regularity upon the set of components. They thus control the complexity associated with the robustness intervention.

As just mentioned, we'll also be looking at system management tools that monitor sets of related components, treating them as groups within which a common management, monitoring, or control policy can be applied. Again, by factoring out something that is true for all system components in a certain class or set of classes, these techniques reduce complexity. What were previously a set of apparently independent objects are now explicitly seen to be related objects that can be treated in similar ways, at least for purposes of management, monitoring, or control.

Broadly, then, we will see that although complexity is a serious threat to reliability, complexity can potentially be controlled by capturing and exploiting regularities in distributed system structure—regularities that are common when such systems are designed to be managed, fault tolerant, secure, or otherwise reliable. To the degree that this is done, the system structure becomes more explicit and hence complexity is reduced. In some ways, the effort of building the system will increase: This structure needs to be specified and needs to remain accurate as the system subsequently evolves. But in other ways, the effort is decreased: By managing a set of components in a uniform way, one avoids the need to do so in an on ad hoc basis, which may be similar for the members of the set but not identical if the component management policies were developed independently.

These observations are a strong motivation for looking at technologies that can support grouping of components in various ways and for varied purposes. However, they also point to a secondary consideration: Unless such technologies are well integrated with system development software tools, they will prove to be irritating and hard to maintain as a system is extended over time. As we will see, researchers have been more involved with the former problem than the latter one, but this situation has now begun to change, particularly with the introduction of CORBA-based reliability solutions, which are well integrated with CORBA development tools. For example, CORBA offers an FTOL architecture for building fault-tolerant active objects. On the downside, these kinds of features remain rather tentative and have yet to be adopted by CORBA's siblings (progeny?), J2EE and .NET. The Web Services community seems to be at the verge of rejecting such mechanisms precisely because the CORBA community has had mixed experience with the specific versions they adopted. None of these developments is especially encouraging for those of us "in the business" of high assurance.

13.5 Detecting Failures

Surprisingly little work has been done on the problem of building failure detection subsystems. A consequence is that many distributed systems detect failures using timeouts—an error-prone approach that forces the application to overcome inaccurate failure detections in software.

Work by Vogels (see Vogels [1996]) suggests that many distributed systems may be able to do quite a bit better. Vogels makes the analogy between detecting a failure and discovering that one's tenant has disappeared. If a landlord were trying to contact a tenant whose rent check is late, it would be a little extreme to contact the police after trying to telephone that tenant once, at an arbitrary time during the day, and not receiving any reply. More likely, the landlord would telephone several times, inquire of neighbors, check to see if the mail is still being collected and if electricity and water are being consumed, and otherwise check for indirect evidence of the presence or absence of the tenant.

Modern distributed systems offer a great number of facilities that are analogous to these physical options. The management information base of a typical computing node (its MIB) provides information on the active processes and their consumption of resources such as memory, computing time, and I/O operations. Often, the network itself is instrumented, and indeed it may sometimes be possible to detect a network partition in an accurate way by querying MIBs associated with network interface and routing nodes. If the operating system on which the application in question is running is accessible, one can sometimes ask it about the status of the processes it is supporting. In applications designed with fault-tolerance in mind, there may be the option of integrating self-checking mechanisms directly into the code, so that the application will periodically verify that it is healthy and take some action, such as resetting a counter, each time the check succeeds. Through such a collection of tactics, one can potentially detect most failures rapidly and accurately and even distinguish partitioning failures from other failures such as crashes or application termination. Vogels has implemented a prototype of a failure investigator service that uses these techniques, yielding much faster and better failure detection than is traditionally assumed possible in distributed systems. Unfortunately, however, this approach is not at all standard. Many distributed systems rely entirely on timeouts for failures; as one might expect, this results in a high rate of erroneous detections and a great deal of complexity in order to overcome their consequences.

Vogels has gone beyond this initial point in his most recent work on the problem (see Vogels [2003]). He is now arguing that Web Services systems should include a module, WS_MEMBERSHIP, implementing the failure detection functionality and guaranteeing system-wide consistency. As noted earlier, it is not at all clear how industry views this proposal, although he is certainly seen as a leader in the Web Services architecture community.

13.6 Hostile Environments

The discussion in this chapter has enumerated a great variety of reliability threats, which a typical distributed system may need to anticipate and deal with. The problems considered, however, were all of a nature that might be considered "routine," in the sense that they all fall into the category of building software and hardware to be robust against anticipated classes of accidental failures and to be self-managed in ways that anticipate system upgrades and maintenance events.

Just a few years ago, it seemed unnatural to think of the Internet as a hostile environment, and one steadily growing more so. Today, after a decade of viruses and "denial of service" attacks, only a very trusting individual would still see the network as a benign place. Modern computer networks are shared with a huge population of computer-literate users, whose goals and sense of personal ethics may differ tremendously from those of the system developer. Whether intentionally or otherwise, these network users represent a diffuse threat; they may unexpectedly probe a distributed system for weaknesses or even subject it to a well-planned and orchestrated assault without prior warning. Even applications as innocent as personal e-mail have become targets for everything from pornographic spam to viruses embedded in active content.

The intentional threat spectrum is as varied as the accidental threat spectrum reviewed earlier. The most widely known of the threats are computer viruses, which are software programs designed to copy themselves from machine to machine and to do damage to the machines on which they manage to establish themselves. (A benign type of virus that does no damage is called a *worm,* but because the mere presence of an unanticipated program can impact system reliability, it is perhaps best to take the view that all undesired intrusions into a system represent a threat to reliable behavior.) A virus may attack a system by violating assumptions it makes about the environment or the network, breaking through security codes and passwords, piggybacking a ride on legitimate messages, or any of a number of other routes. Attacks that exploit several routes at the same time are more and more common—for example, simultaneously compromising some aspect of the telecommunication infrastructure on which an application depends while also presenting the application with an exceptional condition that it can only handle correctly when the telecommunication subsystem is also functioning.

Other types of intentional threats include unauthorized users or authorized users who exceed their normal limitations. In a banking system, one worries about a rogue trader or an employee who seeks to divert funds without detection. A disgruntled employee may seek to damage the critical systems or data of an organization. In the most extreme case, one can imagine hostile actions directed at a nation's critical computing systems during a period of war or terrorism. Today, this sort of *information warfare* may seem like a suitable topic for science fiction writers, yet, as society shifts increasingly critical activities onto computing and communication technology, the potential targets for attack will eventually become rich enough to interest military adversaries.

A distributed denial of service (DDoS) attack occurs when a collection of machines, often subverted by hackers who have broken in over the network, are directed to barrage some server or data center with a tremendous load of costly messages, such as the first-phase messages for establishing a TCP connection. Often, origin data is concealed for such messages so as to prevent the server from using a simple filtering mechanism to weed out the bad connections. The server grinds to its knees and legitimate users are unable to connect. The basic DDoS attack has many variants, some aimed at key services such as DNS, some at routers or "weak links" in the network, and some aimed at other kinds of infrastructure or even the application itself. Moreover, DDoS attacks can be effective, but the good news is that they have limits.

For example, when Metallica unveiled its new Web site in early 2003, the band attracted the attention of the music swapping community, which had previously been attacked by Metallica and its lawyers through an organization called the RIAA. Metallica's site fielded some 6M requests per minute for several days, until network providers worldwide devised a strategy for blocking the problematic packets. Surprisingly, though, rather few Metallica fans were actually disrupted by the event: the DDoS traffic made it hard to register with their Web site but because the actual Web content was cached on a huge data center maintained by Akamai, once a user was registered, the DDoS traffic had little impact. Thus the attackers were only able to shut down one aspect of the overall system, and only for a few days.

Later in this part of the book we'll be looking at issues of scalability, and we'll see that some high availability techniques have overheads that are potentially quite significant when certain "rare" events occur. A clever attacker might even launch a denial of service attack by triggering an unusually high frequency of these kinds of events, knowing that the system will pay a steep price dealing with them. Yet because the events are normal ones, albeit normally not so frequent, the system administrator may have a tough time even noticing that a problem has occurred. For example, in a replication protocol one could repeatedly add, then remove, some process—again and again. The group membership protocol will have to run each time, and while this happens, updates can be delayed, effectively degrading the group. Peer-to-peer protocols are often sensitive to churn, the analogous problem but on a large scale. Thus an attack might not even be predicated on the use of some sort of really abnormal traffic pattern!

Clearly, no computing system can be protected against every conceivable form of internal and external threat. Distributed computing can, however, offer considerable benefits against a well-known and fully characterized threat profile. By distributing critical functionality over sets of processes that must cooperate and coordinate their actions in order to perform sensitive functions, the barrier against external threats can be formidable. For example, Metallica's decision to host content on a Web server farm maintained by Akamai meant that DDoS attacks would have had to shut down all of Akamai's thousands of computers to really shut down Metallica itself. Similarly, a terrorist who might easily overcome a system that lacks any defenses at all would face a much harder problem overcoming firewalls, breaking through security boundaries, and interfering with critical subsystems designed to continue operating correctly even if some limited number of system components crash or are compromised. Later we will discuss virtual private network technologies, which take such approaches even further, preventing all communication within the network except that initiated by authenticated users. Clearly, if a system uses a technology such as this, it will be relatively hard to break into. However, the cost of such a solution may be higher than most installations can afford.

As the developer of a critical system, the challenge is to anticipate the threats that it must overcome and to do so in a manner that balances costs against benefits. Often, the threat profile that a component subsystem may face will be localized to that component— hence, the developer may need to go to great lengths in protecting some especially critical subsystems against reliability and security threats, while using much more limited and less-costly technologies elsewhere in the same system. One goal of this part of the book involves a corresponding issue—that of understanding not just how a reliability problem can be solved, but also how the solution can be applied in a selective and localized manner, so that a developer who faces a specific problem in a specific context can draw on a solution tailored to that problem and context, without requiring that the entire system be reengineered to overcome a narrow threat.

Today, we lack a technology with these attributes. Most fault-tolerant and security technologies demand that the developer adopt a fault-tolerant or secure computing and communication architecture starting with the first lines of code entered into the system. With such an approach, fault tolerance and security become very hard to address late in the game, when substantial amounts of technology already exist. Unfortunately, however, most critical systems are built up out of preexisting technology, which will necessarily have been adapted to the new use and hence will necessarily be confronted with new types of reliability and security threats that were not anticipated in the original setting. What is needed, then, is a technology base that is flexible enough to teach us how to overcome a great variety of possible threats, but that is also flexible enough to be used in a narrow and selective manner (so that the costs of reliability are localized to the component being made reliable), efficient (so that these costs are as low as possible), and suitable for being introduced *late in the game,* when a system may already include substantial amounts of preexisting technology.

The good news, however, is that current research is making major strides in this direction. In the following chapters, we will be looking at many of the fundamental challenges that occur in overcoming various classes of threats. We will discuss computing models that are dynamic, self-managed, and fault tolerant, and will see how a technology based on *wrapping* preexisting interfaces and components with look-alike technologies that introduce desired robustness features can be used to harden complex, pre-existing systems, albeit with many limitations. Finally, we will consider some of the large-scale system issues raised when a complex system must be managed and controlled in a distributed setting. While it would be an overstatement to claim that all the issues have been solved, it is clear that considerable progress towards an integrated technology base for hardening critical systems is being made.

I have few illusions about reliability: Critical computing systems will continue to be less reliable than they should be until the customers and societal users of such systems demand reliability, and the developers begin to routinely concern themselves with understanding the threats to reliability in a given setting—planning a strategy for responding to those threats and for testing the response. However, there is reason to believe that in those cases where this process does occur, a technology base capable of rising to the occasion can be provided.

13.7 Related Reading

On dramatic system failures and their consequences: (see Gibbs, Peterson [1995]).
    How and why systems fail and what can be done about it: (see Birman and van Renesse [1996], Borr and Wilhelmy, Chilaragee, Gray [1990], Gray and Reuter, Gray et al.).
    On the failure investigator: (see Vogels [1996], Vogels [2003]).
    On understanding failures: (see Cristian [1996]).

14

Overcoming Failures in a Distributed System

14.1 Consistent Distributed Behavior

In this and the next two chapters, we'll be focused on mechanisms for *replicating data and computation* while guaranteeing some form of consistent behavior to the end-user. For example, we might want to require that even though information has been replicated, the system behaves as if that information wasn't replicated and instead resides at a single place. This is an intuitively attractive model, because developers find it natural to think in terms of non-distributed systems, and it is reasonable to expect that a distributed system should be able to mimic the behavior of a non-distributed one. At the same time, though, it isn't a minor undertaking to ensure that a distributed system will behave just like a non-distributed one.

Distributed systems are inherently concurrent: actions occur at multiple places, and if we start to replicate data, we need to acknowledge the possibility that access will occur simultaneously at more than one replica. Yet it is hard to visualize concurrent behaviors of a system, because one needs to think about all the things that can be happening at all the locations in the system, and the possible execution scenarios generally grow in number as the cross product of the numbers of possible local scenarios. It isn't hard to see how concurrency can be a source of serious bugs. Far preferable would be to not only think of a system as if it didn't have any kind of replicated data, but to go further and also be able to think about it as if any concurrency that occurs is of the type that can happen when building a conventional multi-threaded application.

With this in mind, in what follows we'll work our way up to a model called "virtual synchrony," in which one thinks about a system as if it isn't using replicated data and doesn't exhibit concurrency. The model lets us substitute groups of processes or objects where we might have used a single one in our conceptual design, in effect offering the developer an incremental way to introduce replication and to achieve a high degree of concurrency.

Virtual synchrony is supported by some popular communications packages, including several that should be available to readers of this text (Horus, Ensemble and Spread). Although Web Services development tools don't yet provide integrated support for these kinds of mechanisms, down the road that type of integrated solution will almost certainly become available. Meanwhile, for those who need high assurance, there are practical ways to apply the ideas in this and the subsequent chapter to real systems, by using standard Web Services development tools and integrating them with communication libraries implementing the mechanisms we'll be studying.

Although our "real" goal is to support replicated data and replicated computation for high availability and improved performance, we'll tackle the problem a little bit at a time. In particular, the main topic on which we'll focus in this chapter concerns the best options for tracking the set of members of a distributed system. Monitoring membership in a system may not seem all that central to replicating data, but in fact plays a fundamental role: after all, it makes no sense to talk about replicating information unless we can explain precisely *where* the replicas are supposed to be! Moreover, it turns out that the way we solve the membership problem has stunning performance implications. Getting membership "right" can result in replicated update rates thousands of times superior to those seen in systems that approach the membership problem naively. Indeed, while there are many who would suggest that "agreeing on something" is the most fundamental distributed computing problem, the author of this text could make a pretty strong argument that agreeing on *membership* is perhaps at the real core.

Why worry about *agreement* on system membership? Why not simply trust processes to make their own decisions, in accordance with the end-to-end philosophy, perhaps using timeouts?[6] Readers may recall that in the introduction of this book, we saw that when timeout is used to detect failures, events unrelated to failure such as network congestion, brief disconnections of some computers from the network, or routing changes can trigger timeouts and thus fool the system into believing that such-and-such a node has crashed. Worse still, this can happen in wildly inconsistent ways. Perhaps process p will conclude that processes q, r, and s are up but that process t has crashed, while process q thinks that all five are healthy, and process t believes that it is the only survivor of some sort of massive outage. Such problems can percolate up to the user, resulting in confusing or even unsafe behavior. For example, in the introduction, we saw a "split brain" scenario, where an air traffic control system might partition into two side-by-side systems, each claiming to be in control—and each unaware of the other. It isn't hard to see why confusion about membership will translate to trouble if we want to replicate data. Suppose that our five processes are part of an air traffic control service that needs to maintain information about which planes are in the sky and where they are going, and the data in question is updated when controllers give

---

[6]Of course, one can interpret almost any distributed system built without changes to the core Internet protocols as an "end-to-end" system. But the end-to-end approach is often understood to refer to a model in which properties are enforced *pairwise*, between cooperating end-points. If we understand the model in this strong sense, the introduction of new services that play a role such as membership tracking throughout the entire system represents a major departure.

instructions to the planes, or when a plane changes its course. If the system isn't consistent about which members are operational, it may neglect to update one of the replicas, in which case that replica will start to give incorrect information to the pilots and controllers who are unlucky enough to query it. Conversely, if we can trust a membership service to tell us which processes "belong" to the system, we'll be in a position to use that information in support of simple tools, like libraries that maintain replicated data and provide ways to lock items for exclusive use, and then in higher level algorithms, for example to rapidly "fail over" from a process that crashes to one that remains healthy so as to maintain near-continuous availability. In many ways, *agreement on membership* is thus at the center of the universe, at least insofar as high assurance computing is concerned.

14.1.1 Static Membership

There are many ways to obtain consistency in a distributed system, and not all boil down to the use of a group membership tracking subsystem. For example, many systems start with a list of the possible constituent computers that might be operational, and rather than continuously tracking the state of each node, deal with availability on an operation-by-operation manner. Such a system would basically have a list, readily available to all the processes in the system, listing the places where replicas *might* be found. In this "static" model, one has an unchanging list of members, but at any given point in time, only a subset of them will typically be available.

Let's think for a moment about how one might support replicated data on a static membership model. We have our five processes and we would like to maintain some sort of information—for simplicity, we'll focus on just a single variable x and assume that it takes integer values. Obviously any real system might have more elaborate data structures, but it turns out that a method that works for a single integer can usually be generalized to handle more complex information in a straightforward manner.

Now, if x were a non-replicated variable, living in some place that never fails, we could track its values over time and in this manner, build a history. It might look like this: from time 0 to 20, x was zero. Then, an update occurred at time 21 and x took on the value 17. An additional update occurred at time 25, changing x to 97, and so forth.

In our real system, processes p, q, r, s and t need to maintain replicas of x. For this purpose, let's require that each process in the system keep a single copy of x and also record the time at which it was lasted updated. When we start the system up, we'll assume that all five know that at time 0, the value of x was zero. Now, at time 21, p wants to initiate an update. How should it do so?

Recall that in a static membership model, p knows the identities of the other processes in the system, but doesn't know which ones are currently operational. It may be that if p sends an update request to each of its counterparts, asking them to record a new value for x, only some will get the message and of those, perhaps only some of the replies will get back to p. (On top of this, one needs to worry about concurrent updates, but for the purposes of this part of the chapter, one update is already quite adequate to understand the basic issues.)

We also need a way to read the value of x. Suppose that s wants to read x. If it simply looks at its own value, how can it be sure that nobody else has a more "recent" update that didn't get through, perhaps because of a network problem?

There is an obvious way to work around such problems, and almost all systems that use the static membership model employ it. The idea is to make sure that each operation reaches a majority of the processes in the system. Suppose that we know that if p wants to update x it always makes sure that at least three out of the five processes in the system record that update (since it can't be sure how many will respond in advance of trying to do the operation, this means than an update has multiple phases—an initial attempt, then some sort of decision as to whether the operation was successful, and then a second phase in which the processes learn the outcome). If s similarly reads copies from a majority of members, at least one process is guaranteed to overlap any successful update and the read, hence at least one process will know the most current value of x!

Generalizing, this way of designing systems leads to what are called *quorum update* and *read* architectures (see Gilford, Skeen [February 1982], Thomas). Rather than requiring that reads and updates both reach a majority, we instead define a minimum number of copies that must be read, QR, and a minimum number of copies that must be updated, QW, and ensure that QR + QW is greater than the size of the system. For example, in a system with n processes, we might set QW $= n - 1$ and QR $= 2$. In this way, we can successfully update our variable even if one of the group members is faulty, and any read will definitely "see" the most current update.

Returning to our example, process p thus updates x as follows. First, it does a read operation to find the most current value of x and the associated time—and to do this, it issues an RPC-style read requests to one replica after another until it has QR replies. The current version of x will be the one with the largest time, and the value is the value associated with that version. (Several processes may report the same version and value).

Process p now computes a time at which the new version will become active—any value will do as long as it is larger than the maximum number it read from the group, and the new value. And it issues RPCs to at least QW members, asking them to "prepare" to update x. (In practice, of course, it would probably just issue requests to all group members, but the rule allows a bit more flexibility.)

The processes in the group now respond, acknowledging that they are prepared to do the update. Process p looks to see if it has a write quorum. If the number of acknowledgements is QW or larger, p allows the update to *commit*, and otherwise, it must be *aborted*, meaning that the members don't change their replica's value. We'll revisit the protocol later and pin down some of the details, but this should already give the basic sense of how it works.

Notice that in a fault-tolerant system, QW will necessarily have to be smaller than n. As a result, even if p only wants to read x it *still* needs to do an RPC to some other process, because QR > 1! This means that read operations can't run any faster than the speed of an RPC. Similarly, to do an update, p needs to perform two rounds of RPCs. Obviously, this is going to be at least as slow as the slowest respondant, and while one can shift the costs around with clever programming, static membership does tend to incur significant costs. In practice, one finds that systems built in this manner would be able to sustain tens of updates per second in a "real" group of five processes, but perhaps not much more.

We'll call this the "static membership" model. The set of potential system members is fixed, even though the operational subset varies, and the algorithms are quorum based. Moreover the members are typically denoted by the names of the computers on which they run, since process-ids change if a machine fails, then restarts. Obviously, networks evolve over time, and even static systems will need to update the membership list now and then, but the presumption is that this can be treated as an offline activity.

14.1.2 Dynamic Membership

When we introduce a group membership service, things brighten up considerably. Protocols that trust such a service to monitor the system state are able to avoid doing much of the work done in the static case and this translates to dramatic speedups, at least for operations like updating replicated data. The "dynamic group membership" model is concerned with systems built this way. In experiments with one of the systems we'll talk about later in this part of the book, called Horus, it was possible to send as many as 80,000 update operations per second within a group of five members—literally thousands of times faster than in the static case. The core issue here is that even for the cheapest category of operations (those that change the "internal state" of a service), a quorum-based system can't perform an operation until a majority of its members have seen the operation, while a system like Horus can perform an operation as soon as the multicast describing it is received. This limits the quorum system: pending operations impose overhead on the initiating system. The larger such a system gets, the longer an operation will be pending before it can be executed, and the higher the impact of these overheads. Thus quorum systems will usually slow down at least linearly in the system size. In fact, the situation is often quite a bit worse: Jim Gray, winner of the ACM Turing Award, has reported on studies that found the slowdown to be roughly $O(n^2)$ where n is the number of members in the service. Thus, if you accept his analysis, a system with 2 nodes will be roughly half as fast as one with 1 node, but a system with 4 nodes will be 1/16th the speed of the single-node system. As a practical matter, it is extremely uncommon to talk about quorum systems having more than about 5 members[7].

Horus will also turn out to have scaling limits, but the issue is of a different nature. The Horus protocols scale well up to some bounded group size (usually around 32 members); over a multicast layer such as IP multicast, throughput may be roughly constant in this range (and similarly for other such systems, including Spread). Moreover, because Horus and Spread don't need to wait for acknowledgements on these cheapest operations, the delay seen in quorum systems is avoided. However, as Horus or Spread configurations get

---

[7]There has been recent work on so-called "Byzantine Quorum" systems, in which we think of the server as having n^2 members organized as a square array; a read quorum would be any row and a write quorum any column. Jim Gray actually argues that the costs of replication will often rise as $O(n)$ due to concurrency control conflicts and, independently, will also rise as $O(n)$ due to the cost of the quorum operations. Thus Byzantine Quorum systems, in his analysis, would slow down as $O(n^*\sqrt{n})$. This is still quite severe and any practical application would need to keep n as small as possible.

very large, they too begin to slow down; detailed studies suggest that this degradation in throughput is at first linear, but that eventually a quadratic factor dominates. The problem is initially one of flow control (it is easy to see why collecting acknowledgements from a set of n members should take time proportional to n if n is large enough), but then becomes more complex, involving overheads associated with retransmission of lost messages and membership health tracking. Thus, for smaller configurations, Horus and Spread will vastly outperform quorum systems, and they can also be used in somewhat larger group settings than can the quorum schemes. But all of these classes of systems do hit limits. Later in the book, we'll ask what can be done in really large systems, with hundreds of processes, where those limits aren't acceptable.

In fairness, our performance claims should be taken with a grain of salt for other reasons too: the messages in question were very small ones, the protocol has some optimizations that can't be used if network partitioning is a concern, and the quoted data rate doesn't include any time that might be required to process these messages (for example, even a single disk update would limit the achieved data rate to 1,000 events per second or less). A user building an application that does something on receipt of messages, such as logging them, might not be able to achieve anything like these data rates. Still, there are many situations in which data structures are maintained entirely within memory, in which network partitioning really isn't a risk, and for which it isn't unreasonable to talk about an update that can be represented by just a few bytes of information. Thus, there are practical settings in which these data rates can really be achieved. Forcing such an application to run over a protocol designed for the static case and limited to hundreds of updates per second would impose a staggering performance penalty.

In dynamic membership models, we usually assume that individual processes are the members of the system, rather than focusing on the computers hosting those processes. Processes come and go, and we'll model them as "joining" and "leaving" the system. Sometimes a process fails and hence "leaves" without warning. The model is quite flexible, and in fact when working with it, one often mixes it with elements of the static approach. For example, one can build applications composed of dynamic groups, but with the restriction that no group can be formed without having members on such and such a set of servers. This flexibility, combined with the higher speed of applications built using the model, is a strong argument in its favor.

These aren't the only two consistency models that have been proposed. We'll touch on some of the others later in this chapter. For example, the static and dynamic system models assume that when a machine fails, it does so by crashing, and this of course simplifies matters in important ways. If we introduce the possibility that data is corrupt or that group members might behave maliciously, the most appropriate consistency model changes to one called the "Byzantine" model. Byzantine fault tolerance is a powerful idea and is increasingly useful in systems concerned with obtaining very strong guarantees (for example, security mechanisms), but not many developers actually work with such subsystems. For this reason, we limit ourselves to a brief mention of the Byzantine model, and similarly for several other well-known but less practically significant approaches to high assurance distributed computing.

Our basic goal, then, is to explore two kinds of systems. The static ones assume a pre-specified set of servers but are able to handle failures of minority subsets. These solutions tend to be easy to describe but rather slow. The dynamic systems use a software group membership service to track membership, resulting in a more flexible but somewhat more complex architecture. The main merit of this architecture is the tremendous speedup it brings. It also brings some limitations, and we'll touch on those, but in practice, they don't seem to represent real problems for users.

14.2 Formalizing Distributed Problem Specifications

As anyone who has taken courses in computer science quickly learns, the field has deep connections to the area of mathematics concerned with logic and formal reasoning. When developing an algorithm we often talk about specifying its safety and liveness properties, proving partial and total correctness, etc. The distributed systems community has long sought to do similar things, but with mixed success.

In what follows, we won't delve very deeply into the mathematics of distributed computing, but the reader may still run into the consequences of what has been a somewhat uneasy marriage. Our real goal here is practical: there exists a class of systems, including the Horus and Spread systems mentioned earlier, and many others in the same class (for example Ensemble, Transis, Eternal, Phoenix, Relacs—a complete list can be found in Chapter 27) any of which can be used as tools to build highly assured distributed applications such as high assurance Web Services. They work very well in practical settings, and the essential message of the book is that Web Service builders should begin to use them where appropriate.

But for the more theoretical community, the precise characterization of these systems and the situations under which they can guarantee to remain operational is anything but a minor detail. It turns out that the three systems mentioned, and indeed all systems that use dynamic membership models, are fairly hard to model using temporal logic, while static membership systems (the best known one is called Paxos; see Lamport [2001]) is quite a bit easier to model. This has triggered considerable debate and quite a bit of confusion. At the time of this writing, it seems safe to say that the confusion has mostly settled. Rigorous theoretical work has been done in both models and the average theoretician understands how the two are related (both are subject to a famous limitation called the FLP Impossibility Result) and how they differ (the dynamic model provides a slightly weaker "agreement" condition in the event of failures, and this is how it manages to run so much faster than the static one). Perhaps the best paper to have tackled this overall area is Chockler [2001].

As we mentioned, however, static membership leads to slow systems. Thus we have a bit of a tension: if we want speed and flexibility, dynamic membership is the way to go. But if we want simple mathematics, we should abandon speed and go with static membership. The good news is that if we are willing to accept somewhat messy mathematics, the theory of dynamic membership is (by now) understood fairly well; there is nothing intrinsically incorrect or bad about this model. It is just harder to write down, harder to work with in a formal sense, and less familiar to the theoretical community.

At any rate, we'll try to avoid theoretical digressions here, but the reader should be aware that doing so is a question of taste. Others might delve deeply into that material, or choose to avoid it entirely. Our goal is to be rather practical—we're working up to some rather concrete options for hardening Web Services applications and similar systems—but to give the reader the underpinnings to delve deeper if the need to do so ever arises.

14.3 Time in Distributed Systems

In discussing the two views of system membership, we made casual reference to temporal properties of a system. For example, we said that processes should "agree" on the membership in a system—but when should they agree? Clearly, the concept of time represents a fundamental component of any distributed computing model. In the simplest terms, a distributed system is any set of processes that communicates by message passing and carrying out desired actions over time. Specifications of distributed behavior often include such terms as "when," "before," "after," and "simultaneously," and we will need to develop the tools to make this terminology rigorous.

In nondistributed settings, time has an obvious meaning—at least to non-physicists. The world is full of clocks, which are accurate and synchronized to varying degrees. Something similar is true for distributed systems: All computers have some form of clock, and clock synchronization services are a standard part of any distributed computing environment. Moreover, just as in any other setting, these clocks have limited accuracy. Two different processes, reading their local clocks at the same instant in (real) time, might observe different values, depending on the quality of the clock synchronization algorithm. Clocks may also drift over long periods of time.

The use of time in a distributed system raises several problems. One obvious problem is to devise algorithms for synchronizing clocks accurately. In Chapter 23 we will look at several such algorithms, although the use of inexpensive GPS hardware can obviate the need for complex protocols in many settings. However, even given very accurate clocks, communication systems operate at such high speeds that the use of physical clocks for fine-grained temporal measurements can only make sense for processes sharing the same clock—for example, by operating on the same computer. This leads to something of a quandary: In what sense is it meaningful to say that one event occurs and then another does so, or that two events are concurrent, if no means are available by which a program could label events and compare their times of occurrence?

Looking at this question in 1978, Leslie Lamport proposed a model of logical time that answers this question (see Lamport [July 1978, 1984]). Lamport considered sets of processes (they could be static or dynamic) that interact by message passing. In his approach, the execution of a process is modeled as a series of atomic events, each of which requires a single unit of logical time to perform. More precisely, his model represents a process by a tuple $(E_p, <_p)$, where E_p is a set of events that occurred within process p, and $<_p$ is a partial order on those events. The advantage of this representation is that it captures any concurrency available within p. Thus, if a and b are events within p, $a <_p b$ means that a happens before b, in some sense meaningful to p—for example, b might be an operation that reads a value written by a, b could have acquired a lock that a released, or p might be executing sequential code in which operation b isn't initiated until after a has terminated.

Notice that there are many levels of granularity at which one might describe the events that occur as a process executes. At the level of the components from which the computer was fabricated, computation consists of concurrent events that implement the instructions or microinstructions executed by the user's program. At a higher level, a process might be viewed in terms of statements in a programming language, control-flow graphs, procedure calls, or units of work that make sense in some external frame of reference, such as operations on a database. Concurrency within a process may result from interrupt handlers, parallel programming constructs in the language or run-time system, or from the use of lightweight threads. Thus, when we talk about the events that occur within a process, it is understood that the designer of a system will typically have a granularity of representation that seems natural for the distributed protocol or specification at hand and that events are encoded to this degree of precision. In this book, most examples will be at a very coarse level of precision, in which we treat all the local computation that occurs within a process, between when it sends or receives a first message, and when it sends or receives a second message, as a single event or even as being associated with the send or receive event itself.

Lamport models the sending and receiving of messages as events. Thus, an event a could be the sending of a message m, denoted $snd(m)$; the reception of m, denoted $rcv(m)$; or the delivery of m to application code, denoted $deliv(m)$. When the process at which an event occurs is not clear from context, we will add the process identifier as a subscript: $snd_p(m)$, $rcv_p(m)$ and $deliv_p(m)$, as seen here:

Figure 14.1. Process send, receive and deliver events.

The reasons for separating receive events from delivery events are to enable us to talk about protocols that receive a message and do things to it, or delay it, before letting the application program see it. Not every message sent will necessarily be received, and not every message received will necessarily be delivered to the application; the former property depends upon the reliability characteristics of the network, and the latter upon the nature of the message.

Consider a process p with an event $snd(m)$ and a process q in which there is a corresponding event $rcv(m)$ for the same message m. Clearly, the sending of a message precedes its receipt. Thus, we can introduce an additional partial order that orders send and receive events for the same messages. Denote this communication ordering relation by $<_m$ so that we can write $snd_p(m) <_m rcv_q(m)$.

This leads to a definition of logical time in a distributed system as the transitive closure of the $<_p$ relations for the processes p that comprise the system and $<_m$. We will write $a \rightarrow b$ to denote the fact that a and b are ordered within this temporal relation, which is often called the potential causality relation for the system. In words, we will say that a happened before b. If neither $a \rightarrow b$ nor $b \rightarrow a$, we will say that a and b occur *concurrently*.

Potential causality is useful in many ways. First, it allows us to be precise when talking about the temporal properties of algorithms used in distributed systems—for example, when we have used phrasing such as "at a point in time" or "when" in relation to a distributed execution, it may not have been clear just what it means to talk about an instant in time that spans a set of processes composing the system. Certainly, the discussion at the start of this chapter, in which it was noted that clocks in a distributed system will not often be sufficiently synchronized to measure time, should have raised concerns about the concept of simultaneous events. An instant in time should correspond to a set of simultaneous events, one per process in the system, but the most obvious way of writing down such a set (namely, writing the state of each process as that process reaches some designated time) would not physically be realizable by any protocol we could implement as a part of such a system.

Consider, however, a set of concurrent events, one per process in a system. Such a set potentially represents an instantaneous snapshot of a distributed system, and even if the events did not occur at precisely the same instant in real time, there is no way to determine this from within the system, nor do we care. We will use the term *consistent cut* to refer to a set of events with this property (see Chandy and Lamport). A second term, *consistent snapshot*, is commonly used in the literature to refer to the full set of events that happen before or on a consistent cut; we won't make use of snapshots here, but readers who explore the topic in more detail will want to be aware of the concept, which is a bit like a checkpoint but includes all the processes in the system and the contents of all the communications channels between them. The messages in the channels of a snapshot will be those for which the snapshot contains a *snd* event but lacks a corresponding *rcv* event.

Figure 14.2 illustrates both the notion of causal time and also the concept of a consistent cut. With respect to potential causality, one can easily see that, for example, event a is prior (in a potentially causal sense) to events c and f, whereas events a and b are concurrent— even though b "looks" like it happens after a in the figure. The point is that, as just explained, no information could have reached b from a hence the ordering in this case is essentially arbitrary.

What about the various cuts shown in Figure 14.2? The gray cuts are inconsistent because they include message receive events but exclude the corresponding send events. The black cuts satisfy the consistency property. If one thinks about process execution timelines as if they were made of rubber, the black cuts correspond to possible distortions of the execution in which time never flows backward; the gray cuts correspond to distortions that violate this property.

If a program or a person were to look at the state of a distributed system along an inconsistent cut (i.e., by contacting the processes one by one to check each individual state and then assembling a picture of the system as a whole from the data obtained), the results

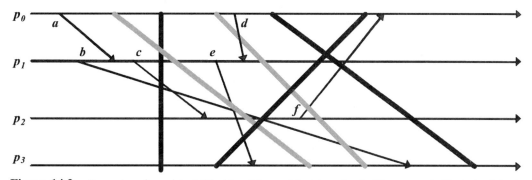

Figure 14.2. Examples of consistent (black) and inconsistent (gray) cuts. The gray cuts illustrate states in which a message receive event is included but the corresponding send event is omitted. Consistent cuts represent system states that could have occurred at a single instant in real time. Notice, however, that a consistent cut may not actually capture simultaneous states of the processes in question (i.e., a cut might be instantaneous in real time, but there are many consistent cuts that are not at all simultaneous) and that there may be many such cuts through a given point in the history of a process.

could be confusing and meaningless—for example, if a system manages some form of data using a lock, it could appear that multiple processes hold the lock simultaneously. To see this, imagine that process p holds the lock and then sends a message to process q in which it passes the lock to q. If our cut happened to show q after it received this message (and hence obtained the lock) but showed p before it sent it (and hence when it still held the lock), p and q would appear to both hold the lock. Yet in the real execution, this state never occurred. Were a developer trying to debug a distributed system, considerable time could be wasted in trying to sort out real bugs from these sorts of virtual bugs introduced as artifacts of the way the system state was collected!

The value of consistent cuts is that they represent states the distributed system might actually have been in at a single instant in real time. Of course, there is no way to know which of the feasible cuts for a given execution correspond to the actual real-time states through which the system passed, but Lamport's observation was that in a practical sense, to even ask this question reveals a basic misunderstanding of the nature of time in distributed systems. In his eyes, the consistent cuts for a distributed system are the *more meaningful* concept of simultaneous states for that system, while external time, being inaccessible within the system, is actually *less* meaningful. Lacking a practical way to make real-time clocks that are accurate to the resolution necessary to accurately timestamp events, he argued that real time is in fact not a very useful property for protocols that operate at this level. Of course, we can still use real time for other purposes that demand lesser degrees of accuracy, and will reintroduce it later, but for the time being, we accept this perspective. For a discussion about some uses of consistent cuts, see Babaoglu and Marzullo.

Potential causality is a useful tool for reasoning about a distributed system, but it also has more practical significance. There are several ways to build logical clocks with which causal relationships between events can be detected, to varying degrees of accuracy.

A very simple logical clock can be constructed by associating a counter with each process and message in the system. Let LT_p be the logical time for process p (the value of p's copy of this counter). Then when a message is sent, LT_p is copied into the message. We'll denote this by LT_m the logical time associated with message m (also called the logical timestamp of m). When m is delivered, or some other event occurs at a process p, the following rules are used to update LT_p.

1. If $LT_p < LT_m$, process p sets $LT_p = LT_m + 1$
2. If $LT_p \geq LT_m$, process p sets $LT_p = LT_p + 1$
3. For important events other than the reception of a message, process p sets $LT_p = LT_p + 1$

The application can decide what an "important" event is—in practice, it only makes sense to track the time of events if the application needs that temporal information for some other purpose, such as concurrency control in a transactional subsystem, or deciding how to order events in ways consistent with causality. For example, some algorithms for updating replicated data generate multicasts that can be delivered out of order, and it is important to put them into timestamp order before applying the updates so as to ensure that the replicate data item ends up with the correct value. Logical timestamps turn out to be a very compact way to label the multicasts so as to achieve this goal. Similarly, some algorithms for replicating a transactional service allow operations to occur concurrently, but need to know if there *might* have been a causal relation between two events, because when this occurs the former transaction will need to be serialized before the one that may have run later. Using logical timestamps, such algorithms are able to efficiently recognize such cases. We'll see additional uses for logical timestamps in the remainder of this chapter and in Chapters 15 through 18.

We will use the notation $LT(a)$ to denote the value of LT_p when event a occurred at process p. It can easily be shown that if $a \rightarrow b, LT(a) < LT(b)$: From the definition of the potential causality relation, we know that if $a \rightarrow b$, there must exist a chain of events $a \equiv e_0 \rightarrow e_1 \ldots \rightarrow e_k \equiv b$, where each pair is related either by the event ordering $<_p$ for some process p or by the event ordering $<_m$ on messages. By construction, the logical clock values associated with these events can only increase, establishing the desired result. On the other hand, $LT(a) < LT(b)$ does not imply that $a \rightarrow b$, since concurrent events may have arbitrary timestamps. This means that in the kinds of applications just mentioned, logical clocks may sometimes indicate a potential ordering relationship when none is present— and if such a situation could be costly, the developer might want a more accurate way of representing time that isn't misleading in this way.

For systems in which the set of processes is static, logical clocks can be generalized in a way that permits a more accurate representation of causality. A vector clock is a vector of counters, one per process in the set (see Fidge, Mattern, Schiper et al.). Similar to the concept of logical clocks, we will say that VT_p and VT_m represent the vector times associated with process p and message m, respectively. Given a vector time VT, the notation VT[p] denotes the entry in the vector corresponding to process p.

The rules for maintaining a vector clock are similar to the ones used for logical clocks, except that a process only increments its own counter. Specifically:

1.   Prior to performing an important event, process p sets $VT_p[p] = VT_p[p] + 1$
2.   When sending a message, process p sets $VT_m = VT_p$
3.   Upon delivering a message m, process p sets $VT_p = max(VT_p, VT_m)$

In the third situation, the function max applied to two vectors is just the element-by-element maximum of the respective entries. We now define two comparison operations on vector times. If $VT(a)$ and $VT(b)$ are vector times, we will say that $VT(a) \leq VT(b)$ *if* $\forall i$: $VT(a)[i] \leq VT(b)[i]$. When $VT(a) \leq VT(b)$ *and* $\exists i$: $VT(a)[i] < VT(b)[i]$, we will write $VT(a) < VT(b)$.

In words, a vector time entry for a process p is just a count of the number of events that have occurred at p. If process p has a vector clock with $Vt_p[q]$ set to six, and $p \neq q$, this means that some chain of events has caused p to hear (directly or indirectly) from process q subsequent to the sixth event that occurred at process q. Thus, the vector time for an event e tells us, for each process in the vector, how many events occurred at that process causally prior to when e occurred. If $VT(m) = [17, 2, 3]$, corresponding to processes $\{p, q, r\}$, we know that 17 events occurred at process p that causally precede the sending of m, two at process q, and three at process r.

It is easy to see that vector clocks accurately encode potential causality. If $a \rightarrow b$, then we again consider a chain of events related by the process or message ordering: $a \equiv e_0 \rightarrow e_1 \dots \rightarrow e_k \equiv b$. By construction, at each event the vector time can only increase (i.e., $VT(e_i) < VT(e_{i+1})$), because each process increments its own vector time entry prior to each operation, and receive operations compute an element-by-element maximum. Thus, $VT(a) < VT(b)$. However, unlike a logical clock, the converse also holds: If $VT(a) < VT(b)$, then $a \rightarrow b$. To see this, let p be the process at which event a occurred, and consider $VT(a)[p]$. In the case where b also occurs at process p, we know that $\forall i$: $VT(a)[i] \leq VT(b)[i]$—hence, if a and b are not the same event, a must happen before b at p. Otherwise, suppose that b occurs at process q. According to the algorithm, process q only changes $VT_q[p]$ upon delivery of some message m for which $VT(m)[p] > VT_q[p]$ at the event of the delivery. If we denote b as e_k and $deliv(m)$ as e_{k-1}, the send event for m as e_{k-2}, and the sender of m by q', we can now trace a chain of events back to a process q'' from which q' received this vector timestamp entry. Continuing this procedure, we will eventually reach process p. We will now have constructed a chain of events $a \equiv e_0 \rightarrow e_1 \dots \rightarrow e_k \equiv b$, establishing that $a \rightarrow b$, the desired result.

For example, referring back to Figure 14.2, if we follow the event chain denoted by a, b, c, e, each successive event increments one counter in the vector: a increments the counter associated with process p_0, and b, c, and e each increment the counter associated with process p_1. We'll be left with a $VT = [1, 3, 0, 0]$. After events a and d at process p_0, the vector timestamp at that process is [2,0,0,0]. And we can see that events d and e were concurrent by comparing these two vectors. Neither vector is less than the other, hence neither event preceded the other in a causal sense. In contrast, if we compare event a at process p_0 (which will have vector timestamp [1,0,0,0]) with event d (vector timestamp [1,3,0,0]), the latter timestamp is larger than the former, pointing to the existence of a causal path from a to d.

The key insight is that if two events are concurrent, there must be causal paths to each of them along which different vector timestamp entries will be incremented. Lacking a causal path from one to the other, neither can "learn" about the updates that occurred on the other's path. So each ends up with a vector timestamp that has some counters larger than in the other—counters for events along these disjoint parts of the causal histories. We see this when the vector timestamp associated with event d is compared with that of event e. In contrast, if an event occurred before some other event, the latter will have learned about all the counter increments that occurred up to the point that the earlier event took place. Since that time, some of these counters may have been incremented, but the resulting vector timestamp will always be recognizable as larger than the one for the earlier event. And this is the case if we compare the time at event e ([1,3,0,0]) with that at events a ([1,0,0,0]), b ([1,1,0,0]) or c ([1,2,0,0]).

This tells us that if we have a fixed set of processes and use vector timestamps to record the passage of time, we can accurately represent the potential causality relationship for messages sent and received, and other events, within that set. Doing so will also allow us to determine when events are concurrent: This is the case if neither $a \rightarrow b$ nor $b \rightarrow a$. For algorithms where we need temporal information but will pay a steep price if that information is inaccurate, vector timestamps can be a good choice. However, they also bring some costs of their own: the vectors are obviously larger than the single counter needed to implement a logical clock, and (as defined above), they only make sense for a system with static membership.

There has been considerable research on optimizing the encoding of vector timestamps, and the representation presented above is far from the best possible in a large system (see Charron–Bost). For a very large system, it is considered preferable to represent causal time using a set of event identifiers, $\{e_0, e_1, \dots e_k\}$ such that the events in the set are concurrent and causally precede the event being labeled (see Peterson [1987], Melliar–Smith and Moser [1993]). Thus if $a \rightarrow b, b \rightarrow d$ and $c \rightarrow d$ one could say that event d took place at causal time $\{b, c\}$ (meaning "after events b and c"), event b at time $\{a\}$, and so forth. In practice the identifiers used in such a representation would be process identifiers and event counters maintained on a per-process basis—hence, this *precedence-order* representation is recognizable as a compression of the vector timestamp. The precedence-order representation is useful in settings where processes can potentially construct the full $\rightarrow$ relation and in which the level of true concurrency is fairly low. The vector timestamp representation is preferred in settings where the number of participating processes is fairly low and the level of concurrency may be high.

As for the membership issue, there turn out to be several ways to work around this. One obvious option is to just list the process identifier associated with each counter in the vector itself. Thus, [1,3,0,0] in our previous example could be written as $[p_0 : 1, p_1 : 3]$, with zero entries omitted. We'll see another option in Chapter 16, when we introduce the idea of process groups that advance through a well-defined set of membership *views*. In that approach, we can associate a vector timestamp with a view; the list of members in the view then tells us which counter in the vector is associated with which process in the group.

Logical and vector clocks will prove to be powerful tools in developing protocols for use in real distributed applications. The method favored in a specific setting will typically depend upon the importance of precisely representing the potential causal order and on the overhead that can be tolerated. We'll use logical clocks when possible, because the overhead is tiny. Vector clocks are useful too, but their larger size can turn out to be a serious problem, for example in systems with large groups and very small messages, where the vector timestamp itself may be much larger than the data in a message.

The remainder of this chapter focuses on problems for which logical time, represented through some form of logical timestamp, represents the most natural temporal model. In many distributed applications, however, some concept of real time is also required, and our emphasis on logical time in this section should not be taken as dismissing the importance of other temporal schemes. Methods for synchronizing clocks and for working within the intrinsic limitations of such clocks are the subject of Chapter 23.

14.4 Failure Models and Reliability Goals

Any discussion of reliability is necessarily phrased with respect to the reliability threats of concern in the setting under study—for example, we may wish to design a system so that its components will automatically restart after crash failures, which is called the *recoverability problem*. Recoverability does not imply continuous availability of the system during the periods before a faulty component has been repaired. Moreover, the specification of a recoverability problem would need to say something about how components fail: through clean crashes, which never damage persistent storage associated with them; in other limited ways; in arbitrary ways, which can cause unrestricted damage to the data directly managed by the faulty component; and so forth. These are the sorts of problems typically addressed using variations on the transactional computing technologies introduced in Section 6.5, and to which we will return in Chapter 24.

A higher level of reliability may entail *continuous availability*, whereby the operational components of a system are guaranteed to continue providing correct, consistent behavior even in the presence of some limited number of component failures—for example, one might wish to design a system so that it will remain available provided that at most one failure occurs, under the assumption that failures are clean ones involving no incorrect actions by the failing component before its failure is detected and it shuts down. Similarly, one might want to guarantee reliability of a critical subsystem up to t failures involving arbitrary misbehavior by components of some type. The former problem would be much easier to solve, since the data available at operational components can be trusted; the latter would require a voting scheme in which data is trusted only when there is sufficient evidence as to their validity, so even if t arbitrary faults were to occur, the deduced value would still be correct.

Failure categories include the benign version, which would be an example of a *halting* failure, and the unrestricted version, which would fall into the *Byzantine* failure model mentioned in Section 14.1. An extremely benign (and in some ways not very realistic) model is the *fail-stop* model, in which machines fail by halting and the failures are *reported* to all surviving members by a notification service (the challenge, needless to say, is implementing a means for accurately detecting failures and turning them into a reporting mechanism that can be trusted not to make mistakes).

In the following sections, we will provide precise definitions of a small subset of the problems that one might wish to solve in a static membership environment subject to failures. This represents a rich area of study and any attempt to exhaustively treat the subject could easily fill a book. However, as noted at the outset, our primary focus in this book is to understand the most appropriate reliability model for realistic distributed systems. For a number of reasons, a dynamic membership model is more closely matched to the properties of typical distributed systems than the static one; even when a system uses a small hardware base that is relatively static, we will see that availability goals frequently make a dynamic membership model more appropriate for the application itself. Accordingly, we will confine ourselves here to a small number of particularly important problems and to a very restricted class of failure models.

14.5 The Distributed Commit Problem

The first step in our development of a good way to replicate data involves a classical problem that arises as a subproblem in several of the replication methods that follow. This is the *distributed commit problem*, which we briefly encountered earlier; now, however, we'll look at it carefully. Distributed commit arises in many settings where one wants to perform an operation in an all-or-nothing manner (see Gray [1979], Gray and Reuter). We're going to start by talking about commit in a static membership model, but in fact we'll later use the commit protocol as our way to *implement* the dynamic membership model. Then we'll use the resulting membership mechanisms to implement replicated data.

The commit problem arises when we wish to have a set of processes that all agree on whether or not to perform some action that may not be possible at some of the participants. To overcome this initial uncertainty, it is necessary to first determine whether or not all the participants will be able to perform the operation and then communicate the outcome of the decision to the participants in a reliable way (the assumption is that once a participant has confirmed that it can perform the operation, this remains true even if it subsequently crashes and must be restarted). We say that an operation can be *committed* if the participants can all perform it. Once a commit decision is reached, this requirement will hold even if some participants fail and later recover. On the other hand, if one or more participants are unable to perform the operation when initially queried, or some can't be contacted, the operation as a whole *aborts*, meaning that no participant should perform it.

Consider a system composed of a static set S containing processes $\{p_0, p_1, \ldots p_n\}$ that fail by crashing and that maintain both *volatile* data, which is lost if a crash occurs, and *persistent* data, which can be recovered after a crash in the same state they had at the time of the crash. An example of persistent data would be information in a disk file; volatile data is any information in a processor's memory, on some sort of a scratch area, that will not be preserved if the system crashes and must be rebooted. It is frequently much cheaper to store information in volatile data—hence, it would be common for a program to write intermediate results of a computation to volatile storage. The commit problem will now occur if we wish to arrange for all the volatile information to be saved persistently. The all-or-nothing aspects of the problem reflect the possibility that a computer might fail and lose the volatile data it held; in this case the desired outcome would be that no changes to *any* of the persistent storage areas occur.

As an example, we might want all of the processes in S to write some message into their persistent data storage. During the initial stages of the protocol, the message would be sent to the processes, which would each store it in their volatile memory. When the decision is made to try to commit these updates, the processes clearly cannot just modify the persistent area, because some process might fail before doing so. Consequently, the commit protocol involves first storing the volatile information into a persistent but temporary region of storage. Having done so, the participants would signal their ability to commit.

If all the participants are successful, it is safe to begin transfers from the temporary area to the real data storage region. Consequently, when these processes are later told that the operation as a whole should commit, they would copy their temporary copies of the message into a permanent part of the persistent storage area. If the operation aborts, they would not perform this copy operation. As should be evident, the challenge of the protocol will be to handle with the recovery of a participant from a failed state; in this situation, the protocol must determine whether any commit protocols were pending at the time of its failure and, if so, whether they terminated in a commit or an abort state.

A distributed commit protocol is normally initiated by a process that we will call the *coordinator;* assume that this is process p_0. In a formal sense, the objective of the protocol is for p_0 to solicit votes for or against a commit from the processes in S and then to send a *commit* message to those processes only if all of the votes are in favor of commit; otherwise an *abort* message is sent. To avoid a trivial solution in which p_0 always sends an abort, we would ideally like to require that if all processes vote for commit and no communication failures occur, the outcome should be commit. Unfortunately, however, it is easy to see that such a requirement is not really meaningful because communication failures can prevent messages from reaching the coordinator. Thus, we are forced to adopt a weaker nontriviality requirement that states that if all processes vote for commit and all the votes reach the coordinator, the protocol should commit.

For a researcher wearing a "theoretician's hat," this solves the problem by separating the obligations on the protocol from the whole question of how the network behaves. Practitioners often find such slight-of-hand annoying: all we've done is to shift any uncertainty into the network. However, one can reconcile these perspectives by recalling that our goal here is just to talk about protocol correctness—does the protocol do the right thing when the means of doing so are "placed in its hands"? A separate but equally important question is "will my network work well enough to ensure that the protocol functions in the desired manner?" Theoreticians rarely worry about that second question; practitioners will typically want to start with a correct protocol, and then take the step of engineering a network so that the overall probability that the system will be reliable satisfies some end-user objective. Thus, our non-triviality condition doesn't sweep the whole issue under the rug, it simply separates the issue into two aspects that can be attacked separately.

A commit protocol can be implemented in many ways. The most standard implementations are called two- and three-phase commit protocols, often abbreviated as 2PC and 3PC. In what follows, we'll focus on 2PC and 3PC, but the reader should keep in mind that the commit "pattern" is sometimes concealed in a protocol that doesn't actually use this specific style of message exchange. When faced with such a protocol—perhaps, a protocol that sends a token twice around a ring of processes, taking actions only on the second pass—it is often helpful to realize that if the protocol "could" have been implemented using a more standard 2PC or 3PC approach, then many of the insights one can have concerning 2PC or 3PC probably apply to that protocol as well. Indeed (to pursue the analogy a little further), if one implements point to point message passing over a token ring network device, what looks to the application like a 2PC protocol might look to the network like a token circulating among a ring of processes, on which varying sets of point to point messages are piggybacked. When confronting such a duality, we should again fall back by recalling our goals.

If the goal is basically theoretical—proving correctness, or proving an impossibility result—the implementation "details" may not matter. Such results often apply to any solution to a given problem and are independent of the way a particular solution operates. If our goals are more practical, we should think of the problem statement as laying out the requirements that any implementation needs to satisfy. Within the space of possible implementations, we can then use clever engineering to maximize performance, minimize cost, and achieve other objectives. The different goals of theoreticians and engineers can sometimes create tensions, but these tensions are rarely fundamental. More often, they reflect poor communication: the theory community sometimes neglects to point out that their problem statements matter far more than the implementation of a protocol they use to illustrate a general principle. And engineers sometimes forget that no matter how a protocol is implemented, the solution may need to live within deeper constraints imposed by the nature of the problem itself. We'll see several examples of this tension in the remainder of the book, including some that have provoked major debates which, seen from the perspective just outlined, turn out to be almost entirely the result of confusion and miscommunication!

14.5.1 Two-Phase Commit

A 2PC protocol operates in rounds of multicast communication. Each phase is composed of one round of messages to the participants and one round of replies from the recipients to the sender. The coordinator initially selects a unique identifier for this run of the protocol—for example, by concatenating its own process ID to the value of a logical clock. The protocol identifier will be used to distinguish the messages associated with different runs of the protocol that happen to execute concurrently, and in the remainder of this section we will assume that all the messages under discussion are labeled by this initial identifier.

The coordinator starts by sending out a first round of messages to the participants. These messages normally contain the protocol identifier, the list of participants (so that all the participants will know who the other participants are), and a message "type" indicating that this is the first round of a 2PC protocol. In a static system, where all the processes in the system participate in the 2PC protocol, the list of participants can be omitted because it has a well-known value. Additional fields can be added to this message depending on the situation in which the 2PC was needed—for example, it could contain a description of the action that the coordinator wishes to take (if this is not obvious to the participants), a reference to some volatile information that the coordinator wishes to have copied to a persistent data area, and so forth. 2PC is thus a very general tool, which can solve any of a number of specific problems sharing the attribute of needing an all-or-nothing outcome as well as the requirement that participants must be queried if they will be able to perform the operation before it is safe to assume that they can do so.

Each participant, upon receiving the first round message, takes such local actions as are needed to decide if it can vote in favor of commit—for example, a participant may need to set up some sort of persistent data structure, recording that the 2PC protocol is underway and saving the information that will be needed to perform the desired action if a commit occurs. In the previous example, the participant would copy its volatile data to the temporary persistent region of the disk and then force the records to the disk. Having done this (which may take some time), the participant sends back its vote. The coordinator collects votes, but also uses a timer to limit the duration of the first phase (the initial round of outgoing messages and the collection of replies). If a timeout occurs before the first-phase replies have all been collected, the coordinator aborts the protocol. Otherwise, it makes a commit or abort decision according to the votes it collects.[8]

Now we enter the second phase of the protocol, in which the coordinator sends out commit or abort messages in a new round of communication. Upon receipt of these messages, the participants take the desired action or, if the protocol is aborted, they delete the associated information from their persistent data stores. Figure 14.3 illustrates this basic skeleton of the 2PC protocol.

Several failure cases need to be addressed. The coordinator could fail before starting the protocol, during the first phase, while collecting replies, after collecting replies but before sending the second-phase messages, or during the transmission of the second-phase messages. The same is true for a participant. For each case we need to specify a recovery action, which will lead to successful termination of the protocol with the desired all-or-nothing semantics.

---

[8]As described, this protocol already violates the nontriviality goal that we expressed earlier. No timer is really safe in an asynchronous distributed system, because an adversary could just set the minimum message latency to the timer value plus one second, and, in this way cause the protocol to abort despite the fact that all processes vote commit and all messages will reach the coordinator. Concerns such as this can seem unreasonably narrow-minded, but are actually important in trying to pin down the precise conditions under which commit is possible. The practical community tends to be fairly relaxed about such issues, while the theory community takes problems of this sort very seriously. It is regrettable but perhaps inevitable that some degree of misunderstanding results from these different points of view.

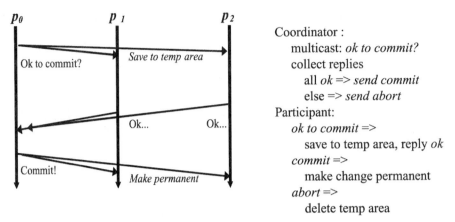

Figure 14.3. Skeleton of two-phase commit protocol.

In addition to this, the protocol described above omits consideration of the storage of information associated with the run. In particular, it seems clear that the coordinator and participants should not need to keep any form of information indefinitely in a correctly specified protocol. Our protocol makes use of a protocol identifier, and we will see that the recovery mechanisms require that some information be saved for a period of time, indexed by protocol identifier. Thus, rules will be needed for garbage collection of information associated with terminated 2PC protocols. Otherwise, the information base in which these data is stored might grow without limit, ultimately posing serious storage and management problems.

We start by focusing on participant failures, then turn to the issue of coordinator failure, and finally discuss the question of garbage collection.

Suppose that a process p_i fails during the execution of a 2PC protocol. With regard to the protocol, p_i may be in any of several states. In its initial state, p_i will be unaware of the protocol. In this case, p_i will not receive the initial vote message; therefore, the coordinator aborts the protocol. The initial state ends when p_i has received the initial vote request and is prepared to send back a vote in favor of commit (if p_i doesn't vote for commit, or isn't yet prepared, the protocol will abort in any case). We will now say that p_i *is prepared to commit*. In the prepared to commit state, p_i is compelled to learn the outcome of the protocol even if it fails and later recovers. This is an important observation because the applications that use 2PC often must lock critical resources or limit processing of new requests by p_i while they are prepared to commit. This means that until p_i learns the outcome of the request, it may be unavailable for other types of processing. Such a state can result in denial of services. The next state entered by p_i is called the *commit* or *abort* state, in which it knows the outcome of the protocol. Failures that occur at this stage must not be allowed to disrupt the termination actions of p_i, such as the release of any resources that were tied up during the prepared state. Finally, p_i returns to its initial state, garbage collects all information associated with the execution of the protocol, and is left in a state that retains only the effects of any committed actions.

From this discussion, we see that a process recovering from a failure will need to determine whether or not it was in a prepared to commit, commit, or abort state at the moment of the failure. In a prepared to commit state, the process will need to find out whether the 2PC protocol terminated in a commit or abort, so there must be some form of system service or protocol outcome file in which this information is logged. Having entered a commit or abort state, the process needs a way to complete the commit or abort action even if it is repeatedly disrupted by failures in the act of doing so. We say that the action must be *idempotent*, meaning that it can be performed repeatedly without ill effects. An example of an idempotent action would be copying a file from one location to another: Provided that access to the target file is disallowed until the copying action completes, the process can copy the file once or many times with the same outcome. In particular, if a failure disrupts the copying action, it can be restarted after the process recovers.

Not surprisingly, many systems that use 2PC are structured to take advantage of this type of file copying. In the most common approach, information needed to perform the commit or abort action is saved in a *log* on the persistent storage area. The commit or abort state is represented by a bit in a table, also stored in the persistent area, describing pending 2PC protocols and indexed by protocol identifier. Upon recovery, a process first consults this table to determine the actions it should take, and then uses the log to carry out the action. Only after successfully completing the action does a process delete its knowledge of the protocol and garbage collect the log records that were needed to carry it out. (See Figure 14.4.)

Up to now, we have not considered coordinator failure—hence, it would be reasonable to assume that the coordinator itself plays the role of tracking the protocol outcome and saving this information until all participants are known to have completed their commit or abort actions. The 2PC protocol thus needs a final phase in which messages flow back from participants to the coordinator, which must retain information about the protocol until all such messages have been received.

Coordinator:	Participant:
multicast: *ok to commit?*	*ok to commit =>*
collect replies	save to temp area, reply *ok*
all *ok =>log "commit" to "outcomes" table*	*commit =>*
send commit	make change permanent
else *=>send abort*	*abort =>*
collect acknowledgments	delete temp area
garbage-collect protocol outcome information	After failure:
	for each pending protocol
	contact coordinator to learn outcome

Figure 14.4. 2PC extended to handle participant failures.

Consider next the case where the coordinator fails during a 2PC protocol. If we are willing to wait for the coordinator to recover, the protocol requires a few changes to deal with this situation. The first change is to modify the coordinator to save its commit decision to persistent storage *before* sending commit or abort messages to the participants.[9] Upon recovery, the coordinator is now guaranteed to have available the information needed to terminate the protocol, which it can do by simply retransmitting the final commit or abort message. A participant not in the precommit state would acknowledge such a message but take no action; a participant waiting in the precommit state would terminate the protocol upon receipt of it.

One major problem with this solution to 2PC is that if a coordinator failure occurs, the participants are blocked, waiting for the coordinator to recover. As noted earlier, preparing to commit often ties down resources or involves holding locks—hence, blocking in this manner can have serious implications for system availability. (See Figure 14.4) Suppose that we permit the participants to communicate among themselves. Could we increase the availability of the system so as to guarantee progress even if the coordinator crashes?

Again, there are three stages of the protocol to consider. If the coordinator crashes during its first phase of message transmissions, a state may result in which some participants are prepared to commit, others may be unable to commit (they have voted to abort and know that the protocol will eventually do so), and still other processes may not know anything at all about the state of the protocol. If it crashes during its decision, or before sending out all the second-phase messages, there may be a mixture of processes left in the prepared state and processes that know the final outcome.

Suppose that we add a timeout mechanism to the participants: In the prepared state, a participant that does not learn the outcome of the protocol within some specified period of time will timeout and seek to complete the protocol on its own. Clearly, there will be some unavoidable risk of a timeout occurring because of a transient network failure, much as in the case of RPC failure-detection mechanisms discussed early in the book. Thus, a participant that takes over in this case cannot safely conclude that the coordinator has actually failed. Indeed, any mechanism for takeover will need to work even if the timeout is set to 0 and even if the participants try to run the protocol to completion starting from the instant that they receive the phase-one message and enter a prepared to commit state!

---

[9]It is actually sufficient for the coordinator to save only commit decisions in persistent storage—this is called the "presumed abort" approach. After failure, a recovering coordinator can safely presume the protocol to have aborted if it finds no commit record; the advantage of such a change is to make the abort case less costly, by removing a disk I/O operation from the critical path before the abort can be acted upon. The elimination of a single disk I/O operation may seem like a minor optimization, but in fact can be quite significant in light of the tenfold latency difference between a typical disk I/O operation (10–25 ms) and a typical network communication operation (perhaps 1–4 ms latency). One doesn't often have an opportunity to obtain an order of magnitude performance improvement in a critical path—hence, these are the sorts of engineering decisions that can have very important implications for overall system performance. Similarly, it is possible to architect systems to "presume commit" and only log abort decisions. If aborts are very rare this can be a good option, although doing so imposes a continuous low-level of costs that can turn out to dominate the cost savings associated with the "trick."

Accordingly, let p_i be some process that has experienced a protocol timeout in the prepared to commit state. What are p_i's options? The most obvious would be for it to send out a first-phase message of its own, querying the state of the other p_j. From the information gathered in this phase, p_i may be able to deduce that the protocol either committed or aborted. This would be the case if, for example, some process p_j had received a second-phase outcome message from the coordinator before it crashed. Having determined the outcome, p_i can simply repeat the second phase of the original protocol. Although participants may receive as many as n copies of the outcome message (if all the participants time out simultaneously), this is clearly a safe way to terminate the protocol.

On the other hand, it is also possible that p_i would be unable to determine the outcome of the protocol. This would occur, for example, if all processes contacted by p_i, as well as p_i itself, were in the prepared state, with a single exception: process p_j, which does not respond to the inquiry message. Perhaps p_j has failed, or perhaps the network is temporarily partitioned. The problem now is that only the coordinator and p_j can determine the outcome, which depends entirely on p_j's vote. If the coordinator is itself a participant, as is often the case, a single failure can thus leave the 2PC participants blocked until the failure is repaired! This risk is unavoidable in a 2PC solution to the commit problem. (See Figure 14.5.)

Earlier, we discussed the garbage collection issue. Notice that in this extension to 2PC, participants must retain information about the outcome of the protocol until they are certain that all participants know the outcome. Otherwise, if a participant p_j were to commit but promptly forget that it had done so, it would be unable to assist some other participant p_i in terminating the protocol after a coordinator failure.

Garbage collection can be done by adding a third phase of messages from the coordinator (or a participant who takes over from the coordinator) to the participants. This phase would start after all participants have acknowledged receipt of the second-phase commit or abort message, and it would simply tell participants that it is safe to garbage collect the protocol

Coordinator:	Participant: first time message received
multicast: *ok to commit?*	*ok to commit* =>
collect replies	save to temp area, reply *ok*
all *ok* =>*log commit to outcomes table*	*commit* =>
wait until safe on persistent store	make change permanent
send commit	*abort* =>
else =>*send abort*	delete temp area
collect acknowledgements	Message is a duplicate (recovering coordinator)
garbage-collect protocol outcome information	*send acknowledgment*
After failure:	After failure:
for each pending protocol in outcomes table	*for each pending protocol*
send outcome (commit or abort)	contact coordinator to learn outcome
wait for acknowledgements	
garbage collect outcome information	

Figure 14.5.   2PC protocol extended to overcome coordinator failures.

information. The handling of coordinator failure can be similar to that during the pending state. A timer is set in each participant that has entered the final state but not yet seen the garbage collection message. Should the timer expire, such a participant can simply echo the commit or abort message, which all other participants acknowledge. Once all participants have acknowledged the message, a garbage collection message can be sent out and the protocol state safely garbage collected.

Notice that the final round of communication, for purposes of garbage collection, can often be delayed for a period of time and then run once in a while, on behalf of many 2PC protocols at the same time. When this is done, the garbage collection protocol is itself best viewed as a 2PC protocol that executes perhaps once per hour. During its first round, a garbage collection protocol would solicit from each process in the system the set of protocols for which they have reached the final state. It is not difficult to see that if communication is first in, first out (FIFO) in the system, then 2PC protocols—even if failures occur—will complete in FIFO order. This being the case, each process need only provide a single protocol identifier, per protocol coordinator, in response to such an inquiry: the identifier of the last 2PC initiated by the coordinator to have reached its final state. The process running the garbage collection protocol can then compute the minimum over these values. For each coordinator, the minimum will be a 2PC protocol identifier, which has fully terminated at all the participant processes that can be garbage collected throughout the system.

We now arrive at the final version of the 2PC protocol shown in Figure 14.6. Notice that this protocol has a potential message complexity which increases as $O(n^2)$ with the

Coordinator:	Participant: first time message received
multicast: *ok to commit?*	*ok to commit =>*
collect replies	save to temp area, reply *ok*
all *ok =>log commit to outcomes table*	*commit =>*
wait until safe on persistent store	log outcome, make change permanent
send commit	*abort =>*
else *=>send abort*	log outcome, delete temp area
collect acknowledgements	Message is a duplicate (recovering coordinator)
	send acknowledgment
After failure:	After failure:
for each pending protocol in outcomes table	*for each pending protocol*
send outcome (commit or abort)	contact coordinator to learn outcome
wait for acknowledgements	After timeout in *prepare to commit* state:
Periodically:	query other participants about state
query each process: *terminated protocols?*	outcome can be deduced =>
for each coordinator: determine *fully*	*run coordinator-recovery protocol*
terminated protocols	outcome uncertain =>
2PC to garbage collect outcomes information	*must wait*

Figure 14.6. Final version of 2PC commit: Participants attempt to terminate protocol without blocking periodic 2PC protocol used to garbage collect outcome information saved by participants and coordinators for recovery.

worst case occurring if a network communication problem disrupts communication during the three basic stages of communication. Further, notice that although the protocol is commonly called a two phase commit, a true two-phase version will always block if the coordinator fails. The version of Figure 14.6 gains a higher degree of availability at the cost of additional communication for purposes of garbage collection. However, although this protocol may be more available than our initial attempt, it can still block if a failure occurs at a critical stage. In particular, participants will be unable to terminate the protocol if a failure of both the coordinator and a participant occurs during the decision stage of the protocol.

14.5.2 Three-Phase Commit

In 1981, Skeen and Stonebraker studied the cases in which 2PC can block (see Skeen [June 1982]). Their work resulted in a protocol called *three-phase commit* (3PC), which is guaranteed to be nonblocking provided that only fail-stop failures occur. (A subsequent generalization by Keidar and Dolev weakens this requirement, making progress whenever a connected majority of processes is achieved). Before we present this protocol, it is important to stress that the fail-stop model is not a very realistic one: This model requires that processes fail only by crashing, and that such failures *be accurately detectable* by other processes that remain operational. As we will see, inaccurate failure detections and network partition failures continue to pose the threat of blocking in this protocol. In practice, these considerations limit the utility of the protocol (because we lack a way to accurately sense failures in most systems, and network partitions are a real threat in most distributed environments). Nonetheless, the protocol sheds light both on the issue of blocking and on the broader concept of consistency in distributed systems; therefore, it is presented here.

As in the case of the 2PC protocol, 3PC really requires a fourth phase of messages for purposes of garbage collection. However, this problem is easily solved using the same method presented in Figure 14.6 for the case of 2PC. For brevity, we focus on the basic 3PC protocol and overlook the garbage collection issue.

Recall that 2PC blocks under conditions in which the coordinator crashes and one or more participants crash, such that the operational participants are unable to deduce the protocol outcome without information that is only available to the coordinator and/or these participants. The fundamental problem is that in a 2PC protocol, the coordinator can make a commit or abort decision, which would be known to some participant p_j and even acted upon by p_j, would be totally unknown to other processes in the system. The 3PC protocol prevents this from occurring by introducing an additional round of communication and delaying the prepared state until processes receive this phase of messages. By doing so, the protocol ensures that the state of the system can always be deduced by a subset of the operational processes, provided that the operational processes can still communicate reliably among themselves.

A typical 3PC protocol operates as shown in Figure 14.7. As in the case of 2PC, the first-round message solicits votes from the participants. However, instead of entering a

Coordinator:	Participant: logs state on each message
multicast: *ok to commit?*	*ok to commit* =>
collect replies	save to temp area, reply *ok*
all *ok* =>*log precommit*	*precommit* =>
send precommit	enter precommit state, *acknowledge*
else =>*send abort*	*commit* =>
collect acks from non-failed participants	make change permanent
all *ack* =>*log commit*	*abort* =>
send commit	delete temp area
collect acknowledgements	After failure:
garbage-collect protocol outcome information	collect participant state information
	all *precommit, or any committed* =>
	push forward to commit
	else =>
	push back to abort

Figure 14.7. Outline of a three-phase commit protocol.

prepared state, a participant that has voted for commit enters an *ok to commit* state. The coordinator collects votes and can immediately abort the protocol if some votes are negative or if some votes are missing. Unlike for a 2PC, it does not immediately commit if the outcome is unanimously positive. Instead, the coordinator sends out a round of *prepare to commit* messages, receipt of which causes all participants to enter the prepare to commit state and to send an acknowledgment. After receiving acknowledgements from all participants, the coordinator sends *commit* messages and the participants commit. Notice that the *ok to commit* state is similar to the *prepared* state in the 2PC protocol, in that a participant is expected to remain capable of committing even if failures and recoveries occur after it has entered this state.

If the coordinator of a 3PC protocol detects failures of some participants (recall that in this model, failures are accurately detectable) and has not yet received their acknowledgements to its *prepare to commit* messages, the 3PC can still be committed. In this case, the unresponsive participants can be counted upon to run a recovery protocol when the cause of their failure is repaired, and that protocol will lead them to eventually commit. The protocol thus has the property of only committing if all operational participants are in the *prepared to commit* state. This observation permits any subset of operational participants to terminate the protocol safely after a crash of the coordinator and/or other participants.

The 3PC termination protocol is similar to the 2PC protocol, and it starts by querying the state of the participants. If any participant knows the outcome of the protocol (commit or abort), the protocol can be terminated by disseminating that outcome. If the participants are all in a prepared to commit state, the protocol can safely be committed.

Suppose, however, that some mixture of states is found in the state vector. In this situation, the participating processes have the choice of driving the protocol forward to a commit or back to an abort. This is done by rounds of message exchange that either move the full set of participants to *prepared to commit* and then to *commit* or that roll them back to *ok to commit* and then abort. Again, because of the fail-stop assumption, this algorithm runs no risk of errors. Indeed, the processes have a simple and natural way to select a new coordinator at their disposal: Since the system membership is assumed to be static, and since failures are detectable crashes (the fail-stop assumption), the operational process with the lowest process identifier can be assigned this responsibility. It will eventually recognize the situation and will then take over, running the protocol to completion.

Notice also that even if additional failures occur, the requirement that the protocol only commit once and that all operational processes are in a *prepared to commit* state and only abort when all operational processes have reached an *ok to commit* state (also called *prepared to abort*) eliminates many possible concerns. However, this is true only because failures are accurately detectable and because processes that fail will always run a recovery

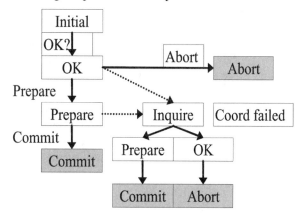

Figure 14.8. States for a nonfaulty participant in 3PC protocol.

protocol upon restarting. (The "inquire" state in Figure 14.8.)

It is not hard to see how this recovery protocol should work. A recovering process is compelled to track down some operational process that knows the outcome of the protocol, and to learn the outcome from that process. If all processes fail, the recovering process must identify the subset of processes that were the last to fail (see Skeen [1985]), learning the protocol outcome from them. In the case where the protocol had not reached a commit or abort decision when all processes failed, it can be resumed using the states of the participants that were the last to fail, together with any other participants that have recovered in the interim.

Unfortunately, however, the news for 3PC is actually not quite as good as this protocol may make it seem, because real systems do not satisfy the fail-stop failure assumption. Although there may be some specific conditions under which failures are detectable by crashes, these most often depend upon special hardware. In a typical network, failures are only detectable using timeouts, and the same imprecision that makes reliable computing difficult over RPC and streams also limits the failure-handling ability of the 3PC.

The problem that occurs is most easily understood by considering a network partitioning scenario, in which two groups of participating processes are independently operational and trying to terminate the protocol. One group may see a state that is entirely *prepared to commit* and would want to terminate the protocol by commit. The other, however, could see a state that is entirely *ok to commit* and would consider abort to be the only safe outcome: After all, perhaps some unreachable process voted against commit! Clearly, 3PC will be unable to make progress in settings where partition failures can occur. We will return to this issue in Section 15.2, when we discuss a basic result by Fisher, Lynch, and Paterson; the inability to terminate a 3PC protocol in settings that don't satisfy fail-stop failure assumptions is one of many manifestations of the so-called "FLP impossibility result" (see Fisher et al., Ricciardi [1996]). For the moment, though, we find ourselves in the uncomfortable position of having a solution to a problem that is similar to, but not quite identical to, the one that occurs in real systems. One consequence of this is that few systems make use of 3PC commit protocols today: Given a situation in which 3PC is less likely to block than 2PC, but may nonetheless block when certain classes of failures occur, the extra cost of the 3PC is not generally seen as bringing a return commensurate with its cost.

Keidar and Dolev at Technion University and Hebrew University, respectfully, did some interesting work with 3PC in 1995 that illustrates a point made earlier: the theoretical structure of a problem and the engineering of a protocol sometimes lead to very different insights. In this effort, the researchers asked how one should build systems that may need to tolerate very long communication outages—extended "partitioning" events. To make the problem as interesting as possible, they focused on the most extreme scenario possible: now and then a pair of processes managed to communicate, but the system was otherwise partitioned. Thus there were never any opportunities for a majority to communicate all at the same time. On the other hand, the group eliminated the notion of communication timeout: processes were either able to communicate, or unable to "reach" one-another. Failures look like long periods of unreachability in this model.

The group was able to show that one can "simulate" a 3PC protocol by piggybacking information on messages exchanged during the brief periods when processes manage to reach one-another, and furthermore that doing so is the optimal availability strategy for replicating data under these extreme conditions. They also showed that relatively little data actually needs to be carried in the messages to accomplish this objective. Up to the present, this work has been of largely academic value. However, with the increasing interest in mobility and widespread use of ad-hoc network routing protocols, one can easily imagine situations in which a "nearly always partitioned" model for data replication could become important in a practical sense, and the Dolev, Keidar and Chockler implementation of 3PC would then be an obvious choice.

14.5.3 Quorum update revisited

Recall the discussion of quorum updates from the start of this chapter. The "actual" algorithm uses 2PC, as seen in Figure 14.9. In the example shown in the figure, we have a group with three members, and the quorum size is set to two for both reads and writes.[10] The read is

---

[10]We've illustrated a scenario in which the read and update protocols optimistically assume that their targets are healthy and will respond. In practice, however, lacking knowledge of the states of the processes in the service, a quorum system might need to send additional messages simply to maximize the likelihood of reaching a quorum of healthy group members. This, of course, makes the protocol even more costly.

done as a one-phase algorithm, collecting values and version numbers from two replicas, picking the correct version, and returning that to the application. The update, in contrast, is done as a read followed by a 2-phase commit protocol— not 3-phase commit, since we don't have an accurate way to detect failures, so the extra phase won't bring any significant benefit. Instead, the first phase proposes a new value,

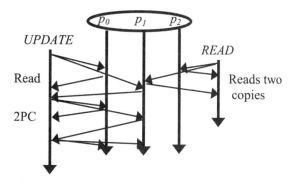

Figure 14.9. Quorum update algorithm uses a quorum read followed by a 2PC protocol for updates.

and the second phase commits or aborts depending on the success of the first. A failed process would need to track down the outcome of any pending commit protocol before it could resume actions in a system built this way, presumably by contacting some form of logging service or some process that has been up long enough to know the status of past updates.

14.6 Related Reading

On logical concepts of time: (see Lamport [July 1978, 1984]).

Causal ordering in message delivery: (see Birman and Joseph [February 1987, November 1987]).

Consistent cuts: (see Babaoglu and Marzullo, Chandy and Lamport).

Vector clocks: (see Fidge, Mattern).

Vector clocks used in message delivery: (see Birman et al., [1992], Schiper et al.).

Optimizing vector clock representations: (see Charron-Bost, Melliar-Smith and Moser [1993]).

Compression using topological information about groups of processes: (see Birman et al. [1991], Rodrigues and Verissimo, Rodrigues et al.).

Static groups and quorum replication: (see Bernstein et al., Birman and Joseph [November 1987], Cooper [1985]).

Two-phase commit: (see Bernstein et al., Gray [1979], Gray and Reuter).

Three-phase commit: (see Skeen [June 1982, 1985]).

Method of Keidar and Dolev: (see Keidar and Dolev 1995, 2000).

15

Dynamic Membership

15.1 Dynamic Group Membership

We now have the tools to develop the dynamic membership tracking service, and ultimately to build the desired high speed data replication protocols. The basic elements of the dynamic membership model are as follows. The system is initialized by starting some set of processes, perhaps by hand or on a pool of servers that have been specially designated by the system administrator—an initial bootstrapping step. For the remainder of the lifetime of the system, new processes are started and *join* the system, while active processes *leave* the system when they terminate, fail, or simply chose to disconnect themselves. Of course, a dynamic membership model doesn't preclude having some static set of resources that play special roles; the basic idea is that the majority of the processes in the system can come and go as they like.

Notice that membership really involves dealing with two related problems. The GMS service itself needs to track its own membership, because it won't otherwise be able to provide consistent responses to applications using it. So, we need a protocol by which GMS servers talk to one-another. The second problem is that GMS servers need to track the states of other (non-GMS) processes in the system. They will use this monitoring mechanism to update their list of system members, and to report events back out to processes in the system as a whole. We end up with a 2-tier architecture.

As a slight digression, notice that even a static system can be treated as a special case of the dynamic membership model. For example, consider a cluster-style data center in which an instance of some database application is to be launched on every node. A static system model may seem to be a good match for such a clustered architecture, but we've seen that it brings high costs. We can just as easily adopt the view that the processes comprising the database application are launched dynamically (when the corresponding node is booted), and that they form a dynamic group whose members "own" the local database stores on their respective computers. This approach will turn out to have important benefits if the database system needs to use replicated data. Thus, our broad approach is to add a group membership service to the system, using the protocol developed below to implement it. Then we can layer groups of various kinds "over" the GMS-supported abstractions, including groups that have special relationships to various kinds of hardware.

15.1.1 GMS and Other System Processes

The interface between the GMS and other system processes provides three operations, shown in Table 15.1, and further illustrated by Figure 15.1. The *join* operation is invoked by a process that wishes to become a system member. The *monitor* operation is used by a process to register its interest in the status of some other process; should that process be dropped from the membership, a callback will occur to notify it of the event. Such a callback is treated as the equivalent of a failure notification in the fail-stop computing model: The process is considered to have crashed, all communication links with it are severed, and messages subsequently received from it are rejected. Finally, the *leave* operation is used by a process that wishes to disconnect itself from the system, or by some other system component that has detected a fault and wishes to signal that a particular process has failed. We assume throughout this section that failure detections are inaccurate in the sense that

Table 15.1. GMS Operations

Operation	Function	Failure handling
Join (process-ID, callback) returns (time, GMS list)	Calling process is added to membership list of system, returns logical time of the join event and a list giving the membership of the GMS service. The callback function is invoked whenever the core membership of the GMS changes.	Idempotent: can be reissued to any GMS process with same outcome
leave (process-ID) returns void	Can be issued by any member of the system. GMS drops the specified process from the membership list and issues notification to all members of the system. If the process in question is really operational, it must rejoin under a new process-ID.	Idempotent: fails only if the GMS process that was the target is dropped from the GMS membership list
monitor (process-ID, callback) Returns callback-ID	Can be issued by any member of the system. GMS registers a callback and will invoke callback (process-ID) later if the designated process fails.	Idempotent: as for *leave*

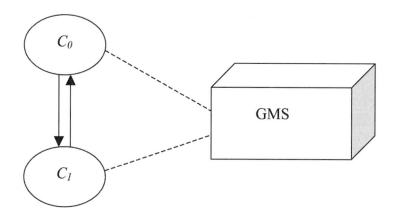

Figure 15.1.   In a system with a GMS, clients (c_0 and c_1) don't monitor one-another's health directly. Instead, they are monitored by the GMS, and trust the GMS to notify them if a counterpart fails. This ensures that members of the system will react in a consistent manner when a failure occurs. We can now separate concerns: one challenge is to build a highly available GMS, and a separate one is to implement the protocols by which clients cooperate, i.e., to replicate data or synchronize actions.

they may result from partitioning of the network, but are otherwise of sufficiently good quality as to rarely exclude an operational process as faulty.

The GMS itself will need to be highly available—hence, it will typically be implemented by a set of processes that cooperate to implement the GMS abstraction. Although these processes would normally reside on a statically defined set of server computers, so that they can readily be located by a process wishing to join the system, the actual composition of the group may vary over time due to failures within the GMS service itself, and one can imagine other ways of tracking down representatives (files, name services, the use of hardware broadcast to poll for a member, etc.). Notice that in order to implement the GMS abstraction on behalf of the rest of the system, a GMS server needs to solve the GMS problem on its own behalf. We will say that it uses a *group membership protocol*, or GMP, for this purpose. Thus, the GMP deals with the membership of a small service, the GMS, which the rest of the system (a potentially large set of processes) employs to track the composition of the system as a whole.

Similar to the situation for other system processes that don't comprise the GMS, the GMP problem is defined in terms of *join* and *leave* events; the latter being triggered by the inability of the GMS processes to communicate with one another. Clearly, such an environment creates the threat of a partitioning failure, in which a single GMS might split into multiple GMS sub-instances, each of which considers the other to be faulty. What should our goals be when such a partitioned scenario occurs?

Suppose that our distributed system is being used in a setting such as air traffic control. If the output of the GMS is treated as being the logical equivalent of a failure notification, one would expect the system to reconfigure itself after such notification to restore full air traffic control support within the remaining set of processes. If some component of the air traffic control system is responsible for advising controllers about the status of sectors of the airspace (free or occupied), and the associated process fails, the air traffic system would probably restart it by launching a new status manager process.

Now, a GMS partition would be the likely consequence of a network partition, raising the prospect that two air traffic sector services could find themselves simultaneously active, both trying to control access to the same portions of the airspace, and neither aware of the other! Such an inconsistency would have disastrous consequences. While the partitioning of the GMS might be permissible, it is clear that at most one of the resulting GMS components should be permitted to initiate new actions.

From this example we see that although one might want to allow a system to remain operational during partitioning of the GMS, we also need a way to pick one component of the overall system as the primary one, within which authoritative decisions can be taken on behalf of the system as a whole (see Malkhi, Ricciardi [1993]). Nonprimary components might report information on the basis of their state as of the time when a partitioning occurred, but would not permit potentially conflicting actions (such as routing a plane into an apparently free sector of airspace) to be initiated. Such an approach clearly generalizes: One can imagine a system in which some applications would be considered primary within a component considered nonprimary for other purposes. Moreover, there may be classes of actions that are safe even within a nonprimary component; an example would be the reallocation of air traffic within sectors of the air traffic service already owned by the partition at the time the network failed. But it is clear that any GMP solution should at least track the primary component, so that actions can be appropriately limited.

The key properties of the primary component of the GMS are that its membership should overlap with the membership of a previous primary component of the GMS and that there should only be one primary component of the GMS within any partitioning of the GMS as a whole. As for the clients of the GMS, they inherit the "primaryness" property of the GMS server to which they are connected. Thus, a client connected to a GMS server in the primary component is also in the primary component, and a client connected to a GMS server that has lost contact with the primary component is itself a non-primary client (even if the vast majority of clients end up in this unhappy state).

In the beginning of this chapter, we discussed concepts of time in distributed settings. In defining the primary component of a partitioned GMS we used temporal terms without making it clear exactly what form of time was intended. In the following text, we have *logical* time in mind. In particular, suppose that process p is a member of the primary component of the GMS, but then suddenly becomes partitioned away from the remainder of the GMS, executing for an arbitrarily long period of time without sending or receiving any additional messages and finally shutting down. From the discussion up to now, it is clear that we would want the GMS to reconfigure itself to exclude p, if possible, forming a new primary GMS component, which can permit further progress in the system as a whole. But now the question occurs as to whether or not p would be aware that this has happened. If not, p might consider itself a member of the previous primary component of the GMS, and we would now have two primary components of the GMS active simultaneously.

There are two ways in which we could respond to this issue. The first involves a limited introduction of time into the model. Where clocks are available, it would be useful to have a mechanism whereby any process that ceases to be a member of the primary component of a partitioned GMS can detect this situation within a bounded period of time—for example, it would be helpful to know that within two seconds of being excluded from the GMS, p knows that it is no longer a member of the primary component. If clocks are synchronized, a process that is taking over some role would be able to delay its first action long enough to ensure that the process that previously had the role has become quiescent. For example, in an air traffic application, if process a was responsible for decisions about air-traffic sector S, and now b is informed that a has either failed or become partitioned away from the primary component, b could delay for an appropriate amount of time. During this period, we would know that a will experience a "loss of connectivity" timeout. By the time that b takes over a's role, any controller still in contact with a will be told that a has lost contact with the primary component of the system. The controller could then shift to some other, operational, machine and would find him or herself in contact with b. Notice that there would never be a point in real time where there are two processes claiming to be in control of S.

The second option involves designing our system so that if a partition does form, any process taking over some role will be able to duplicate the actions of the process that became partitioned away. In this second approach, b takes over the role of a but does so with accurate knowledge of the actions a might have taken prior to losing connectivity to the primary partition. In practice, this involves fully replicating the information a will use within the group before taking any action based on that information.

The two approaches can be combined, and for an application as "mission critical" as air traffic control, normally would be. One would arrive at a system in which, if a process fails, no process takes over from it until the failed (or disconnected) process has quiesced, and moreover, a process taking over from some other process also can reproduce the last actions taken by its quiescent counterpart prior to crashing or becoming disconnected. Of course, this is a costly approach, because every update to the group state needs to be registered with every group member before any action can be taken on the basis of that update. The delay while waiting for acknowledgements that everyone has seen the update will reduce the rate of updates we can do substantially. On the other hand, we'll still be able to operate a small group at a rate of perhaps a few tens or even hundreds of events per second, and for an application like air traffic control, this may be adequate.

In addition to these considerations, we will need a way to capture the sense in which it is legal for p to lag the GMS in this manner, albeit for a limited period of time. Notice that because we wish to require that primary components of the GMS have overlapping membership, if we are given two different membership lists for the GMS, a and b, either $a \rightarrow b$, or $b \rightarrow a$. Thus, rather than say that there should be at most one primary component of the GMS active simultaneously, we will say that any two concurrently active membership lists for the GMS (in the sense that each is considered current by some process) should be ordered by causality. Equivalently, we could now say that there is at most a single sequence of GMS membership lists that is considered to represent the primary component of the

GMS. We will use the term "view" of the GMS membership to denote the value of the membership list that holds for a given process within the GMS at a specified point in its execution.

If the GMS can experience a partitioning failure, it can also experience the *merging* of partitions (see Amir et al.[1992], Malkhi, Moser et al. [1994]). The GMP should therefore include a merge protocol. Finally, if all the members of the GMS fail, or if the primary partition is somehow lost, the GMP should provide for a restart from complete failure or for identification of the primary partition when the merge of two nonprimary partitions makes it possible to determine that there is no active primary partition within the system. We'll discuss this issue at some length in Chapter 18.

The protocol that we now present is based on one that was developed as part of the Isis system in 1987 (see Birman and Joseph [February 1987]), but was substantially extended by Ricciardi in 1991 as part of her Ph.D. dissertation (see Ricciardi [1992, 1993], Ricciardi and Birman). The protocol has the interesting property: All GMS members see exactly the same sequence of join and leave events. The members use this property to obtain an unusually efficient protocol execution.

To avoid placing excessive trust in the correctness or fault tolerance of the clients, our goal will be to implement a GMS for which all operations are invoked using a modified RPC protocol. Our solution should allow a process to issue requests to any member of the GMS server group with which it is able to establish contact. The protocol implemented by the group should stipulate that *join* operations are idempotent: If a joining process times out or otherwise fails to receive a reply, it can reissue its request, perhaps to a different server. Having joined the system, clients that detect apparent failures merely report them to the GMS. The GMS itself will be responsible for all forms of failure notification, both for GMS members and other clients. Thus, actions that would normally be triggered by timeouts (such as reissuing an RPC or breaking a stream connection) will be triggered in our system by a GMS callback notifying the process doing the RPC or maintaining the stream that the party it is contacting has failed. Table 15.1 summarizes this interface.

15.1.2 Protocol Used to Track GMS Membership

We now develop the protocol used to track the core membership of the GMS service itself. These are the processes responsible for implementing the GMS abstraction, but not their clients. For simplicity, we assume that the processes all watch one another using some form of network-level ping operation, detecting failures by timeout. In practice, failure detection doesn't necessarily require an all-to-all pattern of monitoring, but this assumption makes the GMS protocol easier to explain. The only real requirement here is that if a process or a set of processes fail, the survivors will eventually detect all the failures.

Both the addition of new GMS members and the deletion of apparently failed members are handled by the GMS coordinator, which is the GMS member that has been operational for the longest period of time. As we will see, although the GMS protocol permits more than one process to be added or deleted at a time, it orders all add and delete events so that this concept of oldest process is well defined and consistent throughout the GMS. If a process believes the GMS coordinator has failed, it treats the next highest ranked process (perhaps itself) as the new coordinator.

Our initial protocol will be such that any process suspected of having failed is subsequently *shunned* by the system members that learn of the suspected failure. This has the effect of emulating what we called *fail-stop* behavior earlier. Upon detection of an apparent failure, a GMS process immediately ceases to accept communication from the failed process. It also immediately sends a message to every other GMS process with which it is communicating, informing them of the apparent failure; they then shun the faulty process as well. If a shunned process is actually operational, it will learn that it is being shunned when it next attempts to communicate with some GMS process that has heard of the fault; at this point it is expected that the shunned process will rejoin the GMS under a new process identifier. In this manner, a suspected failure can be treated as if it were a real one.

Having developed this initial protocol, we will discuss extensions that allow partitions to form and later merge in Section 15.1.5, and then will return to the topic in Chapter 18, where we present an execution model that makes use of this functionality.

Upon learning of a failure or an addition request, the GMS coordinator starts a protocol that will lead to the updating of the membership list, which is replicated among all GMS processes. The protocol requires two phases when the processes being added or deleted do not include the old GMS coordinator; a third phase is used if the coordinator has failed and a new coordinator is taking over. Any number of add operations can be combined into a single round of the protocol. A single round can also perform multiple delete operations, but here there is a limit: At most a minority of the processes present in a given view can be dropped from the subsequent view (more precisely, a majority of the processes in a given view must acknowledge the next view; obviously, this implies that the processes in question must be alive).

In the two-phase case, the first round of the protocol sends the list of add and delete events to the participants, including the coordinator itself. All acknowledge receipt. The coordinator waits for as many replies as possible, but also requires a majority response from the current membership. If less than a majority of processes are reachable it waits until communication is restored before continuing. If processes have failed and only a minority are available, a special protocol is executed.

Unless additional failures occur at this point in the protocol, which would be very unlikely, a majority of processes acknowledge the first-round protocol. The GMS coordinator now commits the update in a second round, which also carries with it notifications of any failures that were detected during the first round. Indeed, the second-round protocol can be compacted with the first round of a new instance of the deletion protocol, if desired. The GMS members update their membership view upon reception of the second-round protocol messages.

In what one hopes will be an unusual condition, it may be that a majority of the previous membership cannot be contacted because too many GMS processes have crashed. In this case, a GMS coordinator still must ensure that the failed processes did not acquiesce in a reconfiguration protocol of which it was not a part. In general, this problem may not be solvable—for example, it may be that a majority of GMS processes have crashed, and prior to crashing they could have admitted any number of new processes and deleted the ones now trying to run the protocol. Those new processes could now be anywhere in the system. In practice, however, this problem is often easy to solve: The GMS will most often execute within a static set of possible server hosts, and even if this set has some small degree of dynamicism, it is normally possible to track down any GMS server by checking a moderate number of nodes for a representative.

A three-phase protocol is employed when the current coordinator is suspected as having failed and some other coordinator must take over. The new coordinator starts by informing at least a majority of the GMS processes listed in the current membership that the coordinator has failed and then collects their acknowledgements and current membership information. At the end of this first phase, the new coordinator may have learned of pending add or delete events that were initiated by the prior coordinator before it was suspected of having failed. The first-round protocol also has the effect of ensuring that a majority of GMS processes will start to shun the old coordinator. The second and third rounds of the protocol are exactly as for the normal case: The new coordinator proposes a new membership list, incorporating any add events it has learned about, as well as all the delete events, including those it learned about during the initial round of communication and those from the prior coordinator. It waits for a majority to acknowledge this message and then commits it, piggybacking suspected failure information for any unresponsive processes.

Ricciardi has given a detailed proof that the above protocol results in a single, ordered sequence of process add and leave events for the GMS and that it is immune to partitioning (see Ricciardi [1992]). The key to her proof is the observation that any new membership list installed successfully necessarily must be acknowledged by a majority of the previous list, and therefore that any two concurrent protocols will be related by a causal path. One protocol will learn of the other, or both will learn of one another, and this is sufficient to prevent the GMS from partitioning. Ricciardi shows that if the ith round of the protocol starts with n processes in the GMS membership, an arbitrary number of processes can be added to the GMS and at most $\lfloor n/2 \rfloor - 1$ processes can be excluded (this is because of the requirement that a majority of processes agree with each proposed new view). In addition, she shows that even if a steady stream of join and leave or failure events occurs, the GMS should be able to continuously output new GMS views provided that the number of failures never rises high enough to prevent majority agreement on the next view. In effect, although the protocol may be discussing the proposed $i + 2$ view, it is still able to commit the $i + 1$ view.

15.1.3 GMS Protocol to Handle Client Add and Join Events

We now turn to the issues that occur if a GMS server is used to manage the membership of some larger number of client processes, which interact with it through the interface given earlier.

In this approach, a process wishing to join the system will locate an operational GMS member. It then issues a *join* RPC to that process. If the RPC times out, the request can simply be reissued to some other member. When the join succeeds, it learns its logical ranking (the time at which the join took place) and the current membership of the GMS service, which is useful in setting up subsequent monitoring operations. Similarly, a process wishing to report a failure can invoke the *leave* operation in any operational GMS member. If that member fails before confirming that the operation has been successful, the caller can detect this by receiving a callback reporting the failure of the GMS member itself and then can reissue the request.

To solve these problems, we could now develop a specialized protocol. Before doing so, however, it makes sense to ask if the GMS is not simply an instance of a service that manages replicated data on behalf of a set of clients; if so, we should instead develop the most general and efficient solutions possible for the replicated data problem, and then use them within the GMS to maintain this specific form of information. And, indeed, it is very natural to adopt this point of view.

To transform the one problem into the other, we need to understand how an RPC interface to the GMS can be implemented such that the GMS would reliably offer the desired functionality to its clients, using data replication primitives internally for this purpose. Then we can focus on the data replication problem separately and convince ourselves that the necessary primitives can be developed and can offer efficient performance.

The first problem that needs to be addressed concerns the case where a client issues a request to a representative of the GMS that fails before responding. This can be solved by ensuring that such requests are *idempotent*, meaning that the same operation can be issued repeatedly and will repeatedly return the identical result—for example, an operation that assigns the value 3 to a variable x is idempotent, whereas an operation that increments x by adding 1 to it would not be. We can make the client join operation idempotent by having the client uniquely identify itself, and repeat the identifier each time the request must be reissued. Recall that the GMS returns the time of the join operation; this can be made idempotent by arranging it so that if a client join request is received from a client already listed as a system member, the time currently listed is returned and no other action is taken.

The remaining operations are all initiated by processes that belong to the system. These, too, might need to be reissued if the GMS process contacted to perform the operation fails before responding (the failure would be detected when a new GMS membership list is delivered to a process waiting for a response, and the GMS member it is waiting for is found to have been dropped from the list). It is clear that exactly the same approach can be used to solve this problem. Each request need only be uniquely identifiable—for example, using the process identifier of the invoking process and some form of counter (request 17 from process p on host h).

The central issue is thus reduced to replication of data within the GMS or within similar groups of processes. We will postpone this problem momentarily, returning later when we give a protocol for implementing replicated data within dynamically defined groups of processes.

15.1.4 GMS Notifications With Bounded Delay

If the processes within a system possess synchronized clocks, it is possible to bound the delay before a process becomes aware that it has been partitioned from the system. Consider a system in which the health of a process is monitored by the continued reception of some form of "still alive" messages received from it; if no such message is received after delay σ, any of the processes monitoring that process can report it as faulty to the GMS. (Normally, such a process would also cease to accept incoming messages from the faulty process and would also piggyback this information on messages to other processes to ensure that if p considers q to have failed, then any process that receives a message from p will also begin to shun messages from q.) Now, assume further that all processes receiving a "still alive" message acknowledge it.

In this setting, p will become aware that it may have been partitioned from the system within a maximum delay of $2\varepsilon+\sigma$, where ε represents the maximum latency of the communication channels. More precisely, p will discover that it has been partitioned from the system $2\varepsilon + \sigma$ time units after it last had contact with a majority of the previous primary component of the GMS. In such situations, it would be appropriate for p to break any channels it has to system members and to cease taking actions on behalf of the system as a whole.

Notice that the GMS may run its protocol to exclude p as early as 2ε time units before p discovers that it has been partitioned from the main system, hence there is a potentially long window of time during which the exact status of p is unknown. The new primary system component can safely break locks held by p or otherwise takeover actions for which p was responsible after 2ε time units have elapsed, but this event may actually follow a long period during which the system was essentially idle, waiting for this to happen. (See Figure 15.2.) Our only options for narrowing this window are to use as fast a communication network as possible, and to detect failures aggressively, so that ε and σ will be small. If clocks are synchronized, any process q taking over from p will know how long to wait before doing so, and also will know the wall clock time for the last action that p could have initiated. In applications such as air traffic control, these guarantees are sufficient to design a safe take-over protocol.

Reasoning such as this is only possible in systems where clocks are synchronized to a known precision and in which the delays associated with communication channels are also known (if the wall-clock time issue does not arise in the application, it suffices to ensure that the various clocks advance at the same rate—that $2\varepsilon + \sigma$ time units means the same thing system-wide). In practice, such values are rarely known with any accuracy, but coarse approximations may exist. Thus, in a system where message-passing primitives provide expected latencies of a few milliseconds, one might take ε to be a much larger number: one second or ten seconds. Although extremely conservative, such an approach would in practice be quite safe. Later, we will examine real-time issues more closely, but it is useful to keep in mind that very coarse-grained real-time problems are often easy to solve in distributed systems where the equivalent fine-grained real-time problems would be very difficult or provably impossible. At the same time, even a coarse-grained rule such as this one would only be safe if there was good reason to believe that the value of ε was a safe approximation.

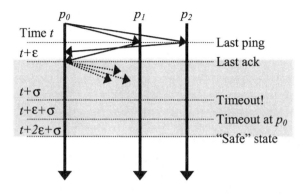

Figure 15.2. If channel delays are bounded, a process can detect that it has been partitioned from the primary component within a bounded time interval, making it safe for the primary component to take over actions from it even if externally visible effects may be involved. The gray region denotes a period during which the new primary process will be unable to take over because there is some possibility that the old primary process is still operational in a nonprimary component and may still be initiating authoritative actions. At the end of the gray period a new primary process can be appointed within the primary component. There may be a period of real time during which no primary process is active, but there is very little risk that two could be simultaneously active. One can also bias a system in the other direction, so that there will always be at least one primary active provided that the rate of failures is limited.

Some systems provide no guarantees of this sort at all, in which case incorrect behavior could result if a period of extreme overload or some other unusual condition caused the ε limit to be exceeded.

To summarize, the core primary partition GMS protocol must satisfy the following properties:

- *C-GMS-1*: The system membership takes the form of system views. There is an initial system view, which is predetermined at the time the system starts. Subsequent views differ by the addition or deletion of processes.
- *C-GMS-2*: Only processes that request to be added to the system are added. Only processes that are suspected of failure or that request to leave the system are deleted.
- *C-GMS-3*: A majority of the processes in view i of the system must acquiesce in the composition of view $i + 1$ of the system.
- *C-GMS-4*: Starting from an initial system view, subsequences of a single sequence of system views are reported to system members. Each system member observes such a subsequence starting with the view in which it was first added to the system and continuing until it fails, when it either leaves the system or is excluded from the system.
- *C-GMS-5*: If process p suspects process q of being faulty, and if the core GMS service is able to report new views, either q will be dropped from the system, or p will be dropped, or both.
- *C-GMS-6*: In a system with synchronized clocks and bounded message latencies, any process dropped from the system view will know that this has occurred within bounded time.

As noted previously, the core GMS protocol will not always be able to make progress: There are patterns of failures and communication problems that can prevent it from reporting new system views. For this reason, *C-GMS-5* is a conditional liveness property: If the core GMS is able to report new views, then it eventually acts upon process add or delete requests. It is not yet clear what conditions represent the weakest environment within which liveness of the GMS can always be guaranteed. For the protocol given above, the core GMS will make progress provided that at most a minority of processes from view *i* fail or are suspected of having failed during the period needed to execute the two- or three-phase commit protocol used to install new views. Such a characterization may seem evasive, since such a protocol may execute extremely rapidly in some settings and extremely slowly in others. However, unless the timing properties of the system are sufficiently strong to support estimation of the time needed to run the protocol, this seems to be as strong a statement as can be made.

We note that the failure detector called ◇W in Chandra and Toueg's work is characterized in terms somewhat similar to this (see Chandra and Toueg [1991], Chandra et al. [1992]). Related work by several researchers (see Babaoglu et al. [1995], Friedman et al., Guerraoui [1995]) has shown that the ◇W failure detector can be adapted to asynchronous systems in which messages can be lost during failures or processes can be killed because the majority of processes in the system consider them to be malfunctioning. Although fairly theoretical in nature, these studies are shedding light on the conditions under which problems such as membership agreement can always be solved and those under which agreement may not always be possible (the theoreticians are fond of calling the latter problems "impossible"). To present this work here, however, is beyond the scope of this book.

15.1.5 Extending the GMS to Allow Partition and Merge Events

Research on the Transis system, at Hebrew University in Jerusalem, has yielded insights into the extension of protocols, such as the one used to implement our primary component GMS, so that it can permit continued operation during partitionings that leave no primary component, or allow activity in a non-primary component, reconciling the resulting system state when partitions later remerge (see Amir et al. [1992], Malkhi). Some of this work was done jointly with the Totem project at University of California, Santa Barbara (see Moser et al.).

Briefly, the approach is as follows. In Ricciardi's protocols, when the GMS is unable to obtain a majority vote in favor of a proposed new view, the protocol basically gets stuck—it ceases to make progress. This ripples up to the application layer, since the application will eventually try to send a multicast or block waiting for a message from some other process, and while the membership protocol is blocked, these operations also will block. Thus, with little delay, the entire portioned portion of the system is likely to grind to a halt waiting until a primary partition can be reestablished, or for some kind of "shut down" action initiated in the application or by a human operator. In practice, such problems should never occur in a local area network, since it is easy to design a LAN so that partitioning will never occur.

However, if an application runs over wide-area links and tries to treat the entire infrastructure as a single, seamless network, partitioning failures could be common. The choice is between designing such applications differently (basically, as a set of loosely interconnected systems, with each system residing within a single LAN), or to extend the communication platform to deal with partitioning. Such an extension needs to start with a partitionable GMS.

In the extended protocol, a GMS experiencing a partitioning failure continues to produce new views, but no longer considers itself to be the primary partition of the system. Of course, there is also a complementary case in which the GMS encounters some other GMS and the two merge their membership views. It may now be the case that one GMS or the other was the primary component of the system, in which case the new merged GMS will also be primary for the system. On the other hand, perhaps a primary component fragmented in such a way that none of the surviving components considers itself to be the primary one. When this occurs, it may be that later, such components will remerge and "primaryness" can then be deduced by study of the joint histories of the two components. Thus, one can extend the GMS to make progress even when partitioning occurs.

Work at the University of Bologna, on a system named Relacs, subsequently refined this approach into one that is notable for its simplicity and clarity. Ozalp Babaoglu, working with Alberto Bartoli and Gianluca Dini, demonstrated that a very small set of extensions to a view-synchronous environment suffice to support EVS-like functionality. They call their model Enriched View Synchrony and describe it in a technical report (see Babaoglu et al. [1996]). Very briefly, Enriched View Synchrony arranges to deliver only *nonoverlapping* group views within different components of a partitioned system. The reasoning behind this is that overlapping views can cause applications to briefly believe that the same process or site resides on both sides of a partition, leading to inconsistent behavior. Then, they provide a set of predicates by which a component can determine whether or not it has a quorum that would permit direct update of the global system state, as well as algorithmic tools for assisting in the state merge problem that occurs when communication is reestablished. I am not aware of any implementation of this model yet, but the primitives are simple and an implementation in a system such as Horus (Chapter 21) would not be difficult.

Having described these approaches, an important question remains: whether or not it is *desirable* to allow a GMS to make progress in this manner. We defer this point until Chapter 19, but the author's belief is that few systems require the ability to continue operation on both sides of a failure that partitions the network, and that the primary partition model (in which the non-primary partition is basically shut down until the problem has been fixed) is preferable because it is much simpler for the user to understand. In addition, as was noted in footnote 3, Keidar, Chockler and Dolev have shown that there are cases in which no component is ever the primary one for the system, and yet dynamically uniform actions can still be performed through a type of gossip that occurs whenever the network becomes reconnected and two nonminority components succeed in communicating. Although interesting, this protocol is costly: Prior to taking any action, a majority of all the processes in the system must be known to have seen the action. Indeed, Keidar and Dolev develop their solution for a static membership model, in which the GMS tracks subsets of a known maximum system membership. The majority requirement makes this protocol costly—hence, although it is potentially useful in the context of wide area systems that experience frequent partition failures, it is not likely that one would use it directly in the local area communication layers of a system. We will return to this issue in Chapter 18 in conjunction with the model called *Extended Virtual Synchrony.*

15.2 Replicated Data with Malicious Failures

In this and the next section we touch on two problems that are basically tangential to the overall topic of interest here, yet important enough so that a well-read student should at least be aware of them. Nonetheless, the contents of Sections 15.2 and 15.3 are not particularly central to the remainder of the book and can be skipped by practitioners focused on building highly assured Web Services but having less of an interest in the broad area.

The discussion in the previous sections assumed a *crash-failure model*, which is approximated in most distributed systems, but may sometimes represent a risky simplification. Consider a situation in which the actions of a computing system have critical implications, such as the software responsible for adjusting the position of an aircraft wing in flight or for opening the cargo door of the Space Shuttle. In settings such as these, the designer may hesitate to simply assume that the only failures that will occur will be benign ones.

There has been considerable work on protocols for coordinating actions under extremely pessimistic failure models, centering on what is called the Byzantine generals' problem, which explores a type of agreement protocol under the assumption that failures can produce arbitrarily incorrect behavior, but that the *number* of failures is known to be bounded. Although this assumption may seem more realistic than the assumption that processes fail by clean crashes, the model also includes a second type of assumption, which some might view as unrealistically benign: It assumes that the processors participating in a system share perfectly synchronized clocks, permitting them to exchange messages in rounds that are triggered by the clocks (e.g., once every second). Moreover, the model assumes that the latencies associated with message exchange between correct processors is accurately known.

Thus, the model permits failures of unlimited severity, but at the same time assumes that the *number* of failures is limited and that operational processes share a very simple computing environment. Notice in particular that the round model would only be realistic for a very small class of modern parallel computers and is remote from the situation on distributed computing networks. The usual reasoning is that by endowing the operational computers with extra power (in the form of synchronized rounds), we can only make their task easier. Thus, understanding the minimum cost for solving a problem in this model will certainly teach us something about the minimum cost of overcoming failures in real-world settings.

The Byzantine generals' problem is as follows (see Lynch). Suppose that an army has laid siege to a city and has the force to prevail in an overwhelming attack. However, if divided, the army might lose the battle. Moreover, the commanding generals suspect that there are traitors in their midst. Under what conditions can the loyal generals coordinate their action so as to either attack in unison or not attack at all? The assumption is that the generals start the protocol with individual opinions on the best strategy: to attack or to continue the siege. They exchange messages to execute the protocol, and if they decide to attack during the ith round of communication, they will all attack at the start of round $i + 1$. A traitorous general can send out any messages he or she likes and can lie about his or her own state, but can never forge the message of a loyal general. Finally, to avoid trivial solutions, it is required that if all the loyal generals favor attacking, an attack will result, and that if all favor maintaining the siege, no attack will occur. Protocols solving this problem are generally referred to as "Byzantine Agreement" protocols.

To see why this is difficult, consider a simple case in which three generals surround the city. Assume that two are loyal, but that one favors attack and the other prefers to hold back. The third general is a traitor. Moreover, assume that it is *known that there is at most one traitor*. If the loyal generals exchange their votes, they will both see a tie: one vote for attack, one opposed. Now suppose that the traitor sends an attack message to one general and tells the other to hold back. The loyal generals now see inconsistent states: One is likely to attack while the other holds back. With the forces divided, they would be defeated in battle. The Byzantine generals' problem is thus seen to be impossible for $t = 1$ and $n = 3$.

With four generals and at most one failure, the problem is solvable, but not trivially so. Assume that two loyal generals favor attack, the third favors retreat, and the fourth is a traitor. Again, it is known that there is at most one traitor. The generals exchange messages, and the traitor sends "retreat" to one, and "attack" to two others. One loyal general will now have a tied vote: two votes to attack, two to retreat. The other two generals will see three votes for attack, and one for retreat. A second round of communication will clearly be needed before this protocol can terminate! Accordingly, we now imagine a second round in which the generals circulate messages concerning their state in the first round. Two loyal generals will start this round knowing that it is safe to attack: On the basis of the messages received in the first round, they can deduce that even with the traitor's vote, the majority of loyal generals favored an attack. The remaining loyal general simply sends out a message that it is still undecided. At the end of this round, all the loyal generals will have one undecided vote, two votes that it is safe to attack, and one message from the traitor. Clearly, no matter what the traitor votes during the second round, all three loyal generals can deduce that it is safe to attack. Thus, with four generals and at most one traitor, the protocol terminates after two rounds.

In the general case, most Byzantine Agreement algorithms operate by having some form of "witnessing" mechanism. In a typical algorithm, during the first round, each process broadcasts its proposed agreement value—its "vote." In a second round, each process broadcasts the list of votes it "witnessed" in the first round, and if a third round occurs, each processes sends messages listing the events it witnessed in the second one, and so forth. The goal is to arrive at a state in which, no matter what the faulty processes do, the correct processes are able to force a unique outcome all by themselves.

By using this model, one can prove what are called lower bounds and upper bounds on the Byzantine generals' problem. A lower bound would be a limit to the quality of a possible solution to the problem—for example, one can prove that any solution to the problem capable of overcoming t traitors requires a minimum of $3t + 1$ participants (hence: $2t + 1$ or more loyal generals). The intuition into such a bound is fairly clear: The loyal generals must somehow be able to deduce a common strategy even with t participants whose votes cannot be trusted. For the others there must be a way to identify a majority decision. However, it is surprisingly difficult to prove that this must be the case. For our purposes, such a proof would represent a digression and is omitted, but interested readers are referred to the excellent treatment in Fisher et al. (August 1985). Another example of a lower bound concerns the minimum number of messages required to solve the problem: No protocol can overcome t faults with fewer than $t + 1$ rounds of message exchange, and hence $O(t * n^2)$ messages, where n is the number of participating processes.

A curious property of Byzantine protocols is the following: they normally assume that when the protocol starts, all the participants know how many processes are in the system, and have worst-case bounds on the number of failures that can occur. These protocols will typically execute to completion under those worst-case assumptions, no matter what actually transpires in a real run—no attempt is made to check for and detect faults, or to somehow exclude processes based on faulty behavior. Up to the limited number of failures that can be tolerated, these protocols simply push forward and overwhelm the attacker with the weight of correct messages they exchange. The attacker, knowing the futility of attacking, might not even bother. Thus, in some sense, these protocols kill a mosquito with a sledge-hammer: most likely, no failure even occurs, and yet the protocol grinds away under worst-case assumptions! (In fairness, we should perhaps note that there are some "early stopping" Byzantine protocols, but they tend to be slower when failures actually *do* occur—in effect, one is damned either way!)

In practical terms, the formulas just cited represent costly findings: Recall that our 2PC protocol is capable of solving a problem much like Byzantine generals' problem in two rounds of message exchange requiring only $3n$ messages, albeit for a simpler failure model. Moreover, the quorum methods permit data to be replicated using as few as $t + 1$ copies to overcome t failures. Later in the book we will discuss even cheaper replication schemes below, albeit with slightly weaker guarantees. Thus, a Byzantine protocol is very costly, and the best solutions are also fairly complex.

An upper bound on the problem would be a demonstration of a protocol that actually solves Byzantine generals' problem and an analysis of its complexity (number of rounds of communication required or messages required). Such a demonstration is an upper bound because it rules out the need for a more costly protocol to achieve the same objectives. Clearly, one hopes for upper bounds that are as close as possible to the lower bounds, but unfortunately no such protocols have been found for the Byzantine generals' problem. The simple protocol illustrated here can easily be generalized into a solution for t failures that achieves the lower bound for rounds of message exchange, although not for numbers of messages required.

In recent years, there has been a flurry of research using Byzantine Agreement protocols as the core of practical data replication systems. Two bodies of work are worthy of special note, although both are best understood as examples of broad areas of research. The first is a project called Phalynx, in which Reiter and Malkhi combined Byzantine Agreement with quorum data replication to replicate information critical to a security architecture. Their approach assumes that each object will be replicated on k^2 nodes, for some suitable value of k (typically, 2 or 3, although larger values are certainly possible). The nodes are assigned coordinates in a $k \times k$ coordinate system. A read quorum is defined to be a row in this "array" of nodes, and a write quorum is defined to be a column. Obviously, reads and writes will overlap. Byzantine Agreement is then used to determine the value actually read or the value to be written.

Subsequent work by Castro and Liskov took Byzantine Agreement in a slightly different direction, by exploring the potential value of the protocol for file or database replication. The idea these researchers addressed involves replicating data over a set of untrusted servers, then using Byzantine Agreement to update or read the values. They actually have two versions of their basic solution: one in which agreement is performed on the entire data object, and a second in which agreement is performed only on a "digital signature," which is a type of encoded checksum that cannot be forged or guessed. By means of a clever analysis of the application, this project showed that for many purposes, one can tolerate Byzantine failures and yet incur very little overhead relative to a less secure solution.

Yet despite these and other success stories, Byzantine Agreement remains a rather costly and relatively unpopular technology. Suppose that we wanted to use Byzantine Agreement to solve a static data replication problem in a very critical or hostile setting. To do so, it would be necessary that the setting somehow correspond to the setup of the Byzantine generals' problem itself—for example, one could imagine using this problem to control an aircraft wing or the Space Shuttle cargo door by designing hardware that carries out voting through some form of physical process. The hardware would be required to implement the mechanisms needed to write software that executes in rounds, and the programs would need to be carefully analyzed to be sure that when operational, all the computing they do in each round can be completed before that round terminates.

On the other hand, one would not want to use a Byzantine protocol in a system where, at the end of the protocol, some single program will take the output of the protocol and perform a critical action. In that sort of a setting (unfortunately, far more typical of real computer systems), all we will have done is to transfer complete trust in the set of servers within which the agreement protocol runs into a complete trust in the single program that carries out their decision.

The practical use of the Byzantine protocol raises another concern: The timing assumptions built into the model are not realizable in most computing environments. While it is certainly possible to build a system with closely synchronized clocks and to approximate the synchronous rounds used in the model, the pragmatic reality is that few existing computer systems offer such a feature. Software clock synchronization, on the other hand, is subject to intrinsic limitations of its own, and for this reason is a poor alternative to the real thing.

Moreover, the assumption that message exchanges can be completed within known, bounded latency is very hard to satisfy in general-purpose computing environments.

Continuing in this vein, one could also question the extreme pessimism of the failure model. In a Byzantine setting the traitor can act as an adversary, seeking to force the correct processes to malfunction. For a worst-case analysis this makes a good deal of sense. But having understood the worst case, one can also ask whether real-world systems should be designed to routinely assume such a pessimistic view of the behavior of system components. After all, if one is this negative, shouldn't the hardware itself also be suspected of potential misbehavior, as well as the compiler and the various prebuilt system components that implement message passing? In designing a security subsystem or implementing a firewall, such an analysis makes a lot of sense. But when designing a system that merely seeks to maintain availability despite failures, and is not expected to come under active and coordinated attack, an extremely pessimistic model would be both unwieldy and costly.

From these considerations, one sees that a Byzantine computing model is of value in applications (or subsystems) demanding the utmost in security provisions, and may be applicable to certain types of special-purpose hardware, but it will rarely be directly useful in more general distributed computing environments where we might raise a reliability goal. As noted above, recent work with the model (see Malkhi and Reiter, Castro et al.) focuses on such uses: in one effort, a "Byzantine Quorums" mechanism is employed to build core components of a high-security architecture (see Malkhi and Reiter [1998], Malkhi [2001], Alvisi [2001], Abraham [2003]), while the other uses Byzantine Agreement to ensure the integrity of data in a replicated file server where the servers themselves aren't very trustworthy (see [Castro and Liskov [2001], Castro and Liskov [2002]). As an aside, it should be noted that Rabin has introduced a set of probabilistic Byzantine protocols that are extremely efficient, but that accept a small risk of error (the risk diminishes exponentially with the number of rounds of agreement executed) (see Rabin). Meanwhile, Avlisi and Dahlin have recently proposed a fast Byzantine Agreement protocol for use in settings like the ones considered by Malkhi, Reiter, Castro and their respective colleagues. But it still isn't especially fast!

15.3 The Impossibility of Asynchronous Consensus (FLP)

We now turn to the second of the two "tangential" topics mentioned at the start of Section 15.2, namely the "impossibility" of achieving agreement in asynchronous distributed systems. Even before tackling the topic, it may be appropriate to remind the reader that this section of the book is covering some rather theoretical material, and that the theory community sometimes defines terms in unexpected ways. In particular, as we'll use it below, the term "impossible" doesn't mean "never possible." Rather, it means "isn't always possible."

To illustrate this definition, consider the challenge of reaching the author of this book by telephone during a busy day filled with meetings, talks by students, classes to teach, and so forth. Perhaps, over the eight hours of an academic working day, I'm actually at my telephone for just four hours. Is it "possible" to reach me? A pragmatic answer is that of course it is: just keep trying. If your call is timed at random, with probability roughly 1/2 you'll reach me. If you make n calls at random times, the likelihood of reaching me will be $1-1/2^n$. These sound like pretty good odds. But a theoretician might not be satisfied with such an analysis. He or she would reason as follows: suppose that the caller makes n extremely brief calls at times specified by a clever adversary who is keeping one eye on my desk through the door. It won't be difficult for that adversary to steer the caller towards times when I'm not at my desk. Indeed, one could formalize a model in which it is provably impossible to reach me; such a result might hold even if I am "almost always" at my desk. The impossibility result considered below is of such a nature: it has limited practical importance yet the result matters because it tells us that there are certain properties our distributed systems simply cannot be shown to possess—notably, liveness guarantees. We'll be able to build systems that are safe, in the sense of "not doing bad things," and that are probabilistically live, in the sense of being "very likely to do a good thing." But we will not be able to build systems that are guaranteed to "*always* do a good thing." Such a goal would violate the theory.

Recall that in Section 15.2, we focused on the *synchronous computing model*. At the other side of the spectrum is what we call the *asynchronous* computing model (see Break-out 15.1), in which a set of processes cooperate by exchanging messages over communication links that are arbitrarily slow and balky. The assumption here is that the messages sent on the links eventually get through, but that there is no meaningful way to measure progress except by the reception of messages. Clearly such a model is overly pessimistic, but in a way that is different from the pessimism of the Byzantine model, which extended primarily to failures—here we are pessimistic about our ability to measure time or to predict the amount of time actions will take. A message that arrives after a century of delay would be processed no differently than a message received within milliseconds of being transmitted. At the same time, this model assumes that processes fail by crashing, taking no incorrect actions and simply halting silently.

One might wonder why the asynchronous system completely eliminates any physical concept of time. We have seen that real distributed computing systems lack ways to closely synchronize clocks and are unable to distinguish network partitioning failures from processor failures, so there is a sense in which the asynchronous model isn't as unrealistic as it may initially appear. Real systems do have clocks and use these to establish timeouts, but generally they lack a way to ensure that these timeouts will be accurate, as we saw when we discussed RPC protocols and the associated reliability issues in Chapter 4. Indeed, if an asynchronous model can be criticized as specifically unrealistic, this is primarily in its assumption of reliable communication links: Real systems tend to have limited memory resources, and a reliable communication link for a network subject to extended partitioning failures will require unlimited spooling of the messages sent. This represents an impractical design point: A better model would state that when a process is *reachable*, messages will be exchanged reliably with it, but if it becomes *inaccessible*, messages to it will be lost and its state, faulty or operational, cannot be accurately determined. In Italy, Babaoglu and his colleagues are studying such a model, but this is recent work and the full implications of this design point are not yet fully understood (see Babaoglu et al. [1994]). Other researchers, such as Cristian, are looking at models that are partially asynchronous: They have time bounds, but the bounds are large compared to typical message-passing latencies (see Cristian [1996]). Again, it is too early to say whether or not this model represents a good choice for research on realistic distributed systems.

Within the purely asynchronous model, a classical result limits what we can hope to accomplish. In 1985, Fischer, Lynch, and Patterson proved that the asynchronous consensus problem (similar to the Byzantine generals' problem, but posed in an asynchronous setting) is impossible if even a single process can fail. Their proof revolves around the use of type of message scheduler that delays the progress of a consensus protocol and holds regardless of the way that the protocol itself works. Basically, they demonstrate that any protocol guaranteed to produce only correct outcomes in an asynchronous system can be indefinitely delayed by a complex pattern of network partitioning failures. More recent work has extended this result to some of the communication protocols we will discuss in the remainder of this chapter (see Chandra et al. [1996], Ricciardi [1996]).

The Fisher, Lynch, and Paterson (FLP) proof is short but quite sophisticated, and it is common for practitioners to conclude that it does not correspond to any scenario that would be expected to occur in a real distributed system—for example, recall that 3PC is unable to make progress when failure detection is unreliable because of message loss or delays in the network. The FLP result predicts that if a protocol such as 3PC is capable of solving the consensus problem, it can be prevented from terminating. However, if one studies the FLP proof, it turns out that the type of partitioning failure exploited by the proof is at least superficially very remote from the pattern of crashes and network partitioning that forces the 3PC to block.

Thus, it is a bit facile to say that FLP predicts that 3PC will block in this specific way, because the proof constructs a scenario that seems to have relatively little to do with the one that causes problems in a protocol like 3PC. At the very least, one would be expected to relate the FLP scheduling pattern to the situation when 3PC blocks, and I am not aware of any research that has made this connection concrete.

Indeed, it is not entirely clear that 3PC *could* be used to solve the consensus problem: Perhaps the latter is actually a more difficult problem, in which case the inability to solve consensus might not imply that 3PC cannot be solved in asynchronous systems.

As a matter of fact, although it is obvious that 3PC cannot be solved when the network is partitioned, if we carefully study the model used in FLP we realize that network partitioning is not actually considered in this model: The FLP result assumes that every message sent will eventually be received, in FIFO order. Thus, FLP essentially requires that every partition eventually be fixed and that every message eventually get through. The tendency of 3PC to block during partitions, which concerned us above, is not captured by FLP because FLP is willing to wait until such a partition is repaired (and implicitly assumes that it will be), while we wanted 3PC to make progress even while the partition was present (whether or not it will eventually be repaired).

15.1   *The Asynchronous Computing Model*

Although we refer to our model as asynchronous, it is in fact more constrained. In the asynchronous model, as used by distributed systems theoreticians, processes communicate entirely by message passing and there is no concept of time. Message passing is reliable but individual messages can be delayed indefinitely, and there is no meaningful concept of failure except for a process that crashes (taking no further actions) or that violates its protocol by failing to send a message or discarding a received message. Even these two forms of communication failure are frequently ruled out.

The form of asynchronous computing environment used in this chapter, in contrast, is intended to be "realistic." This implies that there are clocks on the processors and expectations regarding typical round-trip latencies for messages. Such temporal data can be used to define a concept of reachability or to trigger a failure-detection mechanism. The detected failure may not be attributable to a specific component (in particular, it will be impossible to know if a *process* failed or just the *link* to it), but the fact that some sort of problem has occurred will be detected, perhaps very rapidly. Moreover, in practice, the frequency with which failures are erroneously suspected can be kept low.

Jointly, these properties make the asynchronous model used in this book different than the one used in most theoretical work. And this is a good thing, too: In the fully asynchronous model, it is known that the group membership problem cannot be solved, in the sense that any protocol capable of solving the problem may encounter situations in which it cannot make progress. In contrast, these problems are always solvable in asynchronous environments, which satisfy sufficient constraints on the frequency of true or incorrectly detected failures and on the quality of communication.

To be more precise, FLP tells us that any asynchronous consensus decision can be *indefinitely delayed*, not merely delayed, until a problematic communication link is fixed. Moreover, it says that this is true even if every message sent in the system eventually reaches its destination. During this period of delay the processes may thus be quite active. Finally, and in some sense most surprising of all, the proof doesn't require that any process fail at all: It is entirely based on a pattern of message delays. Thus, FLP not only predicts that we would be unable to develop a 3PC protocol guaranteeing progress despite failures, but that, in actuality, there is no 3PC protocol that can terminate at all, even if no failures actually occur and the network is merely subject to unlimited numbers of network partitioning events. We convinced ourselves that 3PC would need to block (wait) in a single situation; FLP tells us that if a protocol such as 3PC can be used to solve the consensus, then there is a sequence of communication failures that would prevent it from reaching a commit or abort point regardless of how long it executes!

15.3.1   Three-Phase Commit and Consensus

To see that 3PC solves consensus, we should be able to show how to map one problem to the other and back—for example, suppose that the inputs to the participants in a 3PC protocol are used to determine their vote, for or against commit, and that we pick one of the processes to run the protocol. Superficially, it may seem that this is a mapping from 3PC to consensus. But recall that consensus of the type considered by FLP is concerned with protocols that tolerate a single failure, which would presumably include the process that starts the protocol. Moreover, although we didn't get into this issue, consensus has a nontriviality requirement, which is that if all the inputs are 1 the decision will be 1, and if all the inputs are 0 the decision will be 0. As stated, our mapping of 3PC to consensus might not satisfy non-triviality while also overcoming a single failure. Thus, while it would not be surprising to find that 3PC is equivalent to consensus, neither is it obvious that the correspondence is an exact one.

But assume that 3PC is in fact equivalent to consensus. In a *theoretical* sense, FLP would represent a very strong limitation on 3PC. In a *practical* sense, however, it is unclear whether it has direct relevance to developers of reliable distributed software. Previously, we commented that even the scenario that causes 2PC to block is extremely unlikely unless the coordinator is also a participant; thus, 2PC (or 3PC when the coordinator actually is a participant) would seem to be an adequate protocol for most real systems. Perhaps we are saved from trying to develop some other protocol to evade this limitation: FLP tells us that any such protocol will sometimes block. But once 2PC or 3PC has blocked, one could argue that it is of little practical consequence whether this was provoked by a complex sequence of network partitioning failures or by something simple and blunt, such as the simultaneous crash of a majority of the computers in the network. Indeed, we would consider that 3PC has failed to achieve its objectives as soon as the first partitioning failure occurs and it ceases to make *continuous* progress. Yet the FLP result, in some sense, hasn't even kicked in at this point: It relates to *ultimate* progress. In the FLP work, the issue of a protocol being blocked is not really modeled in the formalism at all, except in the sense that such a protocol has not yet reached a decision state.

We thus see that although FLP tells us that the asynchronous consensus problem cannot *always* be solved, it says nothing at all about when problems such as this actually *can* be solved. As we will see, more recent work answers this question for asynchronous consensus. However, unlike an impossibility result, to apply this new result one would need to be able to relate a given execution model to the asynchronous one and a given problem to consensus.

As noted earlier, FLP is frequently misunderstood having proved the impossibility of building fault-tolerant distributed software for realistic environments. At the risk of seeming repetitious, this is not the case at all! FLP doesn't say that one cannot build a consensus protocol tolerant of one failure or of many failures. It simply says that if one does build such a protocol, and then runs it in a system with no concept of global time whatsoever and no timeouts, there will be a pattern of message delays that prevents it from terminating. The pattern in question may be extremely improbable, meaning that one might still be able to build an asynchronous protocol that would terminate with overwhelming probability. Moreover, realistic systems have many forms of time: timeouts, loosely synchronized global clocks, and (often) a good idea of how long messages should take to reach their destinations and to be acknowledged. This sort of information allows real systems to evade the limitations imposed by FLP or at least to create a run-time environment that differs in fundamental ways from the FLP-style of asynchronous environment.

This brings us to the more recent work in this area, which presents a precise characterization of the conditions under which a consensus protocol *can* terminate in an asynchronous environment. Chandra and Toueg have shown how the consensus problem can be expressed using what they call "weak failure detectors," which are a mechanism for detecting that a process has failed without necessarily doing so accurately (see Chandra and Toueg [1991], Chandra et al. [1992]). A weak failure detector can make mistakes and change its mind; its behavior is similar to what might result by setting some arbitrary timeout—declaring a process faulty if no communication is received from it during the timeout period, and then declaring that it is actually operational after all if a message subsequently turns up (the communication channels are still assumed to be reliable and FIFO). Using this model, Chandra and Toueg prove that consensus can be solved provided that a period of execution arises during which all genuinely faulty processes are suspected as faulty, and during which at least one operational process is never suspected as faulty by any other operational process. One can think of this as a constraint on the quality of the communication channels and the timeout period: If communication works well enough, and timeouts are accurate enough, for a long enough period of time, a consensus decision can be reached. Interested readers should also refer to Babaoglu et al. (1995), Friedman et al., Guerraoui and Schiper, Ricciardi (1996). Two relatively recent papers in the area are by Babaoglu et al. (1996) and Neiger.

What Chandra and Toueg have done has general implications for the developers of other forms of distributed systems that seek to guarantee reliability. We learn from this result that to guarantee progress, the developer may need to guarantee a higher quality of communication than in the classical asynchronous model, a degree of clock synchronization (lacking in the model), or some form of accurate failure detection. With any of these, the FLP limitations can be evaded (they no longer hold). In general, it will not be possible to say "my protocol always terminates" without also saying "when such and such a condition holds" on the communication channels, the timeouts used, or other properties of the environment.

This said, the FLP result does create a quandary for practitioners who hope to be rigorous about the reliability properties of their algorithms by making it difficult to talk in rigorous terms about what protocols for asynchronous distributed systems actually guarantee. We would like to be able to talk about one protocol being more tolerant of failures than another, but now we see that such statements will apparently need to be made about protocols in which one can only guarantee fault tolerance in a conditional way and where the conditions may not be simple to express or to validate.

What seems to have happened here is that we lack an appropriate concept of what it means for a protocol to be live in an asynchronous setting. The FLP concept of liveness is rigorously defined and not achievable, but in any case this concept does not address the more relative concept of liveness that we seek when developing a nonblocking commit protocol. As it happens, even this more relative form of liveness is not always achievable, and this coincidence has sometimes led practitioners and even theoreticians to conclude that the forms of liveness are the same, since neither is always possible. This subtle but very important point has yet to be treated adequately by the theoretical community. We need a model within which we can talk about 3PC making progress under conditions when 2PC would not do so without getting snarled in the impossibility of guaranteeing progress for all possible runs in the asynchronous model.

Returning to our data replication problem, these theoretical results do have some practical implications. In particular, they suggest that there may not be much more that can be accomplished in a static computing model. The quorum methods give us a way to overcome failures or damage to limited numbers of data objects within a set of replicas; although expensive, such methods clearly work. While they would not work with a very serious type of failure in which processes behave maliciously, the Byzantine agreement and consensus literature suggest that one cannot always solve this problem in an asynchronous model, and the synchronous model is sufficiently specialized as to be largely inapplicable to standard distributed computing systems.

Our best hope, in light of these limitations, will be to focus on the poor performance of the style of replication algorithm arrived at above. Perhaps a less-costly algorithm would represent a viable option for introducing tolerance to at least a useful class of failures in realistic distributed environments. Moreover, although the FLP result tells us that for certain categories of objectives availability must always be limited, the result does not speak directly to the sorts of tradeoffs between availability and cost seen in 2PC and 3PC. Perhaps we should talk about optimal progress and identify the protocol structures that result in the best possible availability without sacrificing consistency, even if we must accept that our protocols will (at least theoretically) remain exposed to scenarios in which they are unable to make progress.

15.4 Extending our Protocol into the Full GMS

We've developed a protocol by which the GMS can track its own membership, converting potentially inconsistent and hence confusing timeout events into an agreed-upon sequence of join and leave events. But these events pertain only to the members of the GMS per-se. In a typical local area network, one might have a single instance of the GMS service, with perhaps three to five members belonging to it. How then should these servers handle membership information for everything else in the system?

In Chapter 16, we'll tackle this problem as part of a more general one. The basic idea, though, is as follows. Each process in the system will register itself with some member of the GMS service. GMS service members *monitor* other GMS service members (since there aren't very many, this isn't going to be a big load), and also all members registered with them. Since few systems have more than a few thousand processes in them, a typical GMS service member might thus monitor a few hundred or even a thousand processes.

There are many ways to monitor the health of a process, and we leave it to the developer of a GMS on a given platform to pick the best option. Examples include periodically pinging the process, or having each process periodically send an "I'm still fine" event to the GMS, or watching the MIB within the operating system (the Management Information Base, or

MIB, contains a variety of information, normally including the identity of currently active processes), maintaining a TCP connection to the monitored process, and so forth. In a very large system, one could use so-called gossip protocols (we'll explore a number of them in our chapter on peer-to-peer techniques) to gossip about the "most recent signs of life" for processes within the system. Ideally, failure detection should be a sophisticated mechanism which reflects a keen awareness of what it means to say that the application is healthy. The outcome of all of this is that the GMS process should be able to detect, within a few seconds (or perhaps a minute or two) the failure of any of the other members or of any of the processes it as been asked to monitor.

In a system where extremely rapid crash detection is needed, and where it is acceptable to pay a high price to get fast response, one can do better. We can install a health-monitoring *agent* on each node in the system and have it open a very small shared-memory file. Each process that registers with the GMS would be assigned a slot in the shared memory file, and would begin to modify the corresponding entry at an agreed upon rate by copying clock values into that slot. The agent would then scan the file periodically, looking for entries that have not changed since the last scan, and then checking to see if the corresponding failure detection threshold has been reached yet. One could achieve failure detection speeds of a few milliseconds in such a model. As for detecting the failure of the entire operating system, such a system would need to send a steady stream of messages to the GMS server at some agreed upon rate, perhaps ten per second. In this manner, one could push failure detection times down to perhaps 200 ms.

The GMS server that detects a failure would notify other GMS members using a multi-cast. In Chapter 16 we'll discuss various kinds of multicasts, but the "flavor" required here is perhaps the most basic: a totally ordered multicast called *abcast*. Technically speaking, we would want to use what is called a "dynamically uniform" version of this protocol, but the issue is a bit esoteric and we won't digress into it for the time being.

Upon receiving such a multicast, a member of the GMS service would relay the failure notification to the processes registered with it. They can then use these notification events as a trustworthy source of failure information, for example to disconnect TCP channels to the failed process, etc. Such events won't be very common and there is no real need to filter them prior to relaying them to the registered pool of processes, but if scalability is a major concern in a given setting, one could certainly do so.

It is useful to number the GMS events. Since each server sees the same ordering of events, this is trivial.

If a GMS server fails, the processes connected to it should probe some other GMS member to see if their failure detection is accurate. If confirmed, such a process would re-register with a different GMS member. Upon reregistering, it informs the new server that it has seen all events up to some number, and the new server forwards notifications that it may have missed. Since this shouldn't take more than a few seconds, it suffices for each server to maintain a log of events and to keep the last few seconds of the log in memory. A process that is registering for the first time would not need to request any replay, since it will not yet be interested in the status of other processes in the system.

Thus, as we move forward in Chapters 16 to 19, we can presume a simple mechanism for detecting failures promptly and, while mistakes can be made, we can assume that they are converted into a trustworthy input. If a process is "falsely" detected as having failed, it would be dropped from the system anyhow, and would need to reconnect. But such events should be extremely rare and in fact when they occur, would probably reflect real failures that somehow corrected themselves—a machine that hung, for example, or a network link that was broken for a while. The tradeoff evident here is between having the entire distributed application hang waiting to find out if one node has failed or not, and having the system as a whole move forward at the risk that very rarely, some application program may have to reconnect (or just shut down and be restarted from scratch). Since we would like to achieve high availability, the latter scenario is simply a small price we'll have to pay for the benefits of improved responsiveness when failures do occur, which is in any case likely to be the far more common scenario.

15.5 Related Reading

Byzantine protocol: (see Ben-Or, Coan and Thomas, Coan et al., Cristian et al., Rabin, Schneider [1984]).

Byzantine quorum systems: (see Malkhi and Reiter [1998], Malkhi [2001], Alvisi [2001], Abraham [2003]),

Byzantine Agreement in servers: (see [Castro and Liskov [2001], Castro and Liskov [2002]).

Asynchronous Consensus: (see Chandra and Toueg [1991], Fisher et al.); but see also Babaoglu et al. (1995), Friedman et al., Guerraoui and Schiper, Ricciardi (1996).

The method of Chandra and Toueg: (see Babaoglu et al. [1995], Chandra and Toueg [1991], Chandra et al. [1992, 1996], Friedman et al.).

Group membership: (see Chockler [2001], Birman and Joseph [February 1987, November 1987], Chandra et al. [1996], Cristian [April 1991], Melliar-Smith et al. [1991], Mishra [1991], Ricciardi and Birman); but see also Agarwal, Anceaume et al., Babaoglu et al. (1994, 1995), Birman and Glade, Chandra et al. (1996), Cristian and Schmuck, Friedman et al., Golding (1992), Guerraoui and Schiper, Reiter (1994), Ricciardi (1992, 1993, 1996), Rodrigues et al.

Partitionable membership: (see Chockler [2001], Fekete [2001], Amir et al. [1992], Moser et al. [1994]).

Fail-stop illusion: (see Sabel and Marzullo).

16

Group Communication Systems

16.1 Group Communication

As explained at the start of Chapter 14, our goal in this part of the book is to find the very best possible way to implement high-speed data replication and other tools needed for fault-tolerant, highly assured Web Services and other forms of distributed computing. Given the GMS, one option would be to plunge right in and build replicated data over it. However, as we just saw (Section 15.4), one can implement replicated data by implementing a totally ordered communication primitive such as *abcast* and using it to update data within a group that maintains replicas. Doing so is more general, because *abcast* has many uses.

The GMS service uses this approach to replicate the information it needs to track system membership, and the same idea can also be applied to other kinds of replicated data. Accordingly, in this chapter we'll be looking at group multicast. A benefit is that we'll arrive not just at a replication algorithm, but rather at a set of tools that can easily support replicated data while also being useful for other purposes, such as implementing locking, or supporting fancy kinds of load-balancing.

Readers who aren't interested in details may want to skip to Chapter 18. The bottom line is that the *abcast* (or *totally ordered*) virtually synchronous multicast primitive used in Section 16.3 is probably all that one needs in most applications, and Chapter 17 covers "esoteric" topics that only arise if a system supports the creation of large numbers of groups (something platforms for group communication probably should do, but that in fact is often omitted). On the other hand, the topic of multicast reliability and ordering is an interesting one, and it isn't all that hard to understand how the desired properties correspond to protocol mechanisms—one property requires an extra phase of communication before delivery, another requires such-and-such information in each message, etc. Indeed, one can easily come up with new mixtures of properties and can usually implement them by just composing the basic mechanisms we'll explore here in a new but straightforward manner.

In this chapter, we'll discuss the options for implementing quite a few forms of ordering, and some other properties as well. Here's a quick summary for those who plan to skip the details.

1. *fbcast*. This is a "FIFO" ordered multicast. Messages from a sender are delivered in the order they were sent. For example, if process *p* sends message *a* followed by message *b*, all recipients deliver *a* before *b*. Messages sent by different senders can be delivered in different orders at different recipients. In a Web Services setting, a server streaming data to a set of clients might use *fbcast* to do so; the multicast stream would act much like *n* side-by-side TCP connections, but could potentially achieve much higher throughput than is possible with TCP (for example, *fbcast* can exploit IP multicast, if available).

2. *cbcast*. This is a "causally" ordered multicast (in the sense of Lamport's "causal" ordering relation, discussed in Section 14.3). We'll use *cbcast* to implement data replication and locking within process groups, for example when replicating the state of a high-availability server. What makes *cbcast* especially powerful is that it can be used in applications that need a very loosely coupled, asynchronous-style of connectivity for reasons of performance: with *cbcast* it will turn out that we can launch an asynchronous update to a replicated data item, immediately update the local copy (without waiting for messages to be sent or delivered) and then move on to the next task without worrying about a race condition in which some application component might try to access the data and see it "before" that update has been applied.

   With *cbcast*, messages from a single thread of computation are delivered in the order they were sent, and this is true *even when that thread spans multiple processes*. For example, one could have a situation in which process *p* sends message *a* and then asks process *q* to do something, causing *q* to send message *b*. Notice that *a* and *b* are ordered (after all, *p* asked *q* to take the action), yet they are not ordered in the eyes of *fbcast*, since *p* and *q* are different processes. In object-oriented systems, such situations arise very often and may not even be obvious to the developer, since object invocation can sometimes cross a process boundary transparently. Even so, *cbcast* would say that *b* came after *a* and deliver *a* before *b* at any destinations they have in common. Messages sent concurrently by different senders, where there is no implicit causal ordering, can be delivered in different orders at different recipients. Some people find *cbcast* confusing, but it is easy to understand if one just thinks of it as a version of *fbcast* fixed to work properly in a world of remote procedure calls and cross-address space object invocations! Indeed, *fbcast* is in some ways the more confusing primitive, especially in platforms like Microsoft .NET, where object invocations can occur without the programmer even realizing that one was requested!

3. *abcast*. Within any single group of processes, the system sorts messages into a total ordering and delivers them to group members in this order (historically, this primitive was also called "atomic broadcast"). The *abcast* primitive is usually understood to also

share the same property as *fbcast:* messages from a single source will be delivered in the order they were sent. In many settings, *abcast* is the easiest multicast primitive to work with, although it can be slower than *cbcast* if it isn't used carefully. Just the same, if in doubt, a developer can't really go wrong by using *abcast* to send multicasts, update replicated data, inform other group members of state changes, etc.

Token passing is a common way to actually implement a protocol such as *abcast*. Without getting into the details of how failures are handled, the basic idea is to associate a token with the group. The holder of the token can take actions on behalf of the group, such as deciding the ordering to use for a set of concurrent multicasts. The idea is to have senders send their messages using *fbcast*. On reception, the delivery is delayed. The token holder sends an *fbcast* of its own from time to time, giving the official ordering to use; recipients then sort their delayed *abcast* messages into order and deliver them accordingly. Of course one can make such a protocol fancier, and there are issues of how often to send the ordering messages and how to recover the token if the process holding it fails. We'll tackle those later in this chapter.

4. *cabcast*. Same as *abcast* but shares the *cbcast* property: if the sending events for some messages are causally ordered, the messages are delivered in a total order consistent with that causal order. This primitive isn't widely used, although there have been some fairly obscure academic arguments suggesting that it is an even safer choice than *abcast*.

5. *gbcast*. Ordered with respect to all other kinds of communication (historically, this was also called "globally atomic broadcast"). If a group of processes delivers a *gbcast* while other multicasts are being transmitted, any given multicast is delivered entirely before or entirely after the *gbcast*. The protocol is used mostly by a communications platform, for updating the membership of a group of processes. In principle, developers and other end-users shouldn't need to use *gbcast* unless they have made very sophisticated use of the other primitives and need a way to take some action atomically (ordered with respect to all of them).

6. *Failure atomicity*. This is a term that can mean different things for different communities, and we won't use in the remainder of the book. As "normally" defined, failure atomicity refers to a multicast that is delivered in the same order at all destinations, and that will be delivered to all operational processes if it is delivered to any, even in the event of a crash. For our purposes, the former property is really an ordering property—the one associated with *abcast*. As for the handling of crashes, we'll break this down into two cases: *dynamically uniform* and *non-uniform* failure handling, as seen below.

7. *Dynamically uniform and non-uniform multicasts.* In addition to ordering, multicasts can also differ in their guarantees in the event that a failure occurs while the multicast is being delivered. A *dynamically uniform* multicast guarantees that if any process delivers a message (even if it fails immediately upon doing so), all destinations that remain operational will deliver a copy of the message too. A *non-uniform* multicast

has a weaker guarantee: a multicast that has been delivered to a subset of the members of a group which (all) fail might not be delivered to the surviving members.

For example, suppose a sends a non-uniform multicast to group G and process b receives and delivers that multicast. If a and b both crash, it is possible that the group will repair itself and resume execution, but that no other members will deliver a's message! Had the multicast been uniform, such a condition couldn't arise. Non-uniformity can pose problems for developers. Say that the group is implementing a replicated bank account: a is an application withdrawing some cash and b is the ATM machine. With a non-uniform multicast, we could get into a situation where the customer withdraws $100 from the ATM machine, then unplugs it (very) quickly, and the main servers at the bank's data center never find out about the transaction. Using a dynamically uniform multicast, that kind of problem just can't arise.

Dynamic uniformity is sometimes called *safe* delivery, in the sense that when a dynamically uniform message is delivered, it is "safe" to take actions that leave externally visible effects with respect to which the remainder of the system must be consistent. However, a non-uniform multicast isn't necessarily *unsafe*. Often, it is perfectly safe for applications in which the action taken upon receipt of the message has only internal effects on the system state or when consistency with respect to external actions can be established in other ways—for example, from the semantics of the application. Moreover, this use of the term "safe" may confuse theoreticians, who prove protocols correct by establishing that they are "safe and live." Accordingly, we avoid using this term.

Given that it offers stronger failure guarantees, why not just insist that all multicast primitives be dynamically uniform? Here, the right answer depends somewhat on whether one wears a theoritician's or a practitioner's hat. From a theory perspective, it makes sense to do precisely this. Dynamic uniformity is a simple property to formalize, and applications using a dynamically uniform multicast layer are easier to prove correct.

But the bad news is that dynamic uniformity is *very costly*. It shouldn't be hard to see why this is the case: to achieve dynamic uniformity, we need to make sure that there is a copy of the message buffered at every group member before any member can be allowed to deliver it (otherwise, just kill all the processes with copies and clearly, the dynamic uniformity property will be violated, no matter what protocol we use to clean up after failure). This means that the slowest member of the group delays delivery of a message to all the other members.

Our bias in this book is pretty practical, especially where huge performance factors arise, as turns out to be the situation here. Accordingly, we won't make much use of the dynamic uniformity property in the algorithms presented later in the book. On the other hand, there are major systems (notably Paxos, the group management protocol favored in some recent Microsoft products and platforms) in which an *abcast* primitive with dynamic uniformity is the default. Such a primitive is very slow and expensive but can be used safely for almost any purpose. On the other hand, the cost is potentially so high that the resulting applications may be unacceptably sluggish compared to versions coded to use one of the cheaper primitives, particularly a non-uniform *abcast* that was implemented using token passing and *fbcast*.

Experts in the field have debated the pros and cons of a Paxos-like guarantee of dynamic uniformity versus a weaker "Isis-like" non-uniform multicast until all concerned have reached utter exhaustion. There simply isn't any agreement on the matter. Many engineers are convinced that replication is far too costly to use in settings like Web Services systems; they point to the CORBA fault tolerance standard, which was implemented using a dynamically uniform *abcast* primitive as proof of their basic point, and to database replication as further evidence supporting it. But all of these are examples in which the cost of dynamic uniformity is at the core of the performance problems they cite. In effect, dynamic uniformity is an appealing choice on conceptual and esthetic grounds, but once you decide to use it, you'll end up using it very sparingly or rejecting it as too slow. Non-dynamically uniform multicast is a bit harder to work with, but gives much faster solutions. Engineers have been quite successful using these primitives in the field; we'll see examples such as the New York and Swiss Stock Exchange systems, the French Air Traffic Control system, the US Naval AEGIS warship, and many others (these are Isis success stories, but Spread has lots of stories of its own).

8. *Flush*. This is more of an algorithm than a property of a multicast primitive; we'll need it as an antidote to the non-uniformity problems just described. In a system where multicasts are non-uniform, *flush* provides the application with a way to pause until multicasts it has sent (or received prior to calling *flush)* have actually reached their destinations and hence can't be lost even if a failure occurs. That is, a non-uniform multicast becomes uniform if a receiver calls *flush* before processing (delivering) it! Thus we can have our cake (higher performance) and eat it too (achieve dynamic uniformity where we really need this costly guarantee), by using a non-dynamically uniform multicast "most of the time" and calling flush now and then, when dynamic uniformity is really needed.

16.2 A Closer Look at Delivery Ordering Options

Let's look carefully at multicast delivery ordering, starting with a multicast that offers no guarantees whatsoever. Using such a multicast, a process that sends two messages, m_0 and m_1, concurrently would have no assurances at all about their relative order of delivery or relative atomicity—that is, suppose that m_0 was the message sent first. Not only might m_1 reach any destinations that it shares with m_0 first, but a failure of the sender might result in a scenario where m_1 was delivered atomically to all its destinations, but m_0 was not delivered to any process that remains operational (Figure 16.1). Such an outcome would be atomic on a per-multicast basis, but might not be a very useful primitive from the perspective of the application developer! Thus, while we should ask what forms of order a multicast primitive can guarantee, we should also ask how order is connected to atomicity in our failure-atomicity model.

As just summarized, we will be studying a hierarchy of increasingly ordered delivery properties. The weakest of these is usually called "sender order" or "FIFO order" and requires that if the same process sends m_0 and m_1 then m_0 will be delivered before m_1 at any destinations they have in common (see Figure 16.2). A slightly stronger ordering property, "causal delivery order," ensures that if $send(m_0) \rightarrow send(m_1)$, then m_0 will be delivered before m_1 at any destinations they have in common (see Figure 16.3). Still stronger is an order whereby any processes that receive the same two messages receive them in the same order: If at process p, $deliv(m_0) \rightarrow deliv(m_1)$, then m_0 will be delivered before m_1 at all destinations they have in common. This is sometimes called a totally ordered delivery protocol, but this is something of a misnomer, since one

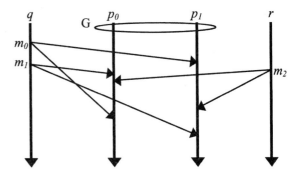

Figure 16.1. An unordered multicast provides no guarantees. Here, m_0 was sent before m_1, but is received after m_1 at destination p_0. The reception order for m_2, sent concurrently by process r, is different at each of its destinations.

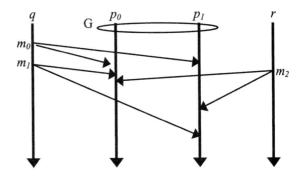

Figure 16.2. Sender ordered or FIFO multicast. Notice that m_2, which is sent concurrently, is unordered with respect to m_0 and m_1.

can imagine a number of ordering properties that would be total in this respect without necessarily implying the existence of a single system wide total ordering on all the messages sent in the system. The reason for this is that our definition focuses on delivery orders where messages overlap, but it doesn't actually relate these orders to an acyclic system wide ordering. The Transis project calls this type of locally ordered multicast an "agreed" order, and we like this term too: The destinations agree on the order, even for multicasts that may have been initiated concurrently and that may be unordered by their senders (Figure 16.4). However, the agreed order is more commonly called a "total" order or an "atomic" delivery order in the systems that support multicast communication and in the literature.

One can extend the agreed order into a causal agreed order (now one requires that if the sending events were ordered by causality, the delivery order will respect the causal send order) or into a system-wide agreed order (one requires that there exists a single system

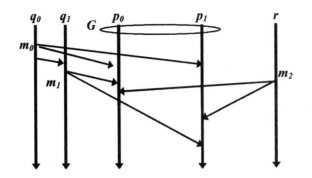

Figure 16.3. Causally ordered multicast delivery. Here m_0 is sent before m_1 in a causal sense, because a message is sent from q_0 to q_1 after m_0 was sent, and before q_1 sends m_1. Perhaps q_0 has requested that q_1 send m_1. m_0 is consequently delivered before m_1 at destinations that receive both messages. Multicast m_2 is sent concurrently and no ordering guarantees are provided. In this example, m_2 is delivered after m_1 by p_0 and before m_1 by p_1.

wide total order on messages, such that the delivery ordering used at any individual process is consistent with the message ordering in this system's total order). Later we will see why these are not identical orderings. Moreover, in systems that have multiple process groups, the issue of how to extend ordering properties to span multiple process groups will occur.

It has been proposed that total ordering be further classified as *weak* or *strong* in terms analogous to the dynamically uniform and nonuniform delivery properties. A weak total ordering property would be one guaranteed to hold only at *correct* processes, namely those remaining operational until the protocol terminates. A strong total ordering property would hold even at faulty processes, namely those that fail after delivering messages but before the protocol as a whole has terminated.

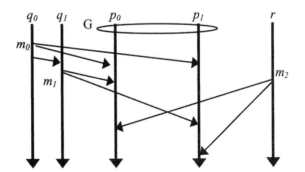

Figure 16.4. When using a totally ordered multicast primitive, p_0 and p_1 receive exactly the same multicasts, and the message are delivered in identical order. Hence, the order happens to also be causal, but this is not a specific guarantee of the primitive.

Suppose that a protocol fixes the delivery ordering for messages m_1 and m_2 at process p, delivering m_1 first. If p fails, a weak total ordering would permit the delivery of m_2 before m_1 at some other process q that survives the failure, even though this order is not the one seen by p. Like dynamic uniformity, the argument for strong total ordering is that this may be required if the ordering of messages may have externally visible consequences, which could be noticed by an external observer interacting with a process that later fails, and then interacts with some other process that remained operational. Naturally, this guarantee has a price, though, and one would prefer to use a less costly weak protocol in settings where such a guarantee is not required.

Let us now return to the issue raised briefly above, concerning the connection between the ordering properties for a set of multicasts and their failure-atomicity properties. To avoid creating an excessive number of possible multicast protocols, we will assume here that the developer of a reliable application will also want the specified ordering property to extend into the failure-atomicity properties of the primitives used. That is, in a situation where the ordering property of a multicast

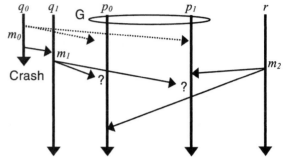

Figure 16.5. In this undesirable scenario, the failure of q_0 leaves a causal gap in the message delivery order, preventing q_1 from communicating with members of G. If m_1 is delivered, the causal ordering property would be violated, because $send(m_0) \rightarrow send(m_1)$. But m_0 will never be delivered. Thus, q_1 is logically partitioned from G. Process r, in contrast is free to communicate with G (message m_2).

would imply that message m_0 should be delivered before m_1 if they have any destinations in common, we will require that if m_1 is delivered successfully, then m_0 must also be delivered successfully, whether or not they actually do have common destinations. This is sometimes called a *gap-freedom* guarantee: It is the constraint that failures cannot leave holes or gaps in the ordered past of the system. Such a gap is seen in Figure 16.5.

Notice that this rule is stated so that it would apply even if m_0 and m_1 have no destinations in common. The reason is that ordering requirements are normally transitive: If m_0 is before m_1, and m_1 is before m_2, then m_0 is also before m_2, and we would like both delivery ordering obligations and failure-atomicity obligations to be guaranteed between m_0 and m_2. Had we instead required that "in a situation where the ordering property of a multicast implies that message m_0 should be delivered before m_1, then if they have any destinations in common, we will also require that if m_1 is delivered successfully, then m_0 must be too," the delivery atomicity requirement might not apply between m_0 and m_2.

Lacking a gap-freedom guarantee, one can imagine runs of a system that would leave orphaned processes that are technically prohibited from communicating with one another—for example, in Figure 16.5, q_1 sends message m_1 to the members of group G causally after m_0 was sent by q_0 to G. The members of G are now required to deliver m_0 before delivering m_1. However, if the failure-atomicity rule is such that the failure of q_0 could prevent m_0 from ever being delivered, this ordering obligation can only be satisfied by *never* delivering

m_1. One could say that q_1 has been partitioned from G by the ordering obligations of the system! Thus, if a system provides ordering guarantees and failure-atomicity guarantees, it should normally extend the latter to encompass the former.

Yet an additional question arises if a process sends multicasts to a group while processes are joining or leaving it. In these cases the membership of the group will be in flux at the time that the message is sent, and one can imagine several ways of interpreting how a system could implement group atomicity.

16.2.1 Nonuniform Failure-Atomic Group Multicast

Consider the following simple, but inefficient group multicast protocol. The sender adds a header to its message listing the membership of the destination group at the time that it sends the message. It now transmits the message to the members of the group, perhaps taking advantage of a hardware multicast feature (such as IP multicast) if one is available, and otherwise transmitting the message over stream-style reliable connections to the destinations. However, unlike a conventional stream protocol, here we will assume that the connection is only broken if the GMS reports that one of the end points has left the system.

Upon receipt of a message, the destination processes deliver it immediately, but also resend it to the remaining destinations. Again, each process uses reliable stream-style channels for this retransmission stage, breaking the channel only if the GMS reports the departure of an end point. A participant will now receive one copy of the message from the sender and one from each nonfailed participant other than itself. After delivery of the initial copy, it discards any duplicates. We will now argue that this protocol is failure-atomic, although not dynamically uniform.

To see that it is failure-atomic, assume that some process p_i receives and delivers a copy of the message and remains operational. Failure-atomicity tells us that all other destinations that remain operational must also receive and deliver the message. It is clear that this will occur, since the only condition under which p_i would fail to forward a message to p_j would be if the GMS reports that p_i has failed, or if it reports that p_j has failed. But we assumed that p_i does not fail, and the output of the GMS can be trusted in this environment. Thus, the protocol achieves failure atomicity. To see that the protocol is not dynamically uniform, consider the situation if the sender sends a copy of the message only to process p_i and then both processes fail. In this case, p_i may have delivered the message and then executed for some extended period of time before crashing or detecting that it has been partitioned from the system. The message has thus been delivered to one of the destinations and that destination may well have acted on it in a visible way; however, none of the processes that remain operational will ever receive it. As we noted earlier, this often will not pose a problem for the application, but it is a behavior that the developer must anticipate and treat appropriately.

As can be seen in Figure 16.5, this simple protocol is a costly one: To send a message to n destinations requires $O(n^2)$ messages. Of course, with hardware broadcast functions, or if the network is not a bottleneck, the cost will be lower, but the protocol still requires each process to send and receive each message approximately n times.

But now, suppose that we delay the retransmission stage of the protocol, retransmitting only if the GMS informs the participants that the sender has failed. This change yields a less-costly protocol, which requires n messages (or just one, if hardware broadcast is an option), but in which the participants may need to save a copy of each message indefinitely. They would do this just in case the sender fails.

Recall that we are transmitting messages over a reliable stream. It follows that within the lower levels of the communication system, there is an occasional acknowledgment flowing from each participant back to the sender. If we tap into this information, the sender will know when the participants have all received copies of its message. It can now send a second-phase message,

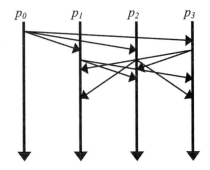

Figure 16.6. A very simple reliable multicast protocol. The initial round of messages triggers a second round of messages as each recipient echoes the incoming message to the other destinations.

informing the participants that it is safe to delete the saved copy of each message, although they must still save the message identification information to reject duplicates if the sender happens to crash midway through this stage. At this stage the participants can disable their retransmission logic and discard the saved copy of the message. Later, the sender could run still a third phase, telling the participants that they can safely delete even the message identification information, because after the second phase completes there will be no risk of a failure that would cause the message to be retransmitted by the participants.

But now a further optimization is possible. There is no real hurry to run the third phase of this protocol, and even the second phase can be delayed to some degree. Moreover, most processes that send a multicast will tend to send a subsequent one soon afterwards: This principle is well known from all forms of operating systems and database software. It can be summarized by this maxim: *The most likely action by any process is to repeat the same action it took most recently.* Accordingly, it makes sense to delay sending out messages for the second and third phase of the protocol in the hope that a new multicast will be initiated; this information can be piggybacked onto the first stage of an outgoing message associated with that subsequent protocol!

In this manner, we arrive at a solution, illustrated in Figure 16.7, that has an average cost of n messages per multicast, or just one if hardware broadcast can be exploited, plus some sort of background cost associated with the overhead to implement a reliable stream channel. When a failure does occur, any pending multicast will suddenly generate as many as n^2 additional messages, but even this effect can potentially be mitigated. Since the GMS provides the same membership list to all processes and the message itself carries the list of its destinations, the participants can delay briefly in the hope that some jointly identifiable lowest-ranked participant will turn out to have received the message and will terminate the protocol on behalf of all. We omit the details of such a solution, but any serious system for reliable distributed computing would implement a variety of such mechanisms to keep costs down to an absolute minimum and to maximize the value of each message actually transmitted using piggy-backing, delaying tactics, and hardware broadcast.

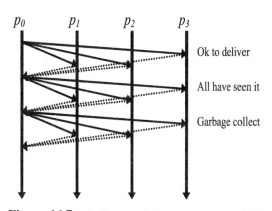

Figure 16.7. An improved three-phase protocol. Ideally, the second and third phases would be piggybacked onto other multicasts from the same sender to the same set of destinations and would not require extra messages.

Notice that because the protocol in figures 16.7 delivers messages in the first phase, it is *non*-uniform.

16.2.2 Dynamically Uniform Failure-Atomic Group Multicast

We can extend the above protocol to one that is dynamically uniform. Doing so requires that no process deliver the message until it is known the processes in the destination group all have a copy. (In some cases it may be sufficient to know that a majority have a copy, but we will not concern ourselves with these sorts of special cases now, because they are typically limited to the processes that actually run the GMS protocol.) Earlier, we mentioned the Paxos system and commented that it, and other similar systems that provide dynamic uniformity, tend to be quite slow. The problem is precisely the one just cited, namely the need to wait until a majority of processes have a copy of each message before that message can be delivered.

We could accomplish our goal with the original inefficient protocol of Figure 16.6, by modifying the original nonuniform protocol to delay the delivery of messages until a copy has been received from every destination that is still present in the membership list provided by the GMS. However, such a protocol would suffer from the inefficiencies that led us to optimize the original protocol into the one in Figure 16.7. Accordingly, it makes more sense to focus on that improved protocol.

Here, it can be seen that an additional round of messages will be needed before the multicast can be delivered initially; the rest of the protocol can then be used without change (Figure 16.8). Unfortunately, though, this initial round also delays the delivery of the messages to their destinations. In the original protocol, a message could be delivered as soon as it reached a destination for the first time—thus, the latency to delivery is precisely the latency from the sender to a given destination for a single hop. Now the latency might

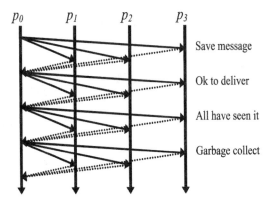

p_0 p_1 p_2 p_3

Save message

Ok to deliver

All have seen it

Garbage collect

Figure 16.8. A dynamically uniform version of the optimized, reliable multicast protocol. Latency to delivery may be much higher, because no process can deliver the message until all processes have received and saved a copy. Here, the third and fourth phases can piggyback on other multicasts, but the first two stages may need to be executed as promptly as possible to avoid increasing the latency still further. Latency is often a key performance factor.

be substantially increased: For a dynamically uniform delivery, we will need to wait for a round trip to the slowest process in the set of destinations, and then one more hop until the sender has time to inform the destinations that it is safe to deliver the messages. In practice, this may represent an increase in latency of a factor of ten or more. Thus, while dynamically uniform guarantees are sometimes needed, the developer of a distributed application should request this property only when it is genuinely necessary, or performance (to the degree that latency is a factor in performance) will suffer badly.

16.2.3 Dynamic Process Groups

When we introduced the GMS, our system became very dynamic, allowing processes to join and leave at will. But not all processes in the system will be part of the same application, and the protocols presented in the previous section are therefore assumed to be sent to groups of processes that represent subsets of the full system membership. This is seen in Figure 16.9, which illustrates the structure of a hypothetical trading system in which services (replicated for improved performance or availability) implement theoretical pricing calculations. Here we have one big system, with many small groups in it. How should the membership of such a subgroup be managed?

In this section, we introduce a membership management protocol based on the idea that a single process within each group will serve as the coordinator for synchronizing the delivery of events reporting membership changes with the delivery of events reporting new multicast messages. If a process wishes to join the group, or voluntarily leaves the group, this coordinator will update the group membership accordingly. (The role of coordinator will really be handled by the layer of software that implements groups, so this won't be visible

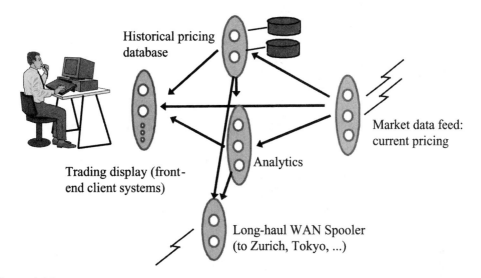

Historical pricing
database

Market data feed:
current pricing

Analytics

Trading display (front-
end client systems)

Long-haul WAN Spooler
(to Zurich, Tokyo, ...)

Figure 16.9. Distributed trading system may have both static and dynamic uses for process groups. The historical database, replicated for load-balancing and availability, is tied to the databases themselves and can be viewed as static. This is also true of the market data feeds, which are often redundant for fault tolerance. Other parts of the system, however, such as the analytics (replicated for parallelism) and the client interface processes (one or more per trader), are highly dynamic groups. For uniformity of the model, it makes sense to adopt a dynamic group model, but to keep in mind that some of these groups manage physical resources.

to the application process itself.) Additionally, the coordinator will monitor the members (through the GMS and by periodically pinging them to verify that they are still healthy), excluding any failed processes from the membership (much as in the case of a process that leaves voluntarily).

In the approach we present here, all processes that belong to a group maintain a local copy of the current membership list. We call this the "view" of the group and will say that each time the membership of the group changes, a new view of the group is reported to the members. Our protocol will have the property that all group members see the identical sequence of group views within any given component of a partitioned system. In practice, we will mostly be interested in primary component partitions, and, in these cases, we will simply say that all processes either see identical views for a group or, if excluded from the primary component, cease to see new views and eventually detect that they are partitioned, at which point a process may terminate or attempt to rejoin the system much like a new process.

The members of a group depend upon their coordinator for the reporting of new views and consequently monitor the liveness of the coordinator by periodically pinging it. If the coordinator appears to be faulty, the member or members that detect this report the situation to the GMS in the usual manner, simultaneously cutting off communication to the coordinator and starting to piggyback or gossip this information on messages to other members, which similarly cut their channels to the coordinator and, if necessary, relay this information to the GMS. The GMS will eventually report that the coordinator has failed, at which point the lowest ranked of the remaining members takes over as the new coordinator.

Interestingly, we have now solved our problem, because we can use the nonuniform multicast protocol to distribute new views within the group. In fact, this hides a subtle point, to which we will return momentarily—namely, the way to deal with ordering properties of a reliable multicast, particularly in the case where the sender fails and the protocol must be terminated by other processes in the system. However, we will see below that the protocol has the necessary ordering properties when it operates over stream connections that guarantee FIFO delivery of messages, and when the failure-handling mechanisms introduced earlier are executed in the same order that the messages themselves were initially seen (i.e., if process p_i first received multicast m_0 before multicast m_1, then p_i retransmits m_0 before m_1).

16.2.4 View-Synchronous Failure Atomicity

We have now created an environment within which a process that joins a process group will receive the membership view for that group as of the time it was added to the group. It will subsequently observe any changes that occur until it crashes or leaves the group, provided only that the GMS continues to report failure information. Such a process may now wish to initiate multicasts to the group using the reliable protocols presented earlier. But suppose that a process belonging to a group fails while some multicasts from it are pending? When can the other members

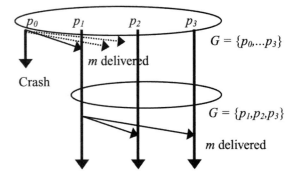

Figure 16.10. Although m was sent when p_0 belonged to G, it reaches p_2 and p_3 after a view change reporting that p_0 has failed. The earlier (at p_1) and later (p_2, p_3) delivery events thus differ in that the recipients will observe a different view of the process group at the time the message arrives. This can result in inconsistency if, for example, the membership of the group is used to subdivide the incoming tasks among the group members.

be certain that they have seen all of its messages, so that they can take over from it if the application requires that they do so?

Up to now, our protocol structure would not provide this information to a group member—for example, it may be that process p_0 fails after sending a message to p_1 but to no other member. It is entirely possible that the failure of p_0 will be reported through a new process group view before this message is finally delivered to the remaining members.

Such a situation would create difficult problems for the application developer, and we need a mechanism to avoid it. This is illustrated in Figure 16.10.

It makes sense to assume that the application developer will want failure notification to represent a final state with regard to the failed process. Thus, it would be preferable for all messages initiated by process p_0 to have been delivered to their destinations before the failure of p_0 is reported through the delivery of a new view. We will call the necessary protocol a *flush* protocol, meaning that it flushes partially completed multicasts out of the system, reporting the new view only after this has been done. The reader may recall from section 16.1 that *flush* is also useful in "converting" non-uniform multicasts to uniform ones, so as to take an external action safely. In fact the same protocol can address both requirements.

In the example shown in Figure 16.10, we did not include the exchange of messages required to multicast the new view of group G. Notice, however, that the figure is probably incorrect if the new-view coordinator of group G is actually process p_1. To see this, recall that the communication channels are FIFO and that the termination of an interrupted multicast protocol requires only a single round of communication. Thus, if process p_1 simply runs the completion protocol for multicasts initiated by p_0 before it starts the new-view multicast protocol that will announce that p_0 has been dropped by the group, the pending multicast will be completed first. This is shown in Figure 16.11.

We can guarantee this behavior even if multicast m is dynamically uniform, simply by delaying the new-view multicast until the outcome of the dynamically uniform protocol has been determined.

On the other hand, the problem becomes harder if p_1 (which is the only process to have received the multicast from p_0) is not the coordinator for the new-view protocol. In this case, it will be necessary

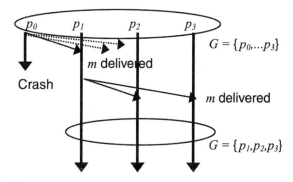

Figure 16.11. Process p_1 flushes pending multicasts before initiating the new-view protocol.

for the new-view protocol to operate with an additional round, in which the members of G are asked to flush any multicasts that are as yet unterminated, and the new-view protocol runs only when this flush phase has finished. Moreover, even if the new-view protocol is being executed to drop p_0 from the group, it is possible that the system will soon discover that some other process, perhaps p_2, is also faulty and must also be dropped. Thus, a flush protocol should flush messages *regardless of their originating process*, with the result that all multicasts will have been flushed out of the system before the new view is installed.

These observations lead to a communication property that Babaoglu and his colleagues have called *view synchronous communication*, which is one of several properties associated with the *virtual synchrony model* introduced by Thomas Joseph and the author in 1985. A view-synchronous communication system ensures that any multicast initiated in a given view of some process group will be failure-atomic with respect to that view and will be terminated before a new view of the process group is installed.

One might wonder how a view-synchronous communication system can prevent a process from initiating new multicasts while the view installation protocol is running. If such multicasts are locked out, there may be an extended delay during which no multicasts can be transmitted, causing performance problems for the application programs layered over the system. But if such multicasts are permitted, the first phase of the flush protocol will not have flushed *all* the necessary multicasts!

A solution for this problem was suggested independently by Ladin and Malkhi, working on systems called Harp and Transis, respectively. In these systems, if a multicast is initiated while a protocol to install view i of group G is running, the multicast destinations are taken to be the future membership of G when that new view has been installed—for example, in the Figure 16.11, a new multicast might be initiated by process p_2 while the protocol to exclude p_0 from G is still running. Such a new multicast would be addressed to $\{p_1, p_2, p_3\}$ (not to p_0), and would be delivered only after the new view is delivered to the remaining group members. The multicast can thus be initiated while the view change protocol is running and would only be delayed if, when the system is ready to deliver a copy of the message to some group member, the corresponding view has not yet been reported. This approach will often avoid delays completely, since the new-view protocol was already running and will often terminate in roughly the same amount of time as will be needed for the new multicast protocol to start delivering messages to destinations. Thus, at least in the most common case, the view change can be accomplished even as communication to the group continues unabated. Of course, if multiple failures occur, messages will still queue up on receipt and will need to be delayed until the view flush protocol terminates, so this desirable behavior cannot always be guaranteed.

The Horus and Ensemble systems use a slightly different approach. In these systems, the sender of a message is guaranteed that the message will be delivered in the same view that it finds itself in when it performs the send operation. However, these systems also implement a form of interlock between the view installation layer and the application. When membership will be changed, the system first asks the application to stop sending new multicasts, and the application acknowledges the request. Next, the system delivers the new view. Finally, the application can resume sending multicasts, using the new view.

16.2.5 Summary of GMS Properties

The following is an informal (English-language) summary of the properties that a group membership service guarantees to members of subgroups of the full system membership. We use the term "process group" for such a subgroup. When we say "guarantees" the reader should keep in mind that a GMS service does not, and in fact cannot, guarantee that it will remain operational despite all possible patterns of failures and communication outages.

Some patterns of failure or of network outages will prevent such a service from reporting new system views and will consequently prevent the reporting of new process group views. Thus, the guarantees of a GMS are relative to a constraint—namely, that the system provides a sufficiently reliable transport of messages and that the rate of failures is sufficiently low.

1. *GMS-1:* Starting from an initial group view, the GMS reports new views that differ by addition and deletion of group members. The reporting of changes is by the two-stage interface described previously, which gives protocols an opportunity to flush pending communication from a failed process before its failure is reported to application processes.

2. *GMS-2:* The group view is not changed capriciously. A process is added only if it has started and is trying to join the system, and deleted only if it has failed or is suspected of having failed by some other member of the system.

3. *GMS-3:* All group members observe continuous subsequences of the same sequence of group views, starting with the view during which the member was first added to the group and ending either with a view that registers the voluntary departure of the member from the group or with the failure of the member.

4. *GMS-4:* The GMS is fair in the sense that it will not indefinitely delay a view change associated with one event while performing other view changes. That is, if the GMS service itself is live, join requests will eventually cause the requesting process to be added to the group, and leave or failure events will eventually cause a new group view to be formed that excludes the departing process.

5. *GMS-5:* The GMS permits progress only in a primary component of a partitioned network. In fact we'll see that *GMS-5* can be weakened; some group communication systems permit operation despite partitioning failures, and offer extensions to the GMS-5 property so that a recipient of a message can also learn whether it (the recipient) is still connected to the primary partition. But such extensions haven't been very popular with developers, who either don't often run into partitioning scenarios or find it too difficult to work with such extensions.

Although we will not pursue these points here, it should be noted that many networks have some form of critical resources on which the processes reside. Although the protocols given above are designed to make progress when a majority of the processes in the system remain alive after a partitioning failure, a more reasonable approach would also take into account the resulting resource pattern. In many settings, for example, one would want to define the primary partition of a network to be the one that retains the majority of the servers after a partitioning event. One can also imagine settings in which the primary should be the component within which access to some special piece of hardware remains possible, such as the radar in an air traffic control application. These sorts of problems can generally be solved by associating weights with the processes in the system and redefining the majority rule as a weighted majority rule. Such an approach recalls work in the 1970s and early 1980s by Bob Thomas of BBN on weighted majority voting schemes and weighted quorum replication algorithms (see Gifford, Thomas).

16.2.6 Ordered Multicast

Earlier, we observed that our multicast protocol would preserve the sender's order if executed over FIFO channels and if the algorithm used to terminate an active multicast was also FIFO. Of course, some systems may seek higher levels of concurrency by using non-FIFO-reliable channels, or by concurrently executing the termination protocol for more than one multicast, but, even so, such systems could potentially number multicasts to track the order in which they should be delivered. Freedom from gaps in the sender order is similarly straightforward to ensure.

This leads to a broader issue of what forms of multicast ordering are useful in distributed systems and how such orderings can be guaranteed. In developing application programs that make use of process groups, it is common to employ what Leslie Lamport and Fred Schneider call a *state machine* style of distributed algorithm (see Schneider [1990]). Later, we will see reasons that one might want to relax this model, but the original idea is to run identical software at each member of a group of processes and to use a failure-atomic multicast to deliver messages to the members in identical order. Lamport's proposal stated that Byzantine protocols should be used for this multicast, and, in fact, he also uses Byzantine protocols on messages output by the group members. The result of this is that the group as a whole gives the behavior of a single ultra-reliable process, in which the operational members behave identically and the faulty behaviors of faulty members can be tolerated up to the limits of the Byzantine protocols. One limitation is that this method requires deterministic programs and thus could not be used in applications that are multithreaded or that accept input through an interrupt-style of event notification. Both are common in modern software, so the restriction is a serious one.

As we will use the concept, however, there is really only one aspect that is exploited—namely that of building applications that will remain in identical states if presented with identical inputs in identical orders. Here we may not require that the applications actually be deterministic, but merely that they be designed to maintain identically replicated states. This problem, as we will see, is solvable even for programs that may be very nondeterministic in other ways and very concurrent. Moreover, we will not be using Byzantine protocols, but will substitute various weaker forms of multicast protocols. Nonetheless, it has become usual to refer to this as a variation on Lamport's state machine approach, and it is certainly the case that his work was the first to exploit process groups in this manner.

FIFO Order

We've talked about the FIFO multicast protocol, *fbcast* (the "b" comes from the early literature, which tended to focus on static system membership and hence on "broadcasts" to the full membership; "fmcast" might make more sense here, but would be non-standard). Such a protocol can be developed using the methods previously discussed, provided that the software used to implement the failure-recovery algorithm is carefully designed to ensure that the sender's order won't get lost when a crash occurs and processes other than the original sender step in to ensure that all group members will receive copies.

There are two variants on the basic *fbcast*: a normal *fbcast*, which is nonuniform, and a safe *fbcast*, which guarantees the dynamic uniformity property at the cost of an extra round of communication.

The costs of a protocol are normally measured in terms of the latency before delivery can occur, the message load imposed on each individual participant (which corresponds to the CPU usage in most settings), the number of messages placed on the network as a function of group size (this may or may not be a limiting factor, depending on the properties of the network), and the overhead required to represent protocol-specific headers. When the sender of a multicast is also a group member, there are two latency metrics that may be important: latency from when a message is sent to when it is delivered, which is usually expressed as a multiple of the communication latency of the network and transport software, and the latency from when the sender initiates the multicast to when it learns the delivery ordering for that multicast. During this period, some algorithms will be waiting—in the sender case, the sender may be unable to proceed until it knows when its own message will be delivered (in the sense of ordering with respect to other concurrent multicasts from other senders). And in the case of a destination process, it is clear that until the message is delivered, no actions can be taken.

In all of these cases, *fbcast* and *safe fbcast* are inexpensive protocols. The latency seen by the sender is minimal: In the case of *fbcast*, as soon as the multicast has been transmitted, the sender knows that the message will be delivered in an order consistent with its order of sending. Still focusing on *fbcast,* the latency between when the message is sent and when it is delivered to a destination is exactly that of the network itself: Upon receipt, a message is deliverable as soon as any prior messages have been delivered—hence, if message loss is rare, immediately upon receipt. The protocol requires only a single round of communication, and other costs are hidden in the background and often can be piggybacked on other traffic. And the header used for *fbcast* needs only to identify the message uniquely and capture the sender's order—information that may be expressed in a few bytes of storage.

For *safe fbcast*, on the other hand, these costs would be quite a bit higher, because an extra round of communication is needed to find out if all the intended recipients have a copy of the message. Suppose that the network has latency σ and the slowest destination adds an additional delay of δ. Then *safe fbcast* has a latency at the sender of roughly $2\sigma + \delta$. The non-sender processes need to learn that the message is safe from the sender, so they see a delay of $3\sigma + \delta$. Notice that even the fastest destinations are limited by the response times of the slowest destinations, although one can imagine partially safe implementations of the protocol in which a majority of replies would be adequate to permit progress.

Notice that although *fbcast* can also be converted into *safe fbcast* by invoking *flush* after sending the multicast, doing so would be even more costly. Thus if *safe fbcast* will be used often, one should implement the optimized version just described. The *fbcast* and *safe fbcast* protocols can be used in a state-machine style of computing under conditions where the messages transmitted by different senders are independent of one another, and hence the actions taken by recipients will commute—for example, suppose that sender p is reporting trades on a stock exchange and sender q is reporting bond pricing information.

Although this information may be sent to the same destinations, it may or may not be combined in a way that is order sensitive. When the recipients are insensitive to the order of messages that originate in different senders, *fbcast* is a strong enough ordering to ensure that a state machine style of computing can safely be used. However, many applications are more sensitive to ordering than this, and the ordering properties of *fbcast* would not be sufficient to ensure that group members remain consistent with one another in such cases.

Causal Order

An obvious question to ask concerns the maximum amount of order that can be provided in a protocol that has the same cost as *fbcast*. At the beginning of this chapter, we discussed the causal ordering relation, which is the transitive closure of the message send/receive relation and the internal ordering associated with processes. In 1985, Thomas Joseph and the author developed a causally ordered protocol with costs similar to that of *fbcast* and showed how it could be used to implement replicated data. We named the protocol *cbcast*. Soon thereafter, Schmuck was able to show that causal order is a form of maximal ordering relation among *fbcast*-like protocols (see Schmuck). More precisely, he showed that any ordering property that can be implemented using an asynchronous protocol can be represented as a subset of the causal ordering relationship. This proves that causally ordered communication is the most powerful protocol possible with cost similar to that of *fbcast*.

The basic idea of a causally ordered multicast is easy to express. Recall that a FIFO multicast is required to respect the order in which any single sender sends a sequence of multicasts. If process p sends m_0 and then later sends m_1, a FIFO multicast must deliver m_0 before m_1 at any overlapping destinations. The ordering rule for a causally ordered multicast is almost identical: if $send(m_0) \rightarrow send(m_1)$, then a causally ordered delivery will ensure that m_0 is delivered before m_1 at any overlapping destinations. In some sense, causal order is just a generalization of the FIFO sender order. For a FIFO order, we focus on events that happen in some order at a single place in the system. For the causal order, we relax this to events that are ordered under the "happens before" relationship, which can span multiple processes but is otherwise essentially the same as the send order for a single process. A causally ordered multicast simply guarantees that if m_0 is sent before m_1, then m_0 will be delivered before m_1 at destinations they have in common.

The first time one encounters the concept of causally ordered delivery, it can be confusing because the definition doesn't look at all like a definition of FIFO ordered delivery. In fact, however, the underlying idea is extremely similar. Most readers will be comfortable with the idea of a thread of control that moves from process to process when RPC is used by a client process to ask a server to take some action on its behalf. We can think of the thread of computation in the server as being part of the thread of the client. In some sense, a single computation spans two address spaces. Causally ordered multicasts are simply multicasts ordered along such a thread of computation—they are FIFO ordered, but along computational threads rather than by individual processes. When this perspective is adopted one sees that FIFO ordering is in some ways the less natural concept: *fbcast* tracks ordering of events only when they occur in the same address space. If process p sends message m_0

and then asks process q to send message m_1, it seems natural to say that m_1 was sent after m_0. Causal ordering expresses this relation, but FIFO ordering only does so if p and q are in the same address space.

There are several ways to implement multicast delivery orderings that are consistent with the causal order. We will now present two such schemes, both based on adding a timestamp to the message header before it is initially transmitted. The first uses a logical clock; the resulting change in header size is very small but the protocol itself has high latency. The second uses a vector timestamp and achieves much better performance. Finally, we discuss several ways of compressing these timestamps to minimize the overhead associated with the ordering property.

Causal ordering with logical timestamps.   Suppose that we are interested in preserving causal order within process groups and in doing so only during periods when the membership of the group is fixed (the flush protocol that implements view synchrony makes this a reasonable goal). Finally, assume that all multicasts are sent to the full membership of the group. By attaching a logical timestamp to each message, maintained using Lamport's logical clock algorithm, we can ensure that if $send(m_1) \rightarrow send(m_2)$, then m_1 will be delivered before m_2 at overlapping destinations. The approach is extremely simple: Upon receipt of a message m a process p_i waits until it knows that there are no messages still in the channels to it from other group members, p_j that could have a timestamp smaller than $LT(m)$.

How can p_i be sure of this? In a setting where process group members continuously emit multicasts, it suffices to wait long enough. Knowing that m will eventually reach every other group member, p_i can reason that eventually every group member will increase its logical clock to a value at least as large as $LT(m)$ and will subsequently send out a message with that larger timestamp value. Since we are assuming that the communication channels in our system preserve FIFO ordering, as soon as any message has been received with a timestamp greater than or equal to that of m from a process p_j, all future messages from p_j will have a timestamp strictly greater than that of m. Thus, p_i can for a message from every other process in the group with a timestamp greater than that of m. If there are messages with timestamps less than or equal to $LT(m)$, they can be delivered in timestamp order. If two messages have the same timestamp, they must have been sent concurrently, and p_i can either deliver them in an arbitrary order or can use some agreed-upon rule (e.g., by breaking ties using the process-ID of the sender or its ranking in the group view) to obtain a total order. With this approach, it is no harder to deliver messages in an order that is causal and total than to do so in an order that is only causal.

Of course, in many (if not most) settings, some group members will send to the group frequently while others send rarely or participate only as message recipients. In such environments, p_i might wait in vain for a message from p_j, preventing the delivery of m. There are two obvious solutions to this problem: Group members can be modified to send a periodic multicast simply to keep the channels active, or p_i can ping p_j when necessary—in this manner flushing the communication channel between them.

Although simple, this causal ordering protocol is too costly for most settings. A single multicast will trigger a wave of n^2 messages within the group, and a long delay may elapse before it is safe to deliver a multicast. For many applications, latency is the key factor that limits performance, and this protocol is a potentially slow one because incoming messages must be delayed until a suitable message is received on every other incoming channel. Moreover, the number of messages that must be delayed can be very large in a big group, creating potential buffering problems.

Causal ordering with vector timestamps.   If we are willing to accept a higher overhead, the inclusion of a vector timestamp in each message permits the implementation of a much more accurate message-delaying policy. Using the vector timestamp, we can delay an incoming message m_i precisely until any missing causally prior messages have been received. This algorithm, like the previous one, assumes that all messages are multicast to the full set of group members.

Again, the idea is simple. Each message is labeled with the vector timestamp of the sender as of the time when the message was sent. This timestamp is essentially a count of the number of causally prior messages that have been delivered to the application at the sender process, broken down by source. Thus, the vector timestamp for process p_1 might contain the sequence [13,0,7,6] for a group G with membership $\{p_0, p_1, p_2, p_3\}$ at the time it creates and multicasts m_i. Process p_1 will increment the counter for its own vector entry (here we assume that the vector entries are ordered in the same way as the processes in the group view), labeling the message with timestamp [13,1,7,6]. The meaning of such a timestamp is that this is the first message sent by p_1, but that it has received and delivered 13 messages from p_0, seven from p_2 and six from p_3. Presumably, these received messages created a context within which m_i makes sense, and if some process delivers m_i without having seen one or more of them, it may run the risk of misinterpreting m_i. A causal ordering avoids such problems.

Now, suppose that process p_3 receives m_i. It is possible that m_i would be the very first message that p_3 has received up to this point in its execution. In this case, p_3 might have a vector timestamp as small as [0,0,0,6], reflecting only the six messages it sent before m_i was transmitted. Of course, the vector timestamp at p_3 could also be much larger: The only "hard" upper limit is that the entry for p_1 is necessarily 0, since m_i is the first message sent by p_1. The delivery rule for a recipient such as p_3 is now clear: It should delay message m_i until both of the following conditions are satisfied:

1   Message m_i is the *next* message, in sequence, from its sender.
2   Every causally prior message has been received and delivered to the application.

We can translate rule 2 into the following formula: If message m_i sent by process p_i is received by process p_j, then we delay m_i until, for each value of k different from i and j, $VT(p_j)[k] \geq VT(m_i)[k]$. Thus, if p_3 has not yet received any messages from p_0, it will not deliver m_i until it has received at least 13 messages from p_0. Figure 16.12 illustrates this rule in a simpler case, involving only two messages.

We need to convince ourselves that this rule really ensures that messages will be delivered in a causal order. To see this, it suffices to observe that when m_i was sent, the sender had already received and delivered the messages identified by $VT(m_i)$. Since these are precisely the messages causally ordered before m_i, the protocol only delivers messages in an order consistent with causality.

The causal ordering relationship is acyclic—hence, one would be tempted to conclude that this protocol can never delay a message indefinitely. But, in fact, it can do so if failures occur. Suppose that process p_0 crashes. Our flush protocol will now run, and the 13 messages that p_0 sent to p_1 will be retransmitted by p_1 on its behalf. But if p_1 also fails, we could have a situation in which m_i, sent by p_1 causally after having received 13 messages from p_0, will never be safely deliverable, because no record exists of one or more of these prior messages! The point here is that although the

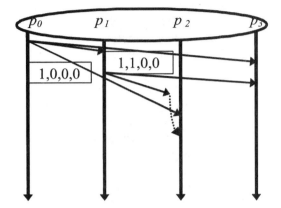

Figure 16.12. Upon receipt of a message with vector timestamp [1,1,0,0] from p_1, process p_2 detects that it is too early to deliver this message, and delays it until a message from p_0 has been received and delivered.

communication channels in the system are FIFO, p_1 is not expected to forward messages on behalf of other processes until a flush protocol starts when one or more processes have left or joined the system. Thus, a dual failure can leave a gap such that m_i is causally orphaned.

The good news, however, is that this can only happen if the *sender of m_i* fails, as illustrated in Figure 16.13. Otherwise, the sender will have a buffered copy of any messages that it received and that are still unstable, and this information will be sufficient to fill in

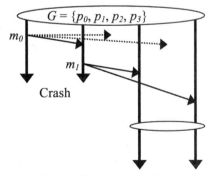

Figure 16.13. When processes p_0 and p_1 crash, message m_1 is causally orphaned. This would be detected during the flush protocol that installs the new group view. Although m_1 has been received by the surviving processes, it is not possible to deliver it while still satisfying the causal ordering constraint. However, this situation can only occur if the sender of the message is one of the failed processes. By discarding m_1 the system can avoid causal gaps. Surviving group members will never be logically partitioned (prevented from communicating with each other).

any causal gaps in the message history prior to when m_i was sent. Thus, our protocol can leave individual messages that are orphaned, but it cannot partition group members away from one another in the sense that concerned us earlier.

Our system will eventually discover any such causal orphan when flushing the group prior to installing a new view that drops the sender of m_i. At this point, there are two options: m_i can be delivered to the application with some form of warning that it is an orphaned message preceded by missing causally prior messages, or m_i can simply be discarded. Either approach leaves the system in a self-consistent state, and surviving processes are never prevented from communicating with one another.

Causal ordering with vector timestamps is a very efficient way to obtain this delivery ordering property. The overhead is limited to the vector timestamp itself and to the increased latency associated with executing the timestamp ordering algorithm and with delaying messages that genuinely arrive too early. Such situations are common if the machines involved are overloaded, channels are backlogged, or the network is congested and lossy, but otherwise they would rarely be observed. In the best case, when none of these conditions are present, the causal ordering property can be assured with essentially no additional cost in latency or messages passed within the system! On the other hand, notice that the causal ordering obtained is definitely not a total ordering, as was the case in the algorithm based on logical timestamps. Here, we have a genuinely cheaper ordering property, but it is also less ordered.

Timestamp compression. The major form of overhead associated with a vector-timestamp causality is that of the vectors themselves. This has stimulated interest in schemes for compressing the vector-timestamp information transmitted in messages. Although an exhaustive treatment of this topic is well beyond the scope of this book, there are some specific optimizations that are worth mentioning.

Suppose that a process sends a burst of multicasts—a common pattern in many applications. After the first vector timestamp, each subsequent message will contain a nearly identical timestamp, differing only in the timestamp associated with the sender itself, which will increment for each new multicast. In such a case, the algorithm could be modified to omit the timestamp: A missing timestamp would be interpreted as being the previous timestamp, incremented in the sender's field only. This single optimization can eliminate most of the vector timestamp overhead seen in a system characterized by bursty communication. More accurately, what has happened here is that the sequence number used to implement the FIFO channel from source to destination makes the sender's own vector-timestamp entry redundant. We can omit the vector timestamp because none of the other entries were changing and the sender's sequence number is represented elsewhere in the packets being transmitted.

An important case of this optimization occurs if all the multicasts to some group are sent along a single causal path—for example, suppose that a group has some form of token, which circulates within it, and only the token holder can initiate multicasts to the group. In this case, we can implement *cbcast* using a single sequence number: the first *cbcast*, the second *cbcast*, and so forth. Later, this form of *cbcast* will turn out to be important. Notice, however, that if there are concurrent multicasts from different senders (i.e., if senders can transmit multicasts without waiting for the token), the optimization is no longer able to express the causal ordering relationships on messages sent within the group.

A second optimization is to reset the vector-timestamp fields to zero each time the group changes its membership, and to sort the group members so that any passive receivers are listed last in the group view. With these steps, the vector timestamp for a message will tend to end in a series of zeros, corresponding to those processes that have not sent a message since the previous view change event. The vector timestamp can then be truncated: The reception of a short vector would imply that the missing fields are all zeros. Moreover, the numbers themselves will tend to stay smaller and hence can be represented using shorter fields (if they threaten to overflow, a flush protocol can be run to reset them). Again, a single very simple optimization would be expected to greatly reduce overhead in typical systems that use this causal ordering scheme.

A third optimization involves sending only the difference vector, representing those fields that have changed since the previous message multicast by this sender. Such a vector would be more complex to represent (since we need to know which fields have changed and by how much) but much shorter (since, in a large system, one would expect few fields to change in any short period of time). This generalizes into a run-length encoding.

This third optimization can also be understood as an instance of an ordering scheme introduced originally in the Psync, Totem, and Transis systems. Rather than representing messages by counters, a precedence relation is maintained for messages: a tree of the messages received and the causal relationships between them. When a message is sent, the leaves of the causal tree are transmitted. These leaves are a set of concurrent messages, all of which are causally prior to the message now being transmitted. Often, there will be very few such messages, because many groups would be expected to exhibit low levels of concurrency.

The receiver of a message will now delay it until those messages it lists as causally prior have been delivered. By transitivity, no message will be delivered until all the causally prior messages have been delivered. Moreover, the same scheme can be combined with one similar to the logical timestamp ordering scheme of the first causal multicast algorithm to obtain a primitive that is both causally and totally ordered. However, doing so necessarily increases the latency of the protocol.

Causal multicast and consistent cuts. At the outset of chapter 14, we discussed concepts of logical time, defining the causal relation and introducing the definition of a consistent cut. Notice that the delivery events of a multicast protocol such as *cbcast* are concurrent and can be thought of as occurring at the same time in all the members of a process group (Figure 16.14). In a logical sense, *cbcast* delivers messages at what may look to the recipients like a single instant in time. Unfortunately, however, the delivery events for a single *cbcast* do not represent a consistent cut across the system, because communication that was concurrent with the *cbcast* could cross it. Thus, one could easily encounter a system

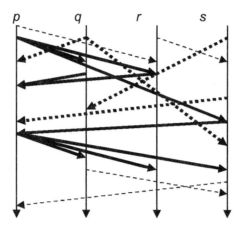

Figure 16.14. A protocol for creating a consistent cut or snapshot. In this figure, processes are sending point-to-point messages (dashed lines) when process p initiates the protocol by sending a multicast to q, r, and s (dark lines). The delivery of the multicast is closed under causality and hence is a consistent cut. A second phase of multicasts can be used to flush communication channels (any pending message in a channel will be causally prior to the second multicast and hence delivered before it is delivered; the four messages in this category are shown in a darker dashed line style). Notice that during the period between delivery of the two multicasts, the sending of other messages is temporarily inhibited.

in which a *cbcast* is delivered at process p, which has received message m, but where the same *cbcast* was delivered at process q (the eventual sender of m) before m had been transmitted.

With a second *cbcast* message, it is actually possible to identify a true consistent cut, but to do so we need to either introduce a concept of an epoch number or inhibit communication briefly. The inhibition algorithm is easier to understand. It starts with a first *cbcast* message that tells the recipients to inhibit the sending of new messages. The process group members receiving this message send back an acknowledgment to the process that initiated the *cbcast*. The initiator, having collected replies from all group members, now sends a second *cbcast* telling the group members that they can stop recording incoming messages and resume normal communication. It is easy to see that all messages that were in the communication channels when the first *cbcast* was received will now have been delivered and that the communication channels will be empty. The recipients now resume normal communication. (They should also monitor the state of the initiator, in case it fails!) The algorithm is very similar to the one for changing the membership of a process group, discussed previously.

Noninhibitory algorithms for forming consistent cuts are also known. One way to solve this problem is to add *epoch numbers* to the multicasts in the system. Each process keeps an *epoch counter* and tags every message with the counter value. In the consistent cut protocol, the first phase message now tells processes to increment the epoch counters (and not to inhibit new messages). Thus, instead of delaying new messages, they are sent promptly but with epoch number $k + 1$ instead of epoch number k. The same algorithm now works to allow the system to reason about the consistent cut associated with its kth epoch even as it exchanges new messages during epoch $k + 1$. Another well-known solution takes the form of what is called an *echo protocol*, in which two messages traverse every communication link in the system (see Chandy and Lamport). For a system with all-to-all communication connectivity, such protocols will transmit $O(n^2)$ messages, in contrast with the $O(n)$ required for the inhibitory solution.

This *cbcast* algorithm provides a relatively inexpensive way of testing the distributed state of the system to detect a desired property. In particular, if the processes that receive a *cbcast* compute a predicate or write down some element of their states at the moment the message is received, these states will fit together cleanly and can be treated as a glimpse of the system as a whole at a single instant in time. To count the number of processes for which some condition holds, it is sufficient to send a *cbcast* asking processes if the condition holds and to count the number that return *true*. The result is a value that could in fact have been valid for the group at a single instant in real time. On the negative side, this guarantee only holds with respect to communication that uses causally ordered primitives. If processes communicate with other primitives, the delivery events of the *cbcast* will not necessarily be prefix closed when the send and receive events for these messages are taken into account. Marzullo and Sabel have developed optimized versions of this algorithm.

Some examples of properties that could be checked using our consistent cut algorithm include the current holder of a token in a distributed locking algorithm (the token will never appear to be lost or duplicated), the current load on the processes in a group (the states of members will never be accidentally sampled at different times yielding an illusory load that is unrealistically high or low), the wait-for graph of a system subject to infrequent deadlocks (deadlock will never be detected when the system is in fact not deadlocked), and the contents of a database (the database will never be checked at a time when it has been updated at some locations but not others). On the other hand, because the basic algorithm inhibits the sending of new messages in the group, albeit briefly, there will be many systems for which the performance impact is too high and a solution that sends more messages but avoids inhibition states would be preferable. The epoch-based scheme represents a reasonable alternative, but we have not treated fault-tolerance issues; in practice, such a scheme works best if all cuts are initiated by some single member of a group, such as the oldest process in it, and a group flush is known to occur if that process fails and some other takes over from it.

Exploiting topological knowledge.   Many networks have topological properties, which can be exploited to optimize the representation of causal information within a process group that implements a protocol such as *cbcast*. Within the NavTech system, developed at INESC in Portugal, wide area applications operate over a communication transport layer implemented as part of NavTech. This structure is programmed to know of the location of wide area network links and to make use of hardware multicast where possible (see Rodriguez and Verissimo, Rodrigues et al.). A consequence is that if a group is physically laid out with multiple subgroups interconnected over a wide area link, as seen in Figure 16.15, the message need only be sent once over each link.

In a geographically distributed system, it is frequently the case that all messages from some subset of the process group members will be relayed to the remaining members through a small number of relay points. Rodriguez exploits this observation to reduce the amount of information needed to represent causal ordering relationships within the process group. Suppose that message m_1 is causally dependent upon message m_0 and that both were sent over the same communication link. When these messages are relayed to processes on the other side of the link, they will appear to have been sent by a single

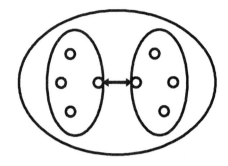

Figure 16.15. In a complex network, a single process group may be physically broken into multiple subgroups. With knowledge of the network topology, the NavTech system is able to reduce the information needed to implement causal ordering.

sender and the ordering relationship between them can be compressed into a single vector-timestamp entry. In general, this observation permits any set of processes that route through a single point to be represented using a single sequence number on the other side of that point.

Stephenson explored the same question in a more general setting involving complex relationships between overlapping process groups (the multigroup causality problem) (see Stephenson). His work identifies an optimization similar to this one, as well as others that take advantage of other regular layouts of overlapping groups, such as a series of groups organized into a tree or some other graph-like structure.

Total Order

In developing our causally ordered communication primitive, we really ended up with a family of such primitives. The cheapest of these are purely causal in the sense that concurrently transmitted multicasts might be delivered in different orders to different members. The more costly ones combined causal order with mechanisms that resulted in a causal, total order. We saw two such primitives: One was the causal ordering algorithm based on logical timestamps, and the second (introduced very briefly) was the algorithm used for total order in the Totem and Transis systems, which extend the causal order into a total one using a canonical sorting procedure, but in which latency is increased by the need to wait until multicasts have been received from all potential sources of concurrent multicasts.[11]

---

[11]Most ordered of all is the flush protocol used to install new views: This delivers a type of message (the new view) in a way that is ordered with respect to all other types of messages. In the Isis Toolkit, there was actually a *gbcast* primitive, which could be used to obtain this behavior at the request of the user, but it was rarely used and more recent systems tend to use this protocol only to install new process group views.

In this section we discuss totally ordered multicasts, known by the name *abcast*, in more detail.

There are many ways to implement total ordering, and it may be best to start by just describing the most commonly used approach, partly for reasons of brevity, but partly because this has become prevalent. The idea can be traced to work by Chang and Maxemchuk, which then was simplified and refined over time by Frans Kaashoek in his PhD. thesis and finally by Robbert van Renesse in his work on the Horus system. An ordering "token" is associated with some member of the group (usually, the first member in the current list of group members—the least ranked process in the group's current "view"). The token holder is in charge of deciding the *abcast* ordering. To send an *abcast* a process uses *fbcast* to send it out, but on receipt, members delay the message briefly. The token holder, however, sends a tiny *fbcast* giving ordering information: "deliver message 1234 from process p_1 as your 20'th message. (Obviously, you can make this fancier by delaying the ordering message and trying to batch a few notifications up). All recipients just follow the instructions: they reorder messages according to the specified order and then deliver them. If a failure happens, the "flush" mechanism discussed later in this chapter ensures that everyone remaining operational gets a copy of these *fbcasts*. Thus, after a failure, all surviving group members will have delivered identical sequences of messages. A new token holder is selected if the old one was the process that failed, and it just takes over the role of sending ordering messages. This is a simple and efficient way to implement total ordering, and can be extremely fast if the developer takes care to optimize the critical paths. Notice also that a big message is sent directly to its destinations; some early versions of this protocol relayed all messages through the token holder, but with big messages, I/O bandwidth at that process becomes a serious bottleneck. By sending messages directly and sending ordering information separately, this can be avoided.

As described above, we end up with a version of *abcast* capable of violating causal ordering. Suppose that process p_i sends an *abcast*, and then sends some other point to point message or multicast (not an abcast) which process p_j receives. Now process p_j sends an *abcast* "in response" to that message. Since the *abcast* is implemented as a protocol over *fbcast* there is no reason to assume that the token holding process will order the one from p_i before the one from p_j. Yet the message sent by p_j could be a form of response to the one sent by p_i. For example, perhaps p_i is a message asking group members to create a new slot in the employees table for a recently hired employee, and p_j reacts by sending out some default security information. If the messages arrive out of causal order, applications may receive the "second" message, look up the employee, and then throw an exception when they are unable to find an entry for that employee in their current-employees tables. Thus we might prefer a stronger guarantee.

It is also possible to use the causally ordered multicast primitive to implement a token-based ordering scheme that is simultaneously causal and totally ordered. Such a primitive would respect the delivery ordering property of *cbcast* when causally prior multicasts are pending in a group, similar to *abcast* when two processes concurrently try to send a multicast.

Rather than present this algorithm here, however, we defer it until Chapter 18, when we present it in the context of a method for implementing replicated data with locks on the data items. We do this because, in practice, token-based total ordering algorithms are more common than the other methods. The most common use of causal ordering is in conjunction with the specific replication scheme presented in Chapter 18; therefore, it is more natural to treat the topic in that setting.

Yet an additional total ordering algorithm was introduced by Leslie Lamport in his very early work on logical time in distributed systems (see Lamport [July 1978]) and later adapted to group communication settings by Skeen during a period when he and the author collaborated on an early version of the Isis totally ordered communication primitive. The algorithm uses a two-phase protocol in which processes vote on the message ordering to use, expressing this vote as a logical timestamp.

The algorithm operates as follows. In the first phase of communication, the originator of the multicast (we'll call it the coordinator) sends the message to the members of the destination group. These processes save the message but do not yet deliver it to the application. Instead, each proposes a delivery time for the message using a logical clock, which is made unique by appending the process-ID. The coordinator collects these proposed delivery times, sorts the vector, and designates the maximum time as the *committed* delivery time. It sends this time back to the participants. They update their logical clocks (and hence will never propose a smaller time) and reorder the messages in their pending queue. If a pending message has a committed delivery time, and this time is smallest among the proposed and committed times for other messages, it can be delivered to the application layer.

This solution can be seen to deliver messages in a total order, since all the processes base the delivery action on the same committed timestamp. It can be made fault tolerant by electing a new coordinator if the original sender fails. One curious property of the algorithm, however, is that it has a non-uniform ordering guarantee. To see this, consider the case where a coordinator and a participant fail and that participant also proposed the maximum timestamp value. The old coordinator may have committed a timestamp that could be used for delivery to the participant, but that will not be reused by the remaining processes, which may therefore pick a different delivery order. Thus, just as dynamic uniformity ("safety") is costly to achieve as an atomicity property, one sees that a dynamically uniform ordering property may be quite costly. It should be noted that dynamic uniformity and dynamically uniform ordering tend to go together: If delivery is delayed until it is known that all operational processes have a copy of a message, it is normally possible to ensure that all processes will use identical delivery orderings

This two-phase ordering algorithm, and a protocol called the "born-order" protocol, which was introduced by the Transis and Totem systems (messages are ordered using unique message identification numbers that are assigned when the messages are first created, or "born"), have advantages in settings with multiple overlapping process groups, a topic to which we will return in Chapter 17. Both provide what is called "globally total order," which means that even *abcast* messages sent in different groups will be delivered in the same order at any overlapping destinations they may have.

16.3 Communication from Nonmembers to a Group

Up to now, all of our protocols have focused on the case of group members communicating with one another. However, in many systems there is an equally important need to provide reliable and ordered communication from nonmembers into a group. This section presents two solutions to the problem—one for a situation in which the nonmember process has located a single member of the group but lacks detailed membership information about the remainder of the group, and one for the case of a nonmember that has cached group membership information.

Before launching into this topic, we should note that there is a class of systems for which this problem doesn't really arise. When using a system such as Spread, which consists of a core set of long-running daemons to which all application processes connect (or Ensemble in its "outboard" mode), the application itself isn't really responsible for group communication. Instead, all group operations are passed to the servers, which implement multicast among themselves, then relay messages up to the appropriate application processes. Since the daemons "know" the membership of the groups, communication by a non-member to a group is no different than communication from a member to a group: the request is forwarded through a daemon. However, there are performance and "single point of failure" concerns with this kind of 2-tier architecture. Many systems implement multicast directly, as an end-to-end protocol, and these are the ones for which the mechanisms described below are useful.

In the first case, our algorithm will have the nonmember process ask some group member to issue the multicast on its behalf, using an RPC for this purpose. In this approach, each such multicast is given a unique identifier by its originator, so that if the forwarding process fails before reporting on the outcome of the multicast, the same request can be reissued. The new forwarding process would check to see if the multicast was previously completed, issue it if not, and then return the outcome in either case. Various optimizations can then be introduced, so that a separate RPC will not be required for each multicast. The protocol is illustrated in Figure 16.16 for the normal case, when

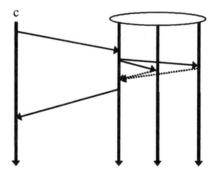

c

Figure 16.16. Nonmember of a group uses a simple RPC-based protocol to request that a multicast be done on its behalf. The ID of the message can be assigned by the sender. This protocol becomes complex when ordering considerations are added, particularly because the forwarding process may fail during the protocol run.

the contact process does not fail. Not shown is the eventual garbage collection phase needed to delete status information accumulated during the protocol and saved for use in the case where the contact eventually fails.

Our second solution uses what is called an *iterated* approach, in which the nonmember processes cache possibly inaccurate process group views. Specifically, each group view is given a unique identifier, and client processes use an RPC or some other mechanism to obtain a copy of the group view (e.g., they may join a larger group within which the group reports changes in its core membership to interested non-members). The client then includes the view identifier in its message and multicasts it directly to the group members. Again, the members will retain some limited history of prior interactions using a mechanism such as the one for the multiphase commit protocols.(See Figure 16.17.)

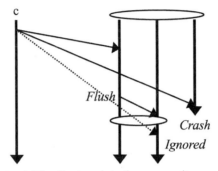

Figure 16.17.   An iterated protocol. The client sends to the group as its membership is changing (to drop one member). Its multicast is terminated by the flush associated with the new-view installation (message just prior to the new view), and when one of its messages arrives late (dashed line), the recipient detects it as a duplicate and ignores it. Had the multicast been so late that all the copies were rejected, the sender would have refreshed its estimate of group membership and retried the multicast. Doing this while also respecting ordering obligations can make the protocol complex, although the basic idea is quite simple. Notice that the protocol is cheaper than the RPC solution: The client sends directly to the actual group members, rather than indirectly sending through a proxy. However, while the figure may seem to suggest that there is no acknowledgment from the group to the client, this is not the case: The client communicates over a reliable FIFO channel to each member—hence, acknowledgements are implicitly present. Indeed, some effort may be needed to avoid an implosion effect, which would overwhelm the client of a large group with a huge number of acknowledgements.

There are now three cases that may occur. Such a multicast can arrive in the correct view, it can arrive partially in the correct view and partially late (after some members have installed a new group view), or it can arrive entirely late. In the first case, the protocol is considered successful. In the second case, the group flush algorithm will push the partially delivered multicast to a view-synchronous termination; when the late messages finally arrive, they will be ignored as duplicates by the group members that receive them, since these processes will have already delivered the message during the flush protocol. In the third case, all the group members will recognize the message as a late one that was not flushed by the system and all will reject it. Some or all should also send a message back to the nonmember warning it that its message was not successfully delivered; the client can then retry its multicast with refreshed membership information. This last case is said to iterate the multicast. If it is practical to modify the underlying reliable transport protocol, a convenient way to return status information to the sender is by attaching it to the acknowledgment messages such protocols transmit.

This protocol is clearly quite simple, although its complexity grows when one considers the issues associated with preserving sender order or causality information in the case where iteration is required. To solve such a problem, a nonmember that discovers itself to be using stale group view information should inhibit the transmission of new multicasts while refreshing the group view data. It should then retransmit, in the correct order, all multicasts that are not known to have been successfully delivered in while it was sending using the previous group view. Some care is required in this last step, however, because new members of the group may not have sufficient information to recognize and discard duplicate messages.

To overcome this problem, there are basically two options. The simplest case occurs when the group members transfer information to joining processes, including the record of multicasts successfully received from nonmembers prior to when the new member joined. Such a state transfer can be accomplished using a mechanism discussed in the next chapter. Knowing that the members will detect and discard duplicates, the nonmember can safely retransmit any multicasts that are still pending, in the correct order, followed by any that may have been delayed while waiting to refresh the group membership. Such an approach minimizes the delay before normal communication is restored.

The second option is applicable when it is impractical to transfer state information to the joining member. In this case, the nonmember will need to query the group, determining the status of pending multicasts by consulting with surviving members from the previous view. Having determined the precise set of multicasts that was dropped upon reception, the nonmember can retransmit these messages and any buffered messages and then resume normal communication. Such an approach is likely to have higher overhead than the first one, since the nonmember (and there may be many of them) must query the group after each membership change. It would not be surprising if significant delays were introduced by such an algorithm.

16.3.1 Scalability

The preceding discussion of techniques and costs did not address questions of scalability and limits. Yet clearly, the decision to make a communication protocol reliable will have an associated cost, which might be significant. Different studies have reached conflicting findings on this topic (see Birman [1999], Amir [2003], Rowston [2001], Gupta [2001]); we treat the topic in more detail in Section 21.8. The reader is cautioned to keep in mind that reliability does have a price, and many of the most demanding distributed applications, which generate extremely high message-passing loads, must be split into a reliable subsystem that experiences lower loads and provides stronger guarantees for the subset of messages that pass through it, and a concurrently executed unreliable subsystem, which handles the bulk of communication but offers much weaker guarantees to its users. Reliability properties can be extremely valuable but one shouldn't make the mistake of assuming that reliability properties are *always* desirable or that such properties should be provided everywhere in a distributed system. Used selectively, these technologies are very powerful; used blindly, they may actually compromise reliability of the application by introducing undesired overheads and instability in those parts of the system that have strong performance requirements and weaker reliability requirements.

16.4 Communication from a Group to a Nonmember

The discussion of the preceding section did not consider the issues raised by transmission of replies from a group to a nonmember. These replies, however, and other forms of communication outside of a group, raise many of the same reliability issues that motivated the ordering and gap-freedom protocols presented previously—for example, suppose that a group is using a causally ordered multicast internally, and that one of its members sends a point-to-point message to some process outside the group. In a logical sense, that message may now be dependent upon the prior causal history of the group, and if that process now communicates with other members of the group, issues of causal ordering and freedom from causal gaps will arise.

This specific scenario was studied by Ladin and Liskov, who developed a system in which vector timestamps could be exported by a group to its clients; the client later presented the timestamp back to the group when issuing requests to other members, and in this way the client was protected against causal ordering violations. The protocol proposed in that work used stable storage to ensure that even if a failure occurred, no causal gaps will occur.

Other researchers have considered the same issues using different methods. Work by Schiper, for example, explored the use of an $n \times n$ matrix to encode point-to-point causality information (see Schiper et al.), and the Isis Toolkit introduced mechanisms to preserve causal order when point-to-point communication was done in a system. We will present some of these methods in Chapter 19.

16.5 Summary of Multicast Properties

Table 16.1. Terminology

Concept	Brief description
abcast	View-synchronous totally ordered group communication. If processes p and q both receive m_1 and m_2, then either both deliver m_1 prior to m_2, or both deliver m_2 prior to m_1.
	As noted earlier, *abcast* comes in several versions. Throughout the remainder of this book, we will assume that *abcast* is a locally total and nondynamic uniform protocol—that is, we focus on the least costly of the possible *abcast* primitives, unless we specifically indicate otherwise.

Table 16.1. Continued

cabcast	Causally and totally ordered group communication. The delivery order is as for *abcast*, but it is also consistent with the causal sending order.
cbcast	Causally ordered group communication. If $send(m_1) \to send(m_2)$, then processes that receive both messages deliver m_1 prior to m_2.
fbcast	View-synchronous FIFO group communication. If the same process p sends m_1 prior to sending m_2, then processes that receive both messages deliver m_1 prior to m_2.
gap freedom	The guarantee that if message m_i should be delivered before m_j and some process receives m_j and remains operational, m_i will also be delivered to its remaining destinations. A system that lacks this property can be exposed to a form of logical partitioning, where a process that has received m_j is prevented from (ever) communicating to some process that was supposed to receive m_i but will not because of failure.
gbcast	A group communication primitive based upon the view-synchronous flush protocol. Supported as a user-callable API in the Isis Toolkit, but very costly and not widely used. *gbcast* delivers a message in a way that is totally ordered relative to all other communication in the same group.
group client	A nonmember of a process group that communicates with it and that may need to monitor the membership of that group as it changes dynamically over time.
member (of a group)	A process belonging to a process group.
process group	A set of processes that have joined the same group. The group has a *membership list*, which is presented to group members in a data structure called the *process group view*. This lists the members of the group and other information, such as their ranking.
Safe (or dynamically uniform) multicast	A multicast having the property that if any group member delivers it, then all operational group members will also deliver it. This property is costly to guarantee and corresponds to a *dynamic uniformity* constraint. Most multicast primitives can be implemented in a safe or an unsafe version; the less costly one is preferable. In this book, we are somewhat hesitant to use the term "safe," because a protocol lacking this property is not necessarily "unsafe." Consequently, we will normally describe a protocol as being dynamically uniform (safe) or nonuniform (unsafe). If we do not specifically say that a protocol needs to be dynamically uniform, the reader should assume that we intend the nonuniform case.

Table 16.1. Continued

View-synchronous multicast	A way of sending a message to a process group so all the group members that don't crash will receive the message between the same pair of group views. If a process sends a multicast when the membership consists of $\{p_0, \ldots p_k\}$ and it doesn't crash, the message will be delivered while the view is still $\{p_0, \ldots p_k\}$.
Virtual synchrony	A distributed communication system in which process groups are provided, supporting view-synchronous communication and gap freedom, and in which algorithms are developed using a style of closely synchronous computing in which all group members see the same events in the same order and consequently can closely coordinate their actions. Such synchronization become virtual when the ordering properties of the communication primitive are weakened in ways that do not change the correctness of the algorithm. By introducing such weaker orderings, a group can be made more likely to tolerate failure and can gain a significant performance improvement.

16.6 Related Reading

On logical concepts of time: (see Lamport [July 1978, 1984]).

Causal ordering in message delivery: (see Birman and Joseph [February 1987, November 1987]).

Consistent cuts: (see Babaoglu and Marzullo, Chandy and Lamport).

Vector clocks: (see Fidge, Mattern).

Vector clocks used in message delivery: (see Birman et al., [1992], Schiper et al.).

Optimizing vector clock representations: (see Charron-Bost, Melliar-Smith and Moser [1993]).

Compression using topological information about groups of processes: (see Birman et al. [1991], Rodrigues and Verissimo, Rodrigues et al.).

Static groups and quorum replication: (see Bernstein et al., Birman and Joseph [November 1987], Cooper [1985]).

Two-phase commit: (see Bernstein et al., Gray [1979], Gray and Reuter).

Three-phase commit: (see Skeen [June 1982, 1985]).

Byzantine protocol: (see Ben-Or, Coan and Thomas, Coan et al., Cristian et al., Rabin, Schneider [1984]).

Asynchronous Consensus: (see Chandra and Toueg [1991], Fisher et al.); but see also Babaoglu et al. (1995), Friedman et al., Guerraoui and Schiper, Ricciardi (1996).

The method of Chandra and Toueg: (see Babaoglu et al. [1995], Chandra and Toueg [1991], Chandra et al. [1992, 1996], Friedman et al.).

Group membership: (see Birman and Joseph [February 1987, November 1987], Chandra et al. [1996], Cristian [April 1991], Melliar-Smith et al. [1991], Mishra [1991], Ricciardi and Birman); but see also Agarwal, Anceaume et al., Babaoglu et al. (1994, 1995), Birman and Glade, Chandra et al. (1996), Cristian and Schmuck, Friedman et al., Golding (1992), Guerraoui and Schiper, Reiter (1994), Ricciardi (1992, 1993, 1996), Rodrigues et al.

Partitionable membership: (see Amir et al. [1992], Moser et al. [1994]).

Fail-stop illusion: (see Sabel and Marzullo).

Token-based total order: (see Chang and Maxemchuk, Kasshoek).

Lamport's method: (see Birman and Joseph [February 1987], Lamport [July 1978]).

Communication from nonmembers of a group: (see Birman and Joseph [February 1987], Wood [1991]).

Point-to-point causality: (see Schiper et al.).

On the timestamp technique used in Harp: (see Ladin et al. [1992], Liskov et al.).

On preserving causality in point-to-point message-passing systems: (see Schiper et al.).

On the associated controversy: (see Cheriton and Skeen), and on the responses (see Birman [1994], Cooper [1994], van Renesse [1993]).

17

Point to Point and Multi-group Considerations

As noted at the start of Chapter 16, researchers have carried the idea of group communication to something of an extreme. This chapter tackles some of the more esoteric topics that arise when building a group-communication platform that permits the creation of large numbers of groups without requiring (as in the Spread system) that they all be subgroups of a single encompassing group. The questions raised by such a model are quite interesting, but aren't necessarily very important, since existing group communication platforms such as Ensemble and Spread focus on supporting a small number of groups, although permitting the creation of subgroups within them. Yet if group communication begins to be applied in Web Services settings, the very nature of those platforms may force them to support much larger numbers of groups and preclude the assumption that larger enclosing groups will generally be present. Thus the material that follows is of limited importance in existing systems but may become more significant down the road.

Multi-group communication protocols have a way of becoming both complex and costly, and this should send up warning flags for developers seeking elegant, high-performance solutions to reliability in large systems. Certainly, if a system will support large numbers of groups, any special properties it offers to the user who works with multiple groups should be "selectable": capable of being enabled or disabled quite easily under program control. Moreover, the defaults should generally be set to achieve the lowest possible costs, much as we have opted for non-uniform failure behavior rather than safe, dynamically uniform behavior, despite the relative conceptual simplicity of the latter: at the end of the day, if a property is very costly, it shouldn't be the default.

17.1 Causal Communication Outside of a Process Group

Although there are sophisticated protocols in guaranteeing that causality will be respected for arbitrary communication patterns, the most practical solutions generally confine concurrency and associated causality issues to the interior of a process group—for example, at the end of Section 16.3, we briefly cited the replication protocol of Ladin and Liskov (see Ladin et al. [1992], Liskov et al.). This protocol transmits a timestamp to the client, and the client later includes the most recent of the timestamps it has received in any requests it issues to the group. The group members can detect causal ordering violations and delay such a request until causally prior multicasts have reached their destinations, as seen in Figure 17.1.

Client

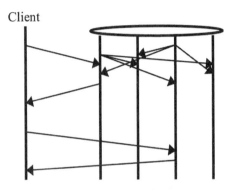

Figure 17.1. In the replication protocol used by Ladin and Liskov in the Harp system, vector timestamps are used to track causal multicasts within a server group. If a client interacts with a server in that group, it does so using a standard RPC protocol. However, the group timestamp is included with the reply and can be presented with a subsequent request to the group. This permits the group members to detect missing prior multicasts and to appropriately delay a request, but omits the client's point-to-point messages from the causal state of the system. Such tradeoffs between properties and cost seem entirely appropriate, because an attempt to track causal order system-wide can result in significant overheads. A system such as the Isis Toolkit, which enforces causal order even for point-to-point message passing, generally do so by delaying after sending point-to-point messages until they are known to be stable—a simple and conservative solution that avoids the need to represent ordering information for such messages.

An alternative is to simply delay messages sent out of a group until any causally prior multicasts sent within the group have become stable—in other words, have reached their destinations. Since there is no remaining causal ordering obligation in this case, the message need not carry causality information. Moreover, such an approach may not be as costly as it sounds, for the same reason that the *flush* protocol introduced earlier turns out not to be terribly costly in practice: Most asynchronous *cbcast* or *fbcast* messages become stable shortly after they are issued—long before any reply is sent to the client. Thus, any latency is associated with the very last multicasts to have been initiated within the group, and will normally be small. We will see a similar phenomenon (in more detail) in Section 19.5, which discusses a replication protocol for stream protocols.

There has been some work on the use of causal order as a system-wide guarantee, applying to point-to-point communication as well as multicasts. Unfortunately, representing such ordering information requires a matrix of size $O(n^2)$ in the size of the system (one for each sender-receiver pair). Moreover, this type of ordering information is only useful if messages are sent asynchronously (without waiting for replies). But, if this is done in systems that use point-to-point communication, there is no obvious way to recover if a message is lost (when its sender fails) after subsequent messages (to other destinations) have been delivered. Cheriton and Skeen discuss this form of all-out causal order in a well-known paper and conclude that it is probably not desirable (see Birman [1994], Cheriton and Skeen, Cooper [1994], Schiper et al., van Renesse [1993]). If point-to-point messages are treated as being causally prior to other messages, it is best to wait until they have been received before sending causally dependent messages to other destinations.[12] (We'll discuss Cheriton and Skeen's paper in Chapter 19.)

Early versions of the Isis Toolkit solved this problem without actually representing causal information at all, although later work replaced this scheme with one that waits for point-to-point messages to become stable (see Birman and Joseph [February 1987], Birman et al. [1993]). The approach was to piggyback pending messages (those that are not known to have reached all their destinations) on *all* subsequent messages, regardless of their destination (Figure 17.2)—that is, if process p has sent multicast m_1 to process group G and now wishes to send a message m_2 to any destination other than group G, a copy of

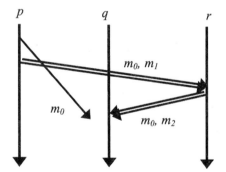

Figure 17.2. After sending m_0 asynchronously to q, p sends m_1 to r. To preserve causality, a copy of m_0 is piggybacked on this message. Similarly, when r sends m_3 to q a copy of m_0 is included. q will receive m_0 by the first causal path to reach it. A background garbage collection algorithm cleans up copies of messages that have become stable by reaching all of their destinations. To avoid excessive propagation of messages, the system always has the alternative of sending a message directly to its true destination and waiting for it to become stable, or it can simply wait until the message reaches its destinations and becomes stable.

---

[12]Notice that this issue doesn't occur for communication to the same destination as for the point-to-point message: One can send any number of point-to-point messages or individual copies of multicasts to a single process within a group without delaying. The requirement is that messages to *other* destinations be delayed until these point-to-point messages are stable.

m_1 is included with m_2. By applying this rule system-wide, p can be certain that if any route causes a message m_3, causally dependent upon m_1, to reach a destination of m_1, a copy of m_1 will be delivered too. A background garbage collection algorithm is used to delete these spare copies of messages when they do reach their destinations, and a simple duplicate suppression scheme is employed to avoid delivering the same message more than once if it reaches a destination several times.

This scheme may seem wildly expensive, but it rarely sends a message more than once in applications that operate over Isis. One important reason for this is that Isis has other options available for use when the cost of piggybacking becomes too high—for example, instead of sending m_0 piggybacked to some destination far from its true destination, q, any process can simply send m_0 to q, in this way making it stable. The system can also wait for stability to be detected by the original sender, at which point garbage collection will remove the obligation. Additionally, notice that m_0 only needs to be piggybacked once to any given destination. In Isis, which typically runs on a small set of servers, this meant that the worst case is just to piggyback the message once to each server. For all of these reasons, the cost of piggybacking is never excessive in Isis. The Isis algorithm also has the benefit of avoiding any potential gaps in the causal communication order: If q has received a message that was causally after m_1, then q will retain a copy of m_1 until m_1 is safe at its destinations.

The author is not aware of any system other than Isis that has used this approach. Perhaps the strongest argument against it is that it has an *unpredictable* overhead: One can imagine patterns of communication for which its costs would be high, such as a client/server architecture in which the server replies to a high rate of incoming RPCs. In principle, each reply will carry copies of some large number of prior but unstable replies, and the garbage collection algorithm will have a great deal of work to do. Moreover, the actual overhead imposed on a given message is likely to vary depending on the amount of time since the garbage collection mechanism was last executed. Recent group communications systems, such as Horus, seek to provide extremely predictable communication latency and bandwidth and steer away from mechanisms that are difficult to analyze in a straightforward manner.

17.2 Extending Causal Order to Multigroup Settings

Additional issues occur when groups can overlap. Suppose that a process sends or receives multicasts in more than one group—a pattern that is commonly observed in complex systems that make heavy use of group computing. Just as we asked how causal order can be guaranteed when a causal path includes point-to-point messages, we can also ask how causal and total order can be extended to apply to multicasts sent in a series of groups.

Consider first the issue of causal ordering. If process p belongs to groups g_1 and g_2, one can imagine a chain of multicasts that includes messages sent asynchronously in both groups—for example, perhaps we will have $m_1 \rightarrow m_2 \rightarrow m_3$, where m_1 and m_3 are sent asynchronously in g_1 and m_2 is sent asynchronously in g_2. Upon receipt of a copy of m_3, a process may need to check for and detect causal ordering violations, delaying m_3 if necessary until m_1 has been received. Actually, this example illustrates two problems, since we also need to be sure that the delivery atomicity properties of the system extend to sequences of multicasts sent in a different group. Otherwise, scenarios can occur whereby m_3 becomes causally orphaned and can never be delivered.

In Figure 17.3, for example, if a failure causes m_1 to be lost, m_3 can never be delivered. There are several possibilities for solving the atomicity problem, which lead to different possibilities for dealing with causal order. A simple option is to delay a multicast to group g_2 while there are causally prior multicasts pending in group g_1. In the example, m_2 would be delayed until m_1 becomes stable. Most existing process group systems use this solution, which is called the *conservative scheme*. It

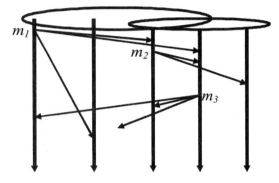

Figure 17.3. Message m_3 is causally ordered after m_1, and therefore may need to be delayed upon reception if m_1 has not yet been delivered when m_3 is received.

is simple to implement and offers acceptable performance for most applications. To the degree that overhead is introduced, it occurs within the process group itself and hence is both localized and readily measured.

Less-conservative schemes are riskier in the sense that safety can be compromised when certain types of failures occur and they require more overhead; this overhead is less localized and consequently harder to quantify—for example, a *k-stability* solution might wait until m_1 is known to have been received at $k + 1$ destinations. The multicast will now be atomic provided that no more than k simultaneous failures occur in the group. However, we now need a way to detect causal ordering violations and to delay a message that arrives prematurely to overcome them.

One option is to annotate each multicast with multiple vector timestamps. This approach requires a form of piggybacking: Each multicast carries with it only timestamps that have changed or (if timestamp compression is used) only those with fields that have changed. Stephenson has explored this scheme and related ones and has shown that they offer general enforcement of causality at low average overhead. In practice, however, I am not aware of any systems that implement this method, apparently because the conservative scheme is so simple and because of the risk of a safety violation if a failure causes k processes to fail simultaneously.

Another option is to use the Isis style of piggybacking *cbcast* implementation. Early versions of the Isis Toolkit employed this approach, and, as noted earlier, the associated overhead turns out to be fairly low. The details are essentially identical to the method presented in Section 16.3. This approach has the advantage of also providing atomicity, but it has the disadvantage of having unpredictable costs.

In summary, there are several possibilities for enforcing causal ordering in multigroup settings. One should ask whether the costs associated with doing so are reasonable. The consensus of the community has tended to accept costs that are limited to within a single group (i.e., the conservative mode delays) but not costs that are paid system-wide (such as those associated with piggybacking vector timestamps or copies of messages). Even the conservative scheme, however, can be avoided if the application doesn't actually *need* the guarantee that this provides. Thus, the application designer should start with an analysis of the use and importance of multigroup causality before deciding to assume this property in a given setting.

17.3 Extending Total Order to Multigroup Settings

The total ordering protocols presented in Section 16.3 guarantee that messages sent in any one group will be totally ordered with respect to one another. However, even if the conservative stability rule is used, this guarantee does not extend to messages sent in different groups but received at processes that belong to both. Moreover, the local versions of total ordering permit some surprising global ordering problems. Consider, for example, multicasts sent to a set of processes that form overlapping groups, as shown in Figure 17.4. If one multicast is sent to each group, we could easily have process q receive m_1 followed by m_2, process r receive m_2 followed by m_3, process s receive m_3 followed by m_4, and process s receive m_4 followed by m_1. Since only a single multicast was sent in each group, such an order is total if only the perspective of the individual group is considered. Yet this ordering is clearly cyclic in a global sense.

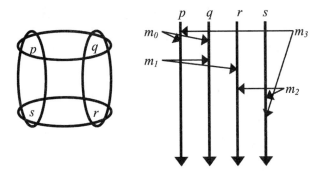

Figure 17.4. Overlapping process groups, seen from above and in a time-space diagram. Here, m_0 was sent to $\{p, q\}$, m_1 to $\{q, r\}$ and so forth, and since each group received only one message, there is no ordering requirement within the individual groups. Thus, an *abcast* protocol would never delay any of these messages. But one can deduce a global ordering for the multicasts. Process p sees m_0 after m_3, q sees m_0 before m_1, r sees m_1 before m_2, and s sees m_2 before m_3. This global ordering is thus cyclic, illustrating that many of our *abcast* ordering algorithms provide locally total ordering but not globally total ordering.

A number of schemes for generating a globally acyclic total ordering are known, and indeed one could have qualms about the use of the term "total" for an ordering that now turns out to sometimes admit cycles. Perhaps it would be best to say that previously we identified a number of methods for obtaining *locally total* multicast ordering whereas now we consider the issue of *globally total* multicast ordering.

The essential feature of the globally total schemes is that the groups within which ordering is desired must share some resource that is used to obtain the ordering property— for example, if a set of groups shares the same ordering token, the ordering of messages assigned using the token can be made globally total as well as locally total. Clearly, however, such a protocol could be costly, since the token will now be a single bottleneck for ordered multicast delivery.

In the Psync system an ordering scheme that uses multicast labels was first introduced (see Peterson [1987], Peterson et al.); soon after, variations of this were proposed by the Transis and Totem systems (see Amir et al. [July 1992], Melliar-Smith and Moser [1989]). All of these methods work by using some form of unique label to place the multicasts in a total order determined by their labels. Before delivering such a multicast, a process must be sure it has received all other multicasts that could have smaller labels. The latency of this protocol is thus prone to rise with the number of processes in the aggregated membership of groups to which the receiving process belongs.

Each of these methods, and in fact all methods with which the author is familiar, has performance that degrades as a function of scale. The larger the set of processes over which a globally total ordering property will apply, the more costly the ordering protocol. When deciding if globally total ordering is warranted, it is therefore useful to ask what sort of applications might be expected to notice the cycles that a local ordering protocol would allow. The reasoning is that if a cheaper protocol is still adequate for the purposes of the application, most developers would favor the cheaper protocol. In the case of globally total ordering, there are very few applications that really need this property.

Indeed, the following explanation may be the only widely cited example of a problem for which locally total order is inadequate and globally total order is consequently needed. Suppose that we wish to solve the dining philosophers' problem. In this problem, which is a classical synchronization problem well known to the distributed system community, a group of philosophers gather around a table. Between each pair of philosophers is a single shared fork, and at the center of the table is a plate of pasta. In order to eat, a philosopher must have one fork in each hand. The life of a philosopher is an infinite repetition of the sequence *think, pick up forks, eat, put down forks.* Our challenge is to implement a protocol that solves this problem and avoids deadlock.

Suppose that the processes in our example are the forks and that the multicasts originate in philosopher processes arrayed around the table. The philosophers can now request their forks by sending totally ordered multicasts to the process group of forks to their left and right. It is easy to see that if forks are granted in the order that the requests arrive, a globally total order avoids deadlock, but a locally total order is deadlock prone. Presumably, there is a family of multigroup locking and synchronization protocols for which similar results would hold. However, to repeat the point made above, the author has never encountered a *real-world* application in which globally total order is needed. This being the case, such strong ordering should perhaps be held in reserve as an option for applications that specifically request it, but not as a default. If globally total order were as cheap as locally total order, the conclusion would be reversed.

17.4 Causal and Total Ordering Domains

We have seen that when ordering properties are extended to apply to multiple heavyweight groups, the costs of achieving ordering can rise substantially. Sometimes, however, such properties really are needed, at least in subsets of an application. If this occurs, one option may be to provide the application with control over these costs by introducing what are called *causal and total ordering domains*. Such a domain would be an attribute of a process group: At the time a group is created, it would be bound to an ordering domain identifier, which remains constant thereafter. We can then implement the rule that when two groups are in different domains, multicast ordering properties do not need to hold across them—for example, if group g_1 and group g_2 are members of different ordering domains, the system could ignore causal ordering between multicasts sent in g_1 and multicasts sent in g_2. More general still would be a scheme in which a domain is provided for each type of ordering: Two groups could then be in the same causal ordering domain but be in different total ordering domains. Implementation of ordering domains is simple if the corresponding multi-group ordering property is available within a system—for example, if group g_1 and group g_2 are members of different causal ordering domains, the conservative rule would be overlooked when a process switched from sending or receiving in one group to sending in the other. Delays would only occur when two groups are explicitly placed in the same ordering domain, presumably because the application actually requires multi-group ordering in this case.

It can be argued that the benefits associated with preserving causal order throughout a large system, as was done in the Isis Toolkit, are significantly greater than those for supporting globally total order. The reasoning is that causal order is needed to implement asynchronous data replication algorithms, and, since these have such a large performance advantage over other schemes, the benefits outweigh the costs of needing to enforce causal order across group boundaries. However, the conservative causality scheme is an adequate solution to this particular problem, and has the benefit of providing a system-wide guarantee with a local method. When combined with causal domains, such a mechanism has a highly selective cost. This said, however, it should also be noted that the *flush* primitive proposed earlier offers the same benefits and is quite easy to use. Thus, many real systems opt for causal ordering, do not delay when sending messages outside of a group, and provide a *flush* primitive for use by the application itself when causal ordering is needed over group boundaries. Such a compromise is visible to the user and is easily understood.

Similar reasoning seems to argue against globally total order: The primitive has a significant cost (mostly in terms of latency) and limited benefit. Thus, my work has stopped providing this property, after initially doing so in the early versions of the Isis Toolkit. The costs were simply too high to make globally total ordering the default, and the complexity of supporting a very rarely used mechanism argued against having the property at all.

17.5 Multicasts to Multiple Groups

An additional multigroup issue concerns the sending of a single multicast to a set of process groups in a single atomic operation. Until now, such an action would require that the multicast be sent to one group at a time, raising issues of nonatomic delivery if the sender fails midway. One can imagine solving this problem by implementing a multigroup multicast as a form of nonblocking commit protocol; Schiper and Raynal have proposed such a protocol in conjunction with their work on the Phoenix system (see Schiper and Raynal). However, there is another option, which is to create a new process group superimposed on the multiple destination groups and to send the multicast in that group. Interestingly, the best implementations of a group-creation protocol require a single *fbcast*—hence, if one creates a group, issues a single multicast in it, and then deletes the group, this will incur a cost comparable to doing a multiphase commit over the same set of processes and then garbage collecting after the protocol has terminated!

This last observation argues against explicit support for sending a multicast to several groups at the same time, except in settings where the set of groups to be used cannot be predicted in advance and is very unlikely to be reused for subsequent communication—that is, although the application process can be presented with an interface that allows multicasts to be sent to sets of groups, it may be best to implement such a mechanism by creating a group in the manner described previously. In the belief that most group communication patterns will be reused shortly after they are first employed, such a group could then be retained for a period of time in the hope that a subsequent multicast to the same destinations will reuse its membership information. The group can then be torn down after a period during which no new multicasts are transmitted. Only if such a scheme is impractical would one need a multicast primitive capable of sending to many groups at the same time, and I am not familiar with any setting in which such a scheme is clearly not viable.

17.6 Multigroup View Management Protocols

A final issue that occurs in systems where groups overlap heavily is that our view management and flush protocol will run once for each group when a failure or join occurs, and our state transfer protocol will only handle the case of a process that joins a single group at a time. Clearly, these will be sources of inefficiency (in the first case) and inconvenience (in the second case) if group overlap is common. This observation, combined with the delays associated with conservative ordering algorithms and the concerns raised above in regard to globally total order, has motivated research on methods of collapsing heavily overlapped groups into smaller numbers of larger groups. Such approaches are often described as resulting in *lightweight* groups, because the groups seen by the application typically map onto some enclosing set of *heavyweight* groups.

Glade explored this approach in Isis and Horus (see Glade et al.). His work supports the same process group interfaces as for a normal process group, but maps multicasts to lightweight groups into multicasts to the enclosing heavyweight groups. Such multicasts are filtered on arrival, so that an individual process will only be given copies of messages actually destined for it. The approach essentially maps the fine-grained membership of the lightweight groups to a coarser-grained membership in a much smaller number of heavyweight groups.

The benefit of Glade's approach is that it avoids the costs of maintaining large numbers of groups (the membership protocols run just once if a process joins or leaves the system, updating multiple lightweight groups in one operation). Moreover, the causal and total ordering guarantees of our single-group solutions will now give the illusion of multigroup causal and total ordering, with no changes to the protocols themselves. Glade argues that when a system produces very large numbers of overlapping process groups, there are likely to be underlying patterns that can be exploited to efficiently map the groups to a small number of heavyweight ones.

17.7 Related Reading

On multiple groups in Isis: (see Birman and Joseph [February 1987], Birman et al.).

On communication from a nonmember of a group to a group: (see Birman and Joseph [February 1987], Wood [1993]).

On graph representations of message dependencies: (see Amir et al. [July 1992], Melliar-Smith and Moser [1989], Peterson [1987], Peterson et al.).

On lightweight process groups: (see Glade et al.).

18

The Virtual Synchrony Execution Model

We finally have the basics out of the way and can put things together into a comprehensive platform for group communication! The process group communication primitives introduced in the previous chapters create a powerful framework for algorithmic development. When the properties of the model are combined with these primitives, we will say that a *virtually synchronous* execution environment results (see Birman and Joseph [February 1987, November 1987], Birman and van Renesse [1994]). In chapters 14–16 of the book we built up our primitives from basic message passing, but for this chapter, it is probably easier to understand the idea behind virtual synchrony in a top-down treatment. We'll then use the approach to develop an extremely high performance replicated data algorithm, as well as several other tools for consistent distributed computing.

18.1 Virtual Synchrony

Suppose that we want to use a process group (or a set of process groups) as a building block in a distributed application. The group members will join that group for the purpose of cooperation, perhaps to replicate data or to perform some operation in a fault-tolerant manner. The issue now arises of designing such algorithms with a high degree of confidence that they will operate correctly.

Recall the discussion of transactional serializability from Section 6.5 and 6.6. In that context, we encountered a similar problem: a set of concurrently executed programs that share files or a database and want to avoid interference with one another. The basic idea was to allow the developer to code these applications as if they would run in isolation, one by one. The database itself is permitted to interleave operations for greater efficiency, but only in ways that preserve the illusion that each transaction executes without interruption. The results of a transaction are visible only after it commits; a transaction that aborts is automatically and completely erased from the memory of the system. As we noted at the time, transactional serializability allows the developer to use a simple programming model, while offering the system an opportunity to benefit from high levels of concurrency and asynchronous communication.

Virtual synchrony is not based on transactions, but introduces a similar approach for developers who are programming with process groups. In the virtual synchrony model, the simplifying abstraction seen by the developer is that of a set of processes (the group members) which all see the same events in the same order. These events are incoming messages to the group and group membership changes. The key insight, isn't particularly profound: Since all the processes see the same inputs, they can execute the same algorithm and in this manner stay in consistent states. This is illustrated in Figure 18.1, which shows a process group receiving messages from several nonmembers. It then has a new member join and transfers the state of the group to this new member. Having completed the transfer, one of the old members crashes or terminates (this can accidentally, but would also occur when migrating a task from p_0 to p_2). Notice that the group members see identical sequences of events while they belong to the group. The members differ, however, in their relative ranking within the group membership. There are many possible ways to rank the members of a group, but the most common one, which is used in this chapter, assumes that the rank is based on when members joined—the oldest member having the lowest ranking, and so forth.

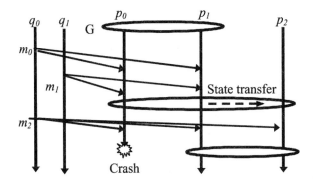

Figure 18.1. Closely synchronous execution: All group members see the same events (incoming messages and new group views) in the same order. In this example only the nonmembers of the group send multicasts to it, but this is just to keep the picture simple. In practice, group members can also multicast to one another, and can send point-to-point messages to the nonmembers—for example, a group RPC could be performed by sending a multicast to the group, to which one or more members reply.

The State Machine approach of Lamport and Schneider first introduced this approach as part of a proposal for replicating objects in settings subject to Byzantine failures (see Schneider [1988, 1990]). Lamport's work made a group of identical replicas of the object in question, and used the Byzantine protocol for all interactions with the group and to implement its interactions with the external world. However, the State Machine approach saw little use when it was first proposed for the same reason that the Byzantine protocol sees limited practical use: Few computing environments satisfy the necessary synchronous computing and communications requirements, and it is difficult to utilize a service that employs a Byzantine fault model without extending the same approach to other aspects of the environment, such as any external objects with which the service interacts and the operating systems software used to implement the communication layer.

A further concern about the State Machine approach arises because all copies of the program see identical inputs in exactly the identical order, and execute each request in exactly the same state. If one copy of a program crashes because of a software bug, so will all the replicas of that program. Unfortunately, as we saw earlier, studies of real-world computing installations reveal that even in mature software systems, bugs that crash the application remain a proportionately important cause of failures. Thus, by requiring correct processes that operate deterministically and in lockstep, the State Machine approach is unable to offer protection against software faults.

Virtual synchrony is similar to the State Machine abstraction, but it moves outside of the original Byzantine setting, while also introducing optimizations that overcome the concerns mentioned previously. The idea is to view the State Machine as a sort of reference model but to implement it in a way that yields better performance and requires less of the environment. The effect of these optimizations is that the true execution of a process group will be very far from the kind of lockstep synchrony that could cause trouble. In effect, just as transactional executions allow operations to be interleaved, provided that the behavior is indistinguishable from some serial execution, a virtually synchronous execution allows operations to be interleaved, provided that the result is indistinguishable from some closely synchronous (State Machine) execution. The benefit of this approach is that the executions of the different replicas will often be different enough to let the group as a whole tolerate software bugs that cause individual members to crash.

To take a very simple example, suppose that we wish to support a process group whose members replicate some form of database and perform load-balanced queries upon it. The operations on the service will be queries and updates, and we will overlook failures (for the time being) to keep the problem as simple as possible.

Next, suppose that we implement both queries and database updates as totally ordered multicasts to the group membership. Every member will have the same view of the membership of the group, and each will see the same updates and queries in the same order. By simply applying the updates in the order they were received, the members can maintain identically replicated copies of the database. As for the queries, an approximation of load-balancing can be had using the ranking of processes in the group view. For example, suppose that the process group view ranks the members in $[0 \ldots n-1]$. Then the ith incoming query can be assigned to the process whose rank is $(i \bmod n)$. Each query will be handled by exactly one process.

We'll call this a *closely synchronous* execution. Frank Schmuck was the first to propose this term, observing that the actions of the receiving processes were closely synchronized but might be spread over a significant period of real time. The synchronous model, as discussed previously, would normally require real-time bounds on the time period over which an action is performed by the different processes. Notice that a closely synchronous execution does not require identical actions by identical processes: If we use the load-balancing idea outlined above, actions will be quite different at the different copies. Thus, a closely synchronous group is similar to a group that uses State Machine replication, but it is not identical.

Having developed this solution, however, there will often be ways to weaken the ordering properties of the protocols it uses—for example, it may be the case that updates are only initiated by a single source, in which case an *fbcast* protocol would be sufficient to provide the desired ordering. Updates will no longer be ordered with respect to queries if such a change is made, but in an application where a single process issues an update and follows it with a query, the update would always be received first and hence the query will reflect the result of doing the update. In a slightly fancier setting, *cbcast* might be needed to ensure that the algorithm will operate correctly—for example, with *cbcast* one would know that if an application issues an update and then tells some other process to do a query, that second process will see the effects of the causally prior updates. Often, an analysis such as this one can be carried very far.

Having substituted *fbcast* or *cbcast* for the original *abcast*, however, the execution will no longer be closely synchronous, since different processes may see different sequences of updates and queries and hence perform the same actions but in different orders. The significant point is that if the original analysis was performed correctly, the actions will produce an effect indistinguishable from what might have resulted from a closely synchronous execution. Thus, the execution appears to be closely synchronous, even though it actually is not. It is *virtually synchronous* in much the same sense that a transactional system creates the illusion of a serial execution even though the database server is interleaving operations from different transactions to increase concurrency—one might say that a transactional—system is "virtually serial."

Our transformation has the advantage of delivering inputs to the process group members in different orders, at least some of the time. Moreover, as we saw earlier, the process groups themselves are constructed dynamically, with processes joining them at different times. Also, the ranking of the processes within the group differs. Thus, there is substantial room for processes to execute in slightly different ways, affording a degree of protection against software bugs that could crash some of the members.

Recall the Gray/Lindsey characterization of Bohrbugs and Heisenbugs from Chapter 13. It is interesting to note that virtually synchronous replication can protect against many Heisenbugs (see Birman and van Renesse [1994, 1996]). If a replica crashes because such a bug has been exercised, the probability that other group members will crash simultaneously is reduced by the many aspects of the execution that differ from replica to replica. Our transformation from a closely synchronous system to a virtually synchronous system increases the natural resiliency of the group, assuming that its constituent members are mature, well-debugged code. Nonetheless, some exposure to correlated failures is unavoidable, and the designer of a critical system should keep this in mind.

Additionally, notice that the *cbcast* primitive can be used asynchronously: There is no good reason for a process that issues a *cbcast* to perform an update to wait until the update has been completed by the full membership of the group. The properties of the *cbcast* protocol ensure that these asynchronously transmitted messages will reliably reach their destinations and that any causally subsequent actions by the same or different processes will see the effects of the prior *cbcasts*. In an intuitive sense, one could say that these *cbcast* protocols look as if they were performed instantly, even when they actually execute over an extended period of time.

In practice, the most common transformation that we will make is precisely the approach just described: the replacement of a totally ordered *abcast* primitive with an asynchronous, causally ordered *cbcast* primitive. In the following sections, this pattern will occur repeatedly.

Notice that in weakening the degree of synchronization within the group, we also transformed a closely synchronous group application, in which the members operate largely in lockstep, into a very asynchronous implementation in which some members can pull ahead and others can lag behind, communication can occur concurrently with other execution, and the group may be able to tolerate software bugs that crash some of its members. Such scheduling flexibility often translates to better overall performance, and weaker multicast primitives are also much faster than the more strongly ordered ones. Thus, our solution is likely to be far faster than the original closely synchronous one.

When an application has multiple process groups in it, an additional level of analysis is often required. As we saw in the previous chapter, multigroup causal (and total) ordering is expensive. When one considers real systems, it also turns out that multigroup ordering is often unnecessary: Many applications that need multiple groups use them for purposes that are fairly independent of one another. Operations on such independent groups can be thought of as commutative, and it may be possible to use *cbcast* to optimize such groups independently without taking the next step of enforcing causal orderings across groups. Where multigroup ordering is needed, it will often be confined to small sets of groups, which can be treated as an ordering domain. In this manner, we obtain a general solution that can scale to large numbers of groups while still preserving the benefits of the asynchronous communication pattern seen in the *cbcast* protocol.

Our overall approach is less effective when dynamic uniformity (safe delivery) is required. The problem arises because asynchronous *cbcast* delivers messages during its first phase of communication, pretty much as soon as the multicast can reach its destination. In contrast, a dynamically uniform protocol will necessarily delay delivery until a second phase because we need to be certain that all processes in the system have received a copy before any process is permitted to deliver the message. Once we've given up on quick delivery, the benefit of replacing *abcast* with *cbcast* has been lost.

Thus, one begins to see a major split between the algorithms that operate synchronously, requiring more than a single phase of message passing before delivery can occur, and those that operate asynchronously, allowing the sender of a multicast to continue computing while multicasts that update the remainder of a group or that inform the remainder of the system of some event propagate concurrently to their destinations. The split corresponds to an enormous performance difference, with asynchronous algorithms frequently outperforming their more synchronous siblings by several orders of magnitude. In effect, the asynchronous protocols can run as fast as the network is able to "pipeline" data from sources to destinations, while the synchronous ones are limited by the slowest round-trip times in the system as a whole!

The following is a summary of the key elements of the virtual synchrony model:

- *Support for process groups*: Processes can join groups dynamically and are automatically excluded from a group if they crash.
- *Identical process group views and mutually consistent rankings*: Members of a process group are presented with identical sequences of group membership, which we call *views* of that process group. If a nonprimary component of the system forms after a failure, any process group views reported to processes in that component are identified as nonprimary, and the view sequence properties will otherwise hold for all the processes in a given component. The view ranks the components, and all group members see identical rankings for identical group views.
- *State transfer to the joining process*: A process that joins a group can obtain the group's current state from some prior member or from a set of members.
- A *family of reliable, ordered multicast protocols*: We have seen a number of these, including *fbcast, cbcast, abcast, cabcast,* the *safe* (dynamically uniform) versions of these, and the group flush protocol, which is sometimes given the name *gbcast*.
- *Gap-freedom guarantees*: After a failure, if some message, m_j, is delivered to its destinations, then any message, m_i, that the system is obliged to deliver prior to m_j will also have been delivered to its destinations.
- *View-synchronous multicast delivery*: Any pair of processes that are both members of two consecutive group views receive the same set of multicasts during the period between those views.[13]
- *Use of asynchronous, causal, or FIFO multicast*: Although algorithms will often be developed using a closely synchronous computing model, a systematic effort is made to replace synchronous, totally ordered, and dynamically uniform (safe) multicasts with less synchronous, less-costly alternatives—notably the asynchronous *cbcast* primitive in its nonuniform mode.

18.2 Extended Virtual Synchrony

Even before launching into a brief discussion of tolerating partitioning events (where a group splits into two components, perhaps because of a network failure), we should warn the reader that what follows is a bit hard to understand and, in fact, is probably *not* a mechanism one would really want to use except in a small category of very demanding applications! The

---

[13] In some systems this is interpreted so that if a process fails, but its failure is not reported promptly, it is considered to have received multicasts that would have been delivered to it had it still been operational.

reader focused on high assurance Web Services might wish to skip directly to Section 18.3. However, other readers have now been warned, and with that out of the way, we tackle partitioning. Notice that, as presented in the previous section, the virtual synchrony model is intolerant of partitioning failures: The model was defined in terms of a single system component within which process groups reside. In this primary component approach, if a network partitioning failure occurs and splits a group into fragments, only the fragment that resides in the primary component of the system is able to continue operation. Fragments that find themselves in the nonprimary component(s) of the system are typically forced to shut down, and the processes within them must reconnect to the primary component when communication is restored.

The basis of the primary component approach lies in a subtle issue, which we first saw when discussing commit protocols. In a dynamic distributed environment there can be symmetric failure modes resulting from communication problems that mimic process failures. In such a situation perhaps process p will consider that process q has failed while process q assumes that p has failed. To make progress, one or the other (or perhaps both) of these events must become official. In a partitioned run of the system, only one of these conflicting states can become official.

At the core of this problem is the observation that if a system experiences a partitioning failure, it is impossible to guarantee that multiple components can remain operational (in the sense of initiating new actions, delivering messages, and new group views) with guarantees that also span both sides of the partition. To obtain strong system-wide guarantees a protocol must always wait for communication to be reestablished under at least some executions in at least one side of the partition. When we resolve this problem using the protocols discussed in the previous chapters, the primary component is permitted to make progress at the expense of inconsistency relative to other components: Within other components, the set of messages delivered may be different from the set in the primary component, and the order may also be different. In the case of the dynamically uniform protocols the guarantees are stronger, but nonprimary components may be left in a state where some dynamically uniform multicasts are still undelivered and where new dynamically uniform ones are completely blocked. The primary component, in contrast, can make progress so long as its GMS protocol is able to make progress.

Some researchers, notably those involved with the Transis and Totem projects, have pointed out that there are applications that can tolerate inconsistency of the sort that could occur if progress were permitted in a nonprimary component of a partitioned system (see Agarwal, Dolev et al., Malkhi). In these systems, any component that can reach internal agreement on its membership is permitted to continue operation. However, only a single component of the system is designated as the primary one. An application that is safe only in the primary component could simply shut down in nonprimary components. Alternatively, the application could remain available in nonprimary components, but buffer any update requests for delayed execution. Later, when the partition is repaired, these buffered requests would be replayed, with the effect of merging information collected by the non-primary component back into the primary component. However, not all applications can be designed in this manner—often, the user needs to see the effect of an update as soon as it is requested, in which case buffering such requests isn't practical.

Carrying this observation even further, the Transis group has shown that there are distributed systems in which no component ever can be identified as the primary one, and yet every action initiated within the system can eventually be performed in a globally consistent manner (see Dolev et al., Keidar, Chockler and Dolev). However, this work involves both a static system model and a relatively costly protocol, which delays performing an action until a majority of the processes in the system as a whole have acknowledged receipt of it. The idea is that actions can be initiated within dynamically defined components, which represent subsets of the true maximal system configuration, but these actions remain in a pending state until a sufficient number of processes are known to have seen them, which occurs when communication is restored between components. Eventually, knowledge of the actions reaches enough processes so that it becomes safe to perform them. The protocol is intended for systems that operate in a partitioned mode over very long periods of time and where there is no special hurry to perform actions. Yair Amir has extended this approach to deal with more urgent actions, but his approach involves weakening global consistency properties (see Amir). Thus, one is faced with a basic tradeoff between ensuring that actions will occur quickly and providing consistency between the primary component of the system and other components. We can have one or the other, but not both at once.

Cornell's most recent systems, Horus and Ensemble, support an extended model of the former sort (see Malkhi). (In fact, this part of Horus was actually implemented by Malkhi, who ported the associated code from Transis into Horus, and then the code was used as the basis for the Ensemble version, which is coded in the O'CaML language.) However, many users complain that the extended model is quite a bit harder to work with than the primary partition model. The merge of states when an arbitrary application resumes contact between a nonprimary and a primary component cannot, in general, be automated. In practice, such an application would use the buffered update approach just described, capturing any update actions on a queue. When a merge becomes possible, a process that joins the primary partition would replace its state with that of the primary component and then replay these updates, if any, for the benefit of the entire group. Experience with Horus and Ensemble suggests that very few applications can operate this way. Moreover, unless dynamically uniform protocols are employed for updates, the nonprimary component's state may be inconsistent with the primary one in significant ways.

On the other hand, the primary component model is awkard in wide area networks where partitioning events occur more easily (see Figure 18.2). Here, the model will in effect shut down parts of the overall system that are physically remote from the main part of the system. Each time these parts manage to restart after a communication failure, a new communication problem may soon cut them off again. (See Figure 18.3.)

Recent work, which we will not discuss in detail, points to yet a third possible mode of operation. In this mode, a computing system would be viewed as a wide area network composed of interconnected local area networks, as was first proposed in the Transis project. Within each of the LAN systems one would run a local subsystem: a complete primary-

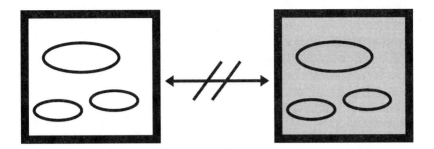

Figure 18.2. When a partitioning failure occurs, an application may be split into two or more fragments, each complete in the sense that it may potentially have a full set of processes and groups. In the primary component model, however, only one set is permitted to remain operational—hopefully one that has a full complement of process and groups. In this figure, the white component might thus be alive after the link breaks, while the members of the gray component are prevented from continuing execution. The rationale underlying this model is that it is impossible to guarantee consistency if both sides of a partitioning failure are permitted to remain available while a communication failure is pending. Thus, we could allow both to run if we sacrifice consistency, but then we face a number of problems: Which side owns critical resources? How can the two sides overcome potential inconsistencies in their states as of the time of the partition failure event? There are no good general answers to these questions.

component system with its own sets of process groups and a self-sufficient collection of services and applications. The WAN layer of the system would be built up by superimposing a second communication structure on the aggregate of LANs and would support its own set of WAN services. At this higher level of the system, one would use a true asynchronous communication model: If a partitioning event does occur, such a WAN system would wait until the problem is resolved. The WAN system would then be in a position to make use of protocols that don't attempt to make progress while communication is disrupted, but rather wait as long as necessary until the exchange of messages resumes and the protocol can be pushed forward. The consensus protocol of Chandra and Toueg or the Paxos protocols developed by Lamport are good examples of protocols one could use at the WAN level of a system structured in this manner, while the virtual synchrony model would be instantiated multiple times separately: once for each LAN subsystem.

In this two-tiered model (see Figure 18.4), an application would typically be implemented as a local part designed to remain available in the local component and to reconfigure itself to continue progress despite local failures. The primary component virtual synchrony model is ideal for this purpose. When an action is taken that has global implications, the local part would initiate a global action by asking the WAN architecture to communicate this message through the WAN system. The WAN system would use potentially slow protocols, which offer strong global ordering and atomicity properties at the expense of reduced progress when partitioning failures occur, delivering the resulting messages back into the various local subsystems. The local subsystems would then apply these updates to their global states.

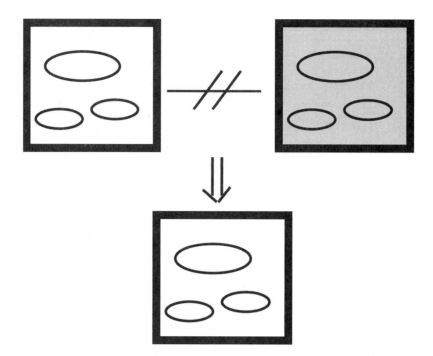

Figure 18.3.   The extended virtual synchrony model allows both white and gray partitions to continue progress despite the inconsistencies that may occur between their states. However, only one of the components is considered to be the primary one. Thus, the white partition might be considered to be authoritative for the system, while the gray partition is permitted to remain alive but is known to be potentially stale. Later, when the communication between the components is restored, the various process group components merge, resulting in a single, larger system component with a single instance of each process group (shown at the bottom of the figure). The problem, however, is that merging must somehow overcome the inconsistencies that may have occurred during the original partitioning failure, and this may not always be possible. Working with such a model is potentially challenging for the developer. Moreover, one must ask what sorts of applications would be able to continue operating in the gray partition knowing that the state of the system may at that point may be inconsistent—for example, it may reflect the delivery of messages in an order that differs from the order in the main partition, having atomicity errors or gaps in the message-delivery ordering.

Danny Dolev has suggested the following simple way to understand such a two-tiered system. In his view, the LAN subsystems run applications that are either entirely confined to the LAN (and have no interest in global state) or that operate by reading the *global* state but updating the *local* state. These applications do not directly update the global system state. Rather, if an action requires that the global state be updated, the LAN subsystem places the associated information on a WAN action queue, perhaps replicating this for higher availability. From that queue, the WAN protocols will eventually propagate the action into the WAN level of the system, from where it will filter back down into the LAN level of the system, in the form of an update to the global system state. The LAN layer will then update its local state to reflect the fact that the requested action has finally been completed. The LAN layer of

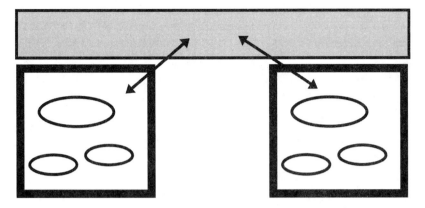

Figure 18.4. In a two-tiered model, each LAN has its own complete subsystem and runs using its own copy of the primary-component virtual synchrony model. A WAN system (gray) spans the LANs and is responsible for distributing global updates. The WAN layer may block while a partitioning failure prevents it from establishing the degree of consensus needed to safely deliver updates, but the local systems continue running even if global updates are delayed. Such a mixed approach splits the concerns of the application into local ones, where the focus is on local consistency and high availability, and global ones, where the focus is on global consistency even if partitioning failures can introduce long delays. This approach is used in the Isis Toolkit's long-haul subsystem and was applied successfully in such Isis applications as its wide area publish-subscribe facility.

such a system would use the primary-component virtual synchrony model, while the WAN layer employs protocols based on the method discussed by Keidar and Dolev.

First introduced in the Isis system's long-haul service by Makpangou, and then extended through Dolev and Malkhi's work on the Transis architecture (which has a "LANsys" and a "WANsys" subsystem), two-tier architectures such as this have received attention in many projects and systems (see [Amir [2000], Keidar [2002], Keidar and Khazan [2002], and also [Zhao 2002], which uses a similar two-level structure, albeit for a different purpose). They are now used in Transis, Horus, NavTech, Phoenix, and Relacs. By splitting the application into the part that can be done locally with higher availability and the part that must be performed globally even if availability is limited, two-tiered architectures do not force a black or white decision on the developer. Moreover, a great many applications seem to fit well with this model. It seems likely that we will soon begin to see programming tools that encapsulate this architecture into a simple-to-use, object-oriented framework, making it readily accessible to a wide community of potential developers.

At the very end of Chapter 14, we discussed partitioning as an issue within the context of the GMS itself. At that time we observed that although a partition-tolerant GMS is certainly practical, it isn't so clear that one should really expose the end-user to the resulting complexity. The same issue arises here. Yes, we can build a group communication system to tolerate partitions and support merge events—Cornell's Ensemble platform, in fact, does so. But users find this very hard to work with. Systems like Horus and Spread,[14] where the

---

[14]In fact, Spread goes further and implements a single non-partitionable "group," within which the user's process groups are actually supported as subgroups. A multicast, for example, is performed by multicasting to the whole

default behavior is to use the primary partition model are *much simpler* for most users. And, realistically, how often do partitioning events occur in local area networks, where these platforms are most commonly employed? The author of this text has slowly come to the conclusion that partitionable group communication is just a bit too much for the average user. Yes, there should be a way to activate such mechanisms—but only a very skilled, knowledgeable user should ever do so!

18.3 Virtually Synchronous Algorithms and Tools

In the following sections, we will develop a set of simple algorithms to illustrate the power and limitations of reliable multicast within dynamic process groups. These algorithms are just a small subset of the ones that can be developed using the primitives, and the sophisticated system designer may sometimes find a need for a causal and total multicast primitive (*cabcast*) or one with some other slight variation on the properties we have focused on here. Happily, the protocols we have presented are easily modified for special needs, and modern group communication systems, such as the Horus system, are designed precisely to accommodate such flexibility and fine-tuning. The following algorithms, then, should be viewed as a form of template upon which other solutions might be developed through a process of gradual refinement and adaptation.

18.3.1 Replicated Data and Synchronization

When discussing the static process group model, we put it to the test by using it to implement replicated data. The reader will recall from Section 14.2 that this approach was found to have a number of performance problems. The algorithm that resulted would have forced group members to execute nearly in lockstep, and the protocols themselves were costly both in latency and messages required. Virtual synchrony, on the other hand, offers a solution to this problem that is inexpensive in all of these aspects, provided that dynamic uniformity is not required. In fact, even when dynamic uniformity is required, the cost is still lower than for the static, quorum-replication methods, but the advantage is less pronounced.

   We start by describing our replication and synchronization algorithm in terms of a closely synchronous execution model. We will initially focus on the nonuniform case. Suppose that we wish to support *READ, UPDATE,* and *LOCK* operations on data replicated within a process group. As a first approximation to a solution, we would use *abcast* to implement the *UPDATE* and *LOCK* operations, while allowing any group member to perform *READ* operations using its local replica of the data maintained by the group.

---

group but then filtering messages on arrival so only the appropriate subset of group members receive a copy. This proves to be an especially easy model to implement and performance is good. On the other hand, the "deliver, then filter and discard" approach imposes considerable overhead if most messages are destined for just a small subset of processes.

Specifically, we will require each group member to maintain a private replica of the group data. When joining a group, the state transfer algorithm (developed below) must be used to initialize the replica associated with the joining process. Subsequently, all members will apply the same sequence of updates by tracking the order in which *UPDATE* messages are delivered and respecting this order when actually performing the updates. *READ* operations, as suggested above, are performed using the local replica (this is in contrast to the quorum methods, where a read must access multiple copies).

An *UPDATE* operation can be performed without waiting for the group members to actually complete the individual update actions. Instead, an *abcast* is issued asynchronously (without waiting for the message to be delivered), and the individual replicas perform the update when the message arrives.

Many systems make use of nonexclusive read locks. If necessary, these can also be implemented locally. The requesting process will be granted the lock immediately unless an exclusive (write) lock is registered at this copy.

Finally, exclusive (write) *LOCK* operations are performed by issuing an *abcast* to request the lock and then waiting for each group member to grant it. A recipient of such a request waits until there are no pending read locks and then grants the request in the order it was received. The lock will later be released either with another *abcast* message or upon reception of a new view of the process group reporting the failure of the process that holds the lock.

This implementation of replicated data will be tolerant of failures and guarantee the consistency of the copies. The individual replicas start in identical states because the state transfer to a joining member copies the state of the replicated data object from some existing member. Subsequent updates and lock operations behave identically at all copies. Thus, all see the same events in the same order, and all remain in identical states.

Now, let us ask how many of these *abcast* operations can be replaced with asynchronous *cbcast* operations. In particular, suppose that we replace *all* of the *abcasts* with asynchronous *cbcast* operations. Remarkably, with just two small changes, the modified algorithm will be correct. The first change is that all updates must be guarded by a lock with appropriate granularity—that is, if any update might be in conflict with a concurrent update, we will require that the application must use locks to obtain mutual exclusion. On the other hand, updates that are independent can be issued concurrently—for example, updates to two different variables maintained by the same process group can be issued concurrently. In groups where all the updates for a specific type of data originate with a single process, no locks are required at all.

The second change is a bit more subtle: It has to do with the way that ordering is established when a series of write locks are requested within the group. The change is as follows. We will say that the first process to join the group, when the group is created, is its *initial writer*. This process is considered to control write access to all the data items managed by the group.

Now, before doing an update, a process will typically request a lock, sending a *cbcast* to inform the group members of its *LOCK* request and waiting for the members to grant the request. In our original closely synchronous algorithm, a recipient of such a request granted it in first-come, first-served order when no local read-lock was pending. Our modified algorithm, however, will wait before granting lock requests. They simply pile up in a queue, ordered in whatever order the *cbcast* messages were delivered.

When the writer for a given lock no longer needs that lock, we will say that it becomes *prepared to pass the lock*. This process will react to incoming lock requests by sending out a *cbcast* that *grants* the first lock request on its copy of the queue. The grant message will be delivered to all group members. Once the grant message is received, a member dequeues the corresponding lock request (the causal ordering properties ensure that the request will indeed be found on the pending lock-request queue) and then grants it when any read locks present for the same item have been released. A writer grants the lock to the process that issued the oldest of the pending lock requests on its version of the lock queue.

Having obtained a grant message for its lock request, as well as individual confirmation messages from each group member that the lock has been acquired locally, the writer may begin issuing updates. In many systems the local read-lock mechanism will not be required, in which case the members need not confirm write-lock acquisition, and the writer need not wait for these messages. The members simply dequeue the pending lock request when the grant message arrives, and the writer proceeds to issue updates as soon as it receives the grant message.

It may at first seem surprising that this algorithm can work: Why should it ensure that the group members will perform the same sequence of updates on their replicas? To understand this, start by noticing that the members actually might not perform identical sequences of updates (Figure 18.5). However, any sequence of *conflicting updates* will be identical at all

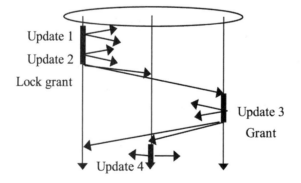

Figure 18.5. A set of conflicting updates is ordered because only one process can write at a time. Each update, and the lock-granting message, is an asynchronous *cbcast*. Because the causal order is in fact a total one along this causal path (shown in bold), all group members see the same updates in the same order. Lock requests are not shown, but they too would be issued using an asynchronous *cbcast*. Notice that lock requests will not be seen in the same order by all processes, but this is not required for the algorithm to behave correctly. All that matters is that the grant operation grant a currently pending lock request, and, in this algorithm, all processes do have a way to track the pending requests, even though they may learn about those requests in different orders.

replicas, for the following reason: Within the group, there can be only one writer that holds a given lock. That writer uses *cbcast* (asynchronously) to issue updates and uses *cbcast* (asynchronously) to grant the write lock to the subsequent writer. This establishes a total order on the updates: One can imagine a causal path traced through the group, from writer to writer, with the updates neatly numbered along it—the first update, the second, the granting of the lock to a new writer, the third update, the granting of the lock to a new writer, the fourth update, and so forth. Thus, when *cbcast* enforces the delivery order, any set of updates covered by the same lock will be delivered in the same order to all group members.

As for the nonconflicting updates: These commute with the others and hence would have had the same effect regardless of how they were ordered. The ordering of updates is thus significant only with respect to other conflicting updates.

Finally, the reader may have noticed that lock requests are not actually seen in the same order by each participant. This is not a problem, however, because the lock-request order isn't used in the algorithm. As long as the grant operation grants a request that is genuinely pending, the algorithm will work.

The remarkable thing about this new algorithm is that it is almost entirely asynchronous. Recall that our *cbcast* protocol delivers messages in the same view of the process group as the one that was in place when the *cbcast* was initiated. This implies that the sender of a *cbcast* can always deliver its own copy of the multicast as soon as it initiates the message. After all, by definition, a causally prior *cbcast* will already have been delivered to the sender, and the flush protocol enforces the view synchrony and causal gap-freedom guarantees. This means that a process wanting to issue an update can perform the update locally, sending off a *cbcast* that will update the other replicas without delaying local computation. Clearly, a lock request will block the process that issues it—unless that process happens to hold the write lock already, as is often the case in systems with bursty communication patterns. But it is clear that this minimal delay—the time needed to request permission to write and for the grant message to travel back to the requesting process—is necessary in any system.

The algorithm can be simplified further. Although we used *cbcast* here, one could potentially replace this with *fbcast* by employing a sequence number: The ith update would be so labeled, and all group members would simply apply updates in sequence order. The token would now represent permission to initiate new updates (and the guarantee that the values a process reads are the most current ones). Such a change eliminates the vector-timestamp overhead associated with *cbcast*, and it is also recognizable as an implementation of one of the *abcast* protocols we developed earlier!

From the perspective of an application, this asynchronous replication and locking scheme may seem astonishingly fast. The only delays imposed upon the application are when it requests a new write lock. During periods when it holds the lock, or if it is lucky enough to find the lock already available, the application is never delayed at all. Read operations can be performed locally, and write operations respond as soon as the local update has been completed. The *cbcast* or *fbcast* (we'll just call it a *cbcast* for simplicity) will be performed asynchronously in communication subsystem. Later, we will see that the Horus system achieves performance that can reach 85,000 such updates per second. Reads are essentially free—hence, millions could be done per second. When this is compared with a quorum read and update technology, in which it would be surprising to exceed 100 reads and updates (combined) in one second, the benefits of an asynchronous *cbcast* are nothing short of astonishing! In practice, quorum schemes are often even slower than this analysis suggests, because of the overheads built into the algorithm. Moreover, a quorum read or update forces the group members into lockstep, while our asynchronous replication algorithm encourages them to leap ahead of one another, buffering messages to be transmitted in the background.

However, this algorithm is not identical to the quorum replication scheme, because that scheme provides the equivalent of a dynamic uniformity guarantee and a strong total ordering. The algorithm described above could be modified to provide such a guarantee by using a safe *cbcast* in place of the standard *cbcast*. But such a change will make the protocol dramatically slower, because each *UPDATE* will now be delayed until at least a majority of the group members acknowledge receipt of the update message. Thus, although the algorithm would continue to perform *READ* operations from local replicas, *UPDATE* operations will now be subject to the same performance limits as for a quorum update. The advantage of this scheme over a quorum scheme would be much reduced.

In the author's experience, dynamic uniformity is rarely needed. If an application is about to take an externally visible action and it is important that in the event of a failure the other replicas of the application be in a consistent state with that of the application taking the action, this guarantee becomes important. In such cases, it can be useful to have a way to *flush* communication within the group, so that any prior asynchronous multicasts are forced out of the communication channels and delivered to their destinations. A *cbcast* followed by a *flush* is thus the equivalent of a *safe cbcast* (stronger, really, since the *flush* will flush all prior *cbcasts*, while a safe *cbcast* might not provide this guarantee). Many process group systems, including Horus and Ensemble, adopt this approach rather than one based on a *safe cbcast*. The application developer is unlikely to use *flush* very frequently—hence, the average performance may approximate that of our fully asynchronous algorithm, with occasional short delays when a *flush* pushes a few messages through the channels to their destinations. Unless large backlogs develop within the system, long delays are unlikely to occur. Thus, such a compromise can be very reasonable from the perspective of the application designer.

By way of analogy, many system developers are familiar with the behavior of operating systems that buffer disk I/O. In such settings, to increase performance, it is common to permit the application to continue operation as soon as a disk write is reflected in the cache contents—without waiting for the data to be flushed to the disk itself. When a stronger guarantee is required, the application explicitly requests that the disk buffer be flushed by invoking an appropriate primitive, such as the UNIX *fsync* system call. The situation created by the asynchronous *cbcast* is entirely analogous, and the role of the *flush* primitive is precisely the same as that of *fsync*.

What about a comparison with the closely synchronous algorithm from which ours was derived? Interestingly, the story here is not so clear. Suppose that we adopt the same approach to the dynamic uniformity issue, by using a *flush* primitive with this property if required. Now, the performance of the closely synchronous *abcast* algorithm will depend entirely on the way *abcast* is implemented. In particular, one could implement *abcast* using the *cbcast*-based lock and update scheme described in this section or using a rotating token (with very similar results). Indeed, if the lock (token) never moves unless the holder fails, we can use *fbcast* to implement the desired primitive.

Such an *abcast* solution would push the logic of our algorithm into the communication primitive itself. In principle, performance could converge to that of an algorithm using *cbcast* explicitly—this level of performance has been achieved in experiments with the Horus system. The major issues is that to use the approach just outlined, one needs to use an *abcast* algorithm well matched to the communication pattern of the user, and this is not always possible: Many developers lack information at design time that would be required to predict such patterns accurately.

18.3.2 State Transfer to a Joining Process

There is often a need to transfer information about the current state of a process group to a joining member at the instant it joins. In a replicated data algorithm, for example, there is clearly a need to transfer a current copy of the data in question to the joining process.

The most appropriate representation of the state of the group, however, will be highly dependent on the application. Some forms of state may be amenable to extreme compression or may be reconstructable from information stored on files or logs using relatively small amounts of information at the time the process joins. Accordingly, we adopt the view that a state transfer should be done by the application itself. Such a transfer is requested at the time of the join. The mechanism looks very much like the creation of a checkpoint file.

The basic idea is to introduce state transfer as a mechanism within the protocol for group flush. At the time a process first requests that it be added to the group, it should signal its intention to solicit state from the members. The associated information is passed in the form a message to the group members and is carried along with the join protocol to be reported with the new group view after the members perform the flush operation.

Each member now faces a choice: It can stop processing new requests at the instant of the flush, or it can make a copy of its state as of the time of the flush for possible future use, in which case it can resume processing. The joining process will solicit state information RPC-style, pulling it from one or more of the prior members. If state information is needed from all members, they can send it without waiting for it to be solicited (Figure 18.6), although this can create a burst of communication load just at the moment when the flush protocol is still running, with the risk of momentarily overloading some processes or the network. At the other extreme, if a transfer is needed from just a single member, the joining process should transmit an asynchronous multicast, *terminating* the transfer after it has successfully pulled the state from some member. The remaining members can now resume processing requests or discard any information saved for use during the state transfer protocol.

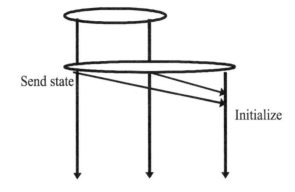

Figure 18.6. One of several state transfer mechanisms. In this very simple scheme, the group members all send their copies of the state to the joining member and then resume computing. The method may be a good choice if the state is known to be small, since it minimizes delay, is fault tolerant (albeit sending redundant information), and is very easy to implement. If the state may be large, however, the overhead could be substantial.

Perhaps the best among these options, if one single approach is desired as a default, is for the joining process to pull state from a single existing member, switching to a second member if a failure disrupts the transfer. The members should save the state in a buffer for later transfer, and should use some form of out-of-band transfer (e.g., over a specially created TCP channel) to avoid sending large state objects over the same channels used for other forms of group communication

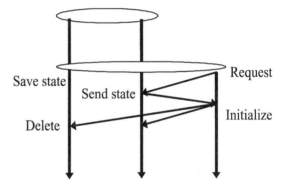

Figure 18.7. A good state transfer mechanism for cases where the state is of unknown size—the joining member solicits state from some existing member and then tells the group as a whole when it is safe to delete the saved data.

and request processing. When the transfer is completed, the joining process should send a multicast telling the other members it is safe to delete their saved state copies. This is illustrated in Figure 18.7.

Developers should be wary of one possible problem with this approach to state transfer. In many systems, the group state can be so large that transferring it represents a potentially slow operation—for example, in a file system application, the state transferred to a joining process might need to contain the full contents of every file modified since that process was last operational. Clearly, it would be a terrible idea to shut down the request processing by existing group members during this extended period of time! Clearly, if state becomes large enough so that the system could pause for an unacceptable amount of time while recording it and reloading it at the joining member, both operations need to be forked off as asynchronous tasks that can be performed while still accepting new requests.

Such considerations lead to three broad recommendations. First, if the state is very large, it is advisable to transfer as much of it as possible before initiating the join request. A mechanism can then be implemented by which any last-minute changes are transferred to the joining process—without extended delays. Second, the state transfer should be done asynchronously—in a manner that will not lead to congestion or flow-control problems impeding the normal processing of requests by the service. A service that remains available, but is inaccessible because its communication channels are crammed with data to a joining process may seem very unavailable to other users. Finally, where possible, the approach of jotting down the state is preferable to one that shuts down a server even briefly during the transfer. Again, this reflects a philosophy whereby every effort is made to avoid delaying the response by the server to ongoing requests during the period while the join is still in progress.

18.3.3 Load-Balancing

One of the more common uses of process groups is to implement some form of load-balancing algorithm, whereby the members of a group share the workload presented to them in order to obtain a speedup from parallelism. It is no exaggeration to say that parallelism of this sort may represent the most important single property of process group computing systems: The opportunity to gain performance while also obtaining fault-tolerant benefits on relatively inexpensive cluster-style computing platforms is one of the main reasons that developers turn to such architectures.

There are several broad styles of load-balancing algorithms. The first style involves multicasting the client's request to the full membership of the group; the decision as to how the request should be processed is left for the group members to resolve. This approach has the advantage of requiring little trust in the client, but the disadvantage of communicating the full request (which may involve a large amount of data) to more processes than really need to see this information. In the second style, the client either makes a choice among the group members or is assigned a preferred group member to which its requests are issued. Here, some degree of trust in the behavior of the clients is accepted in order to reduce the communication load on the system. In this second style, the client may also need to implement a *fail-over policy* by which it reissues a request if the server to which it was originally issued turns out to be faulty or fails while processing it. A third style of load-balancing is the replicated load-balancer. Here, the server state is replicated on multiple machines and the client requests are sprayed over them, often randomly. It should perhaps be noted that in commercial practice, this third style is the most common, particularly for Web sites that have unchanging or very slowly changing content, since such content is easy to replicate.

Load-balancing algorithms of the first sort require some form of deterministic rule by which incoming requests can be assigned within the server group. As an example, if incoming requests are issued using an *abcast* protocol, the group can take advantage of the fact that all members see the requests in the same order. The ith request can now be assigned to the server whose rank within the group is i *(mod n)*, or the servers can use some other deterministic algorithm for assigning the incoming work. (See Figure 18.8.)

If group members period-ically send out load reports to one another, also using *abcast*, these load measures can be used to balance work in the fol-lowing manner. Suppose that the servers in the group mea-sure their load on a simple numeric scale, with 0 repre-senting an unloaded server, 1 representing a server currently handling a single request, and so forth. The load on a group of n servers now can be repre-

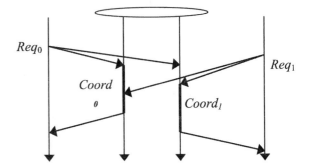

Figure 18.8. Load-balancing based on a coordinator scheme using ranking. Ideally, the load on the members will be fairly uniform.

sented as a vector $[l_0, \dots l_n]$. Think of these load values as intervals within a line segment of total length $L = (l_0 + \dots l_n)$ and assume that the group members employ an algorithm for independently but identically generating pseudorandom numbers—the seed of which is transferred as part of the state passed to a joining process when it joins the group. Then, as each new request is received, the group members can independently pick the same random number on the segment $[0, L]$, assigning the request to the process corresponding to the interval within which that number falls. Such an approach will tend to equalize load by randomly spreading it within the group, and it has the benefit of working well even if the load values are approximate and may be somewhat inaccurate.

The same methods can be used as the basis for client affinity load-balancing schemes. In these, the group members provide the client with information that it uses to select the server to which requests will be sent—for example, the group can statically assign clients to particular members at the time the client first interacts with the group. Such an approach risks overloading a server whose clients happen to be unusually active, but it can also be advantageous if caching is a key determinate of request processing performance, since this server is more likely to benefit from the use of a caching algorithm. Alternatively, the client can randomly select a server for each new request within the group membership, or it can use the same load-balancing scheme outlined above to spread requests over the group member-ship using approximate load information, which the members would periodically broadcast to the clients. Any of these methods represents a viable option for distributing work, and the best choice for a given setting will depend on other information available only to the application designer, such as the likely size of the data associated with each request, fault-tolerant considerations (discussed in the next section), or issues such as the balance between queries (which can often be load-balanced) and update requests (which generally cannot).

18.3.4 Primary-Backup Fault Tolerance

Earlier, we illustrated the concept of primary-backup fault tolerance, in which a pair of servers are used to implement a critical service. Virtually synchronous process groups offer a good setting within which such an approach can be used (see Budhiraja et al.).

Primary-backup fault tolerance is most easily understood if one assumes that the application is completely deterministic—that is, the behavior of the server program will be completely determined by the order of inputs to it and is therefore reproducible by simply replaying the same inputs in the same order to a second copy. Under this assumption, a backup server can track the actions of a primary server by simply arranging that a totally ordered broadcast be used to transmit incoming requests to the primary-backup group. The client processes should be designed to detect and ignore duplicate replies to requests (by numbering requests and including the number in the reply). The primary server can simply compute results for incoming requests and reply normally, periodically informing the backup of the most recent replies known to have been received safely. The backup mimics the primary, buffering replies and garbage collecting them when such a status message is received. If the primary fails, the backup resends any replies in its buffer.

Most primary-backup schemes employ some form of checkpoint method to launch a new replica if the primary process actually does fail. At some convenient point soon after the failure, the backup turned primary makes a checkpoint of its state, and simultaneously launches a new backup process[15]. The new process loads its initial state from the checkpoint and joins a process group with the primary. State transfer can also be used to initialize the backup, but this is often harder to implement because many primary-backup schemes must operate with old code, which is not amenable to change and in which the most appropriate form of state is hard to identify. Fortunately, it is just this class of server that is most likely to support a checkpoint mechanism.

The same approach can be extended to work with nondeterministic primary servers, but doing so is potentially much harder. The basic idea is to find a way to *trace* (keep a record of) the nondeterministic actions of the primary, so that the backup can be forced to repeat those actions in a trace-driven mode—for example, suppose that the only nondeterministic action taken by the primary is to request the time of day from the operating system. This system call can be modified to record the value so obtained, sending it in a message to the backup. If the backup pauses each time it encounters a time-of-day system call, it will either see a copy of the value used by the primary (in which case it should use that value and ignore the value of its local clock), or it will see the primary fail (in which case it takes over as primary and begins to run off its local clock). Unfortunately, there can be a great many sources of nondeterminism in a typical program, and some will be very hard to deal with: lightweight thread scheduling, delivery of interrupts, shared memory algorithms, I/O ready notifications through system calls such as "select," and so forth. Moreover, it is easily seen that to operate

---

[15]Interested readers may also want to read about log-based recovery techniques, which we do not cover in this book because these techniques have not been applied in many real systems. Alvisi gives a very general log-based recovery algorithm and reviews other work in the area in his Ph D. dissertation and in a paper with Marzullo.

a primary-backup scheme efficiently, the incoming requests, the corresponding replies, and these internal trace messages will need to be transmitted as asynchronously as possible, while respecting causality (See Figure 18.9.). Our causal ordering algorithms were oriented towards group multicast, and this particular case would demand nontrivial analysis and optimization. Thus, in practice, primary-backup replication can be very hard to implement when using arbitrary servers.

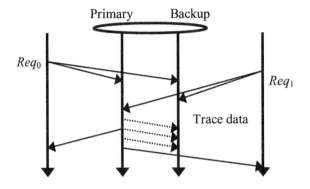

Figure 18.9. Primary-backup scheme for nondeterministic servers requires that trace information reach the backup. The fundamental requirement is a causal gap-freedom property: If a reply or some other visible consequence of a primary's actions is visible to a client or the outside world, all causally prior inputs to the primary, as well as trace information, must also be delivered to the backup. The trace data contain information about how nondeterministic actions were performed in the primary. The ordering obligation is ultimately a fairly weak one, and the primary could run far ahead of the backup, giving good performance and masking the costs of replication for fault tolerance. The complexity of the scheme is fairly high, because it can be hard to generate and use trace information—hence, it is rare to see primary-backup fault tolerance in nondeterministic applications.

Another drawback to the approach is that it may fail to overcome software bugs. As we can see, primary-backup replication is primarily appealing for deterministic applications. But these are just the ones in which Heisenbugs would be carefully repeated by a primary-backup solution, unless the fact of starting the backup from a state checkpoint introduces some degree of tolerance to this class of failures. Thus, the approach is likely to be exposed to correlated failures of the primary and backup in the case where it can be most readily applied.

18.3.5 Coordinator-Cohort Fault Tolerance

The coordinator-cohort approach to fault tolerance generalizes the primary-backup approach in ways that can help overcome the limitations previously mentioned. In this fault-tolerant method, the work of handling requests is shared by the group members. (The same load-sharing mechanisms discussed previously are used to balance the load.) The handler for a given request is said to be the *coordinator* for processing that request and is responsible for sending any updates or necessary trace information to the other members, which are termed the *cohorts* for that request. As in the primary-backup scheme, if the coordinator fails, one of the cohorts takes over.

Unlike the primary-backup method, there may be many coordinators active in the same group for many different requests. Moreover, the trace information in a primary backup scheme normally contains the information needed for the backup to duplicate the actions of the primary, whereas the trace data of a coordinator-cohort scheme will often consist of a log of updates the coordinator applied to the group state. In this approach, the cohorts do not actively replicate the actions of the coordinator, but merely update their states to reflect its updates. Locking must be used for concurrency control. In addition, the coordinator will normally send some form of copy of the reply to its cohorts, so that they can garbage collect information associated with the pending requests for which they are backups. The approach is illustrated in Figure 18.10.

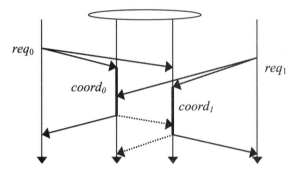

req_0 req_1

$coord_0$

$coord_1$

Figure 18.10. Coordinator-cohort scheme. The work of handling requests is divided among the processes in the group. Notice that as each coordinator replies, it also (atomically) informs the other group members that it has terminated. This permits them to garbage collect information about pending requests that other group members are handling. In the scheme, each process group member is active handling some requests while passively acting as backup for other members on other requests. The approach is best suited well for deterministic applications, but it can also be adapted to nondeterministic ones.

Some practical cautions limit the flexibility of this style of load-balanced and fault-tolerant computing (which is quite popular among users of systems such as the Isis Toolkit and Horus, we should add!). First, it is important that the coordinator selection algorithm do a good job of load-balancing, or some single group member may become overloaded with the lion's share of the requests. In addition to this, the method can be very complex for requests that involve nontrivial updates to the group state or that involve nondeterministic processing that the cohort may be expected to reproduce. In such cases, it can be necessary to use an atomic protocol for sending the reply to the requesting client and the trace information or termination information to the cohorts. Isis implements a protocol for this purpose: It is atomic and can send to the members of a group plus one additional member. However, such protocols are not common in most systems for reliable distributed computing. Given appropriate protocol support, however, and a reasonably simple server (e.g., one processing requests that are primarily queries that don't change the server state), the approach can be highly successful, offering scalable parallelism and fault-tolerance for the same price.

18.4 Related Reading

On virtual synchrony: (see Birman and van Renesse [1994, 1996,] Powell [1996]); but see also Birman and Joseph (February 1987, November 1987), Birman and van Renesse (1996), Dolev and Malkhi, Schiper and Raynal.

On extended virtual synchrony: (see Malkhi); but see also Agarwal, Amir, Keidar and Dolev, Moser et al. (1996).

On uses of the virtual synchrony model: (see Birman and Joseph [November 1987], Birman and van Renesse [1994]).

On primary-backup schemes: (see Budhiraja et al.).

A discussion of other approaches to the same problems can be found in Cristian (1996).

19

Consistency in Distributed Systems

We now tackle the last of the "process group internals" topics that will be covered in this textbook. As mentioned at the start of Chapters 14, a reader focused primarily on high assurance for Web Services doesn't really need to read the material that follows in any detail. The questions tackled here are a bit esoteric and while they do matter, platforms like Horus, Spread and Ensemble address these issues in a simple, standardized manner reflecting a sensible tradeoff between performance and guarantees. If your goal is to just use a group communication tool, it isn't necessarily important to understand precisely how that tool was implemented, just as one can use TCP without understanding the details of TCP "slow start" and the so called additive-increase multiplicative-backoff congestion control used in that protocol. On the other hand, we cite TCP as an example of why readers might want to be familiar with this information just the same. If you use TCP in a mission-critical application, the behavior of the protocol might really matter; it can be hard to get good performance without understanding how TCP itself is designed. Sometimes, what you don't know can surprise you, and certainly for those readers building an elaborate or very critical application, understanding exactly how a platform behaves can avoid nasty misunderstandings. In a similar spirit, this chapter seeks to pull together what we've learned in Part III into a single synthesized overview.

In the previous chapters, we examined options for implementing replicated data in various group membership models and looked at protocols for ordering conflicting actions under various ordering goals. We then showed how these protocols could be used as the basis of a computational model, virtual synchrony, in which members of distributed process groups see events that occur within those groups in consistent orders and with failure-atomicity guarantees and are consequently able to behave in consistent ways. All that is lacking is a more general synthesis, which we provide in this chapter. Key ideas underlying virtual synchrony are:

- Self-defining system and process group membership, in which processes are excluded from a system, if necessary, to permit continued progress.
- Tools for joining a group, state transfer, communication, and reporting new membership views.
- Depending on the model, a concept of primary component of the system.
- Algorithms that seek to achieve internal (as opposed to dynamically uniform) consistency.
- Distributed consistency achieved by ordering conflicting replicated events in consistent ways at the processes that observe those events.

The remainder of this chapter reviews these points relative to the alternatives we touched upon in developing our protocols and tools.

19.1 Consistency in the Static and Dynamic Membership Models

In the static model, the system is understood to be the set of places at which processes that act on behalf of the system execute. Here, the system is a relatively fixed collection of resources, which experience dynamic disruptions of communication connectivity, process failures, and restarts. Obviously, a static system may not be static over very long periods of time, but the time scale on which membership changes is understood to be long compared to the time scale at which these other events occur. The protocols for adding new members to the static set or dropping them are treated as being outside of the normal execution model. In cases where the system is symmetric, meaning that any correct execution of the system would also have been correct if the process identifiers were permuted, static systems rely on agreement protocols within which the majority of the statically defined composition of the full system must participate, directly or indirectly.

The dynamic model employs a concept of system membership that is self-defined and turns out to be more complex to support but cheaper than the static one. Dynamic systems add and lose members on a very short time scale compared to static ones. In the case where the system is symmetric, the set of processes that must participate in decisions is based on a majority of a dynamically defined group; this is a weaker requirement than for the static model and hence permits progress under conditions when a static system would not make progress. (See Figure 19.1)

These points are already significant when one considers what it means to say that a protocol is live in the two settings. However, before focusing on liveness, we review the question of consistency.

Consistency in a static model is typically defined with regard to an external observer, who may be capable of comparing the state and actions of a process that has become partitioned from the other processes in the system with the states and actions of the processes that remained connected. Such an external observer could be a disk that contains a database that will eventually have to be reintegrated and reconciled with other databases maintained by

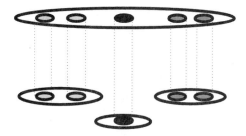

Figure 19.1. Static and dynamic views of a single set of sites. From a static perspective, the set has fixed membership but changing connectivity and availability properties—for example, the black nodes may be available and the gray ones treated as not available. Depending upon how such a system is implemented, it may be impossible to perform certain types of operations (notably, updates) unless a majority of the nodes are available. The dynamic perspective treats the system as if it were partitioned into a set of components whose membership is self-defined. Here, the black component might be the primary one and the gray components nonprimary. In contrast to the static approach, the primary component remains available, if primaryness can be deduced within the system. If communication is possible between two components, they are expected to merge their states in this model. Neither perspective is more correct than the other: The most appropriate way to view a system will typically depend upon the application, and different parts of the same application may sometimes require different approaches to membership. However, in the dynamic model, it is frequently important to track one of the components as being primary for the system, restricting certain classes of actions to occur only in this component (or not at all, if the primaryness attribute cannot be tracked after a complex series of failures).

the processes remaining in the connected portion of the system, an external device or physical process with which the system processes interact, or some form of external communication technology that lacks the flexibility of message passing but may still transfer information in some way between system processes.

Consistency in a dynamic system is a more internal concept (see Figure 19.2). In essence, a dynamic form of consistency requires that processes permitted to interact with one another will never observe contradictions in their states, which are detectable by comparing the contents of messages they exchange. Obviously, process states and the system state evolve through time, but the idea here is that if process p sends a message to process q that in some way reflects state information shared by them, process q should never conclude that the message sent by process p is impossible on the basis of what q itself has seen in regard to this shared state. If the state shared by p and q is a replicated variable, and q has observed that variable to increment only by 2s from 0 to its current value of 40, it would be inconsistent if p sent a message, ostensibly reflecting a past state, in which the variable's value was 7. For q such a state would not merely be stale, it would be impossible, since q believes itself to have seen the identical sequence of events, and the variable never had the value 7 in $q's$ history.

Although this example is unrealistic, it corresponds to more realistic scenarios in which dynamic consistency is precisely what one wants—for example, when a set of processes divides the work of performing some operation using a coordinator-cohort rule, or by exploiting a mutually perceived ranking to partition a database, dynamic consistency is required for the partitioning to make sense. Dynamic consistency is also what one might

$$x = 2, 4, 6, 8 \qquad x = 2, 4, 7, 9$$

Figure 19.2. Dynamic (or interactive) consistency is the guarantee that the members of a given system component will maintain mutually consistent states (here, by agreeing upon the sequence of values that a variable, x, has taken). If a protocol is not dynamically uniform, it may allow a process that becomes partitioned from a component of the system to observe events in a way that is inconsistent with the event ordering observed within that component. Thus, in this example, the component on the right (consisting of a single process) observes x to take on the values 7 and 9, while the larger component on the right sees x pass through only even values. By pronouncing at most one of these components to be the primary one for the system, we can impose a sensible interpretation on this scenario. Alternatives are to use dynamically uniform protocols with external consistency guarantees. Such protocols can be supported both in the dynamic membership model and the static one, where this guarantee is almost always required. However, they are far more costly than protocols that do not provide dynamic uniformity.

desire from the Web proxies and servers that maintain copies of a document: They should agree on the version of the document that is the most current one and provide guarantees to the user that the most current document is returned in response to a request.

The significance of the specific example described above is thus not that applications often care about the past state of a replicated variable, but rather that cooperation or coordination or synchronization in distributed settings all involve cases in which a process, p, may need to reason about the state and actions of some other process, q. When this occurs, p can be understood to be using a form of replicated system state that it believes itself to share with q. Our shared variable has now become the shared concept of the state of a lock or the shared list of members and ranking of members for a process group to which both belong. Inconsistency in these cases means that the system is visibly misbehaving: Two processes both think they have locked the same variable, or each thinks the other holds the lock when neither in fact holds it. Perhaps both processes consider themselves primary for some request, or perhaps neither does. Both may search the first half of a database, each thinking the other is searching the second half. These same issues only get worse if we move to larger numbers of processes.

Of course, as the system evolves through time, it may be that p once held a lock but no longer does. So the issue is not so much one of being continuously consistent, but of seeing mutually consistent and mutually evolving histories of the system state. In effect, if the processes in a system see the same events in the same order, they can remain consistent with one another. This extremely general concept is at the heart of all forms of distributed consistency.

In the purest sense, the dynamic system model is entirely concerned with freedom from detectable inconsistencies in the logically derivable system state. This concept is well defined in part because of the following rule: When a dynamic system considers some process to have failed, communication to that process is permanently severed. Under such a rule, p cannot communicate to q unless both are still within the same component of the possibly partitioned system, and the protocols for dynamic systems operate in a manner that maintains consistency within subsets of processes residing in the same component. The system may allow a process to be inconsistent with the state of the system as a whole, but it does so only when that process is considered to have failed; it will never be allowed to rejoin the system until it has done something to correct its (presumably inconsistent) state.

The ability to take such an action permits dynamic systems to make progress when a static system might have to wait for a disconnected process to reconnect itself or a failed process to be restarted. Thus, a process in the dynamic model can sometimes (often, in fact) make progress while a process in the static model would not be able to do so.

The static model, on the other hand, is in many ways a more intuitive and simpler one than the dynamic one. It is easy to draw an analogy between a static set of resources and a statically defined set of system processes. External consistency constraints, being very strong, are also easy to understand. The dynamic model is in some sense superficially easy to understand, but much harder to fathom upon close study. Suppose we are told that process p is a member of a dynamically defined system component and sets a replicated variable x to 7. In a static system we would have concluded that, since the system guarantees the consistency of this action, p was safe in taking it. In a dynamic system, it may be that it is too early to know if p is a valid member of the system and that setting x to 7 is a safe action in the broader sense. The problem is that future events may cause the system to reconfigure itself in a way that excludes p and leads to an evolution of system state in which x never does take on the value 7. Moreover, the asynchronous nature of communication means that even if in real time p sets x to 7 before being excluded by the other system members as if it were faulty, in the logical system model, p's action occurs *after* it has been excluded from the system.

Where external actions are to be taken, the introduction of time offers us a way to work around this dilemma. Recall our air traffic control example (see Section 15.1.5). Provided that p shares a clock with the remainder of the system, it (p) can be warned with adequate time to avoid a situation where two processes ever own the air traffic space at the same time. Of course, this does not eliminate the problem that during the period after it became disconnected and before the remainder of the system took over, p may have initiated actions. We can resolve this issue by acknowledging that it is impossible to improve on the solution and by asking the application program to take an appropriate action. In this specific example, p would warn the air traffic controller that actions taken within the past δ seconds may not have been properly recorded by the main system, and connection to it has now been lost. With a person in the loop, such a solution would seem adequate. In fact, there is little choice, for no system that takes actions at multiple locations can ever be precisely sure of its state if a failure occurs while such an action is underway.

Faced with such seemingly troubling scenarios, one asks why we consider the dynamic model at all. Part of the answer is that the guarantees it offers are almost as strong as those for the static case, and yet it can often make progress when a static solution would be unable to do so. Moreover, the static model sometimes just doesn't fit a problem. Web proxies, for example, are a very dynamic and unpredictable set: The truth is out there, but a server will not be able to predict in advance just where copies of its documents may end up (imagine the case where one Web proxy obtains a copy of a document from some other Web proxy!). But perhaps the best answer is, as we saw in previous chapters, that the weaker model permits dramatically improved performance, perhaps by a factor of hundreds if our goal is to replicate data.

Both the static and dynamic system models offer a strong form of consistency whereby the state of the system is guaranteed to be consistent and coordinated over large numbers of components. But while taking an action in the static model can require a fairly slow, multiphase protocol, the dynamic system is often able to exploit asynchronous single-phase protocols, such as the nonuniform *fbcast* and *cbcast* primitives, for similar purposes. It is no exaggeration to say that these asynchronous protocols may result in levels of performance that are hundreds of times superior to those achievable when subjected to static consistency and membership constraints—for example, as was mentioned earlier, the Horus system is able to send nearly 85,000 small multicasts per second to update a variable replicated between two processes. This figure drops to about 50 updates per second when using a quorum-style replication scheme such as the one in the Paxos system, and perhaps 1,500 per second when using an RPC scheme that is disconnected from any concept of consistency. As we've seen, the issue is not the quality of implementation (although Horus is a heavily optimized system), but rather the protocols themselves: these latter systems are limited by the need to receive acknowledgements from what may be very slow participants. The latency improvements can be even larger: In Horus, there are latency differences of as much as three orders of magnitude between typical figures for the dynamic case and typical protocols for taking actions in a static or dynamically uniform manner. Other systems using the dynamic model, for example Ensemble or the Spread toolkit from John Hopkins University, achieve similar performance benefits.

In practical work with dynamic system models, we typically need to assume that the system is "usually" well-behaved, despite experiencing some infrequent rate of failures. Under such an assumption, the model is easy to work with and makes sense. If a system experiences frequent failures (relative to the time it takes to reconfigure itself or otherwise repair the failures), the static model becomes more and more appealing and the dynamic one less and less predictable. Fortunately, most real systems are built with extremely reliable components, hence experience infrequent failures. This pragmatic consideration explains why dynamically consistent distributed systems have become popular: The model behaves reasonably in real environments, and the performance is superior compared to what can be achieved in the static model.

Indeed, one way to understand the performance advantage of the dynamic model is that by precomputing membership information, the dynamic algorithms represent optimizations of the static algorithms. As one looks closely at the algorithms, they seem more and more similar in a basic way, and perhaps this explains why that should be the case. In effect, the static and dynamic models are very similar, but the static algorithms (such as quorum data replication) tend to compute the membership information they needed on each operation, while the dynamic ones precompute this information and are built using a much simpler fail-stop model.

Moreover, it is important to realize that the external concept of consistency associated with static models is in some ways much stronger, and consequently more restrictive, than is necessary for realistic applications. This can translate to periods of mandatory unavailability, where a static system model forces us to stop and wait while a dynamic consistency model permits reconfiguration and progress. Many distributed systems contain services of various kinds that have small server states (which can therefore be transferred to a new server when it joins the system) and that are only of interest when they are operational and connected to the system as a whole. Mutual consistency between the servers and the states of the applications using them is all that one needs in such internal uses of a consistency-preserving technology. If a dynamic approach is dramatically faster than a static one, so much the better for the dynamic approach!

These comments should not be taken to suggest that a dynamic system can *always* make progress even when a static one must wait. In subsequent work, Chandra, Toueg and Vassilacos established that a result similar to the FLP result holds for group membership protocols (see Chandra et al. [1996])—hence, there are conditions under which an asynchronous system can be prevented from reaching consensus upon its own membership and therefore prevented from making progress. Other researchers (myself included) have pinned down precise conditions (in various models) under which dynamic membership consensus protocols are guaranteed to make progress (see Babaoglu et al. [1995], Friedman et al., Guerraoui and Schiper, Neiger), and the good news is that for most practical settings the protocols make progress if the probability of failures and message loss is uniform and independent over the processes and messages sent in the system. In effect, only partitioning failures or a very intelligent adversary (one that in practice could never be implemented) can prevent these systems from making progress.

Thus, we know that *all* of these models face conditions under which progress is not possible. As a practical matter, the evidence is that all of these models are perfectly reasonable for building reliable distributed systems. The theoretical impossibility results do not appear to represent practical impediments to implementing reliable distributed software; they simply tell us that there will be conditions that these reliability approaches cannot overcome. The choice, in a practical sense, is to match the performance and consistency properties of the solution to the performance and consistency requirements of the application. The weaker the requirements, the better the performance we can achieve.

Our study also revealed two other issues that deserve comment: the need, or lack thereof, for a *primary component* in a partitioned membership model and the broader but related question of how consistency is tied to ordering properties in distributed environments.

The question of a primary component is readily understood in terms of the air traffic control example we looked at earlier. In that example, there was a need to take authoritative action within a service on behalf of the system as a whole. In effect, a representative of a service needed to be sure that it could safely allow an air traffic control to take a certain action, meaning that it ran no risk of being contradicted by any other process (or, in the case of a possible partitioning failure, that before any other process could start taking potentially conflicting actions, a timeout would elapse and the air traffic controller would be warned that this representative of the service was now out of touch with the primary partition).

In the static system model, there is only a single concept of the system as a whole, and actions are taken upon the authority of the full system membership. Naturally, it can take time to obtain majority acquiescence in an action—hence, this is a model in which some actions may be delayed. However, when an action is actually taken, it is taken on behalf of the full system.

In the dynamic model we lose this guarantee and face the prospect that our concept of consistency can become trivial because of system partitioning failures—a dynamic system could partition arbitrarily, with each component having its own concept of authoritative action. All of this seems to argue that practical systems should limit themselves to supporting a single, primary component. If a partition forms and some process is operating in a non-primary component, an exception should be delivered to the application ("you have become partitioned away from the system"), and the application can deal with this, perhaps by terminating the disconnected process. Progress would be limited to the primary partition.

This isn't really all that restrictive an approach. First, partitions are rare in most systems, so the whole issue of continuing execution while partitioned away from the majority of the system should be very rare. Secondly, some form of read-only behavior may suffice. A nonprimary component may, for example, continue to operate a device that it owns, but that may not be reliable for use in instructing an air traffic controller about the status of air space sectors or other global forms of state-sensitive data unless they were updated using dynamically uniform protocols.

Of course, a dynamic distributed system can lose its primary component, and, making matters still more difficult, there may be patterns of partial communication connectivity within which a dynamic model must block. Suppose, for example, that a system partitions so that all of its members are disconnected from one another. Now we can selectively reenable connections so that over time a majority of a static system membership set are able to vote in favor of an action. Such a pattern of communication could allow progress—for example, there is the protocol of Keidar and Dolev, cited several times previously, in which an action can be terminated entirely on the basis of point-to-point connections. However, as we commented, this protocol delays actions until a majority of the processes in the entire system know about them, which will often take a very long time.

This type of reasoning might not apply in new kinds of systems that deviate from the usual behavior seen in a local network. Frequent periods of partitioned operation *could* occur in very mobile situations, such as when units are active on a battlefield. Thus, there are probably systems that should use a static model with partial communications connectivity as their basic model, systems that should use a primary component consistency model, and perhaps still other systems for which a virtual synchrony model that doesn't track primaryness would suffice. These represent successively higher levels of availability, and even the lowest level retains a meaningful concept of distributed consistency. At the same time, they do provide weaker forms of consistency. This suggests that there are unavoidable tradeoffs in the design of reliable distributed systems for critical applications.

The two-tiered architecture discussed in the previous chapter can be recognized as a response to this impossibility result. Such an approach explicitly trades higher availability for weaker consistency in the LAN subsystems, while favoring strong consistency at the expense of reduced availability in the WAN layer (which might run a protocol based on the Chandra/Toueg consensus algorithm). The LAN level of a system might use nonuniform protocols for speed, while the WAN level uses tools and protocols similar to the ones proposed by the Transis effort or by Babaoglu's group in their work on Relacs.

We alluded briefly to the connection between consistency and order. This topic is perhaps an appropriate one on which to end our review of the models. Starting with Lamport's earliest work on distributed computing systems, it was already clear that consistency and the ordering of distributed events are closely linked. Over time, it has become apparent that distributed systems contain what are essentially two forms of knowledge or information. Static knowledge is that information that is well known to all of the processes in the system at the outset—for example, the membership of a static system is a form of static knowledge. Being well known, it can be exploited in a decentralized but consistent manner. Other forms of static knowledge can include knowledge of the protocol that processes use, knowledge that some processes are more important than others, or knowledge that certain classes of events can only occur in certain places within the system as a whole. (See Figure 19.3.)

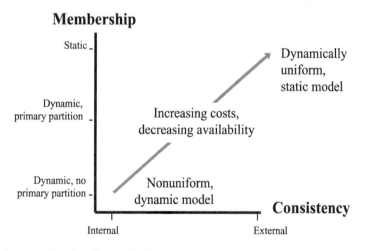

Figure 19.3. Conceptual options for the distributed systems designer. Even when one seeks consistency, there are choices concerning how strong the consistency desired should be and which membership model to use. The least-costly and highest-availability solution for replicating data, for example, looks only for internal consistency within dynamically defined partitions of a system and does not limit progress to the primary partition. This model, as we have suggested, may be too weak for practical purposes. A slightly less available approach, which maintains the same high level of performance, allows progress only in the primary partition. As one introduces further constraints, such as dynamic uniformity or a static system model, costs rise and availability falls, but the system model becomes simpler and simpler to understand. The most costly and restrictive model sacrifices nearly three orders of magnitude of performance in some studies relative to the least-costly one. Within any given model, the degree of ordering required for multicasts introduces further fine-grained cost/benefit tradeoffs.

Dynamic knowledge is information that stems from unpredicted events occurring within the system—either as a consequence of nondeterminism of the members, failures or event orderings that are determined by external physical processes, or inputs from external users of the system. The events that occur within a distributed system are frequently associated with the need to update the system state in response to dynamic events. To the degree that system state is replicated, or is reflected in the states of multiple system processes, these dynamic updates of the state will need to occur at multiple places. In the work we have presented here, process groups are the places where such state resides, and multicasts are used to update such state.

Viewed from this perspective, it becomes apparent that *consistency is order*, in the sense that the distributed aspects of the system state are entirely defined by process groups and multicasts to those groups, and these abstractions, in turn, are defined entirely in terms of ordering and atomicity. Moreover, to the degree that the system membership is self-defined, as in the dynamic models, atomicity is also an order-based abstraction.

This reasoning leads to the conclusion that the deepest of the properties in a distributed system concerned with consistency may be the ordering in which distributed events are scheduled to occur. As we have seen, there are many ways to order events, but the schemes all depend upon either explicit participation by a majority of the system processes or upon dynamically changing membership, managed by a group membership protocol. These protocols, in turn, depend upon majority action (by a dynamically defined majority). Moreover, when examined closely, all the dynamic protocols depend upon some concept of token or special permission, which enables the process holding that permission to take actions on behalf of the system as a whole. One is strongly inclined to speculate that in this observation lies the grain of a general theory of distributed computing, in which all forms of consistency and all forms of progress could be related to membership and in which dynamic membership could be related to the liveness of token passing or leader election protocols. At the time of this writing, I am not aware of any clear presentation of this theory of all possible behaviors for asynchronous distributed systems, but perhaps it will emerge in the not-too-distant future.

19.2 Practical Options for Coping with Total Failure

The reader who follows the above recommendations will be guided towards a style of system in which replication is used to maintain availability in the primary partition of a system that dynamically tracks its own membership. If a machine becomes partitioned away from the primary group, it will detect this and should probably shut down.

But this recommendation raises an obvious concern. What happens if (after some sort of rare event like a power outage), the network itself shuts down, and as a result all the nodes in the system seem to be isolated from the primary partition? Should they all shut down? And more broadly, how can a system recover after a total failure?

To some extent, this problem has been solved by researchers. In a 1985 paper (see Skeen), an algorithm was published for "determining the last process to fail" after a total failure. As one might expect, the processes in a system compare notes and in this way track down the last survivor of the wave of outages. That node restarts first, and the others then join. But in practice, such an approach is unlikely to be satisfactory for several reasons.

The central problem is that in most systems, not all machines are equal. Servers are more important than clients, and if a system includes a mixture (as many do), restarting the system from a client machine is often a nonsensical proposition: one restarts servers. Thus, the "last process to fail" may not be the issue. Furthermore, while an algorithm for picking the last server that failed can be designed, Skeen's solution involves waiting until all the last servers to fail are operational again. In any real-world setting, we may not want to wait so long.

This leads to the following advice. First, if possible, applications partitioned away from the majority should checkpoint their states and then either shut down, or sit idle waiting to connect with the primary partition. Thus when the network goes down, all machines may either shut down, or at least will stop processing new operations.

There are now two cases. The easy one arises when a server in this state manages to connect to the primary partition. It should just discard the checkpointed state and "rejoin" with a state transfer. The second case arises if there is no primary partition. Here, a less than completely automated solution makes sense. The application should simply ask a human operator for help. That human operator will presumably study the system state, pick the "official" last node to fail, and tell it via command to restart (perhaps from its checkpoint). This reestablishes the primary partition and the others now follow the first rule above.

Not all problems can or should be solved in fully automated ways, and the author has become convinced that handling of severe partitionings or total failure are among them. Fortunately, such situations are infrequent, and as long as there is a simple way to restart the system, most application developers should be satisfied by the resulting mechanism.

19.3 General Remarks Concerning Causal and Total Ordering

The entire concept of providing ordered message delivery has been a source of considerable controversy within the community that develops distributed software (see van Renesse [1993]). Causal ordering has been especially controversial, but even total ordering is opposed by some researchers (see Cheriton and Skeen), although others have been critical of the arguments advanced in this area (see Birman [1994], Cooper [1994], van Renesse [1994]). The CATOCS (Causally and Totally Ordered Communication Systems) controversy came to a head in 1993, and although it seems no longer to interest the research community, it would also be hard to claim that there is a generally accepted resolution of the question.

Underlying the debate are tradeoffs between consistency, ordering, and cost. As we have seen, ordering is an important form of consistency. In the next chapter, we will develop a variety of powerful tools for exploiting ordering, especially for implementing and exploiting replicated data efficiently. Thus, since the first work on consistency and replication with process groups, there has been an emphasis on ordering. Some systems, such as the Isis Toolkit, which the author developed in the mid-1980s, made extensive use of causal ordering because of its relatively high performance and low latency. Isis, in fact, enforces causally delivered ordering as a system-wide default, although, as we saw in Chapter 18, such a design point is in some ways risky. The Isis approach makes certain types of asynchronous algorithms very easy to implement, but it has important cost implications; developers of sophisticated Isis applications sometimes need to disable the causal ordering mechanism to avoid these costs. Other systems, such as Ameoba, looked at the same issues but concluded that causal ordering is rarely needed if total ordering can be made fast enough. Moreover, these systems (including Horus, the successor to Isis) often implement total ordering using a token-based scheme in which the token never moves unless a failure occurs; under such conditions, *fbcast* can be used to implement *abcast*.

We have now seen a sampling of the sorts of uses to which ordered group communication can be put. Moreover, earlier sections of this book have established the potential value of these sorts of solutions in settings such as the Web, financial trading systems, and highly available database or file servers.

Nonetheless, there is a third community of researchers (Cheriton and Skeen are best known within this group), who have concluded that ordered communication is almost *never* matched with the needs of the application. These researchers cite their success in developing distributed support for equity trading in financial settings and work in factory automation—both settings in which developers have reported good results using distributed message-bus technologies (TIB is the one used by Cheriton and Skeen), which offer little in the sense of distributed consistency or fault-tolerant guarantees. To the degree that the need occurs for consistency within these applications, Cheriton and Skeen have found ways to reduce the consistency requirements of the *application* rather than providing stronger consistency within a system to respond to a strong application-level consistency requirement (the NFS example from Chapter 7 comes to mind). Broadly, this leads them to a mindset that favors the use of stateless architectures, nonreplicated data, and simple fault-tolerant solutions in which one restarts a failed server and leaves it to the clients to reconnect. Cheriton and Skeen suggest that such a point of view is the logical extension of the end-to-end argument (see Saltzer et al.), which they interpret as an argument that each application must take direct responsibility for guaranteeing its own behavior.

Cheriton and Skeen also make some very specific points. They are critical of system-level support for causal or total ordering guarantees. They argue that communication ordering properties are better left to customized application-level protocols, which can also incorporate other sorts of application-specific properties. In support of this view, they present applications that need stronger ordering guarantees and applications that need weaker ones, arguing that in the former case causal or total ordering will be inadequate, and in the latter case it will be overkill. Their analysis led them to conclude that in *almost all cases*, causal order is more than the application needs (and more costly), or less than the application needs (in which case the application must add some higher-level ordering protocol of its own). They also produced similar arguments for total ordering (see Cheriton and Skeen).

Unfortunately, while making some good points, Cheriton and Skeen's paper also includes a number of questionable claims, including some outright errors, which have been analyzed in other papers (see Birman [1994], Cooper [1994], van Renesse [1994]). For example, Cheriton and Skeen claim that causal ordering algorithms have an overhead on messages that increases as n^2, where n is the number of processes in the system as a whole. As it turns out, multicasts do have scalability issues, although these stem from the way the protocol is implemented and some protocols scale quite well compared to others. But that's not the point made in this paper. They argue that providing causal ordering is especially costly, and this just isn't true. We have seen that causal ordering for group multicasts, which they claim to be discussing, can easily be provided with a vector clock, whose length is linear in the number of active senders in a group (rarely more than two or three processes). In more complex settings, compression techniques can often be used to bound the vector timestamp to a small size; experiments suggest that such vectors tend to be quite short even in very active, large groups. Thus, what is portrayed by the Cheriton and Skeen paper as an n^2 complexity barrier shrinks to an overhead of perhaps two or three counters—maybe 16 bytes in typical experience. This example is just one of several specific points about which Cheriton and Skeen make statements that could be disputed on technical grounds.

The entire approach to causal ordering adopted by Cheriton and Skeen is also unusual. In this chapter, we have seen that causal order is potentially quite useful when one seeks to *optimize* an algorithm expressed originally in terms of totally ordered communication and that total ordering is useful because, in a state machine style of distributed system, by presenting the same inputs to the various processes in a group in the same order, their states can be kept consistent. Cheriton and Skeen never address this use of ordering, focusing instead on causal and total order in the context of a publish/subscribe architecture in which a small number of data publishers send data that a large number of consumers receive and process and in which there are no consistency requirements that span the consumer processes. This example somewhat misses the point of the preceding chapters, where we made extensive use of total ordering primarily for consistent replication of data and of causal ordering as a relaxation of total ordering where the sender has some form of mutual exclusion within the group.

At the other end of the spectrum, it seems strange that Cheriton and Skeen would have such antipathy towards total order. The *abcast* primitive is easy to understand and use, easy to implement, can run at extremely high speeds, and is therefore very popular even with unsophisticated programmers. Cheriton and Skeen develop an elaborate argument that, sometimes, *abcast* will be far too costly. But if we can optimize the protocol to such a high degree, and reduce other costs (such as programmer time, bug rates, maintenance costs), we benefit in many ways that more than compensate for the rare situations where *abcast* is overkill. It happens that their own product (a message bus called TIB) lacked the *abcast* properties, and perhaps this underlies their very strong advocacy for such a curious position!

Cheriton and Skeen's most effective argument is one based on the end-to-end philosophy. They suggest, in effect, that although many applications will benefit from properties such as fault tolerance, ordering, or other communication guarantees, no single primitive is capable of capturing all possible properties without imposing absurdly high costs for the applications that required weaker guarantees. Our observation about the cost of dynamically uniform strong ordering bears this out: Here we see a very strong property, but it is also thousands of times more costly than rather similar but weaker properties! If one makes the weaker version of a primitive the default, the application programmer will need to be careful not to be surprised by its nonuniform behavior; the stronger version may just be too costly for many applications. Cheriton and Skeen generalize from similar observations based on their own examples and conclude that the application should implement its own ordering protocols.

Yet even this argument can be disputed. After all, in what sense is the Isis system, or Horus, or Spread, or Ensemble, *not* an end-to-end solution? The technology is only used in applications that were deliberately linked to the appropriate library. These systems don't replace standard system services, like the Internet DNS or the TCP protocol stack, with non-standard versions. They are implemented, in effect, right in the end-user's address space. How far does the end-to-end concept need to be carried? Must we all program in assembly language, because the use of compilers violates the end-to-end principle?

Their other good point, with the benefit of hindsight, is the argument that the whole concept of causal ordering is too mind-bendingly complex for mere mortals to comprehend. This may be the case. Not that *cbcast* is such a complex idea. But there is no obvious analogy in the real world, in contrast to the *fbcast* or *abcast* properties, which seem very evident even at a glance. Perhaps *cbcast* is perceived as complex because we need to develop an intuition into causal ordering before the primitive starts to seem natural and even obvious. Had Cheriton and Skeen devoted their paper to an attack on causal ordering, it seems likely that the average reader would have concluded that they might be correct.

When we discuss the Horus and Ensemble systems, in upcoming chapters, we'll see that these take Cheriton and Skeen's point to heart, offering a way to match the ordering properties of the application to the guarantees of the system.

In both of these systems, ordering is provided by modules that the user can chose to include in a system or exclude from it (even at runtime), thus adapting the system to provide *only the properties actually required by the application*, and to pay only the associated costs. On the other hand, neither system *precludes* the causal ordering property. The user is left to decide whether or not that property is needed. Cheriton and Skeen, in contrast, state fairly clearly that the property is never desirable.

Setting the user's perspective to the side, however, we have seen that these protocols are not trivial and implementing them would not be an easy undertaking. It also seems unreasonable to expect the average application designer to implement a special-purpose, hand-crafted protocol for each specific need. In practice, if ordering and atomicity properties are not provided by the computing system, it seems unlikely that applications will be able to make any use of these concepts at all. Thus, even if one agrees with the end-to-end philosophy, one might disagree that it implies that each application programmer should implement nearly identical and rather complex ordering and consistency protocols, because no single protocol will suffice for all uses.

Current systems, including the Horus system, usually adopt a middle ground, in which the ordering and atomicity properties of the communication system are viewed as options that can be selectively enabled (Chapter 21). If the user doesn't specify otherwise, they get *abcast,* optimized to give the maximum possible performance with the lowest possible delay and overhead. A sophisticated user can then override the default as needed. One is left with the best of possible worlds: a simple basic option (*abcast*), and a way to make the system do more elaborate tricks when special requirements so dictate.

19.4 **Summary and Conclusion**

There has been a great deal of debate over the concepts of consistency and reliability in distributed systems (which are sometimes seen as violating end-to-end principles) and of causal or total ordering (which are sometimes too weak or too strong for the needs of a specific application that does need ordering). Finally, although we have not focused on this here, there is the criticism that technologies such as the ones we have reviewed do not fit with standard styles of distributed systems development.

As to the first concern, the best argument for consistency and reliability is to simply exhibit classes of critical distributed computing systems that will not be sufficiently "assured" unless data are replicated and will not be trustworthy unless the data is replicated consistently. One would not want to conclude that *most* distributed applications need these properties: Today, the ones that do remain a fairly small subset of the total. However, with the advent of Web Services, this subset is poised for rapid growth. Moreover, even if one believed that consistency and reliability are extremely important in a great many applications, one would not want to impose potentially costly communication properties system-wide, especially in applications with very large numbers of overlapping process groups. To do so is to invite poor performance, although there may be specific situations where the enforcement of strong properties within small sets of groups is desirable or necessary.

Turning to the second issue, it is clearly true that different applications have different ordering needs. The best solution to this problem is to offer systems that permit the ordering and consistency properties of a communication primitive or process group to be tailored to their needs. If the designer is concerned about paying the minimum price for the properties an application really requires, such a system can then be configured to only offer the requested properties. Later in the book, will see that the Horus and Ensemble systems adopt this approach, while others (notably Spread) simply adopt an easily understood multicast and focus on making it as fast as possible. Both approaches make sense, and users seem to find both rather easy to use.

Finally, as to the last issue, it is true that we have presented a distributed computing model that, so far, may not seem very closely tied to the software engineering tools normally used to implement distributed systems. In the next chapter we study this practical issue, looking at how group communication tools and virtual synchrony can be applied to real systems that may have been implemented using other technologies.

19.5 Related Reading

On concepts of consistency in distributed systems: (see Birman and van Renesse [1994, 1996]); in the case of partitionable systems: (see Amir, Keidar and Dolev, Malkhi, Moser et al. [1996]).

On the causal controversy: (see van Renesse [1993]).

On the dispute over CATOCS: (see Cheriton and Skeen); but see also Birman (1994), Cooper (1994), van Renesse (1994) for responses.

The end-to-end argument was first put forward in Saltzer et al.

Regarding theoretical work on tradeoffs between consistency and availability: (see Babaoglu et al. [1995], Chandra et al. [1996], Fisher et al., Friedman et al.).

PART IV

Applications of Reliability Techniques

In this fourth part of the book, we apply the techniques developed in Part III to real problems seen in a wide variety of systems, including Web Services. The techniques on which we focus are fairly practical and a talented student shouldn't have much trouble employing them in conjunction with a platform such as Spread or Ensemble. We pick problems that are interesting in their own terms, but are also representative of broader classes of issues seen in a wide range of settings and systems, in the hope that the examples developed here might serve as templates for developers working on mission-critical problems in production settings.

20

Retrofitting Reliability into Complex Systems

This chapter deals with options for presenting group computing tools to the application developer. Two broad approaches are considered: those involving wrappers that encapsulate an existing piece of software in an environment that transparently extends its properties—for example, by introducing fault tolerance through replication or security—and those based upon toolkits that provide explicit procedure-call interfaces. We will not examine specific examples of such systems now, but will instead focus on the advantages and disadvantages of each approach and on their limitations. At the time of this writing, it remains unclear how best to integrate reliability mechanisms with Web Services, although it *is* clear that doing so would be feasible (and also of considerable commercial value).

Down the road, it seems likely that we'll see a third and perhaps more prevalent option: platforms that include reliability functionality as an integral component. For example, when programming on Microsoft platforms, most developers work with the Visual Studio product, an editing and debugging framework with support for many languages. In Visual Studio, one can literally drag-and-drop complex functionality into an application. To turn a C# application into a Web Services program, it suffices to drag the ASP.NET template onto the application; a dialog box then permits the user to specify which classes should be exported, and to control such aspects as how the interface will appear in a UDDI-compliant name server. Through a combination of dialog boxes associated with the template and implementation of any application-specific methods, the user is led rather directly to a working Web Services program.

Thus one could imagine a path by which industry would embrace the kinds of solutions discussed in this book and even package them to a point where by dragging "replication" onto a Visual Studio application (or doing the analogous action in some other development platform, since many share this style of intentional programming), group communication technology, security tools, or other specialized reliability mechanisms could be requested.

All that we really need is to see broad demand emerge for such functionality, and this may finally be occurring as the Web Services community begins to roll out an increasingly critical class of applications and to encounter the reliability and availability limitations of the initial Web Services architecture and platform technologies.

20.1 Wrappers and Toolkits

The introduction of reliability technologies into a complex application raises two sorts of issues. One is that many applications contain substantial amounts of preexisting software or make use of off-the-shelf components (the military and government favor the acronym COTS for this, meaning "commercial off the shelf." In these cases, the developer is extremely limited in terms of the ways that the old technology can be modified. A *wrapper* is a technology that overcomes this problem by intercepting events at some interface between the unmodifiable technology and the external environment (see Jones), replacing the original behavior of that interface with an extended behavior, which confers a desired property on the wrapped component, extends the interface itself with new functionality, or otherwise offers a virtualized environment within which the old component executes. Wrapping is a powerful technical option for hardening existing software, although it also has some practical limitations. In this section, we'll review a number of approaches to performing the wrapping operation itself, as well as a number of types of interventions that wrappers can enable.

Many developers view Web Services as wrappers, because the Web Services model and interfaces are often used as a gateway between a "new" application and a legacy server to which the Web Services dispatcher has been linked. Unfortunately, however, the notion of wrapping is not currently a first-class part of the Web Services architecture, and wrapping an entire Web Services system is not (yet) a straightforward action. Additionally, because the Web Services request dispatch and routing component often runs on a different computer than does the back-end server, the extra layer between the client and the server can raise availability and reliability issues of its own, for example because it might experience a crash even when the client and server both remain operational; the client would then lose connectivity to the server even though the server is still healthy. As we saw in Part II of the book, the reliability mechanisms of the Web Services architecture focus on this problem but address it in a way that favors a pipelined, very asynchronous style of interaction with the back-end server. High availability for Web Services applications is just not anticipated in the initial architectural designs for the technology.

Were it possible to use the Web Services framework as a reliability wrapper, the approach might represent a natural first step towards providing high assurance in Web Services applications, by offering a path towards replicating first the Web Services front end, and then the server to which it connects. Accordingly, this is one direction we'll discuss here and in Chapter 26, which focuses specifically on Web Services. Indeed, building a prototype of such a Web Services architecture would be an interesting project for students seeking to get a hands-on feel for the technologies covered by this text. However, we need to do some homework before we can tackle such an ambitious question. This chapter focuses on what might be thought of as component technologies that will be needed in Chapter 26.

An alternative to wrapping is to explicitly develop a new application program designed from the outset with the reliability technology in mind—for example, we might set out to build an authentication service for a distributed environment that implements a particular encryption technology and uses replication to avoid denial of service when some of its server processes fail. Such a program would be said to use a *toolkit* style of distributed computing, in which the sorts of algorithms developed in the previous chapter are explicitly invoked to accomplish a desired task. A toolkit approach packages potentially complex mechanisms, such as replicated data with locking, behind easy-to-use interfaces (in the case of replicated data, *LOCK, READ* and *UPDATE* operations). The disadvantage of such an approach is that it can be hard to glue a reliability tool into an arbitrary piece of code, and the tools themselves will often reflect design tradeoffs that limit generality. Thus, toolkits can be very powerful in the hands of a developer with the freedom to use them in the intended manner, and who understands their limitations, but they are also inflexible: They adopt a programming paradigm, and, having done so, it is potentially difficult to use the functionality encapsulated within the toolkit in a setting other than the one envisioned by the tool designer.

Toolkits can also take other forms—for example, one could view a firewall, which filters messages entering and exiting a distributed application, as a tool for enforcing a limited security policy. When one uses this broader interpretation of the term, toolkits include quite a variety of presentations of reliability technologies—even a Web Services system is a toolkit in this very broad sense. In addition to the case of firewalls, a toolkit could package a reliable communication technology as a message bus, a system monitoring and management technology, a fault-tolerant file system or database system, or a wide area name service (Table 20.1). Moreover, one can view a programming language that offers primitives for reliable computing as a form of toolkit.

As we see in Table 20.1, each toolkit would address a set of application-specific problems, presenting an API specialized to the programming language or environment within which the toolkit will be used and to the task at hand. While it is also possible to develop extremely general toolkits, which seek to address a great variety of possible types of users, doing so can result in a presentation of the technology that is architecturally weak and doesn't guide users to the best system structure for solving their problems. In contrast, application-oriented toolkits often reflect strong structural assumptions, which are known to result in solutions that perform well and achieve high reliability.

In practice, many real-world distributed applications are so large and so complex that they require a mixture of toolkit solutions and wrappers. To the degree that a system has new functionality, which can be developed with a reliability technology in mind, the designer is afforded a great deal of flexibility and power through the execution model supported (e.g., transactional serializability or virtual synchrony) and may be able to provide sophisticated functionality that would not otherwise be feasible. On the other hand, in any system that reuses large amounts of old code, wrappers can be invaluable by shielding the

Table 20.1. Types of Toolkits Useful in Building or Hardening Distributed Systems

Toolkit	Description
Server replication	Tools and techniques for replicating data to achieve high availability, load-balancing, scalable parallelism, very large memory-mapped caches, and so forth. Cluster APIs for management and exploitation of clusters.
Video server	Technologies for striping video data across multiple servers, isochronous replay, and single replay when multiple clients request the same data.
WAN replication	Technologies for data diffusion among servers that make up a corporate network.
Client groupware	Integration of group conferencing and cooperative work tools into Java agents, TCL/TK, or other GUI builders and client-side applications.
Client reliability	Mechanisms for transparently fault-tolerant RPC to servers, consistent data subscription for sets of clients that monitor the same data source, and so forth.
System management	Tools for instrumenting a distributed system and performing reactive control. Different solutions might be needed when instrumenting the network itself, cluster-style servers, and user-developed applications.
Firewalls and containment tools	Tools for restricting the behavior of an application or for protecting it against a potentially hostile environment-for example, such a toolkit might provide a bank with a way to install a partially trusted client/server application in order to permit its normal operations while preventing unauthorized ones.

previously developed functionality from the programming model and assumptions of the toolkit.

20.1.1 Wrapper Technologies

In our usage, a wrapper is any technology that intercepts an existing execution path in a manner transparent to the wrapped application or component. By wrapping a component, the developer is able to virtualize the wrapped interface, introducing an extended version with new functionality or other desirable properties. In particular, wrappers can be used to introduce various robustness mechanisms, such as replication for fault tolerance or message encryption for security.

Wrapping at Object Interfaces

Object-oriented interfaces are the best example of a wrapping technology (Figure 20.1), and systems built using CORBA or OLE-2 are, in effect, pre-wrapped in a manner that makes it easy to introduce new technologies or to substitute a hardened implementation of a service for a nonrobust one. Suppose, for example, that a CORBA implementation of a client/server system turns out to be unavailable because the server has crashed. Earlier, when discussing CORBA, we pointed out that the CORBA architectural features in support of dynamic reconfiguration or fail-over are difficult to use. If, however, a CORBA service could be replaced with a process group (object group) implementing the same functionality, the problem becomes trivial. This is the main insight underlying the CORBA Fault Tolerant Objects standard (FTOL), and has been implemented by researchers at UCSD as part of a system they call Eternal. The approach is an older one; technologies such as Orbix+Isis and Electra, described in Chapter 21, also provided this ability; on the other hand, the CORBA standard was the first time that replication was embraced by a major standards body. In effect, the CORBA interface wraps a service in such a manner that any other service providing a compatible interface can be substituted for the original one transparently.

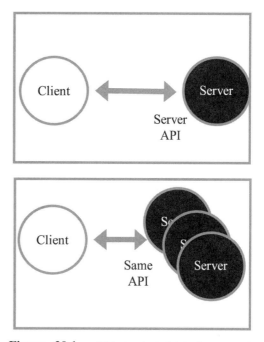

Figure. 20.1. Object-oriented interfaces permit the easy substitution of a reliable service for a less-reliable one. They represent a simple example of a wrapper technology. However, one can often wrap a system component even if it were not built using object-oriented tools.

It should be noted in passing that the CORBA Fault Tolerance standard has not been widely popular. Early in this book, we alluded to the distinction between a standard, and a widely-accepted standard. Simply standardizing a technology doesn't mean that the technology is widely used, or even that it works well—all it tells us is that some community saw value in sitting down and hammering out a political document expressing their agreement as to the interfaces to the technology, its functionality, and the appropriate patterns of use. Only if the standard is embodied into products that become popular does the term take on real importance. On the other hand, commercial users often reject complex, non-standard technologies. Industry needs standards, even though many proposed standards are quickly abandoned.

In the case of CORBA, users apparently find that the standard, which provides for state-machine replication of active (server) objects and the data they maintain, and requires that the server code be completely deterministic, is overly restrictive. Thus while the associated wrapper technology is extremely simple to use and highly transparent, the "positioning" of this standard seems not to accord with a large market. It seems likely that any Web Services

High Availability standard would need to offer greater flexibility to the user (perhaps, integrated with a comprehensive development environment) to gain wider acceptance.

Wrapping by Library Replacement

Even when we lack an object-oriented architecture, similar ideas can often be employed to achieve the same sorts of objectives. As an example, one can potentially wrap a program by relinking it with a modified version of a library procedure that it calls. In the relinked program, the code will still issue the same procedure calls as it did in the past. But control will now pass to the wrapper procedures, which can take actions other than those taken by the original versions. In this sense, an RPC stub is a wrapper.

In practice, this specific wrapping method would only work on older operating systems, because of the way that libraries are implemented on typical modern operating systems. Until fairly recently, it was typical for linkers to operate by making a single pass over the application program, building a *symbol table* and a list of *unresolved external references*. The linker would then make a single pass over the library (which would typically be represented as a directory containing object files or as an archive of object

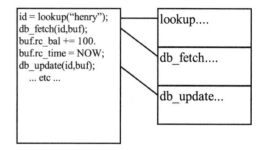

Figure. 20.2. A linker establishes the correspondence between procedure calls in the application and procedure definitions in libraries, which may be shared in some settings.

files), examining the symbol table for each contained object and linking it to the application program if the symbols it declares include any of the remaining unresolved external references. This process causes the size of the program object to grow, and it results in extensions both to the symbol table and, potentially, to the list of unresolved external references. As the linking process continues, these references will in turn be resolved, until there are no remaining external references. At that point, the linker assigns addresses to the various object modules and builds a single program file, which it writes out. In some systems, the actual object files are not copied into the program, but are instead loaded dynamically when first referenced at run time. (See Figure 20.2.)

Operating systems and linkers have evolved, however, in response to pressure for more efficient use of computer memory. Most modern operating systems support some form of shared (also called "dynamically linked") libraries. In the shared library schemes, it would be impossible to replace just one procedure in the shared library. Any wrapper technology for a shared library environment would then involve reimplementing all the procedures defined by the shared library—a daunting prospect if the library is large enough, especially if the documentation available wasn't designed for the developer of such a wrapper. Indeed, many libraries have important but undocumented internal interfaces.

Wrapping by Object Code Editing

Object code editing is an example of a wrapping technology that has been exploited in a number of research and commercial application settings. The approach was originally developed by Wahbe, Lucco, Anderson, and Graham and involves analysis of the object code files before or during the linking process. A variety of object code transformations are possible. Lucco, for example, used object code editing to enforce type safety and to eliminate the risk of address boundary violations in modules that will run without memory protection—a software fault isolation technique. Object code editors for languages such as C# and Java, which compile into an intermediate representation, should be even easier to build, since so much information is preserved about object types and uses.

For purposes of wrapping, object code editing would permit the selective remapping of certain procedure calls into calls to wrapper functions, which could then issue calls to the original procedures if desired (see Figure 20.3). In this manner, an application that uses the UNIX *send to* system call to transmit a message could be transformed into one that calls *filter_sendto* (perhaps even passing additional arguments). This procedure, presumably after filtering outgoing messages, could then call *sendto* if a message sur-

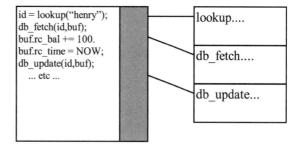

Figure. 20.3. A wrapper (gray) intercepts selected procedure calls or interface invocations, permitting the introduction of new functionality transparently to the application or library. The wrapper may itself forward the calls to the library, but it can also perform other operations. Wrappers are an important option for introducing reliability into an existing application, which may be too complex to rewrite or to modify easily with explicit procedure calls to a reliability toolkit or some other new technology.

vives its output filtering criteria. Notice that an approximation to this result can be obtained by simply reading in the symbol table of the application's object file and modifying entries prior to the linking stage. Of course, this can only be done if the object file format is well documented and isn't protected against such tampering. Unfortunately, modifying programs in this manner could also be done for purposes of attacking a system, hence it is less and less practical to take such a step—many operating systems now support some form of cryptographic signature scheme to detect evidence of "tampering" and will refuse to run a program that has been modified in this manner.

On the other hand, some systems exploit object code editing as a way to secure themselves against a threat. For example, one important application of object code editing, discussed earlier, involves importing untrustworthy code into a client's Web browser. When we discussed this option in Section 10.9, we described it simply as a security enhancement tool. Clearly, however, the same idea could be useful in many other settings. Thus, it makes sense to understand object code editing as a wrapping technology and how specific use of it in Web browser applications might permit us to increase our level of trust in applications that would otherwise represent a serious security threat.

Because programming languages such as C# and Java are compiled into an intermediary language, then "JIT" compiled, they offer new opportunities for code transformation and rewriting. Indeed, Java environments often include powerful rewriters. These would appear to offer substantial opportunities for those seeking ways to automatically introduce replication or fault-tolerance mechanisms.

Wrapping with Interposition Agents and Buddy Processes

Until now, we have focused on wrappers that operate directly upon the application process and that live in its address space. However, wrappers need not be so intrusive.

Interposition involves placing some sort of object or process in between an existing object or process and its users. An interposition architecture based on what are called "coprocesses" or "buddy processes" is a simple way to implement this approach, particularly for developers familiar with UNIX pipes (Figure 20.4). Such an architecture involves replacing the connections from an existing process to the outside world with an interface to a buddy process that has a much more sophisticated view of the external environment—for example, perhaps the existing program is basically designed to process a pipeline of data, record by

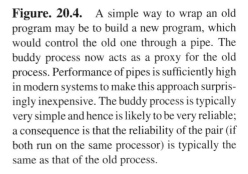

Figure. 20.4.   A simple way to wrap an old program may be to build a new program, which would control the old one through a pipe. The buddy process now acts as a proxy for the old process. Performance of pipes is sufficiently high in modern systems to make this approach surprisingly inexpensive. The buddy process is typically very simple and hence is likely to be very reliable; a consequence is that the reliability of the pair (if both run on the same processor) is typically the same as that of the old process.

record, or to process batch-style files containing large numbers of records. The buddy process might employ a pipe or file system interface to the original application, which will often continue to execute as if it were still reading batch files or commands typed by a user at a terminal; therefore, it may not need to be modified. To the outside world, however, the interface seen is the one presented by the buddy process, which may now exploit sophisticated technologies such as CORBA, Web Services, Spread or Horus, a message bus, and so forth. (One can also imagine imbedding the buddy process directly into the address space of the original application, coroutine style, but this is likely to be much more complex and the benefit may be small unless the connection from the buddy process to the older application is known to represent a bottleneck.) The pair of processes would be treated as a single entity for purposes of system management and reliability: They would run on the same platform and be set up so that if one fails, the other automatically fails too.

Interposition is easier in some settings than in others. In CORBA, for example, any object can be replaced by a link to a remote object, accessed via the CORBA remote object invocation protocol (IIOP). The ability to make this replacement turns out to be the "hook" that permitted developers of the CORBA Fault Tolerance specification to slide group replication into CORBA in a relatively clean manner. Windows, similarly, includes a fairly general way to interpose an object providing identical interfaces where some existing object is used in the system; the author is not aware of that ability having been exploited to introduce high assurance properties, but it is used for other purposes (indeed, within the operating system itself, the Windows virtual memory subsystem is interposed under a number of other mechanisms, including the file system, permitting the developers of the system to reuse functionality and simplifying the core of the operating system). This, then, could be an attractive development path for future work on high assurance Windows-based applications. On the other hand, it would result in proprietary solutions that depend upon features of Windows.

Interposition wrappers may also be supported as a general capability provided by the operating system. Many operating systems provide some form of packet filter capability, which would permit a user-supplied procedure to examine incoming or outgoing messages, selectively operating on them in various ways. Clearly, a packet filter can implement wrapping. The streams communication abstraction in UNIX and Linux supports a related form of wrapping, in which stream modules are pushed and popped from a protocol stack. Pushing a stream module onto the stack is a way of wrapping the stream with some new functionality implemented in the module. The stream still looks the same to its users, but its behavior changes.

Interposition wrappers were elevated to a real art form in the Chorus operating system (see Rozier et al. [Fall 1988, December 1988]), which is object oriented and uses object invocation for procedure and system calls. In Chorus, an object invocation is done by specifying a procedure to invoke and providing a handle referencing the target object. If a different handle is specified for the original one, and the object referenced has the same or a superset of the interface of the original object, the same call will pass control to a new object. This object now represents a wrapper. Chorus uses this technique extensively for a great variety of purposes, including the sorts of security and reliability objectives discussed above.

Wrapping Communication Infrastructures: Virtual Private Networks

Sometime in the near future, it may become possible to wrap an application by replacing the communication infrastructure it uses with a virtual infrastructure. A great deal of work on the Internet and on telecommunication information architectures is concerned with developing a technology base that can support virtual private networks, having special security or quality-of-service guarantees. A virtual network could also wrap an application—for example, by imposing a firewall interface between certain classes of components or by encrypting data so that intruders can be prevented from eavesdropping.

The concept of a virtual private network runs along the following lines. In Section 9.10 we saw how agent languages such as Java permit a server to download special-purpose display software into a client's browser. One could also imagine doing this in the network communication infrastructure itself, so that the network routing and switching nodes would be in a position to provide customized behavior on behalf of specialized applications needing particular, non-standard communication features. We call the resulting structure a virtual private network (VPN)[16] because, from the perspective of each individual user, the network seems to be a dedicated one with precisely the properties needed by the application. This is a virtual behavior, however, in the sense that it is superimposed on a physical network of a more general nature. Uses to which a generalized virtual private network (VPN) could be put include the following:

- Support for a security infrastructure within which only legitimate users can send or receive messages. This behavior might be accomplished by requiring that messages be signed using some form of VPN key, which the VPN itself would validate. This is the most common meaning for the term "VPN."
- Communication links with special video transmission properties, such as guarantees of limited loss rate or real-time delivery (so-called "isochronous" communication).
- Tools for stepping down data rates when a slow participant conferences to individuals who all share much higher-speed video systems. Here, the VPN would filter the video data, sending through only a small percentage of the frames to reduce load on the slow link.
- Concealing link-level redundancy from the user. In current networks, although it is possible to build a redundant communication infrastructure that will remain connected even if a link fails, one often must assign two IP addresses to each process in the network, and the application itself must sense that problems have developed and switch from one to the other explicitly. A VPN could hide this mechanism, providing protection against link failures in a manner transparent to the user.

20.1.2 Introducing Robustness in Wrapped Applications

Our purpose in this text is to understand how reliability can be enhanced through the appropriate use of distributed computing technologies. How do wrappers help in this undertaking? Examples of robustness properties that wrappers can introduce into an application include the following:

- *Fault tolerance*: Here, the role of the wrapper is to replace the existing I/O interface between an application and its external environment with one that replicates inputs so that each of a set of replicas of the application will see the same inputs. The wrapper also plays a role in collating the outputs, so that a replicated application will appear to

---

[16]This uses the term somewhat loosely: a VPN, in platforms like Windows and Linux, is a fairly specific technology packaging focused on providing secure remote access to a corporate network by tunneling through the firewall using a shared-key cryptographic scheme. In contrast, here we are employing the same term to connote a more general idea of overlaying a network with "other properties" on a base network with "base properties." Others might call this an overlay network—but, overlay networks, like VPNs, also have come to have a fairly specific meaning, associated with end-to-end implementations of routing. Rather than invent some completely new term, the book uses VPN in a generalized way.

produce a single output, albeit more reliably than if it were not replicated. To the author's knowledge, the first such use was in a protocol proposed by Anita Borg as part of a system called Aurogen (see Borg et al. [1983, 1985]), and the approach was later generalized by Eric Cooper in his work at Berkeley on a system called Circus (see Cooper [1985], and in the Isis system, which I developed at Cornell University (see Birman and Joseph [November 1987]). Generally, these techniques assume that the wrapped application is completely deterministic, although later we will see an example in which a wrapper can deal with nondeterminism by carefully tracing the non-deterministic actions of a primary process and then replaying those actions in a replica.

- *Caching*: Many applications use remote services in a client/server pattern, through some form of RPC interface. Such interfaces can potentially be wrapped to extend their functionality—for example, a database system might evolve over time to support caching of data within its clients in order to take advantage of patterns of repeated access to the same data items, which are common in most distributed applications. To avoid changing the client programs, the database system could wrap an existing interface with a wrapper that manages the cached data, satisfying requests out of the cache when possible and otherwise forwarding them to the server. Notice that the set of clients managing the same cached data item represents a form of process group, within which the cached data can be viewed as a form of replicated data. Indeed, the Java Jini architecture allows a server stub to specify its own transport protocol for talking to the server, in effect, "wrapping" the notion of communication from client to server. On the other hand, this option hasn't been used very actively, and Jini itself seems to have never gained the degree of acceptance of J2EE, in which such wrapping is impractical.

- *Security and authentication*: A wrapper that intercepts incoming and outgoing messages can secure communication by, for example, encrypting those messages or adding a signature field as they depart and decrypting incoming messages or validating the signature field. Invalid messages can either be discarded silently, or some form of I/O failure can be reported to the application program. This type of wrapper needs access to a cryptographic subsystem for performing encryption or generating signatures. Notice that in this case, a single application may constitute a form of *security enclave*, having the property that all components of the application share certain classes of cryptographic secrets. It follows that the set of wrappers associated with the application can be considered as a form of process group, despite the fact that it may not be necessary to explicitly represent that group at run time or communicate to it as a group.

- *Firewall protection*: A wrapper can perform the same sort of actions as a firewall, intercepting incoming or outgoing messages and applying some form of filtering to them—passing only those messages that satisfy the filtering criteria. Such a wrapper would be placed at each of the I/O boundaries between the application and its external environment. As in the case of the security enclave just mentioned, a firewall can be viewed as a set of processes surrounding a protected application or encircling an application to protect the remainder of the system from its potentially unauthorized behavior. If the ring contains multiple members (multiple firewall processes) the structure of a process group is again present, even if the group is not explicitly represented by the system—for example, all firewall processes need to use consistent filtering policies if a firewall is to behave correctly in a distributed setting.

- *Monitoring and tracing or logging*: A wrapper can monitor the use of a specific interface or set of interfaces and can trigger certain actions under conditions that depend on the flow of data through those interfaces. A wrapper could be used, for example, to log the actions of an application for purposes of tracing the overall performance and efficiency of a system, or, in a more active role, it could be used to enforce a security policy under which an application has an associated behavioral profile and in which deviation from that profile of expected behavior potentially triggers interventions by an oversight mechanism. Such a security policy would be called an *in-depth security mechanism*, meaning that, unlike a security policy applied merely at the perimeter of the system, it would continue to be applied in an active way throughout the lifetime of an application or its access to the system.

- *Quality-of-service negotiation*: A wrapper could be placed around a communication connection for which the application has implicit behavioral requirements, such as minimum performance, throughput, loss rate requirements, or maximum latency limits. The wrapper could then play a role either in negotiation with the underlying network infrastructure to ensure that the required quality of service is provided or in triggering reconfiguration of an application if the necessary quality of service cannot be obtained. Since many applications are built with *implicit* requirements of this sort, such a wrapper would really play the role of making *explicit* an existing (but not expressed) aspect of the application. One reason such a wrapper might make sense would be that future networks may be able to offer guarantees of quality of service even when current networks do not. Thus, an existing application might in the future be wrapped to take advantage of those new properties with little or no change to the underlying application software itself.

- *Language-level wrappers*: Wrappers can also operate at the level of a programming language or an interpreted run-time environment. In Chapter 21, for example, we will describe a case in which the TCL/TK programming language was extended to introduce fault tolerance by wrapping some of its standard interfaces with extended ones. Similarly, we will see that fault tolerance and load-balancing can often be introduced into object-oriented programming languages, such as C++, Ada, or SmallTalk, by introducing new object classes that are transparently replicated or that use other transparent extensions of their normal functionality. An existing application can then benefit from replication by simply using these objects in place of the ones previously used.

The above list is at best very partial. What it illustrates is that given the idea of using wrappers to reach into a system and manage or modify it, one can imagine a great variety of possible interventions that would have the effect of introducing fault tolerance or other forms of robustness, such as security, system management, or explicit declaration of requirements that the application places on its environment.

These examples also illustrate another point: When wrappers are used to introduce a robustness property, it is often the case that some form of distributed process group structure will be present in the resulting system. As previously noted, the system may not need to actually represent such a structure and may not try to take advantage of it per se. However, it is also clear that the ability to represent such structures and to program using them explicitly could confer important benefits on a distributed environment. The wrappers could, for example, use consistently replicated and dynamically updated data to vary some sort of security policy. Thus, a firewall could be made dynamic, capable of varying its filtering behavior in response to changing requirements on the part of the application or environment. A monitoring mechanism could communicate information among its representatives in an attempt to detect correlated behaviors or attacks on a system. A caching mechanism can ensure the consistency of its cached data by updating these dynamically.

Wrappers do not always require process group support, but the two technologies are well matched to one another. Where a process group technology is available, the developer of a wrapper can potentially benefit from it to provide sophisticated functionality, which would otherwise be difficult to implement. Moreover, some types of wrappers are only meaningful if process group communication is available.

20.1.3 Toolkit Technologies

In the introduction to this chapter, we noted that wrappers will often have limitations—for example, although it is fairly easy to use wrappers to replicate a completely deterministic application to make it fault tolerant, it is much harder to do so if an application is not deterministic. And, unfortunately, many applications are nondeterministic for obvious reasons—for example, an application that is sensitive to time (e.g., timestamps on files or messages, clock values, timeouts) will be nondeterministic to the degree that it is difficult to guarantee that the behavior of a replica will be the same without ensuring that the replica sees the same time values and receives timer interrupts at the same point in its execution. The UNIX *select* system call is a source of nondeterminism, since even identically replicated programs presented with identical inputs might detect the availability of data at different times in their execution and thus follow differing execution paths. Interactions with devices are notorious sources of nondeterminism. Any time an application uses *ftell* to measure the amount of data available in an incoming communication connection, this introduces a form of nondeterminism. Asynchronous I/O mechanisms, common in many systems, are also potentially nondeterministic. Parallel or preemptive multithreaded applications are potentially the most nondeterministic of all.

More than twenty years ago, researchers confronted by this problem began to explore mechanisms that would transform nondeterministic inputs into events fielded by one copy of a replicated program, which could then record enough information to allow other replicas to reproduce its actions accurately. For example, suppose that process p issues a *select* system call and discovers that I/O is ready on channel 6. It can record this in a message and send it to process q. If q has the same data available on its 6th channel, and knows when the *select* call returned this value, it can wait until its own code issues that same call and then return the same result that p saw, without even needing to ask the operating system to actually perform the *select* operation. By carrying this concept further, to include thread scheduling, and having q lag the execution of p so that these messages always warn it of future events, q should be in a position to take precisely the same actions that p took. There will still be some cases such an approach can't cover—for example, if p and q try to replicate the behavior of a UDP socket on which incoming packets are received, it can be tricky to deal with cases where a packet is dropped by one but not the other, or where the order of the packets differs. But the vast majority of applications could certainly be replicated in this manner.

Today, as communication systems continue to improve in performance, it may make sense to adopt such an approach. However, the general sense at the time of these early studies was that this form of intervention is simply too costly, in which case there may be no obvious way that a wrapper could be introduced to transparently confer the desired reliability property. Alternatively, it may be possible to do so but impractical in terms of cost or complexity. In such cases, it is sometimes hard to avoid building a new version of the application in question, in which explicit use is made of the desired reliability technology. Generally, such approaches involve what is called a *toolkit* methodology.

In a toolkit, the desired technology is prepackaged, usually in the form of procedure calls (Table 20.2). These provide the functionality needed by the application, but without requiring that the user understand the reasoning that lead the toolkit developer to decide that in one situation *cbcast* was a good choice of communication primitive, but that in another *abcast* was a better option. A toolkit for managing replicated data might offer an abstract data type called a replicated data item, perhaps with some form of name and some sort of representation, such as a vector or an n-dimensional array. Operations appropriate to the data type would then be offered: *UPDATE, READ*, and *LOCK* being the obvious ones for a replicated data item (in addition to such additional operations that might be needed to initialize the object, detach from it when no longer using it, etc.). Other examples of typical toolkit functionality might include transactional interfaces, mechanisms for performing distributed load-balancing or fault-tolerant request execution, tools for publish/subscribe styles of communication, tuple-space tools implementing an abstraction similar to the one in the Linda tuple-oriented parallel programming environment, and so forth. The potential list of tools is really unlimited, particularly if such issues as distributed system security are also considered.

Toolkits often include other elements of a distributed environment, such as a name space for managing names of objects, a concept of a communication end point object, process group communication support, message data structures and message manipulation functionality, lightweight threads or other event notification interfaces, and so forth. Alternatively, a toolkit may assume that that the user is already working with a distributed computing environment, such as the DCE environment or Sun Microsystem's ONC environment. The advantage of such an assumption is that it reduces the scope of the toolkit itself to those issues explicitly associated with its model; the disadvantage being that it compels the toolkit user to also use the environment in question, thus reducing portability.

Table 20.2. Typical Interfaces in Toolkits for Process Group Computing*

Tool	Description
Load-balancing	Provides mechanisms for building a load-balanced server, which can handle more work as the number of group members increases.
Guaranteed execution	Provides fault tolerance in RPC-style request execution, normally in a manner that is transparent to the client.
Locking	Provides synchronization or some form of token passing.
Replicated data	Provides for data replication, with interfaces to read and write data, as well as selectable properties, such as data persistence, dynamic uniformity, and the type of data integrity guarantees supported.
Logging	Maintains logs and checkpoints and provides playback.
Wide area spooling	Provides tools for integrating LAN systems into a WAN solution.
Membership ranking	Within a process group, provides a ranking on the members that can be used to subdivide tasks or load-balance work.
Monitoring and control	Provides interfaces for instrumenting communication into and out of a group and for controlling some aspects of communication.
State transfer	Supports the transfer of group state to a joining process.
Bulk transfer	Supports out-of-band transfer of very large blocks of data.
Shared memory	Tools for managing shared memory regions within a process group. The members can then use these tools for communication that is difficult or expensive to represent in terms of message passing.

*In typical practice, a set of toolkits would be needed, each aimed at a different class of problems. The interfaces listed above would be typical for a server replication toolkit, but might not be appropriate for building a cluster-style multimedia video server or a caching Web proxy with dynamic update and document consistency guarantees.

20.1.4 Distributed Programming Languages

Agent programming languages and other *fourth-generation languages* (4GLs) package powerful computing tools in the form of special-purpose programming environments. Unlike general purpose programming languages such as C# or Java, these languages play specific roles. For example, Java Script is a well known language intended for use in building sophisticated Web Pages. The language (related to Java but quite different in the details) is intended for a setting in which reliability is taken primarily to mean security of the user's system against viruses, worms, and other forms of intrusion. Web Browsers support Java Script because the browser development community has satisfied itself that there are few security issues created by such scripts. Other types of agent-oriented programming languages include TCL/TK (see Ousterhout [1994]) and TACOMA (see Johansen et al. [June 1995]).

Although existing distributed programming languages lack group communication features and few make provisions for reliability or fault tolerance, one can extend many such languages without difficulty. The resulting enhanced language can be viewed as a form of distributed computing toolkit in which the tools are tightly integrated with the language. For example, Java users are fond of a communications package called JBOSS, within which JavaGroups provides group communication functionality that seems natural and quite easy to use in a Java Enterprise context. Of course, JBOSS is more of a package than a language, but it represents a major step in the direction of embedding group communication functionality into a Java context—and this is, after all, the way that one "extends" the Java platform. Indeed there have been programming languages in which group communication was offered as a basic language primitive. If language extension can solve the problem, designing a language around a computational abstraction is perhaps overkill. On the other side of the coin, by extending a language, one can incorporate such ideas as "location" and "replication" into the underlying type system, a fascinating opportunity. As networks continue to spread and non-distributed computing eventually becomes the exception rather than the norm, it is entirely possible that both approaches will become common: in object oriented languages like C# and Java, these sorts of technologies will be available as class libraries (so that the developer who wants to replicate information will simply use a replication class and extend it with the specific methods and data appropriate to the need), while the type theory community slowly presses forward on logical foundations of replication and the mathematics of correctness for highly available applications.

20.2 Wrapping a Simple RPC server

To illustrate the idea of wrapping for reliability, consider a simple RPC server designed for a financial setting. A common problem that occurs in banking is to compute the theoretical price for a bond; this involves a calculation that potentially reflects current and projected interest rates, market conditions and volatility (expected price fluctuations), dependency of the priced bond on other securities, and myriad other factors. Typically, the necessary model and input data is tracked by a server, which clients access using RPC. Note that RPC underlies the Web Services remote method invocation model, hence what follows is also relevant to Web Services design. However, notice also that in a bond pricing setting, each request—each RPC—can be reissued as often as necessary: The results may not be identical (because the server is continuously updating the parameters to its model), but any particular result should be valid for at least a brief period of time. We'll exploit that property below.

To start, suppose that we have developed a bond pricing server using standard out of the box technologies such as the TAO CORBA package or one of the Web Services platforms. Only after putting it into operation do we begin to be concerned about its availability. A typical scenario might be that the server has evolved over time, so that although it was really quite simple and easy to restart after crashes when first introduced, it now uses a large database and restarting after failures it can take twenty minutes or longer. The server doesn't fail often, but when it does, the disruption could be extremely costly.

An analysis of the causes of failure is likely to reveal that the server itself is fairly stable, although a low residual rate of crashes is observed. Perhaps there is a lingering suspicion that some changes introduced to handle the unification of European currencies into the euro are buggy and are causing crashes. The development team is rewriting the entire euro package, and expects to have a new version in a few months, but management, being pragmatic, doubts that this will be the end of the software-reliability issues for this server. Meanwhile, however, routine maintenance and communication link problems are known to be at least as serious a source of downtime. Finally, although the server hardware is relatively robust, it has definitely caused at least two major outages during the past year, and loss of power associated with a minor electrical problem triggered additional downtime recently.

In such a situation, it may be extremely important to take steps to improve server reliability. But rebuilding a server from scratch is often impractical, particularly in light of the evolutionary nature of such software. The rebuilding effort could take months or years, and when traders perceive a problem, they are rarely prepared to wait years for a solution. Management is now demanding that something be done. (If you haven't been in this situation, you haven't worked in the industry!)

The introduction of reliable hardware and networks could improve matters substantially. A dual network connection to the server, for example, would permit messages to route around problematic network components such as faulty routers or damaged bridges. One can purchase off-the-shelf routers with this capability, and they are known to achieve extremely high levels of network robustness. But the software and management failures would remain an issue. Upgrading to a fault-tolerant hardware platform on which to run the server would clearly improve reliability, but only to a degree. If the software is in fact responsible for many of the failures that are being observed, all of these steps will only eliminate some fraction of the outages.

An approach that replicates the server using wrappers might be very appealing in this setting. As stated, the server state seems to be dependent on pricing inputs to it, but not on queries. Thus, a solution such as the one illustrated in Figure 20.5 can be considered. Here, the inputs that determine server behavior are replicated using broadcasts to a process group. The queries are load-balanced by directing the queries for any given client to one or another member of the server process group. The architecture has substantial design flexibility

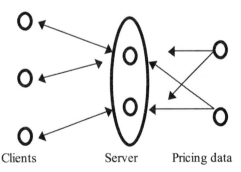

Clients   Server   Pricing data

Figure. 20.5.   A client/server application can be wrapped to introduce fault tolerance and load-balancing with few or no changes to the existing code.

in this regard: The clients can be managed as a group, with their queries carefully programmed to match each client to a different, optimally selected server. Alternatively, the clients can use a random policy to issue requests to the servers. If a server is unreasonably slow to respond, or has obviously failed, the same request could be reissued to some other server (or, if the request itself may have caused the failure, a slightly modified version of the request could be issued to some other server). Moreover, the use of wrappers makes it easy to see how such an approach can be introduced transparently (without changing existing server or client code). Perhaps the only really difficult problem would be to restart a server while the system is already active.

In fact, even this problem may not be so difficult to solve. The same wrappers that are used to replace the connection from the data sources to the server with a broadcast to the replicated server group can potentially be set up to log input to the server group members in the order that they are delivered. To start a new server, this information can be transferred to it using a *state transfer* from the old members, after which any new inputs can be delivered. After the new server is fully initialized, a message can be sent to the client wrappers informing them that the new server is able to accept requests. To optimize this process, it may be possible to launch the server using a checkpoint, replaying only those logged events that changed the server state after the checkpoint was created. If updates aren't all that common and the associated log files can be kept small, these steps would have the effect of minimizing the impact of the slow server restart on perceived system performance.

This discussion is not entirely hypothetical. The author is aware of a number of settings in which problems such as this were solved precisely in this manner. The use of wrappers is clearly an effective way to introduce reliability or other properties (such as load-balancing) transparently, or nearly so, in complex settings characterized by substantial preexisting applications.

20.3 Wrapping a Web Site

The techniques of the preceding section could also be used to develop a fault-tolerant version of a Web server (the kind that serves requests for documents). However, whereas the example presented above concerned a database server used only for queries, many Web servers also offer applications that become active in response to data submitted by the user through a form-fill, a "cgi" script, or some similar interface. To wrap such a server for fault tolerance, one would need to first confirm that its implementation is deterministic. That is, if these operations are invoked in the same order at the replicas, one would need to know that the resulting states would be identical. Given such information, the *abcast* protocol could be used to ensure that the replicas all see the same inputs in the same order. Since the replicas would now take the same actions against the same state, the first response received could be passed back to the user; subsequent duplicate responses can be ignored.

A slightly more elaborate approach is commonly used to introduce load-balancing within a set of replicated Web servers for query accesses, while fully replicating update accesses to keep the copies in consistent states. The HTTP protocol is sufficiently sophisticated to make this an easy task: For each retrieval (*get*) request received, a front-end Web server simply returns a different server's address from which that retrieval request should be satisfied, using a temporary redirection error code. This requires no changes to the HTTP protocol, Web browsers, or Web servers, and although purists might consider it to be a form of hack, the benefits of introducing load-balancing without having to redesign HTTP are so substantial that within the Web development community, the approach is viewed as an important design paradigm. In the terminology of this chapter, the front-end server wraps the cluster of back-end machines.

20.4 Hardening Other Aspects of the Web

A wrapped Web server just hints at the potential that group communication tools may have in future enterprise uses of the Web. As seen in Table 20.3 and Figures 20.6 and 20.7, the expansion of the Web into groupware applications and environments, computer-supported cooperative work (CSCW), and dynamic information publication applications create challenges that the tools we developed in previous chapters could be used to solve. Web Services bring new requirements and new challenges, and indeed represent a fascinating potential area for research.

Today, a typical enterprise that makes use of a number of Web servers treats each server as an independently managed platform and has little control over the cache coherency policies of the Web proxy servers residing between the end user and the Web servers; those policies depend on a mixture of parameter settings that the enterprise *does* control and document properties, which are controlled by the servers that produced the documents. With group replication and load-balancing, we could transform these Web servers into fault-tolerant, parallel processing systems. Such a step would bring benefits such as high availability and scalable performance, enabling the enterprise to reduce the risk of server overload when a popular document is under heavy demand. Web servers will increasingly

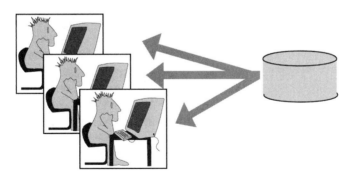

Figure 20.6. Web server transmits continuous updates to documents or video feeds to a group of users. Depending upon the properties of the group-communication technology employed, the users may be guaranteed seeing identical sequences of input, seeing data synchronously, security from external intrusion or interference, and so forth. Such a capability is most conveniently packaged by integrating group communication directly into a Web agent language such as Java or Visual BASIC-for example, by extending the browser with group communication protocols that could then be used through a groupware API.

Table 20.3. Potential Uses of Groups in Internet Systems

Application domain	Uses of process groups
Server replication	• High availability, fault-tolerance • State transfer to restarted process • Scalable parallelism and automatic load-balancing • Coherent caching for local data access • Database replication for high availability
Data dissemination	• Dynamic update of documents in the Web or of fields in documents • Video data transmission to group conference browsers with video viewers • Updates to parameters of a parallel program • Updates to spreadsheet values displayed to browsers showing financial data • Database updates to database GUI viewers • Publish/subscribe applications
System management	• Propagate management information base (MIB) updates to visualization systems • Propagate knowledge of the set of servers that compose a service • Rank the members of a server set for subdividing the work • Detect failures and recoveries and trigger consistent, coordinated action • Coordinate actions when multiple processes can all handle some event • Rebalance of load when a server becomes overloaded, fails, or recovers
Security applications	• Dynamically updating firewall profiles • Updating security keys and authorization information • Replicating authorization servers or directories for high availability • Splitting secrets to raise the barrier faced by potential intruders • Wrapping components to enforce behavior limitations (a form of firewall that is placed close to the component and monitors the behavior of the application as a whole)

be used as video servers, capturing video input (such as conferences and short presentation by company experts on topics of near-term interest, news stories off the wire, etc.), in which case such scalable parallelism may be critical to both data archiving (which often involves computationally costly techniques such as compression) and playback.

Wide area group tools could also be used to integrate these servers into a wide area architecture that would be seamless, presenting users with the abstraction of a single, highly consistent, high-availability Web service—yet internally self-managed and structured. Such a multi-server system might implement data migration policies, moving data to keep them close to the users who demand data most often, and wide area replication of frequently

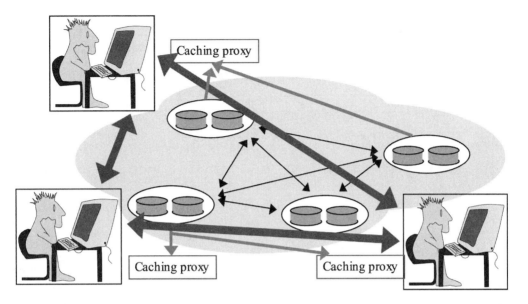

Figure 20.7. Potential group communication uses in Web applications occur at several levels. Web servers can be replicated for fault tolerance and load-balancing or integrated into wide-area structures, which might span large corporations with many sites. Caching Web proxies could be fixed to provide guarantees of data consistency, and digital encryption or signatures could be used to protect the overall enterprise against intrusion or attack. Moreover, one can foresee integrating group communication directly into agent languages such as Java, thereby creating a natural tool for building cooperative groupware applications. A key to successfully realizing this vision will be to design wrappers or toolkit APIs that are both natural and easy to use for the different levels of abstraction and purposes seen here: Clearly, the tools one would want to use in building an interactive multimedia groupware object would be very different from those one would use to replicate a Web server.

requested critical information, while also providing guarantees of rapid update and consistency. Later, we will be looking at security technologies that could also be provided through such an enterprise architecture, permitting a company to limit access to its critical data to just those users who have been authorized.

Turning to the caching Web proxies, group communication tools would permit us to replace the standard caching policy with a stateful coherent caching mechanism. In contrast with the typical situation today, where a Web page may be stale, such an approach would allow a server to reliably send out a message that would invalidate or refresh any cached data that has changed since the data was copied. Moreover, by drawing on CORBA functionality, one could begin to deal with document groups (sets of documents with hyperlinks to one another) and over multidocument structures in a more sophisticated manner. Earlier, we mentioned that one study by IBM researchers C. Mohan and G. Cuomo revealed that Web Services systems are likely to exploit caching in dozens of ways. One common property of all of these mechanisms is that they replicate information, hence group communication tools could be valuable in implementing such structures.

In fact there has been research on "cooperative caching," with very promising initial results. A system called Squirrel, developed using the Pastry platform (a peer-to-peer file sharing service developed at Rice University and Microsoft Research in Cambridge, England) tracks information within client caches and allows one client system to look up objects in the caches of other clients. At Cornell University, the Kelips peer-to-peer indexing technology has been applied to the same problem, again with very encouraging results. However (we'll see this in the chapter on peer-to-peer technologies) neither system implements a true coherent cache, since neither maintains an accurate list of which objects are in which cache—both track this information with a kind of loose consistency guarantee, stemming from the lack of any sort of interlock between the update stream as objects move around and the query stream of requests to find copies of objects. Thus, there is considerable potential to apply group communication mechanisms having stronger guarantees to the problem. Success would enable a style of Web server that deliberately "manages" the caches of its clients, just as the distributed file systems we looked at early in the book manage file caches and buffer pools of their clients to ensure consistency.

Web Services applications using event notification products conforming to the new WS_Eventing specification (basically, a publish-subscribe specification compatible with most publish-subscribe products) can be understood as exploiting a form of group multicast to stream updates to groups of clients who share an interest in some form of dynamically updated data. This raises the question of whether one might build a single basic technology layer offering primitive services such as groups, group communication, overlay routing infrastructures, and event logging, and then employ that single layer to offer a range of technical mechanisms aimed at server availability, system monitoring, event notification, publish-subscribe, system monitoring and management, and so forth. By standardizing the basic layers, the Web Services community could encourage the emergence of a variety of platforms all sharing the same APIs and yet implemented in different ways. The resulting mechanisms could be valuable in a tremendous number of settings. Web Services implementations of financial systems could use them to notify client systems as stock prices change, triggers are reached, or when important news is released. E-commerce systems could use them to notify customers of pricing or availability changes. Large data centers could use these technologies to adjust parameters that client systems employ when talking to the center: the rate at which data should be polled, for example, or security settings, or even security keys.

The same platform might also open the door to new kinds of applications. For example, suppose that a group of soldiers is operating in a dangerous environment. Streams of updates could be used to keep their maps updated about enemy troop movements and activities, or to keep the soldiers current as their orders and mission status evolves. But the same style of system could also be used to inform real-time routing software in our cars as congestion occurs and then clears during rush hour, opening the door to much smarter choices of routes during rush hour. A person shopping in a big city could be sent advertising reporting sales of interesting items in stores within a few blocks walking distance.

We may not perceive these as group communication tools: their presentation will cover a spectrum ranging from monitoring and system management interfaces, to replication for mission-critical components, to publish-subscribe notification architectures. And yet group communication is there, just below the service. These communication patterns will be common in Web Services systems, even if the Web Services architecture lacks explicit support for such patterns.

Obviously, our wrapped Web server represents just the tip of a potentially large application domain. While it is difficult to say with any certainty that this type of system will ever be of commercial importance, or to predict the timeframe in which it might become operational, it seems plausible that the pressures that today are pushing more and more organizations and corporations onto the Web will tomorrow translate into pressure for consistent, predictable, and rapidly updated groupware tools and objects. The match of the technologies we have presented with this likely need is good, although the *packaging* of group communication tools to work naturally and easily within such applications will certainly demand additional research and development. In particular, notice that the tools and APIs one might desire at the level of a replicated Web server will look completely different from those that would make sense in a multimedia groupware conferencing system. This is one reason that systems such as Horus need flexibility, both at the level of how they behave and how they look. Nonetheless, the development of appropriate APIs ultimately seems like a small obstacle.

20.5   Unbreakable Stream Connections

Motivated by the surging interest in high availability Web platforms, in this subsection we will consider a more complex example, involving extensions to Web servers that might make them reliable. Recall that Web Services are based on the same standards as other kinds of Web servers, hence this same mechanism could be used to harden a Web Services system down the road. We can solve part of the problem by replicating the data used by the server using the techniques discussed above. However, to really conceal server failure from the clients, we also need to make the connection from client to server fault-tolerant, and this is the problem tackled in the material that follows.

Our analysis will lead to a mixed conclusion: it will turn out that while replicating servers is definitely a good idea, making TCP fault-tolerant in the manner developed below isn't necessarily a win. A constraint underlying the discussion will be the assumption that only the server can be modified. The client uses a completely standard and unmodified TCP protocol stack, so anything we do on the server side needs to be invisible to the client side. This constraint prevents us from using a solution such as the protocol discussed in Section 17.1, when we explored protocols for sending messages from a non-member of a group into a group. Those assumed that we could do some work on the "non-member" side of the connection, and hence corresponded to modifications of the client's end of the connection.

In practice, the "don't touch the client" constraint is somewhat arbitrary. While there are important benefits in avoiding modification of the client systems, one needs to weigh such benefits against the associated costs: added complexity and reduced performance. Moreover, in a world where servers can download agents to the client, there may be other ways to obtain the desired behavior. A client could talk to a Web site through an applet downloaded from the site, and that applet could use a special protocol. Or, we could introduce a new content retrieval protocol (call it FT-HTTP). A browser extended to "know about" that protocol could be used when accessing high availability web sites, and simply by using an appropriate URL would know when to use the high availability protocol.

Taking such thinking one step further, it is worthwhile to note that even if we do rearchitect TCP to provide improved fault-tolerance, we won't have eliminated all risk of disruption on the client side. After all, the Internet will still adapt its routing slowly, hence a network disruption could impact clients for an extended period of time, even if neither the client nor the servers fail. Our improved protocol won't help in such a situation. Similarly, it won't protect against proxy failures, or DNS problems. Conversely, when using a conventional TCP connection, if the connection is lost a client can often just reconnect and reissue a request. Thus the reliability of TCP is anything but the whole story; one could go to all the trouble of implementing and deploying a high-reliability TCP only to discover that the system is as unreliable as ever!

But the purpose of this section is as much pedagogical as practical. The problem of replicating the server side of a TCP connection is easily understood, and we'll see that it can sometimes be solved quite elegantly, giving a nice illustration of the techniques of Part III. When the solution works best, it does so for reasons that revolve around asynchronous communication patterns that can stream data rapidly from a sender to multiple receivers, a pattern that turns out to be central to high performance in any group communication setting. In situations where the solution doesn't work quite so well, understanding the reasons can help the reader develop intuition into the limitations of group communication and replication. Finally, the solution can actually be implemented and one can come up with scenarios in which it could be of practical value, especially when the client is a computer using the Web Services standards to communicate with a high availability Web server. Thus the question is interesting, informative, and could sometimes be of practical value too.

20.5.1 Reliability Options for Stream Communication

What would it mean to say that a stream connection is "reliable?" Two types of answers make sense. A sensible starting point would recall the discussions of consistency from the preface to this book, later applied in Chapter 3. The idea would be to avoid potential inconsistency in failure-reporting by rewiring the failure TCP to base fault detections on GMS input and output (Figure 20.8).

This type of intervention would be easy if the TCP protocol stack in question is one that runs in the user's address space (for example, the TCP Daytona implementation from MIT), and if we were free to change the client side of the connection as well as the server. We

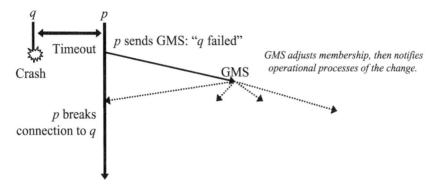

Figure 20.8. Modified stream protocol reports detected failures to the GMS, which breaks all connections to a failed or excluded process simultaneously. To introduce this behavior, the original interfaces by which the protocol detects and reports failures within itself would be wrapped to interconnect the detection mechanism with the GMS and to connect the GMS output back to the stream protocol.

would simply track down the places where the TCP stack decides that the remote endpoint has failed and disable them, then introduce a mechanism whereby each end-point registers itself with the GMS, and cuts the connection if the GMS reports a failure of the remote end-point. A similar approach could be used if the server is running on a Linux platform: Linux is an open-source system, hence one could simply modify the kernel protocol module, rebuild the kernel, and viola: "consistent failure detection."

The practical problem is more complex because most systems use in-kernel TCP implementations, and hence it can be hard to change the protocol. Moreover, we resolved to leave the client side unchanged. In this situation, one can still arrange for user-level code on the server side to disable the automated TCP failure detection mechanism (by setting a parameter called SO_KEEPALIVE to a large value), to register itself with the GMS, and to also register the client with the GMS (since the client is unmodified, we can't count on it to do this on its own). If the client is perceived to have failed, by any server with which it is communicating, the GMS will report the event to *all* such servers. Thus the client will lose all its connections, rather than entering a state in which some break while others remain healthy.

20.5.2   An Unbreakable Stream That Mimics TCP

But can we do more? Recall our assumption that the server itself is a process group that uses replicated data to maintain high availability. Under these circumstances, an appropriately ambitious goal would be to modify TCP so that a client talking to such a group of servers sees what seems to be a conventional TCP endpoint, but where that end-point is actually replicated so that each of the servers holds one of the replicas. Then we could deliver each incoming request to a "primary" server, but if it fails, seamlessly transferring responsibility for any current request *and for the active TCP endpoint* to a backup. The idea is illustrated in Figures 20.9 and 20.10.

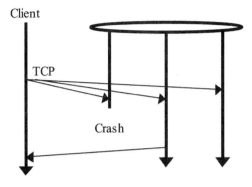

Figure 20.9. A more elaborate solution to the reliable stream problem. In the protocol, the client uses a completely standard stream protocol, such as TCP, but the messages are delivered as reliable broadcasts within the group. Unless all members fail, the client sees an unbroken TCP connection to what appears to be a continuously available server. Only if all members fail does the channel break from the perspective of the client.

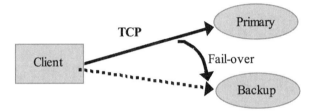

Figure 20.10. The reliable streams protocol provides clients with the illusion of a completely transparent fail-over, under which their TCP connection to a primary server would automatically and seamlessly switch from a primary server to the backup if a failure occurs. To do this, we need mechanisms to keep the primary and backup TCP endpoints in the same state, using multicast. We also need a way to shift the IP address of the endpoint from primary to backup. This can be done if the primary and backup are in the same LAN, or if the IP address is a class-D multicast address. And we need virtual synchrony to coordinate the solution.

The solution to this problem presented below was originally developed in a prior version of this book, published in 1996. However, this is not the only work in which the idea has been explored. For example, a paper by Ekwall et al. published in 2002 implemented and evaluated a protocol called FT-TCP, using methods similar to the ones we present here, but with a series of engineering and optimization decisions that lead to a somewhat different solution. A paper by Alvisi et al. published in 2001 illustrated yet a third approach, also similar in the large but different in the details.

Let's focus on the case of a TCP protocol that runs in the user's address space. At the bottom, the protocol accepts incoming IP packets from the network, probably using what is called a "raw" I/O socket in Linux and other UNIX variants. These packets are processed in the TCP protocol, which sends data up to the application in the normal way, while also sending out IP packets containing acknowledgements, retransmission requests, and outgoing TCP data.

Of course, this isn't the whole story. TCP takes some actions based on the passage of time, hence the protocol module needs an interface to the timer subsystem of the machine on which it is running. It uses time both in its flow control calculations, and to schedule retransmissions. Fortunately, not many protocol implementations of this sort make use of threaded concurrency, but if the user-level protocol in question does so, the interface from it to the subsystem implementing lightweight threads would also have to be considered as part of its

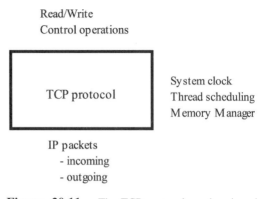

Read/Write
Control operations

System clock
Thread scheduling
Memory Manager

IP packets
 - incoming
 - outgoing

Figure. 20.11. The TCP protocol can be viewed as a black box with interfaces to its environment. Although these interfaces are non-trivial, they are not overwhelmingly so.

interface to the outside world. Finally, there is the interface by which the module interacts with the application process: This consists of its read and write interface and perhaps a control interface (this would implement the UNIX *ioctl, ftell,* and *select* interfaces or the equivalent operations on other operating systems). This environment is illustrated in Figure 20.11.

20.5.3 Nondeterminism and Its Consequences

To use process group replication on a TCP protocol endpoint, we'll need to ensure that the TCP stack is deterministic. And this could be a make-or-break aspect of the solution. The basic idea will be to intercept incoming events by replacing the various interfaces that connect the TCP protocol to the outside world with modified interfaces that will try and keep a set of backup processes in sync with a primary. But this approach won't work unless the primary can write down enough information to enable the backups to track its state.

In effect, our hope is to treat the TCP protocol as a state machine, receiving incoming events from its varied interfaces, computing, and then performing output events. Even access by the protocol to the clock can be thought of as an output event (sent to the clock) followed by an input event (a response from the clock to the protocol). Indeed, even the number of bytes returned when a client does a *read* operation needs to be treated as a kind of a state transition, since TCP can return less than the number of bytes requested by the client: a form of non-determinism.

Obviously, there are sources of nondeterminism that can be very hard to deal with. Interrupt-driven behavior and thread scheduling are two instances of such problems, and any sort of direct access by the driver to hardware properties of the computer or attached peripherals runs the risk of introducing similar problems. Presumably, one would not see such behavior in TCP Daytona, since it runs in the user's address space and hence doesn't communicate directly with the hardware. But a kernel implementation of TCP might be a different matter—in the kernel, anything goes!

To summarize: if we can somehow write down a "script" of the events that occurred in the primary, in such a way that a replica can use the script to track the state of the primary, we'll be in good shape. With TCP Daytona, this wouldn't be all that difficult. But one can easily imagine much harder cases, and those TCP implementations might not be suitable for our overall technique.

20.5.4 Dealing with Arbitrary Nondeterminism

A paper by Bressoud and Schneider suggested a way to extend this trace-driven approach to software fault tolerance to make entire machines fault tolerant, including the operating system and all the applications running on the machine (see Bressoud and Schneider). They do this using special hardware properties of certain classes of modern microprocessors. Their work operates at the level of the CPU itself and involves noting the time at which interrupts occur. Specifically, the method requires a special hardware register, of a type seen on some (but not all) microprocessors.

The register in question plays two roles. In the "normal" mode, the register simply measures time in machine cycles, and is saved as part of the interrupt sequence. One can thus read the value off the stack and know precisely how long a program executed prior to the interrupt.

In the second "slave" mode, an application can *set* the register to a negative value. In this case, an interrupt is generated when the register overflows—when it counts "up" to zero.

Using this feature on the backup, the Bressoud and Schneider solution is able to produce a script covering all the non-determinism that can occur on the entire computer! They do so by recording the times at which interrupts occurred on a master computer, and then setting the cycle counter on a slave computer to the time at which the next interrupt should occur. All other types of interrupts are disabled, and the machine is allowed to execute up to the point when the counter fires. Then, an interrupt indistinguishable from the one that occurred on the primary is generated. Bressoud and Schneider point out that at the end of the day, all non-determinism is caused by interrupts. Thus by reproducing the interrupts that occurred on the master system, the slave can be made to track the master in perfect lock step!

Of course, there are forms of interrupts that simply can't be disabled, such as hardware faults and device interrupts. Bressoud and Schneider can't handle such interrupts, hence their method is most readily applicable to machines with very few I/O connections: ideally, just a communication interface and an interface to the clock.

20.5.5 Replicating the IP Address

Let's assume that we've figured out how to produce a script of all the events that affect the state of TCP in the primary endpoint of a replicated connection. This initial step leaves two questions open.

The first is a simple matter, which is to ensure that the backup will actually receive incoming IP packets after taking over from the primary in the event of a failure. The specific issue is as follows. Normally, the receive side of a stream connection is identifiable by the address (the IP address) to which packets are sent by TCP. This address would normally consist of the IP address of the machine interface and the port number of the TCP protocol. As a consequence, IP packets sent by the client are only received at one site, which represents a single point of failure for the protocol. We need a way to shift the address to a different location to enable a backup to take over after a crash.

If each computer had a single, unique, IP address, it might not be practical to move IP addresses around. Fortunately, this is anything but the story! In fact, any computer with multiple network interfaces will have one IP address for each interface. Thus, it is common for a single computer to have two or more IP addresses.

With that in mind, let's just generate an extra, unused, IP address. The computer currently owning the end-point of our replicated TCP connection will register itself as the owner of that IP address, using the *ifconfig* system call or its equivalent. If the IP address is chosen appropriately, Internet routing will ensure that packets to that address reach the owner. And, if a machine q takes over from machine p, it need only reregister the IP addresses that p was responsible for. As soon as routing tables are updated in the network, q will receive any traffic that p would have received.

Notice that this approach only works if the Internet is able to route the IP address in question to both p and q. This is always the case if p and q are on the same LAN, but might not be possible in a WAN setting. An obvious idea would be to use an IP multicast address, but it turns out that IP multicast isn't well supported in the Internet as a whole. Another option might be to use a network address translation mechanism in the firewall of the data center running the servers. Clearly, if none of these options is feasible, we may get stuck,

20.5.6 Maximizing Concurrency by Relaxing Multicast Ordering

The other lingering problem is concerned with maximizing performance. Had we not intervened to replicate the TCP state machine, it would reside on the critical path that determines I/O latency and throughput from client to server and back. Suddenly, we have modified this path to insert what may turn out to be a large number of multicasts to the replicas. How costly will these be?

To answer this question, we need to understand the conditions under which a replicated TCP stack can perform as well, or nearly as well, as a nonreplicated one. Our answer will reflect two key ideas. First, we'll find that many of the delays associated with replication can be hidden from the client—they don't need to be on the critical path of the modified system. So this leads to a view that what the client isn't aware of won't impact performance. The second part of the answer revolves around the idea of causal ordering: we'll need to make sure that if a client "sees" data from the server, or even an acknowledgement, a replica can get back into the identical state that the primary was in when that data or acknowledgement was sent. And this, it will turn out, means that the replica must have received all parts of the script that were "causally prior" to the message send event by which that data or acknowledgement was sent to the client system.

But let's tackle this one step at a time. So: we have a primary TCP endpoint associated with the server that currently owns the connection. The endpoint is producing a script of important events—a list of the events needed to drive the replicas of the TCP endpoint along the same sequence of state transitions that occurred in the primary. How should we send the script to the replicas?

Notice that all the multicasts in question originate at the same place: in the primary server's TCP protocol stack. Thus we want a reliable multicast primitive that preserves sender order: *fbcast* or *cbcast*. In fact, it will turn out that all we need is *fbcast*.

Accordingly, we can take one tiny step towards our solution. The primary TCP stack will receive events of various kinds, as discussed in Section 20.5.2. It will generate a script of information for replay into the replicas. And it will use *fbcast* to send that script within the process group of endpoints.

Now, how costly will this stream of *fbcast* messages be from the perspective of the remote client? It shouldn't be hard to see that the cost may be very low indeed! After all, we can send the multicasts asynchronously, and get on with the work of processing the user's request while the system is still sending them. Of course we do need to forward the data sent by the client to the server, but few Web operations involve sending huge objects from the client to the server, so the data in question should be small. Thus we won't put more than a few microseconds of delay onto our performance-critical path.

But we aren't out of the woods quite yet. Consider a TCP-level acknowledgment or some other message sent by the TCP protocol from the primary server to the client, perhaps containing some data associated with the server's reply to the client's request (Figure 20.12). When the client receives that message its outgoing window will be updated, clearing frames associated with any data that were acknowledged. If the primary now crashes, there will be no possibility of reconstructing the data that were garbage collected. Thus, before sending any TCP-level message from the primary to the client, we need to be sure that the backup TCP stacks have received the script of events "prior" to the acknowledgement. In the terminology of Chapter 14, we need to be sure that these *causally prior* messages are stable at the backup.

So now we can take another small step towards a solution. It seems that our *fbcasts* can be sent asynchronously from the primary server to its backup replicas, but that we need to wait before the primary server can send any kind of TCP-generated IP traffic back to the client. And what we need to wait for is "multicast stability", a topic discussed in Section 16.3.2. In effect, our solution should invoke the *flush* primitive developed in Section 16 immediately before anything is sent from the primary server to the client. If there are any *fbcast* messages still in the pipeline from the primary to the replicas, *flush* will delay until they get through. If not, it will be a no-op.

How will the *flush* impact performance? There are two cases to consider.

The easy case is that of a one-directional stream from the client to the server—for example, a file upload or some other operation that sends data in, but doesn't involve a reply (or at least, doesn't involve one yet). From the client's perspective, our entire set of changes won't have much impact. After all, their effect is mostly to delay the acknowledgements sent by TCP briefly, and that delay is normally masked by the TCP window.

In the more general case, however, such as an RPC or object invocation that runs over a stream, a *flush* operation will occur before each *send* operation by the server to client. This flush will wait for the prior *fbcasts* to become stable, which in turn involves waiting for an acknowledgement. Round-trip times in typical modern multicast systems, like Horus, are in the range of .7 ms to 1.4 ms for such events. Thus, responses from the server to the client may be delayed by about 1 ms to achieve fault tolerance. Such a cost may seem small to some users and large to others. It can be viewed as the price of transparency, since comparable delays would not have occurred in applications where complete transparency on the client-side was not an objective. This is illustrated in Figure 20.12.

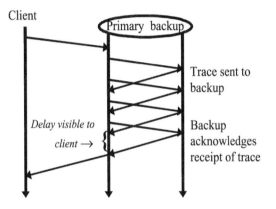

Figure 20.12. The latency introduced by replication is largely invisible to the client. As seen here, most trace information reaches the backup while the primary is still computing. Only the last trace message, sent after the primary issues its reply and before that reply can be sent from primary to client, introduces noticeable latency in the critical path that limits RPC round-trip times over the replicated TCP channel. The problem is that if the trace information causally prior to the reply were lost in a crash, the primary's state could not be reproduced by the backup. Thus, this information must be stable at the backup before the reply is transmitted. Unfortunately, the use of timeouts in the TCP protocol stack implies that such information will be generated. One can imagine other protocols, however, or optimizations to the TCP protocol, in which the primary would have extremely little or no trace information to send to the backup; replication of such protocols for fault tolerance would introduce minimal additional latency.

And this solves our problem. To recap, we've transformed one TCP endpoint into the primary and forced it to write down a script of any non-deterministic information that changes its state. Using *fbcast* we've transmitted that script to the backup endpoints, without needing to wait for confirmation of delivery—they can be sent "asynchronously." But when the primary endpoint sends IP traffic back to the client, we need to compensate for that asynchronous communication pattern, using *flush*. And finally, if the primary fails, the backup taking over must re-register the IP address using *ifconfig*.

Notice that the virtual synchrony model played a quiet but central role here, especially if a server has more than a single backup. The model lets us overlook issues of agreement on membership in the server group and lets us implement an *fbcast* protocol, which will be delivered atomically before failure notifications occur for the primary server, if it fails. These guarantees simplify the protocol.

20.5.7 State Transfer Issues

Our discussion overlooked the issues relating to launching of new servers, and of transferring state information to bring them up to date. For applications and protocols in which state is easily represented, the solution presented here can easily be modified to accommodate joins with state transfer to the joining process. Otherwise, it may be best to launch a sufficient set of replicas at the time the connection is first made, so that even if failures occur, the group will still have an adequate number of servers to continue providing response.

20.5.8 Discussion

Although we presented the unbreakable stream problem as a hypothetical problem, many researchers and students have implemented such protocols. For example, Cho focused on the case of TCP channels to mobile users, whose handheld computers might need to connect to a succession of base stations as the computer was moved around (see Cho and Birman). Cited earlier, Bessoud and Alvisi [2001] and Ekwall [2002] explore related solutions to the basic unbreakable stream problem. All find that performance is quite good.

Our analysis suggests that in situations where we are not limited by bandwidth and where the streams protocol to be modified is available to the developer and has modest nondeterminism, a reliability transformation that uses wrappers to introduce fault tolerance through replication might be worthwhile. The impact on performance and complexity would be reasonably low, and the performance costs may actually be hidden by concurrency. However, if any of these conditions does not hold, the introduced complexity and performance overhead may begin to seem excessive for the degree of transparency such a reliable protocol can afford. Finally, we have observed that there will probably be a small latency impact associated with our transformation in RPC-style interactions, but that this cost would probably be hidden in pipeline-style uses of streams—again, because of the concurrency achieved between the protocol used to transmit trace information to a replica and the computation occurring in the application itself.

Having said all this, it still isn't clear that one would want to use our protocol between a Web browser and a server. As noted earlier, there are other perfectly viable options. However, in Web Services systems the protocol could be attractive. It enables us to hide many kinds of failures from the clients of a highly available server and, if the coverage isn't perfect, the solution is probably adequate for many uses.

These sorts of tradeoffs are inevitable in complex distributed systems, and it is important that the developer keep one eye on the balance. It is very appealing to imagine a technology that would let us replicate a server, making it fault tolerant, in a manner that would be completely transparent to its clients. An unbreakable TCP stream connecting the client to the server seems like a natural and inevitably desirable feature. Yet the alternative of building a protocol whereby the client would know it was communicating to the group, or

Pros	• Totally transparent fail-over
	• Uninterrupted service to client
	• Client system not changed at all
Cons	• With Java, might have a reasonably easy way to modify the client system
	• Solution is complex
	• Performance penalty may be substantial for some patterns of use
	• Doesn't address other causes of failure, such as the ones discussed in Part II of the book

Figure 20.13. Tradeoffs to be considered when looking at the decision to implement a transparently fault-tolerant TCP stream protocol. In many settings, the arguments against doing so would dominate.

that would conceal such interactions beneath a layer of software presenting a stream-like interface, must be weighed against the presumed disadvantages of needing to modify (or at least recompile) the client program. (See Figure 20.13.)

Systems developers often must struggle with tradeoffs between performance and transparency or complexity and transparency. Transparency is a good thing, and the use of wrappers can provide a route for very transparent hardening of a distributed system. However, transparency should generally not be elevated to the level of a religion. In effect, a technology should be as transparent as possible, consistent with the need to keep the software used simple and the overheads associated with it low. When these properties fall into question, a less-transparent solution should be seriously considered.

20.6 Reliable Distributed Shared Memory

During much of the 1990s, distributed shared memories were a "hot topic" in the distributed system research community. Although the enthusiasm ultimately ebbed as the Internet boom gained momentum, the subject remains interesting. Accordingly, in this section we'll look at the idea of implementing a wrapper for the UNIX *mmap* (or *shrmem*) functions, which are used to map files and memory regions into the address space of user applications and shared between concurrently executing processes. The extension we consider here provides for the sharing of memory-mapped objects over a virtually synchronous communication architecture running on a high-speed communication network. One might use such a system as a repository for rapidly changing visual information in the form of Web pages: The provider of the information would update a local mapped copy directly in memory, while the subscribers could map the region directly into the memory of a display device and in this way obtain a direct I/O path between the data source and the remote display. Other uses might include parallel scientific computations, in which the shared memory represents the shared state of the parallel computation; a collaborative workplace or virtual reality environment shared between a number of users; a simulation of a conference or meeting room populated by the participants in a teleconference; or some other abstraction.

As noted, this topic emerges from an area of research in which many operating systems groups worldwide participated (see Ahamad et al., Carter, Feeley et al., Felton and Zahorjan, Gharachorloo et al., Johnson et al., Li and Hudak). Our goals here are simply to look at how a DSM might be implemented in a highly assured manner using process group technology. The resulting solution is interesting for pedagogical reasons, but would certainly not offer performance and latency properties comparable to hardware solutions.

20.6.1 The Shared Memory Wrapper Abstraction

As with the unbreakable TCP connection, our solution will start with an appropriate wrapper technology. In many UNIX-like operating systems (including Linux and Microsoft Windows) there is a mechanism available for mapping a file into the memory of a process, sharing memory between concurrently executing processes or doing both at the same time. The UNIX system calls supporting this functionality are called *shrmem* or *mmap*, depending on the version of UNIX one is using; a related interface called *semctl* provides access to a semaphore-based mutual-exclusion mechanism. By wrapping these interfaces (e.g., by intercepting calls to them, checking the arguments and special-casing certain calls using new code, and passing other calls to the operating system itself), the functionality of the shared memory subsystem can potentially be extended. Our design makes use of such a wrapper.

In particular, if we assume that there will be a *distributed shared memory daemon* process (DSMD) running on each node where our extended memory-mapping functionality will be used, we can adopt an approach whereby certain mapped-memory operations are recognized as being operations on the DSM and are handled through cooperation with the DSMD. The recognition that an operation is remote can be supported in either of two ways. One simple option is to introduce a new file system object called a DSM object, which is recognizable through a special file type, filename extension (such as .dsm), or some other attribute. The file contents can then be treated as a handle on the DSM object itself by the DSM subsystem. A second option is to extend the options field supported by the existing shared memory system calls with extra bits, one of which could indicate that the request refers to a region of the DSM. In a similar manner, we can extend the concept of semaphore names (which are normally positive integers in UNIX) to include a DSM semaphore name space for which operations are recognizable as being distributed synchronization requests.

Having identified a DSM request, that request can then be handled through a protocol with the DSMD process. In particular, we can adopt the rule that all distributed shared memory is implemented as locally shared memory between the application process and the DSMD process, which the DSMD process arranges to maintain in a coherent manner with regard to other processes mapping the same region of memory. The DSMD process thus functions as a type of server, handling requests associated with semaphore operations or events that involve the mapped memory and managing the mapped regions themselves as parts of its own address space. It will be the role of the DSMD servers as a group to cooperate to implement the DSM abstractions in a correct manner; the system call wrappers are thereby kept extremely small and simple, functioning mainly by passing requests through

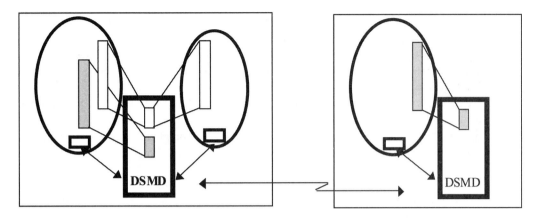

Figure 20.14. Two machines share memory through the intermediary of a distributed shared memory daemon that runs on each. On the left we see that more than one process might employ the same DSMD and might even share memory with one-another (and with remote processes) through it. A wrapper (shown as small boxes) intercepts memory mapping and semaphore system calls, redirecting DSM operations to the DSMD. The DMSD processes sharing a given region of memory belong to a process group and cooperate to provide coherent, fault-tolerant behavior. The best implementation of the abstraction depends upon the expected pattern of sharing and the origin of updates.

to the DSMD or to the local copy of the operating system, depending on the nature of the system call that was intercepted. This is illustrated in Figure 20.14.

It would be inefficient to require that our wrapper see every memory reference to the mapped region. Accordingly, the architecture we favor operates at the granularity of pages and makes use of memory protection features of the hardware, as explained below, to trap operations on pages. The basic idea is to map the full set of pages desired by a process into memory, but to disable access (perhaps just write access, or perhaps both read and write access). If a process doesn't actually access the pages in question, nothing happens. But on its "first" access after a page is locked, a trap will occur. The application catches these events through the wrapper interface.

The wrapper can now forward information to the DSMD, for example asking it to make sure the page is current. Once the DSMD indicates that it is safe to do so, the wrapper unlocks the page and permits the application to resume execution. The sequence of events is exactly the same as when a page fault occurs for a virtual memory region, except that we're handling the fault ourselves in the wrapper and the DSMD, rather than asking the kernel to do it for us.

The sequence of events just described can be implemented more easily on some operating systems than on others. Thus the form of distributed shared memory we'll describe might require kernel changes in some settings, while it could be implemented entirely in the user's address space in others. However, let's view this as an implementation detail. It won't really change the distributed communication issues seen in implementing the DSMD, which is the focus of attention in this book. Indeed, a kernel implementation of a DSM would surely yield material for a fascinating research paper. A paper design, such as the one in this Chapter, is mostly interesting as an academic exercise!

For design simplicity, it will be helpful to consider the DSM architecture as being volatile: DSM regions exist only while one or more processes are mapping them, and there is no persistent disk storage associated with them, except perhaps for purposes of paging if the region is too large to maintain in memory. We can view the DSM as a whole as being a collection of objects or *regions*, each having a base address within the DSM, a size, and perhaps access restrictions and security properties. A region might be associated with a file system name, or could be allocated using some form of DSM region manager server; we will not address this issue here.

Our design reduces the issue to one of maintaining replicated data and performing synchronization with a collection of superimposed process groups (one on behalf of each shared memory region). The DMSD processes that map a given region would also belong to the corresponding process group. The properties of that process group and the algorithms used to maintain the data in it can now be tuned to match the patterns of access expected from the application processes using it.

20.6.2 Memory Coherency Options for Distributed Shared Memory

In any distributed memory architecture, memory coherence is one of the hardest issues to address. Abstractly, the coherence properties of memory characterize the degree to which that memory is guaranteed to behave like a single, nonshared memory that handles every memory access directly. Because our memory is not resident at any single location, but is shared among the processes that happen to be mapping it at a given time, there are a number of options in regard to the degree to which these copies should be coherent. The choices correspond to the options for shared memory on parallel processors, and consist of the following:

- *Strong consistency*: In this model, the DSM is expected to behave precisely as a single nonreplicated memory might have behaved. In effect, there is a single global serialization order for all read and write operations.
- *Weak consistency*: In this model, the DSM can be highly inconsistent. Updates propagate after an unspecified and possibly long delay, and copies of the mapped region may differ significantly for this reason.
- *Release consistency (DASH project)*: This model assumes that conflicting read or update accesses to memory are always serialized (protected) using mutual-exclusion locks, such as the semaphore system calls intercepted by our wrapper. The model requires that if process p obtains a lock associated with a region from process q, then p will also observe the results of any update that q has performed. However, if p tries to access the DSM without properly locking the memory, the outcome can be unpredictable.
- *Causal consistency (Neiger and Hutto)*: In this model, the causal relationship between reads and updates is tracked; the memory must provide the property that if access b occurs after access a in a causal sense, then b will observe the results of access a.

The developer who implements an application (or a parallel computing platform, like PVM or MPI) needs to be aware of the consistency properties of the shared memory, and to code accordingly. Strongly consistent memory can be accessed very much in the same way that memory is shared by concurrent threads running in a single address space on a multiprocessor system. This turns out to be an unrealistically expensive "positioning" in the technology stack because strong consistency is hard to implement efficiently, whether in hardware or, as in our case, in software. Weak consistency suffers from the opposite problem. Here, applications just can't trust the data they read from the shared memory: someone wrote the values, but there is no way to be certain that they are at all consistent from copy to copy. Of course, weak consistency is easy to implement, but it isn't very useful. Release consistency turns out to be the most popular option: it fits well with a style of programming in which the application knows about page boundaries and locks each page before modifying the data within it (some models use read and write locks; others only have write locks). Finally, causal consistency offers an interesting extention to the release consistency model, but hasn't been adopted by developers; apparently, release consistency is "good enough."

This list is not comprehensive, but these four options already represent a sufficient variety of options to present us with some reasonable design choices. To implement strong consistency, it will be necessary to order all update operations, raising the question of how this can be accomplished. The memory protection mechanisms of a virtual memory system offer the needed flexibility: by write-protecting pages managed by the DSMD, we can force an interrupt when those pages are updated and the DSMD can then take any needed action to gain exclusive access. Similarly, by read-protecting a page, we can give the DSMD an opportunity to fetch a current copy if that page might be stale.

For example, to implement strong consistency, we can just protect all the mapped pages against both read and write access. Each time a read or write occurs, we intercept the resulting page fault. The DSMD can then use the replication protocol developed in Section 18.3 to manage the pages, obtaining read and write locks and unprotecting pages at a process during periods of time when that process holds the lock on that page. In effect, we have "wrapped" the mapped file and turned it into a shared memory. However, the solution could be costly. (Without locks, the solution gets much cheaper ... but only provides weak consistency).

The release consistency model can be implemented in a similar manner, except that in this case, we only need to protect pages against writes. We use *cbcast* to implement semaphore operations in the manner of Section 18.3, and also to send updated copies of pages. Notice that there is no need to communicate changes to a page until the corresponding semaphore is released, hence those update messages can be delayed, and only one will need to be sent even if many writes are done on a page (keep in mind that we have one semaphore for each page). Of course, there may be performance considerations that favor transmitting updates *before* the semaphore is released, but the release consistency model itself does not require us to do so.

Asynchronous *cbcast* is a fast protocol: very efficient, suitable for implementations that stream messages without delaying the sender, and yet delaying a process precisely when needed to prevent violations of causal order. Thus we end up with quite an efficient

DSMD in this case. Moreover, if the application obtains read as well as write locks, this implementation will satisfy the causal consistency properties!

Consider now the degree of match between these design options and the expected patterns of use for a DSM. It is likely that a DSM will either be updated primarily from one source at a time or in a random way by the processes that use it, simply because this is the pattern seen for other types of distributed applications that maintain replicated data. For the case where there is a primary data source, both the strong and release consistency models will work equally well: The update lock will tend to remain at the site where the updates are done, and other copies of the DSM will passively receive incoming updates. If the update source moves around, however, there may be advantages to the release consistency implementation: Although the programmer is compelled to include extra code (to lock objects in a way that guarantees determinism), these locks may be obtained more efficiently than in the case of strong consistency, where the implementation we proposed might move the update lock around more frequently than necessary, incurring a high overhead in the process. Further, the release consistency implementation avoids the need to trap page faults in the application, and in this manner avoids a potentially high overhead for updates. (See Figure 20.15)

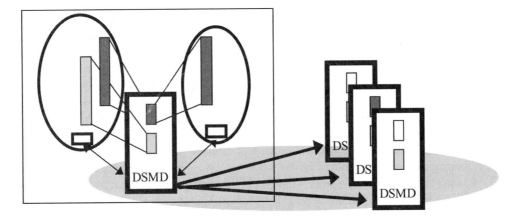

Figure 20.15. The proposed solution maps the DSM problem to a more familiar one: replicated data with locking within a virtually synchronous process group. Only one of several overlapped groups is shown; another group would be used for the dark gray memory region, another for the white one, and so forth. Virtual synchrony provides us with simple solutions for what would otherwise be tricky problems, such as ensuring the coherence of the distributed memory, handling failures and dynamic join events, and dealing with protection.

These considerations make release consistency an appealing model for our DSM, despite its dependence on the use of semaphore-style locking. Of course, should an application desire a weak consistency model or need strong consistency, we now know how both models can be implemented.

However, there are also issues that the consistency model overlooks and that could be quite important in a practical DSM. Many applications that operate on shared memory will be sensitive to the latency with which updates are propagated, and there will be a subset in which other communication patterns and properties are needed—for example, video algorithms will want to send a full frame at a time and will need guarantees of throughput and latency from the underlying communication architecture. Accordingly, our design should include one additional interface by which a knowledgeable application can specify the desired update properties to the DSM. This *dsmctl* system call would be used to specify both the pattern of updates that the application will generate (random, page based, isochronous) and also the maximum latency and other special requirements for acceptable performance. The DSMD can then use this information to schedule its communication appropriately. If available, the *page dirty bit* provided by the virtual memory hardware can be checked periodically by the DSMD; if not available, shared regions that are mapped for update can be transmitted in their entirety at the frequency requested by the user.

20.6.3 False Sharing

False sharing is a phenomenon seen on parallel shared memory machines that triggers a form of thrashing, similar to the kind of thrashing sometimes seen in a virtual memory architecture. False sharing arises when multiple logically unrelated objects are mapped to the same shared memory region or page by an accident of storage allocation. When these objects are updated in parallel, the memory subsystem is unable to detect that the updates are independent ones and treats the situation as one in which the processes doing the updates are contending for the same object. In our implementation of strong consistency, the update token would bounce around in this case, resulting in a huge overhead for token passing and page fault handing on the client systems. Yet the problem also points to an issue in our proposed release consistency scheme—the *granularity of locking*. In particular, it becomes clear that the semaphores used for locking must have the same granularity as the objects the DSMD transmits for updates—most likely a page. Otherwise, because the DSMD lacks a fine-grained concept of data access, when an object is updated on a page and the semaphore locking that object is released, the entire page will be transmitted to other processes mapping the page, potentially overwriting parts of the page that the semaphore was not considered to lock and which are in fact not even up-to-date on the node that held the lock.

Our DSM architecture can only work if the granularity of locking is at the page level or region level, and, in either case, false sharing could now occur as a visible problem for the developer. Rather than trying to overcome this problem, it may be best to simply caution the user: The DSM architecture we have proposed here will perform poorly if an application is subject to false sharing; hence, such applications may need to be redesigned to arrange for concurrently updated but logically unrelated objects to reside in different regions or at least on different pages, and in the case of release consistency, must be locked by separate semaphores.

20.6.4 Demand Paging and Intelligent Prefetching

We cited the case of frequent and time-critical updates, but there is another style of DSM use that will require more or less the opposite treatment. Suppose that the DSM region is extremely large and most applications access it in a sparse manner. Then, even if a region is mapped by some process, it may not be necessary or even desirable to actively update that region each time some process updates some part of the data area. In such cases, a demand paging model, whereby a portion of the DSM is maintained as current only if the process holding that region is actually accessing it, makes more sense.

Although we will not tackle the problem here, for reasons of brevity, it would be desirable for large regions to be managed as multiple subregions, shrinking the process group for a given subregion to include only those processes that are actively updating it or reading it. With such an approach, one arrives at a form of *demand paging*, in which a process, upon attempting to access a subregion not currently mapped into its address space, experiences a page fault. To resolve the fault the DSMD would join the process group for that subregion, transferring the current state of the subregion (or just those updates that have occurred since the process was last a memory) and then enabling read or update access to the subregion and resuming local computation.

Notice that the virtual synchrony properties of the state transfer make it easy to describe a solution to what would otherwise be a tricky synchronization problem! Lacking the virtual synchrony model, it would not be at all simple to coordinate the addition of a new memory to a subregion group and to integrate the state transfer operation with updates that may be occurring dynamically. The virtual synchrony model makes it easy to do so and still be able to guarantee that release consistency or strong consistency will be observed by the DSM user. On the other hand, recall that virtual synchrony comes with no guarantees of real-time performance, and hence support for dynamically adjusting the members of a process group that maps a given region or subregion may be incompatible with providing real-time performance and latency guarantees. For situations in which such guarantees are desired, it may be wise to disable this form of dynamicism unless the requirements are fairly weak ones.

Demand paging systems perform best if the relatively costly operations involved in fetching a page are performed shortly before the page fault actually takes place, so as to overlap useful computation with the paging-in activity and to minimize the delay associated with actually servicing the page fault when it occurs. Accordingly, it would be advisable to implement some form of prefetching policy, whereby the DSMD, recognizing a pattern of access (such as sequential access to a series of subregions), would assume that this pattern will continue into the future and would join subregion groups in anticipation of the future need. For example, the DSMD could include one or more "prefetchers": threads that wait for a pattern of accesses to occur that seems to predict some future access, and then acquire the corresponding semaphore in anticipation that it may soon be needed. Our architecture creates a convenient context within which to implement such a policy.

20.6.5 Fault Tolerance Issues

A DSM implemented by a process group has a natural form of fault tolerance, arising directly from the fault tolerance of the virtual synchrony model used by the DSMD processes to form process groups and propagate updates. The issues that arise are primarily ones associated with the possibility of a failure by a process while it is doing an update. Such an event might leave the DSM corrupted and a semaphore in the locked state (the token for the group would be at the process that failed).

A good way to solve this problem would be to introduce a new kind of page fault exception into the DSM model; this could be called a *page corruption* exception. In such an approach, when a process holding an update lock or semaphore for a page or region fails, any subsequent access by some other process mapping that region would result in a corruption trap. The handler for such a trap would be granted the update lock or semaphore and would be required to restore the page to a consistent state. The next update would be understood to clear the corruption bit, so that processes not attempting to access the page during the period of corruption would be completely unaware that a problem had occurred.

20.6.6 Security and Protection Considerations

The reliability of a DSM should extend beyond issues of fault tolerance and detecting potential corruption to also include guarantees of protection and security or privacy if desired. We have not yet treated security issues in this book and defer discussion of the options until later. In brief, one could arrange for the data on the wire to be encrypted so that eavesdroppers lacking an appropriate key would be unable to map a protected segment and unable to make sense of any intercepted updates. Depending on the degree to which the system implementing virtual synchrony is trusted, weaker security options might include some form of user-ID-based access control in which unauthorized users are prevented from joining the group. Because the DSMD must join a process group to gain access to a DSM segment, the group join operation can include authorization keys for use in determining whether or not access should be granted. Alternatively, if the DSMD process itself can be trusted, it can perform a mapping from local user-IDs on the host machine where it is running to global user-IDs in a protection domain associated with the DSM, permitting access under UNIX-style restrictions.

20.6.7 Summary and Discussion

The previous examples in this chapter illustrated some of the challenges that can be encountered when using group structures in implementing a distributed system. We've seen that not all problems lend themselves to elegant solutions: nondeterminism, for example, seems to create a great deal of complexity in replication algorithms. In contrast, replicating a deterministic state machine can be child's play. We saw that where there is a close match between the application programming model and our primitives, as in the case of "release consistency" and *cbcast*, one can sometimes map even a fairly elaborate programming model into a simple and elegant solution. Moreover, these solutions turn out to be easy to understand when the the match of problem and tool is close, although they become complex when that is not the case.

With respect to the DSM architecture, it seems clear that the practicality of the proposed solution depends upon having a suitable shared memory subsystem available for use between the DSMD and its clients. The scheme discussed above would be easy to implement on Unix or Linux but less so on Windows, where access to the memory protection mechanisms isn't as simple in the case of shared memory regions. Perhaps this explains why distributed shared memory is such an uncommon computing tool; after all, one would expect the simplicity of the abstraction to carry tremendous end-user appeal. The area certainly seems ripe for further research.

20.7 Related Reading

On wrappers and technologies that can support them: (see Jones, Rozier et al. [Fall 1988, December 1988], Wahbe et al.).

On wrapping TCP: (see Birman [1996], Alvisi [2001], Ekwall [2002]).

On the Isis Toolkit: (see Birman and Joseph [November 1987], Birman and van Renesse [1994]). (Information on the most current APIs should be obtained directly from the company that markets the Isis product line; their Web page is http://www.isis.com.)

On agents: (see Gosling and McGilton [1995a, 1995b], Johansen et al. [June 1995], Ousterhout [1994]).

On virtual fault tolerance: (see Bressoud and Schneider).

On shared memory: (see Ahamad et al., Carter, Feeley et al., Felton and Zahorjan, Gharachorloo et al., Johnson et al., Li and Hudak). Tanenbaum also discusses shared memory: (see Tanenbaum), and Coulouris treats the topic as well: (see Coulouris et al.).

21

Software Architectures for Group Communication

The purpose of this chapter is to shift our attention away from protocol issues to architectural considerations associated with the implementation of process group computing solutions. Although there has been a great deal of work in this area, we focus on the Horus system[19], because that system is well matched to the presentation of this book. Horus is still available for researchers in academic or industrial settings (there are no fees, but some years ago the most active community of users migrated to Ensemble and Spread, hence a potential user of Horus might need to start by dusting the software off).

It should be stressed that Horus is just one of many systems a developer might consider working with. At Cornell, the Ensemble system was developed as a successor to Horus and is available for free download too; unlike Horus, Ensemble has an active user community and is supported by some of the major developers involved in building the system (http://www.cs.cornell.edu/Info/Projects/Ensemble). Indeed, one developer (Mark Hayden) has created a series of commercial follow-on products for the system. Ensemble is more widely used than Horus, despite being coded in the O'CaML language, a variant of ML which is widely praised for its elegant handling of mathematical constructs and its powerful type system. Users, of course, shouldn't be aware of the underlying language—they can work in C, C++, C#, or whatever.

---

[19]The ancient Egyptian religion teaches that after the world was created, the gods Osiris and Seth engaged in an epic battle for control of the earth. Osiris, who is associated with good, was defeated and hacked to pieces by the evil Seth, and his body scattered over the Nile Delta. The goddess Isis gathered the fragments and magically restored Osiris to life. He descended to rule the Underworld and, with Isis, fathered a child, Horus, who went on to defeat Seth. When we developed the Isis Toolkit, the image of a system that puts the pieces together after a failure appealed to us, and we named the system accordingly, although the failures that the toolkit can handle are a little less extreme than the one that Osiris experienced! Later, when we developed Horus, it seemed appropriate to again allude to the Egyptian myth. However, it may take some time to determine whether the Horus system will go on to banish unreliability and inconsistency from the world of Web sites and Web Services!

Mentioned earlier, the Spread Toolkit, built by a great team at John Hopkins University (http://www.spread.org/), is an excellent option for those who seek to build real systems, particularly if support is required. Spread is simpler than Ensemble, is supported commercially and offers many advantages, notably exceptional efficiency and simplicity of the user interface. Users concerned about the complexity of group communication will find a happy option in Spread, which was deliberately designed to be as foolproof as possible. Still other options include Eternal, a technology developed at UCSB in support of the CORBA fault-tolerance architecture and JavaGroups, a part of the JBOSS communications platform.

Our decision to drill down on Horus, then, is not a judgment about the relative merits of the various options available to the developer. We do so simply because Horus is a real system, still available for users willing to invest the time needed to recompile it, rather elegantly structured, and widely known as the first system to offer a valuable form of design flexibility, on which the remainder of this chapter will be focused.

21.1 Architectural Considerations in Reliable Systems

The reader may feel that Part II of this book and the first chapters of Part III have lost one of the important themes of Part I—namely, the growing importance of architectural structure and modularity in reliable distributed systems and, indeed, in structuring distributed systems of all types. Our goal in this chapter, in part, is to reestablish some of these principles in the context of the group computing constructs introduced in Part III. Specifically, we will explore the embedding of group communication support into a modular systems architecture.

Historically, group computing and data replication tools have tended to overlook the importance of architectural structure. These technologies have traditionally been presented in what might be called a flat architecture: one in which the APIs provided by the system are fixed, correspond closely to the group construct and associated communication primitives, and less uniformly accessible from any application making use of the group communication environment anywhere in the system.

In practice, however, the use of group communication will vary considerably depending upon what one is attempting to do. Consider the examples that arose in Chapter 20, when we discussed group computing in the context of enterprise Web applications:

- Groups used to replicate a Web server for load-balancing, fault tolerance, or scalable performance through parallelism.
- Groups used to interconnect a set of Web servers, giving the illusion of a single, corporate-wide server within which objects might migrate or be replicated to varying degrees, depending on usage patterns.
- Groups corresponding to the set of Web proxy servers that cache a given data item and are used to invalidate those cached copies or to refresh them when they change.
- Groups used to distribute Java applets to users cooperating in conferencing applications or other groupware applications (we gave a number of examples in Chapter 20 and won't repeat them here).

- Groups used to distribute updates to documents, or other forms of updates, to Java applets running close to the client browsers.
- Groups formed among the set of Java applets, running on behalf of clients, for the purpose of multicasting updates or other changes to the state of the group session among the participants.
- Groups associated with security keys employed in a virtual private network.

Clearly, these uses correspond to applications that would be implemented at very different levels of programming abstraction and for which the most appropriate presentation of the group technology would vary dramatically. Several of these represent potential uses of wrappers, but others would match better with toolkit interfaces and still others with special-purpose, high-level programming languages. Even within those subclasses, one would expect considerable variation in terms of what is wrapped, the context in which those tools or languages are provided, and the nature of the tools themselves. No single solution could possibly satisfy all of these potential types of developers and uses. On the contrary, any system that offers just a single interface to all of its users is likely to confuse its users and to be perceived as complex and difficult to learn, because that API is unlikely to match with the other APIs and major programming paradigms used in the parts of the system where one might want to exploit groups. For example, if one developer is thinking about publish-subscribe, and another about replicating a server, neither may see a group join/leave/multicast interface as a "natural" fit to their needs. If one steps back and looks at the broad history of the field, the tendency to offer group communication tools through a flat interface (one that looks the same to all applications and that offers identical capabilities no matter where it is used in the system) has proved to be an obstacle to the adoption of these technologies, because the resulting tools tend to be conceptually mismatched with the developer's goals and mindset.

The insight here recalls the point made by Cheriton and Skeen in their criticism of "causal and total ordering." Not all applications need all properties. The list of properties that a group *could* offer is almost endless. By picking this one and deciding not to offer that one, the developer of a platform gradually disenfranchises larger and larger subgroups of the potential user community.

Indeed, the lesson goes further than this. Although we have presented group communication as a natural and elegant step, the experience of programming with groups can be more challenging. Obtaining good performance is not always an easy thing, and the challenge of doing so increases greatly if groups are deployed in an unstructured way, creating complex patterns of overlap within which the loads placed on individual group members may vary widely from process to process. Thus, what may seem elegant to the reader, can start to seem clumsy and complex to the developer, who is struggling to obtain predictable performance and graceful scalability.

Cheriton and Skeen concluded from this that one should build systems around a loosely coupled paradigm such as publish-subscribe. Their approach doesn't provide any form of strong guarantee in the usual case, although a "logged" event stream is available as a more costly option for those who need absolute reliability. Thus they prefer a positioning in which the basic primitive offered to the user is rather weak (a best-effort publish-subscribe mechanism), and anything stronger is achieved through end-to-end mechanisms. The Isis Toolkit went the other way, offering publish-subscribe interfaces to group communication tools, so that one could exploit the stronger properties of those tools as needed.

Stepping back, the author's research group concluded that these observations argue for a more *structured* presentation of group computing technologies: one in which the tools and APIs provided are aimed at a specific class of users and will guide those users to a harmonious and simple solution to the problems anticipated for that class of users. If the same technology will also support some other community of users, a second set of tools and APIs should be offered to them. Thus, the tools provided for developers of highly assured Web Services might look very different from those available to the developer of a highly assured database system, even if both are basically forms of replication similar to the functionally found group communication subsystems. I believe that far too little attention has been given to this issue up to the present and that this has emerged as a significant obstacle to the widespread use of reliability technologies.

Functionality of a client-level API:

    Fault-tolerant remote procedure call

    Reliable, unbreakable streams to servers

    Publish-subscribe interfaces, with the possibility of guaranteed reliability or ordering

    Tools for forming groupware sessions involving other client systems

Functionality of a WAN server API:

    Tools for consistently replicating data within wide area or corporate networks

    Technology for updating global state and for merging after a partitioning failure is corrected

    Security tools for creating virtual private networks

    Management tools for control and supervision

Functionality of a cluster-server API:

    Tools for building fault-tolerant servers (ideally, as transparently as possible)

    Load-balancing and scalable parallelism support

    Management tools for system servicing and automatic reconfiguration

    Facilities for on-line upgrade

Other cases that might require specialized APIs:

    Multimedia data transport protocols (special quality-of-service or real-time properties)

    Security (key management and authentication APIs)

    Debugging and instrumentation

    Very large scale data diffusion

Figure 21.1. Different levels of a system may require different styles of group computing support. A simple client/server architecture gives rise to three levels of API (levels in the sense that we start with client issues, then push closer and closer to a server and finally to "platform" uses internal to the operating system and network). Further structure might be introduced in a multimedia setting (where special protocols may be needed for video data movement or to provide time-synchronous functionality), in a transactional database setting (where client's may expect an SQL-oriented interface), or in a security setting (where API's will focus on authentication and key management).

At a minimum, focusing only on issues associated with communication (as opposed to security, system management, or real time), it would appear that three layers of APIs are needed (Figure 21.1). The lowest layer is the one aimed at uses within servers, the middle layer focuses on interconnection and management of servers within a WAN setting, and the third layer focuses on client-side issues and interfaces. Such layers may be further subdivided: Perhaps the client layer offers a collection of transactional database tools and a collection of C# or Java groupware interfaces, while the server layer offers tools for multimedia data transmission, consistent replication and coordinated control, and fault tolerance through active replication. This view of the issues now places unusual demands upon the underlying communication system: not only must it potentially look different for different classes of users, but it may also need to offer very different properties for different classes of users. Security and management subsystems would introduce additional APIs, which may well be further structured. Real-time subsystems are likely to require still further structure and interfaces.

21.2 Horus: A Flexible Group Communication System

The observations in the preceding section may seem to yield an ambiguous situation. On the one hand, we have seen that process group environments for distributed computing represent a promising step toward robustness for mission-critical distributed applications. Process groups have a natural correspondence with data or services that have been replicated for availability or as part of a coherent cache, such as might be used to ensure the consistency of documents managed by a set of Web proxies. They can been used to support highly available security domains. Also, group mechanisms fit well with an emerging generation of intelligent network and collaborative work applications.

Yet we have also seen that there are many options concerning how process groups should look and behave. The requirements that applications place on a group infrastructure vary and there may be fundamental tradeoffs between semantics and performance. Even the most appropriate way to present the group abstraction to the application depends on the setting.

The Horus system responds to this observation by providing an unusually flexible group communication model to application developers. This flexibility extends to system interfaces; the properties provided by a protocol stack; and even the configuration of Horus itself, which can run in user space, in an operating system kernel or microkernel, or be split between them. Horus can be used through any of several application interfaces. These include toolkit-style interfaces and wrappers, which hide group functionality behind UNIX communication system calls, the TCL/TK programming language, and other distributed computing constructs. The intent is that it be possible to slide Horus beneath an existing system as transparently as possible—for example, to introduce fault tolerance or security without requiring substantial changes to the system being hardened (see Bressoud and Schneider).

For example, one could slide Horus beneath a publish-subscribe API of the sort favored
by Cheriton and Skeen. To do this, we use a hashing function to map subjects into a smaller
set of process groups (the objective being to limit the number of groups; systems like Horus
scale to tens of groups but not tens of thousands). A publish event becomes a multicast to
the appropriate group. A subscriber joins the group or group to which their subscription
hashes ("groups" in the case of wildcard subscription patterns).

A basic goal of Horus is to provide efficient support for the virtually synchronous
execution model. However, although often desirable, properties such as virtual synchrony
may sometimes be unwanted, introduce unnecessary overheads, or conflict with other objectives such as real-time guarantees. Cheriton and Skeen, for example, would grimace at the
concept of a publish-subscribe system that offers any properties at all, beyond a best effort
delivery guarantee and some end-to-end mechanism for recovering data if an application
really needs to do so. So while we can map publish-subscribe onto groups, it isn't obvious
that we would want those groups to run over the protocols we've developed so painstakingly
over the past five chapters of the book! Yet we wouldn't want to be too quick to dismiss
the value of causal or total order, or virtual synchrony, either: a publish-subscribe system in
which processes are replicating system state and want strong guarantees would obviously
need stronger group communication properties.

Moreover, the optimal implementation of a desired group communication property
sometimes depends on the run-time environment. In an insecure environment, one might
accept the overhead of data encryption but wish to avoid this cost when running inside
a firewall. On a platform such as an IBM SP scalable supercomputer, which has reliable
message transmission, protocols for message retransmission would be superfluous.

Accordingly, Horus provides an architecture whereby the protocol supporting a group
can be varied, at run time, to match the specific requirements of its application and environment. Virtual synchrony is only one of the options available, and, even when it is selected,
the specific ordering properties that messages will respect, the flow-control policies used,
and other details can be fine-tuned. Horus obtains this flexibility by using a structured
framework for protocol composition, which incorporates ideas from systems such as the
UNIX stream framework and the x-Kernel, but replaces point-to-point communication with
group communication as the fundamental abstraction. In Horus, group communication
support is provided by stacking protocol modules having a regular architecture, where each
module has a separate responsibility. A process group can be optimized by dynamically
including or excluding particular modules from its protocol stack.

21.2.1 A Layered Process Group Architecture

It is useful to think of Horus's central protocol abstraction as resembling a Lego block; the
Horus system is thus similar to a box of Lego blocks. Each type of block implements a micro-
protocol, which provides a different communication feature. To promote the combination
of these blocks into macroprotocols with desired properties, the blocks have standardized
top and bottom interfaces, which allow them to be stacked on top of each other at run time

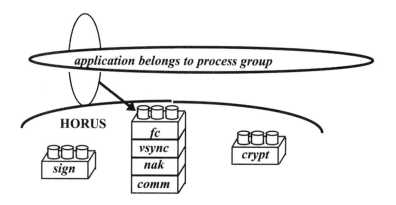

Figure 21.2. Group protocol layers can be stacked at run time like Lego blocks and support applications through one of several application programmer interfaces. Shown is an application program belonging to a single process group, supported by a Horus protocol stack of four layers: "fc," the flow-control layer; "vsync," the layer implementing virtually synchronous process group views; "nak," a layer using negative acknowledgements to overcome communication failures; and "comm," which interfaces Horus to a network. The application would often use Horus through a wrapper, which might conceal this group functionality, but it can also do so using a toolkit. The layers illustrated here are imaginary; some real layers are shown in Table 21.1. Horus supports many layers, but not all need be used in any particular stack: Shown here are two security layers (one for signing messages and one for encrypting their contents), which were not used for this particular application.

in a variety of ways (see Figure 21.2). Obviously, not every sort of protocol block makes sense above or below every other sort. But the conceptual value of the architecture is that where it makes sense to create a new protocol by restacking existing blocks in a new way, doing so is straightforward.

Technically, each Horus protocol block is a software module with a set of entry points for downcall and upcall procedures—for example, there is a downcall to send a message and an upcall to receive a message. Each layer is identified by an ASCII name and registers its upcall and downcall-handlers at initialization time. There is a strong similarity between Horus protocol blocks and object classes in an object-oriented inheritance scheme, and readers may wish to think of protocol blocks as members of a class hierarchy.

To see how this works, consider the Horus *message_send* operation. It looks up the message send entry in the topmost block and invokes that function. This function may add a header to the message and will then typically invoke *message_send* again. This time, control passes to the message send function in the layer below it. This repeats itself recursively until the bottommost block is reached and invokes a driver to actually send the message.

The specific layers currently supported by Horus solve such problems as interfacing the system to varied communication transport mechanisms, overcoming lost packets, encryption and decryption, maintaining group membership, helping a process that joins a group obtain the state of the group, merging a group that has partitioned, flow control, and so forth. Horus also includes tools to assist in the development and debugging of new layers.

Each stack of blocks is carefully shielded from other stacks. It has its own prioritized threads and has controlled access to available memory through a mechanism called *memory channels*. Horus has a memory scheduler, which dynamically assigns the rate at which each stack can allocate memory, depending on availability and priority, so that no stack can monopolize the available memory. This is particularly important inside a kernel or if one of the stacks has soft real-time requirements.

Besides threads and memory channels, each stack deals with three other types of objects: end-points, groups, and messages. The end-point object models the communicating entity. Depending on the application, it may correspond to a machine, a process, a thread, a socket, a port, and so forth. An end-point has an address and can send and receive messages. However, as we will see later, messages are not addressed to end-points, but to groups. The end-point address is used for membership purposes.

A *group object* is used to maintain the local protocol state on an end-point. Associated with each group object is the *group address*, to which messages are sent, and a *view*: a list of destination end-point addresses believed to be accessible group members. An end-point may have multiple group objects, allowing it to communicate with different groups and views. A user can install new views when processes crash or recover and can use one of

Table 21.1. Microprotocols Available in Horus

Layer	Description
COM	The COM layer provides the Horus group interface to such low-level protocols as IP, UDP, and some ATM interfaces.
NAK	This layer implements a negative acknowledgement-based message retransmission protocol.
CYCLE	Multimedia message dissemination using Smith's cyclic UDP protocol
PARCLD	Hierarchical message dissemination (parent-child layer)
FRAG	Fragmentation and reassembly of large messages
MBRSHIP	This layer provides each member with a list of end-points believed to be accessible. It runs a group membership consensus protocol to provide its users with a virtually synchronous execution model.
FC	Flow-control layer
TOTAL	Totally ordered message delivery
STABLE	This layer detects when a message has been delivered to all destination end-points and can consequently be garbage collected.
CRYPT	Encryption and decryption of message body
MERGE	Location and merging of multiple group instances

several membership protocols to reach some form of agreement on views between multiple group objects in the same group.

The message object is a local storage structure. Its interface includes operations to push and pop protocol headers. Messages are passed from layer to layer by passing a pointer and never need be copied.

A thread at the bottom-most layer waits for messages arriving on the network interface. When a message arrives, the bottom-most layer (typically COM) pops off its header and passes the message on to the layer above it. This repeats itself recursively. If necessary, a layer may drop a message or buffer it for delayed delivery. When multiple messages arrive simultaneously, it may be important to enforce an order on the delivery of the messages. However, since each message is delivered using its own thread, this ordering may be lost, depending on the scheduling policies used by the thread scheduler. Therefore, Horus numbers the messages and uses *event count* synchronization variables (see Reed and Kanodia) to reconstruct the order where necessary.

21.3 Protocol stacks

The microprotocol architecture of Horus would not be of great value unless the various classes of process group protocols we might wish to support could be simplified by being expressed as stacks of layers perform well and share significant functionality. The experience with Horus in this regard has been very positive.

The stacks shown in Figure 21.3 all implement virtually synchronous process groups. The left-most stack provides totally ordered, flow-controlled communication over the group membership abstraction. The layers FRAG, NAK, and COM, respectively, break large messages into smaller ones, overcome packet loss using negative acknowledgements, and interface Horus to the underlying transport protocols. The adjacent stack is similar, but provides weaker ordering and includes a layer supporting state transfer to a process joining a group or when groups merge after a network partition. To the right is a stack that supports scaling through a hierarchical structure, in which each parent process is responsible for a set of child processes. The dual stack illustrated in this case represents a feature whereby a message can be routed down one of several stacks, depending on the type of processing required. Additional protocol blocks provide functionality such as data encryption, packing small messages for efficient communication, isochronous communication (useful in multimedia systems), and so forth.

In order for Horus layers to fit like Lego blocks, they each must provide the same down-call and upcall interfaces. A lesson learned from the x-Kernel is that if the interface is not rich enough, extensive use will be made of general-purpose control operations (similar to *ioctl*), which reduce configuration flexibility. (Since the control operations are unique to a layer, the Lego blocks would not fit as easily.) The *Horus Common Protocol Interface* (HCPI), therefore supports an extensive interface, which supports all common operations in group communication systems, going beyond the functionality of earlier layered systems such as

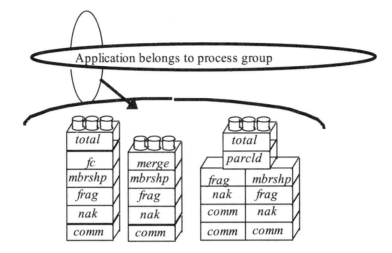

Figure 21.3. The Horus stacks are shielded from each other and have their own threads and memory, each of which is provided through a scheduler. Each stack can be thought of as a small program executing inside Horus. Although this feature is not shown, a stack can be split between the user's address space and the kernel, permitting the user to add customized features to a stack while benefiting from the performance of a kernel-based protocol implementation.

the *x*-Kernel. Furthermore, the HCPI is designed for multiprocessing and is completely asynchronous and reentrant.

Broadly, the HCPI interfaces fall into two categories. Those in the first group are concerned with sending and receiving messages and the stability of messages.[20] The second category of Horus operations is concerned with membership. In the down direction, it lets an application or layer control the group membership used by layers below it. As upcalls, these report membership changes, communication problems, and other related events to the application.

While supporting the same HCPI, each Horus layer runs a different protocol—each implementing a different property. Although Horus allows layers to be stacked in any order (and even multiple times), most layers require certain semantics from layers below them, imposing a partial order on the stacking. Given information about the properties of the network transport service, and the properties provided by the application, it is often possible to automatically generate a minimal protocol stack to achieve a desired property. Indeed, one of the major reasons that Cornell developed Ensemble, the successor to Horus, was that by reimplementing the system in the O'CaML language, it became possible to use a single mathematical formalism to express constraints, properties, and protocols, enabling the use

---

[20]It is common to say that a message is *stable* when processing has completed and associated information can be garbage collected. Horus standardizes the handling of stability information, but leaves the actual semantics of stability to the user. Thus, an application for which stability means "logged to disk" can share this Horus functionality with an application for which stability means "displayed on the screen."

of mathematical theorem proving tools to establish the correctness of the system in a formal way (see Liu et al., 1999).

Layered protocol architectures sometimes perform poorly: the layering limits opportunities for optimization and imposes excessive overhead. Clark and Tennenhouse have suggested that the key to good performance rests in *Integrated Layer Processing* (ILP) (see Abbott and Peterson, Braun and Diot, Clark and Tennenhouse, Karamcheti and Chein, Kay and Pasquale). Systems based on the ILP principle avoid interlayer ordering constraints and can perform as well as monolithically structured systems. Horus is consistent with ILP: There are no intrinsic ordering constraints on processing, so unnecessary synchronization delays are avoided. Moreover, as we will see, Horus supports an optional protocol accelerator, which greatly improves the performance of the layered protocols making use of it.

21.4 Using Horus to Build a Publish-Subscribe Platform and a Robust Groupware Application

Earlier, we commented that Horus can be hidden behind standard application programmer interfaces, giving the example of a publish-subscribe "mapping" of subjects down to groups. Clearly, the core issue in implementing such a publish-subscribe system involves the mapping itself. If we map each subject to a distinct group, we get a very natural implementation of publish-subscribe, but run into the problem that Horus itself wasn't implemented with membership in large numbers of groups as one of its primary goals. The software would "bog down" when a process joins or leaves the system and triggers membership changes in large numbers of groups nearly simultaneously.

If we want to pursue such a mapping, the most obvious idea is to just simplify the job Horus is faced with by applying some sort of a function to reduce the size of the group space. For example, suppose that each subject is somehow hashed to a small space of (just for the sake of argument) about 75 groups, e.g., by taking the first alphanumeric character of the subject name as the group name. Thus "/equities/nyse/ibm" would be mapped to group "e" while "/bonds/fixed/ ... " to group "b". (Obviously this is not a particularly intelligent mapping since all the equity symbols end up in one group, but that's a technicality). A subscription would be implemented by a join; a subscription to a pattern such as "/equities/nyse/*" by joining all the groups that the pattern might match.

Now, this subscription scheme is inefficient, since a subscriber might end up receiving some publications not intended for it. But the data rates would presumably be 75-times reduced relative to the full flow of data into the system, and the extra cost of reevaluating the match and tossing out non-matching incoming events shouldn't be prohibitive. All that remains is to pick an appropriate Horus stack for these groups, and voila: instant publish-subscribe. In the example given, Horus could be configured without the virtual synchrony and ordering layers if one accepts the Cheriton and Skeen argument, or could be set up with stronger ordering and reliability guarantees if the setting demands them.

A second way of exploiting group communication involves the use of groups as a more basic distributed computing "architectural element." Here, the groups become a structural construct visible in the application itself.

A good illustration of this second idea arose some years ago, when colleagues at Cornell interfaced the TCL/TK graphical programming language to Horus. A challenge posed by running systems such as Horus side by side with a package such as X Windows or TCL/TK is that such packages are rarely designed with threads or Horus communication stacks in mind. To avoid a complex integration task, we therefore chose to run TCL/TK as a separate thread in an address space shared with Horus. Horus intercepts certain system calls issued by TCL/TK, such as the UNIX *open* and *socket* system calls. We call this resulting mechanism an *intercept proxy*; it is a special type of wrapper oriented toward intercepting this type of system call. The proxy redirects the system calls, invoking Horus functions, which will create Horus process groups and register appropriate protocol stacks at run time. Subsequent I/O operations on these group I/O sockets are mapped to Horus communication functions.

To make Horus accessible within TCL applications, two new functions were registered with the TCL interpreter. One creates end-point objects, and the other creates group addresses. The end-point object itself can create a group object using a group address. Group objects are used to send and receive messages. Received messages result in calls to TCL code that typically interpret the message as a TCL command. This yields a powerful framework: a distributed, fault-tolerant, whiteboard application can be built using only eight short lines of TCL code over a Horus stack of seven protocols.

To validate the approach, we ported a sophisticated TCL/TK application to Horus. The Continuous Media Toolkit (CMT) (see Rowe and Smith) is a TCL/TK extension providing objects that read or output audio and video data. These objects can be linked together in pipelines and are synchronized by a *logical timestamp* object. This object may be set to run slower or faster than the real clock or even backwards. This allows stop, slow motion, fast forward, and rewind functions to be implemented.

Architecturally, CMT consists of a multimedia server process, which multicasts video and audio to a set of clients. We decided to replicate the server using a primary-backup approach, where the backup servers stand by to back up failed or slow primaries.

The original CMT implementation depends on extensions to TCL/TK. These implement a master-slave relationship between the machines, provide for a form of logical timestamp synchronization between them, and support a real-time communication protocol called Cyclic UDP. The Cyclic UDP implementation consists of two halves: a sink object, which accepts multimedia data from another CMT object, and a source object, which produces multimedia data and passes it on to another CMT object (see Figure 21.4a). The resulting system is distributed but intolerant of failures and does not allow for multicast.

By using Horus, it was straightforward to extend CMT with fault tolerance and multicast capabilities. Five Horus stacks were required. One of these is hidden from the application and implements a clock synchronization protocol (see Cristian [1989]). It uses a Horus layer

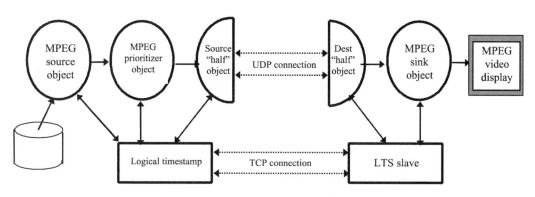

(a) Continuous Media Toolkit: before Horus

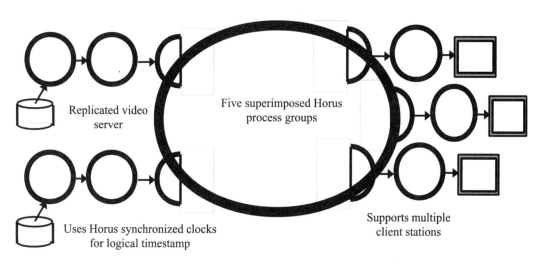

(b) Horus used to introduce fault tolerance and groupware capabilities

Figure 21.4. This illustrates an example of a video service implemented using the Continuous Media Toolkit. MPEG is a video compression standard. In (a), a standard, fault-intolerant set-up is depicted. In (b), Horus was used to implement a fault-tolerant version that is also able to multicast to a set of clients.

called MERGE to ensure that the different machines will find each other automatically (even after network partitions), and it employs the virtual synchrony property to rank the processes, assigning the lowest-ranked machine to maintain a master clock on behalf of the others. The second stack synchronizes the speeds and offsets with respect to real time of the logical timestamp objects. To keep these values consistent, it is necessary that they be updated in the same order. Therefore, this stack is similar to the previous one, but includes a Horus protocol block, which places a total order on multicast messages delivered within the group.[21] The third stack tracks the list of servers and clients. Using a deterministic rule based on the process ranking maintained by the virtual synchrony layer, one server is selected to multicast the video, and one server, usually the same, is picked to multicast the audio. This setup is shown in Figure 21.4b.

To disseminate the multimedia data, we used two identical stacks—one for audio and one for video. The key component in these is a protocol block, which implements a multimedia generalization of the cyclic UDP protocol. The algorithm is similar to FRAG, but it will reassemble messages arriving out of order and drop messages with missing fragments.

One might expect that a huge amount of recoding would have been required to accomplish these changes. However, all of the necessary work was completed using 42 lines of TCL code. An additional 160 lines of C code support the CMT frame buffers in Horus. Two new Horus layers were needed, but were developed by adapting existing layers; they consist of 1,800 lines of C code and 300 lines of TCL code, respectively (ignoring the comments and lines common to all layers). Moreover, performance of the resulting system was quite good; the primary bottleneck at the time was associated with the Internet itself, not the protocols, and a substantial user community emerged over a period of a few years before the developers moved on to other challenges and the software fell into disrepair. Thus, with relatively little effort and little code, a complex application written with no expectation that process group computing might later be valuable was modified to exploit Horus functionality.

21.5 Using Electra to Harden CORBA Applications

The introduction of process groups into CMT required sophistication with Horus and its intercept proxies. Many potential users would lack the sophistication and knowledge of Horus required to do this; hence, we recognized a need for a way to introduce Horus functionality in a more transparent way. This goal evokes an image of plug-and-play robustness; it leads one to think in terms of an object-oriented approach to group computing.

Early in this book, we looked at CORBA, noting that object-oriented distributed applications that comply with the CORBA ORB specification and support the IOP protocol can invoke one another's methods with relative ease. This work resulted in a CORBA-compliant interface to Horus, which we call Electra (see Maffeis). Electra can be used without Horus, and vice versa, but the combination represents a more complete system. This work preceeded the development of the CORBA Fault Tolerance architecture, and differs from what the CORBA community ultimated opted to do in many details—the Eternal ORB is a much more "faithful" implementation of the CORBA specification. However, Electra

---

[21] This protocol differs from the *Total* protocol in the Trans/Total (see Moser et al. [1996]) project in that the Horus protocol only rotates the token among the current set of senders, while the Trans/Total protocol rotates the token among all members.

is interesting in part because it has more flexibility than the CORBA specification allows, and we'll present it here in that spirit. (Readers who might consider working with CORBA and using Eternal should keep in mind that the standard is quite a bit more restrictive, and that this code long ago ceased to be supported)

In Electra, applications are provided with ways to build Horus process groups and to directly exploit the virtual synchrony model. Moreover, Electra objects can be aggregated to form object groups, and object references can be bound to both singleton objects and object groups. An implication of the interoperability of CORBA implementations is that Electra object groups can be invoked from *any* CORBA-compliant distributed application, regardless of the CORBA platform on which it is running, without special provisions for group communication. This means that a service can be made fault tolerant without changing its clients.

When a method invocation occurs within Electra, object-group references are detected and transformed into multicasts to the member objects (see Figure 21.5). Requests can be issued either in transparent mode, where only the first arriving member reply is returned to the client application, or in non-transparent mode, permitting the client to access the full set of responses from individual group members. The transparent mode is used by clients to communicate with replicated CORBA objects, while the nontransparent mode is employed

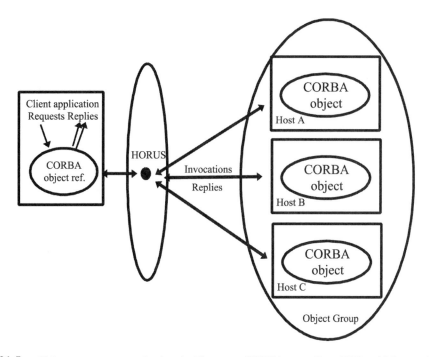

Figure 21.5. Object-group communication in Electra, a CORBA-compliant ORB, which uses Horus to implement group multicast. The invocation method can be changed depending on the intended use. Orbix+Isis and the COOL-ORB are examples of commercial products that support object groups.

with object groups whose members perform different tasks. Clients submit a request either in a synchronous, asynchronous, or deferred-synchronous way.

The integration of Horus into Electra shows that group programming can be provided in a natural, transparent way with popular programming methodologies. The resulting technology permits the user to plug in group communication tools anywhere that a CORBA application has a suitable interface. To the degree that process group computing interfaces and abstractions represent an impediment to their use in commercial software, technologies such as Electra suggest a possible middle ground, in which fault tolerance, security, and other group-based mechanisms can be introduced late in the design cycle of a sophisticated distributed application.

21.6 Basic Performance of Horus

A major concern of the Horus architecture is the overhead of layering. Layering was the key to most of the applications described above, and the essence of our response to the Cheriton and Skeen criticism. To paraphrase them, the criticism is that no matter what standard properties a system elects to offer, individual developers may object to some of those properties (and hence will pay an undesired cost) while needing others (and hence need an end-to-end mechanism of their own, anyhow). Horus responds by offering a framework for building the software implementing properties (layers) and allowing the user to mix and match so that the application runs over precisely the protocol stack it prefers. Most developers should agree that in doing so, Horus offers a good response to the criticism. But this flexibility would be far less interesting if it brings excessive costs.

This section presents the overall performance of Horus on a system of Sun SPARC10 workstations running SunOS 4.1.3, communicating through a loaded Ethernet. We used two network transport protocols: normal UDP and UDP with the Deering IP multicast extensions (see Deering [1988]) (shown as "Deering"). These performance figures are fairly old, and were one to re-run the same experiments today, hardware advances would certainly result in better raw numbers—a Sparc 10 was a 100MIP processor, and the Ethernet on which Horus was tested ran at 10Mbits/second (the ATM was about ten times faster). Thus, a ten-fold performance increase should be possible today. Yet these figures also represent a kind of "speed record," in the sense that Horus was (and perhaps still is) the fastest of the group communication systems. Subsequent to the development of this technology, the academic research community moved on to other topics, and there has been little attention to multicast performance over the ensuing five years—perhaps because there aren't any obvious ways to take dramatic steps beyond the performance levels achieved in the work described below.

To highlight some of the performance numbers: Horus achieves a one-way latency of 1.2 ms over an unordered virtual synchrony stack (over ATM, this dropped to 0.7 ms) and, using a totally ordered layer over the same stack, 7,500 one-byte messages per second. Given an application that can accept lists of messages in a single receive operation, we can drive up the total number of messages per second to over 75,000 using the FC flow-control layer, which buffers heavily using the message list capabilities of Horus (see Freidman and van Renesse [July 1995]). Horus easily reached the Ethernet 1,007 KB/sec maximum bandwidth with a message size smaller than 1 KB.

The performance test program has each member do exactly the same thing: Send k messages and wait for $k * (n - 1)$ messages of size s, where s is the number of members. This way we simulate an application that imposes a high load on the system while occasionally synchronizing on intermediate results.

Figure 21.6 depicts the one-way communication latency of one-byte Horus messages. As can be seen, hardware multicast is a big win, especially when the message size goes up. In this figure, we compare fbcast to abcast. For small messages we get a FIFO one-way latency of about 1.5 ms and a totally ordered one-way latency of about 6.7 ms. A problem with the totally ordered layer is that it can be inefficient when senders send single messages at random, and with a high degree of concurrent sending by different group members. With just one sender, the one-way latency drops to 1.6 ms. Of course, as noted earlier, computers are much faster than when these experiments were performed in 1996; today, a ten-fold or better speedup would be likely, simply because the hardware has become faster.

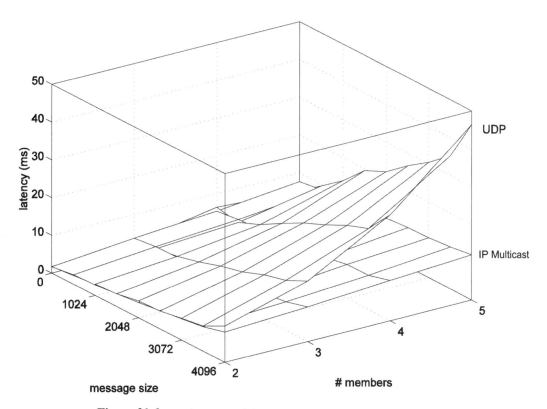

Figure 21.6. Performance of the Horus system, with/without IP multicast

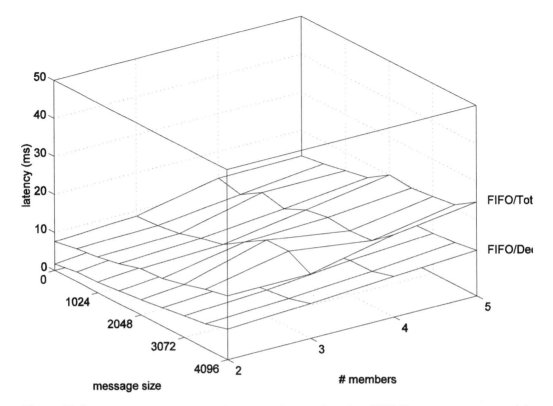

Figure 21.6. The upper graph compares the one-way latency of one-byte FIFO Horus messages over straight UDP and IP multicast. The lower one compares the performance of abcast and fbcast in Horus, both over IP multicast. Technology has advanced since this experiment was run; on modern machines a ten-fold (or more) speedup would be expected.

Figure 21.7 shows the number of one-byte messages per second that can be achieved for three cases. For normal UDP and Deering UDP the throughput is fairly constant. For totally ordered communication we see that the throughput becomes better if we send more messages per round (because of increased concurrency). Perhaps surprisingly, the throughput also becomes better as the number of members in the group goes up. The reason for this is threefold. First, with more members there are more senders. Second, with more members it takes longer to order messages, and thus more messages can be packed together and sent out in single network packets. Third, the ordering protocol allows only one sender on the network at a time, thus introducing flow control and reducing collisions.

In the text, we noted several times that Horus has been "clocked" at 80,000 small multicasts per second in a four-process group. Here we can see how that figure came about. With each packet carrying a separate multicast, Horus is already running at approximately 1,000 multicasts per second. But when Horus has an opportunity to pack multiple small messages into a single packet, it will do so. A stream of asynchronous multicasts can easily

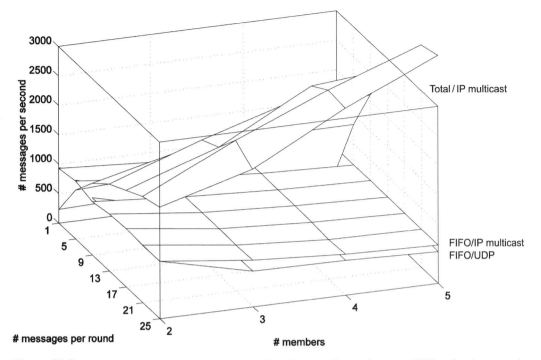

Figure 21.7. This graph depicts the message throughput for virtually synchronous, FIFO-ordered communication (fbcast) over normal UDP and IP multicast, as well as for totally ordered communication (abcast) over IP multicast. The number of application messages packed into each network message is shown on the "z" axis. If very small multicasts are sent in an asynchronous stream, Horus can pack as many as 250 multicasts into each message and hence can achieve throughputs as much as ten times that seen in the single message case. Today one might anticipate throughputs approaching 1,000,000 small, asynchronous messages per second.

achieve a packing ratio of 30 or 40 multicasts per packet, and when conditions are optimal (very small messages, sent with almost no delay at all) the ratio can reach 250 to one. Again, the numbers are bit old, and merely by moving to modern hardware we could easily obtain a ten-fold speedup. Thus, at least for small asynchronous messages, we may be entering an era in which data rates of 1,000,000 messages per second will be achievable. It isn't obvious what applications can be expected to generate small messages at these data rates, but the capability is there.

In contrast, protocols seeking "safe" (dynamically uniform) guarantees will not benefit as much from the technology advances of the past decade, which have yielded much higher bandwidths and processor speed, but not reduced latency all that much. These protocols are limited by worst-case latency and worst-case processing delay, and while their first phase can exploit IP multicast, the acknowledgement phase will still be a many-to-one protocol using point-to-point messages. Thus while our "hundred events a second" estimate for such protocols may be conservative on modern hardware, it isn't excessively so.

21.7 Masking the Overhead of Protocol Layering

Although layering of protocols can be advocated as a way of dealing with the complexity of computer communication, it is also criticized for its performance overhead. Work by van Renesse yielded considerable insight regarding best way to mask the overhead of layering in Horus. The fundamental idea is very similar to client caching in a file system. With these new techniques, he achieves an order of magnitude improvement in end-to-end message latency in the Horus communication framework, compared to the best latency possible using Horus without these optimizations. Over an ATM network, the approach permits applications to send and deliver messages with varied properties in about $85\mu s$, using a protocol stack written in ML, an interpreted functional language. In contrast, the performance figures given in the previous section were for a version of Horus coded in C—carefully optimized by hand but without use of the protocol accelerator.[22]

Having presented this material in seminars, the author has noticed that the systems community seems to respond to the very mention of the ML language with skepticism, and it is perhaps appropriate to comment on this before continuing. First, the reader should keep in mind that a technology such as Horus is simply a tool used to harden a system. It makes little difference whether such a tool is internally coded in C, assembly language, LISP, or ML if it works well for the desired purpose. The decision to work with a version of Horus coded in ML is not one that would impact the *use* of Horus in applications that work with the technology through wrappers or toolkit interfaces. However, as we will see here, it does bring some important benefits to Horus itself, notably the potential for us to harden the system using formal software analysis tools. Moreover, although ML is often viewed as obscure and of academic interest only, the version of ML used in our work on Horus is not really so different from LISP or C++ once one becomes accustomed to the syntax. Finally, as we will see here, the performance of Horus coded in ML is actually better than that of Horus coded in C, at least for certain patterns of communication. Thus, we would hope that the reader will recognize that the work reported here is in fact very practical.

As we saw in earlier chapters, modern network technology allows for very low latency communication—for example, the U-Net (see von Eicken et al. [1995]) interface to ATM achieves $75\mu s$ round-trip communication as long as the message is 40 bytes or smaller. Technologies such as Infiniband, switched fiber-optic Ethernet, and other ultra-high speed communication devices have pushed well beyond these limits. On the other hand, focusing just on ATM, if a message is larger, it will not fit in a single ATM cell, significantly increasing the latency. This points to two basic concerns: first, that if you really want to squeeze overhead to a minimum, systems such as Horus need to be designed to take full advantage of the potential performance of the communication technology on which they run, and, second, that to do so, it may be important to use small headers and introduce minimal processing overhead. Perhaps these observations are less important in a world of faster and faster processors and communications devices. Yet for those concerned with performance,

---

[22]This version of Horus ultimately evolved into the Ensemble system, but the two are not identical. Ensemble was a complete rewrite by Mark Hayden and Ohad Rodeh.

dismissing the issue makes little sense: new generations of technology should open the door to new applications, not simply serve to paper over the costs and overheads of inefficient software!

Unfortunately, these properties are not typical of the protocol layers needed to implement virtual synchrony. Many of these protocols are complex, and layering introduces additional overhead of its own. One source of overhead is interfacing: crossing a layer costs some CPU cycles. The other is header overhead. Each layer uses its own header, which is prepended to every message and usually padded so that each header is aligned on a four- or eight-byte boundary. Combining this with a trend to very large addresses (of which at least two per message are needed), it is impossible to have the total amount of header space be less than 40 bytes.

The Horus Protocol Accelerator (Horus PA) eliminates these overheads almost entirely and offers the potential of one to three orders of magnitude of latency improvement over the protocol implementations described in the previous subsection—for example, we looked at the impact of the Horus PA on an ML (see Milner et al.) implementation of a protocol stack with five layers. The ML code is interpreted (Ensemble, its successor, is compiled) and is therefore relatively slow compared to compiled C code. Nevertheless, between two SunOS user processes on two SPARC20s connected by a 155 MB/sec ATM network, the Horus PA permits these layers to achieve a roundtrip latency of $175\mu s$, down from about 1.5 ms in the original Horus system (written in C).

The Horus PA achieves its results using three techniques. First, message header fields that never change are only sent once. Second, the rest of the header information is carefully packed, ignoring layer boundaries, typically leading to headers that are much smaller than 40 bytes and thus leaving room to fit a small message within a single U-Net packet. Third, a semiautomatic transformation is done on the send and delivery operations, splitting them into two parts: one that updates or checks the header but not the protocol state, and the other vice versa. The first part is then executed by a special packet filter (both in the send and the delivery path) to circumvent the actual protocol layers whenever possible. The second part is executed, as much as possible, when the application is idle or blocked.

21.7.1 Reducing Header Overhead

In traditional layered protocol systems, each protocol layer designs its own header data structure. The headers are concatenated and prepended to each user message. For convenience, each header is aligned to a four- or eight-byte boundary to allow easy access. In systems such as the x-Kernel or Horus, where many simple protocols may be stacked on top of each other, this may lead to extensive padding overhead.

Some fields in the headers, such as the source and destination addresses, never change from message to message. Yet, instead of agreeing on these values, they are frequently included in every message and used as the identifier of the connection to the peer. Since addresses tend to be large (and they are getting larger to deal with the rapid growth the Internet), this results in significant use of space for what are essentially constants of the connection. Moreover, notice that the connection itself may already be identifiable from other information. On an ATM network, connections are named by a small four-byte VPI/VCI pair, and every packet carries this information. Thus, constants such as sender and destination addresses are implied by the connection identifier and including them in the header is superfluous.

The Horus PA exploits these observations to reduce header sizes to a bare minimum. The approach starts by dividing header fields into four *classes*:

- *Connection identification*: Fields that never change during the period of a connection, such as sender and destination.
- *Protocol-specific information*: Fields that are important for the correct delivery of the particular message frame. Examples are the sequence number of a message, or the message type (Horus messages have types, such as "data," "ack," or "nack"). These fields must be deterministically implied by the protocol state—not on the message contents or the time at which it was sent.
- *Message-specific information*: Fields that need to accompany the message, such as the message length and checksum or a timestamp. Typically, such information depends only on the message—not on the protocol state.
- *Gossip*: Fields that technically do not need to accompany the message but are included for efficiency.

Each layer is expected to declare the header fields that it will use during initialization, and it subsequently accesses fields using a collection of highly optimized functions implemented by the Horus PA. These functions extract values directly from headers, if they are present, or otherwise compute the appropriate field value and return that instead. This permits the Horus PA to precompute header templates that have optimized layouts, with a minimum of wasted space.

Horus includes the protocol-specific and message-specific information in every message. Currently, although not technically necessary, gossip information is also included, since it is usually small. However, since the connection identification fields never change, they are only included occasionally, since they tend to be large.

A 64-bit miniheader is placed on each message to indicate which headers it actually includes. Two bits of this are used to indicate whether or not the connection identification is present in the message and to destinate the byte ordering for bytes in the message. The remaining 62 bits are a *connection cookie*, which is a magic number established in the connection identification header, selected randomly, to identify the connection.

The idea is that the first message sent over a connection will be a connection identifier, specifying the cookie to use and providing an initial copy of the connection identification fields. Subsequent messages need only contain the identification field if it has changed. Since the connection identification fields tend to include very large identifiers, this mechanism reduces the amount of header space in the normal case significantly—for example, in the version of Horus that van Renesse used in his tests, the connection identification typically occupies about 76 bytes. It is interesting to note that a similar style of header compression has become common in adapting the IP protocol stack for communication over slow wireless links (see RFC 2507 for details).

21.7.2 Eliminating Layered Protocol Processing Overhead

In most protocol implementations, layered or not, a great deal of processing must be done between the application's send operation and the time that the message is actually sent out onto the network. The same is true between the arrival of a message and the delivery to the application. The Horus PA reduces the length of the critical path by updating the protocol state only after a message has been sent or delivered and by precomputing any statically predictable protocol-specific header fields, so that the necessary values will be known *before* the application generates the next message (Figure 21.8). These methods work because the protocol-specific information for most messages can be predicted (calculated) before the message is sent or delivered. (Recall that, as noted above, such information must not depend on the message contents or the time on which it was sent.) Each connection maintains a predicted protocol-specific header for the next send operation and another for the next delivery (much like a read-ahead strategy in a file system). For sending, the gossip information can be predicted as well, since this does not depend on the message contents. The idea is a bit like that of prefetching in a file system.

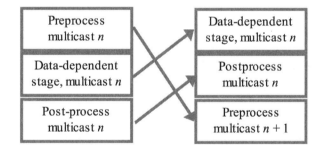

Figure 21.8. Restructuring a protocol layer to reduce the critical path. By moving data-dependent code to the front, delays for sending the next message are minimized. Post-processing of the current multicast and preprocessing of the next multicast (all computation that can be done before seeing the actual contents of the message) are shifted to occur after the current multicast has been sent and hence concurrently with application-level computing.

Thus, when a message is actually sent, only the message-specific header will need to be generated. This is done using a *packet filter* (see Mogul et al.), which is constructed at the time of layer initialization. Packet filters are programmed using a simple programming language (a dialect of ML), and they operate by extracting information from the message information needed to form the message-specific header. A filter can also hand-off a message to the associated layer for special handling—for example, if a message fails to satisfy some assumption that was used in predicting the protocol-specific header. In the usual case, the message-specific header will be computed, other headers are prepended from the precomputed versions, and the message transmitted with no additional delay. Because the header fields have fixed and precomputed sizes, a header template can be filled in with no copying, and scatter-send/scatter-gather hardware used to transmit the header and message as a single packet without copying them first to a single place. This reduces the computational cost of sending or delivering a message to a bare minimum, although it leaves some background costs in the form of prediction code, which must be executed before the next message is sent or delivered

21.7.3 Message Packing

The Horus PA as described so far will reduce the latency of individual messages significantly, but only if they are spaced out far enough to allow time for postprocessing. If not, messages will have to wait until the postprocessing of every previous message completes (somewhat like a process that reads file system records faster than they can be prefetched). To reduce this overhead, the Horus PA uses *message packing* (see Freidman and van Renesse [July 1995]) to deal with backlogs. The idea is a very simple one. After the postprocessing of a send operation completes, the PA checks to see if there are messages waiting. If there are more than one, the PA will pack these messages together into a single message. The single message is now processed in the usual way, which takes only one preprocessing and postprocessing phase. When the packed message is ready for delivery, it is unpacked and the messages are individually delivered to the application.

Returning to our file system analogy, the approach is similar to one in which the application could indicate that it plans to read three 1 KB data blocks. Rather than fetching them one by one, the file system can now fetch them all at the same time. Doing so amortizes the overhead associated with fetching the blocks, permitting better utilization of network bandwidth.

21.7.4 Performance of Horus with the Protocol Accelerator

The Horus PA dramatically improved the performance of the system over the base figures described earlier (which were themselves comparable to the best performance figures cited for other systems). With the accelerator, one-way latencies dropped to as little as $85\mu s$ (compared to $35\mu s$ for the U-Net implementation over which the accelerator was tested). As many as 85,000 one-byte messages could be sent and delivered per second over a protocol stack of five layers implementing the virtual synchrony model within a group of two members. For RPC-style interactions, 2,600 round-trips per second were achieved. These latency figures, however, represent a best-case scenario in which the frequency of messages was low enough to permit the predictive mechanisms to operate; when they become overloaded, latency increases to about $425\mu s$ for the same test pattern. This points to a strong dependency of the method on the speed of the code used to implement layers.

The Horus PA does suffer from some limitations. Message fragmentation and reassembly is not supported by the PA—hence, the preprocessing of large messages must be handled explicitly by the protocol stack. Some technical complications result from this design decision, but it reduces the complexity of the PA and improves the maximum performance achievable using it. A second limitation is that the PA must be used by all parties to a communication stack. However, this is not an unreasonable restriction, since Horus has the same sort of limitation with regard to the stacks themselves (all members of a group must use identical or at least compatible protocol stacks).

21.8 Scalability

Up to the present, this book has largely overlooked issues associated with protocol scalability. Although a serious treatment of scalability in the general sense might require a whole book in itself, the purpose of this section is to set out some general remarks on the subject, as we have approached it in the Horus project. It is perhaps worthwhile to comment that, overall, surprisingly little is known about scaling reliable distributed systems.

For example, we commented earlier that Horus doesn't scale well if a system uses large numbers of overlapping process groups (e.g., a typical process might join ten or even a hundred groups, and the system as a whole might include tens of thousands of them). The Isis Toolkit was an even worse choice for such configurations; indeed, both systems offer a mechanism in which a large group can be presented to users as a collection of smaller ones (multicasts are sent in the large group and then filtered prior to delivery—a simple hack that works, but imposes high overhead). The problem with this approach, needless to say, is that group overlap won't always yield a simple containment pattern, and the overhead of receiving and discarding unwanted multicasts could become prohibitive.

It isn't just Horus and Isis that work this way. Ensemble and Spread also address the multiple group scalability problem in the same manner. Thus there are dimensions in which Isis, Horus, Ensemble and Spread don't scale—not because the problem can't be solved, but because we simply haven't explored the dimension carefully yet!

But what of scalability in a single group? If one looks at the scalability of Horus protocols, as we did earlier in presenting some basic Horus performance figures, it is clear that Horus performs well for groups with small numbers of members and for moderately large groups when IP multicast is available as a hardware tool to reduce the cost of moving large volumes of data to large numbers of destinations. Yet although these graphs are correct, they may be misleading. In fact, as systems like Horus are scaled to larger and larger numbers of participating processes, they experience steadily growing overheads in the form of acknowledgements and negative acknowledgements from the recipient processes to the senders. A consequence is that if these systems are used with very large numbers of participating processes, the backflow associated with these types of messages and with flow control becomes a serious problem.

A simple thought experiment suffices to illustrate that there are probably fundamental limits on reliability in very large networks. Suppose that a communication network is extremely reliable, but that the processes using it are designed to distrust that network and to assume that it may actually malfunction by losing messages. Moreover, assume that these processes are in fact closely rate-matched (the consumers of data keep up with the producers), but again that the system is designed to deal with individual processes that lag far behind. Now, were it not for the backflow of messages to the senders, this hypothetical system might perform very well near the limits of the hardware. It could potentially be scaled just by adding new recipient processes and, with no changes at all, continue to provide a high level of reliability.

However, the backflow messages will substantially impact this simple and rosy scenario. They represent a source of overhead, and, in the case of flow-control messages, if they are not received, the sender may be forced to stop and wait for them. Now, the performance of the sender side is coupled to the timely and reliable reception of backflow messages, and, as we scale the number of recipients connected to the system, we can anticipate a traffic jam phenomenon at the sender's interface (protocol designers call this an acknowledgement "implosion"), which will cause traffic to get increasingly bursty and performance to drop. In effect, the attempt to protect against the mere risk of data loss or flow-control mismatches is likely to slash the maximum achievable performance of the system. Now, obtaining a stable delivery of data near the limits of our technology will become a tremendously difficult juggling problem, in which the protocol developer must trade the transmission of backflow messages against their performance impact.

Graduate students Guerney Hunt and Michael Kalantar have studied aspects of this problem in their Ph.D. dissertations at Cornell University—both using special-purpose experimental tools (i.e., neither actually experimented on Horus or a similar system; Kalantar, in fact, worked mostly with a simulator). Hunt's work was on flow control in very large scale system. He concluded that most forms of backflow were unworkable on a large scale, and he ultimately proposed a rate-based flow-control scheme in which the sender limits the transmission rate for data to match what the receivers can accomodate (see Hunt). Kalantar looked at the impact of multicast ordering on latency, asking how frequently an ordering property such as causal or total ordering would significantly impact the latency of message delivery (see Kalantar). He found that although ordering had a fairly small impact on latency, there were other, much more important, phenomena that represented serious potential concerns.

In particular, Kalantar discovered that as he scaled the size of his simulation, message latencies tended to become unstable and bursty. He hypothesized that in large-scale protocols, the domain of stable performance becomes smaller and smaller. In such situations, a slight perturbation of the overall system—for example, because of a lost message—could cause much of the remainder of the system to block due to reliability or ordering constraints. Now, the system would shift into what is sometimes called a *convoy* behavior, in which long message backlogs build up and are never really eliminated; they may shift from place to place, but stable, smooth delivery is generally not restored. In effect, a bursty scheduling behavior represents a more stable configuration of the overall system than one in which message delivery is extremely regular and smooth, at least if the number of recipients is large and the presented load is a substantial percentage of the maximum achievable (so that there is little slack bandwidth with which the system can catch up after an overload develops).

Hunt and Kalantar's observations are not really surprising ones. It makes sense that it should be easy to provide reliability or ordering when far from the saturation point of the hardware and much harder to do so as the communication or processor speed limits are approached.

Over many years of working with Isis and Horus, the author has gained considerable experience with these sorts of scaling and flow-control problems. Realistically, the conclusion can only be called a mixed one. On the positive side, it seems that one can fairly easily build a reliable system if the communication load is not expected to exceed, say, 20 percent of the capacity of the hardware. With a little luck, one can even push this to as high as perhaps 40 percent of the hardware. However, as the load presented to the system rises beyond this threshold, or if the number of destinations for a typical message becomes very large (hundreds), it becomes increasingly difficult to guarantee reliability and flow control. The good news is that in most settings, a shared switched Ethernet is so much faster than any computer's interface that these properties are easily achievable. The bad news, however, is that even in such configurations one observers infrequent conditions under which a few machines essentially jam the medium and disrupt performance to such a degree that only the epidemic protocols we'll discuss in Chapter 21 have any hope of overcoming the problem.

A fundamental tradeoff seems to be present: One can send data and hope that these data will arrive, and, by doing so, one may be able to operate quite reliably near the limits of the hardware. But, of course, if a process falls behind, it may lose large numbers of messages before it recovers, and no mechanism is provided to let it recover these messages from any form of backup storage. On the other hand, one can operate in a less demanding performance range and in this case provide reliability, ordering, and performance guarantees. In between the two, however, lies a domain that is extremely difficult in an engineering sense and often requires a very high level of software complexity, which will necessarily reduce reliability. Moreover, one can raise serious questions about the stability of message-passing systems that operate in this intermediate domain, where the load presented is near the limits of what can be accomplished. The typical experience with such systems is that they perform well, most of the time, but that once something fails, the system falls so far behind that it can never again catch up—in effect, any perturbation can shift such a system into the domain of overloads and hopeless backlogs.

21.9 Performance and Scalability of the Spread Toolkit

The Spread toolkit is a group communication system available from www.spread.org. Spread provides a range of reliability, ordering and stability guarantees for message delivery. Spread supports a rich fault model that includes process crashes and recoveries and network partitions and merges under the extended virtual synchrony semantics. The standard virtual synchrony semantics are also supported.

Spread is highly configurable, allowing the user to tailor it to their needs. Spread can be configured to use a single daemon in the network or to use one daemon in every computer running group communication applications. Figure 21.9 illustrates a case where each

each computer executes one Spread daemon. As can be seen in the figure, all the physical communication is handled by the daemon. The Spread daemons keep track of the computers' heavyweight membership. Each daemon keeps track of processes residing on its machine and participating in group communication. This information is shared between the daemons, creating the lightweight process group membership. The benefits of this client-daemon architecture are significant:

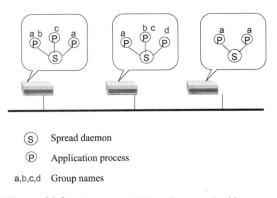

(S) Spread daemon

(P) Application process

a,b,c,d Group names

Figure 21.9. The Spread Client-Daemon Architecture.

- The membership algorithm is invoked only if there is a change in the daemons' membership. Otherwise, when a process joins or leaves a group, the Spread daemon sends a notification message to the other daemons. When this message is ordered, the daemons deliver a membership notification containing the new group membership to the members of the group.
- Order is maintained at the daemons' level and not on a group basis. Therefore, for multi-group systems, message ordering is more efficient in terms of latency and excessive messages. Moreover, message ordering across groups is trivial since only one global order at the daemons' level is maintained.
- Implementing open groups, where processes that are not members of a group can multicast messages to the group is easily supported.
- Flow control is maintained at the daemons' level rather than at the level of the individual process group. This leads to better overall performance in multi-group systems.

Several performance and scalability evaluations of the Spread toolkit are included below. The tests were conducted by the developers of the system (Yair Amir and his team) on 20 Pentium III 850Mhz Linux computers connected by a 100Mbps Fast Ethernet network. Figure 21.10 presents the total order throughput achieved by Spread as a function of the size of the network (number

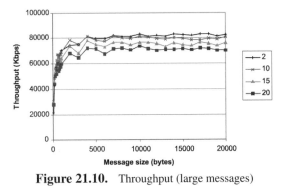

Figure 21.10. Throughput (large messages)

of daemons, each running on a separate computer) and the size of the multicast messages. Note that in all of these graphs, the curves "stack" quite nicely and the key is ordered to correspond to the curves: the top-most curve matches the top-most key entry, etc. In this experiment, half of the participating daemons serve a single local process each that multicasts to a specific group. Each of the other daemons serves a single local process that is a member of that group. For configurations ranging from 2 to 20 computers and message size

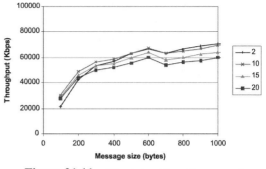

Figure 21.11. Throughput (small messages)

above 1Kbytes a throughput of 60-80Mbits is achieved with a slight degradation as the number of participating computers is increased. Figure 21.11 presents the same experiment focusing on small messages. It is interesting to note the performance dip for messages around 700 Bytes that happens when messages can no longer be packed into one network packet. Similar but less pronounced fragmentation effects can also be noticed in Figure 21.11 for larger message sizes.

In a different experiment, Spread was run on 20 computers. On each computer a receiving application joins a certain number of groups, from 1 to 10,000. All the receiving applications on the different computers join the same set of groups. On one of the computers, a test application sends messages at a constant rate of 500 Kbps, each message to a different group joined by the receiv-

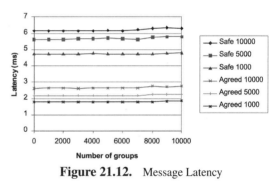

Figure 21.12. Message Latency

ing applications. The one-way latency of each message received is recorded by the receiving applications. The clocks of the computers are accurately synchronized through a separate process similar to NTP. Figure 21.12 presents the message latency as a function of the number of groups joined by the receiving applications, the size of the multicast messages, and the type of the service (Agreed delivery for total order, or Safe delivery for stability). The latency of Agreed delivery (total order) ranges between 1.7 ms to 2.8 ms depending on the size of the message (1000, 5000 and 10000 bytes). The latency for Safe delivery (stability) ranges between 4.7 ms to 6.4 ms. The higher latency incurred by larger messages is mostly attributed to the time it takes to send them on a 100 Mbits network. The figure shows that the number of groups in the system does not affect the message latency much. This is achieved thanks to a skip list data structure that provides $\log(n)$ access to the lightweight group structures in Spread.

In the last experiment, Spread runs on 20 computers. Each computer runs between 1 and 50 instances of a test application, each joining the same group. Therefore, in the group communication system as a whole there are between 20 to 1000 participating processes. A separate application joins and leaves the same group 100 times and the latency of each join and leave operation is measured. Figure 21.13 presents the average latency of the join and leave operations as a function of the group size. This experiment shows that joining a group that has 1000

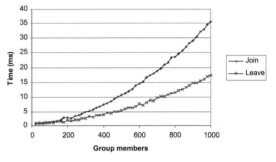

Figure 21.13. Lightweight Membership Latency

members takes less than 40 ms (including membership notifications to all 1000 members). As the number of members in the group increases, the size of the membership notification increases linearly (each member contributes about 32 bytes to the size of the notification), and the number of notifications per daemon also increases linearly. This explains the quadratic shape of the graph. The scalability with the number of groups and number of group participants in the system is attributed to the client-daemon architecture of Spread.

Note: In all of the above figures, the ordering of items in the key matches the ordering of the curves. For example, in Figure 21.13 the top curve corresponds to "Join" and the one below it to "Leave".

21.10 Related Reading

Chapter 27 includes a review of related research activities, which we will not duplicate here.

On the Horus system: (see Birman and van Renesse [1996], Friedman and van Renesse [July 1995], van Renesse et al.). Rodriguez [2000] tackled the overlapping groups problem in Horus, but Glade [1993] was probably the first to propose the "lightweight" group mechanism described here.

On Horus used in a real-time telephone switching application: (see Friedman and Birman).

On virtual fault tolerance: (see Bressoud and Schneider).

On layered protocols: (see Abbott and Peterson, Braun and Diot, Clark and Tennenhouse, Karamcheti and Chien, Kay and Pasquale).

On event counters: (see Reed and Kanodia).

On the Continuous Media Toolkit: (see Rowe and Smith).

On U-Net: (see von Eicken et al. [1995]).

PART V

Related Technologies

In this fifth and final part of the book, we review additional technologies relevant to our broad reliability theme: security mechanisms, transactions, and real-time systems. This part of the book also surveys some of the research underway in academic and commercial laboratories world-wide.

There is a tremendous degree of interest in peer-to-peer computing today, and we treat the topic in Chapter 24. However, our review is tempered by some skepticism about the field. Much of the work being done related to file sharing of the type done in Gnutella and Napster, an application that violates intellectual property laws and hence is illegal. On the other hand, there are some exciting non-filesharing applications for these kinds of protocols; these are of interest because peer-to-peer technologies permit a degree of scalability never previously available and also offer reliability guarantees that can help the developer ensure that solutions will be stable even under stress and may actually be able to self-reorganize and self-repair ("regenerate") if a disruption occurs. Accordingly, our emphasis in the chapter will be on the power of peer-to-peer protocols in these kinds of unconventional settings.

With one eye on length, we'll draw the line at the network layer, although one can make a very strong argument that developers who seek to build secure, reliable applications over the current Internet will ultimately be frustrated by the experience. The author has been promoting a type of overlay network architecture recently, in which the Internet is more or less partitioned into multiple side-by-side networks, only one of which would actually run the Internet protocols. Other networks could run different routing and security protocols, dedicate resources for specific needs, and even implement different queuing policies in the router layer. The resulting "League of Supernets" (see Birman [2003], Birman

[2001] and Birman and Glade [1997]) might let us blast through the barriers imposed by the current Internet. Nonetheless, the current book needs to draw a line somewhere, and topics like network overlays and ad-hoc routing would simply make the treatment too long. Accordingly, despite the author's personal conviction that the future may hold some big surprises at the network level, the book won't pursue what would ultimately be very speculative digressions.

22

Security Options for Distributed Settings

22.1 Security Options for Distributed Settings

The use of distributed computing systems for storage of sensitive data and in commercial applications has created significant pressure to improve the security options available to software developers. Yet distributed system security has many possible interpretations, corresponding to very different forms of guarantees, and even the contemporary distributed systems that claim to be secure often suffer from basic security weaknesses. In Chapter 9, we pointed to some of these limitations. The current chapter looks at the available security technologies, the nature of their guarantees and their limitations and discusses some of the issues raised when we require that a security system also guarantee high availability.

The constraints of brevity make it difficult to do justice to security in a setting such as ours; the topic is deserving of entire textbooks in its own right. Yet it is also difficult to treat security as a problem orthogonal to reliability: if a system is designed to withstand failures, one must anticipate the possibility that those failures will be provoked by an attacker, or by a software bug or operator error that can seem like an attack from within the system. Similarly, while there is a long tradition of tackling security and ignoring reliability, it makes little sense to talk about securing a system if reliability is not addressed. Is a system "secure" if the attacker can shut it down by crashing a component? Accordingly, the text adopts a middle ground: we've treated reliability in detail, and now offer a very skimpy review of security, not so much with the intent that a reader could learn the area from this single chapter, but just to expose the reader to some of the major options and issues.

The technologies we consider here span a range of approaches. At the low end of the spectrum are firewall technologies (often with an integrated network address translation capability, which will block access to machines behind the wall unless a mapping is established first) and other *perimeter defense mechanisms*, which operate by restricting access or communication across specified system boundaries. These technologies are extremely popular and clearly necessary, but very limited in their capabilities. Once an intruder has found a way to work around the firewall or to log into the system, the protection benefit is lost. For example, a common kind of computer virus operates by relaying messages received on a non-traditional path into the local area network behind a firewall. Once a machine becomes infected, such a virus permits intruders to tunnel through the firewall, opening the door to unrestricted access to data within the local area network and permitting the intruder to work on breaking into machines on that network. Worse still, machines behind a firewall are sometimes poorly protected; presumably, the administrators reason that since the firewall deals with security issues, within the firewalled environment there is no need to fuss over it!

Internal to a distributed system one typically finds *access control mechanisms*, which are often based on user and group IDs employed to limit access to shared resources such as file systems. When these are used in stateless settings, serious problems occur, and we'll touch upon several of them here. Access control mechanisms rarely extend to communication, and this is perhaps their most serious security exposure. In fact, many communication systems are open to attack by a clever intruder able to guess what port numbers will be used by the protocols within the system: Secrecy of port numbers is a common security dependency in modern distributed software. Security by secrecy is always a poor idea: far preferable are schemes that can be openly described, and yet retain their security because the mechanism is simply very difficult to break. As we will see, Unix and Linux systems are particularly vulnerable in this regard because of their continued use of a stateless file system technology, NFS.

Stateful protection mechanisms operate by maintaining strong concepts of session and channel state and authenticating use at the time that communication sessions are established. These schemes adopt the approach that after a user has been validated, the difficulty of breaking into the user's session will represent an obstacle to intrusion. Microsoft's Windows systems are an example of an architecture based on a form of stateful protection. (As often happens, Windows remains vulnerable in other ways, even if the Windows file system is relatively more secure than NFS).

Authentication-based security systems employ some scheme to authenticate the user running each application; the method may be highly reliable or less so, depending on the setting (see Denning, Needham and Schroeder). Individual communication sessions are protected using a key, which is negotiated using a trusted agent. Messages may be encrypted or signed in this key, resulting in very strong security guarantees. However, the costs of the overall approach can also be high, because of the intrinsically high costs of data encryption and signature schemes. Moreover, such methods may involve nontrivial modifications of the application programs being used, and they may be unsuitable for embedded settings in which no user would be available to periodically enter passwords or other authentication data. The best-known system of this sort is Kerberos, developed by MIT's Project Athena, and our review will focus on the approaches used in that system (see Schiller, Steiner et al.). (See Figure 22.1.) Initially Kerberos was based on shared secrets (DES keys), but it evolved over time to exploit public keys where those were available.

Today, echoes of this second-generation Kerberos architecture can be seen in many settings: In the Internet's SSL security architecture, a system can use built-in keys to request

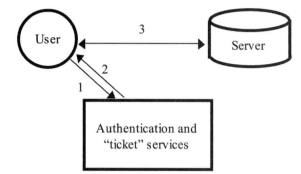

Figure 22.1. MIT's Project Athena developed the Kerberos security architecture. Kerberos or a similar mechanism is found at the core of many distributed system security technologies today. In this approach, an authentication service is used as a trusted intermediary to create secure channels, using DES or public key encryption for security. During step 1, the user employs a password or a secret key to sign a request that a connection be established to the remote server. The authentication server, which knows the user's password or key, constructs a session key, which is sent back in duplicated form—one copy by the user and one encrypted with the server's secret key (step 2). The session key is now used between the user and server (step 3), providing the server with trusted information about user identification. In practice, Kerberos avoids the need to keep user passwords around by trading the user's password for a session to the "ticket granting service," which then acts as the user's proxy in establishing connections to necessary servers, but the idea is unchanged. Kerberos session keys expire and must be periodically renewed—hence, even if an intruder gains physical access to the user's machine, the period during which illicit actions are possible is limited. Kerberos originally used DES throughout, but later was extended to exploit public-key cryptography.

help in establishing a secured connection to a target platform. The basic idea is that the pre-installed key allows the system to talk to a directory server and to establish a trust relationship with it, and the server then generates a certificate containing the information the client needs to create a secure channel. In a modern elaboration of the ideas seen in Kerberos, authentication servers can also vouch for one-another. Thus the user purchasing cheese from www.Fromages.com places trust in Microsoft, which vouches for Verisign's certificate directory, which has a representative at such and such a machine operated by Verisign, from which the user's computer obtained a certificate giving a public key for Fromages.com. We call this a "chain of trust." In the Internet, such chains usually are one-way structures: I can trust Fromages.com to a sufficient degree to convince me that it is safe to provide my credit card information (after all, I can always contest any false charges). Fromages.com, however, is not given any sort of strong information about my identity, although for practical reasons it may require that I provide a user-name and password. But the possession of a password isn't proof that the customer is me. Indeed, the company can't even trust data it generated previously and left on my computer: the cookies on my hard drive might have been moved there from some other machine! Even my IP address may change from time to time.

The broad picture is evolving, but it isn't clear that major changes are in store anytime soon. Intel is promoting an architecture in which keys can be sealed into the hardware and used to countersign messages or to unseal sensitive data, a step that would let a site produce an object that can only be accessed on a specified platform, and perhaps only by a specified application. Such an architecture might let a media company enforce copyrights on digital content, at least to a degree. And even with keys in the hardware, it isn't hard to imagine counterattacks whereby a determined user might steal protected information; short of securing the TV monitor and the speakers, there is always a boundary to the protected realm.

One of the challenges for any form of security system is that once the user's identity is known, a scheme is needed for determining the appropriate set of policies to enforce. Should "Ken Birman" be permitted to order raw-milk Brie for shipment into the United States? Should FBI agent "Bob Anthony" be permitted to review the hospital records for patient Jane Jones? Notice that many factors enter into answering such policy questions: policies associated with the user, with the parties to the transaction, and with their respective countries. In a microcosm, this points to one of the more difficult issues seen even in mundane business-to-business transactions: corporation A has one set of policies, corporation B a second set, and now users a and b wish to share information. Should this be allowed? How can we write down the rules and verify that the desired transaction is safe under both sets? Best known among the security policy languages is a logic-based language called SPKI/SDSI, which uses a kind of deductive reasoning to manage trust and permission relationships. However, for practical reasons, SPKI/SDSI is not nearly elaborate enough to solve the full range of problems seen in real settings. We'll touch on these issues below; they point to an exciting research opportunity.

Multilevel distributed system security architectures are based on a government security standard developed in the mid-1980s. The basic idea is to emulate the way that secrets are handled in the military and in other government settings. This security model is very strong, but it has proven to be difficult to implement and it requires extensive effort on the part of application developers. Perhaps for these reasons, the approach has not been widely successful. Moreover, the pressure to use off-the-shelf technologies made it difficult for the government to build systems that enforce multilevel security. Accordingly, we won't discuss this issue here.

Traditional security technologies have not considered availability when failures occur, creating exposure to attacks whereby critical system components are shut down, overloaded, or partitioned away from application programs that depend upon them. However, when one considers failures in the context of a security subsystem, the benign failure models of earlier chapters must be called into question. Thus, work in this area has included a reexamination of Byzantine failure models, questioning whether extremely robust authentication servers can be built that will remain available even if Byzantine failures occur. Researchers are actively working to overcome these concerns, and one can now see the first signs of a new generation of highly available security technologies (the BASE system, which employs a "practical" form of Byzantine replication [see Castro and Liskov] is most often cited in this context, but the Byzantine Quorum approach of Malkhi and Reiter is also noteworthy). Interestingly, these projects use process groups, although do not employ the virtual synchrony model.

In the future, technologies supporting digital cash and digital commerce are likely to be of increasing importance and will often depend upon the use of trusted banking agents and strong forms of encryption, such as the RSA or DES standards (see Desmedt, Diffie and Hellman, Rivest et al.). Progress in this area has been very rapid and we will review some of the major approaches. Another area in which there has been a great deal of progress recently involves secured peer-to-peer file sharing mechanisms, used in settings ranging from storage and sharing of music (often illegally) to long-term archival preservation in digital library systems. Here, security involves such topics as hiding the identity of the individual who stored or who retrieves a file, hiding the contents of the file, or overcoming "bit rot" that might occur over long periods of time in library settings where files could be preserved for decades.

Yet, if the progress in distributed system security has been impressive, the limitations on such systems remain quite serious. We saw this in Chapter 9, when first reviewing security requirements for future Web sites and Web Services systems (Table 9.1). We identified a wide range of problems that fall outside of the prevailing security model for existing distributed systems, and as a result, are in essence not solvable today. Many of these related to representation of security policy or associating other kinds of "meaning" with security mechanisms; other limitations stem from such issues as security rules that depend upon the roles an individual is playing, or that arise when corporations collaborate in some ways while competing in others. Yet as noted above, policy languages are a weak point of modern security architectures.

On the whole, it remains difficult to secure a distributed system and very hard to add security to a technology that already exists and must be treated as a form of black box. The best-known technologies, such as Kerberos, are still used only sporadically. SSL security will let user a make a secure connection to company b, but really doesn't tackle problems outside of that narrow domain. This makes it hard to implement customized security mechanisms, very difficult to deal with issues of policy representation and enforcement, and leaves the average distributed system quite open to attack.

Break-ins and security violations are extremely common in the most standard distributed computing environments and if anything, each new wave of advances in operating systems and environments has made the security situation worse than in the previous generation of systems: Clearly, the very mechanisms that make it possible for systems to cooperate and interoperate also expose them to attack. Until distributed system security is difficult to *disable*, as opposed to being difficult to enable, we may continue to read about intrusions of increasingly serious nature, and will continue to be at risk for serious intrusions into our personal medical records, banking and financial systems, and personal computing environments.

22.2 Perimeter Defense Technologies

It is common to protect a distributed system by erecting barriers around it. Examples include the password control associated with dial-in ports; dial-back mechanisms, which some systems use to restrict access to a set of predesignated telephone numbers; and firewalls through which incoming and outgoing messages must pass. Each of these technologies has important limitations.

Password control systems are subject to attack by password-guessing mechanisms and by intruders who find ways to capture packets containing passwords as they are transmitted over the Internet or some other external networking technology. So-called password "sniffers" became a serious threat to system security in the mid-1990s and illustrate that the general Internet is not the benign environment it was in the early days of distributed computing, when most Internet users knew each other by name. Typical sniffers operate by exhibiting an IP address for some other legitimate machine on the network or by placing their network interfaces into a special mode, in which all passing packets will be accepted. They then scan the traffic captured for packets that might have originated in a log-in sequence. With a bit of knowledge about how such packets normally look, it is not hard to reliably capture passwords as they are routed through the Internet. Sniffers have also been used to capture credit card information and to break into e-mail correspondence.

In a world that makes increasing use of wireless connectivity and broad-band technologies, it may seem strange to talk about dial-up connections. Yet dial-up systems are often perceived as being more secure than direct network connections, presumably because the user cannot establish the connection without authenticating him or herself at the time it is established. For many reasons, dial-up security is ultimately illusory. The major problem is that many systems use their dial-up connections for data and file transfer and as a sending and receiving point for fax communications—hence, the corresponding telephone numbers are stored in various standard data files, often with connection information. An intruder who breaks into one system may in this manner learn dial-up numbers for other systems and may even find log-ins and passwords, which will make it easy to break in to them, as well. Moreover, the telephone system itself is increasingly complex and, as an unavoidable side-effect, increasingly vulnerable to intrusions. There have been many break-ins in which intruders started by wiretapping a dialup communications link, then dialed in and established a connection by replaying pre-recorded authentication information. The telephone system itself is wide-open to clever hackers, and treating the telephone network as a form of secure perimeter can be dangerously naïve if enough is at stake. Worst of all, even a system in which high speed network access has long been the norm may still have a bank of old dialup modems connected to it somewhere down in the basement. The best firewall in the world won't help if a hacker stumbles on a telephone number and password combination that will permit him to dial in.

Dial-back mechanisms, whereby the system calls the user back, clearly increase the hurdle an intruder must cross to penetrate a system relative to one in which the caller is assumed to be a potentially legitimate user. However, such systems also depend for their security upon the integrity of the telephone system, which, as we have noted, can be subverted. In particular, the emergence of mobile telephones and the introduction of mobility mechanisms into telephone switching systems create a path by which an intruder can potentially redirect a telephone dial-back to a telephone number other than the intended one. Such a mechanism is a good example of a security technology that can protect against benign attacks but would be considerably more exposed to well-organized malicious ones.

Firewalls (often integrated with network address translators) have become popular as a form of protection against communication-level attacks on distributed systems. This technology operates using *packet filters* and must be instantiated at all the access points to a distributed network. Each copy of the firewall will have a *filtering control policy* in the form of a set of rules for deciding which packets to reject and which to pass through; although firewalls that can check packet content have been proposed, typical filtering is on the basis of protocol type, sender and destination addresses, and port numbers. Thus, for example, packets can be allowed through if they are addressed to the e-mail or FTP server on a particular node; otherwise they are rejected. Often, firewalls are combined with *proxy* mechanisms, which permit file transfer and remote log in through an intermediary system enforcing further restrictions. The use of proxies for the transfer of public Web pages and FTP areas has also become common: In these cases, the proxy is configured as a mirror of some protected internal file system area, copying changed files to the less-secure external area periodically.

Other technologies commonly used to implement firewalls include application-level proxies and routers. With these approaches, small fragments of user-supplied code (or programs obtained from the firewall vendor) are permitted to examine the incoming and outgoing packet streams. These programs run in a loop, waiting for the next incoming or outgoing message, performing an acceptance test upon it, and then either discarding the message or permitting it to continue. The possibility of logging the message and maintaining additional statistics on traffic, or routing certain messages to specialized systems designed to diagnose and protect against intrusions, are also commonly supported.

Yet this cuts both ways. Network address translation is sometimes claimed to increase security, because NATs make it physically hard for an intruder to access machines behind the NAT interface. However, once an intruder breaks into a system through a NAT, that security evaporates: it then suffices to introduce an application-level "router" and, in effect, tunnel messages through the NAT and then retransmit them from behind it. Thus, while a NAT does secure a system in some ways, once a chink in the security architecture has been identified, the NAT protection may collapse.

For example, a common pattern of intrusion starts when the user downloads some form of application. This happens all the time: we extend our web browser with a codec, or download a file decompression utility, or a child who shares the computer downloads a game. Suppose that in additional to doing the tasks that program was designed to do, it also makes a connection out through the network filewall. That connection can now function as a tunnel by which an intruder can gain access to the local network and subvert the system. Yet as long as the downloaded code functions normally, the user may be completely unaware that his or her system has been compromised! This type of "Trojan horse" technique has become very common.

The major problem associated with firewall technologies is that they represent a single point of compromise: If the firewall is breached, the intruder essentially could gain free run of the enclosed system. And yet there are a tremendous number of ways to break through even the best firewall. Firewalls are thus central to modern distributed systems security architectures, and yet are simulateously the weakest point in many systems.

The need to support remote connectivity through firewalls is leading many corporations to implement what are called *virtual private networks* (see Figure 22.2). In the most general case, a VPN is a kind of network in which communication is authenticated (typically using a digital signature scheme) so that all messages originating outside of the legitimately accepted sources will be rejected. The idea is that one can run a VPN on top of a public network without fear; intruders won't be able to compromise packets and may not even be able to read them.

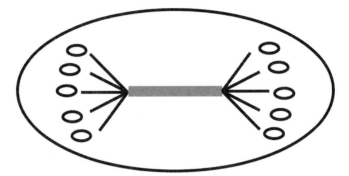

Figure 22.2.   A long-haul connection internal to a distributed system (gray) represents a potential point of attack. Developers often protect systems with firewalls on the periphery but overlook the risk that the communication infrastructure itself may be compromised, offering the intruder a backdoor approach into the protected environment. Although some corporations are protecting themselves against such threats by using encryption techniques to create virtual private networks, most mundane communication systems are increasingly at risk.

More often, VPN security is used to create a secure tunnel through a firewall, as a way to allow a mobile user to connect to his home network. In this common use, the VPN becomes a surprisingly serious security *risk*, because it makes it so easy for a machine that often lives outside the corporate firewall to tunnel through from time to time. Suppose that Dr. Welby is given a PC for home use by the hospital at which he works. At home, his son sometimes uses it to connect to the Internet, and the machine becomes infected with a virus. Dr. Welby may be completely unaware that his computer is compromised, but the next time he uses his machine at work, or connects to the hospital with a VPN connection, any viruses on his machine can gain access to the internal LAN.

Thus, while the prospects for strong security may be promising in certain settings, such as military systems or electronic banking systems, the more routine computing environments, on which the great majority of sensitive applications run, remain open to a great variety of attacks and are likely to continue to have such exposure well into the next decade, if not indefinitely. The core problem is really a social one: the ways we use computers are at odds with strong security.

This situation may seem pessimistic; however, in many respects, the other shoe hasn't even fallen. Although it may seem extremely negative to think in such terms, it is probable that future information terrorists and warfare tactics will include some of these forms of attack and perhaps others that are hard to anticipate until they have first been experienced. One day, terrorist hackers may manage to do significant damage through a coordinated cyber-attack, for example using a virus that spreads rapidly and also wipes disks. Up to the time of this writing, we've seen nasty viruses and we've seen viruses that spread quickly, but not both at once. Perhaps for this reason, our exposure to such risks is only increasing.

Although we will now move on to other topics in security, we note that defensive management techniques can be coupled with security-oriented wrappers to raise the barriers in systems that use firewall technologies for protection.

22.3 Access Control Technologies

Access control techniques operate by restricting use of system resources on the basis of user or group identifiers, which are typically fixed at log-in time—for example, by validation of a password. It is typical that these policies trust the operating system, its key services, and the network. In particular, the log-in program is trusted to obtain the password and correctly check it against the database of system passwords, granting the user permission to work under the user-ID or group-ID only if a match is detected. The log-in system trusts the file server or Network Information Server to respond correctly with database entries that can be used safely in this authentication process, and the resource manager (typically, an NFS server or database server) trusts the ensemble, believing that all packets presented to it as "valid NFS packets" or "valid XYZbase requests" originated at a trusted source.[23] (Microsoft's PC File System uses a stronger model and is not quite as "trusting" in this respect).

These dependencies are only rarely enforced rigorously. Thus, one could potentially attack an access control system by taking over a computer, rebooting it as the root or superuser, directing the system to change the user-ID to any desired value, and then starting work as the specified user. An intruder could replace the standard log-in program with a modified one—introducing a false NIS, which would emulate the NIS protocol but substitute invalid password records. One could even code one's own version of the NFS client protocol, which, operating from user space as a normal RPC application, could misrepresent itself as a trusted source of NFS requests. All these attacks on the NFS have been used successfully at one time or another, and many of the loopholes have been closed by one or more of the major vendors. Yet the fact remains that file and database servers continue to be largely trusting of the major operating system components on the nodes where they run and where their clients run.

---

[23]Not all file systems are exposed to such problems—for example, the AFS file system has a sophisticated stateful client/server architecture, which is also much more robust to attack. AFS has become popular, but it is less widely used than NFS.

Perhaps the most serious limitation associated with access control mechanisms is that they generally do not extend to the communication subsystem: typically, any process can issue an RPC message to any address it wishes to place in a message and can attempt to connect to any stream end point for which it possesses an address. In practice, these exposures are hard to exploit, because a process that undertakes to do so will need to guess the addresses and ports being used by the applications it attacks. Precisely to reduce this risk, many applications exploit *randomly generated* end-point addresses, so that an intruder would be forced to guess a pseudorandom number to break into a critical server. However, pseudorandom numbers may be less random than intended. Moreover, an intruder with a packet sniffer may be able to pull all sorts of "secrets" off the wire: MAC addresses of trusted computers, port numbers, etc.

Such break-ins are more common than one might expect—for example, in 1994 an attack on X11 servers was discovered in which an intruder found a way to deduce the connection port number that would be used. Sending a message that would cause the X11 server to prepare to accept a new connection to a shell command window, the intruder managed to connect to the server and to send a few commands to it. Not surprisingly, this proved sufficient to open the door to a full-fledged penetration. Moreover, the attack was orchestrated in such a manner as to trick typical firewalls into forwarding these poisoned messages, even though the normal firewall protection policy should have required that they be rejected. Until the nature of the attack was understood, the approach permitted intrusion into a wide variety of firewall-protected systems. In 2003, a rather similar attack occurred, but this time involved the Microsoft remote procedure call mechanism at the center of the Windows implementation of distributed object invocations. In both cases, the core problem is that it is difficult to inexpensively validate a packet as it arrives on a machine, hence a faked packet may sometimes slip through.

To give a sense of how exposed typical distributed systems currently are, Table 22.1 presents some of the assumptions made by the NFS file server technology when it is run without the security technology available from some vendors (in practice, NFS security is rarely enabled in systems that are protected by firewalls; the security mechanisms are hard to administer in heterogeneous environments and can slow down the NFS system significantly). We have listed typical assumptions of the NFS, the normal reason that this assumption holds, and one or more attacks that operate by emulation of the normal NFS environment in a way that the server is unable to detect. The statelessness of the NFS server makes it particularly easy to attack, but most client/server systems have similar dependencies and are similarly exposed.

One can only feel serious concern when these security exposures are contemplated against the backdrop of increasingly critical applications that trust client/server technologies such as NFS—for example, it is very common to store sensitive files on unprotected NFS servers. As we noted, there is an NFS security standard, but it is vendor-specific and may be impractical to use in heterogeneous environments. A hospital system, for example, is necessarily heterogeneous: The workstations used in such systems must interoperate with a great variety of special-purpose devices and peripherals, produced by many vendors. Thus, in precisely the setting one might hope would use strong data protection, one typically finds

Table 22.1. NFS Security Assumptions

NFS assumption	Dependent on. . .
O/S integrity	**NFS protocol messages originate only in trusted subsystems or the kernel**
	Attacks: Introduce a computer running an open operating system; modify the NFS subsystem. Develop a user-level program to implement the NFS client protocol; use it to emulate a legitimate NFS client issuing requests under any desired user-ID
Authentication	**Assumes that user- and group-ID information is valid**
	Attacks: Spoof the Network Information Server or NFS response packets so that authentication will be done against a falsified password database. Compromise the log-in program. Reboot the system or log-in using the root or superuser account; then change the user-ID or group-ID to the desired one and issue NFS requests.
Network integrity	**Assumes that communication over the network is secure**
	Attacks: Intercept network packets, reading file system data and modifying data written. Replay NFS commands, perhaps with modifications.

proprietary solutions or unprotected use of standard file servers! Indeed, many hospitals might be prevented from using a strong security policy, because, since so many individuals need access to a patient's record, any form of restriction would effectively be nullified.

Thus, in a setting where protection of data is not just important but is actually legally mandated, it may be very easy for an intruder to break in. While such an individual might find it hard to walk up to a typical hospital computing station and break through its password protection, by connecting a portable laptop computer to the hospital Ethernet (potentially a much easier task), it would be easy to gain access to the protected files stored on the hospital's servers. Such security exposures are already a potentially serious issue, and the problem will only grow more serious with time.

When we first discussed the NFS security issues, we pointed out that there are other file systems that do quite a bit better in this regard. The Microsoft NT File System protocol is far more secure than NFS. The AFS system, developed originally at Carnegie Mellon University and then commercialized by Transarc (an IBM division) has been widely adopted. But most systems combine these kinds of secured technologies with other less secure ones. Attackers simply focus on the weakest link that they can find, and since few system operators can even account for the majority of programs running in the background on the typical computer in their installation, the intruder will often have many options to pick from!

22.4 Authentication Schemes, Kerberos, and SSL

The weak points of typical computing environments are readily seen to be their authentication mechanisms and their blind trust in the security of the communication subsystem.

Best known among the technologies that respond to these issues is MIT's Kerberos system, developed as part of Project Athena, and SSL security, the standard used in the Internet.

Both schemes make use of encryption, albeit in slightly different ways, hence we start by reviewing the existing encryption technologies and their limitations. Although a number of encryption schemes have been proposed, the most popular ones at the time of this writing are the RSA public key algorithms and a version of the DES encryption standard in which one creates 3 DES keys and then encrypts information three times (called triple DES, the effect is comparable to DES with a single triple-length key). Kerberos was originally designed to use (single) DES, then extended to use triple-DES and finally "ported" to run on RSA. SSL, in contrast, was designed to use RSA but with provisions for the use of other non-RSA schemes; to the author's knowledge, SSL over RSA is far more prevalent than any other mix.

The cryptographic community has generated far more "tools" than these basic schemes, including message digest and signature algorithms, ways of splitting secrets into n portions so that any k out the n can be used to reconstruct the secret (but fewer "shares" are inadequate to do so), techniques for hiding information so that a third-party can counter-sign it without actually seeing it, etc. However, none of these are widely used in the Internet today, and hence they are beyond the limited scope of the present chapter.

22.4.1 RSA and DES

RSA (see Rivest et al.) is an implementation of a public key cryptosystem (see Diffie and Hellman), which exploits properties of modular exponentiation. In practice, the method operates by generating pairs of *keys*, which are distributed to the users and programs within a distributed system. One key within each pair is the *private* key and is kept secret. The other key is *public*, as is an encryption function, *crypt(key, object)*. The encryption function has a number of useful properties. Suppose that we denote the public key of some user as K and the private key of that user as K^{-1}. Then $crypt(K, crypt(K^{-1}, M)) = crypt(K^{-1}, crypt(K, M)) = M$—that is, encryption by the public key will decrypt an object encrypted previously with the private key and vice versa. Moreover, even if keys A and B are unrelated, encryption is commutative: $crypt(A, crypt(B, M)) = crypt(B, crypt(A, M))$.

Although a number of mechanisms can be used to implement RSA, the scheme actually used is based on modular exponentiation and is secure under the assumption that very large composite integers are computationally hard to factor. In the scheme, if one knows the factors of a large integer, it is easy to decode messages. The public key is the large integer itself, and the private key is its factorization. RSA keys are typically very large, indeed— 512 or 1024 bits are common at the time of this writing. With the best known factoring algorithms, a 512-bit key would still require some six months of computer time on a grid of processors to factor, and a 1024-bit key is effectively impossible to factor. However, a 512 bit key seemed absurdly long even a few years ago, hence one must wonder if this implementation of RSA has a limited lifetime and, if so, it is not at all clear what might replace it!

At any rate, in typical use, public keys are published in some form of trusted directory service (see Birrell). If process A wants to send a secure message to process B (this message could only have originated in process A and can only be read by process B), A sends $crypt(A^{-1}, crypt(B, M))$ to B, and B computes $crypt(B^{-1}, crypt(A, M))$ to extract the message. Here, we have used A and A^{-1} as shorthand for the public and private keys of processes A and B. A can send a message that only B can read by computing the simpler $crypt(B, M)$ and can sign a message to prove that the message was seen by A by attaching $crypt(A^{-1}, digest(M))$ to the message, where $digest(M)$ is a function that computes some sort of small number reflecting the contents of M, perhaps using an error-correcting code for this purpose. Upon reception, process B can compute the digest of the received message and compare this with the result of decrypting the signature sent by A using A's public key. This message can be validated by verifying that these values match (see Denning).

A process can also be asked to encrypt or sign a blinded message when using the RSA scheme. To solve the former problem, process A is presented with $M' = crypt(B, M)$. If A computes $M'' = crypt(A^{-1}, M')$, then $crypt(B^{-1}, M'')$ will yield $crypt(A^{-1}, M)$ without A having ever seen M. Given an appropriate message digest function, the same approach also allows a process to sign a message without being able to read that message.

In contrast, the DES standard (see *Data Encryption Standard*, Diffie and Hellman) is based on shared secret keys, in which two users or process exchanging a message will both have a copy of the key for the messages sent between them. Separate functions are provided for encryption and decryption of a message. Similar to the RSA scheme, DES can also be used to encrypt a digest of a message as proof that the message has not been tampered with. However, there is no standard blinding mechanism for DES.

DES is the basis of a government standard, which specifies a standard key size and can be implemented in hardware. Although the standard key size is large enough to provide security for most applications, the key is still small enough to permit it to be broken using a supercomputing system or a large number of powerful workstations in a distributed environment. This is viewed by the government as a virtue of the scheme, because it provides the possibility of decrypting messages for purposes of criminal investigation or national security. When using DES, it is possible to convert plain text (such as a password) into a DES key; in effect, a password can be used to encrypt information so that it can only be decrypted by a process that also has a copy of that password. As will be seen, this is the central feature that makes possible DES-based authentication architectures such as Kerberos (see Schiller, Steiner et al.).

One way to work within the DES standard and yet avoid the weakness of the 48-bit key standard is to apply DES three times to each message, using different keys. This approach, called "triple DES," is believed to offer roughly the same cryptographic security as would DES with a single triple-length key.

During the early 1990's, a security standard was proposed for use in telecommunication environments. This standard, Capstone, was designed for telephone communication but is not specific to telephony; it involves a form of key for each user and supports what is called *key escrow*, whereby the government is able to reconstruct the key by combining two portions of it, which are stored in secure and independent locations (see Denning and Branstad). The objective of this work was to permit secure and private use of telephones while preserving the government's right to wiretap with appropriate court orders. A product called the Clipper chip, which implements Capstone in hardware, was eventually produced, and incorporated into some secure telephones. The same mechanism was also adapted for use in computer networks and implemented in a PCMCIA card called Fortezza. However, after a brief period of experimentation with the card, the commercial sector lost interest in it, making it harder and harder for the government to procure Capstone-based solutions. The stunning advances in wireless communication and telephony created a tough choice for the government: either to go it alone, at great cost, or to accept defeat and simply work with commercially available off-the-shelf technologies, layering mechanisms "over" the COTS base to harden it. Faced with a mixture of budget stress and the impossibility of competing for "lowest cost bidder" contracts, both Clipper and Fortezza vanished from the market. At the time of this writing, a number of mobile telephone security products can be found, but there seem to be no generally accepted security standards. On the other hand, a new computer security architecture called Palladium, based on the idea of hard-wiring a security key into a protected read-only register internal to an Intel CPU, is gaining considerable attention, and may eventually offer some of the same opportunities.

Setting aside their limited commercial impact, both DES and Capstone security standard remain the subjects of vigorous debate. On the one hand, such methods limit privacy and personal security, because the government is able to break both schemes and indeed may have taken steps to make them easier to break than is widely known. On the other hand, the growing use of information systems by criminal organizations clearly poses a serious threat to security and privacy as well, and it is obviously desirable for the government to be able to combat such organizations. Meanwhile, the fundamental security of methods such as RSA and DES is not known—for example, although it is conjectured that RSA is very difficult to break, in 1995 it was shown that in some cases, information about the amount of time needed to compute the *crypt* function could provide data that substantially reduce the difficulty of breaking the encryption scheme. Moreover, clever uses of large numbers of computers have made it possible to break DES encryption. For example, when the first version of this textbook came out in 1997, a "state of the art" DES key seemed fairly secure. Today, most DES systems use triple DES.

Thus we face many kinds of challenges. Should systems be "genuinely" secure, or should they have weaknesses that would allow intelligence agencies to crack messages? Is security even possible? And to the extent that it is, will the commercial sector embrace the needed technologies? Up to the present, we lack a compelling story that addresses all of these issues at the same time.

22.4.2 Kerberos

The Kerberos system is a widely used implementation of secure communication channels, based on the DES encryption scheme (see Schiller, Steiner et al.). Integrated into the DCE environment, Kerberos is quite popular in the UNIX community. The approach genuinely offers a major improvement in security over that which is traditionally available within UNIX . Its primary limitations are, first, that SSL security dominates in the Internet and Web, making Kerberos increasingly "non-standard." Secondly, applications using Kerberos must be modified to create communication channels using the Kerberos secure channel facilities. Although this may seem to be a minor point, it represents a surprisingly serious one for potential Kerberos users, since application software using Kerberos is not yet common. Nonetheless, Kerberos has had some important successes.

In what follows, we'll discuss the original DES-based Kerberos protocol, although an RSA version of Kerberos was introduced many years ago. Kerberos per-se is perhaps less important than the basic ideas it illustrates. The basic Kerberos protocols revolve around the use of a trusted authentication server, which creates session keys between clients and servers upon demand. The basic scheme is as follows. At the time the user logs in, he or she presents a name and password to a log-in agent, which runs in a trusted mode on the user's machine, and establishes a secured channel to the Kerberos authentication server at boot time. Having logged in, the user is able to connect securely to various applications using Kerberos as an intermediary. The role of Kerberos is to mediate during connection setup, helping the client and server to authenticate one-another and to agree on a key for use to protect their shared communication channel.

Suppose that a user wants to connect to Fromages.com to purchase a wheel of finest French brie cheese. The first step is to request help from Kerberos. The agent on the user's machine creates a "connection request" message (it says, more or less, that "Ken Birman wishes to connect to Fromages.com"), signs this message using the user's password, encrypts it using the authentication server's key, and sends it to the server. (A few extra pieces of information are used to avoid "replay" attacks, such as the time of the request and a randomly generated number – a "nonce" in the parlance of the cryptographic community).

The Kerberos authentication server keeps a database of user names and passwords, and of course also remembers the key it negotiated with the log-in agent at boot time. It decrypts the request, verifies that Ken Birman's password was really used to sign it, and then creates a "certificate" containing information by which each end-point can validate the other, encrypting the piece destined for use by Fromages.com with a secret key known only to Fromages.com, and the piece destined for the user's computer with the session key employed by the log-in agent. It sends this back to the log-in agent, which decrypts it and extracts the two pieces of the certificate.

Now the user's computer presents the remote half of the certificate to Fromages.com. The Fromages.com server can easily validate the request, since it has been encrypted with its own secret key, which could only have been done by the authentication server. The session key also contains trustworthy information concerning the identification of the person who is making the request (in our example, me), the workstation-ID, and the expiration time of the key itself. Thus, the server knows that it is being used by someone with my password, knows which machine I'm on, and knows how long the session can remain open without a refreshed session key.

In UNIX, a "super user" with access to the debugger can potentially read information out of memory, including the memory of the log-in agent. Thus a risk associated with this method is that it needs the user's password as an encryption key and hence must keep it in the memory of the agent for a long period of time. Kerberos tries to minimize this threat by exchanging the user's password for a type of one-time password, which has a limited lifetime and is stored only at a *ticket granting service* with which a session is established as soon as the user logs in. In effect, the user's password is only employed very briefly, to obtain a temporary "one-time" password that will be employed on the user's behalf for a little while. The human user will be prompted to re-enter his or her password if the session lasts very long, or if the machine goes idle for more than a few minutes.

Once a session exists, communication to and from the file server can be done in the clear, in which case the file server can use the user-ID information established during the connection setup to authenticate file access, or it can be signed, giving a somewhat stronger guarantee that the channel protocol has not been compromised in any way, or even encrypted, in which case data exchange are only accessible by the user and the server. In practice, the initial channel authentication, which also provides strong authentication guarantees for the user-ID and group-ID information to be employed in restricting file access, suffices for most purposes. An overview of the protocol is seen in Figure 22.1 on page 469.

The Kerberos protocol has been proven secure against most forms of attack (see Lampson et al.); one of its few dependencies is its trust in the system time servers, which are used to detect expiration of session keys (see Gong). Moreover, the technology has been shown to scale to large installations using an approach whereby authentication servers for multiple protection domains can be linked to create session keys spanning wide areas. Perhaps the most serious exposure of the technology is that associated with partitioned operation. If a portion of the network is cut off from the authentication server for its part of the network, Kerberos session keys will begin to expire, and it will be impossible to refresh them with new keys. Gradually, such a component of the network will lose the ability to operate, even between applications and servers residing entirely within the partitioned component. In applications requiring support for mobility, with links forming and being cut very dynamically, the Kerberos design would require additional development.

A less obvious exposure to the Kerberos approach is that associated with active attacks on its authentication and ticket granting server. The server is a software system operating on standard computing platforms, and those platforms are often subject to attack over the network. A knowledgeable user might be able to concoct a poison pill by building a message, which will look sufficiently legitimate, to be passed to a standard service on the node; this message will then provoke the node into crashing by exploiting some known intolerance to incorrect input. The fragility of contemporary systems to this sort of attack is well known to protocol developers, many of whom have the experience of repeatedly crashing the machines with which they work during the debugging stages of a development effort. Thus, one could imagine an attack on Kerberos or a similar system aimed not at breaking through its security architecture, but rather at repeatedly crashing the authentication server, with the effect of denying service to legitimate users.

Kerberos supports the ability to prefabricate and cache session keys (tickets) for current users, and this mechanism would offer a period of respite to a system subjected to a denial of service attack. However, after a sufficient period of time, such an attack would effectively shut down the system.

Within military circles, there is an old story (perhaps not true) about an admiral who used a new generation of information-based battle management system in a training exercise. Unfortunately, the story goes, the system had an absolute requirement that all accesses to sensitive data be logged on an audit trail, which for that system was printed on a protected line printer. At some point during the exercise the line printer jammed or ran low on paper, and the audit capability shut down. The admiral's command was crippled by shutdown of the computer system, and the admiral himself developed such a dislike for computers that henceforth, he decreed, no computing system could be installed in his unit without first having its security subsystem disabled. Basically, he felt that having access to data when he needed it was a far higher priority than ensuring that bad guys would be kept away from that data.

And this illustrates an important point. The developer of a secure system often thinks of his or her task as being that of protecting critical data from the "bad guys." But any distributed system has a more immediate obligation, which is to make data and critical services available to the "good guys." Denial of service in the name of security may be far worse than providing service to an unauthorized user!

As noted earlier, Kerberos has been extended to also run over RSA. In this approach, the server becomes a directory managing public keys for applications in the system. Knowing a public key, it is possible to make a secure connection to that server. Of course, one can argue that such a system is no longer Kerberos, but we'll leave semantics to the experts and simply observe that Kerberos, and its progeny, have been hugely important systems.

22.4.3 ONC Security and NFS

Sun Microsystems, Inc., has developed an RPC standard, which it calls Open Network Computing (ONC), around the protocols used to communicate with NFS servers and similar systems. ONC includes an authentication technology, which can protect against most of the spoofing attacks previously described. Similar to a Kerberos system, this technology operates by obtaining unforgeable authorization information at the time a user logs into a network. The NFS is able to use this information to validate accesses as being from legitimate workstations and to strengthen its access control policies. If desired, the technology can also encrypt data to protect against network intruders who monitor passing messages.

ONC security shares the strengths and weaknesses of Kerberos, but is also considered to have suffer from some important practical limitations. For example, a set of restrictions limits export of strong cryptographic-based security. As a result, it is impractical for Sun to enable the NFS protection mechanisms by default or to envision an open standard, allowing complete interoperability between client and server systems from multiple vendors (the major benefit of NFS), which, at the same time, would be secure. A second worry related to heterogeneity: Sun systems need to "play" in settings where hardware and software from other vendors will also be used. Security can be a barrier to setting up such configurations, and when this happens, the user often disables security. He or she may never get around to figuring out how to re-enable it.

Beyond the heterogeneity issue is the problem of management of a security technology in complex settings. Although ONC security works well for NFS systems in fairly simple systems based entirely on Sun products, serious management challenges occur in complex system configurations, where users are spread over a large physical area, or in systems using heterogeneous hardware and software sources. With security disabled, these problems vanish. Finally, the same availability issues raised in our discussion of Kerberos pose a potential problem for ONC security. Thus, it is perhaps not surprising that these technologies have not been adopted on a widespread basis. Such considerations raise the question of how one might wrap a technology such as NFS, which was not developed with security in mind, so that security can be superimposed without changing the underlying software. One can also ask about monitoring a system to detect intrusions as a proactive alternative to hardening a system against intrusions and then betting that the security scheme will in fact provide the desired protection. We discuss these issues further in Chapter 26.

22.4.4 SSL Security

The Secure Sockets Layer (SSL) standard defines a scheme for obtaining security over a TCP channel, typically between a Web browser and a secure Web server to which it connects. SSL consists of two elements: a chain of trust model used to find a trustworthy authentication server, and a protocol by which a client system can obtain security certificates containing a security key (normally, an RSA public key) from that authentication server and then use it to create a secured TCP connection to the target platform. In the SSL model, unlike Kerberos, the focus is on establishing trust in the client that it is talking to the correct server; the server is expected to authenticate the client using some other end-to-end mechanism (a password, or a visa card, etc).

The chain of trust model works as follows. A client system is pre-loaded with a security key and network address for an initial directory server. For example, the Microsoft Windows platform has a preinstalled public key and network address by which it can contact a Microsoft security directory service, and the Netscape browser has a preinstalled key and address for a Netscape directory service. This information is maintained using a mechanism designed to be as tamper-proof as possible.

Microsoft (and Netscape) maintains a directory of trusted authentication servers: Verisign, for example. And Verisign can maintain a directory of its own – perhaps, machines within its data center. Thus through a chain of authorizations, we can work our way down from Microsoft to a company that makes part of its money by maintaining a database of certificates on behalf of corporate clients. Our client system, seeking a secured connection to Fromages.com, determines from Fromages.com that it uses Verisign as a directory server, then traverses the chain to establish contact with a Verisign authentication server, and then retrieves a trusted certificate for Fromages.com from that server.

The certificate, as might be expected, includes identification information for the issuer of the certificate and for the target server, expiration time, a public key for the target, and perhaps additional information concerning the possible uses of the key. In effect, the client system learns that "Microsoft trusts Verisign, and Verisign vouches for this certificate for the Fromages.com secure transactional server." Unlike a Kerberos certificate, the SSL one does not include information about the specific client; this is either a strength of the scheme or a weakness, depending upon one's priorities.

Given the public key of the target server, the client system can now create a secure connection to the target system. It does this by creating a TCP connection but then exchanging a series of messages over that connection, using the public key of the server to ensure that the endpoint of the channel is in possession of the same private key that it held when the certificate for the server was first registered. In principle, SSL can use RSA keys, DES keys, or other cryptographic systems, and can sign or encrypt messages. The "mode" of connection is negotiated by the client and server in the first messages of the authentication handshake.

Why do we need to exchange messages at all, given the certificate? It turns out there even with keying information for the target system, a bit more work must be done. To illustrate both the protocol and these additional issues, we'll imagine a dialog between two people, Alice and Bob, who wish to create a connection. Bob has a pair of keys, one public and one private. Bob's public key has been obtained by Alice from a trustworthy third party. Suppose that Alice tackles this problem by first generating a random message and sending it to Bob:

```
A->B random-message
```

In an SSL-like protocol, Bob could use his private key to encrypt Alice's message and return the encrypted result:

```
B->A {random-message}bobs-private-key
```

Alice receives this message and decrypts it by using Bob's previously published public key. She compares the decrypted message with the one she originally sent to Bob; if they match, she knows she's talking to Bob. As long as Alice doesn't reuse the same random message, an imposter lacking Bob's private key would be unable to properly encrypt the random message for Alice to check.

There is a problem with the above protocol. Bob may not be comfortable simply signing an unknown message with his key, because keys are often used for many purposes and Alice may be trying to trick Bob into signing something he didn't intend to sign, like a loan guarantee. Thus we need to enhance this simple protocol to offer Bob a bit more protection. Here's a modified protocol in which Bob generates the messages he signs (hence he doesn't need to trust Alice), and uses digital signatures instead of outright encryption. (We'll represent a signature as an encrypted message digest):

```
A->B ''Hello, are you Bob?''
B->A ''Alice, This Is Bob'' {digest[Alice, This Is Bob]}
bobs-private-key
```

When he uses this protocol, Bob knows what message he is sending to Alice, and he doesn't mind signing it. He sends the unencrypted version of the message first, "Alice, This Is Bob." Then he sends a signature: a digest of the string, encrypted with his private key. Alice can easily verify that Bob is Bob, and Bob hasn't signed anything he doesn't want to. Recall that in the certificate for Bob, Alice has a secure version of Bob's name, and she can check this against the name in the message to make sure everything matches up. She needs to trust the source of the certificate, of course, but if that source hands out legitimate certificates, Alice has a secure way to convince herself she is talking to Bob.

Once Alice has authenticated Bob, she can send Bob a message that only Bob can decode:

```
A->B {secret}bobs-public-key
```

The only way to find the secret is by decrypting the above message with Bob's private key. Exchanging a secret is another powerful way of using public key cryptography. Even if the communication between Alice and Bob is being observed, nobody but Bob can get the secret.

When working with SSL, the secret is typically a freshly generated key that will now be used between Alice and Bob to sign or encrypt subsequent data on their shared connection. This technique strengthens Internet security by allowing Alice and Bob to switch from RSA to a symmetric cryptographic algorithm (such as triple-DES, RC4, or IDEA). The advantage here is that symmetric cryptography is *much faster* than public-key cryptography. Alice knows the secret because she generated it before sending it to Bob. Bob knows the secret because Bob has the private key and can decrypt Alice's message. Because they both know the secret, they can both initialize a symmetric cipher algorithm and then start sending messages encrypted with it.

SSL includes one extra mechanism, intended to prevent an intruder from interposing himself between Alice and Bob and interfering with their connection. This is done by introducing what is called a message authentication code (MAC) into the protocol. A MAC is a piece of data that is computed by using a secret and some transmitted data. The digest algorithm described earlier has just the right properties for building a MAC function that can defend against an intruder:

```
MAC := Digest[some message, secret]
```

Because the intruder doesn't know the secret, he can't compute the right value for the digest. Even if the intruder randomly garbles messages, his chance of success is small if the digest data is large. For example, by using MD5 (a good cryptographic digest algorithm invented by RSA), Alice and Bob can send 128-bit MAC values with their messages. No intruder could guess such a large, essentially random, number.

Here's the SSL protocol as Netscape implements it, with all of these refinements:

```
A->B    hello
B->A    Hi, I'm Bob, bobs-certificate (the certificate
        contains bob's key, and is signed by a CA that Alice
        trusts)
A->B    Prove it
B->A    Alice, This Is Bob {digest[Alice, This Is Bob]}
        bobs-private-key
A->B    Bob, here is a secret {secret} bobs-public-key {some
        message}secret-key
```

Finally, SSL protects against "playback" attacks, in which an intruder doesn't try to understand messages or to modify them, but just passively replays them in the hope of getting something to happen. For example, if the intruder can capture a sequence by which Alice asks Bob to unlock a door, the intruder might replay the sequence later without needing to understand the details, in the hope that Bob will unlock the door again. The solution is to introduce random elements, called "nonce" values, from both sides of the conversation. Thus, each interaction between Alice and Bob will be different from any previous one, and any replay attack will fail almost immediately.

If the SSL protocol is placed side-by-side with the Kerberos protocol, one can see that the SSL approach is simultaneously similar and different from the Kerberos one. Both rely upon a trusted certificate authority, which provides certificates that can be used to establish connections to a server whose identity can be trusted, to the extent that the CA itself can be trusted. In Kerberos, the client authenticates itself to the CA, and the resulting certificate allows the server to authenticate the client as well as vice-versa. SSL doesn't worry about this, and in fact doesn't bother to authenticate the client at all: the goal is to convince a human client that it is safe to give his or her credit card information to Fromages.com. If we are in a situation where the identity of the client is also an issue, the server might require a login prior to permitting transactions, so we can enhance the basic SSL guarantees fairly easily.

One interesting question concerns the way that hardware like the Intel Palladium architecture, in which the processor itself possesses a secret key, could integrate with SSL security. With this type of hardware, it becomes feasible for the client to "prove" to the server that he or she is using such-and-such a platform. The server could then use this information as part of its policies, for example by granting access to certain media files and denying access to others, on the basis of the client's previously negotiated access permissions and the rules applicable to that particular platform. Exploiting this option opens all sorts of avenues for the research community, and one can anticipate a flurry of results over the next few years.

22.5 Security Policy Languages

An important and active research topic concerns the challenge of representing a non-trivial *security policy* and using it to determine whether or to authorize an action at runtime. To understand this issue, consider the way that security works in the real world, say in a hospital. Certain people are authorized to access the pharmacy stockroom, for example. These people were first cleared by the hospital security manager, who issued them with an appropriate badge. The manager reports to the Vice President for Operations, and this person reports to the CEO and Board of Directors. They, in turn, have legal responsibilities defined under the state charter that incorporated the hospital as a non-profit health center.

This example traces just one chain of authority within the organization – from the top down, we could say that the state gave the hospital certain rights, such as the right to stockpile medications, and the right to authorize individuals to access that stockpile. The hospital delegated rights in a chain that ultimately authorizes such and such a pharmacist to enter that room to retrieve a needed medication.

Complex organizations have many forms of trust. In addition to the hierarchical trust delegation example we've just seen, many organizations have an internal structure in which divisions have distinct roles. Perhaps, the consulting division is allowed to make stock evaluations, but must be kept completely independent of the investment division, which invests in stocks. In our hospital, the records-keeping division shouldn't be accessible to the computer systems used by patients, visitors and volunteers for routine tasks such as finding out what room a patient is in and when she can be visited.

When organizations compete in some spheres of activity while cooperating on others, we get even more complex kinds of rules. IBM competes with SAP in some respects, but perhaps SAP runs IBM computers internally and needs to allow IBM service representatives in to service those systems, run diagnostic tests on them, etc. In Section 9, Table 9.1 illustrated some of the subtle issues raised by such situations. Is this service representative here for a legitimate reason? Did IBM really designate him to repair the problem? Is he doing the appropriate thing and nothing else?

Existing security policy languages are far more useful for representing and dealing with chains of authorization than with these complex security scenarios. To represent a chain of authority or a delegation of rights we can use what are called "authentication logics." A well-known example is Rivest's SPKI/SDSI language (pronounced "spooky and sudsy"). The language allows one to write down simple rules such as "John is authorized to open the safe," or "John trusts Sally to operate the cash register." SPKI/SDSI also allows inference—given an elaborate rules database, one can ask a question such as "Should John open the safe for Sally to deposit the cash receipts for the evening?" and arrive at a sensible answer (hopefully, "yes"). However, SPKI/SDSI has limitations (for example, it doesn't deal all that well with situations involving mutually distrustful organizations that must cooperate for a specific task without revealing more about their security policy than desired or authorizing one-another to have broader rights than intended), and in any case has not been accepted by any very large community as a standard.

Making matters far more complex, many organizations are reluctant to share their security policies except on a need to know basis. Suppose that John presents himself at the FBI and states that he works for the CIA and has been asked to review the FBI's records associated with a terrorism investigation. Not only do we see all the issues just mentioned, but this "disclosure" question now also arises. The CIA will have a mechanism by which the FBI can confirm that John is a legitimate CIA representative and has been tasked to perform the study in question, but won't want to disclose other "unrelated" information, such as John's roles within the CIA, or those of other CIA agents unrelated to John. SPKI/SDSI, however, and other security languages too, assumes that the policy "database" will be placed into the public. Applied to our situation, the CIA would need to publish a complete list of all its agents and all their security permissions. Clearly, such an approach won't fly – yet we don't have any real alternatives today.

We run into the problem that unless a technology is very powerful, very sensitive to the possible concerns of its users, and also widely used as a standard, it won't be all that useful. After all, any one developer, say of a Web Services application, deals with just a tiny corner of the system. Unless everyone uses the same security language and standards, nobody will have the ability to even express their little corner of the security requirements and policies. At the time of this writing, any comprehensive security policy language seems remote.

Readers interested in learning more about SPKI/SDSI should consult the Web Site maintained by the MIT group that developed the system: http://theory.lcs.mit.edu/~cis/sdsi.html.

22.6 On-The-Fly Security

A rather popular style of security applies some form of security policy on the fly. We see this in a firewall, where as messages travel in or out of a system, the firewall checks them against a database of security rules and decides, on-the-fly, whether to allow the message through or to block it. Similarly, languages such as Java and C# enforce security rules at runtime, limiting the active program to only access objects for which it has valid handles. These mechanisms can be quite effective in dealing with what might be called low-level security considerations. They are less useful in dealing with complex requirements arising from the security needs of the application itself. For example, if an application is allowed to create files, one could run into a security issue if some kinds of files, such as files with an extension named ".lock," have a special meaning for some programs. Particularly if the security concern arises from an application that was developed by a third party, one runs into problems using vendor-supplied security mechanisms to enforce the special rules associated with the application's security needs.

Some researchers have begun to experiment with tackling this problem by extending the mechanisms seen in firewalls for use in running programs. The idea can be traced to work by Steve Lucco and Brian Bershad. Lucco's work was concerned with editing already compiled programs at the object code layer to insert behavioral checks, for example to prevent a piece of code from accessing objects outside its legitimate address space. Brian Bershad's project, SPIN, was concerned with protecting the operating system from malicious (or buggy) behavior by applications that need to be downloaded into the kernel, such as a device driver. Both systems aim at allowing the user to benefit from high performance by loading untrusted code right into the address space of some sort of sensitive system service and yet protecting themselves against undesired behavior.

Fred Schneider has taken this idea even further in work underway at Cornell. Schneider's approach is to represent security policy in a simple database that can be used to insert protective mechanisms (firewall style) right into applications, intervening at the layer where the application interacts with the network or the surrounding environment. If the policy says, for example, that users lacking security clearance must not access classified documents, Schneider would modify the program itself, at runtime, to ensure that each operation that accesses any kind of object is filtered to ensure that if the actor lacks a clearance, the object isn't a classified one. Since the program was built without knowledge of the security policy and protective mechanisms, the belief is that this sort of fine-grained firewall can give a degree of customized protection not otherwise feasible.

Combined with work on security policy languages and inference systems, like SPKI/SDSI, one can see hope for a truly comprehensive approach to security policy management and enforcement at some point in the future. We're beginning to understand the mechanisms and beginning to sort out the complexity of simply representing security policy and desires. Yet we are also very far from having the whole story in hand. Developer's of Web Services systems will find themselves in the thick of it: They will often need to enforce corporate security policies, but will lack the kind of standardized, powerful, and widely used mechanisms that might make this straightforward. As a result the developer will be on his or her toes, and in fact is likely to overlook important issues. Even if not, security is an evolving concept: the security policy for a small company doing military development under a classified contract may change drastically when that company is acquired by Boeing, a large company doing many kinds of work. An application built by the small company may not be so easily extended to cover the complex scenarios that can arise at the large one later. Thus, new exposures can creep in, even when a system is initially extremely secure. Schneider's approach, in some future mature and widely used form, could address such a need – but again, we are probably decades from that point today.

22.7 Availability and Security

Research on the introduction of availability guarantees into Kerberos-based (or SSL-based) architectures has revealed considerable potential for overcoming the availability limitations of the basic Kerberos approach. As we have seen, Kerberos and SSL are both dependent on the availability of their authentication servers for the generation of new protection keys. Should a server fail or become partitioned away from the applications depending on it, the establishment of new channels and the renewal of keys for old channels will cease to be possible, eventually shutting down the system.

In a Ph.D. dissertation based on an early version of the Horus system, Reiter showed that process groups could be used to build highly available authentication servers (see Reiter [1993, 1994], Reiter et al. [1992, 1995]). His work included a secure join protocol for adding new processes to such a group; methods for securely replicating data and for securing the ordering properties of a group communication primitive (including the causal property); and an analysis of availability issues, which occur in key distribution when such a server is employed. Interestingly, Reiter's approach does not require that the time service used in a system such as Kerberos be replicated: His techniques have a very weak dependency on time.

Process group technologies permitted Reiter to propose a number of exotic new security options as well. Still working with Horus, he explored the use of split secret mechanisms to ensure that in a group of n processes (see Desmedt, Desmedt et al., Frankel, Frankel and Desmedt, Herlihy and Tygar, Laih and Harn), the availability of any $n - k$ members would suffice to maintain secure and available access to that group. In this work, Reiter uses a state machine approach: The individual members have identical states and respond to incoming requests in an identical manner. Accordingly, his focus was on implementing state machines in environments with intruders and on signing responses in such a way that $n - k$ signatures by members would be recognizable as a group signature carrying the authority of the group as a whole.

A related approach can be developed in which the servers split a secret in such a manner that none of the servers in the group has access to the full data, and yet clients can reconstruct these data provided that $n - k$ or more of the servers are correct. Such a split secret scheme might be useful if the group needs to maintain a secret that none of its individual members can be trusted to manage appropriately.

Techniques such as these can be carried in many directions. Reiter, after leaving the Horus project, started work on a system called Rampart at AT&T (see Reiter [1996]). Rampart provides secure group functionality under assumptions of Byzantine failures and is used to build extremely secure group-based mechanisms for use by less stringently secured applications in a more general setting—for example, Rampart could be the basis of an authentication service, a service used to maintain billing information in a shared environment, a digital cash technology, or a strongly secured firewall technology.

More recently, Reiter and Malkhi have worked with Byzantine Quorum methods. These approaches form a group of N processes in such a way that data can be read or updated using just $O(sqrt(N))$ members, and are also able to tolerate Byzantine failures. Authentication services stand out as one of the first settings that could benefit from such a technology.

Cooper, also working with Horus, has explored the use of process groups as a blinding mechanism. The concept here originated with work by Chaum, who showed how privacy can be enforced in distributed systems by mixing information from many sources in a manner that prevents an intruder from matching an individual data item to its source or tracing a data item from source to destination (see Chaum). Cooper's work shows how a replicated service can actually mix up the contents of messages from multiple sources to create a private and secure e-mail repository (see Cooper [1994]). In his approach, the process group-based mail repository service stores mail on behalf of many users. A protocol is given for placing mail into the service, retrieving mail from it, and for dealing with vacations; the scheme offers privacy (intruders cannot determine sources and destinations of messages) and security (intruders cannot see the contents of messages) under a variety of attacks and can also be made fault tolerant through replication. More recently, Mazieres developed a peer-to-peer system using similar ideas. His *Tangler* system mixes data together in ways that maintain privacy of the publisher, privacy of access and security of the data itself.

Intended for large-scale mobile applications, Cooper's work would permit exchanging messages between processes in a large office complex or a city without revealing the physical location of the principals—however, this type of communication is notoriously insecure. Maziere's Tangler system aims at individuals concerned about their right to free speech (and also at individuals hoping to share files in ways that the government might find very hard to regulate). And these are hardly the only such efforts. The emergence of digital commerce may expose technology users to very serious intrusions on their privacy and finances. Work such as that done by Reiter, Chaum, Mazieres and Cooper suggests that security and privacy should be possible even with the levels of availability that will be needed when initiating commercial transactions from mobile devices.

Later in this book we'll discuss some recent work on using Byzantine Agreement protocols to achieve security in certain types of replicated services, and also work on security in peer-to-peer systems. To avoid repetition, we defer these topics until later sections.

22.8 Related Reading

Chapter 9 reviewed limitations of existing security models. See also *Trust in Cyberspace*, a National Academy of Sciences report edited by F. Schneider, which discusses capabilities and limitations of modern security architectures.

On Kerberos: (see Schiller, Steiner et al.).

On associated theory: (see Bellovin and Merritt, Lampson et al.).

On RSA and DES: (see Denning, Desmedt, Diffie and Hellman, Rivest et al.).

On Rampart: (see Reiter [1993, 1994], Reiter et al. [1992,1995]).

On split-key cryptographic techniques and associated theory: (see Desmedt, Desmedt et al., Frankel, Frankel and Desmedt, Herlihy and Tygar, Laih and Harn).

On mixing techniques: (see Chaum, Cho and Birman, Cooper [1994]).

On the Secure Socket Layer protocol: Netscape originally developed this protocol and maintains very clear materials online. The protocol itself is defined by RFC 2246 (Transport Layer Security) and RFC 2818 (HTTPS over TLS).

Interested readers should also revisit Chapter 14, where we discussed Castro and Liskov's recent work on introducing Byzantine fault tolerance in data replication systems. (See Castro and Liskov).

23

Clock Synchronization and Synchronous Systems

Previous chapters of this book have made a number of uses of clocks or time in distributed protocols. In this chapter, we look more closely at the underlying issues. Our focus is on aspects of real-time computing that are specific to distributed protocols and systems

23.1 Clock Synchronization

Clock synchronization is an example of a topic that until the recent past represented an important area for distributed system research (see Clegg and Marzullo, Cristian [1989], Cristian and Fetzer, Kopetz and Ochsenreiter, Lamport [1984], Lamport and Melliar-Smith, Marzullo [1984], Srikanth and Toueg, Verissimo); overviews of the field can be found in Liskov, Simons et al. The introduction of the global positioning system, in the early 1990s, greatly changed the situation. As recently as five years ago, a book such as this would have treated the problem in considerable detail, to the benefit of the reader, because the topic is an elegant one and the clock-based protocols that have been proposed are interesting to read and analyze. Today, however, it seems more appropriate to touch only briefly on the subject.

The general problem of clock synchronization occurs because the computers in a distributed system typically use internal clocks as their primary time source. On most systems, these clocks are accurate to within a few seconds per day, but there can be surprising exceptions to the rule. PCs, for example, may operate in power-saving modes, in which even the clock is slowed down or stopped, making it impossible for the system to gauge real time reliably. At the other end of the spectrum, the global positioning system (GPS) has introduced an inexpensive way to obtain accurate timing information using a radio receiver; time obtained in this manner is accurate to within a few milliseconds unless the GPS signal itself is distorted by unusual atmospheric conditions or problems with the antenna used to receive the signal. Break-out 23.1 discusses the MARS system, which uses clock synchronization for real-time control.

Traditionally, clock synchronization was treated in the context of a group of peers, each possessing an equivalent local clock, with known accuracy and drift properties. The goal in such a system was typically to design an agreement protocol by which the clocks could be kept as close as possible to real time and with which the tendency of individual clocks to drift (either from one another and/or relative to real time) could be controlled. To accomplish this, processes would periodically exchange time readings, running a protocol by which a software clock could be constructed having substantially better properties than that of any of the individual participating programs—with the potential to overcome outright failures whereby a clock might drift at an excessive rate or return completely erroneous values.

Key parameters to such a protocol are the expected and maximum communication latencies of the system. It can be shown that these values limit the quality of clock synchronization achievable in a system by introducing uncertainty in the values exchanged between processes—for example, if the latency of the communication system between p and q is known to vary in the range $[0, \varepsilon]$, any clock reading that p sends to q will potentially be aged by ε time units by the time q receives it. When latency is also bounded below, a method developed by Verissimo (briefly presented here) can achieve clock precisions bounded by the *variation* in latency. In light of the high speed of modern communication systems, these limits represent a remarkably high degree of synchronization: It is rarely necessary to time events to within accuracies of a millisecond or less, but these limits tell us that it would be possible to synchronize clocks to that degree if desired. Indeed, we'll see precisely how it could be done shortly.

Modern computing systems face a form of clock synchronization problem that is easier to solve than the most general version of the problem. If such systems make use of time at all, it is common to introduce two or more GPS receivers—in this manner creating a number of system time sources. Devices consisting of nothing more than a GPS receiver and a network interface can, for example, be placed directly on a shared communication bus. The machines sharing that bus will now receive time packets at some frequency, observing identical values at nearly identical time. (See Figure 23.1.)

If the device driver associated with the network device is able to identify

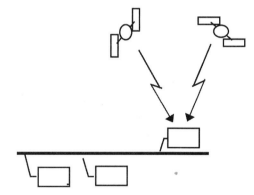

Figure. 23.1.   The global positioning system is a satellite network that broadcasts highly accurate time values worldwide. Although intended for accurate position location, GPS systems are also making accurate real-time information available at low cost.

23.1 MARS: A Distributed System for Real-Time Control

The MARS system uses clock synchronization as the basis of an efficient fault tolerance method, implemented using pairs of processing components interconnected by redundant communication links. The basic approach is as follows (see Damm et al., Kopetz and Ochsenreiter, Kopetz and Verissimo).

A very high quality of clock synchronization is achieved using a synchronization method that resides close to the hardware (a broadcast-style bus). Implemented in part using a special-purpose device controller, clocks can be synchronized to well under a millisecond and, if a source of accurate timing information is available, can be both precise and accurate to within this degree of precision.

Applications of MARS consist of directly controlled hardware, such as robotic units or components of a vehicle. Each processor is duplicated, as is the program that runs on it, and each action is taken redundantly. Normally, every message will be sent four times: once by each processor on each message bus. The architecture is completely deterministic in the sense that all processes see the same events in the same order and base actions on synchronized temporal information in such a way that even clock readings will be identical when identical tasks are performed. Software tools for scheduling periodic actions and for performing actions after a timer expires are provided by the MARS operating system, which is a very simple execution environment concerned primarily with scheduling and message passing.

MARS is designed for very simple control programs and assumes that these programs fail by halting (the programs are expected to self-check their actions for sanity and shut down if an error is detected). In the event that a component does fail, this can be detected by the absence of messages from it or by their late arrival. Such a failed component is taken off-line for replacement and reintegrated into the system the next time it is restarted from scratch. These assumptions are typical of in-flight systems for aircraft and factory-floor process control systems.

Although MARS is not a particularly elaborate or general technology, it is extremely effective within its domain of intended use. The assumptions made are felt to be reasonable ones for this class of application, and although there are limitations on the classes of failures that MARS can tolerate, the system is also remarkably simple and modular, benefiting from precisely those limitations and assumptions. The performance of the system is extremely good for the same reasons.

these incoming time packets, it can be used to set the local clock of the host machine to extremely high precision; if not, an application should be able to do so with reasonable accuracy. Given data for the average access and propagation delays for packets sent over the communication hardware, the associated latency can be added to the incoming time value, producing an even more accurate result. In such a manner, systems in which real time is important can synchronize processor clocks to within fractions of a millisecond, obviating the need for any sophisticated application-level synchronization algorithm. After all, the delays associated with passing a message through an operating system up to the application, scheduling the application process if it were in a blocked state, and paging in the event of a possible page fault are substantial compared with the clock accuracy achievable in this manner. Moreover, it is very unlikely that a GPS time source would fail other than by crashing. If noncrash failures are a concern, a simple solution is to collect sets of readings from three GPS sources, exclude the outlying values, and take the remaining value as the correct one. (See Figure 23.2 for definitions of some useful terms.)

Accuracy is a characterization of the degree to which a correct clock can differ from an external clock that gives the true time. A clock synchronization protocol guaranteeing highly accurate clocks thus provides the assurance that a correct clock will return a value within some known maximum error of the value that the external clock would return. In some settings, accuracy is expressed as an absolute bound; in others, accuracy is expressed as a maximum rate of drift-in this case, the accuracy of the clock at a given time is a function of how long the clock has been free-running since the last round of the synchronization protocol.

Skew is a measure of the difference between clock readings for a pair of processes whose clocks have been sampled at the same instant in real time.

Precision is a characterization of the degree to which any pair of correct clocks can differ over time. As with accuracy, a precision may be given as a constant upper bound on the skew or as a maximum rate of drift of the skews for pairs of correct clocks.

Figure 23.2. Definitions of accuracy, skew, and precision for synchronized clocks in distributed settings.

In light of this development, it has become desirable to consider distributed computing systems as falling into two classes. Systems in which time is important for reliability can readily include accurate time sources and should do so. Systems in which time is not important for reliability should be designed to avoid all use of workstation clock values, using elapsed time on a local clock to trigger timer-based events such as retransmission of messages or timeout, but not exchanging time values between processes or making spurious use of time. For the purposes of such elapsed timers, the clocks on typical processors are more than adequate: A clock that is accurate to a few seconds per day will measure a 100 ms timeout with impressive accuracy.

Where clocks are known to drift, Verissimo and Rodrigues have suggested an elegant method for maintaining very precise clocks (see Verissimo and Rodrigues); see also Clegg and Marzullo. This protocol, call *a-posteriori clock synchronization*, operates roughly as follows. A process other than the GPS receiver initiates clock synchronization periodically (for fault tolerance, two or more processes can run the algorithm concurrently). Upon deciding to synchronize clocks, this process sends out a *resynchronize* message, including its own clock value in the message and setting this value as close as possible to when the message is transmitted on the wire—for example, the device driver can set the clock field in the header of an outgoing message just before setting up the DMA transfer to the network.

Upon arrival in destination machines, each recipient notes its local clock value, again doing this as close as possible to the wire. The recipients send back messages containing their clock values at the time of the receipt. The difference between these measured clock values and that of the initiator will be latency from the initiator to the receivers plus the drift of the recipient's clock relative to the clock of the initiator. For example, suppose the initiator believes it to be three o'clock. It sends out this value over the LAN to a nearby machine. After a latency (communication delay) of 1 ms, that machine receives the clock value and compares it with its own clock, discovering its clock to be smaller by 31 ms. If we "knew" the latency (and we don't), we could now deduce that the recipients clock is running 30 ms slower than that of the initiator. Similarly, a computed difference of 121 ms would correspond to a recipient running 120 ms "ahead" of the initiator, assuming that the latency from initiator to recipient was still 1 ms. Of course in a real LAN, communication latency is somewhat variable. Thus successive runs of the protocol might result in computed "clock skews" varying slightly from these nominal values: perhaps −31.050 ms, or 120.980 ms. And making matters worse, clocks may be drifting as our protocol executes.

In the protocol proposed by Verissimo and Rodriguez, the synchronization algorithm selects one of the participants as the official clock of the system. It does so either by selecting a value returned from a process with a GPS receiver, if one is included, or by sorting the returned differences and selecting the median. It subtracts this value from the other differences. The vector will now have small numbers in it if, as assumed, the latency from initiator to participants if fairly constant over the set. The values in the vector will represent the distance that the corresponding participant's clock has drifted with respect to the reference clock. Given an estimate of the message latency between the reference process and the initiator, the initiator can also compute the drift of its own clock—for example, a process may learn that its clock has drifted by −32 ms since the last synchronization event. Any sort of reliable multicast protocol can be used to return the correction factors to the participants.

To actually correct a clock that has drifted, it is common to use an idea introduced by Srikanth and Toueg. The approach involves gradually compensating for the drift under the assumption that the rate of drift is constant. Thus, if a process has drifted 120 ms over a one-minute period, the clock might be modified in software to introduce a compensating drift rate of −240 ms over the next minute, in this manner correcting the original 120 ms and overcoming the continuing 120 ms drift of its clock during the period. Such an adjustment occurs gradually, avoiding noticeable jumps in the clock value that might confuse an application program.

The above discussion has oversimplified the protocol: The method is actually more complicated because it needs to account for a variety of possible failure modes; this is done by running several rounds of the protocol and selecting, from among the candidate clocks appearing best in each round, that round and clock for which the overall expected precision and accuracy is likely to be best.

Verissimo and Rodrigues's algorithm is optimally precise but not necessarily the best for obtaining optimal accuracy: The best-known solution to that problem is the protocol of Srikanth and Toueg mentioned above. However, when a GPS receiver is present in a distributed system having a standard broadcast-style LAN architecture, the a-posteriori method will be optimal in both respects—accuracy and precision—with clock accuracies comparable in magnitude to the variation in message latencies from initiator to recipients. These variations can be extremely small: Numbers in the tens of microseconds are typical. Thus, in a worldwide environment with GPS receivers, one can imagine an inexpensive software and hardware combination permitting processes anywhere in the world to measure time accurately to a few tens of microseconds. Accuracies such as this are adequate for even very demanding real-time uses.

Unfortunately, neither of these methods is actually employed by typical commercial computing systems. At the time of this writing, the situation is best characterized as a transitional one. There are well-known and relatively standard software clock synchronization solutions available for most networks, but the standards rarely span multiple vendor systems. Heterogeneous networks are thus likely to exhibit considerable time drift from processor to processor. Moreover, the clock synchronization mechanisms built into standard operating systems often run over the Internet, where latencies between the user's computer and a trusted clock can range from tens to hundreds of milliseconds. A result is that the average PC or workstation has a clock that can be trusted at a resolution of seconds or tens of seconds, but not to a higher resolution. This turns out to be fine for such uses as remembering to renew a lease on a network resource or a lock on a file, or timestamping a file when it is accessed or modified; developers tackling problems in which finer-grained temporal information is needed should consider adding GPS units to their machines.

23.2 Timed-Asynchronous Protocols

Given a network of computers that share an accurate time source, it is possible to design broadcast protocols to simultaneously guarantee real-time properties as well as other properties, such as failure-atomicity or totally ordered delivery. The best-known work in this area is that of Cristian, Aghili, Strong, and Dolev and is widely cited as the CASD protocol suite or the Δ-T atomic broadcast protocols (see Cristian et al. [1985, 1990]). These protocols are designed for a static membership model, although Cristian later extended the network model to dynamically track the formation and merging of components in the event of network partitioning failures, again with real-time guarantees on the resulting protocols. In the remainder of this section, we present these protocols in the simple case where processes fail only by crashing or by having clocks that lie outside of the acceptable range for correct clocks—where messages are lost but not corrupted. The protocols have often been called synchronous, but Cristian currently favors the term "timed asynchronous" (see Cristian and Schmuck), and this is the one we use here.

The CASD protocols seek to guarantee that in a time period during which a set of processes is *continuously operational* and *connected*, this set will deliver the same messages at the same time and in the same order. Two caveats apply. First, "same time" must be understood to be limited by the clock skew: Because processor clocks may differ by as much as ε, two correct processors undertaking to perform the same action at the same time may in fact do so as much as ε time units apart. Additionally, and this may seem a bit confusing on first reading, a process may not be able to detect that its own clock is incorrect. In effect, a process may be considered "faulty" by the system and yet has no way to know that this is the case (in contrast, if a virtual synchrony system considers a process faulty, that process is excluded from the system and will certainly find out). The importance of this is that when a process is faulty, the guarantees of the protocol no longer apply to it. So, if process a receives a message m we know that if the system considers a to be healthy, m was delivered to a at the same time that it was delivered to any other healthy process. But if a is considered unhealthy (and as noted before, a has no way to detect this), all bets are off. We'll see how this can complicate the job of the developer who works with CASD shortly.

We start by considering the simple scenario of a network consisting of a collection of n processes, k of which may be faulty. The CASD protocol is designed for a network in which packets must be routed; the network diameter, d, is the maximum number of hops a packet may have to take to reach a destination node from a source node. It is understood that failures will not cause the network to become disconnected. Although individual packets can be lost in the network, it is assumed that there is a known limit on the number of packets that will actually be lost in any single run of the protocol. Finally, multicast networks are not modeled as such: An Ethernet or FDDI is treated as a set of point-to-point links.

The CASD protocol operates as follows. A process (which may itself be faulty) creates a message and labels it with a timestamp, t (from its local clock), and its process identifier. It then forwards the message to all processors reachable over communication links directly connected to it. These processes accept incoming messages. A message is *discarded* if it is a duplicate of a message that has been seen previously or if the timestamp on the message falls outside a range of currently feasible valid timestamps. Otherwise, the incoming message is *relayed* over all communication links except the one on which it was received. This results in the exchange of $O(n^2)$ messages, as illustrated in Figure 23.3.

A process holding a message waits until time $t + \Delta$ on its local clock (here, t is the time when the message was sent) and then delivers it in the order determined by the sender's timestamp, breaking ties using the processor ID of the sender. For suitable validity limits and Δ, this protocol can be shown to overcome crash failures, limited numbers of communication failures, and incorrect clock values on the part of the sender or intermediary relay processes.

The calculation of the parameter Δ is based on the following reasoning: For the range of behaviors possible in the system, there is a corresponding maximum latency after which a message that originates at a faulty process and that has been forwarded only by faulty processes finally reaches a correct process and is accepted as valid. From this point forward, there is an additional maximum latency before the message has reached all correct processes,

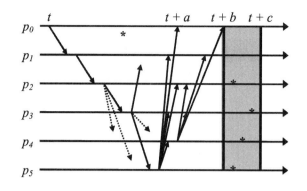

Figure 23.3. In the CASD protocol, messages are delivered with real-time guarantees despite a variety of possible failures. In this example for a fully connected network ($d = 1$), processes p_0 and p_1 are faulty and send the message only to one destination each. p_2 and p_3 are correct but experience communication failures, which prevent the message from being forwarded to the full set of correct processors. Eventually, however, the full set of possible failures has been exhausted and the message reaches all correct destinations even if the execution is a worst-case one. In this example, the message finally reaches its last destination at time $t + a$. The processors now delay delivery of the message under a best-case/worst-case analysis, whereby each process reasons that it may have received the message in the minimum possible time but that others may receive it after the maximum possible time and yet assume that they too had received the message after a minimal delay. When this delay has elapsed, all correct processes know that all other correct processes have the message and are prepared to deliver it; delivery then takes place during a period bounded above and below by the clock synchronization constant e (shown as $[t + b, t + c]$ in the figure). Incorrect processes may fail to deliver the message, as in the case of p_1; may deliver outside of the window, as does p_0; or may deliver messages rejected by all correct processes.

limited by the maximum number of network packet losses that can occur. Finally, any specific recipient may consider itself to be the earliest of the correct processes to have received the message and will assume that other correct processes will be the last to receive a copy. From this analysis, a value can be assigned to Δ such that at time $t + \Delta$, every correct process will have a copy of the message and will know that all other correct processes also have a copy. It is therefore safe to deliver the message at time $t + \Delta$: The other processes will do so as well, within a time skew of ε, corresponding to the maximum difference in clock values for any two correct processes. This is illustrated in Figure 23.3, where time $t + b$ corresponds to $t + \Delta - \varepsilon/2$ and $t + c$ to $t + \Delta + \varepsilon/2$.

Although we will not develop the actual formulas here, because the analysis would be fairly long, it is not hard to develop a basic intuition into the reasoning behind this protocol. If we are safe in assuming that there are at most f faulty processes in the network and that the network itself loses no more than k packets during a run of the protocol, it must follow that a broadcast will reach at least one operational process, which will forward it successfully to every other operational process within $f + k$ rounds. A process using the protocol simply waits long enough to be able to deduce that every other process must have a copy of the message, after which it delivers the message in timestamp order.

Because all the operational processes will have received the same messages and use the same timestamp values when ordering them for delivery, the delivered messages are the same and in the same order at all correct processes. However, this may not be the case at *incorrect* processes—namely, those for which the various temporal limits and constants of the analysis do not hold or those that failed to send or receive messages the protocol requires them to send or receive. (We'll say more about

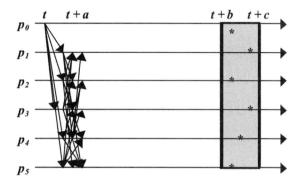

Figure. 23.4. A run of the CASD protocol in which no failures occur. After a flurry of message exchanges during which $O(n^2)$ messages are sent and received, the protocol lies quiescent until delivery occurs. The delay to delivery is unaffected by the good fortune of the protocol in having reached all the participants so rapidly. Notice that as normally presented, the protocol makes no use of broadcast hardware.

this in a moment, but an illustration of the problem can be seen in Figure 23.4.)

Clearly, when a protocol such as this one is used in a practical setting, it will be advantageous to reduce the value of Δ as much as possible, since Δ is essentially a minimum latency for the protocol. For this reason, the CASD protocol is usually considered in a broadcast network for which the network diameter, d, is 1; processes and communication are assumed to be quite reliable (hence, these failure limits are reduced to numbers

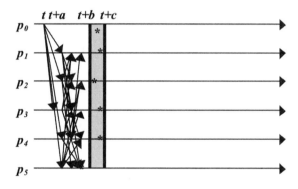

Figure. 23.5. More aggressive parameter settings and assumptions can substantially reduce the delay before delivery occurs.

such as 1); and clocks are assumed to be very closely synchronized for the operational processes in the network. With these sorts of assumptions, Δ, which would have a value of about three seconds in the local area network used by the Computer Science Department at Cornell, can be reduced into the range of 100–150 ms. Such a squeezing of the protocol leads to runs such as the one shown in Figure 23.5.

We noted that there is a subtle issue associated with the definition of "operational" in the goals of the CASD protocol. The problem occurs when we consider a process that is technically faulty because its clock has drifted outside the limits assumed for a correct process; with the clock synchronization methods reviewed above, this is an unavoidable risk, which grows as the assumed limits become tighter. This is also true when using Cristian's recommended clock synchronization protocol (see Cristian [1989])—that is, the same actions that we took to reduce Δ also have the side-effect of making it more likely that a process will be considered faulty.

Such a process is only faulty in a technical sense. Viewed from above, we can see that its clock is slightly too fast or too slow, perhaps only five or ten milliseconds from the admissible range. Internally, the process considers itself quite operational and would be unable to detect this type of fault even if it tried to do so. Yet, because it is faulty in the formal sense of violating our conditions on correct processes, the guarantees of the protocol may no longer hold for such a process: It may deliver messages that no other process delivered, fail to deliver messages that every other process delivered successfully, or deliver messages outside the normal time range within which delivery should have occurred. Even worse, the process may then drift back into the range considered normal and hence recover to an operational state immediately after this condition occurs. The outcome might be a run more like the one shown in Figure 23.6.

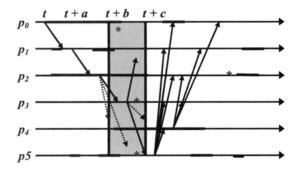

Figure 23.6. In this case, overly aggressive parameter settings have caused many processes to be incorrect in the eyes of the protocol, illustrated by bold intervals on the process timelines (each process is considered incorrect during a bold interval-for example, because its clock has drifted too far from the global mean). The real-time and atomicity properties are considerably weakened; moreover, participating processes have no way to determine if they were correct or incorrect on a given run of the protocol. Here, the messages that arrive prior to time $t + c$ are considered as valid by the protocol; the others arrive too late and are ignored by correct processes.

Thus, although the CASD protocol offers strong temporal and fault-tolerant properties to correct processes, the guarantees of these protocols may appear weaker to a process using them, because such a process has no way to know, or to learn, whether or not it is one of the correct ones. In some sense, the protocol has a concept of system membership built into it, but this information is not available to the processes in the system. The effect is to relax all the properties of the protocol suite, which is perhaps best understood as being probabilistically reliable for this reason.

A stronger statement could be made if failures were detectable so that such a process could later learn that its state was potentially inconsistent with that of other processes. There has been some encouraging work on strengthening the properties of this protocol by layering additional mechanisms over it. Gopal et al., for example, have shown how the CASD protocols can be extended to guarantee causal ordering and to overcome some forms of inconsistency (see Gopal et al.). This, however, slows the protocol down so drastically as to be useless. Another option, explored in Chapter 25, simply embraces the idea of a protocol that gives probabilistic guarantees to its users.

In the Portuguese NavTech project, Almeida and Verissimo have explored a class of protocols that superimpose a background state exchange mechanism on a CASD-like protocol structure (see Figure 23.7). In this approach, processes within the system periodically send snapshots of aspects of their state to one another using unreliable all-to-all message exchanges over dedicated but low bandwidth links. The resulting n^2 message exchange leaves the correct processes with accurate information about one another's states prior to the last message exchange and with

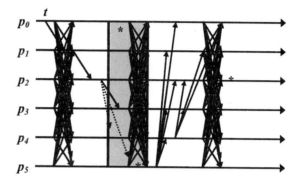

Figure. 23.7. In the NavTech protocol suite developed by Almeida and Verissimo, periodic background exhanges of state (dark intervals) cut through the normal message traffic, permitting such optimizations as early message delivery and offering information for use in overcoming inconsistency. However, short of running a group membership protocol in the background communication channel, there are limits to the forms of inconsistency that this method can actually detect and correct.

partially accurate information as of the current exchange (the limitation is due to the possibility that messages may be lost by the communication subsystem). In particular, the sender of a CASD-style broadcast may now learn that it has reached all its destinations. During the subsequent exchange of messages, information gained in the previous exchange can be exploited—for example, to initiate an early delivery of a timed broadcast protocol. Unfortunately, however, the mechanism does not offer an obvious way to assist the correct processes in maintaining mutually consistent knowledge concerning which processes are correct and which are not: To accomplish that goal, one would need to go further by implementing a process group membership service superimposed on the real-time processes in the system. This limitation is apparent when one looks at possible uses for information that can be gathered through such a message exchange: It can be used to adjust protocol parameters in limited ways, but generally cannot be used to solve problems in which the correct processes must have mutually consistent views of shared parameters or other forms of replicated state.

It would be interesting to explore an architecture in which real-time protocols are knowingly superimposed on virtually synchronous process groups, using a high-priority background channel such as the one introduced in Almeida's work to support the virtually synchronous group. With such a hybrid approach, it would be possible to exclude faulty processes from a system within a known delay after the fault occurs; adjust protocol parameters such as the delay to delivery by correct processes, so that the system will adaptively seek out the best possible delay for a given configuration; or combine the use of coherently replicated data and state with real-time updates to other forms of data and state. An approach that uses reserved-capacity, high-priority channels, such as the ones introduced by Almeida, could be used to support such a solution. At the time of this writing, however the author is not aware of any project that has implemented such an architecture.

This brings us back to the normal implementation of the CASD protocol suite. The user of such a protocol must expect that the distributed system as a whole contains processes that have become contaminated – they didn't realize it, but their clocks had drifted outside of the legal bounds, and as a result messages were delivered differently than at the correct processes. Such a process may have missed some updates to a replicated object, or seen updates out of order.

Now, keep in mind that nobody "knows" which processes are suffering from such problems. CASD doesn't exclude a faulty process from the system in the manner of the virtual synchrony protocols. Accordingly, a process in an incorrect state can still initiate new messages, and those will be delivered just like any other multicasts would be. Indeed, over time, almost any process may be viewed as incorrect for one or another run of the protocol; hence, contamination is likely to be pervasive and is capable of spreading. Mechanisms for ensuring that such a system will converge back into a mutually consistent state should a divergence of states occur are needed when these protocols are used. However, this problem has never received careful study. The most common approach is to simply restrict the use of CASD protocols to forms of information that need not be absolutely correct, or as input to algorithms that are tolerant of some degree of inconsistency. One should never use them as the basis of a safety critical decision that must be made consistently at multiple locations in a system.

The CASD protocols represent an interesting contrast with the virtual synchrony protocols we discussed earlier in this book. The virtual synchrony protocols tolerate similar types of failures, but lack any concept of time and offer no temporal delivery guarantees. On the other hand, they do offer strong logical guarantees. CASD, as we have now seen, lacks this concept of consistency, but has a very strong temporal guarantee when used by processes that are operational within its model. Thus, we have what appears to be a basic tradeoff between logical guarantees and temporal ones. It is intriguing to speculate that such tradeoffs may be fundamental ones.

The tradeoff is also noticeable in the delay of the protocol. For large values of Δ the CASD protocol provides very strong guarantees, but also has a very large latency to delivery. This is the converse of the situation for the virtually synchronous *fbcast* or *abcast* protocol, which does provide very strong guarantees and yet has very low latency to delivery in the usual case. On the other hand, *abcast* does not offer any kind of rigorously specified real-time guarantees, and can sometimes be slow (e.g., if a view change is occurring when the protocol runs, or if some process is very slow to acknowledge receipt of messages). CASD, in contrast, is normally slow to deliver messages but one can formalize its real-time properties. The only way to *guarantee* that *abcast* runs quickly involves classifying many processes as faulty – a high cost. Similarly, if we try to force CASD to deliver messages rapidly by using a small value of Δ, many processes end up inconsistent– also a high cost.

One might characterize the basic difference here as one of pessimism versus optimism. The *abcast* style of protocols is generally optimistic in its expectations from the system: It is expected that failures will be relatively uncommon events and will be optimized for the earliest possible delivery if a failure does occur. These protocols can give extremely low latency (two or more orders of magnitude better than the CASD style of protocol) and can be extremely predictable in their behavior provided that the network load is light, paging and other delays do not occur, and failures are genuinely infrequent. Indeed, if one could be *certain* that these conditions held, a protocol such as *abcast* could be the basis of a real-time system, and it would perform perhaps thousands of times better than the timed-asynchronous style of system. But hoping that a condition holds and proving that it holds are two different matters.

The CASD suite of protocols and other work by Cristian's group on the timed-asynchronous model can be viewed as relatively pessimistic, in the sense that for a given set of assumptions, these protocols are designed to expect and to overcome a worst-case execution. If CASD is used in a setting where it is known that the number of failures will be low, the protocol can be optimized to benefit from this. As we have seen, however, the protocol will only work to the degree that the assumptions are valid and that most operational processes will be considered as correct. When this ceases to be the case, the CASD protocols break down and will appear to behave incorrectly from the point of view of processes that, in the eyes of the system model, are now considered to flicker in and out of the zone of correct behavior. But the merit of this protocol suite is that if the assumptions are valid ones, the protocols are *guaranteed* to satisfy their real-time properties.

As noted above, Cristian has also worked on group membership in the timed-asynchronous model. Researchers in the Delta-4 project in Europe have also proposed integrated models in which temporal guarantees and logical guarantees were integrated into a single protocol suite (see Powell [1991], Rodrigues and Verissimo [1989], Rodrigues et al., Verissimo [1993, 1994]). For brevity, however, we will not present these protocols here.

23.3 Adapting Virtual Synchrony for Real-Time Settings

Friedman has developed a real-time protocol suite for Horus, which works by trying to improve the expected behavior of the virtually synchronous group protocols rather than by starting with temporal assumptions and deriving provable protocol behaviors as in the case of CASD (see Friedman and van Renesse [August 1995]). Friedman's approach yielded a novel extension to the view installation and message-delivery architecture for Horus, loosely motivated by the Transis idea of distinguishing safe from unsafe message delivery states. In Friedman's protocols, "safe" states are those for which the virtual synchrony properties hold, while "unsafe" ones are states for which real-time guarantees can be offered but in which weaker properties than the usual virtual synchrony properties hold.

One way to understand Friedman's approach is to think of a system in which each message and view is delivered twice (the data in a message is only copied to the user's address space a single time). The initial delivery occurs with real-time guarantees of bounded latency from sending to reception or bounded delay from when an event that will change the group view occurs to when that view is delivered. However, the initial delivery may occur before the virtually synchronous one. The second delivery has the virtual synchrony properties and may report a group view different from the initial one, albeit in limited ways (specifically, such a view can be smaller than the original one but never larger—processes can fail but not join). The idea is that the application can now select between virtual synchrony properties and real-time ones, using the real-time delivery event for time-critical tasks and the virtually synchronous event for tasks in which logical consistency of the actions by group members are critical. Notice that a similar behavior could be had by placing a Horus protocol stack running a real-time protocol side by side in the same processes with a Horus protocol stack supporting virtual synchrony and sending all events through both stacks. Friedman's scheme also guarantees that event orderings in the two stacks will be the same, unless the time constraints make this impossible; two side-by-side stacks might differ in their event orderings or other aspects of the execution.

In support of the effort to introduce real-time protocols into Horus, Vogels and Mosse have investigated the addition of real-time scheduling features to Horus, message and thread priorities, and preallocation mechanisms whereby resources needed for a computation can be pinned down in advance to avoid risk of delay if a needed resource is not available during a time-critical task.

One possible application of this real-time, fault-tolerant technology addresses the problem of building a telecommunication switch in which a cluster of computers control the actions taken as telephone calls are received (Figure 23.8). Such an application has a very simple architecture: The switch itself (based on the SS7 architecture) sees the incoming call and recognizes the class of telephone numbers as one requiring special treatment, as in the case of an 800 or 900 number in the United States. The switch creates a small descriptive message, giving the caller's telephone number, the destination, billing information, and a call identification number, and forwards this to a what is called an *intelligent network coprocessor*, or IN coprocessor. The coprocessor (traditionally implemented using a fault-tolerant computer system) is expected to perform a database query based on the telephone numbers and to determine the appropriate routing for the call, responding within a limited amount of time (typically, 100 ms). Typically, the switch will need to handle as many as 10,000 to 20,000 calls per second, dropping no more than some small percentage, and do this randomly even during periods when a failure is being serviced. The switch must never be down for more than a few seconds per year, although individual call may sometimes have a small chance of not going through and may need to be redialed.

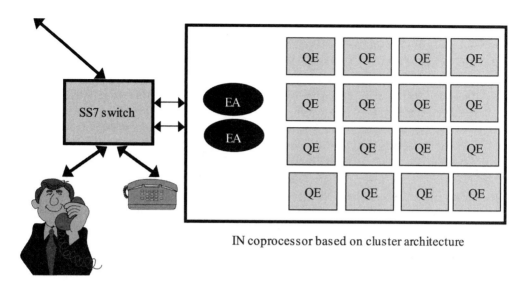

IN coprocessor based on cluster architecture

Figure 23.8.   Friedman has experimented with the use of a cluster of computing systems in support of a demanding real-time telecommunication application. On the left is a single switch, which handles telephone calls in the SS7 switching architecture. Somewhat simplifying the actual setup, we see local telephones connected to the switch from below and lines connecting to other switches above. SS7-compatible switches can be connected to adjunct processors, called IN coprocessors, which provide intelligent routing functionality and implement advanced services on behalf of the switch—for example, if an 800-number call is received, the coprocessor would determine which line to rout the call on, and, if call forwarding were in use, the coprocessor would reroute forwarded calls. Friedman's architecture uses Horus to support a cluster configuration within the IN coprocessor, an approach that provides very large scalable memory for the query elements (which would typically map a telephone directory into memory), load-balancing, and fault tolerance.

The argument in favor of using a cluster of computers for this purpose is that such a system potentially has greater computing power (and much more aggregate main memory) than any single processor could have. This may translate to the ability to keep a very large database in memory for rapid access (spread among the nodes) or of executing a more sophisticated query strategy. Moreover, whereas the upgrading of a fault-tolerant coprocessor may require that the switch be shut down, one can potentially upgrade a cluster-style computer one node or one program at a time.

Without getting into the details, Friedman has demonstrated that systems such as Horus can indeed be used to support such a model. He reports on a system emulating this configuration of telephone switch, servicing 22,000 calls per second while dropping no more than 1 to 3 percent even when a failure or recovery is actually being serviced (and this was back in 1988 – today's hardware is more than ten times faster). Friedman's design involves a pair of external adapter nodes (EAs), which sense incoming calls and dispatch the corresponding query onto pairs of query-processing nodes (QEs). Friedman batches requests and uses an innovative real-time, fault-tolerant protocol to optimize for the very high processing loads characterizing the application (see Friedman and Birman).

To solve this problem, Friedman's work combines the real-time mechanisms cited above with a number of other innovations, and it is fair to say that the application is not a straightforward one. However, the benefits of being able to use a cluster-style computing system in this manner could be dramatic: Such systems are quite inexpensive, and yet they may bring a great deal of performance and flexibility to the application, which would otherwise be very constrained by the physical limitations typical of any single-processor solution.

Although cast in the context of a telephone switching application, it should be noted that the type of real-time, client/server architecture being studied in Friedman's work is much more general. We have seen in earlier chapters of this book that the great majority of distributed systems have a client/server architecture, and this is also true for real-time systems, which typically look like client/server systems with time-critical response deadlines superimposed upon an otherwise conventional architecture. Thus, Friedman's work on telephone switching could also be applicable to process control systems, air traffic control systems, and other demanding applications that combine fault tolerance and real-time constraints.

Other work in this area includes Marzullo's research on the CORTO system, which includes such features as *periodic process groups*. These are process groups whose members periodically and within a bounded period of real time initiate synchronized actions. Marzullo has studied minimizing the communication overhead required in support of this periodic model, integrating real-time communication with other periodic or real-time actions, priority inversion in communication environments, and other topics in the area.

23.4 Related Reading

On clock synchronization, see the review in Simons et al.; other references include Cristian (1989), Kopetz and Ochsenreiter, Lamport (1984), Lamport and Melliar-Smith, Marzullo (1984), Srikanth and Toueg.

On the a-posteriori method: (see Clegg and Marzullo, Verissimo and Rodrigues).

On the CASD protocol: (see Cristian [1996], Cristian and Schmuck, Cristian et al. [1985,1990], Gopal et al.).

On the MARS system: (see Damm et al., Kopetz and Ochsenreiter, Kopetz and Verissimo).

On Delta-4: (see Powell [1991, 1994], Rodrigues and Verissimo [1989], Rodrigues et al., Verissimo [1993, 1994]).

On real-time work with Horus: (see Friedman and Birman, Friedman and van Renesse [August 1995]).

24

Transactional Systems

24.1 Review of the Transactional Model

We first encountered the transactional execution model in Chapter 6, in conjunction with client/server architectures. As noted at that time, the model draws on a series of assumptions to arrive at a style of computing that is especially well matched to the needs of applications operating on databases. In this chapter we consider some of the details that Chapter 6 did not cover: notably the issues involved in implementing transactional storage mechanisms and the problems that occur when transactional architectures are extended to encompass transactional access to distributed objects in a reliable distributed system.

Without repeating the material covered earlier, it may be useful to start by reviewing the transactional model in light of what we have subsequently learned about other styles of distributed computing and distributed state. Notice first that the assumptions underlying the transactional approach are quite different from those underlying the virtual synchrony model. Transactional applications are expected to be structured in terms of the basic transactional constructs: *begin, read, update*, and *commit* or *abort*. They are assumed to have been written in isolation, so that they will operate correctly when applied to an idle database system in an initially consistent state. Each transaction, in effect, is a function transforming the database from a consistent state into a new consistent state. The database, for its part, is a well-defined entity: It manages data objects, has a limited interface by which transactions operate on it, and manages information using operations with well-understood semantics.

General-purpose distributed systems, and many client/server applications, match such a model only to a limited degree. The computations performed may or may not act upon saved data in a database, and even when they do, it will be difficult to isolate data access operations from other types of message-based interactions and operations.

The basic reliability goals of the transactional model are tied closely to its programming model. The transactional reliability guarantees are basically this: If a server or client crashes, prior to the commit point of a transaction, a complete rollback of the server state will occur—it is as if the transaction had never been executed. There is a strong emphasis on recoverability of the database contents after a crash: Any committed transaction will have effects that survive repeated server crashes and restarts. This strong separation of computation from data, coupled with an emphasis on recoverability (as opposed, for example, to continuous availability), distinguishes the transactional approach from the process group replication schemes we have studied in the preceding chapters of this book.

One could ask whether general-purpose distributed programs couldn't be considered as transactional programs, in this manner mapping the general case to the transactional one. This turns out to be very hard to do. General purpose distributed programs lack a well-defined *begin* or *commit* point, and it would not always be practical to introduce such a structure—sometimes one could do so, but often it would be difficult. These programs lack a well-defined separation of program (transactional client) from persistent state (database); again, some applications could be represented this way, but many could not. Indeed, it is not unreasonable to remark that because of the powerful support that exists for database programming on modern computer systems, most database applications are, in fact, implemented using database systems. The applications that are left over are the ones where a database model either seems unnatural, fails to match some sort of external constraint, or would lead to extremely inefficient execution. This perspective agues that the distributed applications of interest to us will probably split into the transactional ones and others, which are unlikely to match the transactional model even if one tries to force them into it.

Nonetheless, the virtual synchrony model shares some elements of the transactional one: The serialization ordering of the transactional model is similar to the view-synchronous addressing and ordered delivery properties of a multicast to a process group.[24] Virtual synchrony can be considered as having substituted the concept of a multicast for the concept of the transaction itself: In virtual synchrony one talks about a single operation that affects multiple processes, while in transaction systems one talks about a sequence of *read* and *update* operations that are treated as a single atomic unit. The big difference is that whereas explicit data semantics are natural in the context of a database, they are absent in the communication-oriented world we considered when studying the virtual synchrony protocols.

As we examine the transactional approach in more detail, it is important to keep these similarities and differences in mind. One could imagine using process groups and group multicast to implement replicated databases, and there have been several research

---

[24]One can imagine doing a multicast by *reading the view of the group and then writing to the group members* and updating the view of the group by *writing to the group view*. Such a transactional implementation of virtual synchrony would address some aspects of the model, such as view synchronous addressing, although it would not deal with others, such as the ordered gap-freedom requirement (Chapter 16). More to the point, it would result in an extremely inefficient style of distributed computing, because every multicast to a process group would now require a database update. The analogy, then, is useful because it suggests that the fundamental approaches are closely related and differ more at the level of how one engineers such systems to maximize performance than in any more basic way. However, it is not an architecture one would want to implement!

projects that have done just this. A great many distributed systems combine transactional aspects with nontransactional ones, using transactions where a database or persistent data structure is present and using virtual synchrony to maintain consistently replicated in-memory structures to coordinate the actions of groups of processes and so forth. The models are different in their assumptions and goals, but are not incompatible. Indeed, there has been work on merging the execution models themselves, although we will not discuss this here.

Perhaps the most important point is the one stated at the start of this chapter: Transactions focus primarily on recoverability and serializability, while virtual synchrony focuses primarily on order-based consistency guarantees. This shift in emphasis has pervasive implications, and even if one could somehow merge the models, it is likely that they would still be used in different ways. Indeed, it is not uncommon for distributed system engineers to try to simplify their lives, by using transactions throughout a complex distributed system as its sole source of reliability, or by using virtual synchrony throughout, exploiting dynamically uniform protocols as the sole source of external consistency. Such approaches are rarely successful.

24.2 Implementation of a Transactional Storage System

In this section we briefly review some of the more important techniques used in implementing transactional storage systems. Our purpose is not to be exhaustive or even try to present the best techniques known; there are several excellent books dedicated to the subject (see Bernstein et al., Gray [1979], Gray and Reuter). Rather, we focus on basic techniques with the purpose of building insight into the reliability mechanisms needed when implementing transactional systems.

24.2.1 Write-Ahead Logging

A *write-ahead log* is a data structure used by a transactional system as a form of backup for the basic data structures that compose the database itself. Transactional systems *append* to the log by writing *log records* to it. These records can record the operations that were performed on the database, their outcome (commit or abort), and can include before or after images of data updated by an operation. The specific content of the log will depend upon the transactional system itself.

We say that a log satisfies a *write-ahead property* if there is a mechanism by which records associated with a particular transaction can be safely and persistently flushed to disk before (ahead of) updates to data records being done by that transaction. In a typical use of this property, the log will record before images (old values) before a transaction updates and commits records for that transaction. When the transaction does an update, the database system will first log the old value of the record being updated and then update the database record itself on disk. Provided that the write-ahead property is respected, the actual order of I/O operations done can potentially be changed to optimize use of the disk.

Should the server crash, it can recover by reviewing the uncommitted transactions in the log and reinstalling the original values of any data records these had modified. The transactions themselves will now be forced to abort, if they have not already done so. Such an event rolls back the transactions that have not committed, leaving the committed ones in place. Later, the log can be garbage collected by cleaning out records for committed transactions (which will never need to be rolled back) and those for uncommitted transactions that have been successfully aborted (and hence need not be rolled back again). (See Figure 24.1.)

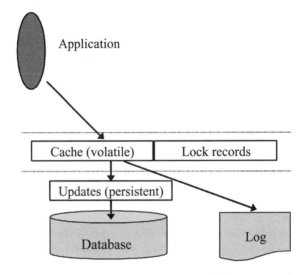

Figure 24.1.   Overview of a transactional database server. Volatile data are used to maintain a high-speed cache of database records and for storage of lock records for uncommitted transactions. An updates list and the database itself store the data, while a write-ahead log is used to enable transactional rollback if an abort occurs and to ensure that updates done by committed transactions will be atomic and persistent. The log saves before or after images of updated data and lock records associated with a transaction running its commit protocol. Log records can be garbage collected after a transaction commits or aborts and the necessary updates to the database have been applied or rolled out.

Although a write-ahead log is traditionally managed on the disk itself, there has been recent research on the use of nonvolatile RAM memory or active replication techniques to replace the log with some form of less-expensive structure (see Liskov et al.). Such trends are likely to continue as the relative performance gap between disks (which seems to have reached a performance limit of approximately 10 ms per disk access for a fast disk and as much as 40 to 50 ms per access for a slow one) and communication continue to grow.

24.2.2 Persistent Data Seen Through an Updates List

Not all transactional systems perform updates to the persistent database at the time they are first issued. The decision to do updates directly depends on several factors; among these are the frequency with which transactions are expected to abort and the likelihood that the transaction will rewrite the same record repeatedly. The major alternative to performing direct updates on the database itself is to maintain some form of *updates list* in which database records that have been updated are saved. Each access to the database is first filtered through this updates storage object, and if the record being accessed has changed, the changed version is returned. The database itself is only accessed if the updates list does not contain the desired item, and any update made to the database is instead applied to this updates list.

The advantage of such a structure is that the database itself can be maintained in a very efficient search and access structure without requiring costly structural updates as each operation occurs. Periodically, the database can be updated to merge the committed updates from the updates list into the persistent part of the database, but this does not need to be done until there is a convenient time, perhaps while the database as a whole is under very light load. Moreover, as we will see shortly, the updates list can be generalized to deal with the nested transactions that occur when transactional databases are constructed using abstract data types.

The updates list data structure, if present, should not be confused with a cache or buffer pool. A database cache is a volatile data structure used to accelerate access to frequently used data items by maintaining them in high-speed memory. The updates list is a persistent data structure, which is logically part of the database itself. Its role is to provide the database system with a way of doing database updates without reorganizing the secondary index and other access structures needed to rapidly access items in the main portion of the database.

24.2.3 Nondistributed Commit Actions

To commit a transaction, it is necessary to ensure that its effects will be atomic even if the database server or client program fails during the commit procedure. In the nondistributed case, the required actions are as follows. First, all log records associated with updates done by the transaction are forced to the disk, as are *lock records* recording the locks currently held by the transaction. Once these actions are taken, the transaction is *prepared to commit*. A log record containing the *commit bit* is now written to disk; once it is recorded in a persistent manner in the log, the transaction is said to have *committed*.

Next, updates done by the transaction are applied to the updates list or database. In many transactional systems, this updating is done while the transaction is running, in which case this step (and the forcing of log records to disk) may have already occurred before the transaction reached the commit point.

Finally, when the updates have all been performed, the locks associated with the transaction are released and any log records associated with the transaction are freed for reuse by other transactions. The transaction is now said to be *stable*.

To abort a transaction, the log records associated with it are scanned and used to roll back any updates that may have been performed. All locks associated with the transaction are released, and the log records for the transaction are freed.

In the event that the client process should crash before requesting that the transaction commit or abort, the database server may *unilaterally abort* the transaction. This is done by executing the abort algorithm and later, if the client ever presents additional requests to the server, refusing them and returning an *already aborted* exception code.

Finally, in the event that the database server should crash, when it recovers it must execute a log-recovery procedure before reenabling access to the database. During this process, any transactions that are not shown as committed are aborted, and any updates that may have been done are backed out. Notice that if the log stored before images, backing out updates can be done by simply reinstalling the previous values of any records that were written by the transaction; this operation can be done as many times as necessary if the database server crashes repeatedly before recovering (i.e., the recovery operation is *idempotent*, meaning that it can be performed repeatedly with the same effect as if it had been performed only once).

For transactions shown as committed in the log, the database server recovers by completing the commit procedure and then freeing the log records. Abstractly, the database server can be thought of as recovering in a state where the committed transactions continue to hold any locks that they held at the time of the commit; this will be useful in the case of a distributed transaction on multiple databases.

24.3 Distributed Transactions and Multiphase Commit

When a transaction operates on multiple databases, it is said to be a *distributed transaction*. The commit problem now becomes the multiphase commit problem we discussed in Section 14.5. To commit, each participating database server is first asked to *prepare to commit*. If the server is unable to enter this state, it votes for abort; otherwise, it flushes log records and agrees that it is prepared. The transaction commits only if all the participating servers are prepared to commit; otherwise, it aborts. For this purpose, the transactional commit protocols presented earlier can be used without any modifications at all.

In the case of a database server recovery to the prepared state of a transaction, it is important for the server to act as if that transaction continues to hold any locks it held at the time it first became prepared to commit (including read locks, even if the transaction were a read-only one from the perspective of the database server in question). These locks should continue to be held until the outcome of the commit protocol is known and the transaction can complete by committing or aborting. When a transaction has read data at a server that subsequently crashed, upon recovery any read locks it held at that server will be lost. This means the server might grant read or update lock requests that it should have delayed pending the commit or abort of the earlier transaction, a situation easily seen to result in nonserializable executions. Accordingly, the transaction that lost its locks would need to abort. From this we can see that a distributed transaction must include all database servers it has accessed in its commit protocol, not just the ones at which it performed updates, and must verify that locks are still intact at the time of commit, even read locks.

24.4 Transactions on Replicated Data

A transactional system can replicate data by applying updates to all copies of a database, while load-balancing queries across the available copies (in a way that will not change the update serialization order being used). In the most standard approach, each database server is treated as a separate database, and each update is performed by updating at least a quorum of replicas. The transaction aborts if fewer than a quorum of replicas are operational. It should be noted, however, that this method of replication, although much better known than other methods, performs poorly in comparison with the more-sophisticated method described in Section 24.7.

The reality is that few existing database servers make use of replication for high availability; therefore, the topic is primarily of academic interest. Transactional systems that are concerned with availability more often use primary-backup schemes in which a backup server periodically is passed a log of committed action performed on a primary server. Such a scheme is faster (because the backup is not included in the commit protocol), but it also has a window during which updates by committed transactions can be temporarily lost (e.g., if the log records for a committed transaction have not yet reached the backup when the primary crashes). When this occurs, the lost updates are rediscovered later, after the primary recovers, and are either merged into the database or, if this would be inconsistent with the database state, user intervention is requested.

Another popular option is to use a spare computer connected by a dual-ported disk controller to a highly reliable RAID-style disk subsystem. If the primary computer on which the database is running fails, it can be restarted on the backup computer with little delay. The RAID disk system provides a degree of protection against hardware failures of the stored database in this case.

Although database replication for availability remains uncommon, there is a small but growing commercial market for systems that support distributed transactions on data spread over multiple sites within an enterprise. The limiting factor for widespread acceptance of these technologies remains performance. Whereas a nonreplicated, nondistributed transactional system may be able to achieve thousands or tens of thousands of short update and read transactions per second, distributed transactional protocols and replication slow such systems to perhaps hundreds of updates per second. Although the resulting performance is adequate to sustain a moderately large market of customers, provided that they value high availability or distributed consistency more than performance, the majority of the database marketplace remains focused on scalable, high-performance systems. Such customers are apparently prepared to accept the risk of downtime because of hardware or software crashes to gain an extra factor of 10 to 100 in performance. However, it should again be noted that process group technology may offer a compromise: combining high performance with replication for increased availability or scalable parallelism. We will return to this issue in Section 24.7.

24.5 Nested Transactions

Recall that at the beginning of this book, we suggested that object-oriented distributed system architectures are a natural match with client/server distributed system structures. This raises the question of how transactional reliability can be adapted to object-oriented distributed systems.

As we saw in Chapter 6, object-oriented distributed systems are typically treated as being composed of *active objects*, which invoke operations on *passive objects*. To some degree, of course, the distinction is an artificial one, because some passive objects have active computations associated with them—for example, to rearrange a data structure for better access behavior. However, to keep this section simple, we will accept the division. We can now ask if the active objects should be treated as transactional processes and the passive objects as small database servers.

This perspective leads to what are called *nested transactions* (see Moss). The sense in which the transactions are nested is that when an active object invokes an operation on an abstract object stored within an object-oriented database, that object may implement the operation by performing a series of operations on some other, more primitive, database object. An operation that inserts a name into a list of names maintained in a name server, for example, may be implemented by performing a series of updates on a file server in which the name list and associated values are actually stored. One now will have a tree-structured perspective on the transactions themselves, in which each level of object performs a transaction on the objects below it.

In this a tree, the topmost level corresponds to an active object or program in the conventional sense. The intermediate levels of code correspond to the execution of methods (procedures) defined by the passive objects in the database. For these passive objects, transactions begin with the operation invocation by the invoking object and end when a result is returned—that is, procedure executions (operation invocations) are treated as starting with an implicit *begin* and ending with an implicit *commit* in the normal return case. Error conditions can be mapped to an *abort* outcome. The active object at the very top of the tree, in contrast, is said to *begin* a *top-level transaction* when it is started and to *commit* when it terminates normally. A nested transaction is shown in Figure 24.2.

The nested transaction model can be used for objects that are colocated on a single object repository or for objects distributed among multiple repositories. In both cases, the basic elements of the resulting system architecture resemble that of a single-level transaction system. The details differ, however, because of the need to extend the concurrency control mechanisms to deal with nesting.

The easiest way to understand nested transactions is to view each subtransaction as a transaction that runs in a context created by its parent transaction and any committed sibling subtransactions the parent executed prior to it. Thus, operation op_{21} in Figure 24.2

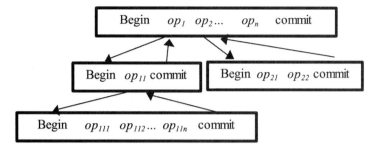

Figure 24.2. Nested transaction. The operations are numbered hierarchically: op_{ijk} thus represents the kth suboperation initiated by the jth suboperation initiated by operation i at the top level. Commit and abort becomes relative in this model, which is the result of work done by Moss and Liskov.

should see a database state that corresponds to having executed the subtransaction below op_1 and committing it, even though the effects of that subtransaction will not become permanent and globally visible until the main transaction commits. This approach can be extended to deal with internal concurrency—for example, if op_1 were executed in parallel with op_2.

Moss proposed a concept of lock and data version inheritance to accomplish this goal. In his approach, each subtransaction operates by creating new versions of data items and acquiring locks, which are *inherited* by the subtransaction's immediate parent when the subtransaction commits or which return to the state prior to when the subtransaction began if it aborts. These inherited locks and data values are accessible to other subtransactions of the parent that now retains them, but they remain inaccessible to transactions outside of its scope. Moss's Ph.D. dissertation includes proof that this approach yields a nested version of two-phase locking, which guarantees serializable executions.

To implement a nested transaction system, it is usual to start by extending the updates list and locking subsystems of the database so that it will know about transactional nesting. Abstracting, the resulting architecture is one in which each lock and each data item are represented as a *stack* of locks or data items. When a new subtransaction is spawned, the abstract effect is to push a new copy of each lock or data item onto the top of the stack. Later, as the subtransaction acquires locks or updates these data items, the copy at the top of the stack is changed. Finally, when the subtransaction aborts, the topmost stack element is discarded; if it commits, the topmost stack item is popped, as well as the one below it, and then the topmost item is pushed back onto the stack. In a similar manner, the stack of lock records is maintained; the one difference is that if a subtransaction obtains a different class of lock than that held by the parent transaction, the lock is left in the more restrictive of the lock modes.

In practice, nested transactional systems are designed to be lazy, so the creation of new versions of data items or new lock records is delayed until absolutely necessary. Thus, the stack of data items and lock records is not actually generated unless it is needed to perform operations.

A similar abstraction is used to handle the commit and abort mechanisms. Abstractly, as a nested transaction executes, each level of the transaction tracks the data servers it visits, maintaining a list of *commit participants*. In order to commit or abort, the transaction will interact with the servers on this list. In practice, however, such an approach would require repeated execution of the multiphase commit protocols, which will have to run once for each internal node in the transaction tree and one more time for the root! Clearly, this would be prohibitively expensive.

To avoid this problem, Liskov's Argus group proposed an approach in which commit decisions are *deferred*, so that only the top-level commit protocol is actually executed as a multiphase protocol (see Ladin et al. [1990], Liskov and Scheifler, Liskov et al. [1987]). Intermediate commits are optimistically assumed successful, while aborts are executed directly by informing the commit participants of the outcome. Now, the issue arises of how to handle an access by a subtransaction to a lock held by a sibling subtransaction or to a data item updated by a sibling. When this occurs, a protocol is executed by which the server tracks down a mutual parent and interrogates it about the outcomes, commit or abort, of the full transaction stack separating the two subtransactions. It then updates the stacks of data items and locks accordingly and allows the operation to proceed. In the case where a transaction rarely revisits data items, the strategy reduces the cost of the nest transactional abstraction to the cost of a flat one-level transaction; the benefit is smaller as the degree of interference increases.

The reader may recall that Liskov's group also pioneered in the use of optimistic (or lazy) concurrency control schemes. These approaches, which are analogous to the use of asynchronous communication in a process group environment, allow a system to achieve high levels of internal concurrency, improving performance and processor utilization time by eliminating unneeded wait states—much as an asynchronous multicast eliminates delay when a multicast is sent in favor of later delays if a message arrives out of order at some destination. At the limit, they converge towards an implementation in which transactions on nonreplicated objects incur little overhead beyond that of the commit protocol run at the end of the top level transaction, while transactions on replicated objects can be done largely asynchronously but with a similar overhead when the commit point is reached. These costs are low enough to be tolerable in many distributed settings, and it is likely that at some future time, a commercially viable, high-performance, object-oriented transaction technology will emerge as a serious design option for reliable data storage in distributed computing systems.

24.5.1 Comments on the Nested Transaction Model

Nested transactions were first introduced in the Argus project at MIT (see Moss) and were rapidly adopted by several other research projects, such as Clouds at the Georgia Institute of Technology and CMU's TABS and Camelot systems (see Spector) (predecessors of Encina, a commercial product marketed by Transarc). The model proved elegant but also difficult to implement efficiently and sometimes quirky. The current view of this technology is that it works best on object-oriented databases, which reside mostly on a single-storage server, but that it is less effective for general-purpose computing in which objects may be widely distributed and in which the distinction between active and passing objects can become blurred.

It is worthy of note that the same conclusions have been reached about database systems. During the mid-1980s, there was a push to develop database operating systems in which the database would take responsibility for more and more of the tasks traditionally handled by a general-purpose operating system. This trend culminated in systems such as IBM's AS/400 database server products, which achieve an extremely high level of integration between database and operation system functionality. Yet there are many communication applications that suffer a heavy performance penalty in these architectures, because direct point-to-point messages must be largely replaced by database updates followed by a read. While commercial products that take this approach offer optimizations capable of achieving the performance of general-purpose operating systems, users may require special training to understand how and when to exploit them. The trend at the time of this writing seems to be to integrate database servers into general-purpose distributed systems by including them on the network, but running nondatabase operating systems on the general-purpose computing nodes that support application programs.

The following example illustrates the sort of problems that can occur when transactions are applied to objects that fit poorly with the database computing model. Consider a file system directory service implemented as an object-oriented data structure: In such an approach, the directory would be a linked list of named objects, associating a name with some sort of abstract object corresponding to what would be a file in a conventional file system. Operations on a directory include searching it, scanning it sequentially, deleting and inserting entries, and updating the object nodes. Such a structure is illustrated in Figure 24.3.

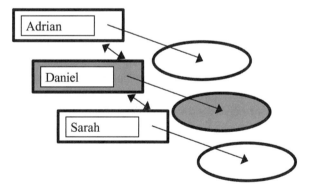

Figure 24.3. While a directory is being updated (in this case, the entry corresponding to "Daniel"), other transactions may be prevented from scanning the associated directory node by locks upon it, even if they are searching for some other record, such as the one corresponding to "Sarah" or "Adrian." Although a number of schemes can be used to work around such problems, they require sophistication by the developer, who must consider cases that can occur because of concurrency and arrange for concurrent transactions to cooperate implicitly to avoid inefficient patterns of execution. Such metadesign considerations run counter to the principle of independent design on which transactions are based and make the overall approach hard to use in general-purpose operating system settings.

A typical transaction in such a system might be a program that displays a graphical interface by which the user enters a name and then looks up the corresponding object. The contents of the object could then be displayed for the user to edit, and the changes, if any, saved into the object when the user finishes. Interfaces such as this are common in modern operating systems, such as Microsoft's Windows or some of the more advanced versions of UNIX.

Viewed as an instance of a nested transaction, this program begins a transaction and then reads a series of directory records looking for the one that matches the name the user entered. The corresponding node would then be locked for update while the user scrutinizes its contents and updates it. The transaction commit would occur when the record is saved in its changed state. An example of such a locked record is highlighted in gray in Figure 24.3.

But now consider the situation if the system has any concurrency at all. While this process is occurring, the entire data structure may potentially be locked against operations by other transactions, even if they are not interested in the same record as the user is preparing to update! The problem is that any simplistic application of the nested transaction concurrency control rules will leave the top-level records that bind names to objects locked for either read or update and will leave all the directory records scanned while searching for the name entered by the user locked for reads. Other transactions will be unable to acquire conflicting forms of locks on these records and may thus be delayed until the user (who is perhaps heading down the hall for a cup of coffee!) terminates the interaction.

Many extensions to the nested transaction model have been proposed to cope with this sort of problem. Argus, for example, offers a way to perform operations outside the scope of a transaction and includes a way for a transaction to spawn new top-level transactions from deep within a nested execution. Weihl argues for a relaxation of the semantics of objects such as directory servers: In his view, overspecification of the interface of the directory service is the cause of this sort of problem, and he suggests extensions, such as unordered queues and nondeterministic interfaces, which correspond to implementations that give better performance. In this approach one would declare the directory to be an unordered semiqueue (an unordered set) and would implement a nontransactional search mechanism in which the search order is nondeterministic and does not need to involve an access to the locked record until all other records have been scanned. Shasha has developed families of concurrent data structures, in which semantic information is exploited to obtain highly concurrent transactional implementations of operations specific to the data type. Still other researchers have proposed that such problems be addressed by mixing transactional and nontransactional objects and have offered various rules to adapt the ACID properties to such an environment.

The example we gave above occurs in a data structure of unsurpassed simplicity. Similar issues would also be encountered in other data structures, such as doubly linked lists where order *does* matter, trees, hash tables, stacks, and so forth. In each case, a separate set of optimizations is needed to achieve optimal levels of concurrency.

Those who have worked with transactions have concluded that although the model works very well for databases, there are problems for which the transactional model is poorly matched. The argument is basically this: Although the various solutions suggested in the literature do work, they have complicated side-effects (interested readers may want to track down the literature concerned with terminating what are called "orphans of an aborted nested transaction," a problem that occurs when a nested transaction having active subtransactions aborts, eliminating the database state in which those subtransactions were spawned and exposing them to various forms of inconsistency). The resulting mechanisms are complex to work with, and many users might have problems using them correctly; some developers of nested transaction systems have suggested that only experts would be likely to actually build transactional objects, while most real users would work with libraries of preconstructed objects. Thus, even if mechanisms for overcoming these issues do exist, it seems clear that nested transactions do not represent an appropriate general-purpose reliability solution for nondatabase applications.

The commercial marketplace seems to have reached a similar decision. Transactional systems consist largely of relational databases (which may be used to store abstract data types, but in which the relationships between the objects are represented in the transactional tables) or transactional file-structured systems. Although many distributed, object-oriented, transactional systems have been developed, few seem to have made the transition from research prototype to commercial use.

Intriguingly, many of the problems that are most easily solved using process groups are quite hard to solve using transactional solutions. The isolation property of transactions runs counter to the idea of load-balancing in a service replicated at several nodes or of passing a token within a group of cooperating processes. Conversely, however, transactional mechanisms bring a considerable infrastructure to the problem of implementing the ACID properties for applications that act upon persistent data stored in complex data structures, and this infrastructure is utterly lacking in the virtual synchrony model.

The implication is that while both models introduce reliability into distributed systems, they deal with very different reliability goals: recoverability on the one hand and availability on the other. While the models can be integrated so that one could use transactions within a virtual synchrony context and vice versa, there seems to be little hope that they could be merged into a single model that would provide all forms of reliability in a single, highly transparent environment. Integration and coexistence are, therefore, a more promising goal, which seems to be the one favored by industry and research groups.

24.6 Weak Consistency Models

There are some applications in which one requires most aspects of the transactional model, but where serializability in the strict sense is not practical to implement. Important among these are distributed systems in which a database must be accessed from a remote node, which is sometimes partitioned away from the system. In this situation, even if the remote node has a full copy of the database, it is potentially limited to read-only access. Even worse, the impossibility of building a nonblocking commit protocol for partitioned settings potentially prevents these read-only transactions from executing on the most current state of the database, since a network partitioning failure can leave a commit protocol in the prepared state at the remote site.

In practice, many distributed systems treat remote copies of databases as a form of second-class citizen. Such databases are often updated by periodic transfer of the log of recently committed transactions and are used only for read-only queries. Update transactions execute on a *primary copy* of the database. This approach avoids the need for a multiphase commit but has limited opportunity to benefit from the parallelism inherent in a distributed architecture. Moreover, the delay before updates reach the remote copies may be substantial, so that remote transactions will often execute against a stale copy of the database, with outcomes that may be inconsistent with the external environment—for example, a remote banking system may fail to reflect a recent deposit for hours or days.

In the following text, we briefly present some of the mechanisms that have been proposed as extensions to the transactional model to improve its usefulness in settings such as these.

24.6.1 Epsilon Serializability

Originally proposed by Pu, *epsilon serializability* is a model in which a preagreed strategy is used to limit the possible divergence between a primary database and its remote replicas (see Pu). The epsilon is supposed to represent the degree to which reported data may depart from the "actual" result, and is best understood where the database contains numeric data. In this case, the model guarantees that any value read by a transaction will be within ε of the exact answer.

Suppose, for example, that a remote transaction is executed to determine the current value of a bank balance, and the result obtained is $500. If $\varepsilon = \$100$, the model allows us to conclude that the exact balance in the database (in the primary database server for the bank) is no less than $400 and no more than $600. The benefit of this approach is that it relaxes the need to run costly synchronization protocols between remote copies of a database and the primary: Such protocols are only needed if an update might violate the constraint.

Continuing with our example, suppose we know that there are two replicas and one primary copy of the database. We can now allocate ranges within which these copies can independently perform update operations without interacting with one another to confirm that it is safe to do so. Thus, the primary copy and each replica might be limited to a maximum cumulative update of $50 (larger updates would require a standard locking protocol). Even if the primary and one replica perform maximum increments to the balance of $50, respectively, the remaining replica would still see a value within $100 of the true value, and this remains true for any update that the third replica might undertake. In general, the minimum and maximum cumulative updates done by other copies must be bounded by ε, to ensure that a given copy will see a value within ε of the exact answer.

24.6.2 Weak and Strong Consistency in Partitioned Database Systems

During periods when a database system may be completely disconnected from other replicas of the same database, we will in general be unable to determine a safe serialization order for transactions originating at that disconnected copy.

Suppose that we want to implement a database system for use by soldiers in the field, where communication may be severely disrupted. The database could be a map showing troop positions, depots, the state of roads and bridges, and major targets. In such a situation, one can imagine transactions of varying degrees of urgency. A fairly routine transaction might be to update the record showing where an enemy outpost is located, indicating that there has been no change in the status of the outpost. At the other extreme would be an emergency query seeking to locate the closest medic or supply depot capable of servicing a given vehicle.

Serializability considerations underlie the consistency and correctness of the real database, but one would not necessarily want to wait for serializability to be guaranteed before making an informed guess about the location of a medical team. Thus, even if a transactional system requires time to achieve a completely stable ordering on transactions, there may be cases in which one would want it to process at least certain classes of transactions against the information presently available to it.

In his Ph.D. dissertation, Amir addressed this problem using the Transis system as a framework within which he constructed a working solution (see Amir); see also Amir et al., Davidson et al., Terry et al. His basic approach was to consider only transactions that can be represented as a single multicast to the database, which is understood to be managed by a process group of servers. (This is a fairly common assumption in transactional systems, and in fact most transactional applications indeed originate with a single database operation, which can be represented in a multicast or remote procedure call.) Amir's approach was to use *abcast* (the dynamically uniform or safe form) to distribute update transactions among the servers, which were designed to use a serialization order deterministically related to the incoming *abcast* order. Queries were implemented as local transactions requiring no interaction with remote database servers.

As we saw earlier, dynamically uniform *abcast* protocols must wait during partitioning failures in all but the primary component of the partitioned system. Thus, Amir's approach is subject to blocking in a process that has become partitioned away from the main system. Such a process may, in the general case, have a queue of undeliverable and partially ordered *abcasts*, which are waiting either for a final determination of their relative ordering or for a guarantee that dynamic uniformity will be achieved. Each of these *abcasts* corresponds to an update transaction, which could change the database state, perhaps in an order-sensitive way, and which cannot be safely applied until this information is known.

What Amir does next depends on the type of request presented to the system. If a request is urgent, it can be executed either against the last known completely safe state (ignoring these incomplete transactions) or against an approximation to the correct and current state (by applying these transactions, evaluating the database query, and then aborting the entire transaction). A non-urgent update, on the other hand, can simply wait until the safe and global ordering for the corresponding transaction is known, which may not occur until communication has been reestablished with remote sites. As mentioned when we discussed the commit problem, Keidar and Dolev later showed that it is not necessary to achieve simultaneously connectivity in order to push such a protocol forward; it suffices that over a period of time, a majority of processes in the system manage to exchange enough messages to discover a safe event ordering.

Amir's work is not the only effort to have arrived at this solution to the problem. Working independently, a group at Xerox PARC developed a very similar approach to disconnected availability in the Bayou system (see Peterson [1997]). Their work is not expressed in terms of process groups and totally ordered, dynamically uniform, multicast, but the key ideas are the same. In other ways, the Bayou system is more sophisticated than the Transis-based one: It includes a substantial amount of constraint checking and automatic correction of inconsistencies that can creep into a database if urgent updates are permitted in a disconnected mode. Bayou is designed to support distributed management of calendars and scheduling of meetings in large organizations: a time-consuming activity, which often requires approximate decision making because some participants may be on the road or otherwise unavailable at the time a meeting must be scheduled.

24.6.3 Transactions on Multidatabase Systems

The Phoenix system (see Malloth), developed by Malloth, Guerraoui, Raynal, Schiper, and Wilhelm, adopts a similar philosophy but considers a different aspect of the problem. Starting with the same model used in Amir's work and in Bayou, where each transaction is initiated from a single multicast to the database servers, which form a process group, this effort asked how transactions operating upon multiple objects could be accommodated. Such considerations led them to propose a generalized multigroup atomic broadcast, which is totally ordered, dynamically uniform, and failure-atomic over multiple process groups to which it is sent (see Schiper and Raynal). The point of using this approach is that if a database is represented in fragments managed by separate servers, each of which is implemented in a process group, a single multicast would not otherwise suffice to do the desired updates. The Phoenix protocol used for this purpose is similar to the extended three-phase commit developed by Keidar for the Transis system and is considerably more efficient than sending multiple concurrent and asynchronous multicasts to the process groups and then running a multiphase commit on the full set of participants. Moreover, whereas such as multistep protocols would leave serious unresolved questions insofar as the view-synchronous addressing aspects of the virtual synchrony model are considered, the Phoenix protocol can be proved to guarantee this property within all of the destination groups.

24.6.4 Linearizability

Herlihy and Wing studied consistency issues from a more theoretical perspective (see Herlihy and Wing). In a paper on the *linearizability* model of database consistency, they suggested that object-oriented systems may find the full nested serializability model overly constraining, and yet could still benefit from some forms of ordering guarantees. A nested execution is *linearizable* if the invocations of each object, considered independently of other objects, leave that object in a state that could have been reached by some sequential execution of the same operations, in an order consistent with the causal ordering on the original invocation sequence. In other words, this model says that an object may reorder the operations upon it and interleave their execution provided that it behaves as if it had executed operations one by one, in an order consistent with the (causal) order in which the invocations were presented to it.

Linearizability is thus a sort of stripped down transactional property. In fact, once one gets used to the definition, the property is rather simple and almost obvious. Nonetheless, there are many distributed systems in which servers might not be guaranteed to respect this property. Such servers can allow concurrent transactions to interfere with one another or may reorder operations in ways that violate intuition (e.g., by executing a read-only operation on a state that is sufficiently old to be lacking some updates issued before the read by the same source). At the same time, notice that traditional serializability can be viewed as an extention of linearizability (although serializability does not require that the causal order of invocations be respected, few database systems intentionally violate this property). Herlihy and Wing argue that if designers of concurrent objects at least prove them to achieve linearizability, the objects will behave in an intuitive and consistent way when used in a complex distributed system; should one then wish to go further and superimpose a transactional structure over such a system, doing so simply requires stronger concurrency control.

24.6.5 Transactions in Real-Time Systems

The option of using transactional reliability in real-time systems has been considered by a number of researchers, but the resulting techniques have apparently seen relatively little use in commercial products. There are a number of approaches that can be taken to this problem. Davidson is known for work on transactional concurrency control subject to real-time constraints; her approach involves extending the scheduling mechanisms used in transactional systems (notably, timestamped transactional systems) to seek to satisfy the additional constraints associated with the need to perform operations before a deadline expires.

Broadly, the complexity of the transactional model makes it ill-suited for use in settings where the temporal constraints have fine granularity with regard to the time needed to execute a typical transaction. In environments where there is substantial breathing room, transactions may be a useful technique even if there are real-time constraints to take into account, but as the temporal demands on the system rise, more and more deviation from the pure serializability model is typically needed in order to continue to guarantee timely response.

24.7   Advanced Replication Techniques

Although the need for brevity precludes a detailed treatment of the topic, readers of this text may be interested to know that there has been a flurry of research on combining various group replication techniques with transactional database systems to obtain scalable high performance database servers (see Holiday [1999, 2002], Pedone [1998]). To the author's taste, the most interesting work in the area uses an idea originating in what has come to be known as "optimistic" concurrency control, an approach in which a transaction is permitted to execute without locks or with only some of the locks it needs, and then subjected to a "validation" test before being permitted to commit.

In this approach, a database is replicated at multiple servers, each of which has a full copy. Each server is willing to perform transactions against its local replica, with locking performed locally and reads and writes served entirely from the local replica. Later, as each transaction reaches its commit point, any updates performed by the transaction are propagated to other copies. Prior to letting the transaction commit, a test is performed to validate that transactions can commit in the order of delivery of the first-phase commit message, which is transmitted using a totally ordered multicast. This validation test involves applying the same updates and checking to make sure that the reads would be valid against the local committed replica. Agarwal has explored this technique in some detail and his results suggest that it could be quite effective. The commercial community is only beginning to take a serious look at the approach.

For example, suppose that the transactional server manages two variables, x and y and supports transactions that read and write these variables. Now suppose that we replicate the server on nodes a and b so that each has a full copy of the database.

When a read request is received, say at server a, it can be processed in the same manner as if a was the sole server in the system. The transaction obtains local read locks on the variables it accesses (waiting, if necessary, for write locks to be released if a desired data object is locally write-locked), then computes the desired result and returns.

An update transaction, however, is handled in a slightly more elaborate manner. Suppose that at server a an update transaction reads y and then modifies x and at server b a concurrent transaction reads x and then modifies y. Each is executed *locally* at the corresponding server. That is, write locks are acquired at that server, and a log is maintained of the changes made by the transaction (the new value of x in the case of the transaction on a, and of y in the case of the transaction on b). When the two transactions are preparing to commit, the system can be understood as including the locking information and the update logs in the commit messages and using *abcast* to transmit them. Thus, both servers will see these commit requests in an identical order and will process them, one by one, in that order.

Notice that if nothing else is happening in the system, these transactions will be mutually exclusive. They need to be serialized, and because we've allowed them to run concurrently against different copies of the database, one or the other will now need to be aborted.

The commit requests are evaluated relative to the committed system state to determine whether or not any committed transaction may have "invalidated" the read or write set of the transaction under consideration. The issue is as follows. While the transaction that updated x was running on server a some other transaction could have been running at server b and performing an action that would invalidate the transactional serialization order presumed at a. For example, perhaps the update transaction reads y. Recall that at server b we assumed a transaction was updating y, and its commit request may have been ordered by *abcast* ahead of that of the update to x. If that transaction committed successfully, all servers will now have updated y in their committed database. When validating the update to x we now discover that subsequent to the "time" when the x transaction was executed at a, an update to y was committed, and that the x update read the old copy of y. Agarwal suggests a very simple way to test for validity based on a notion of virtual time and an inexpensive mechanism that tracks read and write sets for transactions. At any rate, the update to x is thus discovered to have been invalidated by the concurrent update of y which already committed, and the x update is therefore aborted and forced to re-execute.

Had the *abcast* delivered the commit requests in the opposite order, the converse outcome would have occurred. Notice that because the servers ignore the currently active transactions and use only the committed database state to make decisions, and because the *abcast* ordering is the same at all replicas, all servers reach the same decision when validating each transaction. At server a we discover that the transaction to update x has aborted, roll it back, and restart it. At server b the cost is lower: upon receiving the *abcast*, that server just tests for validity, discovers that the transaction is invalid, and ignores it. Had the transaction committed, we would have applied its updates to the committed database state. Any transaction running locally that read one of these updated variables will later abort, when its own commit request is multicast to the server group.

The costs of this basic scheme, then, are rather low: we need to track the lock set (both read and write), maintain an update log, and transmit copies of this information in the commit request. And, of course, we do need to roll back and restart transactions invalidated by concurrent activity at some other server.

How well would the basic scheme scale? Here, the answer depends entirely on the mix of updates and read-only transactions, and on the amount of data each update produces. If the system sees rather few updates, and they don't touch a tremendous amount of data, Agarwal's replication algorithm will scale almost linearly in the number of servers. The cost of the commit requests would, in this case, be negligible.

On the other hand, if a large amount of data is modified by the update, transmitting the log could be a problem; in such cases, executing the same transaction in parallel on the various servers would be a much more efficient strategy. Worse still, if transactions often conflict and aborts become common, the scheme would face a high overhead – and in such a scenario, it seems likely that the rate of conflicts would rise roughly linearly in the number of servers. This is because one would normally assume that each server sees essentially the identical workload; thus, the more servers we add, the more transactions will be at risk of conflict.

Beyond Agarwal's basic idea one could do more. For example, a smart load-balancing system might try to partition update transactions, so that transactions likely to experience concurrency control conflicts go to the same server, and only transactions likely to be independent are dispatched to different servers. Although such a load-balancing agent would need to look "inside" each request to make an appropriate guess, for many applications it should be possible to do this. The frequency of update conflicts would drop accordingly.

We could do still better. Suppose that while transactions run, we use an asynchronous multicast to *lazily* inform replicas of locks held locally and to pretransmit update logs. For example, long before the transaction to update x tries to commit, we might already have informed the other servers that the transaction has a read lock on y and a write-lock on x, and has modified x to new value 24. When this information arrives, the server receiving it can stash the log of updates for later use at commit time, but can also try and obtain the identical locks locally. If no other transaction holds locks on x and y this will register the corresponding locks, with the effect that when the transaction finally tries to commit, it is far more likely to succeed. Moreover, having pretransmitted its updates, the commit message itself will be far smaller, hence faster to send. (One could even go further and pre-apply the log of updates).

In this modified scheme, we reduce the window during which a conflict can arise. However, we don't close it, since server b may learn of the activity at server a only to find that a conflicting activity has already started locally; server a will, symmetrically, discover this shortly after. But keep in mind that not all transactions commit in any case, and of course we can ultimately trust the *abcast* ordering to pick a winner if a true conflict arises and persists to commit time.

With such extensions, it seems possible that at least for databases with a mostly-read workload, a replicated system could perform read-only transactions at close to the speed of a non-replicated database, while performing updates only slightly slower. This holds the promise of near linear speedup in the sustainable read load as the database is run on more and more compute nodes, with relatively minor degradation as a function of scale (since multicast performance for small process groups of the size this might yield tends to be relatively independent of group size – up to a group of perhaps 32 members, that is). Of course, once the server pool gets large enough, the costs of transmitting update logs and handling aborts become to dominate, but this would already represent a substantial opportunity for speedup!

24.8 Related Reading

Chapter 27 includes a review of some of the major research projects in this area, which we will not attempt to duplicate here. For a general treatment of transactions: (see Bartlett et al., Gray and Reuter).

On the nested transaction model: (see Moss).

On disconnected operation in transactional systems: (see Amir, Amir et al., Davidson et al., Terry et al.).

On log-based transactional architectures: (see Birman and van Renesse [1994], Joseph, Liskov et al. [1991], Seltzer).

As part of Cornell's course on "Advanced Replication Techniques, CS734, offered in Fall of 2001, Alan Demers assembled an outstanding bibliography of techniques for replicating database systems (www.cs.cornell.edu/courses/cs734/2001fa).

25

Peer-to-Peer Systems and Probabilistic Protocols

In this chapter, we consider a number of protocols representative of a new wave of research and commercial activity in distributed computing. The protocols in question share two characteristics. First, they exploit what are called *peer-to-peer* communication patterns. Peer-to-peer computing is in some ways a meaningless categorization, since all of the protocols we've discussed in this book involve direct exchanges of messages between "peers." A better term might be "client to client" protocols, because most peer-to-peer systems emerge from a world of client/server computing, but replace some or all functions of the servers by functionality hosted on the clients themselves. For example, in what has become the most standard example of peer-to-peer computing, individuals willing to share music might copy MP3 files onto their machines, then advertise their availability in some form of directory that others can query. To obtain a song, one would look for someone with a copy, then download the file from that machine. Space permitting, the user who downloads a song would then become an alternative source for the file, so that over time, a great many copies would become available. The benefit is that the workload of serving files will be spread over a number of machines proportional to the popularity of each file, so that the system should scale well (although we'll soon need to qualify this statement with all sorts of caveats!).

P2P communication arises in many settings other than this canonical file-sharing one. We'll look at P2P protocols for building distributed indicies (for use in finding resources or data in large systems), for multicast and for monitoring the state of a large system. Yet we'll be forced by the need for brevity to overlook all sorts of other P2P protocols, aimed at problems as varied as database concurrency control and replication, tracking the membership of a system, failure detection, and even such basic functions as estimating the size of a system. And this is probably a good thing, too, since the file sharing problem arises primarily in an illegal context, where individuals are sharing music or movies in ways that violate the intellectual property restrictions imposed by the licensor. It would be unfortunate to think that the most active area of contemporary distributed systems research is primarily useful to those seeking to break the law!

Setting legalities to the side, the appeal of these kinds of protocols is dual. An often-cited reason to favor them is that some P2P solutions are remarkably scalable, stable under stresses that debilitate other kinds of solutions, and self-repairing when a disruptive failure occurs. However, we'll also see that these properties only hold for *some* P2P protocols, and that many (perhaps even most) are at risk of melting down if the system experiences rapid membership changes, a problem known as *churn*. This is a common pattern in large distributed systems, unfortunately, stemming from the behavior of their human users: a student, perhaps, who connects briefly to his preferred music swapping service, downloads a song or two, then disconnects. Even if that student is happy to share files with others, his machine is only on the network briefly, and any attempts to fetch files from it will probably fail later because the machine will no longer be available. Thus we should view scalability of P2P solutions with some skepticism, and not accept the claim that a system scales well until we've undertaken an analysis that includes costs associated with churn. Nonetheless, even if only a small subset of P2P systems really do scale well, that subset will be an important one, because many of the protocols we've reviewed in previous chapters are intended for relatively small systems and perform poorly when a system scales up.

We should note in passing that churn is a serious issue in P2P settings concerned with music sharing, although perhaps not in P2P systems constructed for other purposes. Systems like Napster must contend with a vast population of users, the great majority of whom appear suddenly, then vanish almost as quickly. Accordingly, it is important that systems such as these not incur substantial costs, such as file migration or extensive data structure changes, until a client system has been resident for a sufficiently long period of time to make it likely that the client will be around "for the duration." Such thinking causes P2P systems to distinguish between three classes of nodes. True clients are external to the system, connected to system members in some way but not actively participating in the P2P protocols. Peers are client systems that have been around long enough, and seem powerful and well-connected enough, to participate in the protocols used by the system itself, for example as file-sharing hosts. Finally, server nodes are machines either owned by the entity providing the P2P service or very powerful, very stable client nodes that have been promoted to play a major role on behalf of the service as a whole. Not all systems have all three categories of nodes, but some (such as Napster and Kazaa) do distinguish between the full range of possible behaviors in their protocols and data placement policies. P2P systems that treat all nodes identically are typically either targeted at settings in which the machines are owned by some enterprise (perhaps, "digital libraries in the United States" or "military intelligence databases") and hence known to be stable, highly available, and cooperative players, or else are basically research platforms intended for experiments but not ready for prime-time use.

Returning to our overview, a second reason for the strong appeal of P2P protocols is that many of them are amenable to a style of formal analysis that lets us predict their large-scale behavior to some degree. Usually, these predictions yield probabilistic conclusions: that the worst case lookup time for an object will be proportional to the log of the size of the system, for example, or that with high probability, healthy nodes will converge to agree on the state of the system after a delay proportional to the log of system size. Logarithmic factors figure strongly in these analyses, and while a system can never promise that every single node in the system will have the identical experience, these properties are still useful in developing highly assured applications.

We'll see two kinds of probabilistic results. The most common involves a protocol that is always "safe" in the sense that it always does the correct thing, but in which the time required to perform a desired action is probabilistically related to the size of the system or some other property, as in the case of the expected time to find an object for the P2P lookup systems mentioned above. The less common case involves a protocol in which the behavior of the protocol itself is probabilistic. For example, we'll be looking at a means of replicating data for large-scale system management in which each participant sees the same system state with probability that rises exponentially as time passes after an update, but where some participants may see an inconsistent state with low probability. The big challenge, of course, is to design applications so as to make effective use of such guarantees! But we'll see that in many cases, this is possible.

25.1 Peer-to-Peer File Sharing

As we mentioned above, the peer-to-peer area first became popular as a consequence of a revolutionary new way to distribute music and, to a lesser degree, other kinds of media files. Peer-to-peer file sharing technologies allow users to share their own music with others and to download music others are providing. Beyond this basic set of properties, such systems may have additional ones. For example, OceanStore is designed for long-term file storage and concerns itself with the danger of slow "bit rot" in situations where a file may be needed decades after it was first stored. Several recent systems, not covered here for reasons of brevity, look at such problems as sharing data in such a manner as to obscure the identity of the individual who first stored the data, the identity of those retrieving the data, or the contents of the data objects – all of this information is either obscured through encryption or hidden by the nature of the storage scheme itself. A recent generation of solutions even seeks to provide robustness against distributed denial of service attacks. These are presumably designed to defend themselves against retaliation from a music industry that believes itself to have suffered serious damage at the hands of peer-to-peer computing!

Peer-to-peer music sharing has been extremely popular – in one six-month period, some five million copies of Napster were downloaded, and it had as many as half a million simultaneous users. During 2003, one study of network usage patterns at the University of Washington in Seattle found that between 40 and 90% of the Internet bandwith from the University to the public network was generated by file sharing applications, and that within this set, almost 75% was associated with sharing entire movies – enormous files produced by copying entire DVDs from site to site.

As one might expect, the vast majority of the shared music and other media is covered by copyright restrictions and Napster and its siblings thus emerged as an enormous challenge to the recording industry, which fought back both in court and within the network itself, mounting denial of service attacks against the services themselves. As this battle advanced, the recording industry gained the upper hand on both fronts. Legally, courts have sided with the industry, agreeing that artists and their record labels have an absolute right to regulate the use of their materials. Technically, it has proved very difficult to build file sharing systems that cannot be disrupted by a motivated opponent who also has the resources to purchase substantial numbers of machines, or the capability of "spoofing" a large number of servers with a small number of powerful machines.

But even without attacks by the music industry, the technology of P2P music sharing has also proved less successful (in some ways) than one might have expected. The major systems sometimes do enormous amounts of file copying even when very little actual use is being made of the available music, and the user experience is often poor because some users have low capacity computers or poor network connections. In practice, it may be very hard to find any available node from which a "less popular" music file can be downloaded, although the current top ten files are easy to find and will probably download rapidly from a nearby location. Thus, while P2P systems might sound like the ideal way to share really obscure kinds of music, in practice one finds that they work best for the more popular artists and much less so for artists associated with more esoteric styles and less popular music.

25.1.1 Napster

Napster was the first and most popular of the P2P file sharing systems, at least until it was found to violate copyright law late in 2001. In fact, however, the Napster technology is only peer-to-peer "in part." Although file serving occurs on the clients, Napster uses a centralized directory mechanism to control the selection of peers, to generate advertising and to coordinate other kinds of revenue-generating activities.

Without becoming overly detailed, the basic structure of Napster is as follows. The core of Napster is a rather conventional server, on which a list of regional servers is maintained. When a Napster user first connects to the system, his or her machine contacts the central server and is redirected to one of these regional servers. Subsequently, the regional machine handles requests on behalf of the user.

The client system, having downloaded the basic Napster software, runs a form of file system proxy program that monitors the contents of a "shared files" folder, registering these files with the Napster system through the regional server. The folder also provides a file lookup and retrieve operation whereby the user can find a file with a desired name and then download it from any of a list of systems offering copies. Anecdotal reports suggest that several tries are often required before a suitable download peer can be identified.

Napster uses a number of mechanisms to try and work around the constraints imposed by firewalls and network address translators. In general, if both peers are behind firewalls or network address translators, lacking an implementation of the STUN mechanism mentioned in Chapter 4, it will not be possible to establish a TCP connection. However, UDP communication may still be possible, and TCP connections can be established from behind a firewall or NAT box to a machine in the public Internet. These options leave Napster with several possibilities. At the time a user's machine first connects, Napster's servers probe it to determine which connection modes will work. The system can then filter the list of possible sources for a desired file to list only machines for which connection establishment should be feasible.

Napster has no control over its users, who are motivated to "misbehave" in many ways. Users may want to download large amounts of music without serving the files back to the network, so as to minimize network traffic. They may be motivated to claim that Napster has access to more storage on their machines than is actually available (or they may use up storage nominally available to Napster subsequent to first registering). And a user may connect to Napster for such brief periods of time that they are essentially never available as hosts from which others can download files.

Napster, of course, seeks a good user experience and hence needs to do what it can to protect itself against such abuse of the cooperative model. A client machine is not reported as a possible host until it has been operational for a sufficiently long time, and the company is said to have implemented a number of other proprietary mechanisms to test the quality of client host systems and bias downloads towards good hosts with fast network connections, and also to load-balance among this set. However, relatively little detail has been published on these mechanisms and their efficacy, hence we will not discuss them in further detail here.

25.1.2 Gnutella and Kazaa

Gnutella and Kazaa are second generation Napster-like systems. Gnutella emerged as a quick-and-dirty public-domain response to the problems Napster encountered when it was found to be violating copyright law. Napster has a central server structure, and this was called out in the court proceedings as evidence that the owners of the system were deliberately encouraging copyright violation. Gnutella was designed as a pure P2P system in which all peers were completely equal, each taking responsibility for its own actions.

Gnutella serves files much as Napster does, but uses a different algorithm to find them. The Gnutella approach is based on a form of *anycast*. The protocol involves two aspects. One is concerned with ensuring that each user system is connected to a few Gnutella nodes, and with updating this connection list as nodes come and go (the details are rather "ugly" and will not concern us here, but are a part of the Gnutella specification and hence easily available to readers who wish to learn more). The second part of the scheme handles file search and works by flooding requests to all hosts within a distance designated by the client's machine. For example, if the distance limit is specified as 4, all machines within 4 hops of the client will be probed. (In practice, a download will typically iterate, first searching just nearby nodes and then widening the search to include more and more machines.) Within this set, any machine that happens to match the query will respond, and the user will typically download the file either from the first that responded or concurrently from the first two or three, since download speeds may otherwise be a problem. Many Gnutella implementations are available and some push beyond this basic download functionality by trying to download different portions of a file from different hosts, in parallel, thus reducing the performance impact of a slow choice of peer.

Experience with Gnutella suggests that as the system scales up, the *anycast* mechanism becomes extremely costly and perhaps prohibitively so. The core problem is almost certainly associated with searches for less popular files, since these will burden very large numbers of machines and it is reasonable to assume that the frequency of such requests is basically linear in the number of user (that is, the percentage of users likely to request an obscure file is probably constant, so as the number of users rises, the rate with which the system must serve requests for hard-to-find files rises too).

Kazaa is a more sophisticated second-generation commercial service, competing directly with Gnutella and Napster. The system avoids a central directory structure using a search based on what are called "Plaxton trees." When we discuss Pastry in Section 25.3.2, we'll see an example of such a structure and how it can be searched, hence we defer details until later.

25.1.3 CAN

The Content Addressable Network, or CAN (see Ratnasamy [2001]), was one of the first academic projects to tackle peer-to-peer file storage. For reasons of brevity, we won't treat it in much detail, but the basic idea was as follows. Each object is expected to have a unique system-wide name or identifier. For example, the identifier could be a fully qualified name of a track from a music CD, the name of a file in some sort of a global file system space, or any other name on which users can agree. This name is then *hashed* into a *d-tuple*. By hashing, we mean that the identifier is converted into a random-looking number using some sort of well-known, agreed upon function (often, cryptographic hashing functions are employed for this purpose, since they produce extremely uniform output distributions – as we'll see, any sort of clustering of the outputs could overload a server and force it to do more than its share of the work).

If we consider the case where CAN is used in a 2-dimensional space, an example might be a mapping under which "Spears: I'm not so innocent" is mapped to (2701, 6589) and "Doors: Riders on the Storm" is mapped to (7162, 1232).

Now, CAN repeats the identical process with the identifiers of the computers participating in the system. Perhaps, my computer is mapped to (123, 9876) and your computer to (4567, 543).

CAN's basic policy is to recursively subdivide the space of possible d-dimensional identifiers, storing each object at the node owning the part of the space (the "zone") into which that object's identifier falls, and routing queries to the node. Suppose that there is initially just a single CAN node. It will own all objects and serve all requests. If we now add an additional node to the system, that node starts by looking itself up (naturally, the lookup "finds" the single existing node). The new node and the existing node now agree to divide the existing zone, and objects that need to be moved to the joining node are moved (during this period, if a query arrives, it may still be served by the old node). When a node leaves, it hands off its objects to the node that will now own the corresponding portion of the space. Once the dust settles, the objects will have been distributed between the two nodes. We omit a detailed description of the rule used to split a node, but Figure 25.1 illustrates a possible CAN space after a number of nodes have joined and some have departed.

Clearly, the costs associated with redistribution of data within the system can become substantial, particularly if the amount of data stored in the system becomes large over time, and some joining nodes have slow links. Moreover, it is vital that any node joining a CAN system have the capacity to store the objects that will now map into its space. The author of this text is not aware of any detailed studies of the practical implications of these observations.

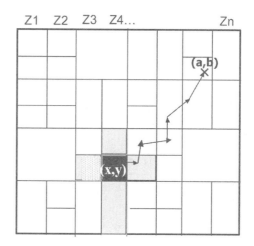

Figure 25.1. Routing in the d-dimensional space of "zones" defined by the CAN peer-to-peer storage protocol.

Navigation in the space is relatively simple. A request is provided by the user to one of the CAN nodes, and that node simply routes it to a node "closer" to the specified ID. The search will reach the node responsible for the desired object after a number of hops proportional to $(d/4) * N^{1/d}$, where N is the number of nodes in the system. For example, in our 2-dimensional space, paths will be of length proportional to the square-root of N – an intuitive result, if computers spread "uniformly" within the overall space. Notice, though, that if some fluke of placement puts lots of computers in one corner of the space, we could end up with abnormally long paths in that area.

Additionally, it is important to realize that a system running the CAN algorithm is capable of "losing" data – the node on which an object is stored could crash without having time to hand off its objects to neighbors. Thus the CAN user is expected to refresh any stored objects periodically, and may also implement a policy of storing backup copies: rather than just storing one copy of the Stone's song, CAN could be asked to store "Riders on the Storm:1", etc. A system that is unable to locate a desired copy could increment the copy number and try again, and might even initiate multiple concurrent searches.

As we just mentioned, the CAN search structure can become sub-optimal if many nodes join or leave, hence periodically a "rebuilding" algorithm is launched to clean the structure up. An interesting question would arise if conditions were such that the need for reconstruction of the data structure began to arise faster than the running time of this cleanup algorithm, since CAN might then degenerate, endlessly trying to rebuild its search structure and never quite cleaning up. The author is not aware of any detailed study of the conditions under which such a problem might actually arise. Should this happen, CAN would "thrash" much as a file system can thrash, working very hard but accomplishing very little useful work.

25.1.4 CFS on Chord and PAST on Pastry

A number of recent systems, notably CFS and PAST (see Dabek [2001], Rowston [2001]), operate by separating "storage" from lookup. These systems make use of indexing systems (Chord and Pastry, respectively), to locate nodes on which they store objects or from which they retrieve copies. We'll be looking closely at both Chord and Pastry below, so we limit ourselves to a quick summary. These systems both hash identifiers into a 1-dimensional space (that is, into a single number), within which they do a lookup, although using algorithms different from the one employed by CAN.

In both CFS and PAST, files are replicated prior to storage. CFS goes further, treating each file as a list of blocks. Thus, a music file might be stored as a large number of blocks, and each block stored many times. The intent is to ensure that even if nodes join or leave the system, copies of a desired file will still be available. In the case of CFS, the copies are stored at adjacent locations in the hashed-id space; this is convenient because in Chord, if a node handling some part of the ID space fails, a neighbor will become the owner of that part of the space (thus, if information is replicated at that neighbor, a search will still find the desired object). There has also been some exploration of assigning each machine multiple ID's and having itself serve requests under each of these ID's; doing so seems to result in a more uniform distribution of labor within the system as a whole than if each node resides at just a single place in the hashed ID space.

A problem that can arise in CFS or PAST is that if a node fails, the number of replicas remaining in the system will drop. Moreover, if a node joins and takes responsibility for a portion of the ID space, a considerable number of files (or file blocks) may need to be transferred to it. Thus, when nodes join or leave these systems, a long-term cost will often result, as a wave of copying is triggered. Should further joins and leaves occur before this is terminated, one can imagine situations in which CFS or PAST bog down, endlessly shuffling files about and consuming the entire available bandwidth of the network to do so. The user would conclude that the system had begun to thrash in such a situation, observing huge amounts of file I/O and a tremendous amount of network I/O with little evidence that useful work was being accomplished, and might well shut the system down – a meltdown scenario for these two systems.

25.1.5 OceanStore

OceanStore (see Kubiatowicz 2000) is an example of a file system implemented over a peer-to-peer architecture (Chord) but with quite a different objective than in any of the systems mentioned above. Whereas CAN, CFS and PAST focus on file storage for the purpose of sharing, OceanStore is focused on longer term archival storage. This results in a model where files are replicated not to overcome churn, but to ensure that there are enough copies available to compensate in the event that a file server fails either by becoming permanently unavailable or by corrupting file contents. To this end, OceanStore has pioneered in the use of what are called "Erasure Codes," namely a class of error-correcting codes that can reconstruct a valid copy of a file given some percentage of the copies. Studies have shown that even a very small bit overhead is sufficient to provide many hundreds of years of expected availability under modeled server characteristics typical of what is seen in corporate data centers or digital libraries.

OceanStore poses a provocative question: Should we begin to design computing systems that might be capable of continuing to function long after current hardware and software has been outmoded, or is this a meaningless objective? Historical precedent would seem to argue both for and against such a proposition. In the affirmative we need merely think back to the Year 2000 phenomenon, when countless corporations discovered themselves to be dependent upon hundreds of millions of lines of "legacy" software, written as much as 30 or 40 years ago, and running today behind wrappers of various kinds, on emulators simulating the behavior of long-vanished software, or even on the very last instances of classes of servers that were state of the art in the 1970s. Arguing against is the immutable law of technical evolution: over time, no system survives. Hardware is replaced by new generations of hardware, software by new languages and new applications, and ultimately, everything is upgraded. Is it meaningful to talk about storing digital documents for use tens or even hundreds of years in the future, when the operating systems on which the applications capable of reading those documents no longer exist, the applications themselves are no longer available, and the hardware on which they ran is long forgotten?

OceanStore, along with many Digital Library projects, is betting that long term storage really will prove important, and through the innovative combination of P2P technology with erasure codes, showing that there may be ways to solve such problems under relatively modest assumptions about the environment.

25.2 Peer-to-Peer Distributed Indexing

When discussing the PAST and CFS systems, we noted that more and more developers are viewing distributed file systems as having two parts: a lookup mechanism designed to track down the node holding an object, and then a superimposed file system application that knows how to store and retrieve files within a system provide that the file objects can be located efficiently. A distributed "indexing" mechanism does precisely this. The Internet DNS is a good example of an existing distributed indexing tool – we use it to map machine names to IP addresses. Peer to peer indexing tools go one step further, creating indicies that let the user store (*key, value*) pairs, offering great flexibility with respect to the interpretation both of the key (which could be a file name, a machine identifier, the identification of some other sort of object, etc) and the value (which could be the address of a machine responsible for the key, the actual value sought by the user, etc).

Many systems refer to a distributed index of this sort as a *distributed hash table* (although the term *index* is more standard in the database literature and would seem entirely applicable here). A distributed hash table, or DHT, is any system that takes (*key, value*) pairs as input, hashes the key to establish a mapping from keys to machines, then stores the tuple at the location identified in this manner for later retrieval. It is common to assume that updates are rare and reads rather common, and in some systems, one assumes that once written, the value associated with a key will never be changed (although those systems often do provide a means by which the (*key, value*) pair can be deleted).

In what follows, we review several of the major DHT architectures, focusing on Chord because it is simple and extremely well known, Pastry because it is the best known and mostly widely used DHT to employ what are called Plaxton trees, and Kelips, a DHT that accepts a higher storage cost at each node in order to gain much faster lookup times (O(1) instead of O(log(*N*)) in most other systems).

25.2.1 Chord

The idea behind Chord (Stoica [2001], Balakrishnan [2003]) is to form a massive virtual ring in which every node in the distributed system participates, "owning" a portion of the periphery. This is done as follows. Given a key or a node identifier, Chord hashes the value into a large non-negative value space (the actual size of the space is immaterial; 128 bits is typical). A machine is understood to "own" the region of the ring corresponding to hashed values less than or equal to its own value, but greater than the value associated with the next smaller hashed node ID. For example, if nodes *a*, *b*, and *c* hash to locations 10, 90 and 150 respectively, then *b* is responsible for ID's 11–90, *c* for ID's 91–150, and *a* for 151–10.

Chord operates in the obvious way. A machine joining the system computes its node ID, finds some existing node, and requests a lookup of its own ID. This leads the machine to an existing node that owns the region of the ID-space into which the new machine will fall. A state transfer is then performed, moving the (*key, value*) pairs that the new node should handle from their previous owner to the joining node, and it is simultaneously linked into place. Searching can be performed either by a form of hot-potato forwarding of requests around the ring or by a series of probes, whereby the new node issues an RPC to each node around the ring in succession until it finds its place. Of course, such a lookup would be painfully slow: on the average, each request would visit half the nodes in the system.

We should perhaps mention at this juncture that a "hop" in any of these systems – DHTs, P2P file systems, and indeed all of the systems we'll discuss below, can be quite expensive. Having hashed the node IDs we create a situation in which a node located in Kenya is as likely to be located "next" to a node located at MIT as is a node at Harvard (more or less up the block). Sending messages to Kenya isn't particularly fast. Even that node at MIT or Harvard could be on a dreadfully slow modem, a wireless link, or some other odd networking device, and the node itself could be a powerful server, but could equally well be the famous MIT coffee machine (linked to the Web to report the freshness of the current pot of coffee) or some sort of state of the art embedded sensor. Thus when we talk about hops through a DHT, we are rather casually invoking a potentially costly activity. Visiting more than a few nodes in a large system would be lunacy.

Indeed, a back-of-the-envelope calculation reveals two kinds of problems. First, consider the fact that the average path through the Internet, at the time of this writing, was about 22 network hops in length (here we are talking about routers, not DHT participants). Each of those hops introduces some delay, perhaps 500 us, hence the average Internet path is on the order of 10 ms in length, with longer distances corresponding to delays of as much as 50 or 100 ms (cross-ocean links, for example, or paths involving a satellite). Thus if we begin to visit nodes all over the world, each hop could cost a substantial fraction of a second. Next, consider the issue of slow connection devices. If 10% of all nodes are connected to the network by a slow device, than any path of length at least 10 (here we're back to paths within the DHT itself) is extremely likely to visit at least one slow machine. Similarly, if 10% of all machines are slow to respond, any path 10 hops long will probably include at least one slow responder.

The Chord designers recognized this problem and tackled it using two mechanisms. One is aimed at the obvious case where an application repeatedly accesses the same object: Chord nodes cache link information, so that having performed a lookup, each node along the path also learns some downstream (hashed) node ID's and IP addresses and can use them to accelerate future requests. Additionally, when a node joins the Chord system, at hashed location *hash(key)*, it also looks up the node associated with *hash(key)/2, hash(key)/4, hash(key)/8*, etc. Using these cached pointers, Chord has a quick way to perform a kind of binary search within the ring, bounding any search to worst-case $\log(N)$ lookups. Figure 25.2 shows a possible Chord configuration, and Figure 25.3 illustrates the idea of a finger table. In Figure 25.4, we see a possible path that a lookup operation might take through the Chord network.

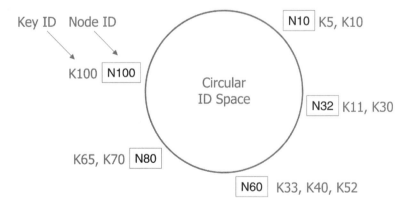

Figure 25.2. The Chord ID space is a ring in which both nodes and keys are mapped to locations along the circumference. Here, five computers are shown (nodes N10, N32, etc) and a few (*key, value*) pairs; the values are omitted since they are application-specific. One way to search the space is to proceed node by node around the periphery, but this will be slow. To ensure robustness of the data structure, each node tracks the ID's of several predecessors and successors.

We should keep in mind that $\log(N)$ isn't necessarily good news. With as few as 100 nodes, $\log(N)$ is already 7, and as noted earlier, we may now be looking at delays of 350 ms or more in the best case – and perhaps much worse if the path is unlucky enough to hit a node or two running with a slow modem or on a slow computer. Chord therefore needs a mechanism to avoid performing lookups entirely. It does this by caching pointer information, in the hope that "cold" lookups will be infrequent events.

This is perhaps a good point to mention that if a node leaves the system or fails,

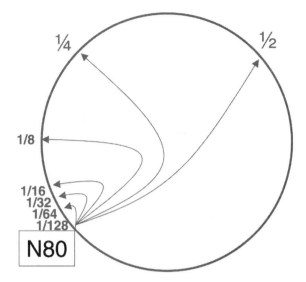

Figure 25.3. Chord maintains a "finger table" at each node in which short-cuts to nodes at various distances within the hashed key space are stored. This supports a form of binary search.

Chord will be left with dangling pointers to it. The system notices these when attempting to follow those pointers. It deletes bad cached pointers, and rebuilds its finger table if a finger pointer goes bad. As mentioned earlier, the frequency of such events is a topic of

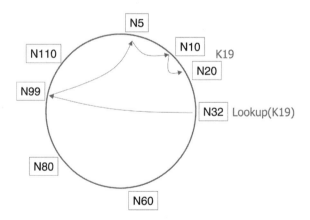

Figure 25.4. A lookup follows a path through the Chord ring using the finger table to approximate a binary search. This lookup must go in a "forward" direction. Thus, node 32 sends the request half-way across the ring, into a region handled by node 99. Node 99 advances by a further quarter, to node 5, and so forth until we reach node 20. Even in a very large network, a Chord lookup shouldn't take more than $\log(N)$ hops to complete unless large numbers of nodes have failed and the finger tables are stale.

hot debate. In systems that experience a great deal of churn, it could be a common phenomenon.

Churn in Chord raises additional issues too. Suppose that the system experiences a
significant rate of nodes joining and leaving the system. Each time this happens, keys
needed to be shuffled (and if those leave events include some crashes, keys could also be
lost). Over time, the binary lookup structure may also degrade, even if relatively few nodes
have departed. For example a pointer to index 1234 could turn out to point to a node owning
keys 5789 through 6781, simply because ownership of keys changes as the membership
in the system changes. Indeed, one can easily see that if nodes have an average lifetime
in the system of τ seconds and each node maintains the addresses of $\log(N)$ other nodes,
then after time $\tau * \log(N)$ most of those pointers will need to be recomputed. To ensure a
high quality of search structure, Chord may need to refresh its pointers with frequency close
to τ! This, of course, means that Chord could have a substantial background overhead in
larger networks or networks subject to churn, in addition to the overhead associated with the
application itself and its own handling of churn. Moreover, when the Chord data structure
degrades, the quality of lookup presumably does too, so that $\log(N)$ may not be the true
worst-case lookup delay for this system.

As a final concern, many researchers have noted that Chord is vulnerable to a number
of styles of attack. For example, a compromised node could simply lie, claiming to own
some part of the space and responding to a request that is actually not destined to it, and
could even insert itself into the ring multiple times. There has been some work by Castro
and others on the use of Byzantine Agreement to overcome such problems, but as a purely
practical matter, the cost implication of doing so appears to be very high.

Despite these concerns, Chord remains an extremely popular system. The software
implementing it is available for free from the developers at MIT, and the architecture is easy
to understand. Few researchers working with P2P systems ever tackle problems involving
more than a few dozen machines, hence the limitations of Chord are not encountered in
most of its current applications. Thus readers of this textbook should give consideration
to downloading and using Chord in their own research, while remaining wary of possible churn-related cost issues if the system ever comes under the kinds of stresses just
mentioned.

25.2.2 Pastry

The Pastry system (Rowston [2001]) is based on an idea first proposed by Vern Plaxton. The
basic concept revolves around the construction of a matrix of pointers ("finger pointers")
at each participating node. The matrix is of size $r \ x \ \log_r(N)$ where r is a *radix* and N, of
course, is the system size. For example, if we were to use base 16, and knew our system to
contain approximately 16^5 nodes, the table would be of size 16×5. Figure 25.5 illustrates
such a Pastry routing table for a node with hashed ID 65a1fc.

Pastry starts by mapping keys into a hashed identifier space, just like Chord, CAN and
the other systems mentioned earlier. By following the pointers, a request is routed closer

0	1	2	3	4	5		7	8	9	A	B	C	D	E	F
X	X	X	X	X	X		X	X	X	X	X	X	X	X	X
6 0 X	6 1 X	6 2 X	6 3 X	6 4 X		6 6 X	6 7 X	6 8 X	6 9 X	6 A X	6 B X	6 C X	6 D X	6 E X	6 F X
6 5 0 X	6 5 1 X	6 5 2 X	6 5 3 X	6 5 4 X	6 5 5 X	6 5 6 X	6 5 7 X	6 5 8 X	6 5 9 X		6 5 B X	6 5 C X	6 5 D X	6 5 E X	6 5 F X
6 5 A 0 X		6 5 A 2 X	6 5 A 3 X	6 5 A 4 X	6 5 A 5 X	6 5 A 6 X	6 5 A 7 X	6 5 A 8 X	6 5 A 9 X	6 5 A A X	6 5 A B X	6 5 A C X	6 5 A D X	6 5 A E X	6 5 A F X

Figure 25.5. A sample Pastry routing table for a node with hashed ID 65a1fc.

and closer to the node owning the corresponding portion of the hashed-key space. The table encodes the node-ID information, with more resolution for nodes close to the key of the process holding the table. The first row of the Pastry routing table represents routing information for keys which have a first digit corresponding to the row index. For example, column 3 in the top row of the routing table gives the node address of a node "closer" than the current node for hashed keys starting with the digit 3.

For the node's own ID, 6 in our example (65a1fc), we get a "match" and this takes us down to the second row of the table, where we find routing information based upon the second digit of the hashed key. A 2-digit match takes us to the third row, and so forth.

Notice that Chord and Pastry are similar in many ways. The Chord finger table has one pointer half way across the system, one pointer a quarter of the way across, etc. A Pastry finger table has one pointer for each possible "first digit" of the hashed key, then one for each possible "second digit." Yet both tables are of size logarithmic in the size of the system, and both are used for a similar style of lookup operation.

The designers of Pastry realized that, like Chord, their system would perform poorly if finger tables were allowed to degrade. To reduce this risk, Pastry periodically probes each finger, and repairs broken or inaccurate links when it notices problems. Studies have shown that the heuristic works well in most settings, although it isn't hard to design "adversarial" scenarios that overwhelm this repair mechanism.

An important use of Pastry is to support application-level multicast (this is needed because IP multicast is poorly supported in WAN settings). Scribe (see Rowston and

Druschel [2001] and [2002]) is a system that uses Pastry to orchestrate the construction of an overlay multicast structure. More recently, van Renesse has been working on Willow, a system that uses aggregation to build such an overlay multicast structure; the work is reported in van Renesse [2004].

25.2.3 Tapestry and Brocade

For completeness, we note that at UC Berkeley, a system similar to Pastry (but differing in the details) has been developed. Called Tapestry (Zhao [2003]), the basic approach used in this system is similar to what is done in Pastry, but there is a second layer of wide-area routing superimposed on the system to minimize the frequency of wide-area "hops" and keep routing as localized as possible. Called Brocade, this wide-area routing infrastructure is a form of network overlay, and the combined system achieves high performance under conditions where Tapestry alone might not. (Pastry seeks to obtain similar results through its link-probing and self-organizing mechanisms).

25.2.4 Kelips

All of the DHTs discussed up to now have logarithmic storage overhead at each node. Yet one might question the value of limiting storage this way. After all, in a system of 1,000,000 nodes, this limits storage to 25 table entries; one might wonder if a bigger table would improve performance. Meanwhile, as the system gets larger, we face potentially crippling communication overheads even when things go well, and some risk of thrashing when churn occurs.

The developers of large systems often consider trading higher storage overhead for a reduced risk of churn and better performance. Kelips, a system developed by the author's research group at Cornell (Gupta [2003]), explores this design point, using $O(sqrt(N))$ storage and achieving O(1) lookup speeds. But this is only one of several tradeoffs within Kelips. Notice that all of the P2P systems mentioned up to now have the potential for bursts of communication when conditions change or churn occurs, and it is difficult to estimate worst case communication costs because these are dependent upon the rate at which relevant events occur. Kelips, in contrast, imposes a constant communication overhead – one that may be higher than in other systems when "nothing is happening" (since others would then quiesce), but that won't surge when conditions degrade. In consequence, Kelips is certain to remain operational under any imaginable conditions. While the quality of data may lag if updates occur very rapidly,[25] Kelips is stable and scalable in ways that other DHTs may be unscalable and/or unstable.

In explaining the Kelips system, we encounter a slight chicken and egg problem. Later in this chapter, in Section 25.3, we'll discuss a protocol called "Bimodal Multicast." Kelips

[25]Liskov has argued that in systems where updates are frequent, Kelips might fall arbitrarily behind, in which case the average query could return stale data. On the other hand, Linga and Gupta have experimented with Kelips in settings that experience considerable churn and that do have high update rates, and their results suggest the problem discussed by Liskov doesn't arise (or at least is hard to provoke).

actually uses this protocol as part of its implementation. However, we don't wish to repeat the protocol in this subsection, and hence will describe its use and properties very briefly here, leaving details for later.

The basic idea behind Kelips is to divide the overall system into $sqrt(N)$ process groups, each having approximately $sqrt(N)$ members. We assume that there is an agreed-upon estimate of N. This need not be extremely accurate as long as everyone knows the nominal value. Assignment of processes to these groups is based upon a hash of the node identifier, just as in the systems reviewed earlier. A (*key, value*) pair is hashed to one of these groups and then a form of multicast is used to fully replicate the tuple among the group members.

Kelips process groups do not use the group membership and multicast protocols discussed earlier. Instead, they use a form of communication based on what is called "gossip." Setting details to the side, the basic idea is that each process has some (perhaps inaccurate) estimate of membership in its group. At a regular interval (but not synchronized with other processes in the system), each process picks some member at random within the ones about which it knows and sends that member a summary of its own state: the members it knows about, and the (*key, value*) pairs it has. If the member to which this gossip is sent is missing some of these tuples, it updates its state, and if it is unaware of some members, it learns about them in this manner. It isn't hard to see that any information known to even a single group member will tend to propagate to all group members within $\log_2 (sqrt(N))$ rounds of gossip. For example, in a system with 10,000 nodes, $sqrt(N)$ is 100 and $\log_2(100)$ is approximately 7. If gossip occurs once every 5 seconds, information will still be fully replicated within about 35 seconds. Each process will send and receive one gossip message, on average, during each "unit" of time. Moreover, Kelips limits the size of these messages; if the information available doesn't fit, each message will contain a random subset of the data the node intended to include. This imposes a strict limit on costs.

But how is information queried in Kelips? As noted above, a process tracks the membership of its own replication group using gossip, and hence maintains a data structure of size $sqrt(N)$. However, we also maintain an additional data structure of size $k \, x \, sqrt(N)$ for some small value of k, perhaps 2 or 3. The system continuously gossips about "recently heard from" system members, hence all members see a slow but steady trickle of reports that *node a recently sent me a message* or *node b recently sent a message to node c*. This communication spans all process groups, and provides all members with a glimpse of the membership of groups other than their own. They sample this stream, picking out k members of each group as representative contacts, using a pseudo-random scheme to do so. More precisely, at random, each node will consider replacing one of its existing contacts with some new contact for group g to which it does not itself belong. It picks a new contact for g and pings that contact, while also pinging its own existing contacts. The best k contacts in the set become the new group g contacts for this process.

Figure 25.6 illustrates the structure of Kelips.

A process queries a group by sending its request to one or more of the group contacts for the group in which the *hkey* falls. Because data is fully replicated by the system, any

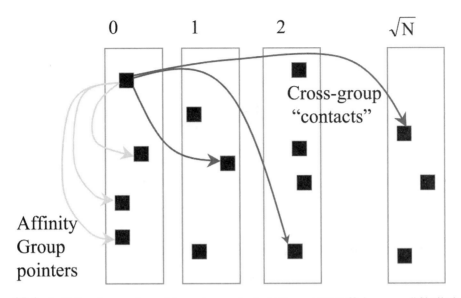

Figure 25.6. In Kelips, the members of the system are hashed into $sqrt(N)$ "affinity groups." Similarly, each *(key, value)* pair is mapped to one such group. A gossip protocol that has a low but continuous and constant cost is used to replicate *(key, value)* data within the affinity group to which a given key maps, so that within a period of time proportional to $\log(sqrt(N))$, all group members know the tuple. To support lookups, each Kelips member maintains pointers to a small number of members of each affinity group. A lookup thus can be done in just one "hop." Kelips thus trades higher costs *($sqrt(N)$ space and constant communication loads)* for fast lookups and good resistance to churn or other disruptive events.

contact that can be reached should be able to respond to such a request, hence there is no need to forward messages or store complex search information. Either the *(key, value)* tuple is known, and the tuple is tracked down, or the tuple is unknown and the application is so informed. The risk of an erroneous result drops exponentially as more group members are queried.

Notice that Kelips, like Pastry, is self-reorganizing. The system continuously monitors changes to its membership using a low-overhead background protocol, and each member periodically probes each of its contacts in other groups. If a member joins or leaves, or a new potential contact is discovered in a group for which one of the existing contacts is slow or unresponsive, Kelips will automatically update its contact list – after all, any contact in a given group is as good as any other from a correctness point of view, so the system might as well optimize for lowest latency.

A consequence of this mechanism is that as conditions change, nodes that fail or have poor performance will tend to be dropped from contact lists and membership lists, while nodes that join or that have good performance will be favored. Similarly, a node that is experiencing some form of churn will tend to be dropped from contact lists system-wide. This happens continuously while the system is healthy, hence if the system comes under sudden stress, it has a good chance of remaining responsive until conditions improve again.

Overheads never surge or even change, hence churn cannot trigger any form of overload. Indeed, Kelips is implemented over UDP, so that if packets don't get through, the system simply moves on.

Linga and Gupta have experimented on Kelips under conditions that might arise in a system experiencing severe churn, and found that in contrast to most other P2P schemes, Kelips continues to give very rapid response to lookup operations. Moreover, they found that the sustainable update rate was high even when the system was under stress – they used a trace-driven evaluation designed to explore Kelips in a hypothetical cooperative Web caching situation similar to the one for which the Squirrel system (built using Pastry) has been used. Kelips is a good example of a P2P system with probabilistic stability, scalability and update-latency properties, in addition to its constant lookup times and constant background costs. See Gupta [2003], Linga [2003] for more details.

25.3 Bimodal Multicast Protocol

Up to now, we have focused on P2P file sharing systems and indexing (DHT) systems. In this section, we shift our focus and look at a class of multicast protocols that use P2P techniques to achieve a high degree of scalability. They are also *probabilistically reliable*. Unlike the protocols presented previously, they are based on a probabilistic system model somewhat similar to the synchronous model, which we considered in our discussion of real-time protocols. In contrast to the asynchronous model, no mechanism for detecting failure is required. Virtual synchrony is not supported "directly" on this model, but we do note that Gupta has shown how to implement a scalable virtual synchrony protocol over the Bimodal Multicast (Birman [1999]), obtaining a solution that is always safe, but may report new views after a delay that rises slowly in group size.

Figure 25.7 illustrates the type of scalability problem we're trying to overcome. In this figure, we've graphed the "steady state" throughput of the basic *abcast* protocol implemented in the Ensemble system. Each line on the graph corresponds to a different group size: 32, 64, and 96 members. The x axis shows how performance is impacted by a "perturbation" at a single member within the overall group, where we stole cycles by forcing the process to sleep for brief intervals of time, thus mimicking the behavior one might see if the process shared the computer with some other workload. With $x = 0$, the process was unperturbed, with $x = .3$, 30% of the time it was sleeping, and so forth.

As can be seen in the figure, this rather minor intervention causes the sustainable throughput to collapse. We should note that the actual throughput numbers aren't very important here – the experiment was performed on an IBM SP2 cluster and used rather large messages, but similar graphs can be obtained for almost any size of message and on any platform.

The problem may at first glance seem specific to the implementation of the protocol: it turns out that when this experiment is running, the sender is forced to choke back (to perform flow control) because messages are piling up in the buffer it uses to retransmit

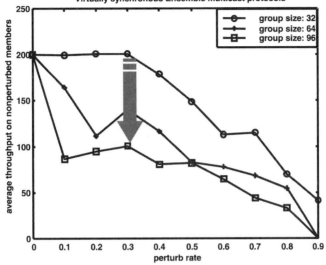

Figure 25.7. Throughput of a virtually synchronous process group suffers when even a single member is perturbed, and the problem gets worse as the group size increases. This suggests that traditional ways of implementing virtual synchrony scale poorly.

lost messages in the event of a communication problem. As the group gets bigger the percentage of messages for which an acknowledgement arrives only after a long delay seems to grow, hence the sender exhausts its buffering space. Studies have shown, however, that this kind of problem is anything but unique to the virtual synchrony reliability model or its implementation in Ensemble. In fact, the great majority of "reliable" multicast protocols share such behavior—regardless of their particular reliability goals. The reasons for the collapse vary from protocol to protocol, but the collapse of achievable throughput seems to be a common phenomenon.

In contrast, the P2P multicast protocols we'll now discuss are scalable in two senses. First, message costs and latencies grow slowly with system size. Second, reliability (the probability of non-atomic delivery of a multicast) falls to 0 exponentially as group size increases. This scalable reliability is achieved through a form of "gossip" protocol, which is strongly self-stabilizing. By this we mean that if the system is disrupted, it will repair itself given a sufficient period of time without failures. Our protocols (particularly for handling replicated data) also have this property.

The basic idea we will work with is illustrated in Figure 25.8, which shows a possible execution for a protocol we call Bimodal Multicast. Bimodal multicast combines a message distribution phase with a *gossip* repair phase, and we see both types of events in the figure (the figure makes it look as if the system runs in synchronous rounds, but that's just to make it clear how things work; the actual protocol isn't at all synchronous and both kinds of rounds are superimposed). The basic idea is as follows. To send a multicast, a process transmits it with some form of quick but not necessarily reliable transport layer, like IP multicast.

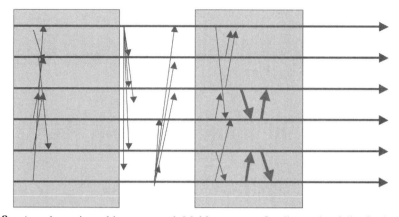

Figure 25.8.   A push gossip multicast protocol. Multicast uses a flooding-style of distribution mechanism, with no effort to achieve reliability (perhaps, IP multicast, perhaps some other scheme). Periodically, each process shares state information with a randomly selected peer, allowing each to catch up with any missed messages that the other received, and within a few rounds, the gaps are filled. Bimodal Multicast will reissue an (unreliable) multicast within a region where it seems likely that several receivers are missing copies, so this gap fill mechanism is used to clean up just the last few gaps in the message sequence.

(If IP multicast isn't available, as is the case in the modern Internet, we can use Scribe trees – a type of overlay built on the Pastry system, or some similar hand-built multicast layer, with no particular reliability guarantees). So this is shown in the unshaded portions of Figure 25.8.

Next, we introduce a form of gossip protocol motivated by work originally done by Demers and others at Xerox PARC (see Demers et al.). After a process receives a message, it begins to "gossip" about the message to a set of peers (in Figure 25.8 this occurs during the shaded periods). The number to which it gossips is said to be the *fanout* of the protocol. Gossip occurs at regular intervals, and offers the members a chance to compare their states and fill any gaps in the message sequence. As mentioned in the caption of the Figure, the actual protocol runs gossip continuously and is unsynchronized.

Even if the initial multicast was a complete failure (and this can happen, although it is unlikely), gossip protocols will typically flood the network within a logarithmic number of rounds. This behavior is very similar to that of a biological epidemic; hence, such protocols are also known as *epidemic* ones (see Bailey). Notice that although each process may hear about a message many times, it doesn't need to receive multiple copies of the message: the gossip messages typically are very compact lists of messages available at the sender, and the actual copies must be retrieved in a separate RPC-style interaction. In fact, the cost of gossip is basically constant. The randomness of the protocols has the benefit of overcoming failures of individual processes, in contrast with protocols where each process has a specific role to play and must play it correctly, or fail detectably, for the protocol itself to terminate correctly. We say that a gossip *push* occurs if a process, picking some peer, sends information to it, and a gossip *pull* occurs if the peer sends information back. Bimodal Multicast uses a *push-pull epidemic*, in which both forms of exchange occur.

Demers and his colleagues have provided an analysis of the convergence and scaling properties of gossip protocols based on pushing, pulling, and combined mechanisms and have shown how these can overcome failures. They prove that both classes of protocols converge toward flooding at an exponential rate and demonstrate that they can be applied to real problems. The motivation for their work was a scaling problem, which occurred in the wide area mail system developed at PARC in the 1980s. As this system was used on a larger and larger scale, it began to exhibit consistency problems and had difficulties in accommodating mobile users. Demers and his colleagues showed that by reimplementing the e-mail system to use a gossip broadcast protocol they could overcome these problems, helping ensure timely and consistent e-mail services that were location independent and inexpensive. Thus, in their system, the "multicast" is a very slow action – a replicated database update that occurs rarely. We'll focus on the use of gossip in systems running at much higher speeds here, where multicast runs at network speeds and gossip may occur many times per second.

25.3.1 Bimodal Multicast

In the style of protocol explored at Xerox, the actual rate with which messages will flood the network is not guaranteed, because of the risk of failures. Instead, these protocols guarantee that, given enough time, eventually either all or no correct processes will deliver a message. This property is called *eventual convergence*. Although eventual convergence is sufficient for many uses, the property is weaker than the guarantees of the protocols we used earlier to replicate data and perform synchronization, because eventual convergence does not provide bounds on message latency or ordering properties. Hayden was the first to suggest that gossip protocols can be extended to have these properties (see Birman et al. [1999]), and in this section we present the protocol he developed for this purpose. Hayden calls his protocol Bimodal Multicast, but for similarity to the protocol names we've used elsewhere in this book, we'll call it *pbcast*, or *probabilistic broadcast*.

Specifically, *pbcast* is designed for a static set of processes, which communicate synchronously over a fully connected, point-to-point network. The processes have unique, totally ordered identifiers and can toss weighted, independent random coins. Runs of the system proceed in a sequence of rounds in which messages sent in the current round are delivered in the next round. The protocol is basically the same as the one shown in Figure 25.8, but it incorporates a number of optimizations intended to retransmit a multicast quickly using IP multicast if several processes may have dropped their copies, and also to deal with a peculiarity of link load seen in wide-area settings. We'll discuss these optimizations below.

Hayden was able to analyze the behavior of his solution, and this is part of what makes it such an interesting protocol. His model assumes that there are two types of failures. The first is process failure. Hayden assumes an independent, per-process probability of at most f_p that a process has a crash failure during the finite duration of a protocol. Such processes are called faulty. The second type of failure is message omission failure. There is an independent, per-message probability of at most f_m that a message between nonfaulty processes experiences a send omission failure. The union of all message omission failure events and process failure events is mutually independent. In this model, there are no malicious faults, spurious messages, or corruption of messages. We expect that both f_p and f_m are small probabilities (e.g., unless otherwise stated, the values used in the graphs in this chapter are $f_m = 0.05$ and $f_p = 0.001$).

The impact of the failure model can be visualized by thinking of the power that would be available to an adversary seeking to cause a run of the protocol to fail by manipulating the system within the bounds of the model. Such an adversary has these capabilities and restrictions:

- An adversary cannot use knowledge of future probabilistic outcomes, interfere with random coin tosses made by processes, cause correlated (nonindependent) failures to occur, or do anything not enumerated below.
- An adversary has complete knowledge of the history of the current run of the protocol.
- At the beginning of a run of the protocol, the adversary has the ability to individually set process failure rates, within the bounds $[0 \ldots f_p]$.
- For faulty processes, the adversary can choose an arbitrary point of failure.
- For messages, the adversary has the ability to individually set send omission failure probabilities within the bounds of $[0 \ldots f_m]$.

Note that although probabilities can be manipulated by the adversary, doing so can only make the system more reliable than the bounds, f_p and f_m.

Using this model, Hayden developed recurrence relations and solved them to derive predictions of how *pbcast* would behave with various parameter settings. We'll review some of his findings momentarily.

Hayden's probabilistic analysis of the properties of the *pbcast* protocol is only valid in runs of the protocol in which the system obeys the model. In particular, the independence properties of the system model are quite strong and are not likely to be continuously realizable in an actual system—for example, partition failures in the sense of correlated communication failures do not occur in this model. Partitions can be simulated by the independent failures of several processes, but they are of low probability. However, the protocols we develop using *pbcast*, such as our replicated data protocol, remain safe even when the system degrades from the model. In addition, *pbcast*-based algorithms can be made self-healing—for instance, our replicated data protocol has guaranteed eventual convergence properties similar to normal gossip protocols: If the system recovers into a state that respects the model and remains in that state for sufficiently long, the protocol will eventually recover from the failure and reconverge to a consistent state.

At the same time, Hayden's analysis is in some ways very pessimistic. For example, he found that *pbcast* is so reliable if IP multicast succeeds that he ended up focused on the case where IP multicast is sometimes a complete failure and nobody receives the initial multicast. This leads to a sort of extreme scenario in which some messages are essentially delivered reliably system-wide in the first phase, while others aren't delivered at all until the gossip mechanism kicks in. Realistic runs of *pbcast* live somewhere in between these extremes, but are hard to analyze using the style of closed form recurrence relations Hayden employed in his investigation. As a result, in what follows we'll use Hayden's analysis to derive worst case bounds, and experimental studies to understand the normal case that might be seen in real deployments of *pbcast*.

25.3.2 Unordered pbcast Protocol

We begin with an unordered version of *pbcast* with static membership (the protocol shown in Figure 25.9). The protocol consists of a fixed number of rounds, in which each process participates in at most one round. A process initiates a *pbcast* by sending a message to a random subset of other processes using an unreliable multicast primitive such as IP multicast, or a flooding scheme implemented over UDP. No effort is made to detect packet loss or repair missing packets, but obviously, one would hope that many of the packets get through. Notice, though, that the cost of initially disseminating the packet is unrelated to network load or congestion, since the protocol starts with just a single attempt to send each message and never sends extra messages no matter what fate befalls that first attempt.

When other processes receive a message, they begin to gossip about it to their peers for a period of time called the "fanout" of the protocol. Gossip occurs at a constant frequency in this system: each process maintains a timer and at some rate (say, ten times per second), picks a peer and sends it a gossip message. There is no need to synchronize gossip or synchronize clocks, and gossip messages are treated as unreliable, asynchronous packets. Presumably, many will get through, but no attempt is made to detect loss or retransmit a lost packet.

The content of a gossip packet is a *digest* of the state of the sender. This typically includes membership information (thus, as nodes join or leave, information about those events will spread through the system) and also a summary of multicasts that the sender of the gossip message has received. The receiver of a gossip message can react in two ways: it can request a copy of a message it lacks, pulling it from the sender of the gossip message, or can send a copy of a message it received that the sender seems to be missing. (In practice, it can react in a third way, too: by re-multicasting a message, unreliably, if there is evidence that a few processes in the region are missing it; this is done cautiously, but with the goal of ensuring that most processes receive each message in an unreliable multicast, and gossip is used just to plug the last few gaps).

For purposes of analysis, the parameters of the protocol are as follows:

- P : the set of processes in the system: $n = |P|$
- k : the number of rounds of gossip to run
- r : the probability that a process gossips to each other process (the weighting of the coin mentioned earlier)

The behavior of the gossip protocol mirrors a class of disease epidemics, which nearly always infects either almost all of a population or almost none of it. In the following text, we will show that *pbcast* has a bimodal delivery distribution, which stems from the epidemic behavior of the gossip protocol. The normal behavior of the protocol is for the gossip to flood the network in a random but exponential fashion. If r is sufficiently large, most processes will usually receive the gossip within a logarithmic number of rounds.

25.3.3 Adding CASD-style Temporal Properties and Total Ordering

In the protocol shown in Figure 25.9, the *pbcast* messages are unordered. However, because the protocol runs in a fixed number of rounds of fixed length, it is trivial to extend it using the same method as was proposed in the CASD protocols (see Figure 25.10). By delaying the delivery of a message until it is known that all correct processes have a copy of that message, totally ordered delivery can be guaranteed. This yields a protocol similar to *abcast*

```
(* State kept per pbcast: have I received a message regarding this pbcast yet? *)
let received_already = false

(* Initiate a pbcast. *)
to pbcast(msg):
   deliver_and_gossip(msg,k)

(* Handle message receipt. *)
on receive gossip(msg,round):
   deliver_and_gossip(msg,round)

(* Auxiliary function. *)
to deliver_and_gossip(msg,round):
   (* Do nothing if already received it. *)
   if received_already then return

(* Mark the message as being seen and deliver. *)
received_already := true
deliver(msg)

(* If last round, don't gossip. *)
if round = 0 then return

for each p in P:
   do with probability r:
      sendto p gossip(msg,round-1)
```

Figure 25.9.   Unordered *pbcast* protocol. The function time() returns the current time expressed in rounds since the first round. Message receipt and *pbcast* are executed as atomic actions.

(* Local state: message buffer and counter for generating unique identifiers. *)
let buffer = {}
let id_counter = 0

(* Initiate a *pbcast*. *)
to *pbcast*(msg):
   (* Create unique id for each message. *)
   let id = (my_id, id_counter)
   id_counter := id_counter + 1

   do_gossip(time(),id,msg,k)

(* Handle message receipt. *)
on receive gossip (timesent, id, msg, round):
   do_gossip(timesent, id, msg, round)

(* Handle timeouts. *)
on timeout(time):
   (* Check for messages ready for delivery. Assumes buffer is
    * scanned in lexicographic order of (sent, id). *)
   for each (sent, id, msg) in buffer:
     if sent + k + 1 = time then
       buffer := buffer \ (sent, id, msg)
       deliver(msg)

(* Auxiliary function. *)
to do_gossip(timesent, id, msg, rnd):
   (* If have seen message already, do nothing. *)
   if (timesent, id, msg) in buffer then
     return

(* Buffer the message for later delivery, and then gossip. *)
buffer := buffer ∪(timesent, id, msg)
set_timer timesent + k + 1

(* If last round, do nothing more. *)
if rnd = 0 then return

foreach p in P
  with probability r
    send p gossip(timesent, id, msg, rnd-1)

Figure 25.10.   Ordered *pbcast* protocol, using the method of CASD.

in that it has totally ordered message delivery and probabilistically good reliability within the fixed membership of the process group invoking the primitive. It would not be difficult to introduce a further extension of the protocol for use in dynamic process groups, but we will not address that issue here.

25.3.4 Scalable Virtual Synchrony Layered Over Pbcast

Indranil Gupta has shown that virtual synchrony can be layered over the *pbcast* protocol. Without getting into the details, he does this using a scheme that probabilistically selects a small set of leader processes, which are responsible for deciding on the ordering of messages relative to view changes. Multicasts are sent to the full group "directly," but membership events vector through these processes, which then use the *pbcast* protocol to report each new view and its sequencing relative to the message stream. This permits him to support a token-based *abcast* protocol: total ordering, but not the CASD-style temporal properties of Hayden's method.

Gupta shows that he can preserve the scalability of *pbcast* and yet get the strong guarantees of virtual synchrony in this manner, at the cost of some delay before messages can be delivered. His experiments showed that at least in the range of group sizes seen earlier in Figure 25.7, where virtual synchrony "melted down" under stress, virtual synchrony over *pbcast* should continue to perform quite well.

25.3.5 Probabilistic Reliability and the Bimodal Delivery Distribution

Hayden has demonstrated that when the system respects the model, a *pbcast* is almost always delivered to most or to few processes and almost never to some processes. Such a delivery distribution is called a "bimodal" one and is depicted in Figure 25.11. The graphs show that varying numbers of processes will deliver *pbcast*—for instance, the probability that 26 out of the 50 processes will deliver a *pbcast* is around 10^{-28}. Such a probabilistic guarantee is, for most practical purposes, a guarantee that the outcome cannot occur. The bimodal distribution property is presented here informally, but later we discuss the method used by Hayden to calculate the actual probability distributions for a particular configuration of *pbcast*.

The *pbcast* protocol also has a second bimodal characteristic: delivery delays (latency) tends to be bimodal, with one distribution of very low latencies for messages that arrive without packet loss using the basic IP multicast, and a second distribution with higher latencies for messages that had to be remulticast or repaired using the gossip-driven gap-filling mechanism. Hayden's analysis doesn't focus on this aspect and in fact had he done so, his model would do a poor job of predicting the observed behavior. However, the actual implementation of *pbcast* reported by Hayden et al. did explore this question (see Hayden 1999). One finds that the degree to which *pbcast* latencies are bimodal is very much a function of parameter settings; with aggressive settings the protocol overhead is still rather low, and latencies can be squeezed down to within a small constant factor of the average network latency. This is quite an encouraging result.

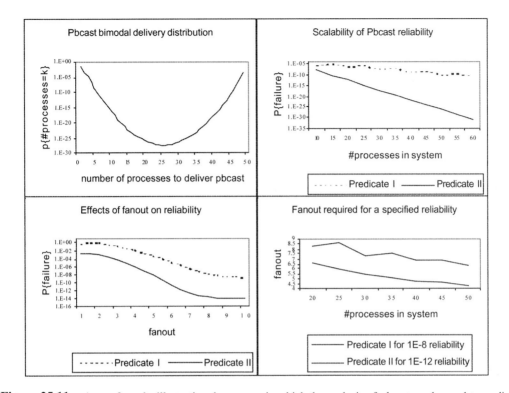

Figure 25.11. A set of graphs illustrating the manner in which the analysis of *pbcast* can be used to predict its reliability and to select parameter settings matched to desired behavior. The graph is drawn from Birman et al (1996).

Most important of all, *pbcast* overcomes the scalability problems we saw in Figure 25.7, where virtual synchrony seemed to melt down. Under precisely the same experimental conditions, *pbcast* is known to continue to deliver messages at a steady rate even while as many as 25% of the participants are intermittently perturbed. Indeed, a tremendously disruptive scenario is required to overload the protocol, and even then, it has been shown to degrade rather gracefully.

The basic reliability of *pbcast* is often all that one needs in an application, in which case it offers a uniquely scalable and stable way to disseminate information. Indeed, studies have shown that *pbcast* will scale essentially without limit, imposing constant cost on the participants (here we assume a constant rate of new multicasts), and with essentially identical latency distributions throughout the system if we factor out the delay of the initial unreliable multicast itself. Indeed, in a healthy network, *pbcast* is so reliable that it can often be substituted for *fbcast* or, when totally ordered, for *abcast*. Nonetheless, there are circumstances under which gaps will not be repaired, and *pbcast* does not support virtually synchronous group membership reporting unless Gupta's extensions are employed.

In practice, one finds that most systems that include a version of *pbcast* integrate the protocol with a form of logging service that captures messages and archives them. Such a service can be used by *pbcast* to overcome failures but can also be used by the application itself, to fill gaps in the delivery sequence not repaired by the protocol itself. For example, at Cornell there has been some recent work on implementing a publish-subscribe system over *pbcast*. In this system, the logging servers are also used by applications that join the system: they can check for "back postings" on subjects of interest, and then are given a stream of updates. The guarantees of this publish-subscribe implementation approximate those of virtual synchrony: the application will see every posting on the subjects of interest to it, both archived and new, won't see any duplicates, and will see events in the same order as everyone else did. QuickSilver, a new multicast platform including this functionality (unrelated to the file system with the same name), should be available for download from Cornell in 2005.

Gupta's work, and Hayden's prior work, point to the other major way of using these protocols. A bimodal distribution is particularly useful for voting-style protocols where, as an example, updates must be made at a majority of the processes to be valid; we saw examples of such protocols when we discussed quorum replication. Problems do occur in these sorts of protocols when failures cause a large number of processes, but not a majority, to carry out an update. *Pbcast* overcomes this difficulty through its bimodal delivery distribution by ensuring that votes will almost always be weighted strongly for or against an update, and will very rarely be evenly divided. By counting votes, it can almost always be determined whether an update was valid or not, even in the presence of some failed processes. Gupta carries this quite far, developing an entire methodology for building solutions to "classical" distributed computing problems over *pbcast* and a few other probabilistic peer-to-peer protocols of his own design.

With *pbcast*, the bad cases are when "some" processes deliver the *pbcast*; these are the cases that *pbcast* makes unlikely to occur. We will call *pbcasts* that are delivered to "some" processes *failed pbcasts* and *pbcasts* delivered to "few" processes *invalid pbcasts*. The distinction anticipates the replicated data protocol presented in the following text, in which invalid *pbcasts* are inexpensive events and failed *pbcasts* are potentially costly.

To establish that *pbcast* does indeed have a bimodel delivery distribution, Hayden used a mixture of symbolic and computational methods. First, he computed a recurrence relation, which expresses the probability that a *pbcast* will be received by a processes at the end of round j, given that the message had been received by b processes at the end of round $j - 1$, c of these for the first time. In the terminology of a biological infection, b denotes the number of processes that were infected during round $j - 1$ and hence are infectious; the difference between a and b thus represents the number of *susceptible* processes that had not yet received a gossip message and that are successfully infected during round j.

The challenge aspect of this analysis is to deal with the impact of failures, which has the effect of making the variables in the recurrence relation random ones with binomial distributions. Hayden arrives at a recursive formula but not a closed form solution. However, such a formula is amenable to computational solutions and, by writing a program to calculate the various probabilities involved, he is able to arrive at the delivery distributions shown in Figure 25.8.

A potential risk in the analysis of *pbcast* is to assume, as may be done for many other protocols, that the worst case occurs when message loss is maximized. *Pbcast*'s failure mode occurs when there is a partial delivery of a *pbcast*. A pessimistic analysis must consider the case where local increases in the message-delivery probability decrease the reliability of the *overall pbcast protocol*. This makes the analysis quite a bit more difficult than the style of worst-case analysis used in protocols such as the CASD one, where the worst case is the one in which the maximum number of failures occurs.

25.3.6 Evaluation and Scalability

The evaluation of *pbcast* is framed in the context of its scalability. As the number of processes increases, *pbcast* scales according to several metrics. First, the reliability of *pbcast* grows with system size. Second, the cost per participant, measured by number of messages sent or received, remains at or near constant as the system grows. Having made these claims, it must be said that the version of *pbcast* presented and analyzed for a network makes assumptions that become less and less realizable for large systems. In practice, this issue could be addressed with a more hierarchically structured protocol, but Hayden's analysis has not been extended to such a protocol. In this section, we will address the scaling characteristics according to the metrics previously listed and then discuss informally how *pbcast* can be adapted for large systems.

Reliability

Pbcast has the following property: As the number of processes participating in a *pbcast* grows, the protocol becomes more reliable. In order to demonstrate this, we present a graph, Figure 25.11(b), of *pbcast* reliability as the number of processes is varied between 10 and 60, fixing fanout and failure rates—for instance, the graph shows that with 20 processes the reliability is about 10^{-13}. The graph almost fits a straight line with slope $= -0.45$, thus the reliability of *pbcast* increases almost tenfold with every two processes added to the system.

Message Cost and Fanout

Although not immediately clear from the protocol, the message cost of the *pbcast* protocol is roughly a constant multiple of the number of processes in the system. In the worst case, all processes can gossip to all other processes, causing $O(n^2)$ messages per *pbcast*. r will be set to cause some expected *fanout* of messages, so that on average a process should gossip to about *fanout* other processes, where *fanout* is some constant, in practice at most 10 (unless otherwise stated, *fanout* = 7 in the graphs presented in Figure 25.11). Figure 25.11(c) shows a graph of reliability versus *fanout* when the number of processes and other parameters held is constant—for instance, the graph shows that with a fanout of 7.0, *pbcast*'s reliability is about 10^{-13}. In general, the graph shows that the fanout can be increased to increase reliability, but eventually there are diminishing returns for the increased message cost.

On the other hand, *fanout* (and hence cost) can be decreased as the system grows, keeping the reliability at a fixed level. In Figure 25.11(d), reliability of at least "twelve nines" (i.e., the probability of a *failed pbcast* is less than or equal to 10^{-12}) is maintained, while the number of processes is increased. The graph shows that with 20 processes a *fanout* of 6.63 achieves "twelve nines" reliability, while with 50 processes a *fanout* of 4.32 is sufficient.

25.3.7 Experimental Results

For reasons of brevity we omit detailed experimental data from the evaluation of *pbcast* reported in Hayden [1999]. To summarize quickly, this work showed that with appropriate parameter settings *pbcast* was able to achieve a message throughput similar to that of the Horus or Ensemble *abcast* protocol *in cases where the sender of the message doesn't hold the group's ordering token*. However, *pbcast* is much slower than *abcast* in small configurations where the application exploits *abcast* in a near-optimal manner. Thus in situations where *abcast* can achieve thousands or tens of thousands of multicasts per second to a group of perhaps 8 to 10 members, *pbcast* rates of one tenth those figures are probably the best that can be expected (both kinds of protocols can benefit from message packing, so we'll set the associated "speedup" to the side here).

The experimental work showed that *pbcast* delivery latency is comparable to that of the Horus *abcast* protocol; both need to repair lost messages, and the bottom line is that both do so with comparable mechanisms. Finally, as noted earlier, under large-scale networking conditions where *abcast* performance collapses, *pbcast* performance remains quite stable.

These findings suggest that production-quality systems may need to implement a protocol like *pbcast* side by side with a more traditional virtual synchrony stack, switching from the traditional stack to the bimodal one when the system size exceeds about 32 members, a point at which *abcast* starts to exhibit pronounced instability. Such an approach should give almost unlimited scalability, stability under all sorts of stresses, and bounded overhead even when the network is exhibiting extreme problems. As mentioned before, Cornell is employing *pbcast* in a new publish-subscribe platform called QuickSilver. The approach just outlined is likely to be the one implemented in the system. The need for Gupta's probabilistic virtual synchrony mechanisms is still being evaluated; it is unclear at the time of this writing that virtual synchrony is really needed on a very large scale, although total ordering and the ability to find missing messages in a logging server does appear to be quite useful.

25.4 Astrolabe

We conclude this chapter with a brief look at a system called Astrolabe (van Renesse [2003]), a system that uses P2P protocols to build a scalable system monitoring, management, control and data-mining framework that has strong probabilistic convergence guarantees. Astrolabe builds a form of virtual database – one that doesn't really exist on a physical server, and yet can be accessed by an application in a manner not unlike a normal database on a real server. This database is structured hierarchically and can be queried using SQL. Astrolabe automatically populates the database with data drawn from the nodes in a distributed system and will automatically update the database as conditions change. The peer-to-peer protocols used by the system scale extremely well and are stable under conditions that would cripple systems built in other ways. Astrolabe is intended for use in monitoring, managing or controlling a system that could have hundreds, thousands or even millions of nodes. Moreover, Astrolabe is well matched to the needs of "data mining" applications, in which a large system is searched for desired data or for the resources best matched to some requirement.

We'll focus on a data mining scenario later in this section as a way to illustrate the power of the system. The basic idea involves configuring Astrolabe to continuously track information of interest to the data miner (perhaps, the team responsible for managing a data center or a set of them, or even the client systems connected to a Web Services platform). The collection of data will occur on the end-nodes, and might even involve asking those nodes to check for something – files matching a search criteria, for example. However, this work is spread over vast numbers of machines, and hence is extremely decentralized and parallel. Astrolabe then combines the information discovered out at the "edges" by continuously computing summaries using on-the-fly *aggregation*. Aggregation is similar to performing a query on a large database, and yields a smaller result that the user can see (or monitor, because the aggregate will be updated regularly as changes occur in the underlying data). The entire protocol has a very light, near-constant, communication and computational overhead on the nodes in the system.

For example, suppose that the manager of a large network notices that performance for a major application has begun to degrade, but has no idea why. Traditionally, she would have little recourse except to run whatever monitoring tools are available in the application. With Astrolabe, as we'll see, she can dynamically change the way the system is instrumented and the way the findings are reported, thus forming a theory, evaluating it (the system can be reconfigured in a few tens of seconds, even on a massive scale), and then perhaps setting that idea to the side and pursuing some other angle. Moreover, rather than being limited to whatever instrumentation was provided by the vendor, she can pursue all sorts of possibilities, even including contents of configuration files, page fault rates, or other kinds of indirect indicators.

To take another example, consider an intelligence analyst working for a government who becomes suspicious that a group of terrorists may be trying to infiltrate chemical or fertilizer supply depots somewhere in Iraq. If monitoring systems have been put in place, he can rapidly configure Astrolabe to look for unusual patterns of activity, then zero in to try and find out who is responsible and precisely what they are up to. Astrolabe offers the analyst a way to search data residing on thousands of computers without downloading all of that data (potentially, terabytes) to a central location. Moreover, the massive parallelism of the network of machines permits him to perform queries that, on any single machine, might take hours to complete. By doing the work out at the edges, the same tasks are finished in seconds.

The need for this type of data mining seems to be increasing rapidly. Corporations and other enterprises can't avoid having large numbers of data centers scattered throughout their organizations: such an approach puts computing where it is needed and administers data close to where it was gathered. Making a centralized copy for purposes of data mining can be very inefficient, and may simply create an overloaded central resource.

Moreover, as the Web Services architecture rolls out, we're starting to see companies that hope to use Web Services to open up their data centers for use in a new kind of 4-tier architecture. Suppose that Amazon.com were to hand out small "serverlets" to assist application developers in embedding point-and-click purchase functionality into their applications. For example, a hospital computing system developer could use these serverlets to integrate the medical system with Amazon's purchasing and delivery mechanisms, so that when the hospital orders supplies, Amazon fills the order. It isn't hard to see why both Amazon.com and the developer might view this as an advantageous arrangement: the developer doesn't need to duplicate Amazon's computing systems (or their network of warehouses and supplier relationships), and Amazon itself gains increased sales volumes. The hospital benefits too, since they are using a widely used supply intermediary that may be able to negotiate volume discounts and other special deals.

But now if a problem occurs – say that hospitals in Pennsylvania suddenly are unable to connect to Amazon's data center in Chicago, we'll need ways to diagnose the problem, to get those serverlets to "fail over" to a different center (maybe New York) in a coordinated way, and to orchestrate the repair. The more one studies such a scenario the more it looks like a decentralized data mining problem. Client systems (serverlets) want to share their current status, diagnose and react in a consistent way, etc. Administrators want to pin down the origin of the problem; perhaps, a problem in the Internet, or in the firewall configuration at the hospital, or at the Amazon data center.

Underlying Astrolabe's powerful data mining and monitoring mechanisms is a principle called *peer-to-peer aggregation*. Aggregation is analogous to computing a dependent cell in a spreadsheet. When the underlying information changes, Astrolabe will automatically and rapidly recompute the associated aggregates and report the changes to applications that have registered their interest. What makes this an aggregation problem is that the underlying data was gathered from many machines in a large networked setting. Astrolabe's protocols ensure that even in huge networks, any change is soon visible everywhere. For example, Astrolabe aggregation can be used to identify sets of sensors which have made related observations – biothreat sensors reading low levels of toxins, coastal traffic sensors reporting vessels matching an Interpol profile of potential concern, and so forth. As a user's needs evolve, Astrolabe can be reconfigured on the fly by changing the set of aggregation queries. Astrolabe uses peer-to-peer protocols to implement aggregation, and this is the "secret" of its power, flexibility and robustness.

25.4.1 How it works

Astrolabe is best understood as a relational database built through a peer-to-peer protocol running between the applications or computers on which Astrolabe is installed. Like any relational database, the fundamental building block employed by Astrolabe is a tuple (a row of data items) into which values can be stored. For simplicity in this paper, we'll focus on the case where each tuple contains information associated with some computer. The technology is quite general, however, and can be configured with a tuple per application, or even with a tuple for each instance of some type of file or database.

Modern computing platforms, such as Microsoft's .NET and J2EE, provide a wealth of instrumentation options. Astrolabe is designed to tap into these. Basically, there are two forms of data available, although both are presented to the user through a single API.

One option is to extract information from the management information base (MIB) of a computer. A MIB is a standardized database maintained by the computer itself, containing such information as load, currently active processes, machine name and IP address, etc. The MIB is an extremely powerful and general source of information, and for a user with appropriate permissions, gives access to almost anything the operating system "knows." On systems such as Linux and Microsoft .NET, the MIB is provided by a server object that can be accessed using an RPC protocol, and Astrolabe taps into this interface to extract data of the type desired by the user, then to monitor that data for changes at a frequency the user controls.

The second major source of data for Astrolabe consists of information that the system extracts directly from a file, database, spreadsheet, or application program. Astrolabe is able to perform this operation by exploiting a recent set of standards (ODBC, JDBC) whereby an application with appropriate permissions can treat the objects on a computer much like databases. For example, Astrolabe could be asked to count the number of image files containing possible matches with a picture of a wanted criminal, or even to report the name of the file having the best match (the image itself would be too large to export into Astrolabe, which limits the data extracted to a few k-bytes per computer). The match with databases or spreadsheets is especially good; in such cases, Astrolabe can perform a "query" on the underlying object and report the result through its own tuple data structure (assuming, that is, that the result can be represented as a single tuple).

Like most modern systems, Astrolabe is flexible about data types, supporting the usual basic types but also allowing the application to supply arbitrary information encoded with XML. The only requirement is that the total size of the tuple be no more than a few k-bytes; much larger objects can be identified by some form of URL or other reference but the data would not reside directly in Astrolabe itself.

The specific data to be pulled into Astrolabe is specified in a *configuration certificate*. Should the needs of the user change, the configuration certificate can be modified and, within a few seconds, Astrolabe will reconfigure itself accordingly. This action is, however, restricted by a security policy.

Astrolabe groups small sets of tuples into relational tables. Each such table consists of perhaps 30 to 60 tuples containing data from sources physically close to one-another in the network; we call this a "zone." This grouping (a database administrator would recognize it as a form of schema) can often be created automatically, using latency and network addresses to identify nearby machines. However, the system administrator can also specify a desired layout explicitly.

Where firewalls are present, Astrolabe employs a tunneling method to send messages to machines residing behind the firewall and hence not directly addressable. This approach also allows Astrolabe to overcome most restrictions associated with network address translation (NAT) filters.

The data collected by Astrolabe evolves as the underlying information sources report updates, hence the system constructs a continuously changing database using information that actually resides on the participating computers. Figure 25.12 illustrates this: we see a collection of small database relations, each tuple corresponding to one machine, and each relation collecting tuples associated with some set of nearby machines. In this figure, the data stored within the tuple includes the name of the machine, its current load, an indication of whether or not various servers are running on it, and the "version" for some application. Keep in mind that this selection of data is completely determined by the configuration certificate. In principle, any data available on the machine or in any application running on the machine can be exported. In particular, spreadsheets and databases can easily be configured to export data to Astrolabe.

Name	Load	Weblogic?	SMTP?	Version
Name	Load	Weblogic?	SMTP?	Version
Name	Load	Weblogic?	SMTP?	Version
swift	2.0	0	1	6.2
falcon	1.5	1	0	4.1
cardinal	4.5	1	0	6.0

Figure 25.12.   Three Astolabe domains.

An application using Astrolabe can access this local data (that is, data associated with machines in its own zone) just as it might access any other table, database or spreadsheet. As updates are reported through Astrolabe, the application receives a form of event notifying it that the table should be rescanned. For example, Astrolabe data can be dragged into a local database, spreadsheet, or even onto a web page. As the data changes, the application will receive refresh events.

Astrolabe is intended for use in very large networks, hence this form of direct access to local data cannot be used for the full dataset: while the system does capture data throughout the network, the amount of information would be unwieldy and the frequency of updates excessive. Accordingly, although Astrolabe does provide an interface with which a remote zone's data can be accessed, the normal way of monitoring remote data is through aggregation queries.

As the name suggests, an aggregation query is just an SQL query that operates on these leaf relations, extracting a single summary tuple from each which reflects the globally significant information within the zone. Sets of summary tuples are concatenated by Astrolabe to form summary relations (again, the size is typically 30 to 60 tuples each), and if the size of the system is large enough so that there will be several summary relations, this process is repeated at the next level up, and so forth. Astrolabe is thus a hierarchical relational database. Each of the summaries is updated, in real-time, as the leaf data from which it was formed changes. Even in networks with thousands or millions of computers, updates are visible system-wide within a few tens of seconds. (Figure 25.13).

A computer using Astrolabe will, in general, have a local copy of the data for its own zone and for aggregation (summary) data for zones above it on the path to the root of this hierarchy. As just explained, the system maintains the abstraction of a hierarchical relational database. Notice that in a physical sense, this hierarchy is an illusion,

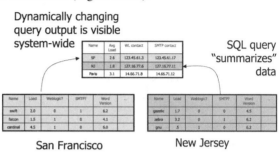

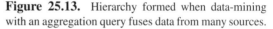

Figure 25.13. Hierarchy formed when data-mining with an aggregation query fuses data from many sources.

constructed using a peer-to-peer protocol of our own design, somewhat like a jig-saw puzzle in which each computer has copies of some of the pieces. The protocols permit the system to assemble the puzzle as a whole when needed. Thus, while the user thinks of Astrolabe as a somewhat constrained but rather general database residing on a conventional server, accessed using conventional programmer APIs and development tools, and updated as information changes, in reality there is no server. The user abstraction is created on the fly.

The peer-to-peer protocol used for this purpose is, to first approximation, easily described. We consider first the case of a single zone. Each Astrolabe system keeps track of the other machines in its zone, and of a subset of *contact* machines in other zones. This subset is selected in a pseudo-random manner from the full membership of the system (a peer-to-peer gossip protocol is used to track approximate membership). At some fixed frequency, typically every 2 to 5 seconds, each participating machine sends a concise state description to a randomly selected destination within this set of neighbors and remote contacts. The state description is very compact and consists of identification of objects available on the system and their timestamps. We call such a message a *gossip* event, because it behaves much like the gossip exchanges described in connection with the *pbcast* protocol. Unless an object is very small, the gossip event contains version information, not actual data.

Upon receiving such a gossip message, an Astrolabe system is in a position to identify information which may be stale at the sender's machine (because timestamps are out of date) or that may be more current at the sender than on its own system. We say *may* because time elapses while messages traverse the network, hence no machine actually has current information about any other. Our protocols are purely asynchronous: when sending a message, the sender does not pause to wait for it to be received and, indeed, the protocol makes no effort to ensure that gossip gets to its destinations.

Through exchanges of gossip messages and data, information should propagate within a network over an exponentially increasing number of randomly selected paths among the participants. That is, if a machine updates its own row, after one round of gossip, the update will probably be found at two machines. After two rounds, the update will probably be at four machines, etc. In general, updates propagate in log of the system size – seconds or tens of seconds in our implementation. In practice, we configure Astrolabe to gossip rapidly within each zone (to take advantage of the presumably low latency) and less frequently between zones (to avoid overloading bottlenecks such as firewalls or shared network links). The effect of these steps is to ensure that the communication load on each machine using Astrolabe and also each communication link involved is bounded and independent of network size.

We've said that Astrolabe gossips about *objects*. In our work, a tuple is an object, but because of the hierarchy used by Astrolabe, a tuple would only be of interest to a receiver in the same region as the sender. In general, Astrolabe gossips about information of *shared interest* to the sender and receiver. This could include tuples in the regional database, but also membership data, and aggregation results for aggregation zones which are common ancestors to the sender and receiver.

So far we've discussed the behavior of Astrolabe within a single zone. To compute the contents of internal zones containing aggregation results, each zone "elects" (using an aggregation query) a small number of representatives to run the Astrolabe gossip protocol on its behalf in the next higher-level zone within the zone hierarchy. These spawn an additional instance of the gossip protocol and, before gossiping, recomputed the zone's contribution to the aggregate. Thus, the average machine within a zone will gossip only with other machines in the same zone, not with representatives of remote zones. Thus, a computer may run gossip on behalf of 1, 2, or as many as $\log_{\text{zone}-\text{size}}(N)$ simultaneous gossip protocols. The zone size in Astrolabe is large (often 64 or 100) hence this will be a small number, rarely more than 3 or 4.

After a round of gossip or an update to its own tuple, Astrolabe informs any local readers of the Astrolabe database that its value has changed, and the associated application rereads the object and refreshes its state accordingly. For example, if an Astrolabe aggregation output is pulled from Astrolabe into a web page, that web server would refresh that page each time it changes. The change would be expected to reach the server within a delay logarithmic in the size of the network, and proportional to the gossip rate. Using a 2-second gossip rate, an update would thus reach all members in a system of 10,000 computers in roughly 25 seconds. Of course, the gossip rate can be tuned to make the system run faster, or slower, depending on the importance of rapid responses and the amount of bandwidth available for our protocols.

Additional details of how Astrolabe is implemented and how it performs can be found in van Renesse, Birman and Vogels (2003).

25.4.2 Peer-to-Peer Data Fusion and Data Mining

Astrolabe is a powerful, flexible technology for data fusion and data mining. The system can be understood as performing data fusion in a continuous manner, since the basic Astrolabe data structure *fuses* designated data into a virtual database for use by the application. The SQL aggregation mechanism permits additional data fusion, and also permits the user to perform a wide variety of data mining actions.

The power of these mechanisms is, however, limited by the physical layout of the Astrolabe database and by our need, as builders of the system, to provide a solution which is secure and scalable. The focus of this section is not so much on the basic ideas but on these limitations and their implications for the Astrolabe user.

Consistency

Although Astrolabe is best understood as a form of hierarchical database, the system doesn't support the transactional consistency model employed by databases. Astrolabe is accessible by read-only operations on the local zone and aggregation zones on the path to the root. Update operations can only be performed by a machine on the data stored in its own tuple. Moreover, the ACID properties do not apply; for example, two different observers will often see updates in different orders and may not even see the identical updates.

If Astrolabe is imagined as a kind of replicated database, a further distinction arises. In a replicated database each update will be reflected at each replica. Astrolabe offers a weaker guarantee: if a participating computer updates its tuple and then leaves the tuple unchanged for a sufficiently long period of time, there is a very high probability that the update will become visible to all non-faulty computers. Indeed, this probability converges to 1.0 in the absence of network partitioning failures. Astrolabe gains a great deal by accepting this weaker probabilistic property: the system is able to scale with constant loads on computers and links, and is not forced to stop and wait if some machine fails to receive an update. In contrast, there is a well-known impossibility result that implies that a database system using the serializability model may need to pause and wait for updates to reach participating nodes, and indeed that a single failure could prevent a replicated database from making progress. Jointly, these results limit the performance and availability of a replicated database. Astrolabe, then, offers a weaker consistency property but gains availability and very stable, predictable performance by so doing.

Aggregation raises a different kind of consistency issue. Suppose that an aggregation query reports some property of a zone, such as the least loaded machine, the average humidity in a region, etc. Recall that aggregates are recomputed each time the Astrolabe gossip protocol runs. One could imagine a situation in which machine A and machine B concurrently update their own states; perhaps, their loads change. Now suppose that an aggregation query computes the average load. A and B will both compute new averages, but the values are in some sense unordered in time: A's value presumably reflects a stale version of B's load, and vice versa. Not only does this imply that the average computed might not be the one expected, it also points to a risk: Astrolabe (as described so far) might report aggregates that bounce back and forth in time, first reflecting A's update (but lacking B's more current data), then changing to reflect B's update but "forgetting" A's change. The fundamental problem is that even if B has an aggregation result with a recent timestamp, the aggregate could have been computed from data which was, in part, more stale than was the data used to compute the value it replaces.

To avoid this phenomenon, Astrolabe tracks minimum and maximum timestamp information for the inputs to each aggregation function. A new aggregate value replaces an older one only if the minimum timestamp for any input to that new result is at least as large as the maximum timestamp for the one it replaces. It can be seen that this will slow the propagation of updates but will also ensure that aggregates advance monotonically in time. Yet this stronger consistency property also brings a curious side-effect: if two different Astrolabe users write down the series of aggregate results reported to them, those sequences of values could advance very differently; perhaps, A sees its own update reflected first, then later sees both its own and B's; B might see its update first, then later both, and some third site, C, could see the system jump to a state in which both updates are reflected. Time moves forward, but different users see events in different order and may not even see the identical events! This tradeoff seems to be fundamental to our style of distributed data fusion.

Security Model and Mechanisms

A related set of issues surround the security of the Astrolabe technology. We noted earlier that many peer-to-peer systems suffer from insecurity and are easily incapacitated or attacked by malfunctioning or malicious users. Astrolabe is intended to run on very large numbers of machines, hence the system itself could represent a large-scale security exposure.

To mitigate such concerns, we've taken several steps. First, Astrolabe reads but does not write data on the machines using it. Thus, while Astrolabe can pull a great variety of data into its hierarchy, the system doesn't take the converse action of reaching back onto the participating machines and changing values within them, except to the extent that applications explicitly read data from Astrolabe.

The issue thus becomes one of trustworthiness: can the data stored in Astrolabe be trusted? In what follows, we assume that Astrolabe is correctly implemented, but that the computers on which it runs could fail, and software bugs (hopefully, rare) could corrupt individual Astrolabe instances. To overcome such problems, Astrolabe includes a public-key infrastructure (PKI) which is built into the code. We employ digital signatures to authenticate data. Although machine B may learn of machine A's updates through a third party, unless A's tuple is correctly signed by A's private-key, B will reject it. Astrolabe also limits the introduction of configuration certificates and aggregation queries by requiring keys for the parent zones within which these will have effect; by controlling access to those keys, it is possible to prevent unauthorized users from introducing expensive computations or configuring Astrolabe to pull in data from participating hosts without appropriate permissions. Moreover, the ODBC and JDBC interfaces by means of which Astrolabe interfaces itself to other components offer additional security policy options.

A limitation on the Astrolabe security mechanism is evident when one considers the way that aggregates are computed. As noted earlier, each zone elects some representatives to run the gossip protocol for the next higher level zone, and this continues up to the layer below the root. Those representatives compute the zone's aggregate function and then gossip about this value, and other cached values from other sibling zones, and in this manner the value of an aggregate zone is assembled.

Now suppose that some node aggregates incorrectly, or even maliciously. For example, it could proclaim itself to have the lowest load in the region and thereby elect itself as the regional aggregation contact, and then incorrectly claim that the region is not reporting and denial of service problems, when in fact many machines are complaining about overloads. The "false" aggregation information might be trusted by other nodes and this can cause problems system-wide. At the time of this writing, work was underway on a type of attestation scheme similar to the one we discussed in conjunction with Byzantine Agreement. The idea (being developed by Kevin Walsh and others) is to require that aggregations be countersigned by multiple nodes; with k counter-signatures, up to k failures can be tolerated.

In fact this idea is harder to put into practice than to describe. For example, Astrolabe's consistency model isn't strong enough to ensure that a node selected to countersign a value can actually do so. To address this, Walsh was forced to add a history mechanism to Astrolabe, whereby each participant would accumulate a history of values for each row. An aggregate can then be pinned down by specifying the row versions used to compute it.

Query Limitations

A final set of limitations arises from the lack of a join feature in the aggregation query mechanism. As seen above, Astrolabe performs data mining by computing summaries of the data in each zone, then gluing these together to create higher level zones on which further summaries can be computed. The approach lacks a way to compute results for queries that require cross-zone joins.

For example, suppose that Astrolabe were used as the basis for a sensor network in a military targeting setting. One might want to express a data fusion query along the following lines: "for each incoming threat, report the weapons system best positioned to respond to that threat." The natural way to express this as a query in a standard database would involve a join. In Astrolabe, one would need to express this as two aggregation queries, one to compute a summary of threats and the other, using output from the first as an input, tracking down the response options. In general, this points to a methodology for dealing with joins by "compiling" them into multiple current aggregation queries. However, at present, we have not developed this insight into a general mechanism; users who wish to perform joins would need to break them up in this manner, by hand. Moreover, it can be seen that while this approach allows a class of join queries to compile into Astrolabe's aggregation mechanism, not all joins can be so treated: the method only works if the size of the dataset needed from the first step of the join, and indeed the size of the final output, will be sufficiently small.

Configuring Astrolabe so that one query will use the output of another as part of its input raises a further question: given that these queries are typically introduced into the system while it is running, how does the user know when the result is "finished"? We have a simple answer to this problem, based on a scheme of counting the number of sub-zones reflected in an aggregation result. The idea is that as a new aggregate value is computed, a period passes during which only some of the leaf zones have reported values. At this stage the parent aggregation zone is not yet fully populated with data. However, by comparing a count of the number of reporting child zones with a separately maintained count of the total number of children, applications can be shielded from seeing the results of an aggregation computation until the output is stable. By generalizing this approach, we are also able to handle failures or the introduction of new machines; in both cases, the user is able to identify and disregard outputs representing transitional states. The rapid propagation time for updates ensures that such transitional conditions last for no more than a few seconds.

25.5 Other Applications of Peer-to-Peer Protocols

This chapter has limited itself to scraping the surface of a thriving area. Recent work suggests that peer-to-peer protocols may also be useful in building scalable publish-subscribe systems, improving the reliability of very large "chat" systems, in managing caches for large Web sites and Web Service applications, and in increasing the robustness of mobile, wireless computing platforms, which often suffer from brief disconnections and other disruptive outages. One very exciting piece of work, by Ion Stoica at Berkeley, proposes to replace the entire Internet with an architecture (called the Internet Indirection Infrastructure, or I3) in which a DHT is used to deliver packets, substituting this for the traditional Internet routing mechanism. Stoica shows that his scheme is able to accommodate such functions as multicast and anycast efficiently, can implement various kinds of packet transformations and pipeline processing, and is even able to provide mobile packet routing under conditions where the standard Internet incurs high overhead.

While it does seem safe to say that peer-to-peer computing is solidly established as an important technology area, it is also important to realize that like most technologies in this third part of the book, peer-to-peer applications remain a somewhat marginalized technology. Only Napster, Gnutella and Kazaa have achieved much success, and of course that was in support of what turns out to have been an illegal application. Whether peer-to-peer solutions ever gain a "first class" role in modern operating systems platforms remains to be determined.

25.6 Related Reading

Peer-to-peer computing is a new and very active area. By far the best way to get the sense of the scope of activities and to learn about some of the very best work is to consult the proceedings of the Workshop on Future Directions in Distributed Computing (see Schiper [2003]), the International Workshop on Peer-to-Peer Computing, which was held at MIT in 2002 and at Berkeley in 2003. Other major outlets for peer-to-peer research include the SIGCOM conference, INFOCOM, and OSDI. Some notable recent papers include: (see Anderson [2001], Balakrishnan [2003], Bhagwan [2003], Castro [2003], Gribble [2001],

Iyer [2002], Kermarrec [2001], Kubiatowicz [2000], Kubiatowicz [2003], Muthitacharoen [2002], Weatherspoon [2002], Zhao [2002])

On gossip protocols: (see Alon et al., Demers et al., Golding [1991], Golding and Taylor).

On the underlying theory: (see Bailey).

Hayden's work (see Birman [1999]), draws on Chandra and Toueg (1990) and Cristian et al. (1985).

26

Prospects for Building Highly Assured Web Services

26.1 Web Services and Their Assurance Properties

In this brief chapter, we review the applicability of the techniques treated previously to the challenge of constructing such a Web Services application. The chapter is structured as a review, with pointers to the various chapters and sections in which the methods that seem most useful were covered within the textbook.

At the outset of the book, it was stressed that not all systems have identical robustness requirements. This is particularly true of Web Services applications, and leads to an important insight: the Web Services vendor community (at least as of the time of this writing) has a rather specific notion of high-assurance systems in mind in its work on reliability standards. Presumably, this reflects a cagey bet that "most" users will be happy with the resulting technology even if "some" are unsatisfied. As a result, while early Web Services systems can certainly achieve a degree of reliability, it will be important to understand precisely what properties the user can count upon, and also to appreciate the limitations of the model. Although we will also find it possible to push beyond the emerging standards, doing so opens the door to concerns about "non-standard" solutions—concerns that are best avoided if possible.

No technology can make everyone happy. Jim Gray, winner of the ACM Turing Award for his groundbreaking work on database systems and his many contributions to other kinds of distributed computing platforms, has observed that if a technology addresses the needs of even 80% of its potential market, the vendor should be very happy with it. It may be that Web Services will never respond to the full range of requirements that users may express relative to applications they wish to port to the technology. The question, though, is whether or not the initial reliability vision of the Web Services development community is ambitious enough to satisfy even a modest percentage of users.

Let's start by summarizing some reliability goals, and then asking whether and how they might be addressed. We'll wrap up by speculating very briefly on where the magic 80% threshold might be found in this emerging market.

Recall from Chapter 10 that a Web Service has three major components: the "back end" servers (which are often legacy components built from some other technology and then wrapped with a connector of some form), the Web Services dispatch module (which also publishes the WSDL document and advertises the service through name spaces supporting the UDDI language), and the Web Services client platform. With this partitioning in mind, a quick summary of reliability goals for High Assurance Web Services is as follows:

- *Recoverability for Web Servers.* We would like to know that the servers used in a Web Services setting are capable of restarting after a crash. For example, servers might use transactional mechanisms to ensure the integrity of critical files and data structures. Notice that our stated goal conflates two aspects: the Web Service "dispatch" module, to which clients connect, and the backend server. Both can fail and both may need to be recoverable. However, the dispatch component is essentially stateless and hence can generally be restarted without much fuss, provided only that it can find the backend server and establish a connection to it. Backend servers (and a single server may be connected to more than one Web Services dispatch module) often have a great deal of state stored in files, logs, databases, etc., and may need to go through an elaborate repair protocol when recovering from a crash.

- *Rapid Server Restart.* In any system, one is interested in maximizing up time, and this entails minimizing downtown. Quick restarts are thus very valuable. However, in some situations, a user is likely to be waiting while the server is down, and in this case a need may arise for an even stronger "high availability" architecture. Thus, we'll want to bring ideas for rapid restart to bear on our solutions, but may also find that this is not enough. (In fact, the author of this book is persuaded that existing systems restart far too slowly and hence that restart will often impose unacceptable delays. Since faster restart is perhaps an unattainable goal, we may have no choice except to press for high availability solutions.)

- *High or Continuous Availability.* Not all Web Services will need to provide rapid responses. However, in situations where a user (or a client computer) is prevented from making progress until a response is received, there will be a need for high or even continuous availability from Web Services platforms. Reiterating the point just made, the author suspects that Web Services will often have impatient clients – computer systems that can't take "wait a while" for an answer. When this happens, high or continuous availability becomes a requirement.

The Web Services architecture currently lacks support for high or continuous availability applications, and this creates a serious concern. With platforms like J2EE and .NET, it is almost trivial to convert a distributed object into a Web Service – it suffices to click a button or apply the ASP.NET template to an object. Thus developers may be tempted to develop a wide variety of small Web Service applications, in which the architecture is used more or less as an interoperability standard as opposed to playing its intended role, which seems to anticipate access to larger back-end server style applications.

But small distributed objects will often bring high availability requirements, and the Web Services architecture's lack of solutions aimed at such applications poses the risk that a new generation of applications may emerge in which the Web Services architecture plays a central role, yet omits features likely to be needed by many users. Below, we'll ask whether the protocols and algorithms developed in prior chapters could be applied to this problem.

- *Reliable Asynchronous Request Streaming*. For some purposes, the client application needs a guarantee that an operation will be performed, but doesn't need to wait for results because no exceptions of an "end-user relevant" nature ever occur. For example, if a banking system successfully provides cash to an ATM user, the "successful withdrawal" transaction that finalizes the operation shouldn't fail, and need not occur instantly. Vendors have argued that a great many Web Services transactions will be of this nature—they will never give error codes, and can be delayed briefly without consequence. For such purposes, a form of reliable request streaming is desirable: a way to enqueue requests for eventual execution (hopefully, quite soon), so that the client system can move on with confidence that the request will not be lost. Once the client has successfully enqueued the request, there is no need to worry about it being executed – the system will contract to carry out the request and, if prevented from doing so, will request help from a (human) systems administrator.

  Asynchronous request streaming systems can be be understood as corresponding to message queuing execution models, in which trustworthy intermediaries accept responsibility for requests, buffering them until a target server is available, and then passing them along. This is the model presumed by the WS_Reliability specification, which is the component of architecture specifically aimed at information assurance issues. However, as discussed further below, such an approach is really very limited. WS_Reliability may make sense for applications streaming requests asynchronously to heavy-weight back-end servers, but is very poorly matched to high availability or notions of reliability that involve some kind of quality of service element, such as fast response times.

- *Consistent Failure Reporting*. When Web Services systems report failures to client systems, we would like those reports to be informative and consistent. For example, when a client performs a request that throws an exception, and the exception reports that a server failure has occurred, this should mean that the server actually failed, not that some sort of muddled event confused the Web Services platform. In Chapter 3 and in Section 10.6.3 we saw that a mixture of events that could involve the server, the network, the client's own machine, or other factors can sometimes mimic a crash in ways that can't easily be sorted out by a platform unless it departs from the so-called "end to end" reliability model (which the Web Services community has adopted). High assurance applications will often need to include fallback plans to deal with such outcomes, even if this means that the Web Services community must revisit its early determination to treat

Web Services like Web sites, which of course often present their users with confusing error reports.

- *Reconnection Capabilities.* Unlike a Web site, the client of a Web Service will often be a computing system that needs the mechanisms provided by that Web Service for its own progress. Accordingly, if a client system is using a Web Service and it fails, that client may need a way to automatically reconnect to the service. In situations that involve a message queuing component, WS_Reliability does tackle reconnection, but doesn't address the issue under other conditions.

- *Resynchronization Capabilities.* Suppose that a client reconnects to the service but operations were underway at the time of the failure. The client may need a way to determine their outcome. For example, if a Web Service is transactional but a failure occurs just as a client issues a commit request, the client may need to query the service to find out if the operation committed or aborted and, if it committed, to learn the result. Since the "client" in this case is a computer, the procedure to use for resynchronization must be fully automated. Again, in situations that involve a message queuing component, WS_Reliability does addresses this issue, but not under other conditions.

- *Manageability.* We would like to have confidence that Web Services can be managed in a highly automated manner, which entails monitoring the system (potentially, not just the servers but also the clients), controlling actions (everything from load-balancing to fail-over), discovering parameter settings and resources automatically, and self-repairing after a disruptive event. Keep in mind that a computer program (an application) will be doing the monitoring and management here, not a human being. The whole point of Web Services is that computers will be talking to other computers – a major shift of mindset away from Web sites in which people use browsers to download Web pages from sites that are document repositories!

- *Defense against Distributed Denial of Service Attacks and other outages.* Our Web Services systems may be hosted on a public network, in which cases DDoS attacks should be considered a possibility. Moreover, even in a well-protected LAN, all sorts of problems can trigger extreme load bursts (for example, a Web Server that rejects a connection request for some reason may soon receive a repeat request, since its clients will often be computer systems that really have no alternative but to wait a little while and then try again). Defense against DDoS attacks usually involves replication of the underlying functionality so that it can be spread over multiple machines, perhaps at multiple physical sites. While attackers may easily be able to muster the resources to cripple a single machine, degrading the performance of a few dozen machines spread over a WAN can be an impractical undertaking. Where DDoS scenarios are a concern, there is much security in numbers! Notice that these same mechanisms will also eliminate the risk of single-point failures capable of bringing down the system. Thus, many of the techniques used to achieve high or continuous availability are also relevant for defending against DDoS scenarios.

- *Documented properties.* Client systems may need a way to examine the reliability properties of a Web Service in order to use it correctly. Thus a need exists for a means of documenting the kinds of properties provided by the architecture, and doing so in a way that can be extended as new properties are introduced in the future. WSDL is extensible and could represent a great range of properties, but the need to do so has not yet been emphasized in the Web Services architectural documents, nor are there standards for documenting most of the properties of interest to us here. This seems like a goal that the Web Services architectural community might want to tackle in coming years.

The above focuses on reliability, but what about security? It is appealing to summarize security for Web Services in terms of "four A's and an E":

- *Authentication.* Web Services systems will need ways to determine the identities of clients, which may be computing systems operated by corporate clients or other agencies. Web sites, of course, focus on identification of human users, which is quite another matter. The Web Services problem is tricky for many reasons, not least of which is that when corporations agree to collaborate for some purpose – perhaps vendor "ACME debugging technologies" has a contract of some form with IBM in Hawthorne, NY, the two companies trust each other only in very limited ways. ACME's relationship may be limited in terms of what ACME has been engaged to do (perhaps, to eliminate a cockroach problem in a storage shed near the parking lot), which subsystems it can communicate with (presumably, the purchase order and invoicing systems at IBM Hawthorne), how long the relationship will last, and so forth. Thus an entity like IBM isn't analogous to a single user of a Web site. Authenticating an organization for a particular role poses a variety of new and rather challenging problems.
- *Authorization.* Having identified the client system that is undertaking some operation, a Web Service will need a way to codify and rapidly check the rules that should be used to determine whether or not that operation is authorized. Web sites leave this open – they tend to either provide access, or deny access, but not to support more elaborate policies. Needed are much more elaborate languages for expressing the logic and restrictions on business relationships and iron-clad mechanisms for validating access rapidly when the need to check authorization arises.
- *Audit.* In secure systems, having the ability to examine the state of the system *after the fact* is a critical element of security. Highly assured Web Services need to be auditable, both to permit post-mortem analysis if an intrusion occurs, and also because for many purposes, auditable security is quite adequate. For example, in a hospital, it is important to know who did what and when they did it – but not necessarily in real-time, and indeed during an emergency, the last thing one wants to do is to pause to type in a password. The topic hasn't received very much attention, either academically or in commercial settings.
- *Anonymity.* For some purposes, concealing user identification data from users not directly participating in a transaction is important. For example, a spy acting on behalf of a terrorist organization may be interested in knowing which user regularly accesses a certain database or receives certain kinds of data. Anonymity isn't always needed and isn't always a good thing – child pornographers, for example, should ideally be exposed and punished. But when we do need this capability, it should be available. Web Services

systems have focused far more on authentication than on anonymity, so applications having this requirement may find the architecture frustrating.

- *Encryption capabilities.* Where information is private or otherwise sensitive, it should be easy to specify that it should be concealed from prying eyes, using strong encryption techniques, with provision to store keys in secure ways. Web Services inherits the secure channel capabilities of SSL, but the architecture lacks a more general ability to create key pairs or to coordinate more complex kinds of shared secret applications, and does not yet standardize the handling of keys stored in hardware components, such as Intel's Palladium architecture. Accordingly, applications that need non-trivial cryptographic mechanisms won't find them in the architecture or in typical platforms complying with it.

Notice also that all of our goals arise at multiple places within the system: on client machines, in the Web Services dispatch module, and in backend machines as well. Many arise at an even higher level – we require consistent behavior *system-wide*, and as we have seen throughout this book, there are forms of system-wide consistency that cannot be achieved with purely end-to-end policies (examples include consistent detection of failures and consistent interpretation of security rules). In what follows, we touch upon the major design options, pointing back to the relevant chapters of the book for readers who want more detail (and who may have skipped those chapters at the time!)

Our objectives split not just between reliability and security, but within each area split further, into two rough groups.

- One group of goal points to constraints on the developer him or herself, who needs to think about assurance requirements when designing a system and be careful to use appropriate mechanisms throughout a system. For example, there is an old adage that security must be designed into a system from the start. A developer who plans to use an authentication scheme, for example, should probably be thinking in those terms right from the outset. Developers who fail to anticipate an eventual security or reliability requirement are unlikely to arrive at a satisfactory solution.
- The second group of goals boil down to technology: we should ask "do we know how to solve the problem?" and then, where the answer is positive, ask whether the Web Services architecture anticipates the technology and provides for appropriate standard interfaces. Unfortunately, the former story is better than the latter: the technology options available to us are considerably richer than the architecture actually anticipates. Thus we face some annoying challenges: we can build, for example, a highly available server, but we may not be able to exploit its high availability features through the intermediary of the Web Services architecture. And sometimes the answers are unsatisfactory in both respects: we lack adequate ways to specify security policies and rules databases, and the Web Services architecture also lacks provision to standardize even the security policy mechanisms currently at our disposal.

The specific issue with which we'll wrestle in the remainder of this chapter is that while Web Services does anticipate that reliability will matter to many users, the type of reliability guarantees available in the architecture are rather narrow ones. Above, we pointed out that Web Services does support transactions, but not other kinds of recovery mechanism. And we noted that Web Services can deal with recoverability in applications structured as asynchronous streams (often with message queuing middleware in the stream), but not for applications where high availability and rapid response times may be needed. Web Services does provide for management and control, but not with scalability – despite the fact that scalability is so often the dominant challenge in building a management or control architecture.

In fact, the bottom line is that Web Services (as currently instantiated) really deals with a few specific cases rather than offering a generic solution for general kinds of applications. These cases are:

1. A legacy server "wrapped" by Web Services, and with message queuing middleware often interposed between the client and the server, leading to a very asynchronous invocation style.

2. A transactional database accessed in the usual "three tier" manner (a client system, possible client code uploaded to the server and running close to it, and the server itself). The model offers two kinds of transactions: standard multiple operation transactions that terminate in a commit or abort, and a long-running "business" transaction, which invokes a sequence of operations and includes exception handling code for each.

3. A distributed object produced using the J2EE, .NET, CORBA, or some other object-oriented development environment and then extended with a Web Services interface by waving whatever magic wand is provided for this purpose.

In what follows, we'll see that the reliability mechanisms for Web Services focus almost entirely on the first two cases. Indeed, one widely referenced essay (by Werner Vogels) asserts that "Web Services are Not Distributed Objects!", arguing that even if platforms like the ones cited make it easy to lose track of the distinction, the architecture itself was clearly conceived with the belief that services are heavy weight, not particularly "interactive," and best accessed in a pipelined asynchronous manner. Figure 26.1 illustrates this kind of system,

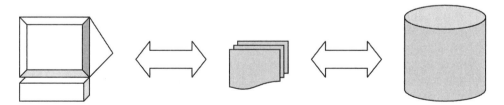

Figure 26.1. Web Services, as currently conceived, may give poor interactive response. This argues for an asynchronous style of requests in which some form of message queuing system is used as a buffer between the application program and the server. Such a message queue might even be programmable using a "business process language," in which case it could automatically translate a single application request into a series of transactions on multiple Web Service platforms. The caller can later collect the reply (perhaps after a substantial delay) by rendezvous with the message queue. Using this approach, server failures can be masked provided that the message queue is highly available.

although omitting Web Services request dispatching (routing) components. In practice, of course, each component in the picture might have a dispatcher of its own.

One is reminded of a period in the late 1980s when major computer vendors, such as DEC and IBM, were perceived as dictating to their customers. Both companies stumbled badly; DEC was acquired by a competitor, while IBM went through a tough period and ultimately reemerged as a company whose central mantra seems to be "listen to the customers." The lesson learned here is that customers ultimately determine the path and the roles a technology needs to play. Wishful thinking doesn't necessarily pan out.

Thus, no matter what the Web Services architecture community may believe, if Web Services looks like a way to access distributed objects, and the platforms make it trivial to generate distributed objects with Web Services interfaces, we're going to see a wave of applications in which developers make use of that functionality. Quite possibly, the majority of major Web Services deployments will include critical subsystems having these attributes. Telling those developers that they've violated a hidden premise of the architecture just isn't going to be acceptable. There may ultimately be little alternative than to tackle the issues head-on.

26.2 High Assurance for Back-End Servers

With these goals in mind, let's start by focusing on the back-end systems that live behind the Web Services dispatching component. Several times, we've quoted Jim Gray in this text. Jim, working with Dennis Shasha and Pat Helland, has offered some rule-of-thumb observations for those interested in developing back-end Web Service servers aimed at demanding applications. Basically, he urges that such systems be hosted on clusters of computers and structured as "RAPS of RACS": Reliable Arrays of Partitioned Servers, where each element is a Reliable Array of Clustered Servers. Whether because of Gray's standing in the community or because the RAPS of RACS concept simply matches existing commercial practice, it is clear that the Web Services architecture anticipates that many servers will in fact be hosted on clusters and that RAPS of RACS will be common.

Let's start by thinking about the partitioning aspect—this is what makes a cluster into RAPS. Jim observes that by far the easiest way to get better performance is to partition the backend server. Consider a financial system providing various operations associated with stock symbols: fetching price history, insider trading records, etc. We can trivially split the work over a large set of servers by simply implementing a mapping function from equity symbol to server. The map could be static (for example, equities starting with letters A-G go to server S1), or dynamic (perhaps, stored directly in DNS records, or implemented using one of the DHT architectures we covered in Section 24.2). Similarly, we could direct traffic associated with "priority gold" customers to a lightly loaded bank of servers, sending other traffic to our main data center. The Web Services dispatching module would, in effect, be connected to the entire pool of servers and would glance at each passing record to decide which server should handle it.

The technology needed here corresponds to the type of content routing discussed in Chapter 11. Products like IBM's Gryphon router (see Aguilera) or the Sarvega XML content router are designed to receive an incoming packet, apply a simple filtering policy to it, and then direct the request to one of a cluster of machines in accordance with the organization's policies. These products are all positioned to help corporate users manage workload in complex data centers organized as RAPS.

What about the "R" in RAPS? The letter stands for reliability, but by now we've seen that reliability is in the eye of the beholder. In the case of Gray's vision, fault-tolerance or high availability issues are the responsibility of a RACS, not a RAPS. The issue for a RAPS is simply to ensure that requests really do get to the appropriate partition of the cluster without being dropped on the floor, and similarly to ensure that the array itself is correctly operational (a very tough problem, since management of a cluster can be the hardest issue that arises on it). Moreover, recall that many kinds of Web Services will be legacy applications, some dating back to the days of batch-style execution, and hence may not be continuously available. A RAPS thus may need some form of reliable message queuing mechanism, so that clients can post requests without actually needing to know that the server is currently ready to process them.

What about the RACS used to implement its various partitions? Here, the challenge relates to the way that the computers comprising the RACS deal with the state of the RACS. In Gray's model, RACS is a group of two or more computers that provide a single, non-partitioned, reliable service. Gray assumes that we are most often talking here about a database or some other form of transactional server, consisting of a server application program and the files in which it stores persistent data. RACS is a mapping of such a service to a small cluster of computers providing high availability, quick restart, or other high assurance properties. The cluster may be as small as two nodes (a primary-backup style of fault-tolerance then comes to mind), or might consist of a somewhat larger number with load balanced among the members.

We should perhaps stress the "transactional" term before saying more. Transactions are a very visible part of the Web Services architecture and there is a strong assumption that "reliability" is linked to transactional processing on the back end. Now, over the course of this book, we've seen many approaches to reliability. Several are based on replication of critical data and functionality and don't involve transactions, and in fact we argued previously that transactions have their place, but can't be the sole technology used in a reliable distributed system. Nonetheless, *transactions actually are the sole reliability story in Web Services back ends*. And this statement carries implications, as we've seen throughout the book. A transactional backend system probably can't provide high availability; more likely will be a recoverability guarantee. Transactional systems can provide tremendously high throughput, but only sometimes rapid response. When a failure does occur, recovery might be a very slow process. Indeed, if a failure occurs at a bad moment, a transactional server might need to wait for a component to be repaired and restarted, and may even need human help in restoring the database.

By buying into this model, the Web Services architecture deliberately sets to the side many of the objectives we enumerated earlier. We may know how to build a fault-tolerant object using replication, but Web Services simply doesn't make use of that technology at this time.

Broadly, the architecture selected when designing a RACS will reflect a tradeoff between the cost of replicating data (and thus having a "hot standby") and the overheads associated with doing so (in terms of system complexity and actual runtime costs). The very simplest RACS typically separate the file storage from the server and simply provide a way to rapidly launch a new copy of the failed service on a healthy node with access to the files the failed copy was using. The idea here is that the new instance will rapidly clean up the mess and then begin to serve requests.

Even this trivial restart architecture raises some non-trivial questions. We'll need a way to accurately detect failures (Section 10.6.3, Chapter 13), and, lacking this, will either need a way to literally "unplug" the server detected as having failed, or will need to introduce a Group Membership Subsystem (Section 14.9, 14.10). The server cluster will probably need to be implemented using transactions against its persistent state (Chapter 24), and faces delicate tradeoffs between the speed of the system and the quality of replication. Using true replication in a transactional setting raises serious problems: the commit protocol will be costly, and there is also no way to avoid the risk of blocking when certain failures occur (Section 14.8, Chapter 18, Section 25.3). By weakening our goals and simply streaming an update log from a primary to a backup server we can achieve higher performance, but at the cost of perhaps "forgetting" some committed transactions when a crash occurs.

All of this starts to sound fairly complex. Making matters worse, it isn't hard to see that our solution won't be able to guarantee high availability because several of the steps mentioned above are slow or capable of blocking. At best, we'll end up with a RACS architecture that, for a "moderate sized" database, can restart itself in a few minutes on a typical computing platform. Meanwhile, client computers will be left twiddling their thumbs – or will have timed out, with potentially serious consequences.

To obtain still higher degrees of availability, we need to turn to some form of active replication. One option is to structure our application into a process group (Chapters 14–20), or to "wrap" an existing server with a front end that uses *abcast* to multicast incoming requests to a set of replicas for independent, concurrent execution (Chapter 20). (If read-only requests can be distinguished from update requests, those can usually be broken out and executed locally, although one must be careful to ensure that the updates will actually be done in the order they are presented to the replicas, and having different read loads at each copy won't help in this regard.)

Another option, particularly promising for developers who find themselves building a new transactional server, would be to use Agarwal's technique, described in Section 23.7. This approach combines group communication with replication of transactional servers to obtain scalability and fault tolerance in small clusters – a perfect technique for use in a RACS.

But the bottom line is fairly negative. Even if one were to build a highly available Web Server, the question arises of whether clients of that server could obtain the same guarantee. The issue here is that the architecture anticipates having many intermediaries between the client and the server: request dispatchers, message queuing subsystems, and perhaps even some form of "engine" for executing business transactions. To say that we've achieved high availability, we would need a story that starts with high availability in the Web Server, but then also tackles issues that could arise in these other components. We'll look at the options below, but to cut to the chase, the Web Services architecture hasn't really thought those kinds of issues through. Thus high availability is not really a priority in Web Services and indeed may not be a practical goal at this time.

What about other aspects of back-end system reliability? Many enterprises are finding that their data centers have grown to include hundreds or thousands of machines, perhaps clustered at multiple locations. Independent of the technology used to implement the servers themselves, the ability of the organization to administer those clusters can emerge as a dominant factor in determining system reliability.

A good goal is to seek systems that are as self-administered as possible and as capable as possible of self-repair after a disruptive failure. For purposes of node management, the author is a great believer in the use of Astrolabe (see Section 24.4), or something similar, such as IBM's Tivoli. The core issue here is that many servers have enormous numbers of parameters, performance tuning knobs, and other kinds of control mechanisms. If we use static values for such things, we'll end up with a system that can easily be disabled by a small failure or even by a minor maintenance action. Worse still, many Web Services systems will consist of a thin layer of front-end wrappers in front of a tangled knot of back-end servers and queuing systems. Lacking some way to monitor the state of this "back-end spaghetti" is a recipe for indigestion!

Once we begin to "light up the dark" by monitoring the state of our RAPS of RACS, it becomes possible to program at least some simple responses in for handling the most common forms of disruptive outages or performance-related adaptations. The front end becomes capable of sensing failures, detecting overloads, and can read parameter values out of Astrolabe, adapting within a few seconds when a server requests a change by posting a new recommended value in its Astrolabe-reported MIB.

The value of using Astrolabe, as opposed (for example) to simply storing such information in an additional database, is that because Astrolabe is a virtual, peer-to-peer technology, we know it to be stable, self-repairing after disruption, and capable of riding out outages. A parameter database would become a single point of failure in most architectures. Of course, for small systems, DNS could be used for many of the same roles as Astrolabe, but DNS would not scale well for a cluster with larger numbers of nodes, nor would it be suitable for parameters that client computers should be able to access and monitor. Astrolabe, in effect, plays the same role as DNS but is designed to scale extremely well.

To summarize, our options seem to be as follows:

1. *Asynchronous pipeline.* Web services encourage us to think of our servers as residing at the back end of a pipeline of message queuing and other intermediaries, which relay requests in and responses out, and can hide server outages by buffering requests reliably and replaying them after the outage is resolved. This method is most effective at masking failures in situations where relatively high average response delays are tolerable and very long (but rare) delays are acceptable.

2. *Use transactions.* Although it is easy to create Web Services that are basically non-transactional distributed objects, the bottom line is that the architecture doesn't favor such an approach. Implicit in the architecture is the assumption that most servers are fairly heavy weight entities that use transactional interfaces for reliability.

3. *Employ a primary-backup fault-tolerance mechanism in the server.* The point here is a reminder of the conclusion reached when we discussed transactional systems in Chapter 24. True replication is very costly in a transactional model. Accordingly, existing systems tend to use one of two approaches. Either one configures a primary and a standby to share a disk, so that if the primary fails the backup can clean up and restart, or one steams a log from the primary to the backup. Log streaming is faster, because the backup won't need to clean up the database after taking over, but the approach can "lose" committed transactions in a crash.

4. *Load balance within the cluster.* If a system will be under heavy demand, the server runs on a small cluster and spreads work over the member nodes to combine high reliability (continuous availability) with better performance through parallelism. Group communication techniques are used to disseminate updates within the cluster, while read-only transactions are distributed over the nodes and performed locally. The approach gives the best performance but is more complex to implement. Chapters 14–20 look at the underlying technologies in the case of non-database servers, while Chapter 24 discusses solutions for transactional database clusters.

5. *Employ process group replication in the Web Server.* Although not currently anticipated in the Web Services architecture, group replication seems to be a natural match with the need and could result in a high availability option for developers of RACS services. A platform extended to offer this option could, for example, begin to tackle the reliability needs of lightweight distributed objects, rather than brushing such objects off by asserting that the Web Services architecture isn't intended to provide such functionality.

26.3 High Assurance for Web Server Front-Ends

In the preceding section, we touched upon the issues encountered in the Web Services dispatch module itself. If we didn't care about high assurance, few issues would arise: the dispatching component would then be a stateless relaying mechanism, and the client would be left to deal with any issues created by a failure.

Matters become more complex if the front end is a message queuing subsystem of the type anticipated by WS_Reliability. Such a component needs to log requests so that they won't be lost in the event that the queuing component experiences a failure and restart, hence it becomes something of a database system itself. Indeed, we run into the "usual" database availability issues. WS_Reliability provides for a variety of request semantics: at least once, at most once, or exactly once. It turns out that the cost of these rises as we go from weaker to stronger properties: to implement at least once semantics, we just need a mechanism that will reissue a request if there is any doubt about it having gotten through. At most once involves remembering enough information to avoid reissuing a request if it "might" have been processed previously. But exactly once semantics are tough; here, not only must the front end take care to not lose requests, but the back end needs the ability to recognize reissued requests and to reply by sending back a copy of the original response. Many systems will lack the technology to do this

In the spirit of suggesting directions that the W3 standards community might consider, it would be worthwhile to explore ways of extending the WSDL language to include standard ways of representing assurance properties of Web Services platforms and requirements upon the client systems. For example, if a Web Services platform is able to provide high availability on the condition that the client uses a given monitoring technology, the WSDL document is an ideal place to capture the availability property and the associated requirements, and to specify the way to download the monitoring functionality and correctly parameterize it. A client needing these properties would then be offered a "recipe" for connecting to the Web Services platform in the appropriate manner.

An intriguing option concerns the use of "non-breakable TCP connections" on Web Services platforms. As noted in Section 21.5.2, it is possible to build a form of replicated TCP connection in which the server, transparent to its clients, shares TCP state with a set of one or more backups. When this is done, those backups can seamlessly take control should the server to which a client was communicating fail. In effect, the message queuing or request dispatch system gains reliability through direct replication of the endpoint of the TCP connection, and hence can avoid logging requests on disk in some form of database. Because most clients will communicate to Web Services using HTTP over TCP, this option provides at least the possibility of concealing failure entirely from the client. There would be a great deal of value in such a technology and vendors seeking a commercial advantage should certainly explore the option.

26.4 Issues Encountered on the Client Side

The limitations of the existing Web Services architecture are most evident in the form of a series of confusing situations that can arise on the client platform. Although the actual technical needs vary depending upon the client system's goals, the fact is that existing Web Services platforms address only the very weakest possible assurance properties.

Let's start with the easiest case. If the client is performing operations that are stateless and idempotent, and each operation is a singleton transaction (a one-shot transaction), high assurance can be treated as an issue faced only on the server side. Moreover, the possibility of using an unbreakable TCP connection on the server side might permit a server to completely mask outages. Although this entails non-trivial use of group communication tools within the server, the commercial value of such an approach is that clients will see far higher availability and have fewer cases to deal with in their application programs.

The problems get tougher if we move away from this simple initial scenario. Above, we anticipated that a message queuing middleware component might use group replication and could hide this behind an unbreakable TCP connection, so that the client sees a standard Web Services interface and yet has a guarantee of availability unless many components fail simultaneously. Similarly, we pointed to ways to make the server itself highly available. But both of these suggestions depart from the Web Services architecture as currently conceived. Indeed, as the architecture is currently designed, the "other" option offered to a client is to employ an asynchronous streaming architecture, placing message queuing intermediaries in the stream if desired, and perhaps using transactions to improve server robustness.

Earlier we suggested that such a constraint may be unworkable for at least some major classes of Web Services developers. Accordingly, today's developer may find that Web Services just doesn't respond to some of the requirements his or her organization may encounter. Short of departing from the standards, such a developer will be in the frustrating situation of using a generally accepted standard and yet arriving at an unacceptable outcome. Unfortunately, it may take the combined voices of quite a few such developers before the vendors take this issue on in a direct way. However, the good news is that when they do, the needed technology seems to be available.

We are left with a number of security issues. As noted earlier, for the time being there is little hope that such problems could be resolved in a standardized manner, and each application may simply need to break new ground in order to obtain the security properties it requires. Over time, however, stronger Web Services standards for system-level security will surely arise, tackling some of the new kinds of enterprise security requirements mentioned earlier. These in turn may impose new kinds of client-side obligations when a problem arises.

26.5 Highly Assured Web Services Need Autonomic Tools!

In Chapter 10 we noted that IBM has launched a major initiative to create a new generation of *Autonomic Computing* technologies. At the risk of some overlap with Section 10.10, what's this about, and why is it relevant to highly assured Web Services?

Many analysts are concerned that Web Services systems could run into trouble as they are deployed in large enterprise settings where there are a great many legacy applications in use. The essence of the concern is as follows: Web Services encourage us to think in terms of rapid response, interactive, RPC interfaces. Earlier, we saw that the architecture really works best for asynchronous, pipelined styles of requests. Yet some systems just can't operate in that manner. Analysts worry that many users will build a Web Services interfaces to corporate servers and services that usually work pretty well, but that sometimes hang or run very slowly for reasons not evident to the outside world.

From the end-user's perspective, such a system will seem flakey. It will appear to be broken during the periods when responses are delayed. Once we begin to connect to a computing system in a given way, we need to make that system work in a predictable manner *all* the time.

But why should we anticipate that delays would arise so frequently? The problem is that many corporate networks are a spaghetti of old, interconnected, batch-style systems, tied together by message oriented middleware queuing systems and using all sorts of quaint technologies to keep the mixture running. For example, Verizon's Michael Brody has made a hobby of tracking the interconnectivity of Verizon's major computing systems. He ends up with a graph that resembles an integrated circuit, with literally hundreds of systems that depend upon each other in thousands of obscure ways.

The worry, in effect, is that even systems that are working perfectly well in the old style may be operating in "surprising" ways if we peek beneath the covers – handling batches of requests once every 15 minutes, for example, or otherwise acting in a surprisingly balky, unpredictable manner. Legacy systems may not adapt easily to new kinds of demands, particular if we expect rapid responses.

Moreover, simply tracking parameter settings and the status of the overall system can emerge as a significant problem. If something causes a service to change its IP address or port number or security key, or any of hundreds of other imaginable parameter settings, client systems may begin to fail for lack of a way to automatically detect this and adapt as necessary. Today, precisely because we lack the tools to automate such responses, corporations often find that the number of people required to administer a computer system grows in proportion to that systems size and interrelatedness – a worrisome formula for executives concerned with the bottom line!

The term *autonomic computing* is intended to evoke the image of the body's autonomic systems: blood pressure, heart and respiratory rate, perspiration, etc. These adapt, silently and automatically, as we go through our daily lives, and unless conditions depart far from the norms, we're completely unaware of them. Could similar mechanisms be developed and integrated into modern computing systems? IBM believes that this is possible, and points to RAID file servers as an example of what they want to accomplish. A RAID system signals failures in a simple, clear way – a red light blinks on the faulty unit, and some systems even send an e-mail to request a visit from a technician. The technician shows up, unplugs the failed disk, plugs in a replacement, and goes home – end of story. If we can get from where we are today to a similar place for Web Services, IBM's effort will have been a huge success!

Clearly, any autonomic computing solution needs to cover several aspects:

1. The key system components need to be closely monitored and we need an instrumentation framework whereby monitoring agents can query applications and the platforms on which they are running for various runtime parameters indicative of health, load, and other aspects of system state.

2. We need a way to collect this data and collate it within some form of system-wide database, both to track actual state and also to watch the system history as it evolves over time.

3. We need to develop rules for analysis of such databases. For example, thinking about the Verizon system, if a billing system is having a problem, it may not be caused by the billing application or database per-se. The problem could stem from some remote location—indeed, Leslie Lamport (we heard about him in Chapter 14) famously remarked that "A distributed computing systems is one in which you can be prevented from carrying out your own work by the failure of a computer that you did not even know existed." In the general case, any single failure can cause a cascade

of downstream events. We need ways to backtrack from the eventual outcome to the original cause.

Today, the picture is somewhat mixed. In some ways, the first item on our list is easiest. We can monitor existing systems without too much trouble, and in fact platforms such as Windows XP include very extensive, standardized, monitoring mechanisms. On the other hand, there are few widely accepted standards for instrumenting application systems, and even if there was a broad standard, application-specific issues enter: perhaps system a is unhealthy when such-and-such a job queue has more than 3 elements on it, but system b is unhealthy when a given table has less than 3 elements on it, and so forth.

IBM currently uses a system called Tivoli to collect instrumentation data into a centralized database for analysis. Tivoli is quite powerful and allows users to define system-specific logic for fault-tree analysis and simply to display system state as it evolves over time. However, it is clear that as systems grow in size and complexity, the load associated with pulling all that data to a central location could become problematic. Delays will be an issue—just when the network falls apart, Tivoli itself may suddenly stop receiving the updates needed to track the state and help the user make sense of the current problem. Moreover, the central system becomes a kind of critical point of failure: if the monitoring and management center is unavailable during a disruption, the remainder of the network may be unable to react to events.

At Cornell, we believe that Astrolabe may be applicable to such problems. With Astrolabe, it is easy to tap into data even on a massive scale, and there is a scalable, resilient, and (loosely) consistent database-like representation available throughout the system. The open question here concerns how to decentralized the kind of control logic that people currently encode into a system like Tivoli, and how to use Astrolabe to create logs for historical trend discovery and post-mortem (offline) analysis. Are there ways to react in a decentralized manner when a system needs to adapt? If this question has a positive answer, than Astrolabe coupled with some sort of control methodology might overcome some of the concerns that a centralized control system like Tivoli poses.

Astrolabe can also endow the operator with powerful new ways to adapt the behavior of the monitoring framework as new challenges arise. With Astrolabe we can change the data being pulled into the system dynamically, and this is effective within seconds even on a huge scale. So, if a system wasn't actively monitoring queue lengths for the ACME systems message bus product but it becomes advisable to do so, the operator can introduce a new "configuration certificate" and, voila, the desired information materializes. Using aggregation, the operator can now narrow in on the nodes where problems seem to be arising. Just as one explores a database with a series of queries, Astrolabe allows the operator to explore a massive system, in real time, while a disruption is occurring, and is very likely to remain healthy even when everything else is seriously messed up! Indeed, depending on how one configures the system, Astrolabe can even be employed to intervene – to track down the servers that have a mistaken configuration, for example, and to initiate a reconfiguration action at those sites. Of course, enabling this functionality also opens security holes, hence there are other issues to keep in mind here. Perhaps, looking at a system and understanding its state is already enough to make a difference, and we should avoid that very last step until we have many years of experience with these first steps.

The very hardest problem of all is the one on which we have the least to say. How does one encode the knowledge of the way a system *should* behave? How can we express the various policies and rules for sorting through a cascade of events to pin down the basic problem: "Ah. Server *a* is having a database problem again. We'll need to shut it down and run the database defragmentation and repair program." These types of insights are hard enough for human operators to arrive at, and in a world of slightly buggy software, we won't soon do away with this role! This is especially true for complex legacy systems where nobody really remembers exactly how things work.

IBM's hope, and one that many in the domain share, is that we don't really need to solve the "whole" problem to achieve a striking success. If we can just enable developers to automate some of the more common scenarios, by providing them with the tools to do so, perhaps we can slash the frequency with which human intervention is needed and show big wins even if our solution only covers perhaps 80% of the cases. Moreover, if we can put more powerful tools into the hands of operators, we can make their jobs easier and more efficient, even if we don't try to automate them at all. After all, even a RAID system needs to be serviced, and in fact, even a RAID system can fail (for example, a sleepy technician could see that blinking bulb and then pull the wrong disk out!) The trick is to not call for service when it isn't needed, and to provide very high quality information to the technician when service is required. A success story doesn't always need to be a 100% success – and in the case of autonomic computing, every small step will save customers money, increase the reliability and adaptiveness of Web Services, and hence help contribute towards a good-news story.

26.6 Summary

We've suggested that high assurance for Web Services may be feasible if the Web Services platform vendors are sufficiently sophisticated about the requirements, are lucky enough to be working in the paradigm the Web Services vendors have in mind, and build their applications in the intended manner (e.g., using message queuing subsystems, content routers, etc). And we made the point that if the Web Services architecture can make 80% of its users happy, it could be quite a success. Developers who either fail to anticipate the needs or who anticipate them but are not working in the right paradigm may find the architecture frustrating. But will they be 20% of the market, or 50% of the market? The author of this text suspects that the group may be very large, and indeed that it could turn out that 80% of the market is after styles of Web Services reliability that depart from what could be called the "standard model" today.

Ultimately, success will require that the Web Services community agree upon standards for such problems as tracking system membership, monitoring system status, reporting appropriate parameter values, and signaling platform "events" to the servers and clients that may need to react. The technologies required already exist—they might, for example, include Astrolabe, Kelips and Bimodal Multicast for the distributed system as a whole, and virtual synchrony as supported in Horus, Ensemble or Spread on the Web Services platform itself. Indeed, these are precisely the technologies Cornell is integrating into its QuickSilver platform, and QuickSilver is intended as one response to the Web Services reliability and assurance problem. Of course, this is a Cornell-dominated list, and the folks at MIT, or the ones at Berkeley, or the ones at IBM or Microsoft or BEA, would surely have some suggestions of their own.

We have the technology. What we lack is the recognition by the community that Web Services actually *are* distributed objects, and a decision to engage the issues head on.

26.7 Related Reading

A great deal has been written about Web Services architectures, although the area is still in its infancy. Good resources include the Web sites maintained by IBM Corporation, Microsoft, and BEA. The Word Wide Web Consortium (W3) is the primary standards body for the area and maintains additional sites documenting the major Web Services specifications and standards, with examples of WSDL documents and the like.

27

Other Distributed and Transactional Systems

In this chapter we review some of the advanced research efforts in the areas covered in this book. The first section focuses on message-passing and group communication systems, and the second section focuses on transactional systems. The review is not intended to be exhaustive, but we do try to include the major activities that contributed to the technology areas stressed in the book.

27.1 Related Work in Distributed Computing

There have been many distributed systems in which group communication played a role. We now review some of these systems, providing a brief description of the features of each and citing sources of additional information. Our focus is on distributed computing systems and environments with support for some form of process group computing. However, we do not limit ourselves to those systems implementing virtually synchronous process groups or a variation on the model. Our review presents these systems in alphabetical order. If we were to discuss them chronologically, we would start by considering V, then the Isis Toolkit and Delta-4, and then we would turn to the others in a roughly alphabetical ordering. However, it is important to understand that these systems are the output of a vigorous research community and that each of the systems cited included significant research innovations at the time it was developed. It would be simplistic to say that any one of these systems came first and that the remainder are somehow secondary. It would be more accurate to say that each system was innovative in some areas and borrowed ideas from prior systems in other areas.

Readers interested in learning more about this subject may want to start by consulting the articles that appeared in *Communications of the ACM* in a special section of the April 1996 issue (vol. 39, no. 4). David Powell's introduction to this special section is both witty and informative (see Powell [1996]), and there are articles about several of the systems discussed in this book (see Cristian [1996], Dolev and Malkhi, Moser et al. [1996], Schiper and Raynal, van Renesse et al. [1996]).

27.1.1 Amoeba

During the early 1990s, Amoeba (see Mullender et al., van Renesse et al., [1988, 1989]) was one of a few microkernel-based operating systems proposed for distributed computing; others include V (see Cheriton and Zwaenepoel), Mach (see Rashid), Chorus (see Rozier [Fall 1988, December 1988]), and QNX (see Hildebrand). The focus of the project when it was first launched was to develop a distributed system around a nucleus supporting extremely high performance communication, with the remaining system services being implemented using a client/server architecture. In our area of emphasis, process group protocols, Amoeba supports a subsystem developed by Frans Kaashoek that provides group communication using total ordering (see Kaashoek). Message delivery is atomic and totally ordered and implements a form of virtually synchronous addressing. During the early 1990s, Amoeba's sequencer protocols set performance records for throughput and latency, although other systems subsequently bypassed these using a mixture of protocol refinements and new generations of hardware and software.

27.1.2 BASE

BASE is an architecture and system for using Byzantine Agreement in small groups as a way to achieve extremely high levels of assurance. Aimed at mission-critical data such as files containing security policies, BASE distributes data among servers and then uses Byzantine Agreement to validate information read by the user. Two forms of agreement are available: a signature-only scheme, which is cheaper, and a more costly scheme in which the full content of each block is subjected to agreement. See Castro [2003].

27.1.3 Chorus

Chorus is an object-oriented operating system for distributed computing (see Rozier et al. [Fall 1988, December 1988]). Developed at INRIA during the 1980s, the technology shifted to a commercial track in the early 1990s and has become one of the major vehicles for commercial UNIX development and for real-time computing products. The system is notable for its modularity and comprehensive use of object-oriented programming techniques. Chorus was one of the first systems to embrace these ideas and is extremely sophisticated in its support for modular application programming and for reconfiguration of the operating system itself.

Chorus implements a process group communication primitive, which is used to assist applications in dealing with services that are replicated for higher availability. When an RPC is issued to such a replicated service, Chorus picks a single member and issues an invocation to it. A feature is also available for sending an unreliable multicast to the members of a process group (no ordering or atomicity guarantees are provided).

In its commercial incarnation, the Chorus operating system was used primarily in real-time settings for applications that occur in telecommunication systems. Running over Chorus is an object request broker technology called Cool-ORB. This system includes a variety of distributed computing services including a replication service capable of being interconnected to a process group technology, such as that used in the Horus system.

27.1.4 Delta-4

Delta-4 was one of the first systematic efforts to address reliability and fault-tolerant concerns (see Powell [1994]). Launched in Europe during the late 1980s, Delta-4 was developed by a multinational team of companies and academic researchers (see Powell [1991], Rodrigues and Verissimo [1989]). The focus of the project was on factory-floor applications, which combine real-time and fault-tolerant requirements. Delta-4 took an approach in which a trusted module was added to each host computer and used to run fault-tolerant protocols. These modules were implemented in software, but they could be included in a specially designed hardware interface to a shared communication bus. The protocols used in the system included process group mechanisms similar to the ones now employed to support virtual synchrony, although Delta-4 did not employ the virtual synchrony computing model.

The project was extremely successful as a research effort and resulted in working prototypes that were indeed fault tolerant and capable of coordinated real-time control in distributed automation settings. Unfortunately, however, this stage was reached as Europe entered a period of economic difficulties, and none of the participating companies were able to pursue the technology base after the research funding for the project ended. Ideas from Delta-4 can now be found in a number of other group-oriented and real-time distributed systems, including Horus.

27.1.5 Ensemble

Ensemble was discussed in considerable detail in Chapter 21. Based on Horus, the system implements virtual synchrony but uses a stackable protocol architecture in which each property is provided by a micro-protocol. Sets of microprotocols are composed to obtain a desired large-scale behavior. Horus performs well and has the flexibility to match properties provided with user requirements. Where Ensemble departs from Horus is in its use of a high level mathematical programming language, O'CaML, for protocol specification. This permits the use of formal theorem proving tools as a part of the development process (see Liu [1999]) and opens the door to provably correct protocol implementations. The system is available for download from Cornell University.

27.1.6 Harp

The "gossip" protocols of Ladin and Liskov were mentioned in conjunction with our discussion of communication from a nonmember of a process group to that group (see Ladin et al. [1992], Liskov et al. [1991]). These protocols were originally introduced in a replicated file system project undertaken at MIT in the early 1990s. The key idea of the Harp system was to use a lazy update mechanism as a way of obtaining high performance and tolerance to partitioning failures in a replicated file system. The system was structured as a collection of file servers consisting of multiple processes, each of which maintained a full copy of the file system, and a set of clients, which issued requests to the servers, switching from server to server to balance load or to overcome failures of the network or of a server process. Clients issued read operations, which the system handled locally at whichever server received the request, and update operations, which were performed using a quorum algorithm. Any updates destined for a faulty or unavailable process were spooled for later transmission when the process recovered or communication to it was reestablished. To ensure that when a client issued a series of requests the file servers performed them at consistent (e.g., logically advancing) times, each response from a file server process to a client included a timestamp, which the client could present on subsequent requests. The timestamp was represented as a vector clock and could be used to delay a client's request if it were sent to a server that had not yet seen some updates on which the request might be dependent.

Harp made extensive use of a hardware feature not widely used in modern workstations, despite its low cost and off-the-shelf availability. A so-called nonvolatile or battery-backed RAM (NVRAM) is a small memory, which preserves its contents even if the host computer crashes and later restarts. Finding that the performance of Harp was dominated by the latency associated with forced log writes to the disk, Ladin and Liskov purchased these inexpensive devices for the machines on which Harp ran and modified the Harp software to use the NVRAM area as a persistent data structure, which could hold commit records, locking information, and a small amount of additional commit-related data. Performance of Harp increased sharply, leading these researchers to argue that greater use should be made of NVRAM in reliable systems of all sorts. However, NVRAM is not found on typical workstations or computing systems, and vendors of the major transactional and database products are under great pressure to offer the best possible performance on completely standard platforms, making the use of NVRAM problematic in commercial products. The technology used in Harp would not perform well without NVRAM storage.

27.1.7 The Highly Available System (HAS)

The Highly Available System (HAS) was developed by IBM's Almaden research laboratory under the direction of Cristian and Strong, with involvement by Skeen and Schmuck, in the late 1980s and subsequently contributed technology to a number of IBM products, including the ill-fated Advanced Automation System (AAS) development that IBM undertook for the American Federal Aviation Agency (FAA) in the early 1990s (see Cristian [February 1991], Cristian and Delancy). Unfortunately, relatively little of what was apparently a substantial body of work was published about this system. The most widely known results include the *timed asynchronous communication model*, proposed by Cristian and Schmuck (see Cristian and Schmuck) and used to provide precise semantics for their reliable protocols. Protocols were proposed for synchronizing the clocks in a distributed system (see Cristian [1989]); managing group membership in real-time settings (see Crisitan [August 1991]); atomic communication to groups (see Cristian et al. [1985, 1990]), subject to timing bounds; and achieving totally ordered delivery guarantees at the operational members of groups. Details of these protocols were presented in Chapter 24. A shared memory model called *Delta-Common Storage* was proposed as a part of this project and consisted of a tool by which process group members could communicate using a shared memory abstraction, with guarantees that updates would be seen by all operational group members (if by any) within a limited period of time.

27.1.8 The Horus System

Horus was discussed in considerable detail in Chapter 21. It implements virtual synchrony but uses a stackable protocol architecture in which each property is provided by a micro-protocol. Sets of microprotocols are compose to obtain a desired large-scale behavior. Horus performs well and has the flexibility to match properties provided with user requirements. See van Renesse [1996].

27.1.9 The Isis Toolkit

The Isis Toolkit was developed by my colleagues and me between 1985 and 1990. It was the first process group communication system to use the virtual synchrony model (see Birman and Joseph [February 1987, November 1987], Birman and van Renesse [1994]). As its name suggests, Isis is a collection of procedural tools that are linked directly to the application program, providing it with functionality for creating and joining process groups dynamically, multicasting to process groups with various ordering guarantees, replicating data and synchronizing the actions of group members as they access that data, performing operations in a load-balanced or fault-tolerant manner, and so forth (see Birman and van Renesse [1996]). Over time, a number of applications were developed using Isis, and it became widely used through a public software distribution. These developments led to the commercialization of Isis through a company, which eventually became a wholly owned subsidiary of Stratus Computer, Inc. Stratus closed down the Isis subsidiary in 1997, when it was acquired by Lucent.

Isis introduced the primary partition virtual synchrony model and the *cbcast* primitive. These steps enabled it to support a variety of reliable programming tools, which was unusual for process group systems at the time Isis was developed. Late in the life cycle of the system, it was one of the first (along with Ladin and Liskov's Harp system) to use vector timestamps to enforce causal ordering. In a practical sense, the system represented an advance merely by being a genuinely useable packaging of a reliable computing technology into a form that could be used by a large community.

Successful applications of Isis include components of the New York and Swiss stock exchanges; distributed control in AMD's FAB-25 VLSI fabrication facility; distributed financial databases such as one developed by the World Bank; a number of telecommunication applications involving mobility, distributed switch management, and control; billing and fraud detection; several applications in air traffic control and space data collection; and many others.

27.1.10 Locus

Locus is a distributed operating system developed by Popek's group at UCLA in the mid-1990s (see Walter et al.). Known for such features as transparent process migration and a uniform distributed shared memory abstraction, Locus was extremely influential in the early development of parallel and cluster-style computing systems. Locus was eventually commercialized and is now a product of Locus Computing Corporation. The file system component of Locus was later extended into the Ficus system, which we discussed earlier in conjunction with other stateful file systems.

27.1.11 Manetho

In writing this book, I was forced to make certain tradeoffs in terms of the coverage of topics. One topic that was not included is that of log-based recovery, whereby applications create checkpoints periodically and log messages sent or received. Recovery is by rollback into a consistent state, after which log replay is used to regain the state as of the instant the failure occurred.

Manetho (see Elnozahy and Zwaenepoel) is perhaps the best known of the log-based recovery systems, although the idea of using logging for fault tolerance is quite a bit older (see Borg et al., Johnson and Zwaenepoel, Koo and Toueg). In Manetho, a library of communication procedures automates the creation of logs, which include all messages sent from application to application. An assumption is made that application programs are deterministic and will reenter the same state if the same sequence of messages is played into them. In the event of a failure, a rollback protocol is triggered, which will roll back one or more programs until the system state is globally consistent—meaning that the set of logs and checkpoints represents a state the system could have entered at some instant in logical time. Manetho then rolls the system forward by redelivery of the logged messages. Because the messages are logged at the sender, the technique is called *sender-based logging*. Experiments with Manetho have confirmed that the overhead of the technique is extremely small. Moreover, working independently, Alvisi has demonstrated that sender-based logging is just one of a very general spectrum of logging methods that can store messages close to the sender, close to the recipient, or even mix these options (see Alvisi and Marzullo).

Although conceptually simple, logging has never played a major role in reliable distributed systems in the field, most likely because of the determinism constraint and the need to use the logging and recovery technique system-wide. This issue, which also makes it difficult to transparently replicate a program to make it fault-tolerant, seems to be one of the fundamental obstacles to software-based reliability technologies. Unfortunately, nondeterminism can creep into a system through a great many interfaces. Use of shared memory or semaphore-style synchronization can cause a system to be nondeterministic, as can any dependency on the order of message reception, the amount of data in a pipe or the time in the execution when the data arrive, the system clock, or the thread scheduling order. This implies that the class of applications for which one can legitimately make a determinism assumption is very small—for example, suppose that the servers used in some system are a mixture of deterministic and nondeterministic programs. Active replication could be used to replicate the deterministic programs transparently, and the sorts of techniques discussed in previous chapters could be employed in the remainder. However, to use a sender-based logging technique (or any logging technique), the entire group of application programs needs to satisfy this assumption—hence, one would need to recode the nondeterministic servers before any benefit of any kind could be obtained. This obstacle is apparently sufficient to deter most potential users of the technique.

I am aware, however, of some successes with log-based recovery in specific applications that happen to have a very simple structure. One popular approach to factoring very large numbers involves running large numbers of completely independent factoring processes that deal with small ranges of potential factors; such systems are very well suited to a log-based recovery technique because the computations are deterministic and there is little communication between the participating processes. Log-based recovery seems to be more applicable to scientific computing systems or problems such as the factoring problem than to general-purpose distributed computing of the sort seen in corporate environments or the Web.

27.1.12 NavTech

NavTech is a distributed computing environment built using Horus (see Birman and van Renesse [1996], van Renesse et al. [1996]), but with its own protocols and specialized distributed services (see Rodrigues and Verissimo [1995], Rodrigues et al., Verissimo [1993, 1994, 1996], Verissimo and Rodrigues). The group responsible for the system is headed by Verissimo, who was one of the major contributors to Delta-4, and the system reflects many ideas that originated in that earlier effort. NavTech is aimed at wide area applications with real-time constraints, such as banking systems involving a large number of branches and factory-floor applications in which control must be done close to a factory component or device. The issues that occur when real-time and fault-tolerant problems are considered in a single setting thus represent a particular focus of the effort. Future emphasis by the group will be on the integration of graphical user interfaces, security, and distributed fault tolerance within a single setting. Such a mixture of technologies would result in an appropriate technology base for applications such as home banking and distributed game playing—both expected to be popular early uses of the new generation of Internet technologies.

27.1.13 Paxos

Paxos (see Lamport [2001]) has been discussed in some detail. This system is similar in spirit to Isis, Horus, Spread, Ensemble, Transis or other group communication architectures, but focuses on the "narrow" problem of supporting atomic broadcast in a static membership model, but where subsets of the full membership might be unavailable. Paxos employs a set of quorum-based protocols to read and update the replicated data maintained by the group, and satisfies the dynamic uniformity property associated with the traditional definition of consensus. The system has been used to develop a distributed file system (Frangiapani; see Thekkath [1997]) and in the Microsoft clustering product. A weakness of the Paxos approach is that it only supports a single, very strong, reliability model, and that model happens to be extremely costly. As a result, Paxos scales poorly and even in a small group can only perform an update after a majority of the system members have acknowledged the operation and the ordering that will be employed.

27.1.14 Phalanx

Phalanx is an object-oriented system that uses Byzantine Quorum protocols (see Malkhi [1998]) to implement extremely high integrity objects, as the basis for secure solutions to problems such as voting, security policy enforcement in organizations of various kinds, or other forms of high-integrity systems.

27.1.15 Phoenix

Phoenix is a distributed computing effort launched by C. Malloth and A. Schiper of the École Polytechnique de Lausanne jointly with O. Babaoglu and P. Verissimo (see Malloth, Schiper and Raynal). Most work on the project occurred at EPFL. The emphasis of this system is on issues that occur when process group techniques are used to implement wide area transactional systems or database systems. Phoenix has a Horus-like architecture, but uses protocols specialized to the needs of transactional applications and has developed an extension of the virtual synchrony model within which transactional serializability can be elegantly treated.

27.1.16 Psync

Psync is a distributed computing system, which was developed by Peterson at the University of Arizona in the late 1980s and early 1990s (see Mishra et al. [1991], Peterson [1987], Peterson et al. [1989]). The focus of the effort was to identify a suitable set of tools with which to implement protocols such as the ones we have presented in the last few chapters. In effect, Psync set out to solve the same problem as the Express Transfer Protocol, but where XTP focused on point-to-point datagrams and streaming-style protocols, Psync was more oriented toward group communication and protocols with distributed ordering properties. A basic set of primitives was provided for identifying messages and for reasoning about their ordering relationships. Over these primitives, Psync provided implementations of a variety of ordered and atomic multicast protocols.

27.1.17 Rampart

Rampart is a distributed system, which uses virtually synchronous process groups in settings where security is desired even if components fail in arbitrary (Byzantine) ways (see Reiter [1996]). The activity was headed by Reiter and resulted in a number of protocols for implementing process groups despite Byzantine failures, as well as a prototype of a security architecture employing these protocols (see Reiter [1993, 1994], Reiter and Birman, Reiter et al. [1992, 1995]). We discuss this system in more detail in Chapter 23. Rampart's protocols are more costly than those we have presented here, but the system would probably not be used to support a complete distributed application. Instead, Rampart's mechanisms could be employed to implement a very secure subsystem, such as a digital cash server or an authentication server in a distributed setting, while other less-costly mechanisms could be employed to implement the applications that make use of these very secure services.

27.1.18 Relacs

The Relacs system is the product of a research effort headed by Ozalp Babaoglu at the University of Bologna (see Babaoglu et al. [1994, 1995]). The activity includes a strong theoretical component, but has also developed an experimental software testbed within which protocols developed by the project can be implemented and validated. The focus of Relacs is on the extension of virtual synchrony to wide area networks in which partial connectivity disrupts communication. Basic results of this effort include a theory that links *reachability* to consistency in distributed protocols, as well as a proposed extension of the view synchrony properties of a virtually synchronous group model to permit safe operation for certain classes of algorithms despite partitioning failures.

27.1.19 RMP

The RMP system is a public-domain process group environment implementing virtual synchrony, with a focus on extremely high performance and simplicity. The majority of the development of this system occurred at the University of California, Berkeley, where graduate student Brian Whetten needed such a technology for his work on distributed multimedia applications (see Callahan and Montgomery, Montgomery, Montgomery and Whetten, Whetten). Over time, the project became much broader, as West Virginia University/NASA researchers Jack Callahan and Todd Montgomery became involved. Broadly speaking, RMP is similar to the Horus system, although less extensively layered.

The major focus of the RMP project has been on embedded system applications, which might occur in future space platforms or ground-based computing support for space systems. Early RMP users have been drawn from this community, and the long-term goals of the effort are to develop technologies suitable for use by NASA. As a result, the verification of RMP has become particularly important, since systems of this sort cannot easily be upgraded or serviced while in flight. RMP has pioneered the use of formal verification and software design tools in protocol verification (see Callahan and Montgomery, Wu), and the project is increasingly focused on robustness though formal methods—a notable shift from its early emphasis on setting new performance records.

27.1.20 Spread

Yair Amir's group at John Hopkins University created the Spread toolkit to provide high performance messaging service that is resilient to faults across external or internal networks. Spread functions as a unified message bus for distributed applications, and provides highly tuned application level multicast and group communication support. Spread services range from reliable message passing to fully ordered messages with delivery guarantees, even in case of computer failures and network partitions.

The basic Spread group communication toolkit is available as a open source from www.spread.org. An enhanced and supported version of the system is being marketed by Spread Concepts Inc. The company provides commercial licensing, customization and support for Spread, enabling the use of open source technology with the support and reliability of a commercial enterprise.

Spread Concepts provides extensions to the basic toolkit that are not in the open source version, including enhanced wide area support and Secure Spread. The company also builds generic infrastructure tools on top of Spread.

27.1.21 StormCast

Researchers at the University of Tromsö, within the Arctic circle, launched this effort, which implemented a wide area weather and environmental monitoring system for Norway. StormCast is not a group communication system per se, but rather is one of the most visible and best documented of the major group communication applications (see Asplin and Johansen, Birman and van Renesse [1996], Johansen, Johansen and Hartvigsen, Johansen et al. [May 1995, June 1995, 1996]). Process group technologies are employed within this system for parallelism, fault tolerance, and system management.

The basic architecture of StormCast consists of a set of data archiving sites, located throughout the Far North. As its peak, StormCast had approximately 50 such sites. Many of these sites simply gather and log weather data, but some collect radar and satellite imagery and others maintain extensive data sets associated with short- and long-term weather modeling and predictions. StormCast application programs typically draw on this varied data set for purposes such as local weather prediction, tracking environmental problems such as oil spills (or radioactive discharges from Russia), research into weather modeling, and other similar applications.

StormCast is interesting for many reasons. The architecture of the system received intense scrutiny (see Johansen, Johansen and Hartvigsen) and evolved over a series of iterations into one in which the application developer is guided to a solution using tools appropriate to the application and following templates that worked successfully for other similar applications. This concept of architecture driving the solution is one that has been lost in many distributed computing environments, which tend to be architecturally flat (presenting the same tools, services, and APIs system-wide even if the applications themselves have very clear architecture, such as a client/server structure, in which different parts of the system need different forms of support). It is interesting to note that early versions of StormCast, which lacked such a strong concept of system architecture, were much more difficult to use than the current one, in which the developer actually has less freedom but much stronger guidance toward solutions.

StormCast also encountered some difficult technical challenges. The very large amounts of data gathered by weather monitoring systems necessarily must be visited on the servers where they reside; it is impractical to move this data to the place where the user requesting a service, such as a local weather forecast, may be working. Thus, StormCast has pioneered in the development of techniques for sending computations to data: the so-called *agent* architecture (see Johansen et al. [1996]) we discussed in Section 9.10 in conjunction with the TACOMA system.

In a typical case, an airport weather prediction for Tromsö might involve checking for incoming storms in the 500-km radius around Tromsö and then visiting one of several other data archives, depending upon the prevailing winds and the locations of incoming weather systems. The severe and unpredictable nature of arctic weather makes these computations equally unpredictable: Data needed for one prediction may be primarily archived in southern Norway, while those needed for some other prediction may be archived in northern Norway or on a system that collects data from trawlers along the coast. Such problems are solved by designing TACOMA agents, which travel to this data, preprocess it to extract needed information, and then return it to the end user for display or further processing. Although such an approach presents challenging software design and management problems, it also seems to be the only viable option for working with such large quantities of data and supporting such a varied and unpredictable community of users and applications.

It should be noted that StormCast maintains an unusually interesting Web page, http://www.cs.uit.no. Readers who have a Web browser will find interactive remote-controlled cameras focused on the ski trails near the university, current environmental monitoring information including data on small oil spills and the responsible vessels, three-dimensional weather predictions intended to aid air traffic controllers in recommending the best approach paths to airports in the region, and other examples of the use of the system. One can also download a version of TACOMA and use it to develop new weather or environmental applications, which can be submitted directly to the StormCast system, load permitting.

27.1.22 Totem

The Totem system is the result of a multiyear project at the University of California, Santa Barbara, focusing on process groups in settings that require extremely high performance and real-time guarantees (see Agarwal, Amir et al., Melliar-Smith and Moser [1989, 1993], Melliar-Smith et al. [1990], Moser et al. [1994, 1996]). The computing model used is the extended virtual synchrony one and was originally developed by this group in collaboration with the Transis project in Israel. Totem has contributed a number of high-performance protocols, including an innovative causal and total ordering algorithm, based on transitive ordering relationships between messages, and a totally ordered protocol with extremely predictable real-time properties. The system differs from a technology such as Horus, since it focuses on a type of distributed system that would result from the interconnection of clusters of workstations using broadcast media within these clusters and some form of bridging technology between them. Most of the protocols are optimized for applications within which communication loads are high and uniformly distributed over the processes in the system or in which messages originate primarily at a single source. The resulting protocols are very efficient in their use of messages, but they sometimes exhibit higher latency than the protocols we presented in earlier chapters of this book. Intended applications include parallel computing on clusters of workstations and industrial control problems.

27.1.23 Transis

The Transis system (see Dolev and Malkhi) was one of the best known and most successful process group-based research projects. The research group contributed extensively to the theory of process group systems and virtual synchrony, repeatedly set performance records with its protocols and flow-control algorithms, and developed a remarkable variety of protocols and algorithms in support of such systems (see Amir [1992, 1993], Friedman et al., Keidar and Dolev, Malkhi). Many of the ideas from Transis were eventually ported into the Horus system. Transis was, for example, the first system to show that by exploiting hardware multicast, a reliable group multicast protocol could scale with almost no growth in cost or latency. The primary focus of this effort was initially partitionable environments, and much of what is known about consistent distributed computing in such setting originated either directly or indirectly from this group. The project is also known for its work on transactional applications that preserve consistency in partitionable settings.

As noted earlier, another interesting topic under study by the Transis group is that of building systems that combine multiple protocol stacks in which different reliability or quality-of-service properties apply to each stack (see Chockler et al.). In this work, one assumes that a complex distributed system will give rise to a variety of types of reliability requirements: virtual synchrony for its control and coordination logic, isochronous communication for voice and video, and perhaps special encryption requirements for certain sensitive data—each provided through a corresponding protocol stack. However, rather than treating these protocol stacks as completely independent, the Transis system (which should port easily into Horus) deals with the synchronization of streams across multiple stacks. This will greatly simplify the implementation of demanding applications that need to present a unified appearance and yet cannot readily be implemented within a single protocol stack.

27.1.24 The V System

Because of the alphabetic sequence of this chapter, it is ironic that the first system to have used process groups is the last that we review. The V system was the first of the microkernel operating systems intended specifically for distributed environments; it also pioneered the RISC style of operating systems that later swept the research community. V is known primarily for innovations in the virtual memory and message-passing architecture used within the system, which achieved early performance records for its RPC protocol. However, the system also included a process group mechanism, which was used to support distributed services capable of providing a service at multiple locations in a distributed setting (see Cheriton and Zwaenepoel, Deering [1988]).

Although the V system lacked any strong process group computing model or reliability guarantees, its process group tools were considered quite powerful. In particular, this system was the first to support a publish/subscribe paradigm, in which messages to a subject were transmitted to a process group whose name corresponded to that subject. As we saw earlier, such an approach provides a useful separation between the source and destination of messages: The publisher can send to the group without worrying about its current membership, and a subscriber can simply join the group to begin receiving messages published within it.

The V style of process group was not intended for process group computing of the types we have discussed in this book; reliability in the system was purely on a best-effort basis, meaning that the group communication primitives made an effort to track current group membership and to avoid high rates of message loss—without providing real guarantees. When Isis introduced the virtual synchrony model, the purpose was precisely to show that with such a model, a V style of process group could be used to replicate data, balance workload, or provide fault tolerance. None of these problems were believed solvable in the V system itself. V set the early performance standards against which other group communication systems tended to be evaluated, however, and it was not until a second generation of process group computing systems emerged (the commercial version of Isis, the Transis and Totem systems, Horus, and RMP) that these levels of performance were matched and exceeded by systems that also provided reliability and ordering guarantees.

27.2 Peer-to-Peer Systems

In this section, we point to some of the major research efforts based on peer-to-peer concepts. Several of these systems were discussed previously, and are included only for completeness.

27.2.1 Astrolabe

Astrolabe was discussed at length in Section 24.4. The system uses a peer-to-peer gossip protocol to construct a virtual database – a hierarchical relational database that doesn't live on any server, but is instead assembled on the fly by means of peer-to-peer message exchanges. The leaf nodes are tuples containing data extracted from application systems in accordance with a configuration certificate, which can be changed on the fly. The inner tables are aggregates formed by evaluating user-defined SQL queries on the leaves. The system is extremely flexible and can be used for distributed monitoring, management and data mining. Information propagates in time logarithmic in the size of the system. See van Renesse et al. 2002, 2003.

27.2.2 Bimodal Multicast

Bimodal Multicast is another name for *pbcast*, the protocol we discussed in Section 24.3. The protocol supports an extremely robust, scalable, multicast primitive that, with high probability (controlled by user-settable parameters) will deliver each message to every recipient. The basic mechanism combines unreliable multicast (such as IP multicast) with a peer-to-peer gossip protocol that recovers data out of logs. See Birman et al. 1999.

27.2.3 Chord/CFS

Chord is the most widely cited and most extensively analyzed peer-to-peer distributed indexing system. It was discussed in Section 24.2. The system constructs a virtual ring and uses a form of lookup similar to a binary search to locate objects within time logarithmic in the size of the system. See Stoica et al. 2001. CFS is a peer-to-peer file system implemented over Chord. See Dabek 2001.

27.2.4 Gnutella/Kazaa

Gnutella and Kazaa are widely used peer-to-peer file sharing technologies. The systems are closely related; at their origins, Kazaa was basically a commercial implementation of Gnutella. Gnutella is a flexible peer-to-peer protocol specification that has been implemented many times on many platforms. The weakness of these systems is generally believed to be their search mechanism, which is costly and scales poorly.

27.2.5 Kelips

Kelips is a recent introduction in the space of peer-to-peer distributed indexing systems. It was discussed in Section 24.2. The system hashes processes and keys into a set of sqrt(N) groups of size sqrt(N) each, and also tracks representatives of each group, in this manner achieving a constant cost lookup. Studies suggest that Kelips is exceptionally resistant to churn. See Gupta [2003].

27.2.6 Pastry/PAST and Scribe

Pastry is a well known peer-to-peer distributed indexing system based on Plaxton trees. It was discussed in Section 24.2. A unique caching architecture gives very fast lookup, with worst-case performance logarithmic in the size of the system. See Rowston and Druschel. 2001a. PAST is a file system that operates over Pastry. See Rowston and Druschel 2001b. Scribe is an architecture for building multicast trees overlaid on the Internet, using Pastry to orchestrate tree formation.

27.2.7 QuickSilver

The QuickSilver system is a platform for publish-subscribe applications, constructed using a mixture of peer-to-peer and traditional reliability mechanism, and targeting systems that might be spread over a wide area and could include thousands or tens of thousands of nodes. Under development at Cornell, QuickSilver will incorporate elements from the virtual synchrony work, Bimodal Multicast and Astrolabe systems developed at that institution, and targets a range of applications that include the Air Force Joint Battelspace Infosphere, the DoD Global Information Grid, and Web Services application in which serverlets might run on vast numbers of client platforms.

27.2.8 Tapestry/Brocade

Tapestry is a Berkeley-developed system with characteristics similar to Pastry. It was discussed in Section 25.2.3. Brocade is a wide-area *overlay network* employed to avoid wide-area "hops" when routing messages in Tapestry. See Zhao.

27.3 Systems That Implement Transactions

We end this chapter with a brief review of some of the major research efforts that have explored the use of transactions in distributed settings. As in the case of our review of distributed communication systems, we present these in alphabetical order.

27.3.1 Argus

The Argus system was an early leader among transactional computing systems that considered transactions on abstract objects. Developed by a team led by Liskov at MIT, the Argus system consists of a programming language and an implementation that was used primarily as a research and experimentation vehicle (see Ladin et al. [1990], Liskov and Scheifler, Liskov et al. [1987]). Many credit the idea of achieving distributed reliability through transactions on distributed objects to this project, and it was a prolific source of publications on all aspects of transactional computing, theoretical as well as practical, during its decade or so of peak activity.

The basic Argus data type is the *guardian*: a software module, which defines and implements some form of persistent storage, using transactions to protect against concurrent access and to ensure recoverability and persistence. Similar to a CORBA object, each guardian exports an interface defining the forms of access and operations possible on the object. Through these interfaces, Argus programs (*actors*) invoke operations on the guarded data. Argus treats all such invocations as transactions and also provides explicit transactional constructs in its programming language, including commit and abort mechanisms, a concurrent execution construct, top-level transactions, and mechanisms for exception handling.

The Argus system implements this model in a transparently distributed manner, with full nested transactions and mechanisms to optimize the more costly aspects, such as nested transaction commit. A sophisticated *orphan termination* protocol is used to track down and abort orphaned subtransactions, which can be created when the parent transaction that initiated some action fails and aborts but leaves active child transactions, which may now be at risk of observing system states inconsistent with the conditions under which the child transaction was spawned—for example, a parent transaction might store a record in some object and then spawn a child subtransaction, which will eventually read this record. If the parent aborts and the orphaned child is permitted to continue executing, it may read the object in its prior state, leading to seriously inconsistent or erroneous actions.

Although Argus was never put into widespread practical use, the system was extremely influential. Not all aspects of the system were successful—many commercial transactional systems have rejected distributed and nested transactions as requiring an infrastructure that is relatively more complex, costly, and difficult to use than flat transactions in standard client/server architectures. Other commercial products, however, have adopted parts of this model successfully. The principle of issuing transactions to abstract data types remains debatable. As we have seen, transactional data types can be very difficult to construct, and expert knowledge of the system will often be necessary to achieve high performance. The Argus effort ended in the early 1990s and the MIT group that built the system began work on Thor, a second-generation technology in this area.

27.3.2 Arjuna

Whereas Argus explored the idea of transactions on objects, Arjuna is a system that focuses on the use of object-oriented techniques to customize a transactional system. Developed by Shrivistava at Newcastle, Arjuna is an extensible and reconfigurable transactional system, in which the developer can replace a standard object-oriented framework for transactional access to persistent objects with type-specific locking or data management objects, which exploit semantic knowledge of the application to achieve high performance or special flexibility. The system was one of the first to focus on C++ as a programming language for managing persistent data, an approach that later became widely popular. Recent development of the system has explored the use of replication for increased availability during periods of failure using a protocol called Newtop; the underlying methodology used for this purpose draws on the sorts of process group mechanisms discussed in previous chapters (see Ezhilhelvan, Macedo et al.).

27.3.3 Avalon

Avalon was a transactional system developed at Carnegie Mellon University by Herlihy and Wing during the late 1980s. The system is best known for its theoretical contributions. This project proposed the *linearizability model*, which weakens serializability in object-oriented settings where full nested serializability may excessively restrict concurrency (see Herlihy and Wing). As noted briefly earlier in the chapter, linearizability has considerable appeal as a model potentially capable of integrating virtual synchrony with serializability. A research project, work on Avalon ended in the early 1990s.

27.3.4 Bayou

Bayou is a recent effort at Xerox PARC that uses transactions with weakened semantics in partially connected settings, such as for the management of distributed calendars for mobile users who may need to make appointments and schedule meetings or read electronic mail while in a disconnected or partially connected environment (see Terry et al.). The system provides weak serialization guarantees by allowing the user to schedule meetings even when the full state of the calendar is inaccessible due to a partition. Later, when communication is reestablished, such a transaction is completed with normal serializability semantics.

Bayou makes the observation that transactional consistency may not guarantee that user-specific consistency constraints will be satisfied—for example, if a meeting is scheduled while disconnected from some of the key participants, it may later be discovered that the time conflicts with some other meeting. Bayou provides mechanisms by which the designer can automate both the detection and resolution of these sorts of problems. In this particular example, Bayou will automatically attempt to shift one or the other rather than requiring that a user become directly involved in resolving all such conflicts. The focus of Bayou is very practical: Rather than seeking extreme generality, the technology is designed to solve the specific problems encountered in paperless offices with mobile employees. This domain-specific approach permits Bayou to solve a number of distributed consistency problems that, in the most general sense, are not even tractable. This reconfirms an emerging theme of the book: Theoretically impossible results often need to be reexamined in specific contexts; what cannot be solved in the most general sense or setting may be entirely tractable in a particular application where more is known about the semantics of operations and data.

27.3.5 Camelot and Encina

This system was developed at Carnegie Mellon University in the late 1980s and was designed to provide transactional access to user-developed data structures stored in files (see Spector). The programming model was one in which application programs perform RPCs on servers. Such transactions become nested if these servers are clients of other servers. The ultimate goal is to support transactional semantics for applications that update persistent storage. Camelot introduced a variety of operating system enhancements for maximizing the performance of such applications and was eventually commercialized in the form of the Encina product from Transarc Corporation. Subsequent to this transition, considerable investment in Encina occurred at Transarc and the system is now one of the leaders in the market for OLTP products. Encina provides both nondistributed and distributed transactions, nested transactions if desired, a variety of tools for balancing load and increasing concurrency, prebuilt data structures for common uses, and management tools for system administration. The distributed data mechanisms can also be used to replicate information for high availability.

Industry analysts have commented that although many Encina users select the system in part for its distributed and nested capabilities, in actual practice most applications of Encina make little or no use of these features. If accurate, this observation raises interesting questions about the true characteristics of the distributed transactional market. Unfortunately, however, I am not aware of any systematic study of this question.

Readers interested in Encina should also look at IBM's CICS technology, perhaps the world's most widely used transactional system, and the Tuxedo system, an OLTP product developed originally at AT&T, which became an industry leader in the UNIX OLTP market. Similar to Encina, CICS and Tuxedo provide powerful and complete environments for client/server-style applications requiring transactional guarantees, and Tuxedo includes real-time features required in telecommunication settings.

27.3.6 Thor

Thor is an object oriented system developed by Liskov et al. at MIT. The technology is presented as an extensible, object-oriented database, but shares many features first introduced in Argus. The programming language used in Thor is syntactically similar to Java.

Appendix: Problems

This book is intended for use by professionals or advanced students, and the material presented is at a level for which simple problems are not entirely appropriate. Accordingly, most of the problems in this appendix are intended as the basis for essay-style responses or for programming projects, which might build upon the technologies we have treated up to now. Some of these projects are best undertaken as group exercises for a group of three or four students; others could be undertaken by individuals.

A number of platforms are suitable for the types of programming problems presented below. At Cornell University, we initially taught this course using Unix or Linux systems, and the students were encouraged to work in C or C++. The language and systems mix worked well, and yield rather efficient systems that, with further tuning, can often push to the limits of the hardware. One could still adopt this approach today, although FreeBSD might be a better choice of platform, particularly because it lends itself to in-kernel protocol implementations. However, at Cornell at least, many students are now finding it preferable to gain as much experience as possible using Java on J2EE or one of the Microsoft languages on .NET. For such students, the author recommends a close look at C# (a Java-like language, although with a different runtime library) on .NET, using Visual Studio .NET as the development environment. Although it can be difficult to squeeze very high performance from this mix, at least at the time of this writing, the package is so powerful and has such good development support that students find themselves launched into such topics as Web Services with almost no learning curve at all. The experience also sells well when looking for a job in the field. Java on J2EE would be almost as good a platform to work on, although one sees less interest in Java on PC and other forms of desktop computing systems than was the case five years ago. For students who want to push further into systems, C or C++ on .NET might be a worthwhile alternative to consider. However, none of these languages will achieve the level of performance possible with a top-quality optimizing compiler running directly on the native instruction set. Thus, performance-oriented students should still be guided towards C or C++ on a Linux or Unix platform.

Professionals may find these problems interesting from a different perspective. Many of them are the sorts of questions that one would want to ask about a proposed distributed solution and hence could be useful as a tool for individuals responsible for the development of a complex system. I am sometimes asked to comment on proposed system designs, and, like many others, have found that it can be difficult to know where to start when the time for questions finally arrives after a two-hour technical presentation. A reasonable suggestion is to begin to pose simple questions aimed at exposing the reliability properties and nonproperties of the proposed system, the assumptions it makes, the dependencies embodied in it, and the cost/benefit tradeoffs reflected in the architecture. Such questions may not lead to a drastically changed system, but they do represent a path toward understanding the mentality of the designer and the philosophical structure of the proposed system. Many of the questions below are of a nature that might be used in such a situation.

1. Write a program to experimentally characterize the packet loss rate, frequency of out-of-order delivery, send-to-receive latency, and byte throughput of the UDP and TCP transport protocols available on your computer system. Evaluate both the local case (source and destination on the same machine) and the remote case (source and destination on different machines).

2. Using one of the major Web Services frameworks (as noted above, the Visual Studio .NET framework is particularly easy to use), build a minimal Web Services application (use the ASP.NET design pattern) supporting two operations: "read" and "update." Do not use any sort of back-end server – have the Web Services application handle these requests directly. Experimentally determine the following basic costs, first with the client and server on the same machine, and then with them on different machines (note: the Internet Information Service, IIS, must be active to do this experiment with multiple machines):

    a. The cost of doing a "null" operation on the Web Service (one with no arguments and no return value).
    b. The per-byte cost of including a byte-string argument. (Graph the result for byte strings of length 10 bytes, 100, 1000, 10,000 and 50,000).
    c. The per-byte cost if your procedure returns a byte-string result.
    d. The cost of including a vector of n32-bit integers. (Again, graph results for various argument lengths.)
    e. The cost of including a vector of double-precision floating point numbers in the argument or result. Does it change the answer if the numbers have simple integer values like 1.0 or 0.0, relative to random double-precision numbers over a large range of values? Why?
    f. Design your Web Service so that it will crash with a zero-divide. Now, have your client application call the Web Service. How long does it take for the failure to be detected? What information is available to the client program? Do you get the same results if the client and Web Service run on different machines?
    g. Same as (f), but now have your Web Service application "freeze up" by calling sleep and never returning a result. What happens?

3. A *broadcast storm* is a problem that can arise when hardware broadcast is used on a shared network, such as an Ethernet. Such a storm is typically triggered by high rates of broadcasts, perhaps for some completely legitimate purpose, and would normally not be seen unless the system contains two or more senders that are each transmitting at near the maximum rate possible. Under these conditions, the broadcasts can keep Ethernet interfaces so busy that legitimate non-broadcast packets just won't get through, creating the impression that the network has become extremely slow. Develop an experiment that will permit you to quantify the conditions under which

such a storm might occur on the equipment in your laboratory. Use your findings to arrive at a set of recommendations that should, if followed, minimize the likelihood of a broadcast storm even in applications that make heavy use of hardware broadcast.

4. Devise a method for rapidly detecting the failure of a process on a remote machine and implement it. How rapidly can your solution detect a failure without risk of inaccuracy? Your work should consider one or more of the following cases: a program that runs a protocol you have devised and implemented over UDP, a program that is monitored by a parent program, and a program on a machine that fails or becomes partitioned from the network. For each case, you may use any system calls or standard communication protocols that are available to you.

5. Suppose that it is your goal to develop a *network radio service*, which transmits identical data to a large set of listeners, and that you need to pick the best communication transport protocol for this purpose. Evaluate and compare the UDP, TCP, and IP multicast transport protocols on your computer (you may omit IP multicast if this is not available in your testing environment). Your evaluation should look at throughput and latency (focusing on variability of these as a function of throughput presented to the transport). Can you characterize a range of performance within which one protocol is superior to the others in terms of loss rate, achievable throughput, and consistently low latency? Your results will take the form of graphs showing how these attributes scale with increasing numbers of destinations.

6. Develop a simple ping-pong program that bounces a UDP packet back and forth between a source and destination machine. One would expect such a program to give extremely consistent latency measurements when run on idle workstations. In practice, however, your test is likely to reveal considerable variation in latency. Track down the causes of these variations and suggest strategies for developing applications with highly predictable and stable performance properties.

7. One challenge to timing events in a distributed system is that the workstations in that system may be running some form of clock synchronization algorithm, which is adjusting clock values even as your test runs—leading to potentially confusing measurements. From product literature for the computers in your environment or by running a suitable experiment, determine the extent to which this phenomenon occurs in your testing environment. Can you propose ways of measuring performance that are immune to distortions of this nature?

8. Suppose you wish to develop a *topology service* for a local area network, using *only* two kinds of information as input with which to deduce the network topology: IP addresses for machines and measured point-to-point latency (for lightly loaded conditions, measured to a high degree of accuracy). How practical would it be to solve this problem? Ideally, a topology service should be able to produce a map showing how your local area network is interconnected, including bridges, individual Ethernet segments, and so forth.

9. (Moderately Difficult.) If you concluded that you should be able to do a good job on the previous problem, implement such a topology service using your local area

network. What practical problems limit the accuracy of your solution? What forms of use could you imagine for your service? Can information available within the MIBs of the machines of your network be used to improve the quality of the topological map?

10. (A current topic of research.) In many applications, it would be helpful to be able to anticipate the costs of operations so as to make intelligent decisions. For example, if a data object can be downloaded from multiple places, one would like to download from the one that will give the fastest transfer, and so forth. Our goal in this problem is to provide an application with a way to estimate such costs. Suppose that your software will be installed in a set of *agent* programs at a large number of nodes in a network (namely, the places where the application in question is running). By looking at IP addresses and measuring round-trip delays for messages exchanged by these agents, as well as the transfer speeds for moving larger amounts of data between them, is it possible to arrive at a reasonably good way to *estimate performance* for operations that the system may wish to do in the future? Develop the least costly mechanism you can (in terms of network load, etc) for tracking the underlying network so that an application running from the same end-points can anticipate the costs associated with its communication events. Since your solution will be used as a kind of "library" by the application, you should provide access to it from a clean, simple API that will be easy for application developers to use.

11. Stream protocols like TCP can fail in inconsistent ways. Develop an application that demonstrates this problem by connecting two programs with multiple TCP streams, running them on multiple platforms and provoking a failure in which some of the streams break and some remain connected. To do this test you may need to briefly disconnect one of the workstations from the network; hence, you should obtain the permission of your network administration staff. Now, develop a wrapper for TCP that disables the TCP KEEPALIVE function and uses your mechanism to break channels. Your wrapper should mimic the API normally supported by TCP; indeed, you might even consider using the "library wrapper" methods discussed in Chapter 20 if you work on UNIX or Linux.

12. Propose a method for passing pointers to servers in an RPC environment, assuming that the source and destination programs are coded in C or C++ and that pointers are an abstract data type. What costs would a user of your scheme incur? Can you recommend programming styles or new programming constructs to minimize the impact of these costs on the running application?

13. Suppose one were building a Web Services system for very long-lived applications. The system needs to remain *continuously operational* for years at a time. Yet it is also expected that it will sometimes be necessary to upgrade software components of the system. Could such a problem be solved in software—that is, can a general-purpose upgrade mechanism be designed as part of an application so that objects can be dynamically upgraded? To make this concrete, you can focus on a system of k objects, $O_1 \ldots O_k$, and consider the case where we want to replace O_i with O_i' while

the remaining objects are unchanged. Express your solution by describing a proposed upgrade mechanism and the constraints it imposes on applications that use it.

14. (A good project for classes in which a large project is required from each student or group.) Suppose that a Web Services system is designed to cache information at the clients of a server. The clients would access the server through a client interface object, and it would handle the interaction with the local cache, the caches of other clients, and the remote server. Notice that we said "caches of other clients" here. Clearly, if caches can be shared, the effective cache size of a system as a whole will be much larger. On the other hand, figuring out what information is in the caches of other clients could be costly, and "side-loading" data from another client's cache might be more expensive than downloading the object itself from the server. Design a scheme whereby clients can track the information in one-another's caches (you may want to think about using Kelips for this), and for deciding when it would be more advantageous to side-load a cached object than to download a copy from the server (you may want to use your own solution to problem 10 here). What would be the best way to validate a cached object to ensure that it has not become stale? Experimentally evaluate the costs and the benefits of your scheme, looking at the average speed for fetching objects, the load on the server and on clients, and also the frequency with which a client request is satisfied using a stale object.

15. (A good project for a class in which a large project is required from each student or group.) Develop a small library for use in a Web Services setting that provides *secure, replicated keys* shared between a Web Services platform and its clients. The package should have a way to authenticate the identity of the client, and should implement two kinds of keys. One form of key would be a symmetric key shared by the Web Service and exactly one client, and used to perform encryption or to sign data in messages transmitted between them. The second form of key, also symmetric, should support a "group" mode in which all clients running under the same ID share the same key. Can you support key refresh, whereby the key currently in use is replaced with a new key, in such a manner that even if the old key is later cracked, and even if the intruder has a complete record of all messages ever sent on the network, the new key will not be compromised?

16. Propose a set of extensions to the WSDL documents used by Web Services for the purpose of specifying reliability properties of a distributed server, such as fault tolerance, real-time guarantees, or security.

17. Discuss options for handling the case where a transactional Web Services application performs operations on a non-transactional server.

18. We discussed the need for a "security rules and policies" management mechanism, whereby the security rules and policies enforced by a system might be stored in a database, then used at runtime to decide whether specific actions should be authorized. Design a mechanism along these lines for use in Web Services settings. The rules should be of the form "client so-and-so is permitted/not-permitted to perform action so-and-so on Web Service such-and-such." How hard would it be to implement the

solution you've designed? Give some examples of problems which this mechanism would solve, and some examples of problems it is not powerful enough to solve.

19. Suppose that a *rebinding* mechanism is to be used to automatically rebind a Web Services or CORBA applications to a working server if the server being used fails. What constraints on the application would make this a safe thing to do without notifying the application when rebinding occurs? Would this form of complete transparency make sense, or are the constraints too severe to use such an approach in practice?

20. A protocol that introduces tolerance to failures will also make the application using it more complex than one making no attempt to tolerate failures. Presumably, this complexity carries with it a cost in decreased application reliability. Discuss the pros and cons of building systems to be robust, in light of the likelihood that doing so will increase the cost of developing the application, the complexity of the resulting system, and the challenge of testing it. Can you suggest a principled way to reach a decision on the appropriateness of hardening a system to provide a desired property?

21. Suppose you are developing a medical computing system using a client/server architecture, in which the client systems control the infusion of medication directly into an IV line to the patient. Physicians will sometimes change medication orders by interacting with the server systems. It is *absolutely imperative* that the physician be confident that an order he or she has given will be carried out or that an alarm will be sounded if there is *any uncertainty whatsoever* about the state of the system. Provide an analysis of possible failure modes (client system crashes, server crashes) and the way they should be handled to satisfy this reliability goal. Assume that the software used in the system is correct and that the only failures experienced are due to hardware failures of the machines on which the client and server systems run or communication failures in the network. Keep in mind that your goal is to ensure that the system is fail-safe but not necessarily to accomplish that goal in a completely automated manner. If the system sometimes needs to ask for help from the doctors using it, or from system operators, doing so is perfectly appropriate.

22. Consider an air traffic control system in which each flight is under the control of a specific individual at any given point in time. Suppose the system takes the form of a collection of client/server distributed networks—one for each of a number of air traffic control centers. Design a protocol for handing off a flight from one controller to another, considering first the case of a single center and then the case of a multicenter system. Now, analyze the possible failure modes of your protocol under the assumption that client systems, server systems, and the communication network may be subject to failures. Keep in mind that your goal is to ensure that the system is fail-safe but not necessarily to accomplish that goal in a completely automated manner. If the system sometimes needs to ask for help from the human air-traffic controllers or system operators, doing so is perfectly appropriate.

23. (Term project; team of two or more.) Explore options for integrating group communication tools (for example, Horus, Ensemble, Spread or Bimodal Multicast) with a Web Services system as a way to implement the kinds of high availability mechanisms

discussed in Chapter 26. Implement what you consider to be the best solution and demonstrate a "before" and "after" version of a Web Service of your own design, in which you've used the technology to build a high assurance database (if you work with Visual Studio on .NET, we recommend using Microsoft's SQL server for the database, since you can then employ the ADO.NET framework to connect the Web Services platform to the database – an otherwise tricky step).

24. (Term project; team of two or more.) Design a wide area service for maintaining directory-style information in very large Web Services deployments, where some sort of Web Services application might run at tens of thousands of locations throughout the Internet. Your solution should support a subset of the UDDI interface, but don't focus on implementing every detail of UDDI (the business rules aspects of UDDI get very complex). Instead, the bulk of your effort should be concerned with the problem of how to match a Web Services application with the "best" resource matching its requirements. We'll interpret "best" to mean closest in the network, least loaded, and having the best bandwidth and lowest latency among the options. (We'll leave it to you to decide how to pick among a set of matching servers where no one server is the "winner" in all of these categories.) You should consider using a P2P technology like Astrolabe or Kelips (or a similar protocol of your own design) in solving this problem.

25. Use Horus, Ensemble or Spread, build an *application level cabcast* protocol that places messages into a total order which is also consistent with the causal event ordering. Since these systems don't provide a *cabcast* protocol, you'll need to implement vector timestamps to represent causal ordering information, and will need to do more work after the basic *abcast* protocol hands messages off to your application layer (for example, you may find that sometimes, the system delivers an *abcast* message out of causal order, in which case your software will need to detect this and delay the message until the causally prior messages have been received and delivered). Now, test your solution under "battle conditions" by setting up a group of four members and, while multicasts are being sent at high speed, killing some members and adding others. You should consider the design of a clever test program to be part of the problem: your test needs to convince a skeptic that even though it may have performed thousands of multicasts and experienced many group view membership changes, any violation of the *cabcast* ordering would have been immediately detected and flagged.

26. Suppose that a Horus or Ensemble protocol stack implementing Cristian's real-time atomic broadcast protocol will be used side by side with one implementing virtual synchronous process groups with *abcast*, both in the same application. To what degree might inconsistency be visible to the application when group membership changes because of failures of some group members? Can you suggest ways that the two protocol stacks might be linked to limit the time period during which such inconsistencies can occur? (Hard problem: Implement your proposal in Horus – not Ensemble unless you are familiar with the ML programming language.)

27. Some authors consider RPC to be an extremely successful protocol, because it is highly transparent, reasonably robust, and can be optimized to run at very high speed—so

high that if an application wants stronger guarantees, it makes more sense to layer a protocol over a lower-level RPC facility than to build it into the operating system at potentially high cost. Discuss the pros and cons of this point of view. In the best possible world, what primitives do you believe should be included into the vendor-supplied communication subsystem, and what primitives should be implemented by the application in an end-to-end manner?

28. Research the *end-to-end argument.* Now, suppose that you are working with mobile computers that use relatively low-reliability wireless links to connect to the Internet, and then run TCP to download Web pages. Does the end-to-end argument suggest that the wireless link should be treated just like the wired part of the Internet? Explain how best to handle such a link, if our goal is rapid download speeds.

29. Review flow-control options for environments in which a Web Service is sending streams of data to large numbers of receivers. Today, TCP doesn't coordinate the actions of one stream relative to those of any other. Yet the one Web Service may be connected to hundreds of clients, and if congestion occurs, there is a good chance that it will impact sets of clients (all of them if the problem is close to the server, and if the problem occurs close to a client, it will probably impact other clients at the same place). Can you suggest ways that a TCP protocol might be modified to make use of this kind of information? (If you are a real hacker, consider using NS/2, which has very accurate TCP simulations built in, to simulate such scenarios and explore the likely impact of your proposed scheme.)

30. A protocol is said to be "acky" if most packets are acknowledged immediately upon reception. Discuss some of the pros and cons of this property. Suppose that a stream protocol could be switched in and out of an acky mode. Under what conditions would it be advisable to operate that protocol with frequent acks?

31. Suppose that a streaming style of multidestination information service, such as the one in problem 30, is to be used in a setting where a small subset of the application programs can be unresponsive for periods of time. A good example of such a setting would be a network in which the client systems run on PCs, because the most popular PC operating systems allow applications to preempt the CPU and inhibit interrupts—a behavior that can delay the system from responding to incoming messages in a timely manner. This might also arise if a client is connected over a wireless link that sometimes "burps." What options can you propose for ensuring that data delivery will be reliable and ordered *in all cases*, but that small numbers of briefly unresponsive machines will not impact performance for the much larger number of highly responsive machines?

32. (Term project.) Suppose you were building a large-scale distributed system for video playback of short video files on demand—for example, such a system might be used in a large bank to provide brokers and traders with current projections for the markets and trading instruments tracked by the bank. Assume that videos are often updated. Design a scheme for getting data to the display servers so as to avoid overloading servers while also giving the best possible user experience. Your solution will probably need to track copies of each video, so that any machine with a copy can be treated as a possible data

source (more or less in the style of Napster and other P2P file sharing protocols). You should provide for a way to update the database of available videos and to play a video on an end-user "playback unit"; beyond this, include such additional functionality as is needed to achieve a high availability, high performance solution.

33. Consider the Group Membership Protocol discussed in Section 14.9. Suppose that this protocol was implemented in the address space of an application program and that the application program contained a bug causing it to infrequently but randomly corrupt a few cells of memory. To what degree would this render the assumptions underlying the GMS protocol incorrect? What behaviors might result? Can you suggest practical countermeasures that would overcome such a problem if it were indeed very infrequent?

34. (Difficult.) Again, consider the Group Membership Protocol discussed in Section 14.9. This protocol has the following property: All participating processes observe *exactly the same sequence* of membership views. The coordinator can add unlimited numbers of processes in each round and can drop any minority of the members each time it updates the system membership view; in both cases, the system is provably immune from partitioning. Would this protocol be simplified by eliminating the property that processes must observe the same view sequence? (Hint: Try to design a protocol that offers this "weaker" behavior. Don't worry about network partitioning failures.)

35. Suppose that the processes in a process group are managing replicated data. Due to a lingering bug, it is known that although the group seems to work well for periods of hours or even days, over very long periods of time the replicated data can become slightly corrupted so that different group members have different values. Discuss the pros and cons of introducing a stabilization mechanism, whereby the members would periodically crash themselves, then restart and rejoin the system as a "new" member. What issues might this raise in the application program, and how might they be addressed?

36. Implement a very simple Web Services banking application supporting accounts into which money can be deposited and withdrawals can be made. (You can easily do this using Visual Studio for .NET with the ASP.NET project design and working in a language such as C#, J++ or C++, with a back-end database such as SQL server, but make sure that your systems administrators have enabled the IIS service and configured SQL server to register itself). Have your application support a form of *disconnected operation* based on the two-tiered architecture, in which each branch system uses its own set of process groups and maintains information for local accounts. Your application should simulate partitioning failures through a command interface. If branches cache information about remote accounts, what options are there for permitting a client to withdraw funds while the local branch at which the account really resides is unavailable? Consider both the need for safety by the bank and the need for availability, if possible, for the user—for example, it would be silly to refuse a user $250 from an account that had thousands of dollars in it moments earlier when connections were still working! Can you propose a policy that is always safe for the bank and yet also

allows remote withdrawals during partition failures? (Hint: this question is motivated by research undertaken by Professor Calton Pu on "epsilon serializability." Although this work was not covered in the textbook in the interest of brevity, you might find it useful to track down Pu's publications on the Web.)

37. Design a protocol by which a process group implemented using Horus or Ensemble or the JHU Spread system can solve the asynchronous consensus problem. Assume that the environment is one in which Horus can be used, processes only fail by crashing, and the network only fails by losing messages with some low frequency. Your processes should be assumed to start with a variable, $input_i$, which, for each process, p_i, is initially 0 or 1. After deciding, each process should set a variable, $output_i$, to its decision value. The solution should be such that the processes all reach the same decision value, v, and this value is the same as at least one of the inputs.

38. In regard to your solution to problem 37, discuss the sense in which your solution solves the asynchronous consensus problem. Would any of these systems (Horus, Ensemble or Spread) be guaranteed to make progress under the stated conditions? Do these conditions correspond to the conditions of the asynchronous model used in the FLP and Chandra/Toueg results?

39. Can the virtual synchrony protocols of a system such as Horus, Ensemble or Spread be said to guarantee safety and liveness in the general asynchronous model of FLP or the Chandra/Toueg results?

40. Group communication systems such as Horus, Ensemble and Spread are usually designed to operate under the conditions seen in clustered computing systems on a local area network. That is, the protocols basically assume low latency, high throughput, and infrequent network disconnections or partitioning events. Consider the challenges of running a group communication platform in a *wireless ad-hoc network*, where connectivity is often disrupted, power considerations may be a factor, and messages need to be relayed to reach their destination, introducing significant latency variations. What sorts of group communication protocols might work best in this setting? If you find it helpful to imagine an application, assume that your solution is aimed at supporting rescue workers who are entering a region that recently experienced a flood or earthquake and need to coordinate their actions, or fire fighters working in a mountainous forest threatened by a fire.

41. (Term project.) Implement your solution to problem 40. You may find it easiest to work with Microsoft Visual Studio .NET, because this platform supports the development of small applications on a wired network that can then be downloaded fairly easily to machines running Windows CE. The other major option would be to work in C on a Linux or FreeBSD platform. MAODV has been implemented for both platforms and we recommend downloading and using a prebuilt version of this routing algorithm. Mobile routing is otherwise a tough problem and if you also try to build and debug a version of MAODV, the resulting project will be too big to complete in a semester!

42. The Horus and Ensemble systems include a stability layer which operates as follows: Each message is given a unique ID, and is transmitted and delivered using the stack

selected by the user. The stability layer expects the processes receiving the message to issue a downcall when they consider the message locally stable. This information is relayed within the group, and each group member can obtain a matrix giving the stabilization status of pending messages originated within the group as needed. Could the stability layer be used in a way that would add the dynamic uniformity guarantee to messages sent in a group?

43. Suppose that a process group is created in which three member processes each implement different algorithms for performing the same computation (so-called "implementation redundancy"). You may assume that these processes interact with the external environment *only using message send and receive primitives*. Design a wrapper that compares the actions of the processes, producing a single output if two of the three or all three processes agree on the action to take for a given input and signaling an exception if all three processes produce different outputs for a given input. Implement your solution using Horus, Ensemble or Spread and demonstrate it for a set of fake processes that usually copy their input to their output, but that sometimes make a random change to their output before sending it.

44. A set of processes in a group monitors devices in the external environment, detecting *device service requests* to which they respond in a load-balanced manner. The best way to handle such requests depends upon the frequency with which they occur. Consider the following two extremes: requests that require long computations to handle but that occur relatively infrequently and requests that require very short computations to handle but that occur frequently on the time scale with which communication is done in the system. Assuming that the processes in a process group have identical capabilities (any can respond to any request), how would you solve this problem in the two cases?

45. Design a locking protocol for a virtually synchronous process group. Your protocol should allow a group member to *request* a lock, specifying the name of the object to be locked (the name can be an integer to simplify the problem), and to *release* a lock that it holds. What issues occur if a process holding a lock fails? Recommend a good, general way of dealing with this case and then give a distributed algorithm by which the group members can implement the *request* and *release* interfaces, as well as your solution to the broken lock case.

46. (Suggested by Jim Pierce.) Suppose we want to implement a system in which n process groups will be superimposed—much like the petals of a flower. Some small set of k processes will belong to all n groups, and each group will have additional members that belong only to it. The problem now occurs of how to handle *join* operations for the processes that belong to the overlapping region and in particular how to deal with state transfers to such a process. Assume that the group states are only updated by "petal" processes, which do not belong to the overlap region. Now, the virtually synchronous state transfer mechanisms we discussed in Chapter 18 would operate on a group-by-group basis, but it may be that the states of the processes in the overlap region are a mixture of information arriving from all of the petal processes. For such

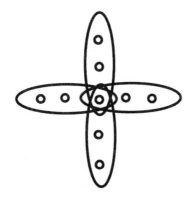

Figure A.1. Overlapping process groups for problem 47. In this example there is only a single process in the overlap region; the problem concerns state transfer if we wanted to add another process to this region. Assume that the state of the processes in the overlap region reflects messages sent to it by the outer processes, which belong to the "petals" but not the overlap area. Additionally, assume that this state is not cleanly decomposed group by group and that it is necessary to implement a single state transfer for the entire structure.

cases one would want to do a *single* state transfer to the joining process, reflecting the *joint state* of the overlapped groups. Propose a fault-tolerant protocol for joining the overlap region and transferring state to a joining process that will satisfy this objective. (Refer to Figure A.1.)

47. Discuss the pros and cons of using an *inhibitory* protocol to test for a condition along a consistent cut in a process group. Describe a problem or scenario where such a solution might be appropriate and one where it would not be.

48. Suppose that the processes in a distributed system share a set of resources, which they lock prior to using and then unlock when finished. If these processes belong to a process group, how could deadlock detection be done within that group? Design your deadlock detection algorithm to be completely idle (with no background communication costs) when no deadlocks are suspected; the algorithm should be one that can be launched when a timeout in a waiting process suggests that a deadlock may have occurred. For bookkeeping purposes, you may assume that a process waiting for a resource calls the local procedure *waiting_for(resource)*, a process holds exclusive access to a resource calls the procedure *holding(resource)*, and a process releasing a resource calls the procedure *release(resource)*, where the resources are identified by integers. Each process thus maintains a local database of its resource status. Notice that you are not being asked to implement the actual mutual-exclusion algorithm here: Your goal is to devise a protocol that can interact with the processes in the system as needed to accurately detect deadlocks. Prove that your protocol detects deadlocks if, and only if, they are present.

49. Suppose you wish to monitor a distributed system for an overload condition, defined as follows. The system state is considered normal if no more than one-third of the processes signal that they are overloaded, heavily loaded if more than one-third but

less than two-thirds of the processes signal that they are overloaded, and seriously overloaded if two-thirds or more of the processes are overloaded. Assume further that the loading condition does not impact communication performance. If the processes belong to a process group, would it be sufficient to simply send a multicast to all members asking their states and then to compute the state of the system from the vector of replies so obtained? What issues would such an approach raise, and under what conditions would the result be correct?

50. (Joseph and Schmuck.) What would be the best way to implement a *predicate addressing* communication primitive for use within virtually synchronous process groups (assume that the group primitives are already implemented and available for you). Such a primitive sends a message to *all the processes in the group for which some acceptance criteria hold* and does so *along a consistent cut.* You may assume that each process contains a predicate, *accept( )*, which, at the time it is invoked, returns *true* if the process wishes to accept a copy of the message and *false* if not. (Hint: It is useful to consider two separate cases here—one in which the criteria that determine acceptance change slowly and one in which they change rapidly, relative to the speed of the multicasting in the system.)

51. Develop a mock-up (or a simulation) of Agarwal's database replication algorithm, described in Chapter 24, for using group communication in transactional database settings. Using the simulation, characterize the scalability of the approach in terms of the speedup it can achieve as a function of the number of servers for various mixtures of read and update transactions under simple assumptions about the frequency of conflicts. Suppose that you were working for a major database company. Would you recommend the use of this replication scheme?

52. (Term project.) Implement Agarwal's architecture, and experimentally evaluate its behavior with a small cluster of side-by-side PC's on a high speed LAN, using a simple hand-built database instead of a full-scale transactional database as the underlying database "system" (for example, you might use a file 100 blocks in length and generate transactions at random to read or write segments of the file, locking each record as it is first accessed).

53. (Schneider.) We discussed two concepts of clock synchronization: *accuracy* and *precision.* Consider the case of aircraft operating under *free-flight* rules, where each pilot makes routing decisions on behalf of his or her plane, using a shared trajectory mapping system. Suppose that you faced a fundamental tradeoff between using clocks with high accuracy for such a mapping system or clocks with high precision. Which would you favor and why? Would it make sense to implement two such solutions, side by side?

54. Suppose that a-posteriori clock synchronization using GPS receivers becomes a world-wide standard in the coming decade. The use of temporal information now represents a form of communication channel that can be used in indirect ways—for example, process p, executing in Lisbon, can wait until process q performs a desired operation in New York (or fails) using timer events. Interestingly, such an approach communicates

information faster than messages can. What issues do these sorts of hidden information channels raise in regard to the protocols we explored in the book? Could temporal information create hidden causality relationships?

55. Show how tightly synchronized real-time clocks can be made to reflect causality in the manner of Lamport's logical clocks. Would such a clock be preferable in some ways to a purely logical clock? Explain, giving concrete examples to illustrate your points.

56. (Difficult.) In discussion of the CASD protocols, we saw that if such protocols were used to replicate the state of a distributed system, a mechanism would be needed to overcome inconsistencies occurring when a process is technically considered incorrect according to the definitions of the protocols and therefore does not benefit from the normal guarantees of atomicity and ordering seen by correct processes. In an IBM technical report, Skeen and Cristian once suggested that the CASD protocols could be used in support of an abstraction called Δ-*common storage*; the basic idea is to implement a distributed shared memory, which can be read by any process and updated using the CASD style of broadcast protocol. Such a distributed shared memory would reflect an update within Δ time units after it is initiated, plus or minus a clock skew factor of ε. How might the inconsistency issue of the CASD protocol be visible in a Δ-common storage system? Propose a method for detecting and eliminating such inconsistencies. (Note: This issue was not considered in the technical report.)

57. (Marzullo and Sabel.) Suppose you wish to monitor a distributed system to detect situations in which a logical predicate defined over the states of the member processes holds. The predicate may state, for example, that process p_i holds a token and that process p_j is waiting to obtain the token. Under the assumption that the states in question change very slowly in comparison to the communication speeds of the system, design a solution to this problem. You may assume that there is a function, *sample_local_state()*, that can be executed in each process to sample those aspects of its local state referenced in the query, and when the local states have been assembled in one place, a function, *evaluate*, can determine if the predicate holds or not. Now, discuss the modifications needed if the rate of state changes is increased enough so that the state can change in the same order of time as your protocol needs to run. How is your solution affected if you are required to detect *every state in which the predicate holds*, as opposed to just detecting *states in which the predicate happens to hold when the protocol is executed*. Demonstrate that your protocol cannot falsely detect satisfying states.

58. There is increasing interest in building small multiprocessor systems for use in inexpensive communication satellites. Such systems might look similar to a rack containing a small number of conventional workstations or PCs, running software that handles such tasks as maintaining the proper orientation of the satellite by adjusting its position periodically, turning on and off the control circuits that relay incoming messages to outgoing channels, and handling other aspects of satellite function. Now, suppose that it is possible to put highly redundant memory modules on the satellite to protect extremely critical regions of memory, but that it is costly to do so. However, unprotected memory

is likely to experience a low level of corruption as a result of the harsh conditions in space, such as cosmic rays and temperature extremes. What sorts of programming considerations would result from using such a model? Propose a software architecture that minimizes the need for redundant memory, but also minimizes the risk that a satellite will be completely lost (e.g., a satellite might be lost if it erroneously fires its positioning rockets and thereby exhausts its supply of fuel). You may assume that the actual rate of corruption of memory is low, but not completely insignificant, and that program instructions are as likely as data to be corrupted. Assume that the extremely reliable memories, however, never experience corruption.

59. Continuing with the topic of problem 58, there is debate concerning the best message-routing architecture for these sorts of satellite systems. In one approach, the satellites maintain a routing network among themselves; a relatively small number of ground stations interact with whatever satellite happens to be over them at a given time, and control and data messages are then forwarded satellite to satellite until they reach the destination. In a second approach, satellites communicate only with ground stations and mobile transmitter/receiver units: Such satellites require a larger number of ground systems, but they do not depend upon a routing transport protocol, which could be a source of unreliability. Considering the conditions cited in problem 60 and your responses, what would be the best design for a satellite-to-satellite routing network? Can you suggest a scientifically sound way to make the design tradeoff between this approach and the one using a larger number of potentially costly groundstations?

60. We noted that the theoretical community considers a problem to be impossible in a given environment if, for all proposed solutions to the problem, there exists at least one behavior consistent with the environment that would prevent the proposed solution from terminating or would lead to an incorrect outcome. Later we considered probabilistic protocols, which may be able to guarantee behaviors to very high levels of reliability—higher, in practice, than the reliability of the computers on which the solutions run. Suggest a definition of *impossible* that might reconcile these two perspectives on computing systems.

61. Suppose that a system is using Chord and has access to the finger tables used by the Chord technology. Devise an efficient protocol for counting the number of nodes actually in the system. How costly is your protocol?

62. Suppose that we wanted to enumerate all *(key,value)* pairs within some range of keys (here, we mean the actual key, not the hashed key). Is there an efficient way to do this using Chord? Explain why or why not.

63. Suppose that we want to do an inverted lookup—for a given value, we would like to find the corresponding key or keys. Can this be done efficiently using Chord? Can you suggest a way to modify Chord to support such an operation?

64. A stock exchange typically reports two kinds of events: actual trades that are completed, and bid-offered pricing. The latter is less important, since bid-offered prices change all the time, whereas information on trades that are consummated is of very high value, because applications predicting pricing trends tend to weight such events

very heavily. Which multicast properties would be most appropriate for reporting each kind of event?

65. Suppose that for reasons of scalability, you are building a stock exchange system that will use bimodal multicast *(pbcast)* for all event reporting. Can you suggest ways to extend the basic protocol so that if a node can tell whether a missing message is one of the "important" ones mentioned in question 64, as opposed to one of the less critical kinds of events?

66. Can Astrolabe aggregators be used to "count" objects in a distributed setting?

    a. Show how Astrolabe can be used to count the number of computers running it (that is, count the number of machines in its own table).

    b. How can Astrolabe be used to count the number of machines reporting load>10.0?

    c. Could Astrolabe be used to count the number of machines having connectivity problems? What issues arise if we try to base an aggregate on data being reported by a machine suffering intermittent connectivity failures?

    d. Suppose that a virus is actively spreading through a network. It modifies a file called C:\FooBar.exe on machines running version 2.1 of Microsoft "Age of Mythology." Can Astrolabe be used to count the number of infected machines? To list them? How would Astrolabe behave if these numbers are changing even as the system operator is looking at the output?

67. Your boss has asked you to estimate the number of downloaded music files on the computers in your company, a multinational corporation with some 25,000 machines on its corporate network. Astrolabe is running on all of these machines.

    a. Would you use a "configuration certificate" or an "aggregation function" to ask each machine to count the files in the "myDownloadedMusic" folder and report the count into Astrolabe?

    b. Assume that Astrolabe is structured with 100 machines per zone and that one gossip message is sent by each participant in a gossip epidemic every 5 seconds. Further, assume that it takes 10 seconds for a machine to count the number of music files it has, once it has been asked to do so. You initiate the action you recommended in (a). How long will it take before all the machines in the network start to report their counts of music files?

    c. How would you design an aggregation query to count the number of files in the system as a whole? Suppose that a time t you ask Astrolabe to begin to compute this aggregate. What issues arise during the period when the aggregation query is known at some machines but not all of them? Could this result in an incorrect reported count? Explain.

    d. Is there a way to set this query up so that you'll know how long to wait until the exact count has been computed? Suppose that starting at time $t + \delta$ the correct count is reported by Astrolabe. Why might the count continue to change long after time $t + \delta$ is reached ?

e.   What if you now want to identify the employee with the largest number of downloaded music files. How could you solve this problem with Astrolabe?

68.   The corporate database center in your company has become overloaded and you want to improve the use of caching by allowing client systems to share their cache contents with one-another. This way, if machine a can obtain a database record from the cache of machine b it will do so, rather than downloading a copy from the database. Assume that staleness of the cached records is not a concern. Which is the best technology for solving this problem: a DHT such as Chord or Pastry, a one-hop DHT such as Kelips, a scalable database-like system such as Astrolabe, or a scalable event reporting system such as a publish-subscribe technology or Bimodal Multicast *(pbcast)*?

69.   In a caching architecture we may want to maintain *coherent caches* by having the server notify nodes that have cached copies of a given record in the event that the record changes. They can then discard or refresh the stale copy. Of course, cache records can also be discarded for other reasons, such as timing considerations or a need to reuse the space for some other purpose. Which would be the best way for the server to track the set of clients that have a given record in their caches? Your answer should focus on the cost of the mechanism and also on how well it is likely to work:

a.   Maintain a collection of dynamic process groups, one group per record.

b.   Use Kelips to advertise copies of the cached record and also to announce that a cached copy has been discarded.

c.   Use some other DHT, such as Pastry, for the same purpose as in (b).

d.   Use Astrolabe for this purpose. One column of the Astrolabe data structure would list the cached records at a given machine, represented as a string of record identifiers separated by semicolons. (Astrolabe would just think of it as a fairly long string).

e.   When downloading a record, tell the server if it will be cached. If so, do an RPC to the server to notify it if and when the cached record is discarded.

f.   Don't explicitly track caching. Use Bimodal Multicast *(pbcast)* to notify all the client systems when a record changes. If a large number of records change, the notifications can be packed into very large messages for greater efficiency.

70.   We are building a military system to monitor the health of soldiers on the battlefield. Each soldier's equipment includes some number of sensors. Although the maximum number of sensors is known and isn't unreasonably large, the actual set of active sensors varies from soldier to soldier.

a.   We would like to use Astrolabe in such a setting, but we don't want its aggregation mechanism to be confused by the cases where a given soldier isn't reporting the sensor value that a given aggregate reads. For example, we might want to list the soldiers who have the lowest reserves of ammunition, but we don't want our list to include a huge number of individuals who either don't have an ammunition counting sensor, or for whom that sensor isn't currently working.

     b.   Suppose that one of the sensors is capable of detecting even traces of VX nerve gas. How might Astrolabe be used to identify the soldiers whose sensors are detecting more than some specified threshold level of VX?

     c.   What if we wanted to use *pbcast* to send a message to all soldiers within 100 meters of any soldier whose VX sensor is reporting an over-threshold level of the gas, for example to warn those soldiers to immediately put on a gas mask. How could we solve this problem? Assume that all soldiers have a GPS location sensor reporting their current coordinates.

71.   OfficeStuff corporation just called to warn that users of OfficeStuff version 2.1 may be at risk of attack by the NimbleFrog virus. Your virus scanning software isn't able to detect this problem, hence you decide to use Astrolabe to do so. How might you tackle this challenge?

72.   Astrolabe can identify machines that match a pattern, as in problem 70, but doesn't take actions on those machines. Suppose that you build an "AstroActor" application intended to run on the same client nodes that use Astrolabe. It's job is to take the actions Astrolabe can't take. For example, in problem 70, AstroAction might be used to initiate a software upgrade to OfficeStuff version 2.2.

     a.   How might you design AstroAction?

     b.   What security issues are raised by such a capability? Keep in mind that Astrolabe and AstroAction may be running on all nodes in a corporate network.

     c.   How might you address these security concerns?

73.   The Kelips and Pastry systems both include mechanisms to track and use the cheapest possible links. For example, Pastry constantly probes the nodes to which its finger tables point, and will substitute a cheaper and more responsive node if one turns out to be slow. Kelips similarly changes the affinity group contacts list to try and use inexpensive contacts that are known to be responsive. What are the pros and cons of such a policy? Think both about the expected performance of the DHT itself and also about the performance overhead of the mechanism.

74.   Suppose that a very large information management system is being designed for surveillance of the airports, train stations, bus stations and borders of a large country. It will have millions of digital camera systems, each associated with a storage device for archival recording of images captured. Now we would like to make this information accessible to authorized law enforcement officials. A small number of locations will be permitted to query the overall system. A typical query involves providing the system with some number of digital pictures of individuals suspected of trying to gain entry into the country, and the goal is to retrieve any possible matches from the archived databases of all of those computers. You can assume that the picture-matching operation is built into the image server, and can be accessed via a secured Web Services interface.

a. Would this problem be better matched to a client/server architecture, a peer-to-peer architecture, or a virtual synchrony process group approach? Why?

b. Suppose that you decide to use a peer-to-peer technology. How could you chose between Astrolabe, Kelips and Chord for the kind of search operation just described? Is one of these a much better "match" with the need than the others? Why?

c. Analyze the ways that a terrorist group might try to compromise the correct behavior of the solution you advocate in part (b). Assume that the group has one person working with them who has gained access to the network on which the system runs, and who is in a position to change the behavior of a few of the nodes collecting data—but just a few. Could such an intruder bring the whole system down? Could he cause the system to report a false result, such as to claim that there have been no sightings of such and such an individual?

75. If a message must take d hops to reach its destination and the worst-case delay for a single link is δ, it is common to assume that the worst-case transit time for the network will be $d * \delta$. However, a real link will typically exhibit a distribution of latencies, with the vast majority clustered near some minimum latency, δ_{min}, and only a very small percentage taking as long as δ_{max} to traverse the link. Under the assumption that the links of a routed network provide statistically independent and identical behavior, derive the distribution of expected latencies for a message that must traverse d links of a network. You may assume that the distribution of delays has a convenient form for your analysis. (This problem is hard to solve in closed form, but using MathLab you should be able to define a regression formula and solve it numerically, then graph the results.)

76. A network address translation box increases the size of the network name space. Suppose that addresses consist of a 32-bit address and a 16-bit port number and that network address translation is used as aggressively as possible. Also, assume that on the average, each application has a single open connection to some remote computer (this is just the average; some may have far more connections and some might not have any connections at all).

a. Characterize this "extreme translation" scenario. How many computers could be connected to the network before we run into situations where some computer. a cannot communicate with some other computer b because we have exhausted the address space?

b. How is your answer impacted if each application has, on the average, 10 open connections?

c. Network address translation is unidirectional: a client behind a NAT can connect to a server on the public Internet, but the server cannot initiate a connection from outside the NAT back through it. How is this reflected in your answer to (a)?

d. Does the answer to this problem change if we allow multiple levels of NAT boxes? E.g., "LayersCorp" might have some application running behind two

        NAT boxes, so that connection requests must pass through first one, then the other.

    e.   Many people consider NAT boxes as a form of security mechanism. What kinds of protection can a NAT provide?

77. (Ethical problem.) Suppose that a medical system does something a person would not be able to do, such as continuously monitoring the vital signs of a patient and continuously adjusting some form of medication or treatment in response to the measured values. Now, imagine that we want to attach this device to a distributed system so that physicians and nurses elsewhere in the hospital can remotely monitor the behavior of the medical system and so that they can change the rules that control its actions if necessary (e.g., by changing the dosage of a drug). In this book we have encountered many practical limits to security and reliability. Identify some of the likely limits on the reliability of a technology such as this. What are the ethical issues that need to be balanced in deciding whether or not to build such a system?

78. (Ethical problem.) You have been asked to participate on a government panel evaluating research proposals submitted to a major funding agency. One of the very strong proposals is focused on a new peer-to-peer file sharing technology with the following properties. First, content is completely anonymous: it is impossible to determine who uploaded a given file into the system. Second, downloads are anonymous: you can tell that data is being accessed, but the underlying system mixes files together in such a way that it is very hard to tell *which* data is being accessed. And third, the identity of the individual downloading the file is also anonymous. (Note: such technologies do exist; they have been developed by a number of researchers and tend to be based on so-called cryptographic "Mixes" (Chaum) and either strong encryption or some other form of steganographic storage (see Cooper and Birman; Mazieres).) The proposal claims that this system is for use by individuals who wish to exchange e-mail and engage in discussions that the government might find objectionable or that might result in discrimination against them by others, and the research group also states that the technology will be available to pro-democracy dissidents in foreign countries. But such a technology could also be used for theft of IP, coordination of spying or terrorist activities, and even for distribution of child pornography. Do you recommend that this work be funded? How would you convince the remainder of the committee to accept your position on the matter?

79. (Ethical dilemma.) The home of an individual suspected of involvement in terrorist activities is searched. No clearly compromising materials are found, but on his laptop computer the investigators discover a program built along the lines discussed in problem 78. The program has created some large files, but they are illegible and, as discussed in problem 78, presumably contain a mixture of encrypted data from many sources. Without the user's cooperation, it is impossible to launch the program or retrieve the files the user himself has stored into the system, or to make sense of any of this data. Should it be possible to compel such an individual to reveal his passwords and access codes? Keep in mind that if such a law were in place and the individual

were to refuse, he would be subject to fines, imprisonment or other penalties. If you find it helpful to do so, you may assume that it is very likely that this individual is guilty, but not certain.

80. (Ethical problem.) An *ethical theory* is a set of governing principles or rules for resolving ethical conflicts such as the one in the previous problem—for example, an ethical theory might stipulate that decisions should be made to favor the maximum benefit for the greatest number of individuals. A theory governing the deployment of technology could stipulate that machines must not replace people if the resulting system is at risk of making erroneous decisions that a person would have avoided. Notice that these particular theories could be in conflict—for example, if a technology that is normally beneficial develops occasional life-threatening complications. Discuss the issues that might occur in developing an ethical theory for the introduction of technologies in life- or safety-critical settings and, if possible, propose such a theory. What tradeoffs are required, and how would you justify them?

Bibliography

Abbott, M., and L. Peterson. Increasing Network Throughput by Integrating Protocol Layers. *IEEE/ACM Transactions on Networking* 1:5 (October 1993): 600–610.

Abraham, I., D. Malkhi. Probabilistic Quorums for Dynamic Systems. In the *17th International Symposium on Distributed Computing (DISC 2003)*, Sorento, Italy, October 2003.

Agarwal, D. A. Totem: A Reliable Ordered Delivery Protocol for Interconnected Local Area Networks. Ph.D. diss., Department of Electrical and Computer Engineering, University of California, Santa Barbara, 1994.

Aguilera, M.K., Strom, R.E., Sturman, D.C., Astley, M., Chandra, T.D. Matching Events in a Content-based Subscription System. *18th ACM Symposium on Principles of Distributed Computing (PODC)*, Atlanta, GA., 1999.

Ahamad, M., J. Burns, P. Hutto, and G. Neiger. Causal Memory. Technical Report, College of Computing, Georgia Institute of Technology, July 1991.

Alon, N., A. Barak, and U. Manber. On Disseminating Information Reliably without Broadcasting. *Proceedings of the Seventh International Conference on Distributed Computing Systems* (Berlin, September 1987). New York: IEEE Computer Society Press, 74–81.

Alonso, R., and F. Korth. Database Issues in Nomadic Computing. *Proceedings of the ACM SIGMOD International Conference on Mannagement of Data* (Washington, DC, May 1993), 388–392.

Alvisi, L., T. Bressoud, A. El-Khasab, K. Marzullo, D. Zagorodnov. Wrapping Server-Side to Mask Connection Failures. *INFOCOMM 2001*, Vol. 1, Anchorage, Alaska, 22–26 April 2001, 329–337.

Alvisi, L., D. Malkhi, E. Pierce, M. Reiter. Fault Detection for Byzantine Quorum Systems. *IEEE Transactions on Parallel and Distributed Systems* 12(9) (2001): 996–1007.

Alvisi, L., and K. Marzullo. Message Logging: Pessimistic, Causal, and Optimistic. *Proceedings of the Fifteenth IEEE Conference on Distributed Computing Systems* (Vancouver, 1995), 229–236.

Amir, O., Y. Amir, and D. Dolev. A Highly Available Application in the Transis Environment. *Proceedings of the Workshop on Hardware and Software Architectures for Fault Tolerance*. Springer-Verlag Lecture Notes in Computer Science, Vol. 774, 125–139.

Amir, Y. Replication Using Group Communication over a Partitioned Network. Ph.D. diss., Hebrew University of Jerusalem, 1995.

Amir, Y., C. Danilov, J. Stanton. A Low Latency, Loss Tolerant Architecture and Protocol for Wide Area Group Communication. *International Conference on Dependable Systems and Networks (DCCA-8)*, New York, June 25–28, 2000.

Amir, Y., D. Dovel, S. Kramer, and D. Malkhi. Membership Algorithms in Broadcast Domains. *Proceedings of the Sixth WDAG (Israel, June 1992)*. Springer-Verlag Lecture Notes in Computer Science, Vol. 647, 292–312.

—— Transis: A Communication Subsystem for High Availability. *Proceedings of the Twenty-Second Symposium on Fault-Tolerant Computing Systems* (Boston, July 1992). New York: IEEE Computer Society Press, 76–84.

Amir, Y. et al. The Totem Single-Ring Ordering and Membership Protocol. *ACM Transactions on Computer Systems* 13:4 (November 1995): 311–342.

Amir, Y., C. Nita-Rotaru, J. Stanton, G. Tsudik. Scaling Secure Group Communication: Beyond Peer-to-Peer *Proceedings of DISCEX3 Washington DC*, April 22–24, 2003.

Anceaume, E., B. Charron-Bost, P. Minet, and S. Toueg. On the Formal Specification of Group Membership Services. Technical Report 95-1534. Department of Computer Science, Cornell University, August 1995.

Andersen, D., H. Balakrishnan, M. F. Kaashoek, R. Morris. Resilient Overlay Networks. *Proceedings of the 8th Workshop on Hot Topics in Operating Systems (HotOS-VIII)*, Schloss Elmau, Germany, May 2001.

Andersen, D., H. Balakrishnan, M. F. Kaashoek, R. Morris. Resilient Overlay Networks. *Proceedings of the Symposium on Operating Systems Principles* 17, Vancouver, CA, Oct. 2001, 131–145.

Anderson, T., B. Bershad, E. Lazowska, and H. Levy. Scheduler Activiations: Effective Kernel Support for the User-Level Management of Parallelism. *Proceedings of the Thirteenth ACM Symposium on Operating Systems Principles* (Pacific Grove, CA, October 1991), 95–109.

Anderson, T. et al. Serverless Network File Systems. *Proceedings of the Fifteenth Symposium on Operating Systems Principles* (Copper Mountain Resort, CO, December 1995). New York: ACM Press, 109–126. Also *ACM Transactions on Computing Systems* 13:1 (February 1996).

Andrews, G. R. *Concurrent Programming: Principles and Practice*. Redwood City, CA, Benjamin/Cummings, 1991.

Architecture Projects Management Limited. The Advanced Networked Systems Architecture: An Application Programmer's Introduction to the Architecture. Technical Report TR-017-00. November 1991.

—— The Advanced Networked Systems Architecture: A System Designer's Introduction to the Architecture. Technical Report RC-253-00. April 1991.

—— The Advanced Networked Systems Architecture: An Engineer's Introduction to the Architecture. Technical Report TR-03-02. November 1989.

Aron, M., P. Druschel Soft timers efficient microsecond software timer support for network processing. *ACM Transactions on Computer Systems (TOCS)* 18(3) (2000): 197–228.

Armand, F., M. Gien, F. Herrmann, and M. Rozier. Revolution 89, or Distributing UNIX Brings It Back to Its Original Virtues. Technical Report CS/TR-89-36-1. Chorus Systemes, Paris, France, August 1989.

Asplin, J., and D. Johansen. Performance Experiments with the StormView Distributed Parallel Volume Renderer. Computer Science Technical Report 95-22. University of Tromsö, June 1995.

Atkin, B. and K.P. Birman. Evaluation of an Adaptive Transport Protocol. ACM INFOCOM 2003, April 1–3 2003, San Francisco.

Babaoglu, O., A. Bartoli, and G. Dini. Enriched View Synchrony: A Paradigm for Programming Dependable Applications in Partitionable Asynchronous Distributed Systems. Technical Report. Department of Computer Science, University of Bologna, May 1996.

Babaoglu, O., R. Davoli, L. A. Giachini, and M. B. Baker. RELACS: A Communications Infrastructure for Constructing Reliable Applications in Large-Scale Distributed Systems. BROADCAST Project Deliverable Report, 1994. Department of Computing Science, University of Newcastle upon Tyne, United Kingdom.

Babaoglu, O., R. Davoli, and A. Montresor. Failure Detectors, Group Membership, and View-Synchronous Communication in Partitionable Asynchronous Systems. Technical Report UBLCS-95-19. Department of Computer Science, University of Bologna, November 1995.

Babaoglu, O., and K. Marzullo. Consistent Global States of Distributed Systems: Fundamental Concepts and Mechanisms. In *Distributed Systems* (2d ed.), S. J. Mullender, ed. Reading, MA: Addison-Wesley/ACM Press, 1993.

Bache, T. C. et al. The Intelligent Monitoring System. *Bulletin of the Seismological Society of America* 80:6 (December 1990): 59–77.

Bailey, N. *The Mathematical Theory of Epidemic Diseases*, 2d ed. London, Charles Griffen and Company, 1975.

Baker, M. G. et al. Measurements of a Distributed File System. *Proceedings of the Thirteenth ACM Symposium on Operating Systems Principles* (Orcas Island, WA, November 1991), 198–212.

Bal, H. E., M. F. Kaashoek, and A. S. Tanenbaum. Orca: A Language for Parallel Programming of Distributed Systems. *IEEE Transactions on Software Engineering* (March 1992), 190–205.

Balakrishnan, H., M.F. Kaashoek, D. Karger, R. Morris, I. Stoica: Looking up data in P2P systems. *Communications of the ACM (CACM)* 46(2) (2003): 43–48.

Bartlett, J., J. Gray, and B. Horst. Fault Tolerance in Tandem Computing Systems. In *Evolution of Fault-Tolerant Computing*. Springer-Verlag, 1987, 55–76.

Bartlett, J. F. A Nonstop Kernel. *Proceedings of the Eighth ACM Symposium on Operating Systems Principles* (Pacific Grove, CA, December 1981). New York: ACM Press, 22–29.

Bellovin, S. M., and M. Merritt. Limitations of the Kerberos Authentication System. *Computer Communication Review* 20:5 (October 1990): 119–132.

Ben-Or, M. Fast Asynchronous Byzantine Agreement. *Proceedings of the Fourth ACM Symposium on Principles of Distributed Computing* (Minaki, Canada, August 1985), 149–151.

Berners-Lee, T., C. J-F. Groff, and B. Pollermann. World Wide Web: The Information Universe. *Electronic Networking Research, Applications and Policy* 2:1 (1992): 52–58.

Berners-Lee, T. et al. *Hypertext Transfer Protocol—HTTP 1.0.* IETF HTTP Working Group Draft 02 (Best Current Practice). August 1995.

—— The World Wide Web. *Communications of the ACM* 37:8 (August 1994): 76–82.

Bernstein, P. E., V. Hadzilacos, and N. Goodman. *Concurrency Control and Recovery in Database Systems.* Reading, MA: Addison-Wesley, 1987.

Bershad, B., T. Anderson, E. Lazowska, and H. Levy. Lightweight Remote Procedure Call. *Proceedings of the Eleventh ACM Symposium on Operating Systems Principles* (Litchfield Springs, AZ, December 1989), 102–113. Also ACM Transactions on Computer Systems 8:1 (February 1990): 37–55.

Bershad, B. et al. Extensibility, Safety, and Performance in the SPIN Operating System. *Proceedings of the Fifteenth Symposium on Operating Systems Principles* (Copper Mountain Resort, CO, December 1995), 267–284.

Bhagwan, R., D. Moore, S. Savage, G. M. Voelker: Replication Strategies for Highly Available Peer-to-Peer Storage. *Future Directions in Distributed Computing*, Springer Verlag (2003): 153–158.

Bhide, A., E. N. Elnozahy, and S. P. Morgan. A Highly Available Network File Server. *Proceedings of the USENIX Winter Conference* (Austin, December 1991), 199–205.

Biagioni, E. A Structured TCP in Standard ML. *Proceedings of the 1994 Symposium on Communications Architectures and Protocols* (London, August 1994).

Biagioni, E., R. Harper, and P. Lee. Standard ML Signatures for a Protocol Stack. Technical Report CS-93-170. Department of Computer Science, Carnegie Mellon University, October 1993.

Birman, K. P.. *Building Secure and Reliable Network Applications.* Manning Publishing Company and Prentice Hall, January 1997.

—— A Review of Experiences with Reliable Multicast. Software Practice and Experience Vol. 29, No. 9, July 1999, 741–774.

—— Next Generation Internet: Unsafe at Any Speed? *IEEE Computer, Special Issue on Infrastructure Protection*, Vol. 33, No. 8, August 2000, 54–88.

—— A Response to Cheriton and Skeen's Criticism of Causal and Totally Ordered Communication. *Operating Systems Review* 28:1 (January 1994), 11–21.

—— The Process Group Approach to Reliable Distributed Computing. *Communications of the ACM* 36:12 (December 1993).

Birman, K.P., R. Constable, M. Hayden, C. Kreitz, O. Rodeh, R. van Renesse, W. Vogels. The Horus and Ensemble Projects: Accomplishments and Limitations. Proc. of the DARPA Information Survivability Conference & Exposition (DISCEX '00), January 25–27 2000 in Hilton Head, South Carolina.

Birman, K. P., and B. B. Glade. Consistent Failure Reporting in Reliable Communications Systems. *IEEE Software*, Special Issue on Reliability, April 1995.

Birman, K.P., Mark Hayden, Oznur Ozkasap, Zhen Xiao, Mihai Budiu and Yaron Minsky. Bimodal Multicast. *ACM Transactions on Computer Systems*, Vol. 17, No. 2, May 1999, 41–88.

Birman, K. P., and T. A. Joseph. Exploiting Virtual Synchrony in Distributed Systems. *Proceedings of the Eleventh Symposium on Operating Systems Principles* (Austin, November 1987). New York: ACM Press, 123–138.

—— Reliable Communication in the Presence of Failures. *ACM Transactions on Computer Systems* 5:1 (February 1987): 47–76.

Birman, K. P., D. Malkhi, A. Ricciardi, and A. Schiper. Uniform Action in Asynchronous Distributed Systems. Technical Report TR 94-1447. Department of Computer Science, Cornell University, 1994.

Birman, K. P., A. Schiper, and P. Stephenson. Lightweight Causal and Atomic Group Communication. *ACM Transactions on Computing Systems* 9:3 (August 1991): 272–314.

Birman, K. P., and R. van Renesse, eds. *Reliable Distributed Computing with the Isis Toolkit*. New York: IEEE Computer Society Press, 1994.

—— Software for Reliable Networks. *Scientific American* 274:5 (May 1996): 64–69.

Birrell, A. Secure Communication Using Remote Procedure Calls. *ACM Transactions on Computer Systems* 3:1 (February 1985): 1–14.

Birrell, A., and B. Nelson. Implementing Remote Procedure Call. *ACM Transactions on Programming Languages and Systems* 2:1 (February 1984): 39–59.

Birrell, A., G. Nelson, S. Owicki, and T. Wobbera. Network Objects. *Proceedings of the Fourteenth Symposium on Operating Systems Principles* (Asheville, NC, 1993), 217–230.

Black, A., N. Hutchinson, E. Jul, and H. Levy. Object Structure in the Emerald System. *ACM Conference on Object-Oriented Programming Systems, Languages, and Applications* (Portland, OR, October 1986).

Borg, A., J. Baumbach, and S. Glazer. A Message System for Supporting Fault Tolerance. *Proceedings of the Ninth Symposium on Operating Systems Principles* (Bretton Woods, NH, October 1983), 90–99.

Borg, A. et al. Fault Tolerance under UNIX. *ACM Transactions on Computer Systems* 3:1 (Febraury 1985): 1–23.

Borr, A., and C. Wilhelmy. Highly Available Data Services for UNIX Client/Server Networks: Why Fault-Tolerant Hardware Isn't the Answer. *Hardware and Software*

Architectures for Fault Tolerance, M. Banatre and P. Lee, eds. Springer-Verlag Lecture Notes in Computer Science, Vol. 774, 385–404.

Brakmo, L., S. O'Malley, and L. Peterson. TCP Vegas: New Techniques for Congestion Detection and Avoidance. *Proceedings of the ACM SIGCOMM '94* (London, 1994).

Braun, T., and C. Diot. Protocol Implementation Using Integrated Layer Processing. *Proceedings of SIGCOMM-95* (September 1995).

Bressoud, T. C., and F. B. Schneider. Hypervisor-based Fault Tolerance. *Proceedings of the Fifteenth Symposium on Operating Systems Principles* (Copper Mountain Resort, CO, December 1995). New York: ACM Press, 1–11. Also *ACM Transactions on Computing Systems* 13:1 (February 1996).

Brockschmidt, K. *Inside OLE-2*. Redmond, WA, Microsoft Press, 1994.

Budhiraja, N. et al. The Primary-Backup Approach. In *Distributed System*, 2d ed., S. J. Mullender, ed. Reading, MA: Addison-Wesley/ACM Press, 1993.

Burrows, M., M. Abadi, and R. Needham. A Logic of Authentication. *Proceedings of the Eleventh ACM Symposium on Operating Systems Principles* (Litchfield Springs, AZ, December 1989). New York: ACM Press, 1–13.

Callahan, J., and T. Montgomery. Approaches to Verification and Validation of a Reliable Multicast Protocol. *Proceedings of the 1996 ACM International Symposium on Software Testing and Analysis*, (San Diego, CA, January 1996), 187-194. Also appears as *ACM Software Engineering Notes*, Vol. 21, No. 3, May 1996, 187–194.

Carter, J. Efficient Distributed Shared Memory Based on Multi-Protocol Release Consistency. Ph.D. diss., Rice University, August 1993.

Carzaniga, A., Rosenblum, D.,Wolf, A. Design and evaluation of a wide-area event notification service. ACM TOCS 19(3), Aug 2001.

Castro, M., P. Druschel, Y. C. Hu, A. Rowstron. Topology-Aware Routing in Structured Peer-to-Peer Overlay Networks. *Future Directions in Distributed Computing* 2003, Springer-Verlag, 2003. 103–107.

Castro, M., B. Liskov: Practical Byzantine Fault Tolerance and Proactive Recovery. *ACM Transactions on Computer Systems (TOCS)* 20(4) (2002): 398–461.

Castro, M., R. Rodrigues, B. Liskov: BASE: Using abstraction to improve fault tolerance. TOCS 21(3) (2003): 236–269.

Chandra, R., V. Ramasubramanian, K.P. Birman. Anonymous Gossip: Improving Multicast Reliability in Ad-Hoc Networks. *International Conference on Distributed Computing Systems* (ICDCS 2001), Phoenix, Arizona, April 2001.

Chandra, T., V. Hadzilacos, and S. Toueg. The Weakest Failure Detector for Solving Consensus. *ACM Symposium on Principles of Distributed Computing* (August 1992), 147–158.

Chandra, T., V. Hadzilacos, S. Toueg, and B. Charron-Bost. On the Impossiblity of Group Membership. *Proceedings of the ACM Symposium on Priciples of Distributed Computing* (Vancouver, May 1996).

Chandra, T., and S. Toueg. Time and Message Efficient Reliable Broadcasts. Technical Report TR 90-1094. Department of Computer Science, Cornell University, February 1990.

—— Unreliable Failure Detectors for Asynchronous Systems. *Journal of the ACM*, in press. Previous version in *ACM Symposium on Principles of Distributed Computing* (Montreal, 1991), 325–340.

Chandy, K. M., and L. Lamport. Distributed Snapshots: Determining Global States of Distributed Systems. *ACM Transactions on Computer Systems* 3:1 (February 1985): 63–75.

Chang, M., and N. Maxemchuk. Reliable Broadcast Protocols. *ACM Transactions on Computer Systems* 2:3 (August 1984): 251–273.

Charron-Bost, B. Concerning the Size of Logical Clocks in Distributed Systems. *Information Processing Letters* 39:1 (July 1991): 11–16.

Chase, J., H. Levy, M. Feeley, and E. Lazowska. Sharing and Protection in a Single-Address-Space Operating System. *ACM Transactions on Computer Systems* 12:4 (November 1994): 271–307.

Chaum, D. Untraceable Electronic Mail, Return Addresses, and Digital Pseudonyms. *Communications of the ACM* 24:2 (February 1981): 84–88.

Chen, P. et al. RAID: High Performance, Reliable, Secondary Storage. *ACM Computing Surveys* 26:2 (June 1994): 45–85.

Cheriton, D., and D. Skeen. Understanding the Limitations of Causally and Totally Ordered Communication. *Proceedings of the Thirteenth ACM Symposium on Operating Systems Principles* (Asheville, NC, December 1993). New York: ACM Press, 44–57.

Cheriton, D., and W. Zwaenepoel. Distributed Process Groups in the V Kernel. *ACM Transactions on Computer Systems* 3:2 (May 1985): 77–107.

Chilaragee, R. Top Five Challenges Facing the Practice of Fault Tolerance. In *Hardware and Software Architectures for Fault Tolerance*, M. Banatre and P. Lee, eds. Springer-Verlag Lecture Notes in Computer Science, Vol. 774, 3–12.

Cho, K., and K. P. Birman. A Group Communication Approach for Mobile Computing. Technical Report TR94-1424. Department of Computer Science, Cornell University, May 1994.

Chockler, G., I. Keidar, R. Vitenberg. Group Communication Specifications: A Comprehensive Study. In *ACM Computing Surveys* 33(4), December 2001, 1–43.

Chockler, G. U., N. Huleihel, I. Keidar, and D. Dolev. Multimedia Multicast Transport Service for Groupware. TINA '96: *The Convergence of Telecommunications and Distributed Computing Technologies* (Heidelberg, September 1996). Berlin: VDE-Verlag.

Chockler, G., D. Malkhi, B. Merimovich, D. Rabinowitz. Aquarius: A Data-Centric approach to CORBA Fault-Tolerance. *The workshop on Reliable and Secure Middle-*

ware, in the 2003 International Conference on Distributed Objects and Applications (DOA), Sicily, Italy, November 2003.

Clark, D., V. Jacobson, J. Romkey, and H. Salwen. An Analysis of TCP Processing Overhead. *IEEE Communications* 27:6 (June 1989): 23–29.

Clark, D., and D. L. Tennenhouse. Architectural Considerations for a New Generation of Protocols. *Proceedings of the 1990 Symposium on Communication Architectures and Protocols* (Philadelphia, September 1990). New York: ACM Press, 200–208.

Clark, D., and M. Tennenhouse. Architectural Considerations for a New Generation of Protocols. *Proceedings of SIGCOMM-87* (August 1987), 353–359.

Clegg, M., and K. Marzullo. Clock Synchronization in Hard Real-Time Distributed Systems. Technical Report. Department of Computer Science, University of California, San Diego, March 1996.

Coan, B., B. M. Oki, and E. K. Kolodner. Limitations on Database Availability When Networks Partition. *Proceedings of the Fifth ACM Symposium on Principles of Distributed Computing* (Calgary, August 1986), 187–194.

Coan, B., and G. Thomas. Agreeing on a Leader in Real Time. *Proceedings of the Eleventh Real-Time Systems Symposium* (December 1990), 166–172.

Comer, D., and J. Griffioen. A New Design for Distributed Systems: The Remote Memory Model. *Proceedings of the 1990 Summer USENIX Conference* (June 1990), 127–135.

Comer, D. E. *Internetworking with TCP/IP.* Vol. I: *Principles, Protocols, and Architecture.* Englewood Cliffs, NJ: Prentice Hall, 1991.

Comer, D. E., and D. L. Stevens. *Internetworking with TCP/IP.* Vol. III: *Client/Server Programming and Applications.* Englewood Cliffs, NJ: Prentice Hall, 1993.

—— *Internetworking with TCP/IP.* Vol. II: *Design, Implementation, and Internals.* Englewood Cliffs, NJ: Prentice Hall, 1991.

Cooper, D. A., and K. P. Birman. The Design and Implementation of a Private Message Service for Mobile Computers. *Wireless Networks* 1:3 (October 1995): 297–309.

Cooper, E. Replicated Distributed Programs. *Proceedings of the Tenth ACM Symposium on Operating Systems Principles* (Orcas Island, WA, December 1985). New York: ACM Press, 63–78.

Cooper, R. Experience with Causally and Totally Ordered Group Communication Support-A Cautionary Tale. *Operating Systems Review* 28:1 (January 1994): 28–32.

Coulouris, G., J. Dollimore, and T. Kindberg. *Distributed Systems: Concepts and Design.* Reading, MA: Addison-Wesley, 1994.

Cristian, F. Synchronous and Asynchronous Group Communication. *Communications of the ACM* 39:4 (April 1996): 88–97.

—— Reaching Agreement on Processor Group Membership in Synchronous Distributed Systems. *Distributed Computing* 4:4 (April 1991): 175–187.

—— Understanding Fault-Tolerant Distributed Systems. *Communications of the ACM* 34:2 (February 1991): 57–78.

—— Probabilistic Clock Synchronization. *Distributed Computing* 3:3 (1989): 146–158.

Cristian, F., H. Aghili, R. Strong, and D. Dolev. Atomic Broadcast: From Simple Message Diffusion to Byzantine Agreement. *Proceedings of the Fifteenth International Symposium on Fault-Tolerant Computing* (1985). New York: IEEE Computer Society Press, 200-206. Revised as IBM Technical Report RJ5244.

Cristian, F., and R. Delancy. Fault Tolerance in the Advanced Automation System. IBM Technical Report RJ7424. IBM Research Laboratories, San Jose, CA, April 1990.

Cristian, F., D. Dolev, R. Strong, and H. Aghili. Atomic Broadcast in a Real-Time Environment. In *Fault-Tolerant Distributed Computing*. Springer-Verlag Lecture Notes in Computer Science, Vol. 448, 1990, 51–71.

Cristian, F., and C. Fetzer. Fault-Tolerant Internal Clock Synchronization. *Proceedings of the Thirteenth Symposium on Reliable Distributed Systems* (October 1994).

Cristian, F., and F. Schmuck. Agreeing on Process Group Membership in Asynchronous Distributed Systems. Technical Report CSE95-428. Department of Computer Science and Engineering, University of California, San Diego, 1995.

Custer, H. *Inside Windows NT*. Redmond, WA: Microsoft Press, 1993.

Dabek, F., M.F. Kaashoek, D. Karger, R. Morris, and I. Stoica, Wide-area cooperative storage with CFS, ACM SOSP 2001, Banff, October 2001.

Damm, A., J. Reisinger, W. Schwabl, and H. Kopetz. The Real-Time Operating System of Mars. *ACM Operating Systems Review* 22:3 (July 1989): 141–157.

Davidson, S., H. Garcia-Molina, and D. Skeen. Consistency in a Partitioned Network: A Survey. *ACM Computing Surveys* 17:3 (September 1985): 341–370.

Deering, S. E. Host Extensions for IP Multicasting. Technical Report RFC 1112. SRI Network Information Center, August 1989.

—— Multicast Routing in Internetworks and Extended LANs. *Computer Communications Review* 18:4 (August 1988): 55–64.

Deering, S. E., and D. R. Cheriton. Multicast Routing in Datagram Internetworks and Extended LANs. *ACM Transactions on Computer Systems* 8:2 (May 1990): 85–110.

Della Ferra, C. A. et al. The Zephyr Notification Service. *Proceedings of the Winter USENIX Conference* (December 1988).

Demers, A. et al. Epidemic Algorithms for Replicated Data Management. *Proceedings of the Sixth Symposium on Principles of Distributed Computing*, (Vancouver, August 1987): 1–12. Also Operating Systems Review 22:1 (January 1988): 8–32.

Dempsey, B., J. C. Fenton, and A. C. Weaver. The MultiDriver: A Reliable Multicast Service Using the Xpress Transfer Protocol. *Proceedings of the Fifteenth Conference on Local Computer Networks* (1990). New York: IEEE Computer Society Press, 351–358.

Denning, D. Digital Signatures with RSA and Other Public-Key Cryptosystems. *Communications of the ACM* 27:4 (April 1984): 388–392.

Denning, D., and D. A. Branstad. Taxonomy for Key Escrow Encryption Systems. *Communications of the ACM* 39:3 (March 1996): 34–40.

Desmedt, Y. Society and Group-Oriented Cryptography: A New Concept. *Advances in Cryptology—CRYPTO '87 Proceedings*. Springer-Verlag Lecture Notes in Computer Science, Vol. 293, 1988, 120–127.

Desmedt, Y., Y. Frankel, and M. Yung. Multi-Receiver/Multi-Sender Network Security: Efficient Authenticated Multicast/Feedback. *Proceedings of the IEEE INFOCOM* (May 1992).

Diffie, W. The First Ten Years of Public-Key Cryptography. *Proceedings of the IEEE* 76:5 (May 1988): 560–577.

Diffie, W., and M. E. Hellman. Privacy and Authentication: An Introduction to Cryptography. *Proceedings of the IEEE* 67:3 (March 1979): 397–427.

Digital Equipment Corporation. A Technical Description of the DECsafe Available Server Environment (ASE). *Digital Equipment Corporation Technical Journal* 7:4 (September 1995): 89–100.

Dolev, D., and D. Malkhi. The Transis Approach to High Availability Cluster Communication. *Communications of the ACM* 39:4 (April 1996): 64–70.

Dolev, D., D. Malkhi, and R. Strong. A Framework for Partitionable Membership Service. Technical Report TR 95-4. Institute of Computer Science, Hebrew University of Jerusalem, March 1995.

Drushel, P., and L. L. Peterson. Fbufs: A High-Bandwidth Cross-Domain Transfer Facility. *Proceedings of the Thirteenth ACM Symposium on Operating Systems Principles* (Pacific Grove, CA, December 1993). New York: ACM Press, 189–202.

Elnozahy, E. N., and W. Zwaenepoel. Manetho: Transparent Rollback-Recovery with Low Overhead, Limited Rollback, and Fast Output Control. *IEEE Transactions on Computers*, Special Issue on Fault-Tolerant Computing, May 1992.

Ekwall, R, Urbán, P, and Schiper, A. Robust TCP Connections for Fault Tolerant Computing *Proceedings of the 9th International Conference on Parallel and Distributed Systems* (ICPDS), Dec. 2002, Taiwan ROC.

Engler, D. R., M. F. Kaashoek, and J. O'Toole. Exokernel: An Operating System Architecture for Application-Level Resource Management. *Proceedings of the Fifteenth Symposium on Operating Systems Principles* (Copper Mountain Resort, CO, December 1995). New York: ACM Press, 251–266.

Ezhilhevan, P., R. Macedo, and S. Shrivastava. Newtop: A Fault-Tolerant Group Communication Protocol. *Proceedings of the Fifteenth International Conference on Distributed Systems* (Vancouver, May 1995).

Feeley, M. et al. Implementing Global Memory Management in a Workstation Cluster. *Proceedings of the Fifteenth ACM SIGOPS Symposium on Operating Systems Principles* (Copper Mountain Resort, CO, December 1995), 201–212.

Felton, E., and J. Zahorjan. Issues in the Implementation of a Remote Memory Paging System. Technical Report 91-03-09. Department of Computer Science and Engineering, University of Washington, March 1991.

Fekete, A., N. Lynch, A. Shvartsman. Specifying and using a partitionable group communication service. *ACM Transactions on Computer Systems* 19(2) (2001): 171–216.

Fidge, C. Timestamps in Message-Passing Systems That Preserve the Partial Ordering. *Proceedings of the Eleventh Australian Computer Science Conference* (1988).

Fisher, M. J., N. A. Lynch, and M. Merritt. Easy Impossibility Proofs for Distributed Consensus Problems. *Proceedings of the Fourth Annual ACM Symposium on Principles of Distributed Computing* (Minaki, Canada, August 1985). New York: ACM Press.

Fisher, M. J., N. A. Lynch, and M. S. Paterson. Impossibility of Distributed Computing with One Faulty Process. *Journal of the ACM* 32:2 (April 1985): 374–382.

Floyd, S., V. Jacobson, S. McCanne, C-G. Liu, and L. Zhang. A Reliable Multicast Framework for Lightweight Sessions and Application-Level Framing. *Proceedings of the '95 Symposium on Communication Architectures and Protocols* (Cambridge, MA, August 1995). New York: ACM Press.

Frank, A., L. Wittie, and A. Bernstein. Multicast Communication on Network Computers. *IEEE Software* (May 1985).

Frankel, Y. A Practical Protocol for Large Group-Oriented Networks. *Advances in Cryptology—EUROCRYPT '89*. Springer-Verlag Lecture Notes in Computer Science, Vol. 434, 56–61.

Frankel, Y., and Y. Desmedt. Distributed Reliable Threshold Multisignature. Technical Report TR-92-0402. Department of EECS, University of Wisconsin, Milwaukee, June 1992.

Friedman, R., and K. P. Birman. Using Group Communication Technology to Implement a Reliable and Scalable Distributed IN Coprocessor. TINA '96: *The Convergence of Telecommunications and Distributed Computing Technologies* (Heidelberg, September 1996), 25–42. Berlin: VDE-Verlag. Also Technical Report. Department of Computer Science, Cornell University, March 1996.

Friedman, R., I. Keider, D. Malkhi, K. P. Birman, and D. Dolev. Deciding in Partitionable Networks. Technical Report 95-1554. Department of Computer Science, Cornell University, October 1995.

Friedman, R., and R. van Renesse. Strong and Weak Virtual Synchrony in Horus. Technical Report 95-1537. Department of Computer Science, Cornell University, August 1995.

—— Packing Messages as a Tool for Boosting the Performance of Total Ordering Protocols. Technical Report 95-1527. Department of Computer Science, Cornell University, July 1995. Submitted to *IEEE Transactions on Networking*.

Ganger, G., McKusick, M., Soules, C. and Patt, Y. Soft Updates: A Solution to the Metadata Update problem in File Systems. *ACM Transactions on Computer Systems, Vol. 18, Num. 2, Pg. 127–153*. May 2000.

Garcia-Molina, H., and A. Spauster. Ordered and Reliable Multicast Communication. *ACM Transactions on Computer Systems* 9:3 (August 1991): 242–271.

Geist, G. A. et al. PVM: *A User's Guide and Tutorial for Networked Parallel Computing*. Cambridge, MA: MIT Press, 1994.

Gharachorloo, K. et al. Memory Consistency and Event Ordering in Scalable Shared-Memory Multiprocessors. *Proceedings of the Seventeenth Annual International Symposium on Computer Architecture* (Seattle, May 1990), 15–26.

Ghemawat, S; Gobioff, H; and Leung, S.T. File and storage systems: The Google file system. *19th ACM Symposium on Operating Systems Principles (SOSP)*, Bolton Landing, NY. October 2003.

Gibbs, B. W. Software's Chronic Crisis. *Scientific American*, September 1994.

Gifford, D. Weighted Voting for Replicated Data. *Proceedings of the Seventh ACM Symposium on Operating Systems Principles* (Pacific Grove, CA, December 1979). New York: ACM Press, 150–162.

Glade, B. B. A Scalable Architecture for Reliable Publish/Subscribe Communication in Distributed Systems. Ph. D. diss., Department of Computer Science, Cornell University, May 1996.

Glade, B. B., K. P. Birman, R. C. Cooper, and R. van Renesse. Lightweight Process Groups in the Isis System. *Distributed Systems Engineering Journal*, July 1993.

Gleeson, B. Fault-Tolerant Computer System with Provision for Handling External Events. U.S. Patent 5,363,503, November 1994.

Golding, R., and K. Taylor. Group Membership in the Epidemic Style. Technical Report UCSC-CRL-92-13. University of California, Santa Cruz, May 1992.

Golding, R. A. Weak Consistency Group Communication and Membership. Ph.D. diss., Computer and Information Sciences Department, University of California, Santa Cruz, 1992.

——Distributed Epidemic Algorithms for Replicated Tuple Spaces. Technical Report HPL-CSP-91-15. June 1991. Concurrent systems project, Hewlett-Packard Laboratories.

Gong, L. Securely Replicating Authentication Services. *Proceedings of the Ninth International Conference on Distributed Computing Systems* (August 1989), 85–91.

Gopal, A., R. Strong, S. Toueg, and F. Cristian. Early-Delivery Atomic Broadcast. *Proceedings of the Ninth ACM Symposium on Principles of Distributed Computing* (Toronto, August 1990). New York: ACM Press, 297–309.

Gosling, J., and H. McGilton. The Java Language Environment: A White Paper. Sun Microsystems, Inc., October 1995a. Available as http://java.sun.com/langEnv/index.html.

——The Java Programmer's Guide: A White Paper. Sun Microsystems, Inc. October 1995b. Available as http://java.sun.com/progGuide/index.html.

Govindran, R., and D. P. Anderson. Scheduling and IPC Mechanisms for Continuous Media. *Proceedings of the Twelfth ACM Symposium on Operating Systems Principles* (Asilomar, CA, October 1991). New York: ACM Press, 68–80.

Gray, J. High Availability Computer Systems. *IEEE Computer*, September 1991.

—— A Census of Tandem System Availability between 1985 and 1990. Technical Report 90.1. Tandem Computer Corporation, September 1990.

—— Notes on Database Operating Systems. Operating Systems: An Advanced Course. Springer-Verlag Lecture Notes in Computer Science, Vol. 60, 1978, 393–481.

Gray, J., J. Bartlett, and R. Horst. Fault Tolerance in Tandem Computer Systems. *The Evolution of Fault-Tolerant Computing*, A. Avizienis, H. Kopetz, and J. C. Laprie, eds. Springer-Verlag, 1987.

Gray, J., Helland, P., and Shasha, D. Dangers of Replication and a Solution. *ACM SIGMOD International Conference on Management of Data*. Montreal, Quebec, Canada. June, 1996.

Gray, J., and A. Reuter. *Transaction Processing: Concepts and Techniques*. San Mateo, CA: Morgan Kaufmann, 1993.

Gribble, S., et. al. The Ninja architecture for robust Internet-scale systems and services. *Computer Networks* 35(4) (2001): 473–497.

Guerraoui, R. Revisiting the Relationship between Nonblocking Atomic Commitment and Consensus. *International Workshop on Distributed Algorithms* (September 1995), 87–100.

Guerraoui, R., and A. Schiper. Gamma-Accurate Failure Detectors. Technical Report APFL. Lausanne, Switzerland: Départment d'Informatique, 1996.

Gupta, I., A.M. Kermarrec, A.J. Ganesh. Efficient Epidemic-Style Protocols for Reliable and Scalable Multicast. Proceedings of the 21st Symposium on Reliable Distributed Systems (SRDS 02), Osaka, Japan. October 2002. pp. 180–189.

Gupta, I., K.P. Birman, P. Linga, A. Demers, R. van Renesse. Kelips: Building an Efficient and Stable P2P DHT Through Increased Memory and Background Overhead. *Proc. 2nd International Workshop on Peer-to-Peer Systems (IPTPS '03)*, Oakland CA, 2003.

Gurwitz, R. F., M. Dean, and R. E. Schantz. Programming Support in the Chronus Distributed Operating System. *Proceedings of the Sixth International Conference on Distributed Computing Systems* (1986). New York: IEEE Computer Society Press, 486–493.

Hagmann, R. Reimplementing the Cedar File System Using Logging and Group Commit. *Proceedings of the Eleventh ACM Symposium on Operating Systems Principles* (Austin, November 1987). New York: ACM Press, 155–171.

Handel, R., H. Huber, and S. Schroder. *ATM Networks: Concepts, Protocols, Applications*. Reading, MA: Addison-Wesley, 1994.

Harper, R., and P. Lee. The Fox Project in 1994. Technical Report CS-94-01. Department of Computer Science, Carnegie Mellon University, 1994.

Hartman, J. H., and J. K. Ousterhout. The Zebra Striped Network File System. *Proceedings of the Thirteenth ACM Symposium on Operating Systems Principles* (Asheville, NC, December 1993). New York: ACM Press, 29–43.

Hayden, M., and K. P. Birman. Achieving Critical Reliability with Unreliable Components and Unreliable Glue. Technical Report TR95-1493. Department of Computer Science, Cornell University, March 1995. (This paper was subsequently substantially revised; a new version was released in September 1996.)

Heidemann, J., and G. Popek. Performance of Cache Coherence in Stackable Filing. *Proceedings of the Fifteenth ACM Symposium on Operating Systems Principles* (Copper Mountain Resort, CO, December 1995), 127–142.

—— File System Development with Stackable Layers. *Communications of the ACM* 12:1 (February 1994): 58–89.

Heinlein, J., K. Garachorloo, S. Dresser, and A. Gupta. Integration of Message Passing and Shared Memory in the Stanford FLASH Multiprocessor. *Proceedings of the Sixth International Conference on Architectural Support for Programming Languages and Operating Systems* (October 1994), 38–50.

Herlihy, M. Replication Methods for Abstract Data Types. Ph.D. diss., Massachusetts Institute of Technology, May 1984. Available as Technical Report LCS-84-319.

Herlihy, M., and J. Wing. Linearizability: A Correctness Condition for Concurrent Objects. *ACM Transactions on Programming Languages and Systems* 12:3 (July 1990): 463–492.

Herlihy, M. P., and J. D. Tygar. How to Make Replicated Data Secure. *Advances in Cryptography—CRYPTO '87 Proceedings*. Springer-Verlag Lecture Notes in Computer Science, Vol. 293, 379–391.

Hildebrand, D. An Architectural Overview of QNX. *Proceedings of the First USENIX Workshop on Microkernels and Other Kernel Architectures* (Seattle, April 1992), 113–126.

Holliday, J., D. Agrawal, A. El Abbadi. The Performance of Database Replication with Group Multicast. FTCS 1999: 158–165.

Holliday, J., D. Agrawal, A. El Abbadi. Partial Database Replication using Epidemic Communication. ICDCS 2002: 485.

Howard, J. et al. Scale and Performance in a Distributed File System. *Proceedings of the Eleventh ACM Symposium on Operating Systems Principles* (Austin, November 1987). New York: ACM Press. Also *ACM Transactions on Computing Systems* 5:1 (February 1988).

Hunt, G. D. Multicast Flow Control on Local Area Networks. Ph.D. diss., Department of Computer Science, Cornell University, February 1995. Also available as Technical Report TR-95-1479.

Internet Engineering Task Force. *Secure Sockets Layer, Version* 3.0. 1995.

Iona Ltd. Information about Object Transaction Services for Orbix. 1995. Available at info@iona.ie.

Iona Ltd. and Isis Distributed Systems, Inc. An Introduction to Orbix+Isis. 1995. Available at info@iona.ie.

Iyer, S., A. Rowstron, P. Druschel. Squirrel: a decentralized peer-to-peer web cache. *Principles of Distributed Computing* (PODC) 2002: 213–222

Jacobson, V. Compressing TCP/IP Headers for Low-Speed Serial Links. Technical Report RFC 114. Network Working Group, February 1990.

—— Congestion Avoidance and Control. *Proceedings of the ACM SIGCOMM '88* (Palo Alto, 1988).

Jalote, P. *Fault Tolerance in Distributed Systems*. Englewood Cliffs, NJ: Prentice Hall, 1994.

Jannotti, J., Gifford, D., Johnson, K., Kaashoek, F., O'Toole, J. Overcast: Reliable Multicasting with an Overlay Network, *4th Symposium on Operating System Design & Implementation (OSDI)*. San Diego, CA. October, 2000.

Johansen, D. StormCast: Yet Another Exercise in Distributed Computing. *In Distributed Open Systems in Perspective*, D. Johansen and Brazier, eds. New York: IEEE Computer Society Press, 1994.

Johansen, D., and G. Hartvigsen. Architecture Issues in the StormCast System. Springer-Verlag Lecture Notes in Computer Science, Vol. 938, 1–16.

Johansen, D., R. van Renesse, and F. Schneider. Supporting Broad Internet Access to TACOMA. Technical Report. February 1996.

—— An Introduction to the TACOMA Distributed System (Version 1.0). Computer Science Technical Report 95-23. University of Tromsö, June 1995.

—— Operating System Support for Mobile Agents. *Proceedings of the Fifth Workshop on Hot Topics in Operating Systems* (Orcas Island, WA, May 1995). New York: IEEE Computer Society Press, 42–45.

Johnson, D. B., and W. Zwaenepoel. Sender-Based Message Logging. *Proceedings of the Seventeenth Annual International Symposium on Fault-Tolerant Computing* (June 1987). New York: IEEE Computer Society Press, 14–19.

Johnson, K., M. F. Kaashoek, and D. Wallach. CRL: High-Performance All Software Distributed Shared Memory. *Proceedings of the Fifteenth ACM Symposium on Operating Systems Principles* (Copper Mountain Resort, CO, December 1995), 213–228.

Jones, M. B. Interposition Agents: Transparent Interposing User Code at the System Interface. *Proceedings of the Fourteenth ACM Symposium on Operating Systems Principles* (Asheville, NC, December 1993). New York: ACM Press, 80–93.

Joseph, A., deLespinasse, A., Tauber, J., Gifford, D. and Kaashoek, F.K. Rover: A Toolkit for Mobile Information Access. *15th ACM Symposium on Operating Systems (SOSP)*. Copper Mountain, CO. December 1995.

Joseph, T. A. Low Cost Management of Replicated Data. Ph.D. diss., Cornell University, 1986. Also Technical Report. Department of Computer Science, Cornell University.

Joseph, T. A., and K. P. Birman. Low Cost Management of Replicated Data in Fault-Tolerant Distributed Systems. *ACM Transactions on Computer Systems* 4:1 (February 1986): 54–70.

Kaashoek, F. Group Communication in Distributed Computer Systems. Ph.D. diss., Vrije Universiteit, 1992.

Kaashoek, M. F., and A. S. Tannenbaum. Group Communication in the Amoeba Distributed Operating System. *Proceedings of the Eleventh International Conference on Distributed Computing Systems.* New York: IEEE Computer Society Press, 222–230.

Kaashoek, M. F. et al. An Efficient Reliable Broadcast Protocol. *Operating Systems Review* 23:4 (July 1978): 5–19.

Kalantar, M. Issues in Ordered Multicast Performance: A Simulation Study. Ph.D. diss., Department of Computer Science, Cornell University, August 1995. Also Technical Report TR-95-1531.

Karamcheti, V., and A. A. Chien. Software Overhead in Messaging Layers: Where Does the Time Go? *Proceedings of the Sixth ACM Symposium on Principles of Programming Languages and Operating Systems* (San Jose, CA, October 1994). New York: ACM Press.

Kay, J., and J. Pasquale. The Importance of Nondata Touching Processing Overheads. *Proceedings of SIGCOMM-93* (August 1993), 259–269.

Kay, J. S. PathIDs: A Mechanism for Reducing Network Software Latency. Ph.D. diss., University of California, San Diego, May 1994.

Keidar, I. Challenges in Evaluating Distributed Algorithms. In *Future Directions in Distributed Computing, Lecture Notes in Computer Science*, Vol. 2584, 40–44.

Keidar, I., and D. Dolev. Increasing the Resilience of Atomic Commit at No Additional Cost. *Proceedings of the 1995 ACM Symposium on Principles of Database Systems* (May 1995), 245–254.

Keidar, I., and D. Dolev. Totally Ordered Broadcast in the Face of Network Partitions. Exploiting Group Communication for Replication in Partitionable Networks. Chapter 3 of *Dependable Network Computing*, pages 51–75, D. Avresky Editor, Kluwer Academic Publications. January, 2000.

Keidar, I., R. Khazan. A Virtually Synchronous Group Multicast Algorithm for WANs: Formal Approach. In *SIAM Journal on Computing (SICOMP)* 32(1) November 2002, 78–130.

Keidar, I., R. Khazan, N. Lynch, A. Shvartsman. An inheritance-based technique for building simulation proofs incrementally. *TOSEM* 11(1) (2002): 63–91.

Keidar, I, K. Marzullo. The Need for Realistic Failure Models in Protocol Design. Position paper in the *4th Information Survivability Workshop (ISW)* 2001/2002, Vancouver, Canada, March 2002.

Keidar, I., J. Sussman, K. Marzullo, D. Dolev. Moshe: A Group Membership Service for WANs. In *ACM Transactions on Computer Systems* (TOCS) 20(3) 2002, August 1–48.

Keleher, P., A. L. Cox, and W. Zwaenepoel. Lazy Release Consistency for Software Distributed Shared Memory. *Proceedings of the Nineteenth Annual International Symposium on Computer Architecture* (May 1992), 13–21.

Kermarrec, A.M., A. Rowstron, M. Shapiro, P. Druschel. The IceCube approach to the reconciliation of divergent replicas. *Principles of Distributed Computing* 2001: 210–218.

Keshav, S. *An Engineering Approach to Computer Networking.* Addison Wesley, New York 1997 (ISBN 0201634422).

Khalidi, Y. A. et al. Solaris MC: A Multicomputer OS. Technical Report 95-48. Sun Microsystems Laboratories, November 1995.

Kistler, J. J., and M. Satyanarayanan. Disconnected Operation in the Coda File System. *Proceedings of the Twelfth ACM Symposium on Operating Systems Principles* (Asilomar, CA, October 1991). New York: ACM Press, 213-225. Also *ACM Transactions on Computing Systems* 10:1 (February 1992): 3–25.

Koo, R., and S. Toueg. Checkpointing and Rollback Recovery for Distributed Systems. *IEEE Transactions on Software Engineering* SE-13:1 (January 1990): 23–31.

Kopetz, H. Sparse Time versus Dense Time in Distributed Systems. *Proceedings of the Twelfth International Conference on Distributed Computing Systems* (Yokohama, June 1992). New York: IEEE Computer Society Press.

Kopetz, H., and W. Ochsenreiter. Clock Synchronization in Distributed Real-Time Systems. *IEEE Transactions on Computers* C36:8 (August 1987): 933–940.

Kopetz, H., and P. Verissimo. Real-Time Dependability Concepts. In *Distributed Systems*, 2d ed., S. J. Mullender, ed. Reading, MA: Addison-Wesley/ACM Press, 1993, 411–446.

Kronenberg, N., H. Levy, and W. Strecker. VAXClusters: A Closely-Coupled Distributed System. *Proceedings of the Tenth ACM Symposium on Operating Systems Principles* (Orcas Island, WA, December 1985). Also *ACM Transactions on Computer Systems* 4:2 (May 1986): 130–146.

Krumvieda, C. Expressing Fault-Tolerant and Consistency Preserving Programs in Distributed ML. *Proceedings of the ACM SIGPLAN Workshop on ML and it Applications* (June 1992), 157–162.

—— DML: Packaging High-Level Distributed Abstractions in SML. *Proceedings of the Third International Workshop on Standard ML* (Pittsburgh, September 1991). New York: IEEE Computer Society Press.

Kubiatowicz, J. Extracting guarantees from chaos. *Communications of the ACM* 46(2) (2003): 33–38.

Kubiatowicz, J. et. al.: OceanStore: An Architecture for Global-Scale Persistent Storage. *Proceedings of Architectural Support for Progamming Languages and Systems* (ASPLOS) 2000, 190–201.

Kubiatowicz, J., D. Bindel, Y. Chen, S. Czerwinski, P. Eaton, D. Geels, R. Gummadi, S. Rhea, H. Weatherspoon, W. Weimer, C. Wells, B. Zhao. OceanStore: An Architecture for Global-Scale Persistent Storage. *Proceedings of ACM* ASPLOS, 2000.

Ladin, R., B. Liskov, L. Shrira, and S. Ghemawat. Providing Availability Using Lazy Replication. *ACM Transactions on Computer Systems* 10:4 (November 1992): 360–391.

—— Lazy Replication: Exploiting the Semantics of Distributed Services. *Proceedings of the Tenth ACM Symposium on Principles of Distributed Computing* (Quebec, August 1990). New York: ACM Press, 43–58.

Laih, C. S. and L. Harn. Generalized Threshold Cryptosystems. *Proceedings of ASIACRYPT '91* (1991).

Lamport, L. Using Time Instead of Timeout for Fault-Tolerant Distributed Systems. *ACM Transactions on Programming Languages and Systems* 6:2 (April 1984): 254–280.

—— Time, Clocks, and the Ordering of Events in a Distributed System. *Communications of the ACM* 21:7 (July 1978): 558–565.

—— The Implementation of Reliable Distributed Multiprocess Systems. *Computing Networks* 2 (March 1978): 95–114.

—— Paxos made simple. *Distributed Computing Column of ACM SIGACT News*, 32(4):51–58, December 2001.

Lamport, L. and P. M. Melliar-Smith. Synchronizing Clocks in the Presence of Faults. *Journal of the ACM* 32:1 (January 1985): 52–78.

Lampson, B. Hints for Computer System Design. *Proceedings of the Ninth Symposium on Operating Systems Principles* (Bretton Woods, NH, October 1993), 33–48.

—— Designing a Global Name Service. Paper presented at the 1985 ACM PODC. Also *Proceedings of the Sixth ACM Symposium on Principles of Distributed Computing* (Calgary, 1986), 1–10.

Lampson, B., M. Abadi, M. Burrows, and E. Wobber. Authentication in Distributed Systems: Theory and Practice. *ACM Transactions on Computer Systems* 10:4 (November 1992): 265–434.

Leffler, S. J. et al. *4.3 BSD UNIX Operating System*. Reading, MA: Addison-Wesley, 1989.

Lenoski, D. et al. The Stanford DASH Multiprocessor. *Computer* 25:3 (March 1992): 63–79.

Leroy, X. *The Caml Light System, Release* 0.7. France: INRIA July 1993.

Li, K., and P. Hudak. Memory Coherence in a Shared Virtual Memory System. *ACM Transactions on Computer Systems* 7:4 (November 1989): 321–359.

Lin, M.J., K. Marzullo, S. Massini. Gossip versus deterministically constrained flooding on small networks. In 14th *International Conference on Distributed Computing (DISC 2000)*, Toledo, Spain, 4–6 Oct. 2000), pp. 253–267.

Liskov, B. Practical Uses of Synchronized Clocks in Distributed Systems. *Distributed Computing* 6:4 (November 1993): 211–219.

Liskov, B., D. Curtis, P. Johnson, and R. Scheifler. Implementation of Argus. *Proceedings of the Eleventh ACM Symposium on Operating Systems Principles* (Austin, November 1987). New York: ACM Press, 111–122.

Liskov, B., M. Day, L. Shrira. Distributed Object Management in Thor. *Proceedings of the International Workshop on Distributed Object Management*, Edmonton, CA (1992), 79–91.

Liskov, B., and R. Ladin. Highly Available Distributed Services and Fault-Tolerant Garbage Collection. *Proceedings of the Fifth ACM Symposium on Principles of Distributed Computing* (Calgary, August 1986). New York: ACM Press, 29–39.

Liskov, B., and R. Scheifler. Guardians and Actions: Linguist Support for Robust, Distributed Programs. *ACM Transactions on Programming Languages and Systems* 5:3 (July 1983): 381–404.

Liskov, B. et al. Replication in the Harp File System. *Proceedings of the Twelfth ACM Symposium on Operating Systems Principles* (Asilomar, CA, October 1991). New York: ACM Press, 226–238.

Liu, X., C. Kreitz, R. van Renesse, J. Hickey, M. Hayden, K.P. Birman, and R. Constable. Building Reliable, High-Performance Communication Systems from Components. *Proc. of the 17th ACM Symposium on Operating System Principles*, Kiawah Island Resort, SC, December 1999.

Liu, X.. Evaluation of the Virtual Interface Architecture (VIA). *Tech Report*. UCSD, June 1998.

Lynch, N. *Distributed Algorithms*. San Mateo, CA: Morgan Kaufmann, 1996.

Lynch, N., A. Shvartsman. Communication and Data Sharing for Dynamic Distributed Systems. *Future Directions in Distributed Computing*, Springer-Verlag (2003): 62–67.

Lyu, M. R., ed. *Software Fault Tolerance*. New York: John Wiley & Sons, 1995.

Macedo, R. A., P. Ezhilchlvan, and S. Shrivastava. Newtop: A Total Order Multicast Protocol Using Causal Blocks. BROADCAST Project Technical Reports, vol. I. Department of Computer Science, University of Newcastle upon Tyne, October 1993.

Maffeis, S. Adding Group Communication and Fault Tolerance to CORBA. *Proceedings of the 1995 USENIX Conference on Object-Oriented Technologies.* (Monterey, CA, June 1995).

Makpangou, M., and K. P. Birman. Designing Application Software in Wide Area Network Settings. Technical Report 90-1165. Department of Computer Science, Cornell University, 1990.

Malkhi, D. Multicast Communication for High Availability. Ph.D. diss., Hebrew University of Jerusalem, 1994.

Malkhi, D., K. P. Birman, A. Ricciardi, and A. Schiper. Uniform Actions in Asynchronous Distributed Systems. Technical Report TR 94-1447. Department of Computer Science, Cornell University, September 1994.

Malkhi, D., M. Reiter, A. Wool and R. Wright. Probabilistic Quorum Systems. *The Information and Computation Journal* 170(2), November 2001.

Malkhi, D., M. K. Reiter: Byzantine Quorum Systems. *Distributed Computing* 11(4) (1998): 203–213.

—— An Architecture for Survivable Coordination in Large Distributed Systems. *IEEE Transactions on Knowledge and Data Engineering*, 12(2) April 2000: 187–202.

Malkhi, D., M. K. Reiter, D. Tulone, and E. Ziskind. Persistent objects in the Fleet system. In *Proceedings of the 2nd DARPA Information Survivability Conference and Exposition (DISCEX II)*, Vol. II, June 2001, 126–136.

Malloth, C. Conception and Implementation of a Toolkit for Building Fault-Tolerant Distributed Applications in Large-Scale Networks. Ph.D. diss., Swiss Federal Institute of Technology, Lausanne (EPFL), 1996.

Malloth, C. P., P. Felher, A. Schiper, and U. Wilhelm. Phoenix: A Toolkit for Building Fault-Tolerant Distributed Applications in Large-Scale Networks. *Proceedings of the Workshop on Parallel and Distributed Platforms in Industrial Products* (held during the Seventh IEEE Symposium on Parallel and Distributed Processing) (San Antonio, TX, October 1995). New York: IEEE Computer Society Press.

Marzullo, K. Tolerating Failures of Continuous Valued Sensors. *ACM Transactions on Computer Systems* 8:4 (November 1990): 284–304.

—— Maintaining the Time in a Distributed System. Ph.D. diss., Department of Electrical Engineering, Stanford University, June 1984.

Marzullo, K., R. Cooper, M. Wood, and K. P. Birman. Tools for Distributed Application Management. *IEEE Computer*, August 1991.

Marzullo, K., and M. Wood. Tools for Constructing Distributed Reactive Systems. Technical Report TR91-1193. Department of Computer Science, Cornell University, February 1991.

Marzullo, K., M. Wood, K. P. Birman, and R. Cooper. Tools for Monitoring and Controlling Distributed Applications. *Spring 1991 Conference Proceedings* (Bologna, Italy, May 1991). EurOpen, 185–196. Revised and extended as *IEEE Computer* 24:8 (August 1991): 42–51.

Mattern, F. Time and Global States in Distributed Systems. *Proceedings of the International Workshop on Parallel and Distributed Algorithms*. Amsterdam: North-Holland, 1989.

McKusick, M.K, Joy, W., Leffler, S., and Fabry, R.S. A Fast File System for UNIX. *Computer Systems*, Vol. 2, Num. 3, Aug 1984, 181–197.

Meldal, S., S. Sankar, and J. Vera. Exploiting Locality in Maintaining Potential Causality. *Proceedings of the Tenth Symposium on Principles of Distributed Computing* (Montreal, August 1991), 231–239.

Melliar-Smith, P. M., and L. E. Moser. Trans: A Reliable Broadcast Protocol. *IEEE Transactions on Communications* 140:6 (December 1993): 481–493.

—— Fault-Tolerant Distributed Systems Based on Broadcast Communication. *Proceedings of the Ninth International Conference on Distributed Computing Systems* (June 1989), 129–133.

Melliar-Smith, P. M., L. E. Moser and V. Agrawala. Membership Algorithms for Asynchronous Distributed Systems. *Proceedings of the IEEE Eleventh ICDCS* (May 1991), 480–488.

—— Broadcast Protocols for Distributed Systems. *IEEE Transactions on Parallel and Distributed Systems* 1:1 (January 1990): 17–25.

Milner, R., M. Tofte, and R. Harper. *The Definition of Standard ML*. Cambridge, MA: MIT Press, 1990.

Mishra, S., L. L. Peterson and R. D. Schlichting. Experience with Modularity in Consul. *Software—Practice and Experience* 23:10 (October 1993): 1050–1075.

—— A Membership Protocol Based on Partial Order. *Proceedings of the IEEE International Working Conference on Dependable Computing for Critical Applications* (February 1991), 137–145.

Mogul, J., R. Rashid, and M. Accetta. The Packet Filter: An Efficient Mechanism for User-Level Network Code. *Proceedings of the Eleventh ACM Symposium on Operating Systems Principles* (Austin, November 1987). New York: ACM Press, 39–51.

Montgomery, T. Design, Implementation, and Verification of the Reliable Multicast Protocol. Master's thesis, Department of Electrical and Computer Engineering, West Virginia University, December 1994.

Montgomery, T., and B. Whetten. The Reliable Multicast Protocol Application Programming Interface. Technical Report NASA-IVV-94-007. NASA/WVU Software Research Laboratory, August 1994.

Morris, R. Scalable TCP Congestion Control. *Proceedings of INFOCOM 2000*, 1176–1183.

Moser, L. E., Y. Amir, P. M. Melliar-Smith and D. A. Agarwal. Extended Virtual Synchrony. *Proceedings of the Fourteenth International Conference on Distributed Computing Sytems* (June 1994). New York: IEEE Computer Society Press, 56–65. Also Technical Report TR-93-22. Department of ECE, University of California, Santa Barbara, December 1993.

Moser, L. E., P. M. Melliar-Smith, D. A. Agarwal, R. K. Budhia, and C. A. Lingley-Papadopoulos. Totem: A Fault-Tolerant Multicast Group Communication System. *Communications of the ACM* 39:4 (April 1996): 54–63.

Moser, L. E., P. M. Melliar-Smith, and U. Agarwal. Processor Membership in Asynchronous Distributed Systems. *IEEE Transactions on Parallel and Distributed Systems* 5:5 (May 1994): 459–473.

Moss, J. E. Nested Transactions and Reliable Distributed Computing. *Proceedings of the Second Symposium on Reliability in Distributed Software and Database Systems* (1982), 33–39.

Mullender, S. J. et al. Amoeba—A Distributed Operating System for the 1990s. *IEEE Computer* 23:5 (May 1990): 44–53.

Mummert, L. B., M. R. Ebling, and M. Satyanarayanan. Exploiting Weak Connectivity for Mobile File Access. *Proceedings of the Fifteenth Symposium on Operating Systems Principles* (Copper Mountain Resort, CO, December 1995). New York: ACM Press, 143–155. Also *ACM Transactions on Computing Systems* 13:1 (February 1996).

Muthitacharoen, A., Chen, B. and Mazieres, D. A low-bandwidth network file system. *18th ACM Symposium on Operating Systems Principles (SOSP '01)*, Chateau Lake Louise, Banff, Canada. October 2001.

Muthitacharoen, A., R. Morris, T. Gil, B. Chen. Ivy: A Read/Write Peer-to-peer File System. *Proceedings of the 5th USENIX Symposium on Operating Systems Design and Implementation (OSDI '02)*, Boston, Massachusetts, December 2002.

National Bureau of Standards. *Data Encryption Standard*. Federal Information Processing Standards Publication 46. Washington, DC: U.S. Government Printing Office, 1977.

Needham, R. M., and M. D. Schroeder. Using Encryption for Authentication in Large Networks of Computers. *Communications of the ACM* 21:12 (December 1988): 993–999.

Neiger, G. A New Look at Membership Services. *Proceedings of the Fifteenth ACM Symposium on Principles of Distributed Computing* (Vancouver, 1996). In press.

Nelson, M., B. Welsh, and J. Ousterhout. Caching in the Sprite Network File System. *Proceedings of the Eleventh ACM Symposium on Operating Systems Principles* (Austin, November 1987). New York: ACM Press. Also *ACM Transactions on Computing Systems* 6:1 (February 1988).

Object Management Group and X/Open. Common Object Request Broker: Architecture and Specification. Reference OMG 91.12.1, 1991.

Oki, B., M. Pfluegl, A. Siegel, and D. Skeen. The Information Bus-An Architecture for Extensible Distributed Systems. *Proceedings of the Thirteenth ACM Symposium on Operating Systems Principles* (Asheville, NC, December 1993). New York: ACM Press, 58–68.

Open Software Foundation. *Introduction to OSF DCE*. Englewood Cliffs, NJ: Prentice Hall, 1994.

Ousterhout, J. *TCL and the TK Toolkit*. Reading, MA: Addison-Wesley, 1994.

—— Why Aren't Operating Systems Getting Faster as Fast as Hardware? *USENIX Summer Conference Proceedings* (Anaheim, CA, 1990), 247–256.

Ousterhout, J. et al. The Sprite Network Operating System. *Computer* 21:2 (February 1988): 23–36.

—— A Trace-Driven Analysis of the UNIX 4.2 BSD File System. *Proceedings of the Tenth ACM Symposium on Operating Systems Principles* (Orcas Island, WA, December 1985). New York: ACM Press, 15–24.

Ozkasap, O., R. van Renesse, K.P. Birman, and Z. Xiao. Efficient Buffering in Reliable Multicast Protocols. *Proceedings of the First Workshop on Networked Group Communication. (NGC99)*. Lecture notes in Computer Science 1736, Springer Verlag, pp 159–169. Pisa, Italy. (November 1999).

Pai, V.S., Druschel, P. and Zwaenepoel, W.. IO-Lite: A Unified I/O Buffering and Caching System. *3rd Symposium on Operating Systems Design and Implementation (OSDI)*. New Orleans, LA, February 1999.

Partridge, C., and S. Pink. A Faster UDP. *IEEE/ACM Transactions on Networking* 1:4 (August 1993): 429–440.

Patterson, D., G. Gibson, and R. Katz. A Case for Redundant Arrays of Inexpensive Disks (RAID). *Proceedings of the 1988 ACM Conference on Management of Data (SIGMOD)* (Chicago, June 1988), 109–116.

Pedone, F., R. Guerraoui and A. Schiper. Exploiting atomic broadcast in replicated databases. *Proceedings EuroPar 98*. 1998.

Pedone, F., A. Schiper. Handling message semantics with Generic Broadcast protocols. *Distributed Computing* 15(2) (2002): 97–107.

Pereira, J., L. Rodrigues, R. Oliveira. Semantically Reliable Multicast: Definition, Implementation, and Performance Evaluation. *IEEE Transactions on Computers* 52(2) (2003): 150–165.

Pereira, J., L. Rodrigues, R. Oliveira. Reducing the Cost of Group Communication with Semantic View Synchrony. *DSN 2002*: 293–302.

Peterson, I. *Fatal Defect: Chasing Killer Computer Bugs*. New York: Time Books/Random House, 1995.

Petersen, K., Spreitzer, M., Terry, D., Theimer, M., and Demers, A. Flexible Update Propagation for Weakly Consistent Replication. *16th ACM Symposium on Operating Systems Principles (SOSP)*. Saint Malo, France. October 1997.

Peterson, L. Preserving Context Information in an IPC Abstraction. *Proceedings of the Sixth Symposium on Reliability in Distributed Software and Database Systems* (March 1987). New York: IEEE Computer Society Press, 22–31.

Peterson, L., N. C. Buchholz, and R. D. Schlicting. Preserving and Using Context Information in Interprocess Communication. *ACM Transactions on Computing Systems* 7:3 (August 1989): 217–246.

Peterson, L., N. Hutchinson, S. O'Malley, and M. Abbott. RPC in the *x*-Kernel: Evaluating New Design Techniques. *Proceedings of the Twelfth Symposium on Operating Systems Principles* (Litchfield Park, AZ, November 1989). New York: ACM Press, 91–101.

Pfister, G. F. *In Search of Clusters*. Englewood Cliffs, NJ: Prentice Hall, 1995.

Pittel, B. On Spreading of a Rumor. *SIAM Journal of Applied Mathematics* 47:1 (1987): 213–223.

Powell, D. Introduction to Special Section on Group Communication. *Communications of the ACM* 39:4 (April 1996): 50–53.

—— Lessons Learned from Delta-4. *IEEE Micro* 14:4 (February 1994): 36–47.

—— ed. *Delta-4: A Generic Architecture for Dependable Distributed Computing*. Springer-Verlag ESPRIT Research Reports, Vol. I, Project 818/2252, 1991.

Pradhan, D. *Fault-Tolerant Computer System Design*. Englewood Cliffs, NJ: Prentice Hall, 1996.

Pradhan, D., and D. Avresky, eds. *Fault-Tolerant Parallel and Distributed Systems*. New York: IEEE Computer Society Press, 1995.

Pu, D. Relaxing the Limitations of Serializable Transactions in Distributed Systems. *Operating Systems Review* 27:2 (April 1993): 66–71. (Special issue on the Workshop on Operating Systems Principles at Le Mont St. Michel, France.)

Qiu, L., V. N. Padmanabhan, G. M. Voelker On the Placement of Web Server Replicas. *Proceedings of INFOCOM 2001*: 1587–1596

Rabin, M. Randomized Byzantine Generals. *Proceedings of the Twenty-Fourth Annual Symposium on Foundations of Computer Science* (1983). New York: IEEE Computer Society Press, 403–409.

Rangan, P. V., and H. M. Vin. Designing File Systems for Digital Video and Audio. *Proceedings of the Twelfth ACM Symposium on Operating Systems Principles* (Asilomar, CA, October 1991). New York: ACM Press, 81–94.

Rashid, R. F. Threads of a New System. *UNIX Review 4* (August 1986): 37–49.

Ratnasamy, S., P. Francis, P., R. Handley, R. Karp, S. Shenker. A Scalable Content-Addressable Network, *Proc ACM SIGCOMM 2001*, San Diego, August 2001.

Reed, D. P., and R. K. Kanodia. Synchronization with Eventcounts and Sequencers. *Communications of the ACM* 22:2 (February 1979): 115–123.

Reiher, P. et al. Resolving File Conflicts in the Ficus File System. *Proceedings of the Summer USENIX Conference* (June 1994), 183–195.

Reiter, M. K., A. D. Rubin. Crowds: Anonymity for Web Transactions. *ACM Transactions on Information and System Security* 1(1): 66–92, November 1998.

Reiter, M. K. Distributing Trust with the Rampart Toolkit. *Communications of the ACM* 39:4 (April 1996): 71–75.

—— Secure Agreement Protocols: Reliable and Atomic Group Multicast in Rampart. *Proceedings of the Second ACM Conference on Computer and Communications Security* (Oakland, November 1994), 68–80.

—— A Secure Group Membership Protocol. *Proceedings of the 1994 Symposium on Research in Security and Privacy* (Oakland, May 1994). New York: IEEE Computer Society Press, 89–99.

—— A Security Architecture for Fault-Tolerant Systems. Ph.D. diss., Cornell University, August 1993. Also Technical Report. Department of Computer Science, Cornell University.

Reiter, M. K., and K. P. Birman. How to Securely Replicate Services. *ACM Transactions on Programming Languages and Systems* 16:3 (May 1994): 986–1009.

Reiter, M. K., K. P. Birman, and L. Gong. Integrating Security in a Group-Oriented Distributed System. *Proceedings of the IEEE Symposium on Research in Security and Privacy* (Oakland, May 1992). New York: IEEE Computer Society Press, 18–32.

Reiter, M. K., K. P. Birman, and R. van Renesse. A Security Architecture for Fault-Tolerant Systems. *ACM Transactions on Computing Systems*, May 1995.

Ricciardi, A. The Impossibility of (Repeated) Reliable Broadcast. Technical Report TR-PDS-1996-003. Department of Electrical and Computer Engineering, University of Texas, Austin, April 1996.

Ricciardi, A., and K. P. Birman. Using Process Groups to Implement Failure Detection in Asynchronous Environments. *Proceedings of the Eleventh ACM Symposium on Principles of Distributed Computing* (Quebec, August 1991). New York: ACM Press, 341–351.

Ricciardi, A. M. The Group Membership Problem in Asynchronous Systems. Ph.D. diss., Cornell University, January 1993.

Riecken, D. Intelligent Agents. *Communications of the ACM* 37:7 (July 1994): 19–21.

Ritchie, D. M. A Stream Input-Output System. *Bell Laboratories Technical Journal, AT & T* 63:8 (1984): 1897–1910.

Rivest, R. L., A. Shamir, and L. Adleman. A Method for Obtaining Digital Signatures and Public Key Cryptosystems. *Communications of the ACM* 22:4 (December 1978): 120–126.

Rodeh, O., K. Birman, D. Dolev. The Architecture and Performance of the Security Protocols in the Ensemble Group Communication System. *Journal of ACM Transactions on Information Systems and Security (TISSEC).*

—— Using AVL Trees for Fault-Tolerant Group Key Management. *International Journal of Information Security (IJIS)*, Vol. 1, No 2, February 2002, 84–99.

Rodrigues, L., K. Guo, P. Verissimo, and K.P. Birman. A Dynamic Light-Weight Group Service. *Journal of Parallel and Distributed Computing*, 60, (2000), 1449–1479.

Rodrigues, L., and P. Verissimo. Causal Separators for Large-Scale Multicast Communication. *Proceedings of the Fifteenth International Conference on Distributed Computing Systems* (May 1995), 83–91.

—— xAMP: A MultiPrimitive Group Communications Service. *Proceedings of the Eleventh Symposium on Reliable Distributed Systems* (Houston, October 1989). New York: IEEE Computer Society Press.

Rodrigues, L., P. Verissimo, and J. Rufino. A Low-Level Processor Group Membership Protocol for LANs. *Proceedings of the Thirteenth International Conference on Distributed Computing Systems* (May 1993), 541–550.

Rosenblum, M., and J. K. Ousterhout. The Design and Implementation of a Log-Structured File System. *Proceedings of the Twelfth ACM Symposium on Operating Systems Principles* (Asilomar, CA, October 1991). New York: ACM Press, 1–15. Also *ACM Transactions on Computing Systems* 10:1 (February 1992): 26–52.

Rowe, L. A., and B. C. Smith. A Continuous Media Player. *Proceedings of the Third International Workshop on Network and Operating Systems Support for Digital Audio and Video* (San Diego, CA, November 1992).

Rowstron, A. and P. Druschel, Pastry: Scalable, distributed object location and routing for *large-scale peer-to-peer systems. IFIP/ACM International Conference on Distributed Systems Platforms* (Middleware), Heidelberg, Germany, pages 329-350, November, 2001.

Rowstron, A., and Druschel, P.. Storage management and caching in PAST, a large scale, persistent peer-to-peer storage utility. *18th ACM Symposium on Operating Systems Principles (SOSP)*, Banff, Canada. October 2001.

Rowstron, A., A.M. Kermarrec, M. Castro, P. Druschel: SCRIBE: The Design of a Large-Scale Event Notification Infrastructure. *Second International Workshop on Networked Group Communication*, Oakland CA, 2001: 30–43.

Rowstron, A., Kermarrec, A.M., Druschel, P., and Castro, M.. SCRIBE: A large-scale and decentralized application-level multicast infrastructure. *IEEE Journal on Selected Areas in communications (JSAC)*, 2002.

—— *Storage management and caching in PAST, a large-scale, persistent peer-to-peer storage utility*, ACM Symposium on Operating Systems Principles (SOSP'01), Banff, Canada, October 2001.

Rozier, M. et al. Chorus Distributed Operating System. *Computing Systems Journal* 1:4 (December 1988): 305–370.

—— The Chorus Distributed System. *Computer Systems*, Fall 1988: 299–328.

Sabel, L., and K. Marzullo. Simulating Fail-Stop in Asynchronous Distributed Systems. *Proceedings of the Thirteenth Symposium on Reliable Distributed Systems* (Dana Point, CA, October 1994). New York: IEEE Computer Society Press, 138–147.

Saito, Y., H. M. Levy. Optimistic Replication for Internet Data Services. *Proceedings of 14th International Conference on Distributed Computing (DISC)*, 2000: 297–314.

Saito, Y., B. N. Bershad, H. M. Levy. Manageability, availability, and performance in porcupine: a highly scalable, cluster-based mail service. *ACM Transactions on Computer Systems* 18(3) (2000): 298.

Saltzer, J. H., D. P. Reed, and D. D. Clark. End-to-End Arguments in System Design. *ACM Transactions on Computer Systems* 39:4 (April 1990).

Saroiu, S., P.K.Gummadi, R. J. Dunn, S. D. Gribble, H. M. Levy. An Analysis of Internet Content Delivery Systems. *Proceedings of 5th Operating System Design and Implementation Conference (OSDI)*, Boston, MA (Dec. 2002).

Satyanarayanan, M. et al. Integrating Security in a Large Distributed System. *ACM Transactions on Computer Systems* 7:3 (August 1989): 247–280.

—— The ITC Distributed File System: Principles and Design. *Proceedings of the Tenth ACM Symposium on Operating Systems Principles* (Orcas Island, WA, December 1985). New York: ACM Press, 35–50.

Schantz, R. E., R. H. Thomas, and G. Bono. The Architecture of the Chronus Distributed Operating System. *Proceedings of the Sixth International Conference on Distributed Computing Systems* (New York, June 1986). New York: IEEE Computer Society Press, 250–259.

Schiller, J. I. Secure Distributed Computing. *Scientific American* (November 1994): 72–76.

Schiper, A., A. A. Shvartsman, H. Weatherspoon, B. Zhao: *Future Directions in Distributed Computing*, Research and Position Papers. Springer-Verlag, 2003.

Schiper, A., J. Eggli, and A. Sandoz. A New Algorithm to Implement Causal Ordering. *Proceedings of the Third International Workshop on Distributed Algorithms* (1989). Springer-Verlag Lecture Notes in Computer Science, vol. 392, 219–232.

Schiper, A., and M. Raynal. From Group Communication to Transactions in Distributed Systems. *Communications of the ACM* 39:4 (April 1996): 84–87.

Schiper A., and A. Sandoz. Uniform Reliable Multicast in a Virtually Synchronous Environment. *Proceedings of the Thirteenth International Conference on Distributed Computing Systems* (May 1993). New York: IEEE Computer Society Press, 561–568.

Schlicting, R. D., and F. B. Schneider. Fail-Stop Processors: An Approach to Designing Fault-Tolerant Computing Systems. *ACM Transactions on Computer Systems* 1:3 (August 1983): 222–238.

Schmuck, F. The Use of Efficient Broadcast Primitives in Asynchronous Distributed Systems. Ph.D. diss., Cornell University, August 1988. Also Technical Report. Department of Computer Science, Cornell University.

Schmuck, F., and J. Wyllie. Experience with Transactions in QuickSilver. *Proceedings of the Twelfth ACM Symposium on Operating Systems Principles* (Asilomar, CA, October 1991). New York: ACM Press, 239–252.

Schneider, F. B. *On Concurrent Programming*. New York: Springer-Verlag, in press.

—— Implementing Fault-Tolerant Services Using the StateMachine Approach. *ACM Computing Surveys* 22:4 (December 1990): 299–319.

—— The StateMachine Approach: A Tutorial. *Proceedings of the Workshop on Fault-Tolerant Distributed Computing* (Asilomar, CA, 1988). Springer-Verlag Lecture Notes on Computer Science, Vol. 448, 18–41.

—— Byzantine Generals in Action: Implementing Fail-Stop Processors. *ACM Transactions on Computer Systems* 2:2 (May 1984): 145–154.

—— Synchronization in Distributed Programs. *ACM Transactions on Programming Languages and Systems* 4:2 (April 1982): 179–195.

Schneider, F. B., D. Gries, and R. D. Schlicting. Fault-Tolerant Broadcasts. *Science of Computer Programming* 3:2 (March 1984): 1–15.

Schwarz, R., and F. Mattern. Detecting Causal Relationships in Distributed Computations. Technical Report 215-91. Department of Computer Science, University of Kaiserslautern, 1991.

Seltzer, M. Transaction Support in a Log-Structured File System. *Proceedings of the Ninth International Conference on Data Engineering* (April 1993).

Shroeder, M., and M. Burrows. Performance of Firefly RPC. *Proceedings of the Eleventh ACM Symposium on Operating Systems Principles* (Litchfield Springs, AZ, December 1989), 83-90. Also *ACM Transactions on Computing Systems* 8:1 (February 1990): 1–17.

Siegal, A. Performance in Flexible Distributed File Systems. Ph.D. diss., Cornell University, February 1992. Also Technical Report TR-92-1266. Department of Computer Science, Cornell University.

Siegel, A., K. P. Birman, and K. Marzullo. Deceit: A Flexible Distributed File System. Technical Report 89-1042. Department of Computer Science, Cornell University, 1989.

Simons, B., J. N. Welch, and N. Lynch. An Overview of Clock Synchronization. In *Fault-Tolerant Distributed Computing*, (B. Simons and A. Spector, eds), Springer-Verlag Lecture Notes in Computer Science, Vol. 448, 1990, 84–96.

Skeen, D. Determining the Last Process to Fail. *ACM Transactions on Computer Systems* 3:1 (February 1985): 15–30.

—— Crash Recovery in a Distributed Database System. Ph.D. diss., Department of EECS, University of California, Berkeley, June 1982.

—— A Quorum-Based Commit Protocol. *Proceedings of the Berkeley Workshop on Distributed Data Management and Computer Networks* (Berkeley, CA, February 1982), 69–80.

—— Nonblocking Commit Protocols. *ACM International Conference on Management of Data (SIGMOD)*, Ann Arbor, MI. May 1981.

Snoeren, A.C., Conley, K., and Gifford, D.K.. Mesh-based Content Routing using XML. *18th ACM Symposium on Operating Systems Principles (SOSP)*, Banff, Canada. October 2001.

Spasojevic, M., and M. Satyanarayanan. An Empirical Study of a Wide Area Distributed File System. *ACM Transactions on Computer Systems* 14:2 (May 1996).

Spector, A. Distributed Transactions for Reliable Systems. *Proceedings of the Tenth ACM Symposium on Operating Systems Principles* (Orcas Island, WA, December 1985), 12–146.

Srikanth, T. K., and S. Toueg. Optimal Clock Synchronization. *Journal of the ACM* 34:3 (July 1987): 626–645.

Srinivasan, V., and J. Mogul. Spritely NFS: Experiments with Cache Consistency Protocols. *Proceedings of the Eleventh ACM Symposium on Operating Systems Principles* (Litchfield Springs, AZ, December 1989), 45–57.

Steiner, J. G., B. C. Neuman, and J. I. Schiller. Kerberos: An Authentication Service for Open Network Systems. *Proceedings of the 1988 USENIX Winter Conference* (Dallas, February 1988), 191–202.

Stephenson, P. Fast Causal Multicast. Ph.D. diss., Cornell University, February 1991. Also Technical Report. Department of Computer Science, Cornell University.

Stoica, I., R. Morris, D. Karger., M.F. Kaashoek, and H. Balakrishnan, Chord: A Scalable Peer-to-peer Lookup Service for Internet Applications, *ACM SIGCOMM 2001*, San Deigo, CA, August 2001, pp. 149–160.

Sussman, J., K. Marzullo. The Bancomat Problem: An Example of Resource Allocation in a Partitionable Asynchronous System. *Journal of Theoretical Computer Science* 291(1), January 2003.

Tanenbaum, A. *Computer Networks*, 2d ed. Englewood Cliffs, NJ: Prentice Hall, 1988.

Tanenbaum, A., and R. van Renesse. A Critique of the Remote Procedure Call Paradigm. *Proceedings of the EUTECO '88 Conference* (Vienna, April 1988), 775–783.

Telecommunications Information Network Architecture Conference, Proceedings of (Heidelberg, September 3–5, 1996). Berlin: VDE-Verlag.

Tennenhouse, D. Layered Multiplexing Considered Harmful. In *Protocols for High Speed Networks*. Elsevier, 1990.

Terry, D. B. et al. Managing Update Conflicts in a Weakly Connected Replicated Storage System. *Proceedings of the Fifteenth Symposium on Operating Systems Principles* (Copper Mountain Resort, CO, December 1995). New York: ACM Press, 172–183.

Thekkath, C. A., and H. M. Levy. Limits to Low-Latency Communication on High-Speed Networks. *ACM Transactions on Computer Systems* 11:2 (May 1993): 179–203.

Thekkath, C. A., T. Nguyen, E. Moy, and E. Lazowska. Implementing Network Protocols at User Level. *IEEE Transactions on Networking* 1:5 (October 1993): 554–564.

Thekkath, C., Mann, T., and Lee, E. Frangipani: A scalable distributed file system. *16th ACM Symposium on Operating Systems Principles (SOSP)*, Saint-Malo, France, October 1997.

Thomas, T. A Majority Consensus Approach to Concurrency Control for Multiple Copy Databases. *ACM Transactions on Database Systems* 4:2 (June 1979): 180–209.

Torrellas, J., and J. Hennessey. Estimating the Performance Advantages of Relaxing Consistency in a Shared-Memory Multiprocessor. Technical Report CSL-TN-90-265. Stanford University Computer Systems Laboratory, February 1990.

Turek, J., and D. Shasha. The Many Faces of Consensus in Distributed Systems. *IEEE Computer* 25:6 (1992): 8–17.

Triantafillou, P. Peer-to-Peer Network Architectures: The Next Step, *SIGCOMM Workshop on Future Directions in Network Architectures* (FDNA-03) August 2003.

van Renesse, R. Why Bother with CATOCS? *Operating Systems Review* 28:1 (January 1994): 22–27.

—— Causal Controversy at Le Mont St.-Michel. *Operating Systems Review* 27:2 (April 1993): 44–53.

van Renesse, R., K.P. Birman and W. Vogels. Astrolabe: A Robust and Scalable Technology for Distributed System Monitoring, Management, and Data Mining. *ACM Transactions on Computer Systems*, May 2003, Vol.21, No. 2, 164–206.

van Renesse, R., K.P Birman, D. Dumitriu, and W. Vogels. Scalable Management and Data Mining Using Astrolabe. *Proceedings of the First International Workshop on Peer-to-Peer Systems (IPTPS)*. Cambridge, Massachusetts. March 2002.

van Renesse, R., K. P. Birman, R. Cooper, B. Glade, and P. Stephenson. Reliable Multicast between Microkernels. *Proceedings of the USENIX Workshop on Microkernels and Other Kernel Architectures* (Seattle, April 1992).

van Renesse, R., K. P. Birman, R. Friedman, M. Hayden, and D. Karr. A Framework for Protocol Composition in Horus. *Proceedings of the Fourteenth Symposium on the*

Principles of Distributed Computing (Ottawa, August 1995). New York: ACM Press, 80–89.

van Renesse, R., K. P. Birman, and S. Maffeis. Horus: A Flexible Group Communication System. *Communications of the ACM* 39:4 (April 1996): 76–83.

van Renesse, R., H. van Staveren, and A. Tanenbaum. The Performance of the Amoeba Distributed Operating System. *Software-Practice and Experience* 19:3 (March 1989): 223–234.

—— Performance of the World's Fastest Operating System. *Operating Systems Review* 22:4 (October 1988): 25–34.

Verissimo, P. Causal Delivery in Real-Time Systems: A Generic Model. *Real-Time Systems Journal* 10:1 (January 1996).

—— Ordering and Timeliness Requirements of Dependable Real-Time Programs. *Journal of Real-Time Systems* 7:2 (September 1994): 105–128.

—— Real-Time Communication. In *Distributed Systems*, 2d ed., 1993, S. J. Mullender, ed. Reading, MA: Addison-Wesley/ACM Press, 1993, 447–490.

Verissimo, P. Uncertainty and Predictability: Can They Be Reconciled? *Future Directions in Distributed Computing*, Springer-Verlag (2003): 108–113.

Verissimo, P., A. Casimiro. The Timely Computing Base Model and Architecture. *IEEE Transactions on Computers* 51(8) (2002): 916–930.

Verissimo, P., L. Rodrigues, A. Casimiro. CesiumSpray: a Precise and Accurate Global Time Service for Large-scale Systems. *Real-Time Systems* 12(3) (1997): 243–294.

Verissimo, P., and L. Rodrigues. A-Posteriori Agreement for Fault-Tolerant Clock Synchronization on Broadcast Networks. *Proceedings of the Twenty-Second International Symposium on Fault-Tolerant Computing* (Boston, July 1992).

Vogels, W. The Private Investigator. Technical Report. Department of Computer Science, Cornell University, April 1996.

Vogels, W. File System Usage in Windows NT 4.0. *Proc. of the 17th ACM Symposium on Operating Systems Principles*, Kiawah Island, SC, December 1999.

W. Vogels, Birman, K., R. van Renesse. Six Misconceptions about Reliable Distributed Computing. Proceedings of the Eighth ACM SIGOPS European Workshop. Sintra, Portugal, September 1998.

von Eicken, T., A. Basu, V. Buch, and W. Vogels. U-Net: A User-Level Network Interface for Parallel and Distributed Computing. *Proceedings of the Fifteenth Symposium on Operating Systems Principles* (Copper Mountain Resort, CO, December 1995). New York: ACM Press, 40–53.

von Eicken, T. and W. Vogels. Evolution of the Virtual Interface Architecture. *IEEE Computer*. November 1998.

von Eicken, T., D. E. Culler, S. C. Goldstein, and K. E. Schauser. Active Messages: A Mechanism for Integrated Communication and Computation. *Proceedings of the Nineteenth International Symposium on Computer Architecture* (May 1992), 256–266.

Voydock, V. L., and S. T. Kent. Security Mechanisms in High-Level Network Protocols. *ACM Computing Surveys* 15:2 (June 1983): 135–171.

Wahbe, R., S. Lucco, T. Anderson, and S. Graham. Efficient Software-Based Fault Isolation. *Proceedings of the Thirteenth ACM Symposium on Operating Systems Principles* (Asheville, NC, December 1993). New York: ACM Press, 203–216.

Walter, B. et al. The Locus Distributed Operating System. *Proceedings of the Ninth ACM Symposium on Operating Systems Principles* (Bretton Woods, NH, October 1993), 49–70.

Weatherspoon, H., J. Kubiatowicz. Erasure Coding Vs. Replication: A Quantitative Comparison. *IPTPS* 2002, 328–338.

Welsh, M., Culler, D. and Brewer, E.. SEDA: An Architecture for Well-Conditioned, Scalable Internet Services. *18th Symposium on Operating Systems Principles (SOSP)*, Banff, Canada. October 2001.

Whetten, B. A Reliable Multicast Protocol. In *Theory and Practice in Distributed Systems*, K. Birman, F. Mattern, and A. Schiper, eds. Springer-Verlag Lecture Notes on Computer Science, Vol. 938, July 1995.

Wilkes, J. et al. The HP AutoRAID Hierarchical Storage System. *Proceedings of the Fifteenth Symposium on Operating Systems Principles* (Copper Mountain Resort, CO, December 1995). New York: ACM Press, 96–108. Also *ACM Transactions on Computing Systems* 13:1 (February 1996).

Wolman, A., G.M. Voelker, N. Sharma, N. Cardwell, A. R. Karlin, H. M. Levy: On the scale and performance of cooperative Web proxy caching. *Proceedings of the 17th Symposium on Operating Systems (SOSP)*, Charleston SC, 1999: 16–31.

Wood, M. D. Replicated RPC Using Amoeba Closed-Group Communication. *Proceedings of the Twelfth International Conference on Distributed Computing Systems* (Pittsburgh, 1993).

—— Fault-Tolerant Management of Distributed Applications Using a Reactive System Architecture. Ph.D. diss., Cornell University, December 1991. Also Technical Report TR 91-1252. Department of Computer Science, Cornell University.

Wu, Y. Verification-Based Analysis of RMP. Technical Report NASA-IVV-95-003. NASA/WVU Software Research Laboratory, December 1995.

Zhao, B., Y. Duan, L. Huang, A. D. Joseph, J. Kubiatowicz. Brocade: Landmark Routing on Overlay Networks. *IPTPS* 2002, 34–44.

Zhao, B., L. Huang, J. Stribling, S. C. Rhea, A. D. Joseph, and J. Kubiatowicz. Tapestry: A Resilient Global-scale Overlay for Service Deployment, *IEEE Journal on Selected Areas in Communication*.

Zhao, B. Y. Duan, L. Huang, A.D. Joseph and J.D. Kubiatowicz. Brocade: landmark routing on overlay networks, *First International Workshop on Peer-to-Peer Systems (IPTPS)*, Cambridge, MA. March 2002.

Index